TURMOIL AND TRADITION

THE FRANCIS PARKMAN PRIZE

The Society of American Historians was founded in 1939 by Allan Nevins and others to stimulate literary distinction in historical writing. In its early years, the Society sought to create a magazine for popular history; this effort culminated in the establishment of *American Heritage* in the early 1950s. The Society then resolved to advance its mission by offering an annual prize for the best-written book in American history. To name the prize after Francis Parkman seemed nearly a foregone conclusion.

Parkman was born in 1823, the grandson of one of Boston's wealthiest merchants. Throughout his life, Parkman was plagued with nervous disorders and problems with his eyes. Yet he loved the outdoors and exulted in sojourns into the wild. "I was haunted with wilderness images day and night," he recalled, one reason why his evocations of frontier life were so powerful.

But he also was drawn to history. As a sophomore at Harvard he resolved on his life's work—a history of the struggle between France and Britain for mastery of North America. But first he trekked to the West and wrote *The Oregon Trail* (1849), a youthful work that exhibited the masterful writing that became his hallmark. The first volume of *France and England in North America* was published in 1865, the ninth and final volume in 1892.

Some of Parkman's judgments have been superseded by modern scholarship, and, in matters of style, he overused the concept of opposition (the most significant being the contrast between authoritarian and Catholic France, and democratic and Protestant Britain). Henry Adams was a more sophisticated thinker, and perhaps a more profound writer, but Parkman was the great American historian of the nineteenth century.

The first Parkman Prize was awarded in 1958 to Arthur M. Schlesinger, Jr., for his *Crisis of the Old Order*, published the previous year. And now the Society of American Historians is pleased to be working together with History Book Club to develop their exclusive new editions of Parkman Prize winners from the past—allowing readers to rediscover what many consider to be some of the best writing on the American story.

Mark C. Carnes
Executive Secretary
The Society of American Historians

TURMOIL AND TRADITION

A STUDY OF THE LIFE AND TIMES
OF HENRY L. STIMSON

Elting E. Morison

Introduction by Dennis E. Showalter

A disposition to preserve, and an ability to improve,
taken together, would be my standard of a statesman.
—Edmund Burke

FRANCIS PARKMAN PRIZE EDITION
HISTORY BOOK CLUB
NEW YORK

TO

WHAT WAS MEANT BY

CONSCIENCE, CHARACTER, WILL

BY THE MEN

WHO USED THESE WORDS

Introduction

by Dennis E. Showalter

H ENRY LEWIS STIMSON was born less than three years after Abraham Lincoln's assassination, and survived Franklin Delano Roosevelt's death by five years. He spent his childhood in an introspective United States, a country looking to its own healing from a fratricidal war and looking to its own frontiers to define its future potential. In forty years of public service, Stimson witnessed and assisted America's transformation into a regional power, then a world power, and finally a superpower whose interests and reach spanned the globe. As a teenaged college student vacationing in Colorado, he carried a rifle for self-defense in the Ute Indians' desperate rising of 1889. A half-century later, as Secretary of War, he played a central role in the dropping of atomic bombs on a Japan that also refused to acknowledge defeat.

Stimson was part of another American paradox as well: the patrician culture of birth, affluence, and talent that grew from earlier, more democratic, roots in the post-Civil War's Gilded Age, blossomed with the Progressive movement at the century's turn, and matured into the American Establishment. Stimson was a model and a mentor for a generation. Dean Acheson and John Foster Dulles, John McCloy, Averill Harriman—these were the "Wise Men, "The Best and the Brightest"—who for good and ill kept firm hands on the tiller of the ship of state in the twentieth century's uncharted and dangerous waters. Like Stimson himself,

most were products of a developing elite private educational system as good as any in the world. Stimson's progress from Andover
through Yale and Harvard Law was typical. Most were born to
affluence, using social connections as earlier aristocracies had used
family links: as leverage into profitable business or professional
opportunities. Stimson again was archetypical: a Wall Street corporate lawyer before he was anything else, but able to live well
enough to be unconcerned with pursuing money for its own sake.
Instead, along with many of his counterparts, he sought personal
and civic fulfillment in public service.

While electioneering might remain beyond the pale, the new
patricians no longer regarded government as the purview of
nonentities and spoilsmen. It was Theodore Roosevelt who
"turned" Stimson, appointing him U.S. Attorney for New York in
1903. He established a distinguished record, both as an administrator and a prosecutor of corporate malefactors. Stimson, like
most of his fellows, identified himself as a Republican: the party
of Union, the party of old-stock America, the party of business,
and the party of principled reform. He saw America as well in
global contexts, as a country with a moral mission to be fulfilled
in a context of power relationships. As Secretary of War for
William Howard Taft, Stimson took on an entrenched and interlocking staff bureaucracy that for decades had thwarted all challenges to its position. If he failed to clean out all the underbrush,
he made the task of his successors under Woodrow Wilson significantly easier.

An unsuccessful try for the governorship of New York in 1910
had confirmed Stimson's growing conviction that electoral politics
were not his métier. He returned to his law practice, then served in
World War I, seeing some combat and acquiring the rank of
colonel, by which he was regularly addressed in later years. As the
Republicans became increasingly isolationist, Stimson stood out
for his retention of the internationalism that had been a hallmark
of patrician Progressivism. President Calvin Coolidge called on
him to negotiate (unsuccessfully) a settlement of the ongoing civil

war in Nicaragua. In 1927 he became Governor General of the Philippines, contributing significantly to developing the policies that guaranteed the islands their independence in 1946. In 1930 Stimson became Herbert Hoover's Secretary of State, and played major roles in the naval limitation conference of 1930 and the Manchurian Crisis of 1931-32, occasioned by Japan's invasion of the province. It was in that context that he authored the "Stimson Doctrine," denying the legitimacy of conquest as a means of transferring territory.

The concept, familiar enough now, remained lawyer's talk in the absence of power and the will to use it. In 1932, Democrat Franklin D. Roosevelt was swept into office by the Great Depression. Stimson became by default a Republican elder statesman, regularly pronouncing on international affairs he could no longer influence directly. That changed in the summer of 1940, when Roosevelt asked him to join the Cabinet as Secretary of War. As usual, the President's motives were mixed. Running for an unprecedented third term, he needed the bipartisan legitimacy a man of Stimson's unquestioned probity and equally unquestioned conservatism would bring his candidacy. Stimson's growing moral distaste for the governing systems of Germany, Japan, and Italy was accompanied by a conviction that they represented a direct threat to the United States. He supported both national rearmament and maximum support for a Britain that in 1940 stood alone in arms against the European Axis. Above all, however, Roosevelt wanted Stimson because Stimson had a reputation for doing well the jobs he took on.

He lived up to that reputation in the next five years. Roosevelt to an extent was his own Secretary of War, as he was his own Secretary of State. Stimson nevertheless was anything but a figurehead. Henry Stimson supervised the most complex mobilization in the history of warfare, a forced-draft process transforming the United States from the military level of Portugal and Bulgaria to the world's greatest military power in a matter of months. Even more remarkably, he did it without transforming American society into a counterpart of those it fought.

Part of this success was institutional. Stimson maintained a positive working relationship with General George Marshall, who was himself committed to preserving civilian control of the war effort. He brought into the War Department a team of young and able civilian assistants, themselves skilled at cooperating with their uniformed counterparts. At the core of Stimson's achievement, however, was his intense commitment to a moral vision of the process of history and the use of power. Stimson believed in moral progress—specifically that the world was moving towards methods of political organization that eschewed war as a valid option. At the same time he accepted the necessity of using force against those who deliberately sought to interrupt that progress. The challenge could not be avoided, Stimson told the bishops of the Methodist Church in 1942: "It was either they or we; 'a house divided against itself could not stand.'" U.S. victory was certain because "there is a power in the universe that makes for righteousness, and that power cannot allow . . . a clear case of right and wrong to go the wrong way."

Fulfilling that moral commitment to total war put Stimson at the center of the two greatest moral crises faced by the U.S. in World War II. The first involved the removal of Japanese civilians from the Pacific Coast in the aftermath of Pearl Harbor. Stimson feared relocation "will make a tremendous hole in our constitutional system." Nevertheless the safety of the nation in an emergency outweighed consideration of individual rights. His opinion was a decisive factor in Roosevelt's final decision. Even more significant was Stimson's support for using the atomic bomb against Japan in 1945. Though Stimson was, certainly by present standards, racially insensitive, racism had nothing essential to do with his approach to the use of nuclear weapons to end the war. Nor was he primarily concerned with intimidating the Soviet Union. At the same time, Stimson's advocacy of nuclear use was not merely a pragmatic desire to avoid the higher levels of casualties and destruction he saw as accompanying alternative strategies. Instead the practical imperative of military victory was an aspect of the higher moral necessity of combating evil.

Stimson believed in what he called "the psychology of combat": taking the initiative and applying unceasing pressure on an opponent's will and capacity. That was the quickest and the surest way not only to end conflict but to prevent its recurrence. An enemy defeated morally and physically was unlikely to seek a rematch. In that context the atomic bomb was an appeal to the rational elements of Japan's decision-making process. The appeal was in the form of a warning: surrender or be destroyed—without even the opportunity for a heroic last stand. The choice was stark and harsh. But Japan surrendered four days after the nuclear strike on Hiroshima—a conclusion putting the use of the atomic bomb well within Stimson's moral universe, with its carefully constructed hierarchies of means and ends.

Henry Stimson was neither a philosopher nor an intellectual. An unusually reticent man in an age when reticence was a supreme virtue, he felt no one's pain—not even his own. Reconstructing the moral compass of such a person is a major challenge. Elting E. Morison met and surmounted that challenge in his biography of Stimson, *Turmoil and Tradition*. Published in 1960, it remains a standard work for its presentation of U.S. foreign policy in the first half of the twentieth century, but even more so for its perceptive analyses of Stimson's character, Stimson's career, and the synergy between them. Critical without being debunking, *Turmoil and Tradition* is a model study of history as great events involving great men, and a worthy recipient of the Parkman Prize.

Foreword

THIS BOOK was written at the suggestion of Arthur W. Page and McGeorge Bundy, the trustees of the papers of Henry L. Stimson. The expense of its preparation was defrayed by grants from the Stimson estate and the Carnegie Corporation of New York. That some such book would be written was the wish of Mrs. Stimson and the expectation of her husband. He had lived long enough, he once said, to know how hard it was to give a full and true report of what had happened. For this reason he expected that the impressive account of his active service which he wrote with McGeorge Bundy would be amplified in due time by others working "in the cold light of history."

Since men must do their work in warmer temperatures, cold light may not be a sufficient condition for the study of men's lives. I suppose this is what a friend of mine, a philosopher, had in mind when he said that though he read much history he could not read the accurate historians. This is slippery ground and of course there are limits to the proposition. William Ellery Channing was thinking of these limits, no doubt, when he told my great-grandfather that "biography was for the most part poor." He went on to say that "no man should undertake to write a biography unless he felt that his subject could *bear* to be presented in an unfavorable light."

In this biography I undertake to write the life of a man who acted, for half a century, in the public interest in a revolutionary time. To find the full meaning of such extended action, the complete truth about such changing fortunes would be hard, whatever the means of illumination. The light that falls here on what has happened was filtered through the beam in my own eye. I hope it is sufficient to reveal that the man and his works, in their sum, can bear the closest scrutiny and that such scrutiny is a useful exercise in days still as disturbing and confusing as his own.

E.E.M.

Contents

PART THREE

The Struggle with Darkness, 1933-1950

Illustrations

xvii

Illustrations

PART ONE

The Ideal Conditions

1867-1917

One of the happiest times that I know of in the history of mankind was the thirty years, roughly, from 1880 to 1910. I am not suggesting that there were not a great many things which needed changing; but we intended to change them and had set about doing so. For people like us, moderately comfortable, the conditions were ideal — not too much money, engrossing work to be done, and a sense of purpose and progress in the world.

— ALFRED NORTH WHITEHEAD

I

The Atmospheric Pressures

ZENO IS supposed to have said that anything real was solid, and therefore God was perfectly solid, and virtue and justice were also "of course, quite solid." In the last half of the last century, in certain places and under certain conditions, a child growing up in this country could learn as much for himself.

Some of it was there to learn in the family where even the past — especially perhaps the past — was also solid. From a picture, a corner cabinet, a locket, a piece of carved ivory, a story told and told again it was possible to obtain the full weight of what had happened. This one had quarreled with his neighbors and gone off to sea in the China trade; that one, a remarkable woman, had supported herself and nine children with her own hands at the loom; this other one had taken his musket off the wall; that other one had left the old farm and gone over the Appalachians; this one here had held his ground in the 2nd Massachusetts at Antietam; and this one here stayed home. One or two had lost themselves, as object lessons, in drink or folly. But by and large they had gone forth to lead lives in which there was something accomplished, something done. And one way or another they all came back.

They came back to join those now on the ground — mothers, fathers, sisters, brothers, uncles, aunts, cousins, grandfathers, grandmothers, a sequence of relations in law and in blood. These met together, ordinarily, on Sundays. In the Sabbath meetings there was something less and something more than intimacy, a binding sense of procedure long settled, as it were, in the common law of the family. According to the ordinances, the members talked with each other in atmospheres made heavy with roast lamb, bric-a-brac, dark cloth and well-considered opinions about their own and each other's welfare.

During the week they were off on their lawful occasions. For the women this meant excursions in the "noiseless vales of private life": the writing of long letters, the paying of calls, the nursing of those relations who were poorly, the ordering of the household. In any household, it was probable, there were two or three women on these active duties — a mother, a grandmother in widowhood, a cousin or an aunt disappointed in some past love or otherwise unmarried. It was theirs to pursue "the beautiful errand" and what that errand was everyone understood.

A woman was there "to raise the man who loves her." As one man said, "There is one thing I do believe with all my heart and intellect, and that is that the hearts of gold in the breasts of these pure women are the vital and moving forces in our civilization. You know what men alone descend to." To exert such an influence, Horace Bushnell told his daughter, it was indispensable to have a "mind and heart . . . perfectly pure as that of infancy." And as for temper, she "should never seem to have any."

A German visitor to the domestic scene in the 1880's found that American ladies were, in fact, "*furchtbar fromm.*" But they were also, he discovered, in many ways "*furchtbar frei.*" Along the avenues of art and literature, of the purely beautiful, they were left free to roam by themselves. Undeterred they could look at pictures, memorize poetry, read novels, listen to music, and reach and express opinions all their own.

They were free to do so because the men were busy about other matters. They worked all day, and harder than men in other countries did, in the market, at the profession, in the plant. They worked to make money, and to get on, and because, in the expanding economy, there was so much to do. They also worked because they knew that "him that doth not work must surely die" and because, as a foreigner noticed, work itself was sacred. But in the home they also had a place and meaning. They were the breadwinners, the husbands, the fathers.

Most of all they were fathers. Whoever was not a strong father, as one of them said, was a very weak man. It was not merely that he knew best; in him there was not only "the voice of his personal authority, but Right and Truth incarnate . . . spoke through him." A father like this, Theodore Roosevelt recalled, was the only man he had ever been afraid of, but he was also the "best" and "finest," loved above all others. The reason was clear enough. Any parent of conscience on this side of the water could, like Philip Gosse in England, "truly aver" that his parental obligations had ever been before him "in my choice of housekeeper, in my choice of a school, in my ordering of your holidays . . . in my choice of an occupation for you, in my choice of a residence for you, and in a multitude of lesser things." Out of these reiterated choices in large and lesser things came in time the definitions of things that were of good report — Right, Truth, Duty.

In the household the virtues made more solid by incarnation — Duty, purity, Right, beauty, Truth — were also, as with men and women, made more separate. They could thus be seen to possess differences in specific gravity and character. In the case of purity and beauty it was enough, as with women, to be; with the others it was necessary to do, and, as one of the great preachers later said, to "do good, do good, do good." Influences and images were in the surrounding air to demonstrate the great necessity.

Tireless men came out of the Old Testament at family prayers to make the point in the sweat of their faces. Other grim old men, some of them ancestors, stood out of the nearer past. They had brought to the stern and rock-bound coast a salvation that had to be, in each generation, renewed by works. Then close at hand was Darwin saying the fit survived, and Huxley saying the great end of life was action, and John Fiske saying "struggle . . . discipline," it is "for him that *overcometh* that the crown of life is reserved." The truth was proved by the endeavor. In the proving, mind and body might sometimes show the sign of strain but, as with Bruce and the Spider, mind and body were subject to the commands of the undefeated will. When Duty whispered low, "thou must," the youth replied, "I can." And he could, even in the last extremity, the parables reported. Whether at Flores in the Azores, or at Ratisbon, or upon a burning deck, or before False Sextus, the imperative remained. 'Twas man's perdition to be safe when for the truth he ought to die.

Out of such exercises and demonstrations came atmospheres "cold and keen as the glacial air." As with the stoics, there was "indifference to heat and cold . . . plainness in matters of food and dress . . . complete independence of all bodily comforts." Things that did not matter were shoved aside or pressed down upon. Imposed on experience was a "propriety" which "forbade all impulsive expression." At the back of the mind there was, perhaps, "heaven knows what world of poetry, hidden away, too inaccessible, too intangible, too unreal in fact ever to be brought into the open." Maybe, as a boy said, they all grew up "missing something."

But much that was quite solid remained. There was energy. No impulsive expressions, no searching for an inaccessible world drained off the wells of individual power. There was also the will, the sense of self and of personal accountability which, once wrested from the control of parental authority, remained one's own. And there was the knowledge that by the will the available energy could be organized in support of saving works. At times, no doubt, there were small confusions at the back of the mind between the work that saved and the work that merely gave advantage, between virtue and success. But, in the ordinary circumstance, such was not the case.

"Good is good and bad is bad and that is all there is about it."
Each man, it was said, had "an innate sense of right and wrong."
And right followed "because I was doing it, I was doing my
best." So can no fountain both yield salt water and fresh.

In the glacial air, in the tryings and the testings and the continuous exertions not all could do their best. Some did not have
the right stuff in them. Weak or merely charming, they lacked
the force to push up through the early truths and duties to burdens independently assumed. In some, whatever stuff there
was proved insufficient against the accidental circumstance.
There was a boy in a book who found his strength had been
"sapped," that "something manly had sickened or died in him"
because a friendly widow had left him, in her will, the money
to go to Yale College. And some with different stuff would not
willingly fulfill the mandates. Thus there were cads and poets
and rotters and surprising spirits and black sheep who were cut
off from the accepted communion. But on the whole the fit
survived.

They came out into the world with the Old Testament or
Calvinist or paternal interest in power and administration, with
minds "dry and direct with few decorative flourishes" and with
the conviction, or so it seemed to Santayana, that women, college clubs, business and country were sacred. They came out
too with a "disposition to apply the maxims of religion to the
conduct of life" and high standards of public duty. Steadied by
the stoic virtues, enlightened by the stoic's ecumenical assumption, they were "idealist[s] working on matter," idealists who
shared with Zeno the further conviction that man was the measure of all things.

In the world they entered they found much to do. All about
them were "shocking contrasts between monstrous wealth and
debasing want." There was also a "huge disorder" produced
by "the play of free and planless energies." Things were always
being "dug up, torn up or blown up." Yet in the turmoil was a
sense of life, of exciting new possibilities, of, almost, "a hilarity

of the sky and air [that] must get into people's blood." To diminish the contrasts, to introduce order into the system opened up great opportunities for idealists who wished to work on vital matter.

There was evidence that the work could be done and was worth doing. The whole society had just been saved by those who had been prepared to take great action. Commanders in the war for union and freedom stood everywhere in flesh and marble as testimony that those who overcame achieved the crown of life. And in most of the several parts of the society, men were busy demonstrating a similar point: Eliot, Harper, Gilman, Osler, Kelly, Welsh, Halstead, Root, Choate, Roosevelt, Carnegie, Rockefeller, Frick and J. P. Morgan. By doing it was possible for men, for individuals, to advance learning, improve conditions, and change the face of nature. The energies and intentions of the single man made a public, general difference. After the great commanders there were also heroes.

But it was not merely great contemporaries and local conditions that gave the sanction. As Zeno and Calvin had said, the course of the universe was predetermined and now, as Darwin seemed to say, the course was determined in a favoring direction. Evolutionary movement took place apparently along an inclined plane. The world that moved onward undoubtedly moved upward and, probably, forever. Where one could discern progress, one could infer a great increasing purpose. To the support and extension of this purpose men trained in the ways of right and duty directly contributed by their individual actions.

In this sustaining synthesis there were no more logical inconsistencies than appear in any human system, and these, on ordinary occasions, could be reduced to symmetry by the power, inherited from the forefathers, to affirm and rationalize. Besides, the essential position was supported by what was happening. The goods piled up, the cities grew, the rails stretched from sea to sea, the expanding energies were brought increasingly within the loose order of custom and the law.

Not everyone in all the country believed in the same kind of right, duty, truth and progress; not all believed the same things were sacred. Some believed in different things and some in none at all. But in spite of the huge terrain and the infinite variety of creed, origin and condition there seemed to some observers to be a common temper, an "ideal essence" of the national character. It may have been no more than a tone set by those who, for reasons political, social or financial, believed they spoke as men having authority. These, it was said, were the "comfortable times," the ideal conditions when, in spite of huge disorders and monstrous contrasts, it was given to men to have the understanding and power to change things that needed changing. Through decades brown, gray or mauve the world did seem to move, in some part propelled by divine inertia, in some part pushed by men themselves, onward and upward in a steady progress.

With human energies and desires confined within the solid virtues, all things seemed possible. And yet, "sometimes, standing in the midst of a great American city, and watching the throngs of eager figures streaming hither and thither . . . knowing that before long a hundred millions of men will be living between ocean and ocean under this one government — a government which their own hands have made, and which they feel to be the work of their own hands," Lord Bryce was "startled by the thought of what might befall this huge yet delicate fabric . . . [if] all these men ceased to believe that there was any power above them, any future before them, anything in heaven or earth but what their senses told them of; suppose that their consciousness of individual force and responsibility . . . were further weakened by the feeling that their swiftly fleeting life was rounded by a perpetual sleep. . . . Would [then] the moral code stand unshaken, and with it the reverence for law, the sense of duty towards the community, and even towards the generations yet to come?"

2

The Small Universe

THERE WERE various ways of looking at it — as a universe bounded on all sides by connecting Stimsons, as a clearinghouse, or, in the words of a young cousin, as a game sanctuary laid off on East 34th Street, New York City. The house where Grandpa and Grandma lived possessed some of the attributes of all three. Thither at frequent intervals the "fifty uncles, aunts and cousins" came to call and to drink tea. Over tea they would bring the reports of their own doings up to date, read the family mail, and exchange information about the Stimsons — those who were absent, who were heavy-laden, who had made their mark, who had received a surprising settlement, who were beginning to feel the heat of the day, who had purchased an unbecoming hat, who were great with child, who were poorly, or who were brokenhearted.

On Sundays and holidays when "the regular family circle" met together the home became a clearinghouse for decisions on policy and administration. In that regular circle were the sons and daughters of Grandpa and Grandma — Henry the minister, Lewis the doctor, Fred the lawyer, Kitty, Mary and Julia. Wives of sons, husbands of daughters, children and grandchildren were also present — more seen, on the whole, than heard and more heard than listened to. There was also son John who had gone off to investigate the world of art, indeed to paint. Save in the family talk he appeared rarely during the Sabbath deliberations. These deliberations dealt ordinarily with family matters — the large and continuous, such as whether to sell the 34th Street house, or the current uses to which Grandma's trust fund should be put; the smaller or nonrecurring, such as the amount of board to be paid by Lewis to his mother for his two children, or the deposition of the suit pressed upon a sister by "the looney [who] talks too damn much."

The canvass of these matters before the taking of decision was thorough and judicious. It was also, at times, painful. After Christmas dinner "there were always tears; somebody's feelings would be hurt by something." But the tears were temporary; they did not serve to dissolve the invisible cords of devotion, mutual dependence and doctrine which held the members of this family securely to one another. Then too the decisions which proceeded from the thorough canvass of the evidence were understood to be taken in the best interest of the individuals concerned, and of the whole, and therefore were understood to be not only sensible but just. These decisions were in their final form, ordinarily, the work of Henry, Lewis and Fred acting, after consultation, together. They brought to bear upon problems, it was said, "the full weight of their collective masculinity" and, in sentences beginning "We feel," announced the manner in which the current domestic issues had been resolved.

If the home was something of a self-contained universe and something of a clearinghouse it was also something of a sanctuary. A Stimson in pain or trouble could always find a shelter within the walls. There lived the daughters before they were married, or after prospects of betrothal had been blasted, or, for suitable intervals, after a marriage to a husband who had turned out to be something less than a good provider. There also lived the sons on those occasions when their wives were ill or when they were looking for new homes for themselves. To this household also, whether on 34th Street or, as later, at West 52nd Street, came at times the children of the sons and daughters in days or weeks of domestic crisis. This household, effectively organized by the clear, firm intelligence of Grandma assisted by her maiden daughter Mary, was also, in some sort, a sanctuary for Grandpa, whose name was Henry Clark Stimson. In these days, his spirit blighted by chronic ill health and the recollection of past disappointments, he brought atmospheres of somberness, almost of gloom, to the hearth and table at 34th Street. But by his achievements in time past he had given the members of his family the situation they now enjoyed.

He had been the first Stimson in several generations to leave the small town of Windham, New York, to seek his fortune in the city. Arriving first in Paterson, New Jersey, he set to work just before the Civil War in a locomotive shop and then, believing that more profit could be found in financing railroads than in constructing engines, he transferred his energies to the lower end of Manhattan. Fortified at first by the small income from the trust fund inherited by his wife Catherine Atterbury, whom he had met in Paterson, he soon rose by his own talents to prominence in the hectic financial environment produced by the Civil War. By 1867 he was the senior partner in Henry C. Stimson and Son of 8 Wall Street, remembered years afterwards as "one of the market's masterful firms." Vanderbilt, it was said, chose him for "super confidential maneuvers." Henry Keep, Jay Gould and the two Jeromes did business with the firm. And Stimson himself lingered long in the memory of Wall Street as the architect of "one classic" market operation — the Prairie du Chien corner. On a Monday in one November, Prairie Dog had opened at 65 and, by Tuesday afternoon, it closed at 225. Throughout that day, "with a face as if cut out of yellow sandstone," "taller and taller, taciturner and yet more taciturn, Henry C. Stimson stood himself on the stock exchange floor" directing and controlling events.

He had indeed a public style — tall, impassive, commanding, utterly contained. It was known that he would dismiss from his presence and his business those who "spoke loosely" or chose "carelessly to treat him a bit too pompously." It was known also that each day he sent a boy around to Delmonico's "for a special brand of cigars which in lavish hospitality he insisted on having office callers share." He was by 1870, with his skill in operations undecorated by any flourish, his home on 34th Street, his reputation for probity and his impressive financial connections, one of "the most respected men in the market."

But to be respected in those days was not enough. Life in an economy where stocks opened at 25 and close at 163, where the firm was in the red by $30,000 at the close of business Wednesday and returned to the black by $7000 on Thursday, was not as secure and satisfying as a face carved out of yellow sandstone appeared to make it. A few of course could achieve a somber distinction as authors of the Erie Chapter, a very few could acquire fame and fortune by putting all the pieces of the New York Central together. But the majority, too respectable or too unimaginative, could only imitate some of the larger gestures by manipulating small, unprofitable railroads like Prairie Dog. They lived precariously at a time when panic "like thunder in a clear sky" could sweep the exchange.

Henry C. Stimson, raised amid simplicities, tutored by his Presbyterian forebears in the stern theory that success was the product of thrift, honesty and decent, hard labor, was not for this life. He "damned speculation and frequently said he wanted to get out." But he had also acquired the Presbyterian interest and pride in election. It was not easy to get out after he had staked his sense of self in the seeking of a larger fortune than could be obtained in Windham, New York.

"But the nature of the business requires that the stocks we are carrying for other parties should be sold to raise money to keep our credit good. . . . At present our shorts have all advanced while our longs have fallen, compounding the difficulties they were to counteract." Days like this and other days when the Commodore sent round a check for $50,000 to tide things over provided for a man like Henry C. Stimson a life of continuous racking strain.

This sense of strain, grimly concealed from his associates, was more fully communicated to those at home. He would brood about selling the 34th Street house, he endured chronic symptoms of insomnia, gastritis and "articula mortis"; he took himself out of the family circle into remote, disturbed self-communions. At table he would recount his great dreams of frustration — how a truss of hay had pinned him helpless to the floor, how he had broken his timepiece and could persuade no watchmaker to repair it. From all these immediate difficulties he was rescued, in a way, by the panic of 1873. Losing most of his money, he withdrew from active participation in the market and retired on his small savings and the proceeds of his wife's modest trust fund.

In the family circle for the next twenty years he remained a kind of force. As the only man in the house, ministered to by his wife and whatever daughters were available, he introduced the sustained drama of semi-invalidism with its special arrangements and its stoic silences. These silences covered, at times insufficiently, the evidence of physical discomfort and of the anguish caused by the incomplete fulfillment of ambition and powers. But if in his case what was called the Stimson reserve could not cover up anxiety and frustration, so also it could not repress persistent impulses of sweetness and generosity. In these declining years there was, both in his situation and in his person, something that roused feelings at once of pathos and respect. When his little grandson Henry Lewis Stimson came to live in the house on 34th Street in the year 1876, he soon discovered that Grandpa was the member of the family with whom he had most in common. Years later he looked back on this grandfather as the one in the whole Stimson family who understood him best.

The small boy of eight, with his sister of six, lived in the house for the better part of five years. In that time they came, inevitably, to know almost everything there was to know about the universe of connecting Stimsons. They listened to the debates about where they would be taken for the summer, they heard about the cousin with the abscess on her breast, and they discovered that Uncle John was wasting his substance with his brushes and oils. On Sunday afternoons they looked on while the Stimson men made their calculations and reached their masterful decisions. But the present of this universe was no more exposed to them than was its past. Stimsons, they discovered, had been in this country a long time — since the seventeenth century — and had worked their way west from the coastal towns of Massachusetts to upper New York State.

How the family seat at Windham had been selected became a thrice-told anecdote. A George Stimson had left his family in Albany sometime in 1790 to search, with his small son named Henry, for a new place to settle. In the wilderness of the Catskills he had found a likely spot. Leaving young Henry, like some Casabianca, to keep watch and ward alone until he returned with the family, George set out for Albany. Weeks later the father came back with his wife and other children to find Henry, obedient to the parent's command, guarding the spot.

At this new settlement of Windham the family had established its permanent base. Members from the time they arrived in this country had set out to lead hard, simple and very long lives. They had fought in King Philip's War, the French and Indian War, the Revolution, and the Civil War. They had contributed regularly to the ministry of the Presbyterian and Congregational churches. On the distaff side the achievements had been, perhaps, more worldly and of greater import. There was, the children heard, Elias Boudinot on their grandmother's side who had been an acting Secretary of Foreign Affairs during the Confederation, and a great-grandmother who knew Washington and Lafayette.

Beyond this record of sound, useful accomplishment on both sides the children heard much about the kind of men and women who had wrought these deeds. There was, for instance, a Stimson who had "as lieve hear a parcel of pigs squeal" as go to a concert; there was another who left his home in Massachusetts "vowing he would not live where justice could not be done him"; there was a third in whom no excitement could "mar the poise of his good sense." In addition to these individual responses or aptitudes, there appeared to be also a dominant characteristic held in common from generation to generation — what was called "a constitutional reserve." Grandma had noticed it in her husband when he fretted that his children "could not make a companion of him." She had watched it descend to her own children — a kind of aloofness, a withdrawal from easy, natural communication with those about them. It seemed worse when Stimsons were dealing with those of their own age and situation than with those younger or older, above or below them. Whatever it was, wherever it came from, as anyone who lived much with Stimsons knew, it was there.

The two children, Henry and Candace, who in 1876 came into the household that was the repository of such information, entered, it was said, as "orphans." This, as far as the facts of the matter were concerned, was not quite true. But they had come to the home on 34th Street after a circuitous and painful journey. They were brought there as a result of a decision taken by their father. This father, Lewis Atterbury Stimson the Doctor, had himself just finished a circuitous and painful journey, in the course of which he had demonstrated unusual qualities of independence and fortitude.

He was indeed an unusual man, "of powerful frame, [with] a superb head, fine vigorous features and an expression in which there [was] no guile." Behind this handsome face there was a powerful intelligence, direct and simple in its operations. These physical and mental capacities were supported, it was said, by a "rugged, militant character." He appeared to have within him the qualities needed to follow with success his mother's advice to him when he was an undergraduate at Yale. In the moral life as in the physical, she had told him, men are "either fuller than is necessary for themselves of electricity or have less than they should." Those with an excess of current could exercise a terrific influence on those about them. "Oh my precious boy," she counseled, "be *sure* you are not the *negative* kind . . . but strive to be a *leader* a *positive character* for good."

The petition was already in early youth in some part answered. The young man had done well at Yale; he had served with distinction during the Civil War in the Army of the James, and as his father's partner in the firm of Henry C. Stimson and Son he had, with barely a dissenting voice ("112 white balls to 7 black"), been elected to a seat on the exchange. In the successful dispatch of these various businesses he had revealed something beyond intellectual clarity and rugged character. To the conduct of the affairs of men he appeared to bring also a certain detachment, a kind of disinterested, even chilling calculation. He had warned his older brother that a minister must think of property as well as person in seeking a happy marriage. He proposed that a younger brother should be put out on his own for a time. "It will toughen him. It will be well for him to learn early in life of how little value one's friends are, & how easy it is to break old ties." At another time he concluded it was wise "to learn to think evil of everyone and everything, and you will be more on a par with the rest of the world." Once at a reception for Ulysses S. Grant he fell out of the line and paused within five feet of the General just to watch the hero's face for some minutes "moving like a piece of machinery" beneath hair that "lies on his forehead like a wig." Then he stepped up, "more to feel of his flipper than for anything else."

Time did not diminish, rather it increased this tendency toward disengagement from human enthusiasms and excitements. When, much later, he reported in a beautifully concise book the events of a cruise he had taken in his small boat the *Fleur-de-Lys* he described in detail the navigational problems and the nature of the coastal terrain, but he made no single mention of the individual people who had sailed with him for three months.

Once, at least, he saw something to startle him out of his controlled reserve. At a picnic in Trenton in October 1865 he looked upon a girl who took "the bird off the bush and no mistake." She sings, he asserted, "like a nightingale, is perfectly self-composed, sensible and as Dickens says, 'a fine woman, sir, with none of your by God nonsense about her.'" Two weeks on shipboard or anywhere else with her would make him "perfectly happy or wretchedly heartbroken." Her name was Candace Wheeler and she was about to depart with her parents for a year in Europe.

Through the ensuing winter months Lewis Stimson discovered he could not rid himself of the memory produced by his single glimpse of this girl. In the spring he decided in his incisive way to go forth in direct pursuit of this source of perfect happiness. He went to Venice and found her standing alone at one of the canal landings, waiting for a Prussian officer who had gone off in search of a gondola. From that time forward he scarcely left her side until, in the fall, in November 1866, they were married at the American Embassy in Paris.

Candace Wheeler, if not as perfectly composed as her husband on his original inspection believed, was an arresting young woman. Others beside Lewis Stimson had been struck by their first sight of her. A delighted Italian had, on meeting her, murmured, *"Bella, per Bacchus,"* while Charlotte Cushman, watching her ride across the Pincio, had stopped her with a word of admiration for her horsemanship and for herself. Thus she had flashed across the vision of many observers, a vivid, urgent little figure fully engaged in a variety of life's doings. She had been brought up in a family which had "a feeling for the unusual idea," for works of speculation and the imagination. Into her mother's and father's house at one time or another came almost everybody who was anybody in the world of art and literature — Booth, Irving, Stockton, Bierstadt, Mrs. Stone, Gilder, Whitman, Oscar Wilde, Herkomer, Mark Twain, Lily Langtry — the list is endless. These parents were forever doing rather remarkable things on the spur of the moment: there was a pageant put together for the diversion of the wild animals that played on a sun-struck slope in the Catskills, and there was a colony — as though the Pre-Raphaelites had come to Brook Farm — precariously maintained for friends. Mrs. Wheeler painted, wrote books, and organized the Associated Artists and Woman's Exchange. Mr. Wheeler worked, at intervals, in his mercantile business and read Shakespeare, Tasso, Goethe and Dante. In between times they traveled endlessly.

Under such rich and varied conditions the daughter Candace developed distinctive talents of her own. She could, as her husband had noted, sing; she could also paint and, from a mind well stored with the findings of constant reading and travel, converse in lively fashion upon a hundred topics. She was passionate in all her endeavors and piquant in her assessment of the works of others and of herself. George Eliot had once asked her so many questions, she reported, that she felt "as limp as a turned out glove"; a friend was found to be taking her broken engagement "like a true Christian, although a very high church one"; her German teacher taught her, to her delight, that only words of "truly, purely German" origin were good strong words — all others were "weak, inexpressive, flat, stale and unprofitable."

This was a spirit out of a different universe from that inhabited by Lewis Stimson; he was and remained utterly captivated. And to him she gave all the love that flowed so unconstrainedly from her heart. Behind the composure, the imperious cast of mind and manners, she discovered — indeed she had touched off — those feelings that made him "the very best husband I ever saw." Shortly, she found, she had need of such a husband.

They came back to New York City after their marriage and remained there four years. In this time their children were born; Henry, with "a chest like a barrel," arrived on September 21, 1867, and the daughter Candace followed two years later. The two babies were the major — almost the only — blessings of this period. Lewis, in his father's firm, found increasingly that he was repelled by the world of finance. The random, precarious state of the market in those days was a source of constant anxiety for one thing. And for another he soon reached the conclusion that "Wall St. men have less knowledge of the world and of human nature than any other class of persons." He came, in time, to believe he would "live on roots and berries if that would save me from hearing a quotation." To these professional dissatisfactions were added soon domestic worries. Candace, not long after Henry's birth, began to be troubled by the onset of a strange disease. In the beginning there were spasmodic attacks when languor and debility would submerge her bright spirits for days at a time. No treatment seemed to abate the symptoms or modify the progressing course of the disturbing malady.

The husband had never been a man to remain inert while difficulties accumulated around him. In the summer of 1871 he decided to act, to drop his life in New York and seek new fortunes in Europe. There, in surroundings she loved, his wife might return to health and he might find in the study of medicine not only a way to assist her, but a new way of life for himself. So at twenty-seven, after six years in the market, he sold his seat on the Exchange and with the proceeds as his only means of support set out for Germany.

For the better part of three years the family moved through Europe — from Berlin to Zurich to Paris. They lived ordinarily in small hotels. In Switzerland Lewis Stimson pursued his preclinical studies before going in 1872 for a surgical internship to Paris. In France he also worked, for a year, with Pasteur. He learned rapidly and, to his delight, discovered in himself not only skill but satisfaction in the work of surgery. But outside the hospital his days were clouded by the rising anxiety he felt about his wife's condition.

They managed a few excursions into the sunlight of the Impressionists. Once or twice they went together to one of the

French beaches, and sat under colored umbrellas, and ate cold chicken and drank a white wine. On a memorable day they rolled out to St. Cloud in two carriages with the children. Candace worked at her sketches, her daughter picked little bouquets of "lovely flowers" and the small boy ran about after butterflies the whole bright afternoon.

Such occasions were rare. Ordinarily the family remained in the hotel rooms where the young mother struggled against the immense weariness that invaded what she called her "poor old weak body." Increasingly sudden, immobilizing attacks followed upon such simple efforts as a tea with friends or the taking of a bath. At such times she lay on a sofa watching her children entertain themselves and each other. Henry would lie all day long, if undisturbed, endlessly drawing pictures of elephants, locomotives and soldiers. In these pictures the watching mother could discover a firm organization of the composing elements, a clear line, and above all a sense of power and of motion. He was, on the whole, a sober little boy, sallow, weak-limbed, hating physical exercise above all things. Also he seemed "a lazy little chap about things he does not fancy"; thwarted, or acting under orders, he took refuge in great shaking rages. But left to his own devices he revealed an "intense purpose in pursuing the things that attracted his one track mind." What attracted him most — "all day long" if permitted — was the organization in pictures of that internal world of elephants, engines and soldiers. Looking down on him, so sober and close-mouthed, his mother thought, "How many times I have failed to do the *best* by him." With the child Candace it was different. She was "a little white witch" who was into everything, beguiling her older brother and his parents with her "little speeches and her winning ways." She flew, like her mother before her, from sight to sight and place to place with a vibrant joy. From the very beginning to the very end she could beguile her older brother out of any solemnity.

These European days drew to a close in 1873. Lewis Stimson

came home to take his degree, after a year of study, at the Bellevue Medical College, and then to begin, at the Presbyterian Hospital, the practice of surgery. His wife on her return found a less satisfying situation awaiting her. She felt, to begin with, the constrictions of family ties. "We were," she confided to a relative, "so American and Presbyterian that we did not go to church at all on Christmas day, but I think it is a mistake . . ." A service and a sermon gave "a deeper meaning" to the day than "the family parties could." Then too she found that "the whirling, crushing American life just kills me, and I feel weak and tired all the time . . ."

Under such conditions the chronic disease, which was probably diabetes, took a stronger hold upon her. She moved through months of slow decline, pitifully and steadily, out of the daily concerns and then, finally, on one June day, out of life itself. Her death blasted the spirit of her husband. He could think apparently of no way out but to cut himself off from all previous recollections — from all those feelings and desires stirred up so short a time ago when he had first looked at this girl and knew it was in her power to make him perfectly happy or wretchedly heartbroken. As with everything else he was thorough about it. He sold his house, broke up his household, took a room to sleep in and buried himself like a monk in "years of constant grinding work" at his calling.

The children — Henry was eight, Candace, six — were taken in at their grandfather's house where, on Sundays, their father came to see them and the others in his family. The children came, in a sense, as the cousin had said, like orphans. But, it is possible, that in the manner of their coming there was something that put them in a plight even more unhappy. In later years, after the boy Henry had grown up, he used, from time to time, to talk with a man who knew him well for forty years, about his youth. At such times it appeared that he labored under an ill-defined impression that his father in some strange way held him accountable for the death of his mother.

The two children lived with Grandma and Grandpa for the next five years. They became the special charge of Aunt Minnie, and for this they could thank such lucky stars as might be found in their firmament. A young, handsome woman, thwarted twice, once providentially and once tragically, in her search for love and a home of her own, she took Henry and Candace under her wing. She tried with impressive fidelity to continue for the children the wishes, spirit and memory of the dead mother as she understood them. Never once did she suggest that she was more than a surrogate. Equally, and perhaps more important, she gave her two charges her whole heart. As her oldest brother Henry said, "She really mothered" them and gave them a care their father "felt inadequate for."

Under her guidance they grew up in a New York where, as the boy Henry later remembered, there were "no recreation grounds, no outdoor place, no grassy meadows" without signs marked "No Trespassing." They also went to school — small private institutions in the neighborhood until Henry was old enough to go to the Sanver School of Languages in Times Square. There, for two years, he studied Greek and Latin with teachers who used to converse with pupils in the antique tongues. It was an experience which he remembered in old age as "beautiful," but also as a failure in the educational sense. Aunt Minnie reached the same conclusion at the time. She talked it over with Aunt Kitty and between them they decided to send Henry, just thirteen, to a school run by a clergyman who was said to have done great things for a cousin. Accordingly, the boy started work in the new classes. But then the word went round the regular family circle that the cousin, after leaving the clergyman's classes, was in trouble at Yale, had in fact "flunked his examinations." Therefore Dr. Stimson came down to his father's house and "overruled everything."

"I am going," he said, "to take him to Andover." It was late in the day for such decisions; Andover had been three weeks in session. But the arrangement was made — and so, not long after his thirteenth birthday, "this little New York City boy, with his narrow shoulders and slender build" entered an entirely new world almost entirely on his own.[1]

[1] In the chapters dealing with Stimson's early life it has been thought sufficient to give a list of principal sources at the end of each chapter. The material for this chapter was drawn primarily from the Stimson Papers described in some detail in the bibliographical note. Of particular use here was an account of his youth dictated in retirement, and a bundle of letters written by members of his family between 1860 and 1890. Most valuable for the present purpose were letters written by Lewis A. Stimson and Candace W. Stimson to various relatives in New York. Many of the quotations in this chapter were taken from the correspondence of these two people. Other information was obtained in conversation with various members of the Stimson family. Of the published works consulted, the following were the most helpful: F. A. Virkus and A. N. Marquis, *The Abridged Compendium of American Genealogy* (Chicago, 1925); Henry Bond, *Genealogies of the Families and Descendants of the Early Settlers of Watertown, Massachusetts* (Boston, 1855); *Bulletin of Yale University, Obituary Record of Yale Graduates, 1917-1918* (New Haven, 1919); *Annals of Medical History*, New Series, Vol. III, No. 1 (New York, 1931); Henry Clews, *Fifty Years in Wall Street* (New York, 1908); *Wall Street Journal*, February 11, 1929; *Civil War Memories of Lewis A. Stimson* (New York, 1918); Candace Wheeler, *Yesterdays in a Busy Life* (New York, 1918); Henry L. Stimson and McGeorge Bundy, *On Active Service in Peace and War* (New York, 1947), hereafter referred to as *Active Service*.

3

Schooling

T HE FOUNDERS had built Phillips Academy at Andover as a school for boys "more especially to learn them the great end and real business of living." In 1880 the Academy was not a place where young men could easily acquire such learning. Only four years earlier the Principal, C. F. P. Bancroft, had told the Trustees that the institution stood in instant need of their efforts and their prayers. The physical plant was inadequate; the faculty of eight included few minds of distinction; the student body, deriving in large part from the Commonwealth, was disturbingly provincial. What confronted the Principal was not a problem of life or death but, in his mind, something much worse — the possibility of a school of the second class. By 1883, the year Stimson graduated, it was clear that this fate had been avoided. The unremitting exertions of Mr. Bancroft, "crowned by a marked blessing from above," had brought the Academy out of its precarious position. In that year the boys who took the Yale examinations had elicited "remarkable commendation and praise" from the professors in New Haven, while the report from "Harvard speaks less disparagingly of our students."

When Henry Stimson arrived in October 1880, the Academy was in the middle of this changing situation which, in the end, produced what the Principal desired, "a national institution" of the first class. It was, in fact, a rather turbulent society the youngest member of the student body entered. Changes and additions in the instructing staff had produced a better faculty, but one without the *esprit* that comes with time and success. The students worked hard enough at their books — many were earning their own tuition — but outside the classroom they turned to less constructive endeavors. There were, in Stimson's time, many crude practical jokes, works of vandalism and, on one or two occasions, impressive acts of crime. Only in the curriculum was the sense of turbulence subdued. Mathematics and the classics were still the two great piers on which the education rested. Amid the austerities of etymology, Greek composition, Xenophon, higher algebra, Latin grammar and trigonometry, small place was found for the flourishes of English literature and the political history of the United States. Over the two principal fields two imposing figures presided — Matthew Scoby Mc-Curdy in mathematics and Edwin Austin Coy in Greek. It was with Mr. Coy, who "seldom unbent, but seemed the very embodiment of unyielding authority," that Stimson went to live when he entered the Academy.

One of the advantages of this arrangement he explained to Aunt Minnie in his first letter home. It meant he did not "have to associate with any bad fellows," and there was a "pretty fair sprinkling of sweaty boys here" — but also "some very nice ones." The fact was he had not been able in the first week to make "any strong friendships yet," but from his point of vantage he was busy "picking out the good boys from the bad." For the rest he was, as Aunt Minnie had asked him to do, praying "every night to God for help the next day" and studying four hours a day "by the watch."

Thus it continued for the first year. He was never once homesick, but he had to work very hard to repair the damages of his earlier education and to keep up with the class. He discovered he could not work well at night — late hours "clouded the mind and upset the stomache" — so he formed the habit of a lifetime by going to bed early and arising before his fellows.

These measures served, and he could feel as the year closed that he had learned to stay on top of his job. He hoped his father would come down to take him home. "If he don't — well, I shan't like it, the idea of his not being able to come up here at all in my first year at school."

His father did not come that first year, nor in the years that followed. He did, however, send his son occasional letters. He told him to take care of his body and advised him "to do nothing of which you are ashamed, and show no shame on account of any honest thing you do." He trusted that such new interests as his son acquired would be accepted "without neglect of the many lesser interests and duties that lie close at hand." He hoped that his son would always be successful and "especially that you will always try to deserve success for success without deserving may easily prove a calamity." He was also glad to hear that his son thought of his mother, "though of course you can remember little in detail about her."

Once the problem of the classroom had been solved by hard work, Henry began in the following two years to expand his horizons. He discovered for the first time the exhilaration of the outdoors, the skating in winter, the tramping and hunting in the woods, the vigorous conflicts of football. He also joined a debating society and a prayer meeting of thirty or forty boys. But his activities remained, on the whole, solitary. In his senior year when he and some classmates walked out in the woods to look for ducks, he reflected that it was one of the very few times in his whole school experience that he went anywhere with boys. But on his own he did some rather remarkable things. The bobsled he built and steered himself was "the fastest bobsled ever on Phillips Hill." He also designed and constructed first a telegraph system and then an electromagnetic telephone by which he sent messages, for a fee, between the dormitories.

The one place he found himself at home with his fellows was in the communion of the prayer meeting. The petitions the boys delivered were better, more simple and earnest, "than those of any minister I ever heard." He found himself constantly surprised by those who "confessed Christ" — for "how different are conceptions from reality." And he found great comfort in the sessions he attended every Wednesday for three years. Without those meetings "each fellow would have to fight more by himself, with them we go like a solid phalanx against the enemy."

And yet despite these associations and accomplishments, despite the fact he was the salutatorian at graduation, he was, as he cast up his three-year accounts, dissatisfied. "The more I notice my position here," he wrote Aunt Minnie, "the more I feel I do not fully share life with my class." Therefore he wished to defer his entry into Yale for a year. He did not wish to be looked down on in New Haven as "a sort of a kid"; he wanted to go to college like a fellow worth something, like one who could hold up his head with anybody. "When you tell papa this," he warned Aunt Minnie, "he will say 'Oh someone has been stuffing him.'" But this was not so; the decision, he assured his aunt, was entirely his own.

And he had his way. That summer he went with his father and Uncle Fred to France, where, to his dismay, he saw men working on a bridge and children playing games just as if there were no such thing as the Sabbath. After a month of travel he returned to New York for six months of tutoring and then returned for the final three months of the academic year at Andover as a special student. To his immense satisfaction he discovered that "boys recognize you have grown a couple of inches and treat you accordingly." He was now ready, he believed, in the year 1884, just turned seventeen, to enter the larger world of Yale College.

As he set out for New Haven he was a boy in knickerbockers who weighed 120 pounds. His spindly frame gave off an impression of frailty, an impression reinforced by the look in the thin face. There was something querulous, too finely drawn, wistful about the countenance. He seemed in fact like what he was — one of the youngest, smallest men in his class.

The college to which he went was one of the best in the country and provided much the same kind of education to be found in the other good institutions. For two years, courses predominantly in mathematics, Latin and Greek were required; in the last two years choices were permitted amid groups of subjects in such fields as modern languages, literature, history, political and natural sciences. Neither at the time nor in later years did Stimson find this course of study particularly rewarding. As a freshman and sophomore he repeated much of the work that had been prescribed at Andover, while in his final two years among a variety of subjects he found only the reading in English literature at all stimulating.

What was true for Stimson was true also for almost all undergraduates. The Yale of that day, like most American institutions of learning at the time, was not an exciting intellectual community. There were remarkable men on the faculty — Dana, Harper, W. G. Sumner — but apparently save in individual cases they did not signify with the majority of students. Professors achieved renown by the reiteration of remarks such as "Those who expectorate need not expect to rate in class." In the *Catalogue*, a course required of all seniors, described as "an essential element" of any education, was also further described as "a somewhat thorough course." It was a time when, as happened in Stimson's sophomore year, the captain of the football team, intent on beating Princeton for the first time in a long interval, could successfully appeal to the faculty for a rearrangement of the academic schedule "to permit more time for practice."

At Yale in these years there appears to have been, as a man who married one of Stimson's cousins later said, "a system of idealism out of which the intellectual structure has evaporated." This may well have been true, but it is not to say that students at New Haven did not learn anything in four years or that they did not emerge, in many instances, profoundly changed by what they had learned. But the instruction was carried on, in large part, outside academic halls and conducted rather more by the students than by the faculty. This education was the product of such varied agencies as "the democracy of the class organization," the eating clubs, Flag Day, "The Lit," the senior societies, the Junior Ex, the campus, which was "the center for seven days a week," the football team, Tap Day, "the cohesive spirit of the class" and the concept of Yale.

What came out of this educational process more often than not was what Santayana called "the Yale man." "Here is sound, healthy principle, but no over-scrupulousness, love of life, trust in success, a ready jocoseness, a democratic amiability and a radiant conviction that there is nothing better than one's self. It is a boyish type of character. But the boyish ideal is a healthy one . . ."

In the class that embarked on this course of instruction in 1884 there were some who bore illustrious names when they arrived — Morison R. Waite, the son of the Chief Justice; W. H. Seward, the grandson of the Secretary of State. There were others who later achieved names for themselves — A. A. Stagg, the football coach, and Irving Fisher, who became not only one of Stimson's best friends, but also one of the few genuinely imaginative, if erratic, American intelligences at work in the field of economics. With these and others like his roommate Sydney Roby, Stimson did all the things undergraduates always do. He engaged occasionally in "college pranks," went off to New York for week ends, and lay with his friends under the elms to investigate the long, long thoughts of youth. In these informal, casual, natural exchanges he demonstrated that at Andover he had learned how to take care of himself. But his classmates soon found that he was not gregarious, that he did not move unguarded through the spontaneous combustions of undergraduate life. One friend remembered that he hated to be touched, disliked any "outlet stronger than a warm handclasp." Another recalled that he fought "shy of expressed emotions," though he possessed stormy feelings "bottled up by a reserve that kept him from going all out for the friendships formed at Yale."

Within the more carefully regulated, institutional forms of undergraduate life Stimson moved with greater ease and, for four years, with growing success. As a freshman he pitted his 120 pounds against the line of the university team until he was persuaded to shift his energies to rowing. His persistence in this sport won him, as a junior, a place on the class crew. For most of the four years he worked in a mission in the "worst quarter of town" among "regular toughs." This proved "a big responsibility" which fell "pretty much on my hands," but it was always a rewarding experience. The class of men were "interesting" and there were satisfactions in getting on the trail of derelicts who, after suitable attentions, "stopped drinking" or "turned over a new leaf entirely."

Other opportunities were offered by the educational process in which he found himself — competitions, elections, prize contests by which a man could more exactly measure his success in undergraduate life. There was the Junior Exhibition in which contestants composed and declaimed their own speeches. For weeks he burned the midnight oil preparing a piece which opened, to his roommate's infinite delight, with the words, "When men sang, they sang the songs of Béranger." Leaving no stone unturned in search of success he went up to Andover to be coached in his gestures by Mr. Churchill who was believed to have put the finishing touches on Matthew Arnold's delivery. The well-laid foundations served their purpose; he won "hands down."

In the following year he obtained the De Forest Prize for his analysis of Sir Henry Vane who was not to be found in the stronghold of Dunbar but afar off in Parliament because he lacked "sturdy manhood." Yet for this he atoned at his execution where "all his natural timidity had been conquered in his inflexible will."

In only one of these competitions did he fail. "The Lit" was one of the most impressive undergraduate ventures. Students obtained membership by writing a number of articles for its pages before submitting themselves to a general election by their fellows in the college. Early in his career he began submitting his contributions — pieces on French literature, a critique of Charlotte Brontë, a study of Mazzini who "erred in not being able to distinguish fully the ideal from the practical." In the winter of his junior year the elections took place — "forty-eight hours [of] agony" during which every point except a man's literary abilities seemed to be discussed. The "long and the short of it" was, he lost. He had not realized "what a tremendous power a little wire pulling is in a popular election, and I had no idea that anyone disliked me enough to spend his time trying to injure me thus." In the days after the election "about a dozen eyes were watching every step, every expression" and he "thought of leaving town." But he did not. Instead — as he wrote Aunt Minnie — he went "around college with a cast iron smile and forced gaiety that would make your heart ache if you saw it." The pain of rejection, thus concealed, remained. Fifty years later he wrote the "Little Lady in Brown" — "The Lit" — that in the depths of his heart he could "still feel the pang of that winter day when you rejected my suit." In the half century "while I have been growing old, you have remained ever young. You have been a very fortunate little lady, my love."

At the moment of defeat, however, his disappointment simply spurred him onward to other achievements — the De Forest Prize and high standing in the class, where "Thank Heaven no chumps can cheat me out. . . ." Taken altogether his success in these undergraduate competitions had been great. But in the end, as he wrote Aunt Minnie, he was not sure whether the effort was worth it. "The incentive is an unnatural one; something beyond the normal desire to do good work for good work's sake . . . still I suppose I shouldn't be contented, and

I'm mighty sure my father would not, unless I was trying some sort of foolishness like this."

These unceasing endeavors, whatever view he might take of them, were seen in favorable perspective by other members of the student body. This was brought home to him when at the end of his junior year he was taken into a senior society. The senior societies, as with any social organisms — cults — artificially contrived out of the larger community, have produced all the classic responses from mirth to dedication, from pure outrage to simple reverence. With their solemn mysteries, their irrational bases for judgment and discrimination, they were, Brockhurst told Dink Stover, dungeons, prisons of the mind. On the other hand, witnesses have not been wanting to attest that "lives have been changed there," the "look in faces transformed."

Young men had to find some way to give body to that system of idealism that Santayana and others discovered to exist at New Haven. There was not much in the classroom, on the evidence, to excite the mind, train it, bring it into useful support of healthy principle. With considerable ingenuity, therefore, the undergraduates turned elsewhere — to the feelings — to find a possible source of energy. They constructed in the senior societies, with admirable insight, a mechanism to mobilize the emotions of the selected few to their high purposes. Exactly how this was done, how in nine months, in weekly meetings, in secret places, whole lives were changed, is past all discovery. Such special election produces no doubt a sense of large responsibility; the compressions of the secret can generate great energy. At any rate, for most of those engaged, it worked. Out of these agencies youthful powers were organized to fortify the love of life, the trust in success, the radiant convictions and the healthy ideals. As the English observer Graham Wallas said, the experience within the senior societies at Yale, in this time, convinced the members that it was a better thing to be and to do than to seem to be and seem to do.

In the legend that has accumulated around these societies the largest place is held by the organization known as Skull and Bones. The special virtues of this sodality were effectively described to Stimson in the fall of his junior year by a girl he had met at a whist party the previous spring. Members of her family, most of her friends in the college were Bones men. She could argue her preference with knowledge and conviction. Stimson's father had been in Keys, but the young woman's arguments weighed with him; he remembered them a long time. He remembered them when he stood alone in the awful excitement of Tap Day, the day on which the societies made public their choices and a fortunate few undergraduates could choose between such propositions as were made to them. In the noise and the milling about and the running past, "I was approached by one of my old classmates. That gave me the hardest turn. He urged me to stay out, and was with me, and it was Tap Day." But then he thought of his independent judgments, and of the arguments the young girl had given to him, and he became a member of Skull and Bones.

This membership, he used to say in later years, was the most important educational experience of his life. By it he was confirmed in his ideals of being and doing and, more specifically, of doing good. But there was more to it than that. Within the society he could take as natural, as confident a place as one could find had he been a member of a family. The institutional secrecy, like family privacy, permitted the disclosure of thoughts and feelings without reserve. In all those undergraduate searchings and ponderings on the point of life, stormy affections elsewhere bottled up could find expression. Here was a place where loyalty had claims prior to those of individual success, where a man was recognized not because he won prizes but because he was himself. The members were a phalanx more solid than he had found at Andover or anywhere else against the enemies of time and chance. And the strength of the phalanx was trust, extended unqualified one to another. It was the great discovery. In later years he made use of it in the formation of policy in many different offices and in the conduct of negotiations with many different peoples. In the last recommendation of his public service he proposed that the country should share its knowledge and control of nuclear energy for peaceful purposes with Russia. He made this proposition, he told the President of the United States, because "the chief lesson I have learned in a long life is that the only way you can make a man trustworthy is to trust him." He had said the same thing often before, and usually when he said it he added that he had learned this thing first when he committed himself to membership in Skull and Bones.

There was a further commitment he made in the closing months of his undergraduate life. From his sophomore year onward he had gone, with increasing frequency, into the homes that lay round and about the college. There he had partaken of buffet suppers, guessed at the meaning of charades, played his hand at whist, and danced in the small dances. The families that lived in these houses, with their "two pillars that might have been labeled Respectability and Reserve," were residents of what H. S. Canby called "the guarded town." This town which was a part of the city was also an extension and enlargement of the college community. The citizens pursued their lawful occasions in New Haven, but they were, as well, members of the Yale society by virtue of ancestral association, or their own diplomas, or marriage or simple propinquity. Frequenting the collegiate precincts for reasons of diversion, enlightenment or personal devotion, they maintained a lively and proprietary interest in the condition of the academic groves.

This community supplied a somewhat larger context for the parochial concerns of students and faculty; it introduced refreshing atmospheres from the outside where people were getting along with the work of the world. But it was itself a small town and therefore, as one observer who took the dark view reported, like any small town with a long history, it was "a little provincial, a little priggish and very much inbred." There is also the more charitable finding. Like so many similar communities it was, within its own shelter, spontaneous, affectionately intimate and generous. These qualities it placed with unquestioning hospitality at the disposal of the students and faculty of Yale.

In this community there was a family named White. There were four brothers — all graduates of the college, all lawyers. One of these brothers had four daughters, the "four lovely White girls" who were, with reason, the object of persistent undergraduate attention. They were a good deal more than pretty. The oldest, it was said, looked the way a duchess ought to look and in each sister there was a similar sense of an individual presence. Certain inherited characteristics were shared in common: the erect carriage, the clean-cut features, the large, confident eyes. But in the daily concerns and sociabilities of their world they revealed quite different temperaments. The second daughter was named Mabel. As Henry Stimson had discovered in his conversation with her about the senior societies, she could express her convictions frankly and forcefully. On matters she knew about, or had made up her mind about, it was clear what she meant and where she stood. The open, resolute countenance reflected accurately the inner spirit. For the aimless frivolity, the gay flirtation she had small use; she was essentially an earnest person. But she entered easily and confidently upon the round of pleasures and duties established for her by the prevailing custom. At the sewing bees, the charitable clubs, the charade parties and the buffet suppers she was a lively companion. To the continuing festivities — a Valentine party, a birthday celebration — she often contributed poems she had written that set off in kindly perspective a person or an occasion. For the amateur theatrical group she contributed plays of her own devising, like the long-remembered "Aunt Laura's Lover." Amid the familiar and affectionate circle that carried forward all these varied endeavors she made the longest, closest friendships of her life.

But she also had a set of solitary concerns. In Shakespeare and in British novels she discovered the deeper matters that she seldom raised for discussion with others. Great reaches of Victorian poetry were systematically committed to memory. These poems she used to quote often; they apparently gave shape and confirmation to her own seriousness of purpose and feeling. In that feeling there was a warmth rarely otherwise disclosed, for she was, whether through diffidence or perplexity, chary of the direct, public expression of any emotion. All her later life, so much of it in a sense public and official, she was to make use of such indirect means — quotation, protocol, the dictates of convention — to expose, and sometimes probably to conceal, how she felt.

How she felt about Henry Stimson in the months after she met him at Professor Whitney's whist party was not, however, difficult for her to know or to communicate. The two found, from that first evening onward, that they could talk easily together about all their common concerns, the light and transient, the weightier and more persistent. They were steadily drawn closer together by attractions that excluded all other possible considerations. In February of his senior year they became engaged. The engagement was not announced at this time out of deference to the wishes of his family. There were those in the family, and especially his father, who felt the young man ought to know what he was going to do with his own life before he assumed any greater obligation. But in their own understanding they had given their word and their love to each other.

Four months later Stimson reached the graduation which put an end to one part of his education. In eight years he had come a long way. At Andover he believed he had reached a turning point in his career. He had learned there for the first time that independently he could survive in a strange environment, and at Yale he had discovered that he could effectively participate in the affairs of his fellows. At the college also he had learned something else which he defined precisely thirty-two years later.

The special glory of the institution, he said, was the spirit of service she fostered. Whether in pulpit, the marts of trade or public life, the Yale spirit had represented the spirit of service to the community, "to spend and be spent in that service." To pass this test, he concluded, "furnishes a more substantial foundation of honor than all the scholarship and all the science of this country."

He was a great believer in institutions and was, therefore, always ready in later life to assign the full credit for what he had learned in these years to the school and college to which he remained devoted. But, obviously, he had advanced in this developing educational process by endeavors of his own. This was made clear to others, if not to himself, at the time of his graduation. Timothy Dwight told him in earnest fashion that he could not give him up; that he must come back; that these were Presidential orders laid upon him. Professor Wright spoke kind words about his Commencement Oration which received also extended notice in the New Haven papers. His father's class of '63 sent for him and each member individually congratulated him. The father himself had not left his surgery to attend the celebrations. From his brother Henry, the boy's uncle, he received the report of his son's success. "I want to tell you," wrote Henry, "how more than sorry I am you did not come up yesterday. You would have had fun in meeting your class at the 25th Anniversary. It would certainly have fortified you to have heard all the complimentary things said about Harry on every side." [1]

[1] The material for this chapter was drawn chiefly from the following sources: Stimson Papers; *Catalogue of Phillips Academy*, 1880-1884; Claude M. Fuess, *An Old New England School* (Boston, 1917); *Yale University Catalogue*, 1884-1888; *Yale University Faculty Books*, 1884-1888 (in which are contained Stimson's grades and course record); *Classbook*, Yale Class of 1888; *The Yale Literary Magazine*, 1884-1888; L. S. Welch and W. Camp, *Yale, Her Campus, Class-Rooms and Athletics* (Boston, 1899); letters to the writer from members of the Class of 1888; conversations with Allen Klots and Harvey Bundy; Henry Seidel Canby, *American Memoir* (Boston, 1947); George Santayana, *Character and Opinion in the United States* (Boston, 1920); Van Wyck Brooks, *America's Coming-of-Age* (New York, 1915).

4

Study in Self-defense

I N THE SUMMER after his graduation from college, Henry
Stimson went out alone to the West. He took with him two
rifles, a volume of Shakespeare's sonnets, and a copy of Canon
Farrar's *The Early Days of Christianity*. The rifles were for
the hunt he was to make through what he called "the old range"
in Colorado. To that range he had first gone four years earlier
with Alden Sampson, a man fifteen years his senior. That first
trip had gotten into his blood, "intoxicated" him. Every summer thereafter in his college years he had gone hunting either in
New Brunswick or in the Far West. These excursions took him
into wild, untenanted land and confronted him with a life not
only rough but perilous. In New Brunswick, as a boy of seventeen, he had been left alone "without grub" for several weeks,
to live off what he trapped and shot, including a bear he ate
"from his toes to his nose." In Colorado once, he was left, also
alone, to defend his tent with his gun against a man who tried,
with threats and a brandishing of rifles, to take it away from
him. And, once again in Colorado, once again alone, he stood
off four Indians who, in the course of a local uprising, had come
upon his campsite.

Out of these experiences, the solitary pitting of his young self
against man and nature, he received, he said, "the whole slant"
of his education. There were things about the western fringes
of civilization that repelled him — the coarse men, with their

cards and their bad liquor. Everywhere he saw "the same dead level of materialism and mercantilism." A war, he thought, would in some ways be "a wonderfully good thing for this country. . . ." Anything "in the shape of a sentiment would be good to lift men out of selfish, individual work." But "the real west" settled "into roots which I had in me very deep down." He learned, of course, how to track, kill and skin game, pursuits that delighted him for the rest of his life. He learned, too, how to live in primitive, dangerous conditions, and most of all, he learned how to live with himself. Out in the wilderness the essential problems were stated clearly and without qualification: "you were up against the great decisions" alone.

As he went West in the summer of 1888, freed for the moment of Eastern encumbrances, he had before him some perplexing problems requiring decision. The volume of Shakespeare's sonnets had been given to him by Mabel White. In these pages he could find evidence of the dark moods produced when to the marriage of true minds impediments have been admitted. The young girl had, out of deference to the wishes of a family she barely knew, been placed in an equivocal position. She was in love and the love remained accepted, but undeclared to others. She was not scathing, or even critical, but she was inevitably unhappy. The young man read the poems, but seeing no way out of the immediate difficulties he could only offer advice drawn from his own experience. "It lies more or less within one whether he or she should be happy or not . . . No one's nature is so hopelessly, irredeemably despondent that it cannot be taken in hand by the will."

There was also a further problem. The work of Canon Farrar he had brought along for Sunday, but it would also serve to cast some light upon what he might do with himself in the future. Professor Harper had suggested the ministry, and to this end the young man was moved by the Professor's opinion, by the example of his Uncle Henry, and by the sense of his own interior impulses. Two other possibilities presented themselves.

He could, like Uncle Fred, become a lawyer or, like his father, a doctor. Throughout the summer by his lonely campfires he thought about these three ways of life without reaching any satisfactory conclusions. As he wrote his Aunt Minnie just before he returned home to seek his further fortune, he was powerfully drawn to the ministry, but he was not sure he had the vocation and there was real doubt that he was sufficiently good. Medicine had its high purpose and an additional advantage. If he entered it and studied alongside his father "that little feeling of restraint" that existed between the two might be got over. And then there was the law. Unhappily, in his own mind "the course which I think my father desires for me, is precisely the one in which I stand in most deadly horror, viz that of a successful New York lawyer." So he came home, in the early fall of 1888, in uncertainty, sure only that he wished a channel "for the right use of strength and influence," sure above all, as he told his aunt, that he wanted "to do good in some way."

The way out of his uncertainty was supplied in a family conference held with Uncle Henry, Uncle Fred and his father. Uncle Henry agreed that in the ministry one could find great satisfactions, but there was the matter of the vocation. Uncle Fred spoke well of the law, but believed his nephew was better fitted for medicine. His father was of the opinion that Henry was not cut out to be a doctor; he could do better elsewhere. In such a pass, Dr. Stimson remarked, "We must not forget that the law is a noble profession," and so, as the young man said, "I finally decided to go to Law School."

This conference had been postponed to wait upon the return of Uncle Fred from Europe. It was now several weeks past the opening of colleges and universities. But a place was found for the tardy candidate — as a special one-year student in search of a master's degree — at the Harvard Law School.

A further decision was reached in these same weeks. The son, as he told Aunt Minnie, agreed that his father was right about the situation in New Haven. The unannounced engagement ought to be rescinded; he and Miss White should return to the condition of things that existed before it. "My duty lies in my work." Members of both families and friends must be able to say honestly, "They are not engaged," until he was able to support a wife. So the conditions were changed, though the original feelings of each to the other remained. But in the changing the young man for the first time was brought to share some of the acute unhappiness felt by Mabel White. These old hopes deferred, this new pursuit of an uncertain professional interest, made the heart sick. A "fearful doubt" was in his mind as he started in the cars for Cambridge. He had come to "loathe second rates," he wanted something "nobler and higher" if he could get into it. And so on a "dreadful evening" he began "the most dismal, hopeless journey" he had ever taken.

Very little that happened to him in the next year altered his state of mind. In the first place there were Cambridge and Boston. "Bah, it's Boston, Boston . . . with its concentrated essence of self-satisfaction. . . ." Even New York, he concluded, seemed "manly alongside of it." He kept running into snobs or "skinny-armed girls" who "can talk music and . . . discuss Matthew Arnold's works," but who withal were not "very deep." Then there were Harvard men, "brutes," it sometimes seemed, or "miserable puppy-faced little ellicks"; at best they were merely "polite to me in their fashion." In their company "real good fellowship" was unknown; they were very different from the "good old Yale set." And finally there was the Harvard Law School itself. This school was in the middle of the transforming administration of the great dean Christopher C. Langdell. He had introduced as "fundamental changes" mock trials and the revolutionary case system of instruction. He had attracted a faculty that included, beside himself, James B. Thayer, John C. Gray, James Barr Ames and William A. Keener. Reviewing these accomplishments in the year Stimson entered the school, President Eliot said in his magisterial way: "Let any who wish to understand the Dean's grounds of legitimate satisfaction" compare the school of 1888 in courses, methods of teaching, library, funds and buildings with what had gone before.

Such satisfaction as the Dean took in his achievements was not shared by the new student who recalled for the rest of his life the "shock and surprise" of his first exposure to the Harvard Law School. There was nothing to do but work, nothing but the simple monotony of constant reading and studying, or working out case after case. "They give you the best facilities and you have to study in self-defense for there isn't another blessed thing to do." Nothing but "to go over to the law library and study." That is the way he spent "the entire time." And the nature of the work was itself unrewarding. There was an enormous difference between the kind of "*sharp* thinking" in which he and his classmates were being trained and the "*deep* thinking" in which he had previously been engaged. He wished he could "catch some of those smart ellicks" on a problem of philosophical import. Sharp thought took him "on my weakest point," for he "never had much of a critical faculty" and was "altogether too lax in little points." Thus he began to feel that he had been plunged into an ocean of new facts without much skill in swimming.

What increased his bewilderment and put him in a "state of rebellion against life, law and Harvard in general" was that he possessed no charted course across this vast new ocean that would take him to some understood destination. He had been used as a lonely boy to making his mark in a community, to demonstrating his value to classmates, friends and family, by the capture of the obvious awards. As he told Mabel White, "the idea of a struggle for prizes, so to speak, has always been one of the fundamental elements of my mind, and I can hardly conceive of what my feelings would be if I ever was put in a position or situation in life where there are no prizes to struggle for." Now, in Cambridge, the prizes lacked precise definition. There was only the law to learn, the aimless chatter on "cultured topics" and the continual "struggling with our own minds against each other." If the unceasing struggle produced in the end no particular good or noble thing, if one's mind was not especially well trained for the conflict, then there was not much use in the whole business.

As the year wore on he became more unhappy with his lot, but he also became "madder and madder." In his irritation he resolved to select his own targets and objectives. He first prepared his class arguments down to the last fact and precedent and then, in the struggle of mind against mind, he went out after the best intelligences in the classroom. In a prolonged contest he convinced the impressive Keener that a particular case had ethical as well as legal connotations, and then, in argument, he proceeded "to black the eye" of Ezra Thayer, "the Harvard valedictorian and genius," with all "his Harvard suave politeness." By this means, repeated more frequently as the year progressed, he improved his situation, but he did not change his state of mind. The narrow confines of professional thinking chafed him and he agreed with a classmate who had observed that Stimson's mind seemed more philosophical than legal in its cast of thought.

To these forlorn reflections on his work in the law were added, in the course of the year, equally unhappy assessments of his personal situation. In New Haven Mabel White was both despondent and unwell. These things, for the most part, she concealed from the man she loved, but friends in New Haven reported her condition and asked Stimson how long she was to be permitted to languish in uncertainty. He replied that the period would be "not a second longer than I can help," that the decision to revoke the undeclared engagement had been taken "simply in deference to the wishes of a Father who has never shown to me anything except the most perfect and wisest kindness." Nevertheless the decision wore on him as well as on Miss White. He went about his tasks, wretched in spirit for weeks together. Time, he wrote to Mabel, seemed "unending" and, on occasion, he was brought to the desolate conclusion that, in his father's words, he had done "the cruelest and wickedest thing in my life" when he had asked her to marry him. Harboring such thoughts, profoundly doubtful of himself and of his prospects in such unwelcome surroundings, he was by the end of the year ready to leave Cambridge. Confused as to what he might do, he was at least sure that he wanted to do something else. When these sentiments were explained to his father in June, Dr. Stimson came immediately to Cambridge. There was a long conversation and the decision was made to return to Harvard in the fall.

What followed surpassed all natural expectations. In the second year of his study the remorseless applications of the previous year began to pay off. He was taken in the Pow Wow to sit alongside the most striking intelligences in the school. There was William Thompson, in after years a United States District Attorney in Boston; William Rand, who became W. T. Jerome's righthand man in New York; Lockwood Honoré, the acid, brilliant brother of Mrs. Potter Palmer; and Ezra Thayer, later the Dean of the Law School. The prospect of the first meeting with these "shining lights" — a mock trial in November — made him "really . . . terribly frightened." He had never before been in such a learned set. As the evening wore on in argument, he found himself reflecting that he used to think Bones men could speak pretty well, but this remarkable crowd left him "fairly paralyzed by [their] fluency and grasp." He hoped he would not make a fool of himself and he did not. Slowly, as the months passed, he got his feet on firm ground; he discovered he was "interested in my work now" or rather "more interested in putting myself up against the other men, whom I think I am getting to admire more and more though not in such a discouraged way as before." By February he was in "a fascinating case" with Thompson and Rand against Honoré, Thayer and Forbes which he thoroughly enjoyed because he "felt like a real scrap." A month later he was sure he was getting to the bottom of all the cases; as he wrote Mabel White, "I never had such a sense of power as I have been having just lately." It was intoxicating, he, who "had been such a nobody and nothing for the last year," had discovered, in the continual struggle "with our minds against each other" how to trust and how to use his own mind.

There were other gratifications also in this year. In time he sat around with Thayer and Thompson in their living quarters discussing the law all evening; he went with Honoré to "swell club rooms" for champagne, chicken and crackers. There and elsewhere he met some of the bloods and found, to his surprise, that, in spite of suave and sophisticated manners, they possessed respectable abilities. Even Boston and Cambridge society emerged in more favorable perspectives. It was not all Matthew Arnold and music, he found. One night he created "a great furor" by betting he could dance with Miss Ames more times than anyone else, and, bolstered by his success in the wager, he began to go regularly to the assemblies to see "the interesting girls." In the spring — with Miss Ames and Miss Thayer and Lloyd Garrison and Ezra Thayer — he became a member of a Shakespeare Club where he greatly enjoyed reading and discussing plays even when he had to keep "pretty mum" because he had not read the plays before.

He would have profited, perhaps, by more of these experiences that brought things like champagne and Shakespeare and bloods and legal talk and interesting girls into a closer kind of juxtaposition. One of his old friends, a Yale man, believed in later years that it would have done him good to belong in his youth to the Porcellian Club at Harvard. There, it was believed, young men sat all night over terrapin and wine, talking indolently about whatever came into their heads — whatsoever things were frivolous, irresponsible, coarse or funny as well as, sometimes, those things that were of good report. Such experiences might have loosened him up, put more play into his system, saved him from the too precise separation of vice from virtue, the flesh from the spirit, the sober truth from the truth that was ridiculous. Bones, for all its great contributions, had, in the opinion of this friend, served primarily to enlarge his already lopsided concern for the pure forms of earnestness and the good.

Whatever the truth of such reflections, it is clear that Stimson entered cheerfully into such out-of-course diversions as came his way in the spring of his second year at the Harvard Law School. In this second year he had also another experience outside his own classrooms that produced far more enduring consequences. For this his roommate Benjamin Tilton was responsible. Stimson had met Tilton, the captain of the football team, the first marshal of his class, the previous year when the two had acted to reduce a rupture in Harvard-Yale athletic relations. Through Tilton, Stimson had been introduced to a decent, responsible, physically sound undergraduate citizenry he had not believed could exist at Harvard. He was also introduced through him to Professor George F. Palmer's course in philosophy and through Palmer's course to Josiah Royce and John Fiske. From these men and their works he discovered for the first time how there could be some intellectual content and, more important, some fusion of the intelligence and the character in the great end and business of life. Heretofore he had been unable to put the things he had learned along with the things he felt in any satisfactory relationship. But here was a scheme into which deep thinking and sharp thinking and Christian endeavor and the work of the world could be fitted together. Like Fiske he found it a concept of matchless romantic interest. The process by which the fit survived had been enlarged beyond mere natural selection. Man in society had with his brains devised regulations and duties in the interest of sound social organization. By reference to these regulations and duties, by recognition of larger standards outside himself, man entered a moral atmosphere. He learned that limits were interposed at which pleasure must be resigned and pain endured. "Ought," "obligation," an idea of "debt" beyond self became governing precepts. Man with the instruments of his trained mind and controlling will worked within the social scheme through struggle, through discipline, through resistance toward the perfection of character. As Fiske later asserted, there was "Below the surface din and clashing of the struggle for life" a deep ethical purpose which "rolls in solemn music through the ages" and this purpose would continue "till in the fulness of time . . . Humanity [would stand] purified and redeemed." This was a tremendous synthesis of all the findings of the past forty years; it gave a place to the intelligence, the spirit and the informed will. Stimson never forgot his debt to Fiske and Palmer; he never forgot the points established; sixty years later he could state the case as clearly as Fiske himself had put these things down in *Through Nature to God*.

While he was discovering these arresting new propositions in the spring of his second year in Cambridge, he was also pondering the problem of his own future. Where and with whom should he enter the practice of law? He thought of the West with all its promise for young men and he thought of New York with all its known confinements. Miss White should make the final choice, he thought at first, but then he thought that "the one wish my father has ever expressed is that I should go to New York" and "that makes the matter much easier . . . in fact takes some of the responsibility off me." So it was decided. He accepted an offer from Sherman Evarts, a Yale graduate and a friend of the Whites, to join him in the fall in his law office at 52 Wall Street.

In June 1890 he left the Harvard Law School to begin, at twenty-two, his work in the world. He took with him an M.A. degree and "a record of excellence in his studies." Twenty years later Ezra Thayer, then Dean of the School, recalled that "he enjoyed in a peculiar degree the respect and esteem of his teachers and his associates who had obtained their law degree in three years of study." The record bears this out. In the graduating class the fourteen top men (ten Harvard, three

Amherst, one Brown) had averaged grades running from 75 to 83. Stimson's two-year average, reduced by a 63 in Equity Pleading, was 76. But the marks were only a partial indication of what he took away with him. Two other things remained in his memory as more important: First, an unexampled mental training and, second, obtained from his ceaseless study of old cases, a steady view of the "long vista of an intelligent past, upon which our present institutions are founded. Nothing else could give such a fundamental grasp of the spirit of our institutions."

He had, as he believed on his departure from the Law School, learned at Andover, Yale and Harvard a great many useful, indeed indispensable, things that would stand him in good stead as he began to work at the great end and business of life.[1]

---

[1] The material for this chapter was drawn chiefly from the following sources: Stimson Papers; *Harvard University Catalogue*, 1888-1890; Harvard Law School Archives; Charles Warren, *History of the Harvard Law School*, 3 vols. (New York, 1908).

5

Coming of Age

SHERMAN EVARTS was assisted in his law practice by an office boy and one stenographer. He worked in chambers at 52 Wall Street where there was neither central heat nor running water. The firm possessed one principal client, the New York and Northern Railway Company, which owned fifty miles of track that stretched from 155th Street on the Harlem River to Brewster, New York. Much of the business produced by this company derived from the accidents that occurred along its short right of way. When peddlers' wagons were hit at crossings, when teams got stuck in trestles, when locomotives ran off rails, there were suits and these suits came in to Sherman Evarts. There was also conducted in his office the small general business of the law — titles traced, notes collected, mortgages foreclosed, wills drawn.

Henry Stimson entered the firm in September 1890 to serve out the year of clerkship that was the prerequisite for the examinations for admission to the bar. He was, in accordance with existing custom, unpaid. For twelve months the new clerk did everything from pasting stamps on envelopes to arguing a motion in court. In between times he read Pollock on Torts and Greenleaf on Evidence in preparation for his examinations, and in the offices of Sherman Evarts there were a good many in-between times. "The Chief" was intelligent and well trained, but he was also a casual man without any very urgent feelings of ambition. The atmosphere of his office was delightful, but it made Stimson restless. After eight months he thought he would go wild if he did not do something right off. "One seems to be standing still," he said, "or even worse than that, rotting, here in such a poky profession as the law in such a stationary place as New York."

This restless irritation was brought to the attention of Dr. Stimson and, through him, to the attention of one of Dr. Stimson's Yale classmates, George Dimmock. Mr. Dimmock was a man of affairs who knew intimately another member of the Yale class of '63, a man of even greater affairs, William C. Whitney. To Mr. Whitney, who was in fact one of the remarkable men of his age, the restlessness of young Stimson was conveyed by both of Whitney's old classmates. It was agreed that something should be done. Mr. Dimmock told the impatient clerk, in the course of an evening call, that he was very fond of Sherman Evarts but that anyone "should have a better chance of 'getting into a big business and becoming a big man' by the right sort of connection with a large office rather than with a small one." About the same time, so Dr. Stimson reported, Mr. Whitney was supposed to have said out of an absolutely clear sky at a dinner party that he had been thinking over young Henry's future for several months. The long and the short of it was the three classmates thought a right sort of connection could be established with Mr. Root, "a prominent lawyer here," on whom apparently Mr. Whitney had "a big hold . . . somehow."

The big hold was, in fact, that Mr. Whitney with all his traction interests was the principal client of Elihu Root; he had felt for some time that his lawyer needed more assistants. So on October 22, 1891, Henry Stimson went round to call on Mr. Root and was very "favorably impressed." The lawyer had "a very quiet polite manner" and "a very sweet sensitive face." He told the clerk, who had passed his bar examinations the previous July, that he could begin any time at a salary of $750.

So on November 1 Stimson began in the Root offices with the hope in his heart that he would not be "a fizzle at his work." The hope was fulfilled; for the rest of his life he practiced his profession where he started out that November day in the Liberty Mutual Building.

At this time, as from the first day of his return to New York, there was an even larger hope in his heart. He had come back "determined to establish a firm relationship" with his father after the long years of his parent's "terrible loneliness." This was, in some ways, a formidable task. That constitutional reserve, discerned so many years ago in the grandfather, had been passed on through the father down to the son. Here they were "craving . . . to share every thought and feeling . . . and yet [with] this strange horrible barrier of reluctance of manner on the part of us both." By what means, if any, could this barrier be demolished?

There were some favorable indications. In the fourteen years since Candace Stimson had died, her husband had worked himself slowly out of his isolating despair. In so doing he had emerged as an eminent physician — a professor at the New York University Medical School and attending surgeon at the Chambers Street House of Relief, the emergency unit of the New York Hospital. In the classroom and on the surgical services Dr. Stimson was unquestioningly looked upon by his students as "the shining example of the master surgeon." His "noble qualities" and "dominating personality" turned the House of Relief into "one of the most noteworthy" teaching services in the country, and also into a place of "devotion, idealism and high adventure." He was "a benevolent autocrat" who insisted in all procedures on the utmost "simplicity and directness of action." Every intern practiced, as a matter of course, in imitation of this powerful intelligence and dedicated spirit. With the achievement of such professional eminence and the passage of time Dr. Stimson extended his range of interest and action well beyond its original, self-imposed, confines. He began to see some of his old friends like the Dimmocks and the Whitneys, he went out occasionally to the theater, he cruised in his small boat, translated a novel by George Sand, and read the Greeks in their own tongue. In spite of the increased cultivation of these natural tastes and interests, in spite of passing time, there was still the hard-defended barren place within him. He would tell his son, for instance, that he "had to go out of town" for the afternoon, and sometime later, in some way, the son would discover that his father had gone out alone to the graveyard in Jamaica where Candace Stimson lay buried.

It was this barren place that the son set himself to penetrate when he returned in 1890 to live with his father in a house on 33rd Street. There for the first time they lived in close, continuous association. Almost every evening they spent together and in their conversations young Henry discovered a great deal he had not known about his father's past in the Civil War and in Wall Street; he also learned much about his father's profession and the reasons why Dr. Stimson preferred the rewards of teaching in an emergency hospital to the financial gains he certainly could have obtained from large private practice. The two reached an increased degree of intimacy, also, in these evenings by reading aloud, each by turns, to the other. The books sometimes were novels like *Lorna Doone*, but more often they were the great texts of the times. In these years they went through Spencer's *Social Dynamism*, Henry George's *Progress and Poverty*, Bellamy's *Looking Backward*, Riis's *How the Other Half Lives*, Fiske's *The Unseen World* and *The Critical Period*. These were great educational sessions in which the younger learned much that he never forgot from his exposure not only to the great works, but also to the acute, vigorous mind of the older man. On Sundays, before the family dinner, they went together, ordinarily, to the church of Dr. Parkhurst where the tremendous sermons lighting up the sin of the city of New York stirred Henry to his very depths and moved him to his first political action, his membership in the City Reform

Club. There were also more cheerful moments, especially when the daughter Candace, or Nan as she was called, came back with all her gaiety on vacation from Wellesley. The three of them would then go off for dinner at Delmonico's before an evening at Pastor's or attendance at some more serious dramatic performance.

In such constant association Dr. Stimson exerted, as his son said, an "influence [that] was perhaps [the] greatest loadstone and guide." There was also a more overt regulation. Not long after Henry came to live at the 33rd Street house, his father gave him "a long talking to . . . on the subject of [his] duties and deficiencies socially." In the city there was a world he did not know; for the first time his "eyes . . . opened" to the necessity of getting about in New York social life. As a beginning Dr. Stimson gave his son lessons to improve his whist because "it was such a fad in society now and a useful thing to know." Then, with the aid of the Dimmocks and the Whitneys, he went forth on these new social excursions. For two years he engaged himself in all the endless celebrated gaieties of those times. He used to call on Mrs. Abram Hewitt in her living room that was "fitted up with perfect taste and wide research"; he shivered in his boots while Mrs. Whitney's butler bawled out his name amid the teacups and the cloisonné. Receptions, the opera, small dances and large balls — all these he attended. Whatever was done, he did, from having a word with Ward McAllister to eating oysters with the whole four hundred while Japanese jugglers did their juggling.

It cannot be said that he enjoyed these things. Save for Susan Dimmock, who accompanied him on most of these excursions, and her family, he found the men and women, their sons and daughters, not only tedious but frivolous. He went about to fulfill his father's "ambition for me, and it seems so funny that he should let it carry him into a region which he has always despised when he himself was concerned, the fashionable life of New York. But he can't bear not to have me at the top of the heap — irrespective of what kind of heap it may be."

What the doctor wanted was that the boy should succeed, make a name for himself. Success, it apparently had been revealed in his Presbyterian youth and verified by his later years of grinding labor, was less a matter of grace than of properly selected works. For the benefit of the son he had painstakingly chosen the tested ways of getting on. Emerging from his surgery at crucial moments to "overrule everything" proposed by those less tutored in the ways of the world, he had, in a series of wise and bracing decisions, determined the course of his child's development. The education, the choice of profession, the surroundings, physical and personal, in which the profession would be practiced, these had all been shaped by his hands. As interns had been quick to imitate the shining example imposed upon them by the master surgeon, so it was natural that a lonely boy, anxious to qualify in the test for his father's affections, would do whatever he could to follow the masterful parental instructions. It was natural also that Dr. Stimson, having acquired by his experience great confidence in his own spirit, should have less confidence in the spirit of others. In the achievement of success the tried procedure was superior, as an instrument, to the wandering of desire. For himself he could marry for love, but it was necessary to warn his older brother that a minister should be moved by reasons more prudential. For himself he could bury his talents away in an emergency hospital, while others must strive to achieve eminence in the more conventional practice of their profession. For himself he could leave his father's brokerage and his father's side in the financial crisis of the seventies to seek his own independent future, but other sons would be better guided by their fathers' wisdom.

Events had thus far justified the calculations of Dr. Stimson. The correct occasional decision inserted at the proper moment was, it might seem, a satisfactory substitute for parental love and understanding more general and more constant in expression. Wherever he had been put, the boy had worked hard, made his mark, qualified, obtained those prizes that those around him set store by. This was the way that men, in time, reached the top of the heap. And for his part, the boy himself had small cause for disagreement. When one knew so little of the world it was steadying to have the counsel of one who knew so much of it; when, for instance, one knew only that he wished to do some ill-defined, generalized good it was reassuring to know that it was possible to do specific good in a noble profession like the law.

But there was a place where the tried procedure was threatened by the wandering of desire; where the sound program of the father collided with the intent of the son. This had to do with the alliance Henry Stimson had established as an undergraduate with Mabel White. There were apparently three reasons why Dr. Stimson looked with small favor upon the alliance. First, it had been conceived at a time when Henry had no money and no prospects. To require a commitment from a girl under such circumstances was unwise and unfair. Then too there was the recollection of the terrible past. Dr. Stimson, so Nan said, was still the captive of his own "past feelings and experience." Marriage, especially a marriage above all things desired, was a time bomb that blew all plans and joys to pieces. And finally there was not the girl herself, but those things which the girl could not be said to represent. In the scheme as drawn — the successful New York lawyer, eminent on any professional, financial, cosmopolitan, sophisticated, influential heap — the natural virtues of New Haven could not be made easily to fit. On the other hand the girl had fitted perfectly into the heart of Henry Stimson. This was the first clear and precise intelligence he had ever had of needs and objectives which were, beyond all shadow of doubt, his very own. And so there was the issue between the father and son, and also, of course, between the father, and the son and the girl together.

The issue — rarely, if ever, overtly stated, discussed often in terms of financial capacity or implied alternatives, never specifically raised for outright resolution — lay open for five and one-

half years. In that time each did what he could. The father
opened the eyes of the son to his social duties and deficiencies;
he put the young man in the field of attractive forces around
him — the Astors, the Whitneys, the Danas, the Delafields, the
Susan Dimmocks — in the apparent hope that a youthful nature might take its usual course in such solicitous surroundings.
The son, determined to establish "a firm relationship" with
his father, gave ground where it was possible. He went out into
the great world; he saw the Susan Dimmocks; he accepted the
principle that, on occasion, the claims of his own family for
his attention were superior to all other claims; he left, for a long
period, his engagement unannounced; he explained as fully as
he could the state of his own feelings and he waited. But he did
not change his intentions. As for Mabel White, she also waited.
In the middle of these bewildering circumstances which she had
not created, throughout the inexplicable negotiations in which
she could take little part, she remained steadfast to her original
commitment. Troubled, baffled, wounded beyond all doubt in
her most natural feelings of self-respect, she continued to trust
absolutely in the word and intent of the man she had fallen in
love with.

Trust, or the giving of ground where possible, could not prevent, in the five and a half years, the occasion that was misunderstood or inopportune or desolating. Visits to New Haven
were canceled because Aunt Julia's child fell desperately ill, or
because, with Grandpa ailing, family reunions in New York
had become infinitely precious. Invitations to the dance were
refused because there were already such "terrible loads on natural desires." There was even a time when the son could not
forgive himself that he had let his "disappointment and his
[father's] inability to change his manner . . . lead me into even
a temporary doubt of his never failing kindness at bottom."
And it was not easy for the girl to be told to bring along some
whist puzzles because she would find it easier to talk to the
father if she did so. It was also not easy for the son to listen

while his father talked as if he were trying "to express as much interest as he can" in his son's plans for marriage.

These occasions, multiplied during the years, threw the young man into fearful moods of depression and the young girl not only into despondency, but into weeks of physical illness. Yet in the end they worked their way through to the desired solution. By 1893 Henry Stimson had demonstrated his capacity to support a wife and home of his own. He had also, he believed, accomplished his larger end "to preserve my self-respect and [the] respect [of the family] for the union I am about to make." Only a few weeks after he wrote these words the two were married in New Haven on July 6, 1893.

For the rest of their lives the people who had lived through this unhappy ordeal had some of the marks to show. In the complicated process it was inevitable that most of the natural irresponsibility of courtship, the gaiety, the sense of rapture had been strained away. It followed that in later years Mr. and Mrs. Stimson would look austerely upon those who fell too easily into or out of marriage. It followed also that they should at all times guard and protect their private feelings about each other from the public gaze or the public knowing. There was, as Henry Stimson said, an outside nature, properly brought up, that shuddered at any demonstration of the workings of the inside nature.

But with the penalties there were also gains. The father had learned something to his advantage. So long deprived of the deepest personal satisfaction, possessed of remarkable powers, he had placed such specific hopes in his son that he had come to believe that only he could design these hopes, that only he, in fact, with benevolent autocracy, could bring these hopes to pass. In the end, in the very end, he gave this common parental misconception up, came to respect the union and the girl who made it possible, and to respect most of all the son who had exerted his "human privilege to fashion his inner life for himself."

And from the exertion of this privilege the son had acquired indispensable experience and self-knowledge. In these five and a half years he might, as an aunt put it, have been "bulldozed" out of his desires. He could have yielded gracefully or just caved in beneath the subtle pressures. On the other hand he might, like an uncle before him, have entered into annihilating rebellion, taking himself out of his father's house and his family. For either course he had large provocation. But it was revealed in these years that on a decision of his own choosing he was not one to give up easily, nor was he one to enter into acts of futile defiance.

He might perhaps have staged another kind of rebellion — a great independent action that would leave him free with his wife to create a whole new life of his own, free of familiar memories and attachments. This was not, however, in his nature. One of his oldest friends, much later, remarked that he had "no philosophy of ecstasy" — no feeling for the undeniable riot of thought and emotion out of which something entirely new and independently beautiful can be created. His was a more prudent interest — to preserve and, by gradual modification, to improve. His interest here apparently was in part to protect the useful values already invested in the total situation; to take into account, for future resolution, the rival influences and conflicting needs; to introduce stabilizing bases for the energies at work. He had set his heart on marrying Mabel White — and this purpose gave him his major organizing principle; but he was also determined to establish for himself a satisfying place, which as a kind of orphan he had never had, in his own family and in his father's regard. In the event he obtained his ends.

It took five and a half years to do so. This is a long time. In the course of these years a load was placed upon Mabel White that many other girls would have found insupportable. What he owed, in the course of this prolonged negotiation, to her fortitude he always recognized though it is doubtful that he ever fully understood at what cost to herself in bewildered pain this fortitude had been purchased. It may also be said that, even if money were wanting, five and a half years is too long a time; it may suggest too faithful attendance upon the father's special desires, if not weakness. Certainly others with a different kind of strength would have resolved the problem in a shorter time, if in a different way. But for the young man the time expended was worth it. By the force of will, patiently and undramatically applied, he sustained his original policy and gained his purpose. And in the end he reached his object without ever having said or done those things that would have broken off the old allegiances or destroyed the familiar environment.

In these five and a half years he was for the first time confronted with the problem which was to engage his primary attention through most of his later years — the relation of force to policy. He revealed here the ability to wait, to calculate the intentions of others, to assess the play of forces within a system, to strike the temporary bargain in the interest of the more enduring point, to apply judiciously the power available behind his intentions, in this case his own will supported by the loyalty of Mabel White, and thus, as in this instance, to reach the saving solution. He found on this occasion that he could come out from the enclosing decision of others and emerge as his own man ready to survive in more dangerous surroundings even than the wilderness. All his life he was to respect those in authority and to wish for their approval, but here he discovered what he remembered afterwards, that there were ways to hold and support his own opinions without placing in jeopardy the relationship between himself and those in greater authority. He and his father lived from that time forward in mutual respect and constructive amity — just as in later administrations he argued differences and stood his ground while serving with great usefulness and in mutual respect along with the highest authorities.

There was a final reward awaiting Mabel White and Henry

Stimson together on July 6, 1893. They obtained the principal object of their common lives. In the courtship there may have been few lyric moments, but at the end of it the title to the ground on which they stood had been thoroughly searched, the unseen cords around them finally proved. They knew that in every season they could trust each other in word and deed. They knew that they had entered upon no unadvised venture, but one which was the central foundation of their lives. So it remained for fifty-seven years.[1]

[1] The material for this chapter was drawn chiefly from the following sources: Stimson Papers; conversations with members of the Stimson and White families.

6

The Noble Profession

LAWYERS IN reminiscence reveal a natural inclination to dwell upon the high points of the profession. They recall the celebrated case, the annihilating witticism in some closing argument; they speak of their priesthood and "the subtile rapture of a postponed power." Accurate as definitions of the splendid moment, such recollections and sentiments are misleading about what happens every day. The law may never be concerned with the smallest things, as the Romans believed, but lawyers often are. If, as Lord Bryce noted, eminent counsel on one day appears before the Supreme Court in Washington, on the next he will be writing "six-and-eight-penny letters from a shopkeeper to an obstinate debtor."

The profession which Henry Stimson entered when he passed his bar examination in July 1891 was not without its high points. Many of these occurred in the courtroom, for it was the day of the great advocate — Edward James, William A. Butler, Wheeler H. Peckham, James C. Carter, William M. Evarts, Frederic Coudert and, of course, Joseph H. Choate. These men dealt with the cases that caught the public attention — the Tweed trials, the constitutionality of the income tax, the bombing of Russell Sage, the Beecher trial, the contested wills of Singer, Tilden, Gould, Vassar, Drake, Fayerweather, and A. T. Stewart. They fought these cases through the courts in a series of tense, dramatic contests against one another. These advocates had come down from a previous generation — most of the men named died in the first decade of the new century — framed in the public eye to a heroic scale. No doubt in many instances they relied more on themselves than upon their legal erudition. The things men remembered about them were "a withering power of sarcasm," "a head of plentiful touselled hair," "a musical voice of tenor quality," "an intuitive insight." There was one who "took refuge from pathos by unexpected transitions to humor," and another in whom "sternness, sadness, and benevolence struggled for supremacy."

Hidden beneath the great public displays was what happened every day, the practice that never, or rarely, reached the courts. Much of this practice consisted, as it always had, of the writing of six-and-eight-penny letters bearing on the collection of debts, the searching of titles, the drawing of wills and all those other small matters of human intercourse and altercation. But, increasingly in these years, the time of lawyers was taken up with the rendering of advice and counsel to men in commercial and industrial enterprise. This kind of work had, of course, always fallen within the province of the lawyer but, because of the extraordinary economic development in the country around the turn of the century, it assumed every year greater significance in the practice of many firms in New York City. One observer concluded that in 1896 "the distinction between the lawyer and the businessman had vanished." He noted with distaste that at least one firm had issued engraved invitations to a dinner for businessmen at which wine was served and "a new business venture" considered. The indefatigable Bryce likewise noticed the trend of affairs, concluding that "on the whole the law acts with probity in controlling big fortunes and corporations"; though, he added, he saw signs of decline in the standards of the lawyer and in his social position as well.

The change in standard and social position was produced, in part perhaps, by the tarnishing connection of the lawyer with commercial enterprise, but also by the fact that many lawyers were left unsupported by proper training for their profession. In 1895 and 1896, 1051 men took the bar examinations in New York. A majority — over 600 — of these had never even been to college; of those without higher education about half had done some work in a law firm, but the others — over 250 — tried to pass the examinations with what they had learned by independent reading.

Those who passed the bar examinations and entered firms in New York City went ordinarily to work in the lower end of the island, in and around Liberty, Nassau, and Wall streets. These firms were small; between 1870 and 1900 it was the rare office that included as many as six partners. At the turn of the century such famous firms as Sullivan and Cromwell had five partners, Strong and Cadwalader four, Shearman and Sterling three. Young law clerks entering these firms received at the beginning more education than money. Not until the middle nineties did it become usual, after the practice had been introduced by that great friend of young lawyers, Walter S. Carter, to pay clerks anything, and then but little. Stimson himself used to recall the managing partner in the Root firm, shocked by the new departure, bellowing out of his office door, "Where is that *paid* law clerk?" Partners themselves rarely made a great deal of money, certainly not as much as they were believed to make in these years. Opportunities were such that "no man who is worth his salt, no man who combines fair talents with reasonable industry fails to earn a competence," but Bryce believed there were not fifteen counsel in the whole country who made more than $50,000 a year, and this seems high. In the year Stimson entered the Root firm, then one of the most respected in the country, the profits distributed among the three partners were $98,000.

But if, for the young clerk, there was not much, if any, remuneration, there was the opportunity to learn a great deal about the general practice of the law. He could, in court, watch the last of the old generation, the great advocates, match wits with each other; in his own office he could serve directly with the members of the rising generation as they worked out the intricacies of the legal arrangements for the expanding industrial ventures. In the small firms of the time they could take part in the large problems presented to the partners and they could obtain extended training in the general practice that still found its way through the doors of most firms. What the clerk ideally received was a thorough apprenticeship in all the branches of his profession.

This apprenticeship for Stimson had begun on November 1, 1891, when at nine o'clock in the morning he arrived at the offices of Root and Clarke on the fourteenth floor of the Liberty Mutual Building at 32 Nassau Street in New York City. He entered a suite of high-studded, white rooms that caught cool breezes off the ocean in summer and were warmed in winter by the small cannel coal fires that burned in iron grates set within white-arched fireplaces. From his own office he could look out at "a beautiful sweep — in so far as a city can ever be beautiful," over the housetops to the East River and Brooklyn Bridge. Beyond his office was a large room for clerical help and beyond that a library where the law clerks did much of their work. Beyond the library were the chambers of the partners. In these high-studded offices, far above the city, there was a sense of space, of light, of quiet and, above all, of simplicity. As a partner remarked, there was and always remained in the rooms the atmosphere of a London solicitor's chambers of 100 years before. In this building, though the address was later changed to 32 Liberty Street, Stimson practiced law for more than half a century.

When Stimson arrived, there were in the office, Elihu Root, Samuel B. Clarke, Joseph Kunzman the managing partner, another law clerk, a bookkeeper, an office boy and one stenographer. Within four days he was "so busy . . . that I really don't know what to do." His first work was to look up points of law in the case of *Belden* vs. *Burke* which had to do with the effort of some stockholders to recover eight million dollars taken from them by the unscrupulous manipulation of a management that controlled coal lands and railroads in Ohio. On and off for many months he continued to work on this case which was in and out of the courts for twenty years. But there were — every day — other matters to attend to: the drawing of a poor widow's will, a preliminary draft for the formation or dissolution of a partnership, the collection of a small debt, the endless reading of the proofs of partners' briefs. Mr. Root asked him to look up some things for the Aqueduct case and took him off on one occasion to hear Wellman cross-examine the witness to an accident. Mr. Clarke went with him to hear Root and Choate oppose each other before a jury that contained Henry George. Every now and then he was given a client of his own: a sailor injured on a ship in Brooklyn, a veteran of both the Union and Confederate armies who wanted a pension for his services to either government or, preferably, to both.

But for most of the time the young clerk was busy on accident cases. Root was counsel for many of the metropolitan traction companies, whose cars frequently damaged men or property. There must have been thirty of these accident cases in Stimson's years of clerkship. They were, for the most part, similar in character and scale to *Ryne* vs. *7th Avenue Railroad Company*. The plaintiff had been struck at 32nd Street by a horsecar. The driver, it was known, had taken a drink before the trip and, as evidence of his drunkenness, had missed a switch at 44th Street. Stimson argued that what happened twelve blocks from the site of the accident was not relevant. Overruled, he argued that the plaintiff should have looked up and down the street before crossing. The judge found that "it has never been held that it was necessary to look both up and down before crossing an ordinary street" where there was no steam railway. The case was lost, appealed, and lost again over a two-year period.

There were many aspects of this work the young man disliked: the dry, detailed labor on small causes; the waiting in court; the personality of Kunzman; the continual representation of the company against the injured member of society. But he got on. Mr. Clarke observed that a memorandum on a point of law read like an essay in equitable jurisprudence and Mr. Root said kind things to his father. Some of these advances, to be sure, were made under forced draft. He obtained the opportunity to try his accident cases only by insisting upon the point to Kunzman who liked to appear in court himself with the findings of the clerks. He refused to work on Saturday afternoon "for anybody." And when Mr. Root, just before going on vacation, presented him with a list of things to do in connection with some cases Root had in hand, Stimson asked if he might, in addition, be assigned some cases of his own to work on. After fourteen months of such activity he had demonstrated his fitness for the profession and for membership in the firm. On January 1, 1893, he became a junior partner in Root and Clarke with a guaranteed return for his labors of $2000 a year.

There were two men in the firm with whom Stimson remained closely associated for a long time. The first was the senior partner. Mr. Root, then forty-eight years old, was a commanding figure in the legal profession. Someone had observed that he had been connected with all the important cases tried in New York since 1880, and it was almost true. But he was not the conventional great advocate; he was, in fact, "far removed from the general idea of a famous pleader brimming over with words and always ready to cite legal maxims." Instead he relied upon a very clear mind, a remarkable power of analysis and tireless preparation. It was said of him that before any trial was finished he knew more about everything in it than anyone else, clients, witnesses, judge or counsels. In presenting his case he was, usually, precisely logical and completely self-contained; but he obviously enjoyed the sense of conflict.

Stimson often noticed when Root was "cross-examining a witness, and suddenly turned to me for a paper, that his eyes seemed to burn with a red glow — a glow which always reminded me of General Forsythe's description of the similar red light which he noticed in General Sheridan's eyes when he went into battle."

But the trial was only part of the satisfaction Root derived from the law. His was an organizing intelligence, a mind more concerned with policy than with the particular incident. In the law he discovered an intellectual device for the stabilization of the energies in his environment. Since his environment was the New York of the late nineteenth century, and since the primary energies were to be found in commerce and industry, he naturally found himself turning to the organization of railroads, banks, traction companies and the other developing enterprises. It does not appear that the money he made by his efforts greatly interested him, but he took his pleasure from the ordering of both men and causes by the intellectual means of the law. As a trial lawyer he could and did teach Stimson much, especially the need for infinite pains in preparation and the virtues of limpid presentation. But the immense satisfaction in the law as a device to supply general patterns for the affairs of men the older man could never fully communicate to the younger.

There was more to Root than his lawyer's skill. As he seemed to know more about a case than anyone else, so he gave off the impression that he understood everything there was to understand in any human situation. He was wise in his own generation, in touch with all earthly considerations, able to appraise the full array of human urges without the unsettling responses of shock, surprise or sentiment. In his dealings with his fellows he was direct and generous, but there remained about him not so much formal aloofness as a kind of disengagement. He was funnier than most of his associates who were indeed members of a sober generation. But in his humors and sardonic asides there is a suggestion of disappointment as well as of muted delight in the odd doings of men.

It is possible that at one time he harbored a larger, warmer faith in human possibilities, a faith that had not been fulfilled by his experiences in his profession or his private life. In any case he was left not so much cynical as without illusion in his calculation of what had to be done or could be done by the human agency. It would never have occurred to him to say that the people was a great beast, but convinced of man's normal ineptitude he was quite ready to accept the necessity of putting things under the direction not of the rich or of the wellborn, but of those who had demonstrated the greatest ability. Since he was one of the able, he stood prepared to take his part in the ordering of his society. He had no conviction that, in so doing, he or anyone else could remold the condition of things much closer to the heart's desire, but he could at least try to make the existing system work a little better. What anyone ought to bring to this task was brains, honesty, and a detachment from the claims of immediate self-interest. What Elihu Root brought besides was an instinct for order and for the way power can be used, with restraint but also with assurance, to introduce order in a system. On Henry Stimson he exerted a profound influence. To no man, save his own father, Stimson frequently acknowledged, did he owe as much intellectually and morally; and the father himself once admitted that, were it not for his own admiration for Root, he would be jealous of the hold he had over his son.

The other man in the firm who was to play a great part in Stimson's career was Bronson Winthrop. The two had met on the threshold of the office in the Liberty Mutual Building on the November day in 1891 when both first reported for work in the Root firm. Winthrop, like Stimson, had been brought to the attention of the senior partner by William C. Whitney. He was an unusual man. Bearing the surname and blood of one of the earliest American families (he was a direct descendant of Governor John Winthrop), he had been born in France and educated at Eton and Trinity College. Just before entering the Root firm, he had obtained his law degree from Columbia. At the Winthrop home in New York Stimson found an atmosphere compounded of history and formality he had never known before. The silver of four generations was on the sideboard; menservants in livery stood in constant attendance. Into these surroundings Bronson Winthrop fitted naturally — Stimson in the first days called him the "Exquisite" — but in their popular connotations they hardly expressed his personality. He was, for one thing, the most unassuming of men, a bachelor pathologically shy. Only on the fiftieth anniversary of their first meeting, after half a century of common service together in the law, could he bring himself to write Stimson of his "respect and love which somehow I never expressed before." By constant small acts of generosity or thoughtfulness, however, he revealed to his associates the feelings he could not find words for. No one gave more time to the young clerks; he would spend hours raising and refining on points of law with them; on week ends he would take them out to his house on Long Island for exercise and sociability.

The surroundings of his family home did not suggest the industry though they did reflect the precision of his mind. It was a patient, subtle intelligence, intent, as a colleague said, on achieving work of quality; indeed the end was perfection. He loved the law as philosophers love metaphysics and occupied himself endlessly with the microscopic examination of every face of a legal problem. Nor did he limit himself to a special kind of law; in his long career he worked with distinction on litigation and reorganizations, in corporate law of all kinds; in his early years he frequently tried jury cases and as he grew older he became "especially learned in the law of wills, estates, and estate management." Root called him the best lawyer in the city. If the law is indeed a priesthood Bronson Winthrop had taken the final vows.

His fascination with the profession as a place where one could reason for reason's sake, Stimson could not really share. But Stimson could learn a great deal from Winthrop. In the early days especially they talked over cases and problems together at great length. From his partner, Stimson picked up a good deal about how to organize a sustained line of argument. As a result of their conversations, he also began to think more about how what he was doing might be placed in a larger context than just the doing of immediate good. Winthrop with his British education embarrassed him greatly by revealing a far fuller understanding of the development of American society and institutions. It was from the example of his friend that he began enlarging his store of information about his country's history. In Winthrop also he had constantly placed before him, but to less effect, the pleasures and profits a man could discover from wide reading in the literature of other times and other civilizations.

Winthrop and Stimson became members of the firm together on New Year's Day 1893. There followed twelve years in which, together, they educated themselves in what Stimson called the business of general practice. For the first six years they had the assistance of Mr. Root in this developing education. Stimson worked directly with the senior partner in the celebrated litigations of the Aqueduct case, the Hamilton Will case and *Metropolitan Street Railway* vs. *3rd Avenue Railroad*. From these labors he learned a great deal about the legal problems faced by the municipal and industrial enterprises the firm represented. Appearing frequently to assist Mr. Root in court, he also learned much about the art of presenting a case before a judge or jury.

But the steadying influence of the senior partner was withdrawn in 1899 when Root went to Washington to become the Secretary of War. The two young men — in their early thirties and with only six years of experience behind them — were then left "pie eyed with the best practice in New York and everybody trying to get it away from us." They changed the name of the firm on May 1, 1901, to Winthrop and Stimson and set out to defend the business they had inherited. It was not easy.

Stimson felt he "never knew what the rough end of life in New York can be until I saw these people trying to grab business away from us." Many of the clients who had been attracted by the great reputation of the senior partner did in fact take their difficulties elsewhere in the next few years. And their departure was made the more serious because neither of the two young lawyers had the happy faculty of attracting new business quickly to the firm. But they proceeded patiently and thoroughly to do the work that was left to them and gradually new clients appeared, drawn by the growing reputation of the two partners for solid, reliable counsel. By 1906 when Stimson took a leave of absence to serve as the United States Attorney for the Southern District of New York they were on firm, independent ground, and Stimson himself was spoken of as a well-known Wall Street corporation lawyer.

This phrase — a Wall Street corporation lawyer — has arresting connotations, not all of which are implicit in the nature of the law practiced by Henry Stimson from 1893 to 1906. He and Winthrop had, to be sure, a good many corporations as clients. Among these were the Continental Rubber Company, the Consolidated Lithograph Company, the Camden Land and Improvement Company, the United States Printing Company, the National Sugar Refining Company, the New York Glucose Company, the Bank of North America, the Mutual Life Insurance Company and the Astoria Power and Light Company. In many instances the contribution of the firm was limited to assisting these companies into life or out of it. Small organizations like the American Perfection Engine Company or the Colorplate Company were, in those days of industrial change, forever beginning or ending their short existences. For them Stimson drew up acts of incorporation, he made plans for the sale of plant and assignment of patents, or worked out a subscription agreement for the sale of bonds to finance a cold storage terminal.

Some of the clients enjoyed a longer life and contributed more frequent business to the firm. As counsel for the Bank of

North America Stimson began in one year fifteen actions to recover on promissory notes. These ranged in size from $10,000 to $53.32. Once, for the bank, he spent the better part of five months, along with lawyers from White and Case and from Sullivan and Cromwell, in bringing a claim against the Oil Seeds Pressing Company, bankrupts for $1579.88. Frequently the time consumed in such matters was even greater; the bank's action to collect the note for $53.32 was in and out of the registers of Winthrop and Stimson for the better part of three years. On another occasion it took a year to settle a difficulty for the Morton Trust Company. The bank, through Stimson, sought to restrain a tenant in one of its buildings from damaging property. Suit was started, accompanied by an offer to discontinue if the tenant would pay $100; a counterproposal of $50 was the basis for a final compromise of $75.

There were, of course, in the field of corporations some more important matters. Stimson, for instance, acted in the reorganization of the Central Washington Railroad and represented the Mutual Life Insurance Company when its high bid for a $10,-000,000 mortgage bond issue was voided on a technicality by the New York, New Haven and Hartford Railroad. The road, after rejecting the life insurance company bid, had sold the issue to J. P. Morgan and Company for less money. After four months of investigation amid the statutes on fraud, bids and contracts, and the personal liabilities of officers and directors, Stimson reached the conclusion that the Finance Committee of the railroad had "committed a breach of duty and violation of trust amounting to a waste of property and assets of the Company." Unless the officers were prepared "to vacate the pretended sale of the bonds," they would be subject to proceedings to hold them "personally liable for all damages sustained by reason of acceptance of the lower bid." Responding to such opinion and pressure the railway canceled the sale to J. P. Morgan and Company and accepted the Mutual Life Insurance Company's proposition.

From time to time Stimson appeared in court on behalf of the corporations he represented. Once he successfully argued a case "important as affecting the interests of the state" for the Astoria Light, Heat and Power Company. The utility had obtained some underwater land from the State Land Board. The City claimed the land could be disposed of only with the permission of the City Dock Board, a claim that was, after Stimson's argument, disallowed. But these appearances in court in the interest of corporate clients were rare. As Stimson said later, the business of the firm in these years was a general practice. There was, naturally, much proving of wills, searching of titles, collecting of bills, foreclosing of mortgages and passings through bankruptcy.

There was also much rendering of counsel on the points of conflict and pain that arise out of mundane human endeavors. The firm advised a woman on how to stop a discharged employee from annoying her present servant; the partners searched for the whereabouts of Herbert Daunt; they arranged a settlement between an employer and an office boy who had stolen watches; they obtained warrants for the arrest of husbands on charges of abandonment; they drew up a standard form for the employment of stable boys and arranged a contract between William C. Whitney and the jockey Hildebrand. They told Miss Booth why she could not collect from the city the cost of grading her own land that abutted on Concord Avenue and they settled a suit between members of a family over the title to premises once owned by the family in common. For two years they were busy with an alleged breach of contract between the prima donna of an opera company and her manager. Much of the evidence was in German and much of it was conflicting. It could be made to seem, for instance, that at different times the prima donna had agreed to appear thirty-five, or forty-five, or fifty-one times before the public. Bronson Winthrop loved every minute of the hard work involved in getting at the truth of this intricate matter, which was resolved after two years by a settlement of $948.83.

This general practice, typical of the small but growing firms in Wall Street at this period, made the two partners in these years what was called "comfortable." From 1898 to 1906 Stimson received somewhere between eight and eleven thousand dollars each year. This was, as he said, "a living," but it was "never thoroughly satisfactory" in other ways. He was constantly vexed by the small and, in any large sense, meaningless transactions that engaged his attention. He disliked the dependence of the lawyer for the nature of his business upon the ineptitudes or defections of others. He was always getting merely fragments and usually unattractive fragments of other people's, other institutions' lives. There was no consistency, no central direction in the career he was developing for himself. "You get a chance, incidentally, to do good in it and to help along someone or some good cause, but primarily, private practice is necessarily devoted, as I suppose most business is, to making your own living." What he disliked most was that in the conflict between private and public interests the former were almost always better served because of the better fees. The long-run effect was bound to be bad. "In this country, it is essential that the rights of property, and the rights of the public, whenever they are threshed out in the law forum, shall be threshed out fairly and with an adequate representation of both sides." The sum of it was that in private practice he did not feel the "ethical side" satisfied; he did not feel close to the "problems of life." As a private lawyer he was still in "the dark places where I had been wandering all my life. . . ."

In his activities outside the office from 1893 to 1906 he took such steps as he could to make the living he made worth the living, to illuminate at least the corners of the dark places.[1]

---

[1] The material for this chapter was drawn chiefly from the following sources: Stimson Papers; files of Winthrop, Stimson, Putnam and Roberts; conversations with George Roberts and Allen Klots; *New York State Reporter*, Vols. 46, 55; *Vicennial Report of the Class of 1888*; James Bryce, *The American Commonwealth*, 2 vols., 2nd edition revised (New York, 1889); T. F. Fenton, "Practice of Law in New York City," *Harvard Law Review*, May 1896; Austin Fox, "Two Years Experience of the New York State Board of Law Examiners," *Harvard Law Review*, November 1896; Philip C. Jessup, *Elihu Root*, 2 vols. (New York, 1938); Otto E. Koegel, *Walter S. Carter* (New York, 1953).

7

Divers Good Causes

ON THE DAY after the presidential election of 1892 Stimson had watched with detached amusement as the sorrowing party workers, seeking aid and comfort, filed into Mr. Root's office. For one thing he and his father had voted for Cleveland. For another, concerned about his progress in his new profession, absorbed in his own private affairs, he had small interest in matters political. For him, as for many of his contemporaries in this period, politics was something other people, a different kind of people, did. Two years in the Liberty Mutual Building changed this attitude. As he said, "I could not live and work in those early years in such an office as that of Root and Clarke without learning the importance of the active performance of his public duties by a citizen of New York."

In the way of public duties there was much that an active citizen could find to do in those days. The things said about New York by Dr. Parkhurst, Jacob Riis, James Bryce, Lincoln Steffens and the others were all, or almost all, true. There were slums, sin and violence. There were also subtler but equally destructive forms of corruption such as the traffic in franchises for public utilities — water, light, fuel, transport. The difficulty was that these vicious or dishonest activities were carried on with the protection or active assistance of members of the municipal government. Beneath nearly every city hall, it was said, "there was a cesspool . . . dug secretly by politicians in the pay of respectable, or at least respected, business men." In the city of New York the leadership of both parties was in the hands of those who, because they profited by the conditions, were reluctant to alter circumstances. There were, for instance, six members of the old Tweed Ring, a convicted murderer, four professional gamblers, and three former prize fighters on the Tammany Executive Committee in 1890. The Republicans under T. C. Platt were scarcely better.

The problem for what was called the better element in the community was what it could do to change the situation. Some went to church on Sunday and listened scandalized to the vivid ministerial reports they heard and let the matter drop there. Others, more active, organized the better element into several independent agencies to bring pressure to bear from outside upon the machinery of government. Since 1870 this had been the most popular procedure. In 1894 these organizations were attempting to secure civic reform by guerrilla tactics: The People's Municipal League; the City Reform Club, founded by John Jay Chapman; the Good Government Clubs, an elaborate federation of high-minded citizens; the Chamber of Commerce Committee of 50; the City Vigilance League; the Home Rule Democracy; the German-American Reform Union; and the Citizens Union.

The men in these organizations were decent and, frequently, dedicated; but they suffered, also frequently, from the sin of the high-minded in suspecting the good intentions of others bent on the same errand. In fact they wasted a great deal of time and energy in counteraccusations and in quarrels over questions of jurisdiction and objective. Also these agencies, whether acting independently or collectively, possessed the fatal defect of every organization on the periphery; they had no secure base for their contemplated operations against the solidly entrenched political parties. Still, with their loud cries and their earnestness, they quickened the metropolitan conscience, defined the civic issues, and, at times, modified where they could not correct the behavior of public officials.

Another way to change matters lay open to the citizen who

wished to perform his duties. He could directly enter the machinery of a political party in the hope of altering the structure and replacing the existing leadership. This was an unattractive and lonely business; it involved talking with as well as about politicians and it involved a certain amount of time on ward pavements. Too few were enthusiastic pilgrims on this particular path of duty in these days, but some, like Theodore Roosevelt, Herbert Parsons and Elihu Root, had demonstrated the path could be taken with success.

And, all things taken together, the remarkable thing about New York municipal politics in this time was not how sinful, in the light of opportunities offered, the party managers were, but how many were the private citizens who devoted a large part of their time, one way and another, to combating the forces of sin. It is true that the moral issues were reassuringly clear and that the conditions were calculated to rouse even sluggish temperaments. It is true also that the situation offered a rich field of operations for those who loved the maneuver of politics. On the other hand the men who joined the clubs or sought to reform from within as party workers were, on the whole, working long and hard at their own professional or commercial pursuits. They had their own lives to live and had, for the most part, very little to gain in a direct way from a change of conditions.

It is therefore interesting that these men have not fared very well in the historical perspective. Those who chose to work on the periphery — the "Goo Goos" — have been often dismissed, sometimes tolerantly, sometimes suspiciously, in a rather odious phrase as "patrician reformers." Those who worked within the parties have been suspected of having larger ambitions and "flexible scruples"; they would even make deals, it has been discovered, with the Easy Boss or Richard Croker in the interests of survival.

The Goo Goos were in fact annoying; John Jay Chapman, Preble Tucker, Fulton Cutting and all the others were often shrill, frequently inept, and, almost always, unattractively self-righteous. The reforming party worker did make certain arrangements; Theodore Roosevelt, Herbert Parsons, Gherardi Davis on their way to power certainly arrived at some understandings with men already in power. And then there is something else. By and large the men who worked to reform the government of the city of New York in these days were well educated and in comfortable circumstances. They were also, in the sense that they knew each other, well connected. They came predominantly, in other words, from the upper level of the community — that is, from a class. Since a class in a society supposedly classless makes for uneasiness, it is found helpful, even in a historical perspective, to suggest that the peculiar virtues of men in their class did not amount to much. These virtues either existed as Goo Goo attitudes without influence on the edge of things, or they simply disintegrated when they came in contact with the common touch of a Thomas Collier Platt.

The thesis has at least the support of nomenclature. Tucker, Cutting, Wickersham, Root, Choate, Roosevelt, Evarts, Parsons, Swayne, Bliss, Jerome, De Forest, Schieffelin, Carter, Burlingham, Taft, Schwab, Hewitt, Low — these are good names. But the thesis does not really satisfy all the data. These good names in the closing decades of the century were attached to good men who in one way or another — as aldermen, members of city commissions, mayors, councilmen and chairmen of county committees — did good work in the city of New York and, later, in some instances, as congressmen, cabinet members, district attorneys, ambassadors and even as Presidents, did good work in the nation.

Henry Stimson was of this class. He was moved by several other considerations to take an active part in the government of the city. Shortly after he began the practice of law the citizenry was shocked by the appointment, as a gross political favor, of a man named Isaac Maynard to the Court of Appeals; and about the same time the Lexow Committee made public its findings of persistent civic corruption. These things moved Stimson to join a Good Government Club but, after a time in the Root office, he concluded that the way to proceed was not around the edges but into the center. Switching his party allegiance he went to work as a Republican in the smallest important political unit in the city, the election district.

The importance of the election district derived from its place in the hierarchy of the Republican organization. Much of the work — determination of party platforms and the selection of candidates for municipal and state offices — was done in conventions. In the election district delegates were selected, by popular suffrage, for the Assembly District Conventions; in the Assembly District Conventions delegates were chosen for the County Conventions; and in the County Conventions delegates were chosen for the State Conventions. Therefore, whoever controlled the popular vote in election districts could exert a determining influence upon the composition of all the party conventions which, in turn, determined the kind of officeholders who represented the party.

When Stimson began to work in 1895 he discovered how T. C. Platt and his executive officer Lemuel P. Quigg dominated his own election district and the others in the 27th Assembly District. It was done by the primitive chicanery of the old days. Votes were bought by small favors or, with less effort, they were manufactured. One district in Stimson's neighborhood was found to have on its check list 220 enrolled Republicans, although a house-to-house canvass revealed only 81 Republicans actually living in the district. This padding of check lists had two advantages for the boss. It enabled him to collect a large number of votes at election time without much expenditure of time and money. It also enabled him to send, on the basis of the presumed population, a far higher number of delegates to the Assembly District Convention than the real population justified. By such simple means the authority of the boss over the various stages of the party hierarchy was, in large part, maintained.

Stimson and his colleagues set out to reduce the power of the machine in several ways from 1895 to 1900. First they did the obvious things; they went from house to house to obtain an honest registration and to rouse the lackadaisical. They printed handbills, gave speeches and held forums to define the issues. On election day they got out the vote. After two years of steady labor they accomplished their first objective; they elected some of their own candidates to the 27th Assembly District Convention in 1897. This convention was called to select a candidate from the district for the state legislature in Albany. When the convention met, Stimson and his fellow delegates contested the seating of delegates from neighboring election districts whom they asserted had been elected by the familiar means. They argued that Quigg had used padded registration rolls to produce nonexistent votes for an inflated number of delegates to the Assembly District Convention.

Quigg absolutely refused to present the registration rolls for investigation. Stimson and his supporters were shouted down. The convention then went on to select Quigg's candidate for the county convention and the state assembly. Thus thwarted, the reform group withdrew and nominated their own candidate for the assembly. In the ensuing election their man beat both the Democratic candidate and Quigg's hand-picked selection. After two years of effort there was one seat in the state legislature to show for their labors.

This was a small return, but it had several consequences. The two years of labor convinced the workers that there ought to be new legislation governing the primary procedures in election districts. Paul D. Cravath and Henry Taft were told to prepare a bill establishing certain qualifications a political organization had to meet to be accepted as a political party. In the bill, also, rules were set forth for the registration of voters and inspection of the check list. The purpose of this bill was to take the power to run primary elections out of the hands of the bosses and thus to reduce at its origin the source of the bosses' power. The bill prepared by Cravath and Taft was then taken to Elihu Root who saw to it that the legislation was presented to the assembly. It was passed in 1898 with the support of Democrats and upstate Republicans who, through the years, had wearied of the power of the city bosses.

Thus encouraged, the men in the 27th District went forward to capitalize on their initial achievement of one man sent to the assembly. Stimson, who had started in 1895 as a captain responsible for about 300 voters in his election district, moved on by 1901 to become president of the 27th Assembly District Republican Club and a year or two later a member of the New York County Republican Committee. He also attended as a delegate the regular district, county and state conventions. He had the further satisfaction of seeing his own assembly district in every election from 1898 to 1902 select the men he supported — able men like Francis Laimbeer and Gherardi Davis — as candidates for public office.

These successes did not please Lemuel Quigg. In each primary he put his own slate of candidates up against the men supported by Stimson and his friends. On each occasion the Quigg nominees, in spite of the support of T. C. Platt, were defeated. But Quigg had further resources; as Platt's executive officer he controlled the distribution of party patronage. Until 1900 the control of patronage in the 27th Assembly District remained, not with the winning candidates, but with John Sabine Smith, thrice defeated for the assembly in these years but Quigg's right-hand man in the district.

On March 8, 1900, Stimson wrote to Governor Theodore Roosevelt to explain this situation. "The liberal Republican organization" had been, he said, "completely ignored." The issue was whether the district was to be run by its own citizens and the men they elected or by the machine created by Platt and Quigg which had been defeated by the citizens. From that time forward Quigg's influence in the 27th Assembly District virtually ceased to exist.

What Stimson thought he was doing by all this political activity he put into a letter to Root on February 16, 1901. He asked the Secretary of War to speak at the annual dinner of the 27th Assembly District Club. The club, he thought, was making "a sensible effort to work out the problems of decent party government with the machinery provided by American custom and law." It was making further "with utmost fidelity and patient work a searching test of the workability of our American party machinery under the conditions which exist in a modern American city." Since he and his fellows had spared "no effort, no expense, no self-sacrifice," if they failed "the chances are the machinery is not workable."

For five more years he took part in municipal and county politics to see what he could do to make the machinery work. When in 1906 he left to devote all his energies to the public service, he could look back with satisfaction at his decade in local politics. He had been part of a movement that produced, year in, year out, winning candidates of character and ability; that had, within the small area of his district, broken the power of the boss. That district presented, no doubt, favorable conditions; what was called "the silk stocking vote" was in a majority. Few other parts of the city were able, in fact, to profit greatly by the example of the 27th District. But the revolt there was used to define the issue of bossism and to pass a bill reducing the power of the bosses to control the primaries and thus to influence the selection of candidates for other offices.

The effect of these experiences upon Stimson himself was considerable. He had acquired an understanding of the political machinery as it was built up from the ward to the state. He had learned, too, a good deal about the political process. There were times, he had discovered, when it was enough to get out the vote and there were other times when even the will of the majority had to be reinforced by the reserves of influence. Others might draw the primary bill, but it was Root who was summoned to negotiate its introduction and arrange its passage. Quigg might try to cut the ground from under his feet by withholding the powers of appointment from successful candidates, but a word to Roosevelt, that governor who, it was said, had reached an understanding with Platt at Montauk, put a stop to Quigg's operations and to all the "underhanded nagging" in the 27th Assembly District.

Most of all, perhaps, he discovered that in politics, as in undergraduate speaking contests, or graduate school, or the practice of the law, it was careful preparation and hard work that did it. Cheering confirmation was to be found here, as elsewhere in that time, that labor at the center of things and the judicious use of power in support of objectives clearly defined and appropriately limited was the inevitable price and certain means of progress.

He was busy also in these years fulfilling other requirements of his time and place. There were, for one thing, the less fortunate. As a young law clerk he had, two or three times a month, brought words of cheer and some of his own money to several poverty-stricken families in the neighborhood of Mott Street. This direct individual attack on the problems of the poor he abandoned when, in the middle nineties, he began to take part in the administration of charitable organizations. Thereafter he was to be found frequently at the board meetings of institutions with arresting names and purposes — The Wayfarers' Lodge; The Order of the King's Daughters, which existed "to develop the spiritual life and increase Christian activities"; The Workroom for Unskilled Women; and the Penny Precedent Fund. He also served as legal counsel for the Lincoln Hospital.

There were others, also unfortunate, who, through the family, friendship, or the Bones association could lay a more direct claim upon his time and interest. These had fallen by the wayside from familiar causes, the purchase of mining stock, lingering illness, incompetence, simple drunkenness. To their calls he always responded, sometimes with a small donation, sometimes with recommendations for a sound investment or the arrangement for a job, never with a cautionary tale.

During these years his own life maintained its gently rising progression. As for its physical circumstances, they were those for which the brownstone has become the symbol. It is the expected inventory: heavy chairs, heavier sofas, silver trays and silver tea caddies, mohair, plush, mauve and dark red, cannel coal fires, massive vibrating shadows thrown by gaslight against high-studded walls, books and pictures telling cheerful stories or improving certain attitudes of mind. On the table and on time, leg of lamb and mint jelly, roast beef and currant jelly, brought in by maids in uniform. Around the table or before the stone mantel black suits, high collars, white shirts and high shoes, all made by little tailors or little cobblers out of stout materials.

The life that took place within these surroundings was well ordered. After an early and large breakfast, the head of the house walked downtown to work from his home at 18 East 32nd Street. At the end of the afternoon he walked back. On his return, after a short rest, he took a bath and changed for dinner. His wife, busy throughout the day with marketing, correspondence, calls and reading, joined with him in the diversions of the evening. One or the other read aloud before the fire from some worth-while book like Churchill's *The Crossing*, or the latest volume of John Fiske. Occasionally, as he lay dozing on the sofa, she recited the works of the nineteenth-century poets she knew by heart. When others were present at dinner or in the evening, they were usually members of the family. Dr. Stimson and his daughter were just around the corner at East 33rd, Grandfather and his wife and unmarried daughter were now at West 48th, Uncle Fred lived on East 39th, and Uncle Henry on East 34th. There was much dropping back and forth between these family stations during the week and a general conclave on Sunday noon. Not infrequently also the Stimson household was augmented by some member of the White family who came on from New Haven for two or three weeks.

If this appears a somewhat spare and staid routine for a young married couple, it was nevertheless what the two profoundly wanted for themselves. Their domestic life was carefully constructed to include and protect the things that gave them mutual satisfaction and to prevent the intrusion of irrelevancies. The diversions of the stage, for instance, attracted them rarely; the solace or excitement of music, never. Not much oftener did they attend the dances, small dinners, or receptions through which the social life of New York was carried forward. Mrs. Stimson knew very few people in the city and, as a young bride raised in a large, simple, cheerful household in a small city where everybody knew everybody else, she doubtless found the more carefully graduated social life of New York somewhat forbidding. In addition, as her husband's wife, she was immediately involved in the affairs of a large and intricately organized family. It did not simplify her task that she had also to acquire, by her own efforts for the most part, some understanding of an imposing body of tribal custom and ritual. Then too, though she was forthright and had a decent respect for her own self, she was without much experience, she was young, and she was also shy. On social occasions it was noticed she labored frequently under some kind of constraint. Throughout her life, in fact, she remained restive under the responsibilities of a hostess. New people — especially those of her own age — troubled her. Only those much younger, or women she had known from childhood, could she ever bring herself to call by their first names. When in later years, for instance, one of her acquaintances, the wife of a cabinet member, suggested the time had come to drop the formal means of address, she replied that she "did not feel quite that way" about her.

In these respects her husband was not much better. Many of his associates noticed that in company "he was not relaxed," that he never took part in general conversation, that he tended to seek out one man and talk earnestly to him, that "he was never really happy with his contemporaries." Neither he nor his wife possessed much skill in the instruments — humor, small talk —

by which inconsequential social intercourse is conducted. Just as neither liked to be touched, it was difficult apparently for either of them to become involved in less obvious forms of casual human contact like the shared joke or the common pursuit of some speculation.

The sources of such unease and constraint are always puzzling, and Stimson's friends were frequently puzzled by him. One associate, citing the facts that Stimson had gone to Andover, Yale, the Harvard Law School and had lived and practiced law in New York, concluded that not even a seventeenth-century Puritan, after such experiences, could continue to hold "as rigid a view of the foibles of man" as Stimson did. Whatever the causes, Stimson did guard himself against the relaxed and careless moment, the unregulated incident, in human experience. This task of interior administration was obviously simplified if he could control the environment in which he acted. Within the family, where loyalties ran with the affections, the situation could be brought to better order than in the wider world where unexpected sympathies sometimes produced confusing issues. Then too, it was easier to organize the energies in support of some known and settled purpose.

No other purpose of his life was as well defined as was his marriage. He and his wife counted themselves fortunate that they shared the same firm convictions on the things that were just, true and of good report. They agreed too on many of the tremendous trifles — such things as the times to eat and to work and to leave off working, and the times to keep silence, and the times to speak. On this large tract of common ground they met together all their lives in perfect trust.

One continuing sorrow brought them ever closer to each other. They soon discovered that the attack of mumps Stimson had suffered not long before the wedding, and from which he thought he had received no ill effect, prevented them from having children. What this meant to each of them and what it did to them they left to others to speculate upon. Some men thought it was as well there were no sons; with all the expectations, imperatives and stern injunctions it would have been too hard to qualify. A woman believed that daughters could easily have modified the stern conditions. Nevertheless, with no life coming up behind them, they were alone and, at times, obviously lonely. At times also the circuits were overloaded. Where there was no one else, where by force of circumstance they had to mean everything to each other, they had, sometimes, to oversympathize, overexpect, overrequire and overprotect. But, it was seen, they never fell into fatal acquiescence. If it had to be a marriage without children, it was nevertheless a family of two distinct and contrasting personalities. He worked, as always, with what lay in him to make the most of the situation in which he found himself. She did no less and probably something more. For instance, someone who knew them both for thirty years discovered, after he had died and she was an old woman thrown on her own devices, that she had a sense of humor of her own.

One of the ways in which she demonstrated not only her solicitude, but her spirit, was in the part she took in his excursions into the wilderness. From 1893 to 1903 he went either to Canada or, more frequently, to the old stamping ground in the West. Once, in 1896, he traveled to Switzerland and climbed the Matterhorn. The skill and courage revealed in this venture so impressed an English observer that thirty years later he wrote an article describing the ascent. In this country Stimson was the first man, so it is said, to climb the rugged heights of Chief Mountain in Montana. These trips — climbing and hunting — meant a great deal to him. He loved the isolation and the independence; he was excited by the hazards. On some headwall or along some trail he was forever putting himself not recklessly, but with calculation, into a dangerous circumstance. To the consternation of friends he would, for instance, go off to hunt a bear alone.

These friends, at times, accompanied him into the West. Gifford Pinchot, the animal sculptor A. Phimister Proctor, Bronson Winthrop once or twice joined his party. They found him, on such occasions, resourceful, tireless and "equable when he had his way." To obtain his way, Amos Pinchot recalled, he had "continually to be killing some poor damned animal or other, and when he was out after grizzly bear, the whole camp was subordinated to his paramount object — a dead bear. Nobody could rest till he got it."

Whatever the hazards and the hardships of such adventures, Mrs. Stimson shared them. Utterly untrained, to begin with, in the procedures of field and stream, disliking animals and not by temperament attached to the specialized charms of "roughing it," she unquestioningly joined her husband in his favorite pursuits. By day, upon occasion, she would remain alone at a remote campsite reading, but she learned to shoot, fish and above all to ride and to do all these things in a way that increased rather than cooled the pleasures of her rather exacting partner. When by force of circumstance she found herself the only source of love and support for her husband in their small household, she set herself to be sufficient. One of the ways she could do this was by her presence and she was to be found at his side in every kind of venture. Of the bonds that held them so closely together, one of the strongest was the sense of shared experience.

These excursions to the wild country were a necessity for Stimson himself. In New York the constant intellectual activity, which he never sustained naturally, but always as an act of the will, the rush and noise of the city itself, its rather aimless diversions, all of these told on him in the course of a year. As fall turned into winter, he usually felt the beginning of a sense of strain that grew with the season. He became troubled with indigestion, remembering breakfast, as he said, all through the day. When he was thirty-three, he began having the insomnia that persisted all his life. By the afternoon he would begin to find his strength ebbing away and the sharpness of his thought blurring around the edges. Then too, about 1900 he began to suffer so acutely from lumbago and rheumatism that he found it hard to stand in court. From time to time he broke out in sudden storms of anger at those around him. Then there were damns to be heard in his office and, indeed, down the corridors. Temporary relief from these accumulating symptoms he could find in exercise, but exercise, save for his daily walks to and from Liberty Street, was difficult to come by in New York.

Not until 1898 did he find a satisfactory outlet for his physical energy. For a variety of reasons, but primarily because he remained indifferent to the events in Cuba until they were almost over, he did not go off to the Spanish-American War. This failure to join the colors caused him, in later years, an uneasiness, a kind of troubled doubt about himself rarely revealed to his associates. At the time he did, however, join the National Guard as a private in Squadron A, Troop 2. There he learned the enduring joys of horses and military routines. He began as a blacksmith, and his first insignia of rank — a horseshoe — remained his most valued military award. The regular weekly drills at the 94th Street armory and the two-week exercises in the field every summer gave him intense satisfaction.

More exciting were the ten days' service he performed in maintaining order during the strike of the workers who were building the Croton Reservoir, and the engagement he always called the Third Battle of Manassas. This was a war game in 1904 when the regular army and the National Guard combined to have a ten-day maneuver on the site of the Civil War battlefield. Stimson, as a corporal in the Blue Army, commanded by General Grant, the son of Ulysses, held captains' horses, captured a member of the 7th Cavalry who was "awfully sore," and took part in a night ride that surrounded a troop of infantry. He remained in the Guard for eight years, retiring in 1906 with the rank of first lieutenant. One of the most satisfying results of this service was "a very gallant little horse" called Bouncer that he bought, on its return from the Spanish-American

War, for twenty dollars. On Bouncer Mrs. Stimson learned to ride, and the horse became the "nucleus of our stable."

The stable, until 1903, was confined to Bouncer and the 94th Street armory. In that year, however, the animal was moved out to West Hills, Long Island. His owner had, for some time before, been searching for a more satisfying and permanent way to mitigate the rigors of urban life. Each summer since 1898 the Stimsons had spent some time in rented houses on Long Island, taking with them ordinarily their nieces, the Gamble children, whose mother was Mrs. Stimson's sister. About 1900 Stimson began looking for land in the area where he could build the kind of home he wanted. By 1903 he felt himself on firm enough financial ground to make his purchase. He bought first about thirty acres on a rise of land in Huntington where there was a small house built in the eighteenth century. To the north there were fugitive glimpses of the Sound. Over the next year he built, on plans that were designed by his cousin Dunham Wheeler, a plain, unassuming frame house that stood 300 feet above the tidewater, which could be seen across low rolling meadows off to the south. On June 21, 1904, he sent with his last payment on a total amount of $7,500, a note to the builder which said that he could not say "how gratified I am at the character of the work you've done." And in return the builder hoped "sincerely that you may spend many happy hours in your new residence."

The builder's hopes were gratified. Highhold was at first the occasional refuge from all the strains of professional and official life; it became in later years the final residence of the couple, and it was at all times the scene of the most deeply satisfying personal activity of the owner. In these years it was used in summer by the Stimsons as a place to gather round them members of the family for the long vacation. In winter it was used on holidays and week ends as an escape from the city and, occasionally, as a quiet place for an uninterrupted week of work on a stubborn law case.

In the years from 1893 to 1906 Stimson achieved many of the things he had set out to do. He became a senior partner in one of the respected law firms of the city. He acquired, if not an impressive financial competence, at least security. His urges to serve some larger cause than his own well-being were partially fulfilled in his political activity and in his contribution to the traditional instruments of public charity. In the vacations, which were always important periods in each year, he was able to do exactly the kind of thing he loved best. At Highhold he had established a base for the kind of life he liked above all others. What a man of his time and place ordinarily set store by, he, in these fourteen years, had achieved by his own hard work. Yet, almost daily, he was stirred by some troubling doubt, frustrated and thwarted by some obstacle which, for all his efforts, he could not fully define or remove. Others toward the end of the year 1905 removed it for him. In December of that year he received an offer that took him out of the dark places and placed him on a height "where I could see the stars and get my bearings once more." [1]

[1] The material for this chapter was chiefly drawn from the following sources: Stimson Papers; New York *Tribune*, 1895-1903; Harold F. Gosnell, *Boss Platt and His New York Machine* (Chicago, 1924); Elting E. Morison, ed., *The Letters of Theodore Roosevelt*, 8 vols. (Cambridge, 1951-1954); Arthur Meier Schlesinger, *The Rise of the City 1878-1898* (New York, 1933).

8

The United States District Attorney

In 1933 STIMSON told a friend that the office of the United States Attorney for the Southern District of New York "has always been my first love. I felt then," he went on, "and I still feel that there is no other public office . . . which makes such a direct and inspiring call upon the conscience and professional zeal of a high-minded lawyer as that office, or in which courageous effort and steady poise bring such a sense of satisfaction to the occupant."[1]

The inspiring call sounded but faintly through the grimy chambers of the office in 1905. It was agreed, for one thing, that the physical conditions were "deplorable." Within the dark confines, witnesses, clerks, assistants and criminals were "all jumbled together." So were the office files; the attorneys lived in "constant anxiety lest valuable papers be lost." Eight lawyers and one stenographer conducted the legal business of the United States in the Southern District. By law they were required to "be in their office every day part of the time." Almost all of them engaged in private practice in an effort to supplement their tiny salaries and limited their official service to grinding "the small daily grist of routine matters."[2]

Supervising their activities in 1905 was the District Attorney, "Lightning Eyes" Burnett, a friend of McKinley, a student of

[1] H.L.S. to Martin Conboy, Nov. 28, 1933.
[2] H.L.S. to W. H. Moody, April 5, Aug. 10, 1906, to C. J. Bonaparte, July 15, 1907. A. G. Langeluttig, *The Department of Justice of the United States* (Baltimore, 1927), 75 ff., describes briefly the duties of U.S. Attorneys in the districts.

the Standard-bred horse, a trial lawyer who by custom did not appear in court for the government. Such time as he did not spend in private practice was devoted to the administration of his office. Like all public servants, he had to file extended reports on his progress each month; he had also to forward to his chief in Washington a record of his expenditures, including the amount he had spent on postage and carfare each month, before he could receive more money. Whenever important or difficult cases came up —"extraordinary matters" they were called — he arranged to have them placed, in accordance with the rules of custom, in the hands of lawyers engaged in private practice. For these duties he was rewarded, not with a salary, but with part of the sums recovered by his office from litigation, particularly in customs cases. The amount obtained by the attorney in this fashion was estimated to be about $100,000 annually, more than four times the amount set aside in 1905 by the government to defray the expenses of his office of eight lawyers and one stenographer. Not far from the chambers of the United States Attorney, in the United States Post Office Building, was the office of the Corporation Counsel for the City of New York. In the same year the Counsel had a staff of twenty-nine assistants and a budget of $138,450.[3]

The general condition of affairs — repeated in every district office of the Department of Justice throughout the country — was not lost on the new Attorney General in Washington, William Henry Moody. It was reported in the fall of 1905 that he was holding conferences with the President and senators about the conditions "that had not been giving satisfaction." One of the results of these conferences was a telegram of December 8, 1905, inviting Stimson to "take lunch" with the President on the following Monday.

Stimson went down to Washington prepared to talk with

[3] "Remarks of Joseph H. Choate" at testimonial dinner, May 20, 1909 (copy of proceedings in Stimson Papers); New York *Tribune*, Jan. 11, 1906; H.L.S. to C. J. Bonaparte, July 15, 1907.

Roosevelt about the pleasures of hunting bear. He knew the President through their mutual membership in the Boone and Crockett Club and through their occasional meetings about political matters in the State of New York. But nothing in their past relationship suggested that Roosevelt might be considering Stimson for a federal office. It is probable that Roosevelt himself would not have thought of the idea if Root had not suggested the name of his former partner as a possible candidate for the position of United States Attorney for the Southern District of New York. When, after lunch, Roosevelt asked if his visitor would be interested in such an appointment Stimson replied that he would like very much to be considered for the place. There were some difficulties, the President said, that might cause delay. Charles E. Hughes was under consideration and there were some "necessary arrangements" to be made with Senator Platt who had a candidate of his own. But the President would see what he could do. So Stimson returned to New York and heard nothing more until January 11, when he read in the papers that his appointment had been confirmed by the Senate. On February 1 he took the oath "as a meet person learned in the law," and went to work.[4]

In the days between his appointment and his assumption of the new duties, he had been told, in several conferences, what he was expected to do. The first task, Moody explained, was to reorganize his office, to build up a staff that would support him in the second task assigned, which was to try all the important cases in court himself. In addition, the Attorney General told him, the fee system would be abolished; instead he would receive a salary of $10,000.[5]

---

[4] H.L.S., "Memorandum of interesting (to me) occasions and events in my life during the past few years," Jan. 17, 1909; "Memorandum on U.S. Attorney of the Southern District of New York" (now part of the Stimson Diary).

[5] "Memo on Southern District"; H.L.S. to W. H. Moody, Jan. 11, 1906. Both Burnett and Judge Thomas, a U.S. District Judge, warned Stimson that he would never be able to appear in court because the paper and administrative work in the office was so "onerous."

The first step obviously was to obtain some new men, and he was not long in finding that there were always plenty of candidates for public office. Many came forward to remind him of the claims on his affection made by the ties of old acquaintance, the Bones association or blood. These he pushed aside with the assertion that his office was "not a political sinecure, but a great professional opportunity" which he was going to "push as hard as I can." Equally, he disregarded the more subtle obligations of politics. To the President he wrote that while he had found Mr. Mahan "attractive and agreeable," and while he shared with Roosevelt an awareness "of the debt that the country owes to his father," still he "does not seem to have made quite the record for force and efficiency. . . ." A congressman who had, in vain, suggested several "bright young faces" was told, "I didn't want you to recommend anyone for the place whom I cannot implicitly rely upon to refuse a $10 bill when an Italian offers it to him, as will happen almost every day."

The disregard of political considerations, sustained through three years of office, did not go unremarked. Herbert Parsons, an old friend and member of Congress, wrote Stimson in 1908 that "Splendidly as you have done, it is my opinion, a distinct misfortune for politics generally in New York that you have not sought to enlist men who politically are active and who come from different parts of the city and different elements in its population." Ruefully, as one who knew Stimson well, he concluded, "This is a matter I have not argued with you inasmuch as you know your own mind and are not likely to change." [6]

[6] H.L.S. to Herbert Parsons, Jan. 11, April 10, 1906, to C. J. Bonaparte, Dec. 22, 1906, to Theodore Roosevelt, April 10, 1908; Herbert Parsons to H.L.S., May 2, 1908. Roosevelt at the time of Stimson's appointment assured him that he would be left alone to run his own office and "almost in the same breath" began suggesting names for Stimson to consider. But he did not ever insist that Stimson take any of the suggested names. He put his assurance that he would not intervene in the affairs of the Southern District this way to Stimson: "My dear fellow, if I had the slightest intention of interfering in your office, I would promise of course; but I have no such intention."

It was one thing to refuse the unlikely candidate, and quite another to attract the properly qualified. An offer to serve the government in a minor position, for a salary that ranged from $750 a year upwards to $1500, would not ordinarily prove irresistible to an experienced man in a New York law firm. Stimson had to think of another solution. Reflecting that law clerks in big firms were not getting much more money than he could offer, and were frequently spending their time in less interesting or exciting areas of the law than he could provide, he wrote off to the law schools for the names of recent able graduates who were serving as clerks in firms in and about New York. Particularly he sought assistance from his old friend, James Barr Ames, at the Harvard Law School. By these means he obtained the names and by his own persuasion he secured the services of a remarkable group of young men — among them Emory Buckner, Goldthwaite Dorr, Winfred Dennison, Wolcott Pitkin, Francis Bird, Thomas Thacher and Felix Frankfurter. Out of this group came in later years illustrious members of the New York Bar, colonial administrators in the Philippines and Puerto Rico, solicitors general of the United States, United States Attorneys of the Southern District of New York, one member of the highest court of New York, and one member of the Supreme Court of the United States. In the years from 1906 to 1909 these young men formed around Stimson a devoted, well-trained, very intelligent staff. They both shared and stimulated his own rather fierce joy in smiting the transgressor. By their youth they contributed "a kind of élan" to the work; the whole office, in Frankfurter's words, was "impregnated with excitement." [7]

Collectively, too, these young men gave something to Stimson he had never really had before: the sense of well-being, the almost physical satisfaction, that comes from working intimately and too hard with others toward a particular, common end.

[7] *Active Service*, 6-7; H.L.S. to J. B. Ames, June 30, 1906, to W. H. Moody, Aug. 10, 1906; conversation with Felix Frankfurter, Sept. 29, 1954.

Some stanzas from an office poem, no shorter or better than any other office poem, suggest the atmosphere with which the assistants surrounded the District Attorney.

Twas a day we'll not forget I think
When Sammy wrote the note
For things got badly on the blink
When Sammy wrote the note
The Chief sprang up and pulled his hair
Went forty feet into the air
Raged like a lion in his lair
When Sammy wrote the note.

He pushed four thousand bells for Fred
When Sammy wrote the note
He raised the hair on Miss Storm's head
When Sammy wrote the note;
Where's Wise, Where's Wise he madly cried
And Frankfurter, where does he hide
Not one damn fool is by my side
When Sammy writes this note.

If Stimson could not enter directly into the high jinks and wreathed smiles of his office, he could display his attitude toward the young men in ways that came more naturally to him. In the course of one trial, some information was published in the papers that a reporter said had been told him by one of Stimson's assistants. In court the opposing counsel asked the judge to cite the assistant for contempt. Stimson arose to say categorically that the reporter was in error, that he was in fact not telling the truth. To his assistant sitting beside him in court he said no word about this matter, but instead drove him to his home in the Bronx every night for the rest of the week. In other ways he constantly revealed, as one of his assistants wrote him, "your disinterestedness and tender fairness, but above all, your thoughtfulness, generosity and loyalty towards your subordinates. . . . An experience such as has been my rare fortune during the last few months becomes a life's possession."

With this staff, recruited for the most part in the first nine months of his new duty, Stimson conducted the business of his office for three years. Much of this business was the "small grist of routine duties." In the records of any district attorney appears the evidence of the trouble men get into or inflict on others because they are weak or perverse or afraid. There one can find, in bald detail, the immemorial schemes devised, in every age, by man's waywardness. Stimson, like those before and after him, caught a man at smuggling Swiss watches, and another in selling women into white slavery. For some months he pursued a Southern railroad that held men, under armed guard, in peonage for indebtedness, contrived and continued by cunning bookkeeping. He put men in prison for giving "faked tips" on horse racing. By "vigorous and successful criminal prosecution," his office prevented José Giordani from shipping gunpowder in food cartons to a revolutionary cabal in Haiti. He tried a man who had taken money to weigh cheese and figs in an inaccurate scale at a customs house, and he tried another who had devised a plan to evade the duties on comfits and marrons sent from France. Before the judges he also brought counterfeiters, the owners of bucket shops, and labor factors who, for a fee, brought in foreigners with "trachoma and other diseases." The investigation and prosecution of the designers of these small and squalid transactions were the daily, unnoticed business of his office.[8]

Other matters placed him, by chance, closer to the public notice by putting him in touch with some of the famous names and events of the period. When soldiers who had served in Brownsville challenged the right of Theodore Roosevelt to order their discharge from the Army, Stimson successfully defended the dismissal as a proper exercise of presidential power. On the appeal of the master of the *General Slocum*, who had been found guilty of negligence, he argued, again successfully, in support of

[8] *Report* from the U.S. Attorney of the Southern District to C. J. Bonaparte, Aug. 14, 1908, JD 1393-98.

the decision of the lower court. To the considerable delight of William Randolph Hearst, he also instituted proceedings against James Gordon Bennett, the publisher of the New York *Herald*. For years the *Herald* had printed in its personal column notices like this: "Thursday, 8:20 P.M. Will lady in blue on platform Broadway Car, 40th St. who noticed gentleman, address Admirer, Herald 146." No one, in all these years, as Mayor Van Wyck confessed in 1898, had cared "to stake up against the New York *Herald*." Stimson was able to establish the responsibility of the publisher for the things that went into this column and Bennett was fined $25,000 by Judge Hough as a man who had, the Judge remarked, maintained "for more years than I can remember . . . a potent aid to local libertines, and a directory of local harlots." [9]

It was not for this kind of work, however, that Moody had asked Stimson to assemble a staff "equal in their combined talents to any office, anywhere, public or private." The Attorney General had come to his office with the determination to enforce the federal laws that had been passed to protect the society from the unregulated actions of large corporations. Three days after Stimson had been invited to lunch at the White House in December, Moody, in a circular of December 8, had made his purpose clear to his subordinates in the districts. He directed them "to diligently investigate all complaints which may come to you from any source . . . and upon your own initiative" of violations of the Elkins Act which prohibited "rebates and other discriminatory practices" on the part of corporations. Since the only penalties assigned by the act were fines, Moody urged his subordinates to seek evidence that would sustain a charge of conspiracy against officers of companies engaged in discriminatory actions. On such a charge it was possible to imprison those found guilty and Moody wished to do everything in his power

[9] H.L.S. to Theodore Roosevelt, May 6, 1908; New York *Tribune*, May 5, 10, 16, 1908; H.L.S. to Ezra Thayer, Feb. 17, 1908, to G. W. Wickersham, May 22, 1909, to Elihu Root, Oct. 8, 1906; New York *Herald*, Oct. 12, 1901; H.L.S. to Attorney General, Feb. 21, 1907, JD 84996.

"to the end that these unlawful practices, which have received almost universal condemnation, may be discouraged and prevented. . . ." [10]

In conversations with Stimson after his appointment in January, Moody described his purpose in great detail. At the time no prosecution under either the Elkins Act or the Sherman Act had been successfully brought to trial in the Southern District. Moody made perfectly clear that his desire was to have his new assistant reorganize his office to the end that successful prosecution under these acts could be undertaken. In another way Moody attempted to make certain that Stimson could get promptly to work in the enforcement of the law against corporate transgressors. The dockets of the district courts in New York were so crowded that in 1905 only 27 out of 650 terminated criminal cases were actually brought to trial. The Attorney General joined with Stimson's friend, Herbert Parsons, the Congressman, in obtaining from Congress a new federal judgeship in New York in 1906. In pushing this through a reluctant legislature, Stimson was also active; and later he and Moody together obtained the support of Taft and Root in a masterful operation by which Roosevelt was persuaded to appoint Charles M. Hough, a man with a mind of "high initial velocity" and "unfaltering" courage as the new Judge before whom Stimson argued many of his cases.[11]

Thus supported by his chief and provided with improved machinery for the administration of federal justice in the Southern District, Stimson, only one hour after he took office, began his operations on what he later called "the new front of great corporate transgression." In the next three years in office he obtained the dissolution of the Manila Paper Manufacturers Asso-

[10] *Circulars* of the Attorney General, Dec. 8, 1905, JD 70192; New York *Tribune*, Dec. 13, 1905.
[11] "Memo on Southern District"; "Remarks of W. D. Guthrie" at testimonial dinner, May 20, 1909; New York *Tribune*, Dec. 7, 1905, May 12, 22, 1906; Herbert Parsons to H.L.S., Feb. 2, 8, 15, 20, March 20, 1906; H.L.S. to Herbert Parsons, April 21, 1906; W. H. Moody to H.L.S., May 25, 29, 1906.

ciation, which was found to be a combination in restraint of trade. He successfully argued in support of a petition of the Interstate Commerce Commission to make E. H. Harriman and Otto Kahn answer questions put by the Commission concerning their transactions. At issue was the constitutional and statutory power of the Commission to investigate the financial operations of an interstate carrier and thus were "involved national questions of vital importance." [12]

Then there were three great cases. In the first of these, Stimson proceeded against the American Sugar Refining Company and a number of railroads for violating the provisions of the Elkins Act. The company had used its dominant position in the sugar trade to set the rates at which its product would be carried by the railroads. Since sugar contributed a large proportion, some said 40 per cent, of all western freight traffic out of New York, the roads were powerless to resist. They thus secretly paid back to the corporation the difference between the published rates established by the I.C.C. and the lower rate arbitrarily set by the sugar company. This was the sin of rebating. In this instance the corporation used the low freight rates it insisted upon to drive out competition of sugar-beet growers in the West. Stimson, in the course of prosecution, proved the payment of rebates, revealed the intricate system by which the sugar company coerced the roads into lower rates, and obtained the conviction of all the parties involved in the system.[13]

Somewhat later he obtained the conviction of Charles W. Morse. This extraordinary man was believed by many at the

[12] H.L.S. to Theodore Roosevelt, Jan. 16, 1908; New York *Tribune*, Nov. 14, 1907, April 26, May 5, June 20, 23, Dec. 15, 1908; H.L.S. to J. W. Taussig, Nov. 17, 1910.
[13] The record of this prosecution is in JD 58-9-13. It includes briefs, transcripts of conversations between Stimson, Moody and witnesses, exchanges of correspondence between Moody's office and Stimson's office. A dramatic account of the rebate system as developed between the railroads and the sugar companies is in the New York *American*, March 8, 1906. A summary of the trial is in Stimson's report, Dec. 20, 1906, to the Attorney General. An accurate condensed account is in *Outlook*, Oct. 27, 1906.

time to be the efficient cause of the panic of 1907. He was famous as the architect of the New York City Ice Trust, the designer of a monopoly of East Coast shipping, the joint creator of a copper pool and the owner of a dozen New York banks. It had been discovered that he obtained some of the money for his remarkable operations by making loans from his banks to the office boy of his brokers. Morse gave the boy's notes to his banks and then kept the boy's money, which he put to work in the market. Stimson uncovered the complicated network of these operations and used his findings not only to put Morse in jail, but also to reveal something of the state of the financial activity in New York in the first decade of the century.[14]

In his last year in office he started proceedings against a combination of sugar companies, dominated by the Havemeyer interests, which had devised a method to avoid paying full duties on imported sugar. The method was simple; scales were rigged to give false, light weights to the drafts of the sugar coming off the ships onto the docks. At the conclusion of the prosecution, the companies were found guilty, fines imposed and back duties recovered. The moneys returned, so the Attorney General asserted in his annual report issued on December 10, 1909, were without much doubt the largest sum "ever secured by the government on a claim of that nature." [15]

All these cases, as argued in the courts, fall into the dramatic form. Each contained within itself the rising excitement produced by an engagement between the hunter and the hunted,

[14] The record of the Morse Case is in JD 120197. The Stimson Papers contain considerable additional correspondence between Stimson and Bonaparte. A good contemporary account is in *The Independent*, Nov. 12, 1908. Henry F. Pringle, *The Life and Times of William Howard Taft*, 2 vols. (New York, 1939), II, 627-31 gives an excellent description of Morse's methods and legal difficulties.

[15] The record of all the sugar trials is in JD 121616. With all the usual material, this contains also an immense correspondence between Stimson and the Attorney General and, further, a series of progress reports to the Attorney General and the President. A summary is in *House Document 901*, 61st Congress, 2nd Session. A good popular account is in "The Case of the Seventeen Holes," *Outlook*, May 1, 1909.

the spell that attends upon the investigation of any human conflict laid bare in all its subtle ramifications and in all its minute and immense detail. As in other trials these prosecutions offer the intellectual satisfaction that can be taken from observing random elements — bills of lading, tally sheets, sailing dates, canceled checks, bills of sale — fitted together into an organized, precise and inescapable situation. As in other trials, the men caught up within the situation revealed in their thought and action the full spectrum of human character, all the classic modes of behavior. There were the disgruntled and informing employees; there were the easy-going and corrupted; there were the cool customers. Rich, guilty men fled off to Europe or into illness. They lied, they forgot, they became confused, they pled the force of customary usage and they pled the extenuating circumstance. Others pled for them in distraction and in tears. And, as in other trials, all these things and more were finally compressed into the small space of the courtroom where Joseph Choate made his indolent witticisms and Stimson walked like "a New England conscience on legs," and Judge Hough spoke in his harsh voice of "these worse than vulgar crimes."

It would, as Goldthwaite Dorr remarked, require a book — or several books — to describe each trial in sufficient detail. To prepare the case against the sugar combination, Stimson interviewed "nearly a thousand men." He traced out in all particulars the history of fifty-four sugar cargoes from the Caribbean docks, through the New York refineries and into the retailers' storerooms. He examined the little books in which each weigher had entered for ten years the record of each shipment of sugar in two columns — one for the false weight on which duty had been paid; one for the real weight sent to the refinery for future sale.

If no full account of these matters can be rendered, some general considerations of method and results may be undertaken. The consideration of method may reveal some interesting things about the administration of federal justice. To begin with, the

conduct of some of these cases was in measurable part determined by very real uncertainty about what was possible under
existing law. When the rebate case began, for instance, neither
Stimson nor Moody knew these things: whether freight from
New York City to Buffalo, which in transit passed through
New Jersey, was considered interstate commerce; whether a rebate paid by a railroad which could not be proved to have
reached the shipper was still a rebate; whether a rebate paid
after the Elkins Act had been passed, on goods transported before the passage of the Act, was punishable under the law;
whether the shipper who received the rebate could be convicted
under the Elkins Act as well as the carrier who paid the rebate.
When Stimson brought the case to trial, no court had ruled on
these implications of the Act passed in 1903. The uncertainty
about these matters was the source of constant correspondence
between Stimson and Moody; it determined the kind of evidence they looked for; it played a part in the way the indictments were drawn; it was the governing factor in the way they
ultimately decided to conduct the prosecution. At one time
Stimson played with the idea of clearing these things up by an
amendment to the Hepburn bill then in Congress. But in the
end he proceeded to indict, prosecute and obtain a charge of
guilty in a lower court against the New York Central for paying a rebate, on the basis of a single transaction for which he
found evidence. Once this decision had been given, with proof
of guilt established, Stimson turned immediately to the sugar
company that had received the rebate and, after obtaining a conviction on one count, obtained pleas of guilty on the remaining
twenty-two counts. Thus armed, he could proceed against all
the remaining roads.[16]

Two other uncertainties dominated the way in which Stimson

[16] The correspondence between Stimson and Moody is especially valuable on
two matters: first, the uncertainty with which the government must ordinarily
proceed in the interpretation and enforcement of a new law; second, the nature
of the relationship, rarely examined, between a powerful attorney general and a
resourceful district attorney.

and Moody thought about these cases. It is surprising to find that in the year 1906 they were both uncertain about the extent of the immunity a corporation could claim for itself from the acts of its agents. Indeed in a conference Moody suggested the prosecution of the sugar company might be put off until the Supreme Court decided the tobacco case, which "we will expect to throw a good deal of light upon the immunity which can be given to the corporation." Stimson replied that the government, under existing conditions, might well be "powerless." However, there "would be no doubt," he continued, "that in case the corporation happened to be an unincorporated association composed of individuals, as it really amounts to in substance, the men in it would not be entitled to that immunity which they claim for the corporation." Finally, he concluded, "if they are to have all the constitutional safeguards that are designed primarily for the individual, the human protection of men and women . . . and [have] the advantage of doing business — I think they ask for more than the immunity of the individual." [17]

Since the purpose of Stimson's endeavor as a government attorney was to prevent corporations from breaking the law, rather than to convict a few agents who could be discharged while the corporation continued in its transgression, the point was transcendently important. In his first case against the sugar company, Stimson and Moody decided they could argue that a rebate check which Stimson had found deposited in the company's account was sufficient evidence of the corporation's, as opposed to an employee's, intent to profit by an illegal transaction. He so argued and obtained from the jury a conviction.

A further uncertainty in all these cases was whether it would be possible to obtain the conviction of officials of these companies for the unlawful acts of their subordinates. A great deal of

[17] Confidential undated transcript, "Inquiry by the Attorney General into the question of rebates by railroads," JD 59-8-13, Section IV. The inquiry took place sometime in January 1906.

time was spent, both in the Morse Case and in the sugar-weighing frauds, obtaining evidence to show the direct involvement of Morse as chairman of the board of the Bank of North America and Heike as president of the American Sugar Refining Company, in the acts committed by their subordinate agents.

Other factors besides points of law determined the shape of these cases. For instance, after Charles J. Bonaparte was appointed Attorney General, a first and ill-conceived attempt in the Eastern District of New York to prosecute the men involved in the sugar frauds failed. When the case was shifted to the Southern District, Stimson was uncertain whether to institute proceedings for the recovery of all the back duties, for the cost of all the sugar lost in the light weighing over ten years, or for a portion of the back duties due on fifty-four specific voyages. He took the latter course, which involved tracing a series of specific transactions and the recovery of $134,000 — on the grounds that these were charges and penalties a jury could understand. The large amounts — over $2,000,000 — for which he could legitimately ask, he rejected since he believed the sum would frighten the members of a jury. Having proved the guilt in the smaller transactions, he went on to recover the full amounts owed the government.

There were still other tactical considerations in the shaping of these cases. As Moody said in one of his first conferences with Stimson, "I regard the full development of this matter in the courts for the public benefit as more important than the conviction of three or four men . . . although I want to convict somebody. We have had the lesson here in New York that, after all, publicity in the insurance investigation is about the best remedy that modern conditions afford. You have seen this tremendous insurance power pulled down like a house of straw — not by any prosecutions, but by public opinion." [18]

This principle was at the bottom of all the cases Stimson tried

[18] Confidential transcript, JD 59-8-13, Section IV.

against the corporations. He and the Attorney General were determined to make clear to everyone the meaning of unregulated and uncontrolled corporate behavior. They were equally determined to show that it was possible to contain and punish the corporate transgressor. It was for this reason more than any other that they were anxious to document fully in court the ways in which corporations broke the law. It was for this reason that they were both so insistent on trying to convict the highest officials as well as their agents. It was for this reason Moody directed Stimson to indict, unsuccessfully, these officials for conspiracy as well as for infraction of the Elkins Act — prison terms he felt had greater educational power than fines. This attitude permeated the conduct of all these trials. In October 1906, Judge Holt found the American Sugar Refining Company guilty on several counts in the indictment drawn for the rebate case. His remarks showed that he viewed the offense "as a very serious one." Counsel for the company then approached Stimson with the offer to change their plea, on the remaining twenty-two counts of the indictment, to guilty in return for greatly reduced fines. Moody was reluctant — every single count which came to trial "hurt the company altogether out of proportion to any punishment"; it produced "a wave of indignation . . . from one end of the land to the other." Only if the company would plead guilty, give up the right of appeal and accept fines of $5000 in each of the twenty-two counts would he agree to accept the guilty plea. And he wished Stimson to be sure beforehand that the proposed fines would be approved of by Judge Holt. Only then would the public know that guilty actions would be punished, under all conditions, by the largest possible penalties.[19]

In the realm of method there is yet another consideration. Sometimes it seems to some people the part of wisdom for a government attorney not to prosecute. Once in September 1908,

[19] H.L.S. to W. H. Moody, Nov. 28, 1906; W. H. Moody to H.L.S., Nov. 29, 1906.

Roosevelt was approached with the suggestion that the proceeding against the companies involved in the sugar customs fraud might "just at this time be" put off. The company had "always felt it had a complete answer to the charges . . . and if the government had accepted its offer of cooperation the matter could have been adjusted without legal controversy." Would not this prosecution, it was asked, "be looked upon as done for political effect?" This query was passed on to Stimson without comment from the White House. At another time Root wrote Stimson that the attack on the *Herald*'s personal column had "really [been] stirred up by Hearst," who was not only Bennett's principal competitor, but who also was running for governor of New York. "Of course," the Secretary of State went on, "the fact that the *Herald* is about the most efficient newspaper at present engaged in fighting Hearst ought not to give it immunity, although it might justify letting the cases stand until after election." "It would," he concluded, "be a pity to allow Hearst to accomplish his purpose through your agency. . . ."

Stimson replied that he was sure that "Hearst will undoubtedly claim credit for everything that has been done." "But," he added, "if I should once permit such political considerations to interfere with the administration of justice in this office, where could I stop? If I should once begin to allow my official conduct to be swayed by considerations such as those, I feel it would end by eventually leading me wholly astray." [20]

One other rather better piece of advice on the methods to be used by a government attorney was offered by Root who, in an earlier time, had also served in the Southern District. In October 1906, just after the New York Central had been found guilty in the lower court in the first rebate case Stimson had prosecuted, Root wrote: "There is a subtle influence which pervades the atmosphere of the Court, the District Attorney's Office and the jury room which makes convictions easy at times and difficult at others; and when one conviction has been ob-

[20] Elihu Root to H.L.S., Oct. 4, 1906; H.L.S. to Elihu Root, Oct. 8, 1906.

tained the tactics of the defense must always be to secure delay by all sorts of dilatory proceedings in the hope of change; while the task of prosecution is to press, press after the first conviction and to follow, follow that up by rapid and strong blows." This was advice Stimson pursued at the time in turning directly to the sugar company and the other roads without waiting to see what the result of the Central's appeal would be. He pressed and pressed and followed and followed until the whole defensive arrangement of the corporations — pleas of not guilty, petitions for delay, demurrers and the like — fell away, and all the companies were convicted.

The foregoing description of method may reveal how inevitably political, legislative and tactical elements interact with the legal element in the administration of federal justice. It may also suggest why the assault on the corporations in the first decade of this century proceeded more slowly than some observers, past and present, believed it should. It takes time to reorganize a moribund office; it takes time to relieve the pressure on the federal courts by creating a new judgeship and appointing, against opposition, a new judge; it takes time to prepare a sound case, especially in the absence of familiar precedents and interpretations.[21]

The description of method, too, may reveal an old and simple truth — the importance of men in the execution of an intent. Moody, for instance, possessed a powerful mind; he was an accomplished administrator and he had a profound understanding of the function of his office. Unlike Bonaparte, Moody knew when and in what way to direct his subordinate and when to leave him alone. He also had, again unlike Bonaparte, a wonder-

[21] In addition to these obstacles, there was the usual shortage of money. In the middle of the rebate case, for instance, Stimson had to take a great deal of time trying to obtain one extra stenographer for the trial period. Each year he had to struggle to get more help for a staff that was "literally swamped." To Moody he once wrote that "your letter indicates that you have a wholly inadequate view of the immense volume of work. . . ." Moody actually tried on several occasions to get more money for his subordinate from a reluctant Congress.

ful feeling for what happens in court. There were others in these years who assisted in the repair of the instruments of justice in the Southern District. Herbert Parsons pushed the new judgeship through the Congress and joined with Root and Taft to support Roosevelt in the appointment of Judge Hough over the considerable opposition of Senator Platt. To these names, which everyone knows and knew at the time, others less well known then may be added — Thacher, Buckner, Frankfurter and Stimson himself in the office of the Southern District. Behind them all stood Theodore Roosevelt. It is not too much to say that every one of these men, from Moody in the Department of Justice to Frankfurter starting out at $750 a year in the District office, were in the government service because of the President of the United States. That his influence extended from the Cabinet down to the lowest levels of his administration, is perhaps the greatest demonstration of his understanding of the uses of executive power.[22]

The results obtained by Stimson in this situation were impressive. He obtained fines of almost half a million dollars for infractions of the Elkins Act; he succeeded in dissolving a combination in restraint of trade; he recovered about $2,500,000 that had been fraudulently withheld from the government; he obtained the punishment, by fine and imprisonment, of the chief officials of several important companies. More important, in his prosecutions he obtained rulings on disputed points of the laws regulating corporations which were sustained in higher courts and thus made the continuation of the effort to regulate corporations easier in the future. Most important, by his successful

[22] The appointment of Judge Hough is in itself a case study of the difficulties of appointing good men to public office and the influence of the President in resolving these difficulties. It took four months for Moody, Stimson and Parsons to find a man mutually satisfying to them and the President, who was searching for a candidate of known "corporation aloofness." It took Roosevelt almost as long to push Hough's name through the hierarchy of the New York Republican Party committees. It took both tact and political courage to thwart the wishes of Senator Platt and his wife, who had a candidate of their own.

prosecutions he informed the public. His cases increased the growing confidence of the citizens that malefactors of great wealth could be not only detected in their wrongdoing, but punished. They also assisted in creating the general climate of opinion which served, in time, as a modifying and stabilizing influence upon the behavior of the great corporations that were the principal source of material strength in the society.

There was one more case, with a special significance, in which Stimson played some part before he left office in 1909. On December 8, 1908, the New York *World* accused Roosevelt of making "deliberate misstatements of fact in his scandalous personal attack upon Delevan Smith." Mr. Smith was the editor of the Indianapolis *News,* which had published a series of stories about what it called "the Panama Canal deal." The burden of these stories was that in purchasing the rights to build the canal the United States had paid an extravagant sum of money and that much of this money — $40,000,000 — had been paid not to the French government but, by devious means and through the intercession of J. P. Morgan and Company, to a syndicate of Americans. Among the Americans were Charles Taft, William Cromwell and Douglas Robinson, the President's brother-in-law. The implication was that the President had been a party to a scheme to enrich friends and relatives at the expense of the taxpayers.[23]

William D. Foulke asked Roosevelt to answer these charges and implications. The President had done so on December 1, 1908, in a long letter which called the principal statements of the *News* both "false" and "too absurd to be discust." It was this letter, made public by Foulke, that the *World* designated a tissue of "deliberate misstatements." The paper then went on to say that the issue was no longer the "Panama exploitation" but "the veracity of the President of the United States."[24]

23 New York *World,* Dec. 8, 1908.
24 *The Letters of Theodore Roosevelt,* Elting E. Morison, ed., 8 vols. (Cambridge, 1951-1954), VI, 1393-97.

The President when he read these words was furious. As he told Congress on December 15 the statements in the *World* and *News* "consist simply of a string of infamous libels." There can be little doubt that Roosevelt's assertions were true. No researches by newspapers at the time, no evidence produced by a congressional investigating committee later supported the main contentions of the *News* or *World* at any point. The newspaper propositions remain not only unproved but, all things considered, incredible.[25]

But the significance of the episode lies elsewhere. Roosevelt was determined to do something; he therefore directed the Attorney General to bring suits of criminal libel against those responsible for the newspaper stories. There were difficulties in fulfilling the presidential desires. Nothing in law or custom directly permitted the federal government to bring such suits; it was therefore necessary to discover some means to claim jurisdiction for the government in the case. A means was found, after some search, which provided what Roosevelt himself called "a very indirect jurisdiction." By court decision and act of Congress, federal courts had been given the power to punish as criminal certain offenses — murder, rape, arson and burglary — if committed on federal property. Punishment of these transgressions was made in accordance with the criminal law of the state in which the federal property lay. Using this accepted authority, the government in this case attempted to claim jurisdiction for itself on the grounds that newspapers containing the alleged libels had been mailed in federal post offices and sold, in some instances, as at West Point, on federal lands. Efforts under this claimed jurisdiction were made to obtain indictments in Indianapolis, the District of Columbia and New York. The cases were, in fact, never brought to trial because both in Indiana and New York the judges ruled that the government's claims to jurisdiction were insufficient.[26]

[25] For a survey of the literature on this subject and a fuller explanation of my conclusions on the question of Roosevelt's involvement, see *Roosevelt Letters,* VI, 1415-16.
[26] *Roosevelt Letters,* VI, 1425-26.

Although nothing came from the President's aborted efforts, they aroused at the time much excitement and have produced since some jaundiced comment. Rooted deep in the structure raised by law and custom for our federal system is the precedent that the power to bring suits for criminal libel lies not with the central government, but with the states. This precedent was originally established in the first days of the republic by those who feared the encroaching authority of the central government. It became, in time, an article of faith for those who maintained the Jeffersonian view of things. When therefore the administration of Theodore Roosevelt tried to proceed against the *World* and *News* there were not wanting men who discerned an ominous effort to extend the power of the federal government to limit the freedom of press and speech. The United States Attorney in Indianapolis, for instance, refused to aid in the attempted prosecutions. He resigned on the ground that the proposed suit was "dangerous, striking at the very foundation of our form of government." Substance was given to such views by the indirectness of the claim of jurisdiction and by the fact that the President, at the very center of the case, seemed to be acting from personal pique. On the other hand, the dangers to civil liberties discovered by some in these proceedings do not appear to be substantial. In the protection of the citizen there is a due process of law which historically has been conducted with at least as great rectitude by the federal government as by the several states. The safety of the society does not seem historically to depend, in this matter, so much upon the question of whether the central government has an equal power with the states to sue for criminal libel as it does upon the general health of the society itself. In England, the source of so many of our civil liberties, the crown and government has always reserved for itself this power. But there are two sides in this issue and in 1909 when Stimson, acting as a United States Attorney, assisted in the preparation of the libel suit against the *World*, it was assumed by many that he was acting as the willing tool of the President in an assault upon the classic freedoms of speech and press.[27]

Stimson was, to begin with, eager to have a suit brought against the newspaper for criminal libel. Ever since the *Herald* personal column case he had been disturbed by the power of an irresponsible press in a democracy. He had been unhappy when Root had proposed that the case against the *Herald* might be set aside and disturbed when Moody had suggested other ways to accommodate the same difficulty. "I have tried," the Attorney General had written, "to write about this matter without any improper bias, but of course we are all cowards about the newspapers who tyrannize over us all." Responses like this from men like Root and Moody on so small a matter as the personal column of the *Herald* had roused Stimson's fears about the influence of newspapers upon the conduct of public affairs. He was predisposed therefore to use the weapons available to force the press into responsible reporting and comment. In January 1909, at the same time the *World* case was under preparation, he urged Root, in the interests of good government, to bring suit against the New York *Evening Journal* for "a whole series of libels of you." It is, he told the Secretary of State, "a great mistake to allow such [a libel] as the enclosed to go unpunished by state authorities." [28]

In the case of Root he was ready to believe that the State of New York was the appropriate instrument for justice. He also believed that Jerome, the attorney for the county of New York, should bring suit against the *World* in the case of the Panama libel. He so informed both Roosevelt and Attorney General Bonaparte. It is quite probable he believed that, if Jerome were permitted to bring suit, a suit by the federal government was unnecessary. But it does not appear that he had doubts about the authority of the national government in the matter. It

---

[27] For an account that views Stimson's part in this case unfavorably, see Richard N. Current, *Secretary Stimson* (New Brunswick, 1954), 20-21.

[28] W. H. Moody to H.L.S., July 26, 1906; H.L.S. to Elihu Root, Jan. 20, 1909.

has been said, apparently with invidious intention, that "he dug up an old statute designed to protect the nation's harbor defenses and other fortifications from 'malicious injury' " to give the government its claim of jurisdiction. There is no direct evidence in the files of the Department of Justice that it was Stimson who discovered the law under which the government proceeded; but it is obvious he looked with others for such a law and it is equally obvious that in so doing he was merely doing what lawyers do every day to give them an opportunity to conduct their cases.[29]

It seems clear on the available evidence that he had no real qualms about the federal government's right to sue for criminal libel, and that he was untroubled by the ways that were discovered to give his government a claim of jurisdiction. But it is also clear that he was annoyed throughout by the way in which both the President and the Attorney General sought to conduct the case. Bonaparte refused to disclose the nature of the government's position before he issued subpoenas and sought to prevent Jerome from bringing a separate libel suit against the *World*. Roosevelt insisted that the proceeding should be against Joseph Pulitzer personally as editor of the paper. These actions created the impression, Stimson wrote his superiors, that "there is something queer about the Federal prosecutions." It was made to look, he told Roosevelt, as though "the Government is doing something unusual . . . under the pressure of your personal desire. . . ." His own desire, he said, was to get the *World* for libel and not to protect the President of the United States. He did not want to prosecute for *lèse-majesté*, or to revive "the alien and sedition acts." This was, he said, "a simple case of a series of alleged libels against the character of a number of gen-

29 H.L.S. to Theodore Roosevelt, Dec. 10, 1908, to C. J. Bonaparte, Jan. 28, 1909; Current, *Secretary Stimson*, 20. JD 10963 contains the entire record. Goldthwaite Dorr, in conversation (May 18, 1959) remembered that Stimson was not enthusiastic about bringing suit. But Stimson's lack of enthusiasm appears to have derived not so much from his doubt about the government's jurisdiction as from his belief that the President was unwise in seeking such recourse.

tlemen, some of whom happen to be in public and some in private life." [30]

Roosevelt's view of things was probably much more personal and specific; at any rate, he by his very presence and the Attorney General by his ineptitudes did create the impression that there was something "queer" about the intended prosecution. Whatever high principle Stimson endeavored by his recommendations to maintain in the case was in fact pretty well concealed from public view by the time the indictments were dismissed by the federal judges. It was not a case that brought him any distinction; indeed it subjected him to criticism as a party to an effort to limit some of the essential freedoms.

Stimson was already out of office before the case was decided. He had decided in the fall of 1908 that he had spent time enough in public service. The things Moody had charged him with, at the outset, had been done. He left his successor with an efficient, well-trained staff of assistants and the tradition that a United States Attorney in the Southern District conducts his own trials in court. He needed, he believed, to make some more money and he felt he had learned as much as he could from his position. He had indeed learned much. For the first time he demonstrated that he knew how to recruit and administer an able staff. For the first time he had a real opportunity to test his abilities as a trial lawyer; in these three years he had met, and defeated, almost every trial lawyer of outstanding ability and reputation in the city. He had also learned in this experience how to prepare and construct a case. The approaches he selected were not perhaps cleverly, surprisingly imaginative, but they revealed marked intellectual resourcefulness. His arguments were always based upon massive evidence produced by extended research. They were well organized, patiently developed and carefully reasoned statements. His practice was to overwhelm the opposition with patiently accumulated, thoroughly mobilized informa-

[30] H.L.S. to Theodore Roosevelt, Jan. 28, Feb. 11, 1909, to C. J. Bonaparte, Jan. 28, 1909.

tion thrown at the weakest points. He learned in these years — as he so frequently said afterwards — "never to ask a question in cross-examination to which you do not already know what the answer has got to be," and he learned also that he was, as so many associates remarked later, a better lawyer with a jury in a case that took two weeks than in one that was over in a day or two. The cumulative effect of his immense evidence, his careful, slow reasoning, his undecorated delivery, his persistence, exerted a peculiar moral influence. If, as one colleague remarked, he knew only one way to win a case, still it was a way that won a great many cases.

Out of this experience also came his enduring love of the public service, the excitement to be discovered in the recognition that individual actions are attended by general implications. This was what he had been looking for all his life — a chance by his private enterprise to do the public good. And in these years, for the first time, he thought seriously about the nature of the society in which he was living. As District Attorney he was introduced to many of the causes, as well as the effects, of the inequities that existed in his environment. As a federal officer he devoted himself primarily to the enforcement of the federal law, but, as well, he reached, in these years, certain general conclusions about the difficulties in American life and arrived at certain decisions about what ought to be done to eliminate them. What these conclusions were belongs more properly to the next chapter of his life.

9

The New Frontiers

ALBERT JAY NOCK used to entertain himself with the idea of writing "a humorous essay on how to recognize the Dark Ages when you are in them." It was his thought that the men of the fourth century took the world of ignorance and violence around them as part of "the day's work," as "pretty much the regular thing." Knowing no history, they "did not recognize the symptoms, or know what they meant, or pay any attention to them." By such means he believed he could show that the men at the turn of the twentieth century, also knowing no history, were equally unaware and unfearful of the dark age that was closing down on them. Virtually all in the "neolithic masses," he concluded, "accept economism's word for it that where you have 'property,' railways, banks, newspapers, industry, trade there of necessity you have civilization."

The trouble with Nock may have been that he knew too much history. His main concern was that the old and valuable world he had never known was being swept away by the rising tides of industrial energy; that he could not, in the America of the twentieth century, live as a citizen had lived in Paris from 1810 to 1885. This preoccupation with a previous condition may well have prevented him from discovering that there were those around who could, in fact, discern the signs of the times. From Edward Bellamy and Henry George down through the years to Frederic Howe and Herbert Croly there were a good many who had been jarred into constructive thought by the bolts of power man had learned to manufacture. Not all of them were detached observers or young men who saw visions; a surprising number held positions of authority and responsibility in the government. During most of the period from 1900 to the beginning of the First World War, the men in national office or in positions of power in America were Republicans; some of their names are still in the public memory — Roosevelt, Taft, Root, Moody, Morton, White, Perkins and all the familiar rest. Together they brought certain common assumptions to the task of governing this country in the opening years of this century.

In the first place, they had some feeling for the symptoms that Nock believed had gone unrecognized. Haymarket and the Homestead had left their mark upon them. There was an uneasy feeling that the society they inhabited had grown, as one of them said, more "fragile"; a premonitory sense that the forces of industry if left to expand at random might blow the civilization apart. Running through the correspondence of the time is a note, subdued but clear, of what Roosevelt called the "horror of anarchy, disorder, wanton bloodshed" if things got out of hand.

But this anxiety was embedded in a general, embracing confidence; it thus served not so much to paralyze as to stimulate the curiosity. One of the sources of confidence was the belief that the principal agency of disruption had been defined and isolated. This agency was taken to be the corporation, that ingenious device which if allowed to grow uncontrolled would, as William Walling said, place in private hands "the greatest power in the world." What Walling called the "problem" of the proper "relation of the state to the corporation" was taken to be the "chief question" put to the society. It was believed that if ways could be devised to place the irresponsible energy of the corporation within substantial containing walls, the problem would, in large part, be solved.

And there was great hope that this could be done. The men of that day assumed that they were taking part in a continuing, evolutionary process. Sensitive to the findings of Charles Darwin, they had put their trust in the idea of the gradual modification and improvement of the social organism. They had great confidence that a society adequately informed of its own situation could, by slow prudence and soft degrees, subdue the disruptive forces to the useful and the good. This assumption that they were part of a continuing process no doubt developed in them a temporal sense different from our own. They were not obsessed by the feeling that there was so little time; if history meant anything, there was time enough. The problem of the corporation did not have to be furnished at once with a comprehensive general solution; it could be solved step by rising step in a future that would obviously continue.

In only one way was this faith in the evolutionary process qualified. By 1900 it had become apparent that industry possessed its own peculiar dynamic. There was, therefore, troubled concern that the anarchic forces would develop so fast that society could not be given the time and opportunity either to comprehend or accommodate to the rapidly changing conditions. In such a pass the civilization that was evolving upon the industrial base might find itself in jeopardy. Joseph Cotton, one of the most sophisticated observers of the contemporary scene, expressed this general concern to Felix Frankfurter. "There exists," he wrote, "in governments abroad as well as here in the last ten years a rather astounding tendency which, in the 70s, would certainly have been regarded as socialistic. It is to better the conditions . . . in the struggle for existence. . . . It is essential, however, that it shall be an *orderly* progress; that it shall not be accompanied by any social, industrial, or political disturbance."

The way to maintain order in the system, to bring the accelerating forces of industry into satisfying consonance with the more lethargic energies of social progress, was the great preoccupation of these days. Through the private correspondence of many men in office such words as stability, efficiency, order and control run like a continuing litany. These are the administrative virtues and the solution to the problem was frequently stated in administrative terms. To obtain what Graham Wallas called, in his contemporary *summa*, "the great society," it would be necessary to impose some man-made controls on the process of evolution. At the center of this great society there had to be, as Wallas insisted, a great and powerful organization, a securely founded executive edifice. In seeking such a structure — superior to the energies of the corporation — the men of this generation turned instinctively to the state.

They recovered, in other words, something of the spirit of Alexander Hamilton. This revealed itself in many little ways. None of their contemporaries, for instance, stirred their continuing irritation and, indeed, disgust as did the shade of Thomas Jefferson, "the most incompetent chief we ever had — not excepting Buchanan." But the Hamiltonian spirit was also present in the larger sense. In the Republican administrations from 1900 to 1912 such matters as the protection of the national resources, the extension of control over the corporate transgressor, the construction of the overseas ramparts, were all done in the Hamiltonian mode by administrators who, like Roosevelt himself, "believe[d] in power."

It has been pointed out that in using this power, not nearly as much was achieved by the men in office as they were wont to claim at the whistle stops and in their memoirs. Certainly not every company that paid a rebate was brought to justice; not every combination in restraint of trade was dissolved. This, at least in part, can be taken as the result of calculation. As in all wars of the nineteenth century after 1815, the assault on the corporations, particularly at the outset, was a campaign with limited objectives. For one thing, it was feared that an unlimited attack might dangerously impair the industrial strength upon which the strength of the society rested. For another thing, it was recognized, as Moody had said, that in the ordering of an industrial society an informed public opinion was as useful an instrument as action by the government. The aim always was not at first to impose by superior authority a nice, general system of controls, but to arrange a new environment in which different and safer corporate responses would be developed and shaped by the pressures of enlightened public opinion. To this end the power of the government was used to set up situations that would inform the public. The prosecutions by Stimson under the Elkins Act, the Northern Securities Case, and the suit against the tobacco trust were skillfully selected, brilliantly cast morality plays, designed to quicken the public conscience and understanding in the meaning of industrial development.

In retrospect it appears that by these small selected means, great general effects were achieved in the first decade of this century. Nothing was done to disturb the essential structure of the existing society, but significant changes in detail took place within the structure. The power of the federal government to deal with the most aggressive malefactors of great wealth was demonstrated. In addition, this power was used to define the principal problems confronting society and to stimulate the community to take an active part in their solution. There was in these years not only confidence but excitement in the idea that society could move itself forward. In this decade, as rarely before or since, the conservative intelligence of the country acted, in power, with both imagination and restraint. Committed to the assumption that the upward lift of the nineteenth century could be projected into an indefinite future, this generation of conservatives accepted without undue pain the idea of gradual change. This idea permitted them to investigate with considerable freedom a wide array of possible solutions to their problems and even to consider modifications in some of the sacred procedures laid down by the founding fathers. It also permitted them to use the preferred instrument of the conservative, administrative authority, with uncommon wisdom.

There is one further thing that might be said. The public acts of this generation were simply the manifestations of the private faiths of the men in office. In these men one discovers a remarkable consistency; rarely did they behave, even those as exuberant as Theodore Roosevelt, in unexpected ways. Their interest in order and efficiency in national affairs was merely a reflection of their interest in form and decency in private life. In private life too, as members of a society that still believed in class distinctions and as members of domestic communities still responsive to the will of "the head of the family," they had a respect and understanding for the uses of authority. The important point was to keep things, personally as well as publicly, under control. Life was better if it was organized, administered in accordance with the dictates of convention and morality.

These were great qualities which made the men who had allegiance to them exceedingly wise in their own generation. But they were also qualities which closed off the possessors from certain other experiences. There was, for instance, nothing very creative in the time. Jefferson was annoying in part because he placidly accepted the disorder out of which new things were often born. His thought that a little rebellion now and then nourished any nation was taken to be irresponsible and dangerous. If there was nothing very creative, there was also nothing intellectually very profound. Brains so directly applied to the solution of existing problems had little time or interest for larger speculations. And there was not much concern, in an age that was aesthetically fulfilled by the bronzes of Frederic Remington or the paintings of Marcius-Simons or the music of Edward MacDowell, for the farthest reaches of the spirit. The concern for order and efficiency and organization is the concern primarily for operational success and the great accomplishment of the country in the first decade of the twentieth century is that it operated, all things considered, so successfully.

How long this might have continued to be true, had the disruption of the First World War not intervened, is not wholly clear. By the end of the decade there was accumulating evidence that the energy of an industrial society, in its rapid and accelerating expansion, kept breaking out of the barriers erected against it. Unexpected inequities and imbalances in the community kept appearing. In such a pass the men of the Hamiltonian persuasion looked increasingly to the state for a solution. Profoundly influenced by the German system of cartels and Lloyd George's budget of 1910, they passed from easy distinctions between good and bad trusts to more sophisticated considerations. Dismissing the possibility of lifting the curse of bigness by breaking up the large concentrations of industrial power, they discussed the possibility of enlarging the sphere of government ownership, considered the wisdom of fixing prices by government action and even, under the influence of "the astounding tendency," examined tentatively the methods of what they called "collectivization." Before the war, none of these procedures was introduced in any systematic way though the power of the central government to regulate the economy was steadily increased.

Thus the more enlightened members of the Republican Party were forced to think about the problem that had so aroused the anxieties of Albert Jay Nock. It had been his fear that in the effort to stabilize the uncertain gyrations of economism, men would invoke the superior power of the central government. That power, steadily increasing, would in time reach the point where, even in a republic, the state existed not so much for the individual as the individual existed for the state. At this point would begin, he predicted, "the Dusk of the nations" marked by the progressive deterioration of taste, manners, education, culture, religion, morals, art. Earlier Matthew Arnold had stated the proposition in different form. If the state were used to direct the operations of railways, coal and iron mines, how could it also sum up "right reason"; how could it, involved in a task exclusively administrative, retain for the society sweetness and light? Fortunately the men of the first decade of the century did not have to answer this question themselves: the First

World War descended upon them to close the nineteenth century and, as well, to postpone, for a season, further examination of the problems of order and value in an industrial society.[1]

From the time Stimson took office as United States Attorney in the Southern District of New York, he found himself directly engaged in working on the principal problems of his period. Forced by his prosecutions to think about the nature of the corporation, he emerged from this experience accepting the importance of the distinction between the good and the bad trust. Whether or not the corporation was, as the Supreme Court had decided, a person, corporate crimes were, in 1906, much like those of the individual thief. A fictitious loan to an office boy, short weights on sugar, the blackmail of the rebate — they were, after all, the tawdry devices of the petty criminal. The differences lay only in scale, system and total impact on society. By preventing the crimes, one could, theoretically, remove the dangers posed by the criminal.

In time, however, Stimson modified this view. Increasingly disturbed by the dislocating influence, he began a patient reconsideration of industry. He read or reread all the great texts of the time — Spencer, George, Bryce and Bellamy. Minor prophets were also consulted. One of these, Frederic Howe, described most clearly for him in *Privilege and Democracy* the nature of the society in which he was living. "Whoever," said Howe, "owns the means of credit controls the industrial life of the nation," and the men who directly or indirectly exerted this control "could be enumerated on the fingers of one hand." The instruments by which this control was maintained were the stock exchange, the banks, private ownership of transport, and the tariff, which was "the mother of many trusts."

---

[1] The literature on the subjects dealt with in the foregoing pages is large and growing. Of particular use in this discussion were Frederic C. Howe, *Privilege and Democracy in America* (New York, 1910); George E. Mowry, *The Era of Theodore Roosevelt* (New York, 1958); Albert J. Nock, *Memoirs of a Superfluous Man* (New York, 1943); Graham Wallas, *The Great Society* (New York, 1914); William English Walling, *Socialism As It Is* (New York, 1912).

Because of the manipulations of this industrial cabal, which retained for itself all increases in profits and power, "the discoveries of the mechanical world pass over society, like a rain-laden cloud over a thirsty desert, leaving humanity but little better off than it was before. We have missed the purpose of organized government. We have perverted the state from its proper ends." [2]

This, in brief, was the view Stimson himself held during the years from 1909 to 1915. Unlike Howe, he did not find in the single tax a sovereign remedy for the current difficulties, though he did speak from time to time of "our antiquated system of land tenure." But he looked elsewhere to discover the true "purpose of organized government" in the existing contingency. Rereading *The Federalist*, he came upon confirming evidence for his position as one of those "who believe in action to overcome present evils, who abhor disorder or anarchy, and stress the need of efficiency in administration [and] advocate a strong central government and a liberal interpretation of the Constitution."

To what end he proposed to use the strong central government he explained in a series of lectures in March 1910 at the Harvard Business School. To this audience he gave the fullest explanation of the position he had gradually developed over the previous two years of study and reflection. "Steam and the telegraph and other machinery," he said, "have required capital greater than any individual can furnish." Financial support for these ventures must therefore come not from a man acting alone, but from the corporation with its "cardinal feature of limited liability." If the corporation as a contemporary institution were destroyed, all "the benefit of the new inventions" would also be destroyed. On the other hand, society in a modern democracy "will not permit unregulated control over production and sale of its necessities." Now that the old forms of regulation through competition had been proved insufficient, what, he

[2] Howe, *Privilege and Democracy*, 61, 63, 69, 231.

asked, would take their place? He found himself "inclining to the belief that the immediate remedy should be . . . to assume that we are not approaching a stage of complete socialism." Instead we should accept the condition of increasing size in industrial organizations and try to regulate industrial behavior through government control in such a way that "the chance of competition" from new capital would be preserved.

To obtain these ends he did not propose, as some years earlier he would have, the general invocation of the Sherman Act. Instead he recommended supplementary legislation that would permit the federal government to incorporate industrial companies engaged in interstate commerce, and to regulate "the financial details of their organization." Further legislation should be enacted that would prevent "in detail the various methods of unfair trade by which competition is destroyed." Two decades of prosecutions under the Sherman Act "had brought to light" the forms of this "unfair competition": boycott, factors' agreements, interfering with contracts by threats or frauds, fictitious independents, favoritism in credit. All these practices should be defined by law and punished in the courts.

To give due weight to this regulatory legislation, a new agency in the government was needed. As a United States Attorney, Stimson had been struck by the fact that he could never tell a businessman who approached him in good faith whether a proposed business action was or was not a violation of the Sherman Act. No one, in fact, could tell until the courts had acted. Legislation would clear up some of the confusion, but what was additionally required was an "essential element — an agency . . . to supervise the working of our laws against monopolistic combinations. . . ." This agency could explain to the business community the meaning of existing laws, it could furnish information to Congress as a basis for new legislation and it could give to the community at large information that would set in motion the tremendous power of publicity.[3]

[3] "Memorandum of Conversation with S. B. Clarke in connection with Harvard lectures, March 31, 1910." See also *Harvard Crimson*, May 6, 7, 1910; Boston

The philosophic basis for these specific recommendations he
explained at greater length before the Republican Club of New
York in 1911. Great inventions of the past, he said, had created
"a large amount of combination on the part of our industries"
that was now economically necessary. Only through the combinations could the country "have reached our present stage
of civilization." But obviously "the old rules . . . under the
common law" were no longer adequate to control the operations of the great corporations. Some way must be discovered
to keep the field of economic activity free for the entry of new
enterprise. Only the central government had the power to
perform this service and it also had the legal right. Hamilton in
1791 had made an argument in behalf of federal corporations
that had never been refuted. Since businesses had become national, the problem was national and therefore the province of
the national government. The "interests of the manufacturer,
the laborer, and the consumer . . . are alike bound up in
common in its solution." The government should therefore attempt "to direct these forces toward a just industrial system,
leaving full play to individual initiative and full scope for individual reward, but at all hazards to secure social and industrial
freedom to the great mass of the people." [4]

Globe, May 10, 1910; Address before the Republican Club, New York City,
Dec. 15, 1911. In an address entitled "National Control and the Public Welfare," delivered at Cooper Union, April 27, 1911, he said that the corporation
was "merely an instrument of man's activities. . . . There is nothing in its own
nature which makes it either national or local." If the purpose for which it
existed, he said at another time, was the distribution of goods across state lines,
it was natural to control that purpose not only by national regulation but by
national incorporation. See also H.L.S. to Alfred Loomis, Nov. 5, 1908, to
Elihu Root, July 1, 1909, to Emory Speer, Dec. 2, 1910, to the editor of the
New York Commercial, Feb. 4, 1911, to Francis Lynde Stetson, March 20, 1911;
Herbert Parsons to H.L.S., April 25, 1911.

[4] In a series of speeches Stimson elaborated his growing conviction that a
strong central government was "inseparably bound up with the individual welfare of the citizen." At Cooper Union in April 1911 he said the task was "to
see that this control and regulation is wisely, conservatively, and yet effectively,
applied." A year later at the University of Pennsylvania he said that "We pay
a sacrifice in efficiency, ordinarily, to the general contentment that comes from
the fact that everybody has a hand in the government. . . ." Two years later,
in 1914, he told an audience at the Academy of Political Science that the Jef-

Stimson was, as he said, one of those who believed in taking action to overcome present evils. Even while he was elaborating his views about the existing difficulties of his society, he was called upon again to consider in what capacity he could best act to serve the community. In March 1909 he had left the District Attorney's office, though he continued for six months to serve as a special counsel for the government to complete the sugar fraud trials. His return to private practice coincided with the beginning of one of the periodic efforts to reform the government of the city of New York. In June 1909 a Committee of 100 was appointed to explore the possibilities of putting a fusion ticket into the city elections in the fall. Throughout the late summer there were murmurs in the newspapers and in the corridors of various political clubs that Stimson would be acceptable as a candidate for mayor to those who sought a fusion program. These elements included the Republican organization, the Citizens Union, and the Independence League of William Randolph Hearst. By the first of September the rumors had become so persistent that Stimson, before leaving for a hunting trip in Canada, wrote to his father to explain his attitude toward the developing situation. From a "purely personal standpoint" he would regard it as "a great misfortune to run for Mayor and still more to be elected." He wanted to spend the next few years in "clinching my position as a trial lawyer" and four years in City Hall might well "completely ruin" his future in the profession. Furthermore, since he knew little of municipal problems it would be a "great waste" both for him and the city to put him in such a position.

---

fersonian error lay in the notion that you must not give a man power to do right for fear he will do wrong. From this error came such further errors as the popular election of all officials, multiple elections, short terms for legislatures and, worst, the too extensive separation of powers — a theory of government "made philosophy by Montesquieu . . . made the language of a gentleman by Blackstone," spread by Jefferson and Andrew Jackson. In taking this position he was not, he said, "a pioneer — merely a humble follower of certain lines." This, as anyone who has read Theodore Roosevelt, Herbert Croly, Graham Wallas, Henry Jones and George Walbridge Perkins knows, was true.

Although these considerations made it difficult for him to conceive of any reason why he should accept the nomination if tendered, he knew that "There are higher things than mere professional success as a lawyer, and one of them is usefulness in a situation like that of New York." The city problem was still "the great National problem of America," and in his own city he was "deeply impressed with the burning disgrace which it is to have the particular Government of New York City so closely allied with crime and vice." Weighing all these things he felt that the need for "a sacrifice" of himself had neither arisen nor been proved, but he wanted his father to know his thoughts if, while he was away hunting, the offer were extended.[5]

Ten days later, two representatives of the Committee of 100 traveled into the Canadian wilderness above Quebec to extend the offer provisionally. Through these emissaries, Stimson sent back a communication to the committee. In effect he said to the members what he had said to his father, that he could not "overstate the personal disappointment" at having to run as a candidate for mayor. He laid down imposing conditions that had to be met before he would consider the proposal and then asked the committee to talk to Root, who knew his "personal life and aims." "He is the man," he continued, "to pass on whether . . . the things I have outlined have been fulfilled or whether the crisis is great enough to make me do this — whether it really is a real public duty." [6]

The committee then turned to Root, who had talked with Dr. Stimson. After much thought, as Root reported to Stimson, he had come to the conclusion "that this duty lies in your path and that you ought to undertake it." If defeated, "so much the better for you personally"; if victorious, "the greatest opportunity in the American struggle for self-government except

5 New York *Tribune*, June 17, Aug. 18, 31, 1909; H.L.S. to L. A. Stimson, Sept. 1, 1909.
6 H.L.S. to E. H. Outerbridge and R. V. Ingersoll, Sept. 14, 1909.

that afforded by the Presidency will lie at your hands." In conclusion, "I would not choose this for you, my dear Harry, but
when duties come to a man he must not dare to refuse them." [7]

This particular duty did not come Stimson's way. At the
last moment, after his name had been agreed upon by all parties
to the fusion movement, Hearst withdrew the support of the
Independence League from all the fusion candidates. Whatever
the reason for this maneuver, and Hearst's explanation that he
did not like some of the names proposed for minor offices in
the Borough of Brooklyn seems hardly adequate, the withdrawal broke up the forces in common cause against Tammany. The Republicans nominated Otto Bannard, a regular
"for whom the party workers would exert themselves," and
Stimson returned to his private practice.[8]

But not for long. In November he was asked to take part in
one of the more complicated and, in any large perspective,
meaningless controversies in our history. Both Gifford Pinchot
and James R. Garfield asked him to act as counsel for the former
in the celebrated contest against Richard A. Ballinger. He
refused but, drawn by his interest in conservation and by a
friendship begun at Yale, he assisted the Chief Forester in several
ways. He was one of the men who proposed that Louis D.
Brandeis should be brought into the case and he persuaded
George Wharton Pepper to serve as Pinchot's attorney. Thereafter he continued to advise both Pinchot and Pepper on the
way in which the case should be developed. He also attempted
in conversation and by correspondence to explain his two
friends to each other. Here he had not much success, for Pepper
ended his service convinced, in a happy phrase, that Pinchot
had "a foible for omniscience," while Pinchot regretted that
Pepper appeared to lack the zeal of the crusader. Much of
Stimson's effort was directed to making Pinchot himself act

[7] Elihu Root to H.L.S., Sept. 18, 1909.
[8] New York *Tribune*, Sept. 20, 21, 22, 23, 24, 1909; Winfred Dennison to H.L.S.,
Sept. 24, 1909.

more like an enlightened public servant and less like a knight with wounded feelings. He warned his old friend that the men around him lacked "poise," that "Amos' judgment is much less valuable in this matter than usual," that Price "has played marplot too much in the past — lovely fellow as he is," and that Pinchot himself should never get into a personal issue with Ballinger "unless you are a great deal more certain than I am that he is a Benedict Arnold." [9]

This sage counsel went, for the most part, unregarded; and in fact Stimson found little but exasperation and trouble in the affair. Before it was over he found himself at odds with the Attorney General, George W. Wickersham, over the merits of the case. Indeed "I have, with deep regret at differing from the conclusions of as good a friend as yourself, reached views which materially diverge from those set forth in your report to the President and which make me feel that it is my duty to comply with Mr. Pinchot's request" to advise him. [10]

While the unpleasant controversy between Pinchot and Ballinger was still in the newspapers, Stimson was drawn off into a more interesting and useful public endeavor. Twice in June 1910 he rode over from Highhold to Sagamore to have long talks with the hunter who had just returned from Africa. In the first of these conversations the two "discussed national and state affairs." After giving his opinion that Taft had probably reached and passed "the nadir of his unpopularity," the Colonel then "opened himself pretty fully," and talked about the possibility that Stimson might be called upon to run as the Republican candidate for governor in the fall elections. Shortly after, Roosevelt went off to the Harvard Commencement where he

[9] Stimson's part in the selection of Brandeis is described in Pringle, *Taft*, I, 510, and in Norman Hapgood, *The Changing Years* (New York, 1930), 184-186. For Stimson's further activity, see H.L.S. to Gifford Pinchot, Aug. 20, 1909, Jan. 5, 1910; Amos Pinchot to H.L.S., Jan. 21, 1910; G. W. Pepper to H.L.S., Feb. 16, 1910; H.L.S. to G. W. Pepper, March 15, 1910.
[10] H.L.S. to G. W. Wickersham, Jan. 21, 1910.

met Charles E. Hughes, then Governor of New York. At the college exercises he promised the Governor to lend his support to Hughes's effort to obtain direct primaries in New York. Thus committed to what seemed a harmless return to political activity, Roosevelt came back to a second talk with Stimson at Sagamore. At that time he gave it as his opinion that his young friend would make the best governor but "not the best candidate." When Stimson replied that he "did not want to run unless a situation came when no honest man could refuse," Roosevelt answered philosophically: "I understand you mean that you don't want to run unless such circumstances should arise as would, for instance, make it necessary for me to run against my will again for President." [11]

Shortly after these talks, Stimson went to Europe for a vacation. Just before he departed he told his father that Roosevelt had obviously "got his dander up" by joining Hughes in the fight for direct primaries, but that he seemed "very sane and cautious." As for himself, he believed that "I shall probably not have to run, although I may." While he was traveling in Europe during July and August, certain things happened in the State of New York that made the probability of his having to run considerably greater than it was on the day of his departure. Most of these things had to do with the deteriorating relationship between Theodore Roosevelt and the President of the United States. This relationship was placed under a special strain by virtue of the situation in New York. The Republican Party in the state in 1910 was split obviously into two parts and then apparently into three. Barnes, Aldridge and Woodruff, the leaders of the oldest of the old guard, were struggling against the more enlightened supporters of President Taft, led by Lloyd C. Griscom, for control of the state organization. In addition, there were men who called themselves liberal or independent Republicans who, in any critical test, would be found

[11] H.L.S., "Personal Recollections of the Convention and Campaign of 1910," undated, now part of the Diary; H.L.S. to L. A. Stimson, July 8, 1910.

more loyal to Roosevelt than to Taft. These, ordinarily, allied
themselves with Griscom in his conflict with the "bosses," but
were subject to the temptations of irregularity that entice so
many independents. In an effort to establish firm control of the
Republican situation, the Griscom forces, in the middle of August, proposed Theodore Roosevelt as the temporary chairman
of the state convention that would meet in Saratoga in the last
week of September. The hope was that with Roosevelt as
chairman, their own forces would control the convention, write
the platform, and select the candidates. To counter this move,
Barnes proposed to the state committee the name of James
Schoolcraft Sherman, the Vice President of the United States,
as temporary chairman; and the committee, subservient to the
wishes of the Albany boss, voted to recommend Sherman's
name to the convention in September. Both Griscom and
Barnes appealed to the President, who, by a series of ineptitudes, succeeded in increasing rather than eliminating the
tensions between the two rival camps. The confusions of this
unresolved situation fatally attracted Theodore Roosevelt. On
August 22 he wrote William Allen White, "One thing I don't
want to become, or rather seem to become, is a factional leader
in New York State politics. But there is of course always the
unpleasant chance that people here may feel so strongly on the
subject that I cannot get out of the fight this Fall." [12]

Shortly after writing this letter, Roosevelt took a trip through
the West and decided on the basis of what he heard and saw
that by unhappy chance people here, there and everywhere
were anxious to force him into the fight in the fall. The electorate, he wrote his friend Lodge, had "become apathetic or sullen"
under the Taft Administration. These impressions, when joined
with the President's failure to act effectively in the question of
the temporary chairmanship, persuaded Roosevelt that the time
had come for him to take some decisive part in the restoration of
liberal Republicanism in the state of New York. At a con-

[12] H.L.S. to L. A. Stimson, July 8, 1910; *Roosevelt Letters*, VII, 107, 116, 119.

ference arranged by Griscom just before the state convention met at Saratoga, Roosevelt explained these considerations and necessities to Taft himself, hoping, but not asking, that the President would support him in his effort to become temporary chairman of the convention. The President again was rather noncommittal, though he did record that "if you were to remove Roosevelt's skull now, you would find written on his brain '1912'." [13]

Into this uncertain situation — a party divided, its two most powerful leaders alienated from each other — Stimson was projected on his return from Europe at the beginning of September. The convention was to meet September 27 at Saratoga; on the 24th Roosevelt and Stimson had a further conversation about the latter's candidacy. Stimson suggested that "If I run and am defeated, as looks now almost certain, it will be made a defeat for you. Our relations have been so close that I will be taken to be your personal candidate, and when I am defeated it will be used to injure your leadership."

Roosevelt said that he realized this and did not care; the important thing in his mind was to raise some standard to which the forces of liberal Republicanism could repair. On the other hand, he recognized the disadvantages of the close relationship and had hoped to find an "upstate man" to fill the place. Unhappily the search had failed; no one could be discovered who "measures up." Again, on the day before the convention met, Stimson rode to Sagamore for a further discussion from which he came away with the thought that the nomination was "more and more imminent." [14]

It was not a view of things that cheered him. Not even sure that he would like to be a successful candidate, he was rather less prepared to accept, without due cause, the more likely lot of the unsuccessful. For several days he had been carrying

[13] *Roosevelt Letters*, VII, 126-28; Archie Butt, *Taft and Roosevelt*, 2 vols. (New York, 1930), II, 516-26; Pringle, *Taft*, II, 575-76.
[14] "Personal Recollections 1910."

around with him "for the comfort of it" a letter in which his father had set forth one of his sensible appraisals of present contingencies and future prospects. In return, the son discovered he could not very adequately express "what I feel about it." "To try to satisfy you," he wrote first and then began again, "To try to satisfy your ambition for me is about the most concrete aim I have had for a good many years, and about as lofty a one as any son could well have before him." [15]

Shortly after writing this letter, he set out with Theodore Roosevelt to Saratoga. At the hotel they found "pandemonium." The lobby was packed with a tired, hot and noisy crowd pushing its way slowly toward the reservation desk. Out of this "howling mob" came Elihu Root. "Isn't this just the kind of thing that you love best?" he asked Stimson in the moment before he was thrust beyond earshot.

Some hours later Root and Stimson met again in Roosevelt's room to discuss the situation. The Colonel's mind initially was on his own difficulties. He was too busy; he had been asked to make 2200 speeches since he left Khartoum, of which, Root added, only 2100 had actually been delivered. Then Roosevelt announced that his mind was made up, that this was his last venture into politics. He would stand it, he said, until after the election and then stop short. "Bet you a dollar," Root said. There was then some discussion about the "curious situation arising out of the uncertainty of the control of the convention." What, in these conditions, Root hoped to do was to find some way "in which we can keep Harry out of this." Roosevelt replied that he was no more anxious than Root to sacrifice Stimson, but that he had "the feeling that with a good fight a licking won't necessarily hurt him."

Root was inclined to believe "a terrible licking" was more probable than a good fight. He then spoke words that were to be, in the years to come, a tremendous comfort to Stimson. The country, he said, had decided to change parties. "It is like a

[15] H.L.S. to L. A. Stimson, Sept. 22, 1910.

man in bed. He wants to roll over. He doesn't know why he wants to roll over, but he just does; and he'll do it." Under such conditions no man could expect to win.

There the matter was left that evening. Next day Stimson and Root took a long walk and once again reviewed the whole subject. Perhaps because of this talk with Root, perhaps for other reasons, he reached the conclusion in the course of the day that his name could be used if "the situation had reached the point where they felt it was my positive duty to go in and get beaten." The situation soon reached that point. Roosevelt was elected temporary chairman and established command of the convention. On the night of September 28 he met with party leaders who, after eliminating from consideration two up-state men, Hinman and Bennett, selected Stimson as the choice for governor. Next day Theodore Roosevelt, calling attention to the candidate's "truculent integrity," placed his name in nomination before a convention that proceeded immediately to ratify the choice of the party leaders. Two days later, when the Democrats nominated a sober, respectable manufacturer of paper, John A. Dix, as Stimson's opponent, the five-weeks campaign began.[16]

For Stimson it began badly. As Roosevelt had reported, the citizens in that year were sullen and apathetic. They were also, in New York, annoyed by the rapidly rising cost of living, which they not unnaturally attributed to the policies of the party in power. And to one of the principal policies of the party — the high-tariff plank agreed upon at Saratoga — Stimson was himself opposed. Then too, he was thought of as Roosevelt's creature, the "hand-picked" candidate of a man whose ultimate objectives by 1910 had become, to many observers, both obscure and disturbing. To these formidable difficulties, others were added. The division within the Republican Party in New York — emphasized when Barnes and Woodruff

[16] "Personal Recollections 1910"; H.L.S. to J. L. Martin, Nov. 22, 1910; *Roosevelt Letters*, VII, 140; *Outlook*, Oct. 22, 1910.

had failed to appear at Stimson's notification ceremony — had left the candidate without effective organization support. Only Lloyd Griscom, a Taft man and chairman of the New York County Republican Committee, came forward from the ranks of those in important political positions to offer assistance in the development of the campaign. And then there were the personal limitations of the candidate himself, unlearned in state politics, unskilled in oratory, remote in manner.[17]

It did not take either the electorate or the papers long to discover that Stimson was not a man to arouse the apathetic quickly to his cause. The *Sun* reported that his "coldness and austerity are more the result of training and environment than part and parcel of his nature," while the *Times* tried to reassure its readers that "the pictures given out . . . have shown him at a disadvantage." Although the upstate press revealed that he liked *Alice in Wonderland*, that he indignantly denied he was an icicle, and that he "had been known to laugh right out loud," the impression of high seriousness remained. He was an "upright," "earnest," "fair," and "hard-working lawyer." [18]

Against these obstacles Stimson proceeded as he had learned to do in the past. To remedy the defect in organization, he gathered round him the able young men who had helped him before — Francis Bird, Felix Frankfurter, Joseph Cotton. With Griscom, this staff, in the first two weeks of October, laid out the plan of the campaign. During this period the candidate applied himself to the preparation of speeches that dealt in a systematic and reasoned way with the problems of the times. Thus equipped, he set off in the middle of the month for a trip around the state in the car "Twilight."

In the cities he talked about the historical development of the corporation and the early history of American political parties. In so doing he presented the voters with a clear view of his own

[17] *Active Service*, 25-26; Jessup, *Root*, II, 168-69; New York *Tribune*, Oct. 23, 1910.
[18] New York *Tribune*, Oct. 2, 1910; *Current Literature*, II, 504-8; *Independent*, Oct. 27, 1910.

maturing political philosophy. The great difference in mankind, he explained, was between the critic and the doer. The doer, he explained, believes that "the Golden Age lies in the future" and thinks "the most important thing is to get the business done." On the other hand, the critic believes the best of times "lies in the present or the past"; he "does not like to move until he is dead sure"; he is "afraid of making a mistake."

At the beginning of the Republic "these two different types at once lined up on opposite sides of the interpretation of our constitution, and formed our first great political parties. The doer necessarily became the liberal constructionist; the critic, necessarily the strict constructionist." "It was the great genius of Alexander Hamilton that he enlisted on the side of the doers, the Federalists, and in behalf of the progressive doctrine of a liberal construction of the Constitution, such of the business interests of our young nation [as] would naturally have been its conservatives." This liberal spirit of Hamilton, under the enlivening influence of Theodore Roosevelt, was still at work in the Republican Party.

In the country towns Stimson talked as one who had a "real" farm of his own, five miles from town on an R.F.D. route. Using some of the ideas of Frederic Howe, who rode for a time on the Twilight, the candidate explained the implications of the closed frontier. In a more complicated and interdependent world the farmer must take "a broader view of governmental duties"; he must have "more diversified interests" and a great "exchange of understanding" with men in the cities. The trained intelligence required to meet the new challenges indicated the need "for more agricultural colleges." [19]

The word came back from the outlying areas to the headquarters at the Hotel Manhattan that this sort of thing simply would not do. The candidate lacked "ginger"; he was too

[19] Extensive notes on these speeches are in the Stimson Papers. New York City newspapers ordinarily gave only brief notice to his talks in upstate New York. The speeches at Carnegie Hall (Oct. 12) and in Brooklyn (Oct. 14) were fully reported.

"precise"; he ought to "thaw out"; he talked of principles and not of the arresting sins of the opposition or of his own impressive virtues. Above all, he was warned, he had to disassociate himself from Theodore Roosevelt. Such advice was hard to accept; to enlarge upon the personality of Dix was distasteful and upon his own, unthinkable. "I can't," he explained, "talk about myself that way. Whatever I did [in the District Attorney's office] was just in line with my work and if that has to be mentioned somebody else ought to do it. I can't be saying I, I, I, all the time." [20]

But he did inject some "ginger," after all. Dix was attacked for the working conditions in his paper mills and accused of privately supporting a high tariff while running for office on a low-tariff program. A man named Skene, who had been the State Engineer in a previous Democratic administration, was cited frequently as the architect of a plan to cheat the state of large sums of money that had been appropriated to build new roads. Stimson argued also that he had made a real effort to reduce the high cost of living by his prosecution of the corporations for evil-doing.

He also developed a paragraph to deal with the Colonel of the Rough Riders. After indicating that he admired the courage and civic righteousness of Theodore Roosevelt, he would conclude to applause — "But . . . if they mean that if you should elect me Governor of this state I would administer this great office according to any other suggestion or any other dictation than my own will and my own oath of office, why then I say to you that I am not only not Mr. Roosevelt's man but I am not any man's man. . . ."

By such means he made himself, "he always insisted, a reasonably competent campaigner." That he was tireless, persistent, and wholly given over to the task of winning the election

---

[20] The advice he received was very specific. "You turned away too quickly at the end of the speech," Lloyd Griscom told him on Oct. 15. The same day George Roberts wished "there was more *I*" in the talks.

is quite beyond doubt. That he delivered from time to time thoughtful disquisitions on political theory and the need for changes in the mechanisms and purposes of government is likewise clear. That by his canvass he won the abiding affection of many hearts or even changed many votes is not so obvious, though one man told him he changed not only his vote but his party because on looking at a picture of Stimson's living room he thought, "Culture's hand is here." But things remained very much in November what they seemed in September at Saratoga. As one of the campaign songs said, there were those who believed,

> *If Stimson came from Africa*
> *If he was a Zulu Chief*
> *If he wore a feather in his hair*
> *And dressed in a fig leaf*
> *We'd vote for Henry just the same*
> *And carry out the plan*
> *Because he's Roosevelt's man.*

There were also those who had tired of Roosevelt and of his party; who were, in Root's words, prepared to roll over. These combined on election day with the Democrats to give Dix 689,700 votes, while Stimson received only 622,229. The entire Republican ticket was defeated although three members ran far ahead of the gubernatorial candidate.[21]

Looking back on this occasion years later, Stimson could not forbear to remark that "victory would almost surely have opened to him a strong possibility of great advancement, even toward the White House." Victory also, he reflected, might

---

[21] *Active Service*, 27; New York *Tribune*, Nov. 10, 1910. The complete election returns are in *The New International Year Book, 1910*. Stimson received about 180,000 votes less than Hughes did two years before. He believed, as he wrote W. D. Washburn, Nov. 14, 1910, that he had reduced the Dix winning margin by "200,000 to 300,000 votes." Some support is given this estimate by the Boston *Herald*, May 13, 1911, which asserted that the "Roosevelt-Stimson combination saved the party in New York from the disasters that overtook it on the eastern seaboard in 1910."

have sustained Theodore Roosevelt "in his original inclination to work out the New Nationalism *within* the Republican party." If in these later speculations he may have miscalculated not only his own capacity to establish a hold over the electorate, but the self-control of Theodore Roosevelt out of power, he nevertheless at the time remained philosophic. "I did," he wrote Seth Low, "the best I could and must rest on that." His achievement, he believed, lay in the fact that he had taken the party out of the hands of the bosses and the stand-patters; that he had put it "on the right side of the big issues." There were other satisfactions accruing from the experience as well. He had, for the first time, learned about the state and the problems of the state and had discovered to his surprise "that a dip into politics is almost as good as a dip into religion." Never before had he known how many unselfish things one's friends would do for a man. It is, he wrote C. C. Burlingham, "a better experience than a revival." Then too, as he returned to the private practice of the law, he had the comforting realization that, in the face of virtually certain defeat from the beginning, he had done his duty.[22]

[22] *Active Service*, 25; H.L.S. to Seth Low, Nov. 14, 1910, to Regis Post, Nov. 21, 1910, to C. C. Burlingham, Nov. 10, 1910.

10

The Secretary of War

S IX MONTHS to the day after Stimson returned to private
  life, Elihu Root "came to town" and told him that once
again he was being considered for public office. The President
wanted him to take the place of Jacob M. Dickinson who had
resigned as Secretary of War. Two days later, May 11, 1911, in
the Hotel Manhattan, Stimson informed Charles D. Hilles,
Taft's private secretary, that he remained loyal to Theodore
Roosevelt and retained a continuing sympathy for the cause of
Gifford Pinchot. These things would make no difference,
Hilles assured him; the President looked upon him as a "mid-
dle-of-the-road progressive." In reply Stimson said he would
have to consult four people — his wife, his father, Bronson
Winthrop and Theodore Roosevelt — before reaching his de-
cision.[1]

During the next twenty-four hours, Roosevelt declared it was
far better to be known as "an ex-secretary than as an ex-de-
feated candidate for governor"; Root suggested that the experience would be broadening; and Dr. Stimson told his son
"to accept if the opportunity for public service justifies personal
loss." In spite of these assurances, Stimson, for a time, remained "confused" by these changes in the horoscope, and
"greatly worried" by "the blow [that had] fallen." He thought
of the pain of "pulling up roots," the "pecuniary embarrass-

[1] H.L.S., *Notes on Experiences in War Department*, March 1913, now part of
Diary; H.L.S. to L. A. Stimson, May 12, 1911.

ment," and the continuing interference with his professional work. But, in the evening of May 12, he called Hilles and told him he would accept.[2]

The news delighted the President for several reasons. He had selected Stimson unexpectedly on Secretary of the Treasury Franklin MacVeagh's suggestion, after rejecting five or six other names. While he was not really very confident that the appointment would "heal the differences in New York" caused by the election of 1910, he believed, correctly, that it would annoy a good many men who had begun to annoy him. Sherman the Vice President and Barnes in New York would, he knew, be furious; while Charles Nagel and George W. Wickersham in his Cabinet and his own brother Henry would be little more enthusiastic. What was even more satisfying, apparently, was the way in which he "scooped the newspaper boys." Chuckling over the tidings Hilles brought him, Taft confided to Archie Butt, "I think I scooped everybody, even Mrs. Taft. I will tell Nellie when I go upstairs to-night, and I don't think she will be any better pleased than were Wickersham and Harry." [3]

A more sober canvass of the merits of the appointment was taken by the press, which on the whole agreed that Taft, in making a sensible effort to "unravel the tangled skein of New York politics," had also selected "a good and able man." Even *The Nation* tempered, for the moment, its irritation with the Taft Administration, though it could not forbear to remark that the position must come as a satisfaction to Stimson "since it gives him the opportunity to demonstrate anew in high office just what his talents are." And it went on to say that the Army stood in need of talent "as never before . . . the whole department is unscientifically managed, over officered and wastefully conducted." [4]

[2] H.L.S., *Notes*, 1913; H.L.S. to L. A. Stimson, May 12, 1911.
[3] Butt, *Taft and Roosevelt*, II, 654-55.
[4] New York *Tribune*, May 14, 1911; *Nation*, May 18, 1911; *Independent*, May 18, 1911; *Outlook*, May 27, 1911; H.L.S., *Notes*, 1913.

This was not what the new Secretary had been told by those who had pressed him to accept the position. Indeed, he had been urged to believe that the Army was "well organized" and "had interesting problems." Whatever the state of its organization, it was, in 1911, at least an interesting, even a curious kind of armed force. The two most powerful general officers had been trained, originally, in the practice of medicine. One of them had made a distinguished contribution to the Army by devising a successful card index file. The troops, about 75,000 in all, were, for the most part, distributed throughout the country in forty-nine posts that had been placed in twenty-four different states and territories in accordance with the strategic requirements of Indian fighting. Each post had a complement of about 650 men. These soldiers, it was said, tended at their remote stations to lose their military bearing and to fill the endless days of peace with tasks of carpentry and landscape gardening.

In this army the largest tactical unit was the regiment. There were not enough field guns for the existing artillery units and not enough ammunition for the existing guns. It was estimated, in December 1910, that at the contemporary appropriation rate, an adequate reserve supply of field artillery material would be obtained in fifty years. To the soldiers of this army more than a million dollars had been paid in excess clothing allowances for uniforms never drawn, and somewhat less for travel never actually taken. Three months before Stimson assumed office, a maneuver took place in Texas designed to reveal how rapidly a force of division strength could be put in the field. Ninety days later, after posts in virtually every part of the continental limits had been drained of manpower, only three-quarters of the desired number of men had found their way to Texas. Other interesting symptoms of our military condition were revealed in these maneuvers. A brigadier with thirty years' service had in this period his first opportunity to command a complement of brigade strength — an opportunity that melted within his grasp as the troops began to fall out after the first three miles of a proposed twenty-mile march.[5]

Such, in brief, was the state of the military establishment in the year 1910. The sources of military ineptitude were many and varied, but three causes appear determining. First, the United States Army had, in half a century, fought only one formal war and that conflict had been fought and finished on remote islands within a single spring. The continuity of a peaceful situation was confirmed by the lessons of history and, in the minds of most Americans, was supported in 1911 by the future prospects.

Then there was the dispersion of the army posts which, as the Texas maneuvers demonstrated, made military training unlikely and the concentration of military force virtually impossible. Two great influences perpetuated this dispersion. In these stations the old Army discovered the nursery of "the distinctive military virtues" and the foundry in which "the bonds of comradeship" were forged. It was pointed out that if young officers were put out of the government quarters at these posts and forced to seek private lodgings in cities, "they must seek well dowered wives," women so rich they "may resign [their] commission[s]," or, on the other hand, they might remain unmarried, and "without a normal domestic life . . . deteriorate."

Other men, for equally compelling reasons, supported the existence of the outposts. In each state where there were forts there were also members of Congress. The $4,925,486 spent on Fort D. A. Russell in the fastnesses of Wyoming was reported not only to have pleased Senator Warren, but to have "grati-

---

[5] *Annual Reports of the War Department, 1911*, 4 vols. (Washington, 1912), I, 7-24; Hermann Hagedorn, *Leonard Wood, A Biography*, 2 vols. (New York, 1931), II, Ch. 5; W. A. Ganoe, *The History of the United States Army* (Revised edition, New York, 1942), 439-45; *McClure's Magazine*, April 1912, 677-83; *Collier's*, April 5, 1911, 17-40; *Nation*, Dec. 2, 1911, 595-96. See also seven articles appearing serially in *Independent*, LXXII, under the general title "What Is the Matter with Our Army?"

fied" his constituents. Other political figures less influential than Warren, and other constituents less fortunate than his, were nevertheless grateful for the opportunities provided by expenditures of the federal government in the development of the forty-nine posts in the twenty-four states and territories.[6]

There was also a third source of weakness in the military establishment; within it could be discovered no real spring of military energy. In time of peace it is occupations essentially civil in character — feeding, clothing, curing, arming, housing the troops — that dominate the thoughts of officers. The attitude of mind created by the performance of the civilian pursuits was, in the Army of 1911, reinforced by two further considerations. The civil functions were divided among several agencies in the War Department called the special staff or simply the bureaus. In charge of these bureaus or divisions — Ordnance, Engineers, Signal Corps, and the like — were senior officers who served without limit of time. Some of them had lived in Washington and presided over their separate duchies for two or three decades. In these years they had not only established complete control over their own civilian enterprises in the War Department, but had created as well permanent and mutually satisfying relationships with members of Congress. These congressmen were at least as interested in the money the Army could bring into congressional districts through army posts, armories, or work on rivers and harbors as they were in preparedness for war. Thus the great tendencies in the military establishment were civil and political rather than military. To protect these tendencies a set of delicate relationships had evolved through the years, a host of associations, a frame of administrative procedures. In 1911 the War Department was a bureaucracy that had lost touch with the real military environment it had been designed to organize and direct.

[6] *Scribner's*, August 1912, 250-51; New York *Tribune*, Jan. 30, 1912; *Nation*, Feb. 1, 1912, 97; *Outlook*, Feb. 17, 1912, 340-41; H.L.S. to Norman Hapgood, Feb. 3, 1912.

As recently as 1903, efforts had been made to correct this situation. Under the urging of Elihu Root, then Secretary of War, the Congress had passed legislation creating a General Staff. Root's great aim had been to introduce an institutional form that would give continuous substance and meaning to the work of military planning and direction. This purpose he had defined in annual reports that revealed his usual mastery of sound administrative principle. What he wanted was a body of informed soldiers who, under the President and Secretary, would prepare plans, train troops and supervise the several bureaus which provided the goods and services of the Army and who would do all these things in the exclusive interest of military efficiency. In the event, though the enabling act was passed, the end was not achieved. For this there were several reasons. The precise extent of the power of the General Staff over the special staff — that is, over the bureaus — was not made clear in the phraseology of the law as originally passed and later amended. Furthermore, whatever the law said, the real conditions often enough prevented the Chief of Staff from a clear exercise of his authority. He represented at best a remote future contingency, war; the bureau chiefs spoke as men having the authority of the present — bridges to build, men to feed, money to spend. And finally, by law, members of the General Staff came and went at four-year intervals, while the men in the bureaus, who had been there before 1903, remained there often enough until retirement. The weight of precedence, fixed organization and continuity all worked, therefore, against the General Staff.[7]

Such difficulties did not prevent the General Staff from struggling to obtain the position Root desired for it. The

[7] Otto L. Nelson, Jr., *National Security and the General Staff* (Washington, 1946), Chs. 1-4; Hagedorn, *Wood*, II, Ch. 5; *General Staff Corps Laws, Regulations, Orders and Memoranda* (Washington, 1912). Root's observations on military organization are to be found in the *Annual Reports of the War Department, 1902, 1903*. They are, said Lord Haldane, "the very last word concerning the *organization* and place of an Army in a democracy."

history of the War Department from 1903 to 1911 is the history of an internal struggle for power between the bureau chiefs and the Chief of Staff. The struggle turned on a series of those curious and recondite matters that beset a society which, in peace, can conjure up no grand divisions over principle. Bitter arguments took place over whether the Chief of Staff or the Adjutant General should have the office next to the office of the Secretary. Innumerable memoranda were exchanged in an effort to establish the meaning of the word "supervise" or the meaning of that greater word "coordinate." Once when the Chief of Staff ordered a soldier to temporary duty in Oregon, an officer of the special staff refused to authorize payment for travel to the temporary duty station. On decisions in matters of this kind turned the question of who would run the United States Army. And in these conflicts, the General Staff — without money, without clear authority, without friends in Congress where it was distrusted as an organ of militarism — ordinarily fought a losing battle. So intense was the conflict, so frustrating the issue, that in these eight years, it was said, one Chief of Staff had been driven from office and another to the hospital.[8]

One officer above all others was the architect of these continuing victories over the General Staff — Major General Fred Ainsworth. In his own right he was "an extraordinary person." The lean, erect figure, cold eye and magnificent cavalry mustache were designed to conceal the fact that he had begun life as a doctor and had never commanded a troop of soldiers in the field. Summoned in Cleveland's first Administration to preside over the Bureau of Records and Pensions, he had begun

[8] For extended accounts of the strife between the General Staff and the bureaus see Hagedorn, *Wood*, II, Ch. 5, and Nelson, *National Security*, Ch. 4. For the kind of dialectical maneuvering that went on over questions of jurisdiction see "Memorandum for the Secretary of War Relative to General Order No. 68," Aug. 8, 1911, prepared in the office of the Adjutant General of the Army, and "Memorandum for the Secretary of War from the Office of the Chief of Staff," Aug. 19, 1911. Copies in the Stimson Papers.

a remarkable administrative career. Before his time a congress-man seeking from this office information for a constituent had been forced to wait six months for an answer. Less than a year after Ainsworth's arrival the reply was forthcoming within a day. The instrument of this revolution was a card index de-signed by the new chief of the office. Using this device to con-solidate his position, the officer through the years worked up the hierarchy of the War Department until he became Adjutant General. On his ascent he established ever more and ever closer bonds with the members of Congress. Since, in his position as Adjutant General, most records and all correspondence passed through his domain, he succeeded, through his control of Army paper and information, in controlling the War Department. With his wonderful administrative sense, he recognized to what uses this power could be put in time of peace. "He under-stood," as General Hagood remarked, ". . . that the War De-partment was . . . something that stood between the Army and Congress; that the way to get legislation for the Army was not to try to educate Congress and the people to Army methods, but to educate the War Department to congressional methods. . . ."

He was a master not only of administrative principle, but of detail as well. When requests came before him that could be approved, he approved them; when requests were to be denied, he forwarded them to the Secretary's office for signature. As the years passed, he acquired by all these means impressive authority within the Department, an authority he used fre-quently wisely, but almost invariably in behalf of the civil in-terests of the Army. Like any sensible man in a bureau, he sought to refine the arts of maintenance, to establish order, keep the peace and continue the flow of appropriations. Also as the years passed he developed not unnaturally a touch of unbecom-ing arrogance — which revealed itself in his memoranda. "Life is too short," he wrote in 1909 in comment on a recom-mendation put forward by a brother officer, "to permit of wasting any portion of it in discussion with . . . anyone whose conception of the underlying principles of military administration is so hazy that he can advocate such a proposition seriously. A proposition of this kind would be regarded as remarkable if advanced by a state militiaman. . . ." This tone, Ainsworth's consuming interest in the arts of simple institutional survival, and the extent of his arbitrary power provoked continuing resentment among officers who wished to prepare the Army for possible war. But he made two significant contributions to the service. By his skill he protected the Army from the ill-informed suspicion that always lies latent in the breasts of congressmen, and by his presence he provided indispensable administrative continuity — "the one fixed point" — in a society that was in theory directed by a series of rapidly changing Secretaries. Therefore in 1911 he was looked upon by almost all men in the Taft Administration, in Congress and even by many in the Army as indispensable.[9]

One man in Washington in 1911 did not share this view of General Ainsworth. This was Leonard Wood, who had been appointed Chief of Staff in 1910. Today Leonard Wood suffers from the strange obsolescence that diminishes most men who, in their own time, have something of the hero about them. Upon many members of his generation Wood cast a kind of spell impossible not to recognize but, at this remove, almost equally impossible to completely comprehend. It may be that what seems now a certain gracelessness of heart and mind was redeemed in life by a demonstration of the stoic virtues that were obviously his. It may be that possessing a degree of sophistication provided by his medical training and, as well, something of the moral concern of his native New England, he seemed to demonstrate what his time believed, that the whole duty of man was fulfilled only if the personal virtues were

[9] Nelson, *National Security*, 84 ff.; Hagedorn, *Wood*, II, 95-98; *Outlook*, Feb. 24, 1912, 378-379; *House Report 508*, Parts 1 and 2, 62nd Congress, 2nd Session, 35. Archie Butt, *Taft and Roosevelt*, II, 780, said, "Ainsworth has more personal influence in Congress than any man in the government, including the President of the United States."

proved in the life of action. Whatever the source of his hold, he came to Washington in 1910, a figure of reputation and influence. He also came with the intent to make the Army a fighting force and to make the General Staff the instrument of that development. He had in mind plans to change the terms of enlistment, to consolidate the dispersed army posts, to build up a trained reserve of military manpower and to reorganize the General Staff. To his new duties and aspirations he brought a clear, if narrow, intelligence, a toughness of spirit and one knows not what further ambitions. With his plans and intentions he came to Washington also with the feeling, as Archie Butt put it, that he was "never at heart's ease as long as he beholds one, not greater, but as great as himself." [10]

It did not take Wood long to discover that in General Ainsworth he beheld one of these. Within a matter of months the program Wood had set for himself became the cause of a struggle for power between the Chief of Staff and the Adjutant General. Wood attempted, by dropping hints to Archie Butt, to enlist the President on his side. There was, for instance, a suggestion that Ainsworth might be sent off on a trip of inspection that would keep him away from the Department for an extended period. To this and to other similar proposals, Taft paid no attention. Wood had been in the past at the center of a complicated row in Cuba; the President had no desire "to supplement my other troubles with a scandal in the War Department." But the collision between the two generals, like so many other unhappy circumstances in the Taft Administration, could not be set aside by the desires for peace of the amiable and intelligent President. In the War Department in the first months of 1911 even casual observers could discern the signs of the times. Some did so with relief. "It's a good thing,"

[10] The fullest description of Wood's career, written in a spirit of friendly respect, is by Hagedorn. See also Butt, *Taft and Roosevelt*, II, 763-64, 780-83. Butt once confided, "When I am away from [Wood] I have a deep suspicion of him and see where he schemes too much for the good of anyone, but when I am with him I find myself quite swept off my feet by his engaging personality."

said General Watson. "Let the two doctors fight it out. They will use more strategy and have more war than in the field." [11]

This was the situation when Stimson entered office at the end of May 1911. Other Secretaries, in earlier times, had found it sensible to rise, benign and inactive, above similar situations. Drawn from civil life in answer more often to the pressing exigencies of politics than of national defense, returning shortly to civil life as ignorant of the peculiar rituals of military society as any tourist can be of tribal customs, the average Secretary has tended to disengage himself — or to be disengaged — from the administration of which he is the directing agency. Such was not the case with Stimson. For the first year in office he was involved with the developing crisis produced by the activities of the two general officers. Because in this time he learned much more about public office and himself, and more especially because in the conflict between Wood and Ainsworth much is revealed about the nature of military administration in a democracy, it is perhaps worth investigating the events of these twelve months at some length.

The first task confronting the new Secretary was to learn something about the nature and needs of the strange organization over which he presided. For seven months he traveled, talked, read and observed in the hope of finding out all he could about the Army. That he found out a great deal was revealed in his first report which, to the surprise of many and the consternation of some, he wrote himself. Promotion by reason of seniority, he reported, had left "much deadwood in the Army." The "scattered" army posts had produced mere "groups of local constabulary" and prevented "a national organization." In the modern nation the standing professional army was a thing of the past; military strength came primarily from a trained reserve filled with citizens aware of the citizen's duty to serve the state. The foundation of sound military administration and policy was the General Staff. Summing up

[11] Hagedorn, *Wood*, II, Ch. 5; Nelson, *National Security*, 133-37; Butt, *Taft and Roosevelt*, II, 780-83.

his findings, he wrote: "For the remote contingency by which a national army must be always judged, namely, the contingency of war with a first class power, the Army is practically unprepared." At the suggestion of Root, who felt these words would create "a false impression of greater delinquency than actually exists," he introduced a somewhat softer impeachment in the published report.[12]

But he nevertheless made himself sufficiently clear to arouse the anxiety and curiosity of Congress. Late in December 1911 the House asked him to furnish the names of "all Army posts which have been located on their present situations for reasons which are now totally obsolete" and of all posts maintained for "purely local" reasons. He replied that of the forty-nine installations, eighteen could be eliminated at once and seven more "ultimately." "From a military point of view," as the New York *Herald* observed on January 30, 1912, it was "not denied" that the recommendations were "a good idea," but they were "very bad from a political point of view." Two posts, it was argued, would have been enough in an election year. Congress agreed. There was, in fact, "much perturbation among members who feared that army posts might be disturbed — for, here as with the tariff and with building appropriations, economy at large is a noble thing; but economy in one's own district is deplorable." [13]

Just at this moment the scandal Taft had feared took place;

[12] H.L.S., *Notes*, 1913; Elihu Root to H.L.S., Dec. 7, 1911; *Annual Report of the Secretary of War, 1911* (Washington, 1911). Root had argued that "our army never can be prepared for a war with a first-class power" since its true function was to prepare the people of the country to put into the field in time of war a far greater army of which the regular army would be only a part. Stimson accepted Root's suggested change verbatim. Root also objected to Stimson's recommendation in his report that Puerto Ricans should be given a guarantee of the rights of American citizens save for the right to participate in the governing process. Root did not like this "Roman idea," preferring a protectorate. Stimson retained his original proposal in his report.
[13] *Congressional Record*, 62nd Congress, 2nd Session, 48, Part 1, 444, 464, 516-22. The House, after debate, asked Stimson in House Resolution 343 to give it information about army posts. His reply, "Mobile Army of the United States," transmitted Jan. 25, 1912, is to be found in House Documents (No. 490), 62nd Congress, 2nd Session.

the conflict between Ainsworth and Wood came out in the open. During the previous fall they had had a falling out over the assignment of some colonels to recruiting stations. Ainsworth had objected on two grounds to the officers nominated by Wood. First, the operation of a modern recruiting depot requires in a commander "a combination of qualities of mind and heart that is not often found in one man either in military or civil life" and could not be discerned in the officers named by the Chief of Staff. Second, since Wood's nominations would in some instances relieve officers who had, in a Congressional hearing, opposed Wood's views, the impression would be created that "the Chief of Staff is endeavoring to punish [officers] because they gave testimony that may be regarded as damaging to his own, and that the solicitude now manifested in behalf of a few superfluous colonels . . . is merely a pretext for a movement whose object is to annoy or humiliate . . ." When the matter was brought to Stimson, he decided in favor of Wood and added, in a letter to Ainsworth: "I greatly regret and reprobate certain passages of your memorandum . . . Nothing is gained by suspecting or intimating ulterior motives on the part of those with whom we have to act in association." [14]

In the office of the Adjutant General this homily went unregarded when, shortly afterwards, the two officers found themselves once again in conflict. The source of trouble was one of those curious issues that arise in the parliamentary novels of Trollope and distinguish the history of all bureaucracy. A Presidential Commission on Economy and Efficiency had discovered that the War Department used too much paper. No doubt this was true. Stimson, in order to have an arm of

[14] Major General Fred Ainsworth to the Secretary of War, Sept. 5, 1911; the Secretary of War to Major General Fred Ainsworth, Sept. 19, 1911. The correspondence bearing on the "Ainsworth affair" is to be found in "Relief of the Adjutant General of the Army from the Duties of His Office," *House Report 508*. Copies of all the important papers bearing on the incident are in the Stimson Papers.

his office chair reglued, had to certify in writing that the work was "necessary for the proper dispatch of the public business." To correct the defect discovered by the Presidential Commission, the Chief of Staff proposed that the information on the muster roll, which contained the service biography of each soldier, should be consolidated with the data on the pay roll and Descriptive List. In December 1911 Wood forwarded this recommendation to the Adjutant General, in whose office the muster roll was prepared.[15]

Two months later, on February 3, 1912, General Ainsworth, after much prodding, replied, reluctantly he said, because "it is recognized that it will be difficult, if not impossible, to formulate any statement that will carry conviction to anyone who is so unmindful of consequences, or so uninformed as to the needs of the Government and the public with regard to the matter in question, as seriously to propose to abolish one of the most important, if not the most important, of all the records of the War Department. However, the statement is submitted in the confident expectation that when other, if not wiser, counsels shall prevail . . . this statement will receive the consideration that may not be given to it now." There was a good deal more about "incompetent amateurs," men with "cool assurance," and the "vital bearing" of the muster roll on the public welfare.[16]

General Wood, upon receiving this memorandum, took it

---

[15] Hagedorn, *Wood*, II, 120-21; Nelson, *National Security*, 152 ff.; H.L.S. to Major General Fred Ainsworth, Feb. 14, 1912. How difficult it might be to act on any of the Commission's proposals to save paper work is suggested by a report made to Stimson on March 7, 1912, by the Chief Clerk of the War Department, W. R. Pedigo. He said that the use of carbon paper instead of "letter press copy books" would not work, that circulars probably could be wrapped by machinery, but the Secretary's Office did not send out circulars, that a dictating machine could be purchased but since the Secretary always had his stenographer read back his dictation a machine was not needed. One thing could be done: the simplification of the salutation and complimentary close in letters, but that in fact was "pretty much done already."

[16] Nelson, *National Security*, 152 ff.; F. C. Ainsworth to the Chief of Staff, Feb. 3, 1912, included in *House Report 508*.

immediately to the Secretary. Stimson, after reading it, said he would attend to it himself and told the officer "to keep his mouth shut." Stimson then went to the Judge Advocate, General Enoch Crowder. Remarking that he proposed to find out "whether the Army was ready to stand for the kind of language" used in the memorandum, he told Crowder he wished to institute court-martial proceedings. This seemed to "stagger" the Judge Advocate, who, "almost frightened," appeared to argue for "administrative punishment" but agreed there were grounds for the more drastic course. Before acting, the Secretary talked with Root, who said something about the necessity of hitting a man who pulls your nose; and with Taft, who ruefully observed that "it has fallen to you to do a dirty job which your predecessors ought to have done before you." [17]

Thus supported, Stimson, on February 14, 1912, wrote a letter relieving General Ainsworth from active duty. Next day, he ordered nine officers to serve as members of a court-martial to be convened March 5. No trial was held. On February 16 Senator Warren brought word to a Cabinet meeting that General Ainsworth wished to retire from the service. Was this, the President asked, "good riddance"? The Secretary of War replied, "Yes, Mr. President, provided it is done at once. . . ." The resignation was then accepted without, to Stimson's regret, an accompanying apology.[18]

It is possible to make both too little and too much of this incident. At first glance it can be made to seem like a piece of jocose satire. As in Ruritania, officers fought, as every civilian suspects, over how the paper work should be prepared and filed because there was nothing else to fight about. This is too simple an interpretation. Beneath the excited words over the muster

[17] H.L.S., *Notes*, 1913; H.L.S. to L. A. Stimson, Feb. 16, 1912.
[18] H.L.S., *Notes*, 1913. Stimson in his letter of Feb. 14, 1912, written with Root's help, reviewed at length the whole altercation, quoting extensively from Ainsworth's earlier letters and memoranda to substantiate his charges of insubordination. Senator Warren told Stimson that Ainsworth had wanted to fight, that the Senator indeed had "great difficulty in getting Ainsworth to retire."

roll there was a genuine and continuing issue — the extent of the power of the Chief of Staff of the United States Army. Wood had always argued that Ainsworth "has no administrative duty," that his was "purely an office of record." The Adjutant General, on the other hand, maintained that by the intent of Congress he was free and independent in the administrative control of his office of records. Since Ainsworth had helped Congress draw the legislation bearing on this point, it is probable he knew the intent of the members. But more important than the interpretation of the confusing law, in this instance, was the meaning of history. General Ainsworth, for a decade, had led the bureau chiefs in the War Department in a successful effort to contain the authority of the Chief of Staff within the narrow limits of planning and coordination, words from which, as any bureau chief knew, all executive strength could be drained away by the interminable work of disquisition. Thus the mean squabble over the muster roll was in fact a conflict for power within the War Department between two divisions of the Department and, in a larger sense, a struggle to determine whether military energy, as represented by the Chief of Staff, or civil and political energy, as represented by the Adjutant General, was to dominate the counsels of the military establishment.[19]

With the relief of Ainsworth, it can be made to seem that the issue was decided in favor of the Chief of Staff and the General Staff as an agency of military energy, and so it has seemed to many observers, both at the time and since. To the biographer of Wood, for instance, this "notable victory" for his hero was also a fulfillment of the requirements of the law and assurance that the War Department would be administered in accordance with "Root's plan of reorganization." Stimson himself, thirty-six years later, believed his action had "insured the power of the Chief of Staff against all bureau chiefs. . . ." Un-

[19] The Chief of Staff to the Secretary of War, Jan. 4, 1912; New York *Herald*, Feb. 16, 17, 18; *Outlook*, Feb. 24, 1912; Nelson, *National Security*, 160-66.

happily these conclusions — and the others like them — are not entirely true. The confusion over the legal power of the General Staff was not cleared away by the decision to relieve General Ainsworth for the kind of language he had used in a memorandum. Nor, in the ensuing years, was the War Department run much more efficiently and wisely than theretofore. The conditions of an armed force in a democracy in peace — the overriding concerns for maintenance, budgetary claims and political convenience — tended frequently to strengthen the hands of the bureau chiefs against the uncertain powers of the General Staff. Twenty-eight years later when Stimson returned to the Department as Secretary of War, he found before him a disorganization and confusion even larger than that he discovered when he took office in 1911.[20]

Yet the action of the Secretary in this instance was both important and impressive. For one thing, by his decision he cleared up, if only temporarily, a situation that had paralyzed the administration of the War Department for a decade. In so doing he contributed greatly to the development of what one historian has called "the forward-looking spirit," which he believes was introduced into the Army in 1911. By his decision also, Stimson created a change not so much in the legal as in the moral atmosphere surrounding the General Staff. The occasion served to add more weight to the Staff's intentions, to give greater significance to its programs, to dignify its very presence in the military hierarchy, and thereby to help in sustaining the principle — only intermittently in these years supported in the sister service of the Navy — that planning and thinking are useful occupations in a military establishment. By his decision also he gave greater dignity and meaning to his office; he nourished the faith in the point and power of the civilian secretary in that most difficult of all administrative relationships — the direction of an armed force in a democracy. No official in

[20] Hagedorn, *Wood*, II, 122; *Active Service*, 36; John J. Pershing, *My Experiences in the World War*, 2 vols. (New York, 1931), I, 17.

the circumstances could do more and few, if any, of those who went before or came after in his office did as much. His action on this occasion remained fixed in the memory of the Army until he came again to take part in the administrative affairs of the War Department.[21]

The influence of General Ainsworth did not, however, end. Eliminated by his resignation from the War Department, it revealed itself forthwith in the House of Representatives. Members of Congress, already alarmed by Stimson's recommendation to close eighteen army posts, asked immediately for all the papers bearing on the case of the Adjutant General. Stimson sent the material to the Capitol but explained that in so doing he was making a gracious gesture and not complying with a request Congress could legitimately make to a member of the executive branch of the government. After studying the evidence for several months, the Democratic majority of the House Military Affairs Committee, over the angry protests of a Republican minority, reached the conclusion that Ainsworth had been the victim of a "Dreyfus-like conspiracy" contrived by the administration.[22]

Much more important was the work of Ainsworth's friends in connection with the Army Appropriation Bill in the spring of 1912. To this bill the Committee on Military Affairs, under the direction of the Chairman, James Hay, had tacked on what Stimson called "vicious substantive legislation." One rider lengthening the term of enlistment was designed to prevent the creation of a military reserve force and thus to preserve the Army as a small society undiluted by civilian strains. Stimson

---

21 Ganoe, *History of the Army*, 441; Nelson, *National Security*, 165 ff.

22 *House Document 619*, 62nd Congress, 2nd Session; *House Report 508*; *Congressional Record*, 48, Part 12, 880-93; New York *Tribune*, April 12, 1912. Stimson's assumption that by sending Congress the papers asked for he was performing a "gracious gesture" aroused James Hay, the Chairman of the House Committee on Military Affairs. The Secretary, Hay said, "has a very erroneous idea as to what his relation is to the Congress of the United States. His office is not a constitutional one. He derives no power from the Executive. He is the creature of the Congress of the United States, and as such is amenable to it."

called this project, dear for years to Ainsworth's heart, a plan to establish "a professional standing army of 150 years ago." Ainsworth's hand was also seen in the proposal to consolidate the Subsistence, Quartermaster and Pay corps under a chief elected not from the line, but from the bureaus. Finally, a rider to the Appropriation Bill provided for placing thirteen officers from the Adjutant General's Office on the General Staff. These officers were to have permanent assignment to this duty while the line officers on the Staff rotated through four-year terms. In the opinion of one observer, the General Staff would be transformed into "a sort of aulic council of bureau chiefs who never serve with troops in the field and who by the very nature of things gradually lose all touch with field soldiers." [23]

This legislation, in effect continuing the domination of the Army by the bureaus, passed the House on the day General Ainsworth resigned. The Senate, after hearing Stimson's arguments before the Committee on Military Affairs, rejected the House riders in April but passed the Appropriation Bill, which was then sent to conference. Word shortly came to the Secretary that the men in conference were planning to add two further riders to the Appropriation Bill. The first would prevent the Secretary from taking any action on army posts until a committee of congressmen and retired generals, some of whom in 1901 had approved the existing distribution of posts, had studied the matter. The second was a provision so drawn that it would disqualify Wood from serving as Chief of Staff. On hearing these things Stimson went to the Capitol, borrowed Henry Cabot Lodge's office, talked to all the Republicans and "progressive democrats" he could find, and "generally made things as warm as possible." Apparently he made things warm

[23] H.L.S. to James Hay, Jan. 4, 1912; *Outlook*, Jan. 20, 1912, 106-7. The appropriation bill as amended by the House is in *House Report 270, 62nd Congress, 2nd Session*. The debates on it appear in the *Congressional Record, 48, Part 2, 1690-1700.* In the course of the discussion Hay said the Chief of Staff was merely a "Congress clerk."

enough. Senator Warren, on June 1, 1912, went round to see the President, told him Stimson had "probably beaten" the new proposals, and suggested a compromise. If, he said, the President would get rid of Wood, he, Warren, would see the bill passed without objectionable riders.[24]

In reporting this proposal to his Secretary, Taft "evinced such lukewarmness on the subject of Wood" that Stimson called in Root to help him. Together they labored to show the President that Warren's idea amounted to a usurpation of the President's power and obligation to choose his own Chief of Staff. Reluctantly Taft agreed and started to dictate a letter in which, after saying he could not accede to the demand for Wood's removal, he went on to say, in effect at least, he could not do so "then and there," though "it might be different later in the fall." Stimson, with some excitement, interrupted to point out that this would be "construed as a back door yielding to their demand in the future." So Taft tried again. In his revised letter he told Warren he could not agree to a proposal that seemed to justify the desire to get rid of Wood for the part he was "supposed to have played" in the relief of Ainsworth. As a matter of fact, Wood "played no part in that business at all" and therefore the President could not "properly yield now" to a request to remove the Chief of Staff. It would look, he thought, "too much like a successful case of 'stand and deliver.' "

Thus revised, the letter said what Root and Stimson wanted and what the President knew was sensible, but it did not express the President's whole feeling. He was obviously "a little sick of Wood," whom he thought of as a disturber of the peace; in writing his first draft he had therefore "just proceeded to think his own thought aloud . . . into his letter." It had been a wearing conference for all three men — prolonged after all

24 H.L.S. to L. A. Stimson, May 24, June 2, 1912; H.L.S., *Notes*, 1913; "Memorandum by Secretary of War for Congressman Robert J. Bulkley," May 30, 1912; "Memorandum of Secretary of War's Objections to the Army Appropriations Bill" (delivered to Senator Hoke Smith, June 1, 1912); *Nation*, June 6, 1912, 554; *Outlook*, June 8, 1912, 280.

was over by the President in a last moment of hesitation before he sent off the letter. As Root and Stimson left the White House, the older man turned to the Secretary and said, with what John Hay had once called his murderous smile, "He isn't very bright about some things." [25]

The men in Congress, annoyed by Taft's resistance to their desire to get rid of Wood, went immediately to work. Out of conference came the Appropriation Bill with many of the original House riders restored, with the Senate's proposal to prevent the Secretary from eliminating army posts added, and finally, with a provision that no one could be selected as Chief of Staff who had not spent ten years as a commissioned officer of the line in grades below that of brigadier. As Root said of this last provision, its meaning could not be more clear if it had read "no man whose initials are L. W. shall be chief of staff." This conference bill, containing almost all the proposals to which Stimson had been originally opposed, passed the Senate and then the House on June 14, 1912.[26]

The press in general expressed itself as mildly unhappy at this Congressional action — especially in the attempt to limit the President's power to choose his Chief of Staff — though *The Nation* pointed out that if Wood were a different kind of man such attacks on him would be "impossible, even if there were a dozen Ainsworths to pull political wires." In spite of the lack of public enthusiasm and of the Congress's disregard of the President's wishes in the matter of Wood, it was not clear that Taft would do anything. Stimson, as he wrote his father, was "not over hopeful," and as he recorded in his notes, "Although [Taft] had always backed me up in Departmental matters, I knew he was at heart indifferent to the issue. . . ." Nevertheless there were several excellent reasons why the President should sign rather than veto the bill. To begin with, a veto

[25] W. H. Taft to Senator F. E. Warren, June 5, 1912, Taft Papers; H.L.S., *Notes,* 1913.
[26] *House Document 835,* 62nd Congress, 2nd Session; H.L.S., *Notes,* 1913; Hagedorn, *Wood,* II, 123.

would leave the Army without money unless Congress took special action to supply funds before an appropriation bill could be passed. Then also, Senator Warren and Senator Du Pont, two powerful Republicans whose support any President needed, had been the principal advocates of the bill as passed. Finally, Taft was not anxious to go to the Republican Convention of 1912 with the public display of difference within his party. Stimson knew Taft was preoccupied with "the exciting political crisis," but he undertook to persuade his chief to veto the legislation. He did so by first trying to rally "my cabinet associates" and then going off with his friend, Major Frank McCoy, to write a draft message.[27]

At the Cabinet meeting the day the bill came out of Congress, Stimson asked permission to discuss an important matter. When he had read his draft message, Taft remarked, "That sounds like authority. . . ." and the Cabinet agreed. The President wished to wait until after the convention, but was persuaded to act immediately on Stimson's argument that Warren and Du Pont would feel "used" if they went to Chicago in support of Taft and returned to find his veto of their legislative handiwork. Thus the President sent Stimson's message immediately to the Congress.[28]

This was not the end of the matter. In August the original bill went back into committee for reconsideration. Stimson, by negotiation with Hay of the House and Du Pont in the Senate, obtained the kind of enlistment terms he wanted — three years instead of five with the colors — in return for acceptance of consolidation of the Supply Corps. All was going smoothly until Stimson heard that once again a "concealed provision" to dis-

---

[27] *Nation*, June 13, 1912, 577; New York *Herald*, June 14, 18, 1912; *Outlook*, June 22, 1912, 372-73; *Literary Digest*, June 22, 1912, 1287-88; H.L.S., *Notes*, 1913.
[28] H.L.S., *Notes*, 1913; H.L.S. to L. A. Stimson, June 21, 1912. In his veto, *House Document 835*, Taft spoke of the dangers of "attaching substantive legislation to appropriation bills," and reported that he found the specific amendments "objectionable."

qualify Wood, "so cleverly drawn that I am still inclined to think that Ainsworth drew it," was being included in the new bill. Upon receiving this intelligence, the Secretary repaired to Chevy Chase to bring this news to the President on the eighteenth green. "Instead of getting angry," Taft remarked in a "rather sad way," "I don't see why they should try and do that to me again."

But they had. Yet when Senator Warren told Taft he "didn't think the provision hit Wood," the President was inclined to believe him because "people" had urged him "to accept it on the ground that it would not hit Wood." Stimson therefore got Hay and Du Pont to come to a conference in the White House at which he asked Hay — who, whatever his faults, "never lied" — whether the provision would disqualify Wood. "Well," said the Chairman of the House Military Affairs Committee, "if you ask me the question, frankly I think it will."

All the President had to do was to say in clear language he would veto a bill which included that provision, but he could not. Instead, he "implied it politely," in a way that made no impression. So next day the Secretary saw him again and persuaded him to tell Senator Warren "flatly" that "if the Wood provision remained in the bill, he would veto it." And so, in the third week of August the Appropriation Bill passed. From it had been excluded all the objectionable features of the legislation proposed the previous February. Included was legislation for the sensible consolidation of the Quartermaster, Subsistence and Pay corps, and enlistment provisions that permitted "the first steps toward creating a regular army reserve." In sum, the Secretary believed, it was at long last a piece of "important and constructive legislation." [29]

In playing his part in obtaining this satisfying result, the Secretary had learned some things he had not known before. He had discovered a good deal about the nature and interests of

[29] H.L.S., *Notes*, 1913; War Department Press Release, Aug. 23, 1912; New York *Tribune*, Aug. 24, 1912; *Harper's Weekly*, Nov. 30, 1912, 23.

the Congress and he had learned something about the ways to deal with congressmen. From the experience he also had acquired some information about the influence of personality in government. His support of Wood, with whom he shared the desire to reform the Army, was unwavering, but he wistfully concluded that his task would be easier if the Chief of Staff had possessed, along with his other qualities, "the ability not to make enemies." The President, he observed, had caused himself and others "enormous unnecessary trouble" because "he would not strike out from the shoulder." The Secretary's sympathy went out to the chief, who had "very little heart in his task." On the other hand he felt it necessary to act at critical moments, "as if I were taking his fist and trying to drive it forward for him." Yet from his association with the Presidency, if not the President, on this occasion, he had learned much about the power of the executive in a situation where lesser powers contended for special interests and supremacy. Rightly — skillfully — used, the power of the executive could reduce the opposition and bring, if not all things desirable to pass, at least order into the confusion of contending forces. Then too, from the preparatory study of the military establishment, his selection of solid ground on which to stand, his negotiations with Hay and Du Pont and Warren, his conversations with members of the Cabinet, his personal applications of judicious pressure upon the President, he reaffirmed something he had for long known: if one is clear on the purpose and if one works longer and harder than others work, then all things may be brought to pass.

The intent behind Stimson's actions in the Ainsworth case and in the passage of the Appropriation Bill was to increase the extent of military energy that flowed in the military establishment. Before he left office he took one further step in this direction. When Congress failed to act on his recommendation to consolidate the army posts, he sought to achieve his aim by other means. In July 1912, officers at the War College were asked to prepare a plan for the tactical reorganization of the

Army. The purpose of this reorganization was to create a divisional structure for the numberless small units spread throughout the country. These dispersed troops were to be assigned to four divisions which were to be given at least administrative existence. The generals in command of these divisions were to provide unity of spirit and purpose for their commands by traveling around the scattered posts to inspect and supervise the tactical training of all elements. It was hoped, once this divisional structure had been given administrative form, that Congress would give substance by supplying funds to bring the troops together for divisional maneuvers.[30]

There were several advantages to this scheme. For the first time in peace a permanent tactical structure larger than a regiment was introduced to the Army. Means were provided to establish uniform training routines for soldiers of the same division. Furthermore, any effort in the past to concentrate forces had produced, as in the Texas maneuvers, a flood of orders from the War Department and a confusing jumble of troops in the field. Under the new plan a single order would, in an emergency, bring units with common training together under general officers who had worked together with their troops in the past.

On January 8, 1913, all the general officers in the United States were summoned to a conference in Washington to discuss the problem. The Secretary presided. At the outset, he discovered "considerable opposition . . . from the older men and more conservative members." But as the week wore on, "general sentiment in favor of the plan" resulted. This favoring sentiment was produced in part by the skill of the presiding officer. He discovered early that "it was very hard on the one side to get the average officer to talk out in meeting in the pres-

[30] H.L.S., *Notes*, 1913; War Department Press Release, Feb. 1, 1913; *Annual Reports of the War Department*, 1912, 4 vols., I, 15-18; John McAuley Palmer, *America in Arms* (New Haven, 1941), 138-39. An excellent brief summary of the reorganization of the Army is given in the *Catalog of Public Documents*, *July 1, 1911-June 30, 1913* (Washington, 1915), 1180.

ence of his superior, and, on the other hand the superior doesn't expect him to do it, and thinks the foundations of the world are shaken if he does." Wood, one of the "superiors" who attended the conference, expected the Secretary to "go through the motions . . . and simply tell these men what the General Staff intended." He was, in fact, "quite horrified" to find that the Secretary intended "to let the flood gates loose and take the chances on controlling them." The procedure, after "the first amazement of finding that views are really wanted," worked well. The War College plan, as revised by the conference recommendations, became, through executive order, the tactical organization of the Army.

General John Palmer, one of the moving spirits behind the original plan, spoke of Stimson's part in the staff discussion as follows: "We have a principle of government that the civil authority is superior to the military. I question whether any other Secretary of War ever applied that principle with greater equity and scientific precision to any important military proposal." The specific results of the work were equally gratifying. A few weeks after the conference ended, Stimson was summoned in the middle of the night to the White House to discuss the crisis created by the insurrection in Mexico against Madero. When the President asked when the Army could be placed in readiness, the Secretary had the satisfaction of assuring Taft he could do so with "only a single order." On February 24, 1913, the 2nd Division was sent to Texas City. It was not a force created by issuing "fifty to sixty orders" from Washington. A five-line letter approved by Stimson started the Division, already established under the tactical reorganization plan, on its way.[31]

In the two years he served as Secretary of War, Stimson obviously was involved with large problems of military admin-

[31] H.L.S. to L. A. Stimson, Jan. 10, Feb. 13, 1913; H.L.S., *Notes*, 1913; Palmer, *America in Arms*, 145; *Outlook*, March 22, 1913; *New York Times*, Feb. 3, 1913.

istration, but like any public official he had, almost every day, to demonstrate that he was faithful also in little things. In the fall he had to arrange for football tickets for congressmen, in the spring he had to defend the playing of baseball on Sunday at Fort Banks against the criticism of some citizens of Winthrop, and in every season he had to send, with his signature, "any picture postcards you may have" for the autograph collections of patriots. At the request of Oscar W. Underwood, he investigated the dismissal of a Jewish student from West Point. Having, as he said, "no anti-semitic prejudices myself," pointing out that he had selected a Jew in his one personal appointment within the Department, he chose on this occasion a Jewish officer to direct the investigation of the case. Examination of the evidence revealed that there were no grounds for believing that the cadet had been dismissed because of his race. On his own initiative, Stimson conducted a canvass of the medical and commissary services of the Army. He also did what he could to return the sale of beer to posts, feeling that by this means he could keep men away "from dives and saloons" and create the atmosphere of "a nice kind of enlisted man's club." In all these matters, great and small, he acted on the assumption that soldiers "form a community by themselves, with different aims, standards, and modes of life from the ordinary civil community." "Enormous harm," he believed, "could be done by" the attempt to impose upon them rules and regulations formulated by other portions of the community not possessed of knowledge and sympathy with their life and temptations.[32]

Not all the time of a Secretary of War is spent on matters exclusively military. The administration of the overseas possessions was under Stimson's general direction. In this he did not find, during his tour of duty, the "interesting problems" others had told him were always present in insular affairs. In the Philippines the procedures of government had been already established. As for the future, "to encourage good business methods

[32] H.L.S. to the Judge Advocate General, Nov. 23, 1911, to Oscar W. Underwood, Nov. 3, 18, 1913, to F. M. White, Aug. 31, 1911.

and the development of merchandising and production, I should
not," he said, "be overafraid of paternalism in these respects.
We as a nation have a tremendous amount to learn, for instance
from the Germans . . . if intelligent cooperation between the
government and the individual merchants is paternalism."

On a visit with his wife to the West Indies, ostensibly to
survey the work of raising the *Maine*, he found in Cuba an
"atmosphere of intrigue and unrest"; he found in "this beautiful island of Santo Domingo, a population" more hopeless
than existed in it 400 years ago. From Puerto Rico, he came
away convinced that the United States should improve sanita-
tion, increase the opportunities for "industrial education,"
and grant the Puerto Ricans citizenship, but not statehood. In
Panama, which he visited with his father, sister and wife, he
left matters largely in the demonstrably competent hands of
General Goethals. From time to time he did act on such
questions as whether wines should be served at the army base,
whether Christian Scientists could practice on the Isthmus,
and whether machinery for the canal should be purchased in
open bidding. His general attitude toward Panama was that in
the canal we had, first, a great commercial waterway which
should be operated, with due regard for American interests, in
behalf of all nations and, second, a military installation of peculiar interest to us. This interest dictated the creation of an "executive" government for the Canal Zone rather than a "local
republic." What he feared was that with the canal finished
there would be no provision for operating it efficiently, that we
might "make a botch in managing it." One decision he made
about Panama after much thought, he later regretted. Before
congressional committees and in memoranda to the President
he took the view that the remission of canal tolls to American
vessels was really a form of justified subsidy, a view he afterwards found "legalistic" and contrary to the sense of the terms
of our treaty with the British.[33]

---

[33] H.L.S. to Cameron Forbes, Sept. 1, 1911, to W. H. Taft, Sept. 13, 1911, to
G. R. Colton, Sept. 19, 1911, to John D. Work, Dec. 23, 1911, to G. W.

As Secretary of War, Stimson also had under his jurisdiction the regulation of water power on navigable rivers. This responsibility brought him into a notable conflict with representatives of private power companies and congressmen of the states-rights persuasion. It had been the custom for the government to give power rights on navigable streams without taking compensation. Stimson, after extended investigation, decided that since dams could aid as well as obstruct navigation, the government, under the commerce clause, could claim jurisdiction in the building of dams. The government therefore could properly set terms and require compensation for the construction of dams by private corporations. With the help of Walter L. Fisher he persuaded the President to accept this interpretation of the commerce clause. When in 1912 a bill was passed enabling a private company to build a dam on the Coosa River without paying compensation to the government, Stimson wrote a veto message and prevailed on the President to sign it. A few months later, he worked out with the firm of Stone and Webster the kind of solution for dam construction he hoped would become a model. The company, in return for a lease, agreed to pay to the government "a share of the net profits"of the power company above 8 per cent, "these moneys to be applied" toward the improvement of navigation on the Connecticut River. Though the Senate proved "unwilling to permit this contribution to be made to the National Treasury," Stimson had the great satisfaction of having the Supreme Court sustain his principle of due compensation in the case of *United States* vs. *Chandler Dunbar Water Power Company* in 1913.[34]

Goethals, July 30, 1912, to Theodore Roosevelt, Nov. 18, 1911; notes on a speech to the Kansas City Commercial Club, Nov. 14, 1911; *Scientific American*, Nov. 9, 1912, 385-99; H.L.S., "The Defence of the Panama Canal," *Scribner's Magazine*, July, 1913, 1-6; *Active Service*, 41.

[34] H.L.S. to W. C. Adamson, Chairman of the House Committee on Interstate Commerce, April 18, 1912, to Chief of Army Engineers, May 20, 1912, to Mark Sullivan, Dec. 9, 1912, Jan. 5, 1913, to Thomas Burke, Dec. 9, 1915; War Department Press Release, Feb. 17, 1913; New York *Tribune*, Aug. 3, 1912; *Senate Document 1067*, 62nd Congress, 3rd Session.

As a member of the administration as well as Secretary of War, Stimson was also active. On two great issues his voice was frequently raised in the Cabinet to support positions not always acceptable to the President or a majority of his colleagues. In the summer of 1911 he offered a good deal of advice on how the administration should deal with the perennial problem of the tariff. Taft had called a special session to act on his reciprocity program. The Congress seized on this opportunity to consider the revision of certain existing tariff schedules. The members, in July, began to construct a wool bill that in Stimson's opinion would be "all dressed up" for the President's veto. Anxious to preserve the reputation of the administration, Stimson, on July 5, wrote Taft urging him to refer the bill, as it had passed the House, immediately to the tariff board. His thought was that Taft could use the arguments that would be forthcoming from the board in support of any Presidential veto he might have to write if the bill passed the Senate. His further thought was that by this means, the significance of the board itself could be made apparent to the public. Indeed, he hoped to demonstrate that the tariff could be taken out of its historic context as a local issue, shot through with regional influences, and placed on a sensible scientific basis by the tariff board.

So strongly did he feel on this matter that in August he and Fisher "ran the President upstairs away from the guests" at a White House reception and "begged him to get busy at once with the tariff board" before the still debating Congress passed a poor bill. The President "hemmed and hawed" and finally agreed. But next day in the Cabinet "he had retrogressed." Because Fisher and Stimson "flew at him tooth and nail," he agreed to call a meeting of congressional leaders with the head of the tariff board. But it was then too late. Just before the meeting took place the House and Senate reached an agreement. When the wool bill passed, the President vetoed it. The best Stimson could do was to recommend in November that the next Presidential message should include a firm statement in support of the tariff board. The message should show, he said, that the board had already "produced scientific information covering all subjects on which Congress attempted to act at haphazard last summer." Rather ruefully he concluded that the actual work of the board "will probably not allow this to be said, but I think it should be done as far as possible." [35]

The other great issue was the Sherman Act. The President and his Attorney General, George Wickersham, were inclined to believe that the trust problem could be dealt with adequately by their prosecutions under this act. To the Secretary of War it appeared that such methods were "mere pounding" without constructive results. The object ought to be to permit combination with regulation. To this end Stimson believed further legislation was necessary to prevent the series of devices — boycotting, the creation of bogus competitors, rebates, false advertising and so forth — by which corporations established monopolies. He also believed in the creation of a bureau "for the permanent, continuous and watchful oversight of corporate business engaged in interstate commerce . . ." These recommendations, he counseled Taft, would give to the Republicans and to the President himself the advantage of offering positive, informed leadership for the solution of the principal problem of the time. Though he did succeed in getting the President to strike out from his annual message in 1912 the thought that the Sherman Act was the most "beneficent legislation" with which the President was acquainted, he discovered that in that message his two proposals were buried away at the end of an eight-page defense of the Sherman Act.[36]

One other idea that he had bore even less fruit at this time. His work with the Appropriations Committees and the Army budget convinced him that it would be a useful thing for cabinet members to sit without vote in Congress and to submit

[35] H.L.S. to W. H. Taft, July 5, Aug. 31, Nov. 3, 1911, to L. A. Stimson, Aug. 5, 1911; W. H. Taft to H.L.S., Aug. 28, 1911.
[36] H.L.S., *Notes*, 1913; address before the New York City Republican Club, Dec. 15, 1911.

to direct questioning by congressmen about departmental programs. He attempted to get his colleagues interested in the idea, citing two earlier congressional reports on the subject, but his recommendation went virtually unnoticed. Later in his career he was to raise the idea again in other circumstances.[37]

In the closing weeks of the Taft Administration he became worried because no one from the Democratic camp had talked with him about the problems his successor would inherit. Therefore he wrote to William Williams, a friend of Wilson's, indicating that he would be happy to help the President-elect "get a clear comprehensive view" of the situation in the War Department. He warned Williams of the presence of "a real Army Congressional ring" which, under an inadequate Secretary, "would probably reinterject a quarrel into the Department." Three weeks later, hearing with consternation that Oswald Garrison Villard had taken Congressman Slayden to see Wilson, he wrote again to say the appointment of James L. Slayden, a congressman opposed to all the reforms of the last two years, would be "a calamity." He hoped therefore that Williams would get in touch with Wilson. A short time later the President-elect did send an emissary, Hugh Wallace, to Stimson. As the Secretary revealed the nature of his office and its problems in a two-hour conversation, Wallace "every few minutes would throw up his hands and say 'Great Heavens! Wilson knows nothing of it.'" Stimson later believed this conversation changed Wilson's plans and led him "to appoint a man like Lindley Garrison," though another story suggests that the new Secretary's name occurred to Colonel House while he was listening to a band playing a tune called "The Garrison March." In any event, it was one of Wilson's finest appointments, though one Wilson himself later much regretted. When Garrison came to Washington, Stimson remained for five days working with him in the War Department. In those five days, Garrison not only learned much about his new responsibility,

[37] H.L.S. to G. W. Wickersham and W. Fisher, Nov. 11, 1912.

but established a relationship with Stimson that continued in frequent discussion of military problems over the next two years.[38]

Not long before Stimson left office he had written to his father that he "felt sometimes as if I have been travelling in blinders ever since I came down here. I have done so many things and the pressure is so great. I am sure I have been a good deal dehumanized." It was true that in these two years he had been made aware of the strains that public office placed on him. He began to ask if he could speak first at any public dinner since he found it "very wearing to my nerves to sit through a long list of prior speakers, particularly when I am rather busy and tired." He also suffered from physical discomforts — rheumatism, gastroenteritis and, more especially, from insomnia. The inconveniences and irritations caused by these chronic symptoms produced in him, at times, feelings of the world's injustice, a sense, stoically borne, that everything happens to me. From time to time, however, he burst out in fits of anger over rather small things. To some the thought occurred that these symptoms were not exclusively produced by physical causes. His friend and associate from the days of the Southern District of New York, Winfred Dennison, proposed once that he see some "mental healer" who, in addition to interests in astronomy, economics and motorcars, had stimulating theories on personality, but the proposal was not well received. It is in any

---

[38] H.L.S. to William Willams, Dec. 31, 1912, Jan. 18, 1913, to L. M. Garrison, March 4, 1913, to J. McA. Palmer, June 2, 1913; *New York Times*, March 4, 9, 1913. Garrison on March 19 issued a statement that he stood "squarely behind" Wood on the need for Army reorganization. There is some evidence to suggest that Hugh Wallace came to Washington at first not so much an emissary from Wilson as an aspirant for the position of Secretary of War. Several days in the Department, together with his conversation with Stimson, apparently convinced him that the job was "too much for him." Wilson, it is said, then told House and Tumulty they must find a good man for the place soon and impressed upon them that he wanted a good equity lawyer. The most important task for the new Secretary, in Wilson's mind, was the administration of the Philippines and for that task he desired a man trained in equity law. Lindley Garrison, however, called to House's attention, fulfilled the Presidential requirement. He had been vice chancellor of New Jersey.

case extremely doubtful that any of his difficulties were severe enough to destroy or even damage the pleasure he took in his position and his work.

He soon discovered he liked soldiers and the soldiers' life. The action, the directness, the interest in form and formality, the atmosphere of a calling in which there was no nonsense — all these gratified him. From the inspection trips to those remote posts in the Far West — with Leonard Wood or that remarkable man and officer Frank McCoy as companions — he took immense satisfaction. Long days in the saddle, a little hunting on the ride, evenings around campfires or in barracks with men who recalled the excitement and dangers of Indian fighting restored in him such health and spirits as he may have lost in Washington. But even in Washington opportunities for living the kind of life he liked were not wanting. Every day he walked down to the State, War and Navy Building from his house at 1149 16th Street. Behind him walked his terrier Punch, who remained his faithful companion throughout the day. In the early morning or late afternoon he rode in Rock Creek Park on Vanguard or Aberdeen, two of the large, hard-mouthed, lively horses he loved. In the evening there was little formal entertainment, partly because for one year of his term he and Mrs. Stimson were in mourning for her mother, partly because no more in Washington than in New York did either of them care for it. At home there was a niece, Frances Gamble, or intermittently some other member of the family to keep the childless household young and lively. There were also *Mr. Dooley* and the *Some Experiences of an Irish R.M.* Only one great moment of anguished choice between different allegiances and hopes had disrupted the essentially satisfying conditions of this time.

II

1912

ONE DAY, in the late fall of 1910, the Stimsons rode Vanguard and Aberdeen over to Sagamore Hill. In the room La Farge had built and the owner had filled with the outward, visible signs of his career, they talked for an hour with Roosevelt. For the first time their host spoke of "an estrangement" between himself and William Howard Taft. The cause, it appeared, was a change in Mr. Taft, a change first noticed by Roosevelt in the summer of 1908, "about the time it became evident that Taft was going to be elected easily." There had been nothing clear and specific; only a "great many small incidents" from which the retiring President had received an impression of "ingratitude," of even "a lack of loyalty" on the part of the heir presumptive. Thinking it over afterward, Stimson reached the conclusion that all personal affection had been "pretty thoroughly killed," but he could not discover that "any real issue of public policy had come between them. . . ."

Again, a few months later, the Stimsons rode over to Sagamore for "one of the most delightful visits that we have ever had with them." This time they discussed whether Stimson should become the Secretary of War in the Taft Cabinet. Mindful of the earlier conversation, Mrs. Stimson expressed the fear that she would find it difficult to feel any great loyalty to the administration. That problem could be easily settled, Roosevelt assured them both, by "Harry's doing his best in the War

Department so as to help make Mr. Taft's administration a success." Then, as they had before when they had talked about whether Stimson should run for governor, they considered what meaning the appointment might have for Stimson's future. From there, as they had before, they turned to the future of Theodore Roosevelt. But this time Mrs. Roosevelt was present and she remarked "laughingly but insistently, 'Put it out of your mind, Theodore, you will never be President of the United States again.' "

The day after this conversation Stimson had called Charles D. Hilles to accept the appointment in Taft's Administration. To help make that administration a success, as Roosevelt advised, was, in 1911, a task to tax superior talents. The President had been described by Senator Jonathan P. Dolliver as "a large amiable island surrounded entirely by persons who knew exactly what they wanted." Charles P. Taft, in a moment of disillusion about his brother and his own plans, supplied some of the supporting details. Wickersham would not appoint a colored man to the Department of Justice, Fisher was seeking a reputation for Fisher, George Von L. Meyer was awaiting the word from Roosevelt, Philander C. Knox would not even stay in Washington, MacVeagh meant well but "ought to be given a bottle of milk and allowed to crawl on the lap of Mrs. MacVeagh and sleep." Stimson's first impression was not much better. The Cabinet, he told his father, were "a bunch of amiable and intelligent gentlemen not one of whom knows much of either what the country is thinking or of the noble art of polemics."

In time, however, he established intellectual accord and useful working relationships with several members of the Cabinet. Shortly after he took office, Wickersham — "always quick-tempered and ready to explode" — took him off for dinner and "had it out on the subject of the campaign of 1910." The Attorney General said that because he did not think Stimson had been loyal to the administration in that campaign, he had advised Taft not to appoint him. He also said he thought it would be impossible for Stimson to be loyal to both Taft and Roosevelt. In his turn, Stimson explained his position, and since the two could not "cherish malice or ill will," they made peace and thenceforth worked "comfortably" together. Equally comfortable was the relationship with Meyer. In time also Fisher, Nagel and Stimson found themselves drawing together at Cabinet meetings in mutual support for their liberal sympathies.

It took a little longer to discover how to work with the President. Not until the special session of Congress in the summer of 1911 did he find out much about the nature of the Chief Executive. Taft, saying he wanted Stimson to have the experience of visiting "in an old-fashioned home," asked him to share bachelor quarters with him in the White House for the last week of the session. The weather was hot, the mosquitoes were active; but the two with Hilles and Butt beguiled the evening hours with "music on the victrola," drives about Washington in search of a cooling breeze, and conversation. Out of the experience Stimson obtained increased understanding of this intelligent, decent, troubled man. He noted with surprise the easy accessibility there was to Taft's private affairs; the lack of reserve, indeed, the complete naturalness with which the President explained, when necessary, the circumstances of his wife's illness. There was also more here than the trained mind of a federal judge, the overt joviality of the fat man. Beneath, as Butt suggested, there was a "coldness," almost "a hardness." It was not, perhaps, so much the hardness of a man who was firm of purpose as of one who sought to protect himself from the purpose of others — of others like his wife and brother who hoped that William Howard Taft could be made into something different and something more than he himself cared to be.

In later months, as Stimson worked more closely with the President, he discovered other interesting manifestations of his character. There was the strange inability of the Chief Executive to hold the ground he had taken by intellectual means, the tendency to slide back into the modifying lights and shadows of his own uncertain feelings. These were the manifestations, Stimson concluded, of a judicial temperament, of a mind whose earnest ponderings more often than not puzzled the executive will.

Sensing all this, Stimson was doubly gratified at the indispensable support the President gave him as he dealt with problems that only fitfully aroused the Presidential interest. In other matters, like the tariff and the trusts and the controversy over compensation for power rights on navigable rivers, Taft, even when he differed with his Secretary of War, came to rely "a good deal on [Stimson's] judgment." Though from time to time there may have been something petulant in the President's way of dealing with the difficulties of his administration, there was nothing mean or bigoted or devious. He was at all times willing, occasionally too willing, to listen and discuss before reaching a decision. On such a mind and character Stimson found it possible to exert some influence and thus to get things done. It is not surprising that at moments he discovered that he was himself "beginning to feel like a Chief Executive." It is also not surprising that when so young and inexperienced a man was given opportunities to act effectively in matters of large public concern, he found himself attached to the administration by bonds of affection and loyalty.

Then there was that other loyalty. Signs had been multiplying in the last six months of 1911 that the unoccupied energy at Oyster Bay would make itself felt in some way in 1912. That the declarations of intent from Sagamore were clouded by a Delphic ambiguity comforted no one, least of all Stimson. He knew that Roosevelt in his views of the Taft Administration had passed from chagrin to contempt. He knew also that Roosevelt's irritation was reaching out to touch others who had served him best in the old days. Root had made one of his funny remarks in a speech during the campaign of 1910. He had said Roosevelt's criticisms of the courts sounded like the judicial criticisms of disappointed litigants and Roosevelt had "grum-

bled" about it ever since. Things like this, when coupled with
the Colonel's failure to disclose any clear intention, profoundly
disturbed Stimson. In the autumn of 1911 he did what he could
to prevent difficulties. He described the support Taft was giving
him; he explained that on important matters the President and
Roosevelt usually felt alike; he took Root over to Sagamore for
a "successful" luncheon. But in December the rumors about
"TR's running for the Presidency had grown so frequent," he
decided to do something more. He and George Von Lengerke
Meyer, equally unhappy about the developments, concluded
they must go and have it out with Roosevelt.

They went to Sagamore together on January 7, 1912. Meyer
began by pointing out that a contest between Taft and Roosevelt would be damaging "from a party standpoint," would be in
fact just what the Democrats wanted. Stimson, worried about
the verdict of history, said, "I do not think you will be regarded
as treating [Taft] fairly if you run against him this year." They
were told in return that their host was "older and quieter"; his
tastes, he believed, were "running to quieter things." The Presidency, the former President went on, "could never again appeal
to him as it had in the past." The general tone of the whole conversation was that "under no circumstances would he be a candidate for the Presidency." What he really wanted to know
from his callers was how he could solve the vexing problem of
what he "should say to people who insisted on pressing him as to
whether he would accept it if it was tendered by the Republican party."

As they left Sagamore, Meyer and Stimson said to each other,
"Why were we ever worried over his attitude? He is just the
same as he has always been and has no thought of becoming a
candidate." Time passed and though Roosevelt may have remained just the same as he always had been, he also gave evidence of thinking about the conditions in which he might become a candidate. So on February 7, 1912, Stimson wrote to
him that he could not "now see on the horizon any reason

which would demand such a sacrifice on your part. After eight months in the cabinet I don't believe there is any issue on official policy between you and Mr. Taft that would justify it."

Two weeks after this letter was written, Theodore Roosevelt went out to Columbus, Ohio, and threw his hat in the ring. Three days later, on February 24, he formally told the seven "little governors" he would "accept the nomination for President if it is tendered to me . . ." The necessity to choose between conflicting loyalties was now, as Wickersham had foreseen, at hand for Stimson. At Chicago on March 5, 1912, he announced his choice. He had entered public life under Theodore Roosevelt, he believed in Roosevelt's national policies, he was his friend, "But I believe that those who are forcing him, contrary to his original intention, into the arena against Mr. Taft, are jeopardizing instead of helping the real cause of progress in the nation."

Before delivery of the speech in which the decision was announced, Stimson had sent it to Sagamore Hill with a letter. In the letter he said he felt that Roosevelt had made "a mistake"; he said also that he felt "as if the horizon of my little world was swimming a good deal and it is hard to look forward to a time when I am not working or thinking with you . . ."

"Heaven's sake!" Roosevelt had replied. "You have so often been right that it is perfectly possible that I am wrong. . . ." But whoever was right, he had always said that Stimson would have to support Taft. In any event, he would not look at the speech and the newspapers would waste their time "if they try to tell me anything that you have said against me." The reporters, however, persevered. After Stimson had spoken at Chicago, they obtained the comment from Theodore Roosevelt that Stimson, after receiving aid and comfort from Roosevelt in 1910, was now revealing his ingratitude. Three years passed before the two men saw each other again.

It will be difficult in this country to forget the year 1912. "What a year it has been," Stimson wrote Robert Bacon on

July 8, 1912. "So many of my old moorings have been cut that I have felt very much lost at times . . ." The nature of that remarkable time was determined for a man in Stimson's position, in great part, by the character and actions of Theodore Roosevelt. What seems to have been the primary cause of 1912 had been defined by Theodore Roosevelt seventeen years before. Sitting one day in the office of the Police Commission of New York City, he was approached by Jacob Riis and Lincoln Steffens, who wished to settle a point of difference between them. What, asked Riis, were Roosevelt's views about his chances for the Presidency at some future time? Leaping from his chair, running around his desk, Roosevelt threw himself toward Riis with a violence that made Steffens fear he was about to "throttle" his questioner. As the two men "cowered amazed," Roosevelt cried out: "Never, never, you must never either of you ever remind a man at work on a political job that he may be president." By the corrupting influence of this temptation a man's capacity to act freely, to judge clearly a situation or himself was destroyed. So wise and self-aware was Theodore Roosevelt in 1895.

Seventeen years later a good many men succeeded in doing what Riis and Steffens had been told no man ought to do. William Kent, the Pinchots, James Garfield and all those others, by means subtle and not so subtle, drew his attention to the Presidency. So did men like Meyer and Stimson by pleading with him to put the vision by. Theodore Roosevelt, out of a political job, had discovered a way in which he had to be reminded that he might be President. He had said he would not lift a hand for the nomination, but he could not with honor refuse it if "the people as a whole desire" it. Only Root, who knew men and this particular man better than all the rest, was content to do no more than define for him what this meant. Where others urged specific courses, he simply said to Roosevelt that he had created a "condition of unstable equilibrium against which your whole nature will frequently cry out." "No thirsty sinner," he went on, "ever took a pledge which was harder for him to keep than it will be for you to maintain this position." The position was not maintained for long. When the seven governors told him that "a large majority of the people favor your election," their voices confirmed the loudest voice within him and he lifted his hand to obtain the nomination.

There was, of course, more to it than that. It was not only, as William Kent said in his jocose way, that "Terrible Ted" had gone "with the girl so long he had to marry her." The problem of succession is always painful and the arbitrary interferences with the processes of natural selection in 1908 had produced additional complications. It created in the predecessor — as it always does — specific expectations, and it laid upon the successor — as it usually does — a sense of undefined and unfulfillable obligation and also, no doubt, a feeling of inadequacy. For weeks in 1909 when someone said "Mr. President," Mr. Taft looked round for Theodore Roosevelt. Events served to play upon these attitudes. As a callous observer remarked, Taft had demonstrated that his bump of political intuition was more like a dent. By ineptitudes he had annoyed Roosevelt, outraged some men who depended upon Roosevelt, and replaced the excitement of the previous administration with a sense of frustration, if not of aimlessness. There can be little doubt that in 1911 the Republican Party, in the absence of skillful leadership, was revealing publicly the differences in point of view that always privately existed within it — or any American political party. This can all be said.

It can be said also that Theodore Roosevelt had some arresting ideas and that, as he told Robert Grant, "I am interested in these ideas of mine and I want to carry them through, and feel that I am the one to carry them through." He did in 1912 foresee that "we are on the verge of an economic revolution . . ." and he had a program to contain the process of that revolution within safe and constructive limits. It is perhaps even possible to say, as O. K. Davis did, that Roosevelt came out of Africa "with a passion for service that outweighed all other considerations, and made that of self the least and last of all."

Yet all these things cannot be made to signify. They suggest as Roosevelt himself said, that the conditions were "complex"; they serve to round out the situation; but they do not, in themselves, demonstrate the necessity to stand at Armageddon. The fact of the matter appears to be that though there were three candidates in 1912, the differences in background, training and intent of these three were smaller than the differences that usually divide the traditional two candidates — as small perhaps as the differences that separate Harvard, Yale and Princeton, from which the three men, in one way or another, came to the Presidency. The fact appears to be that the differences between the three party platforms were at least no greater than those which usually divide the two traditional parties. Wilson in his first term obtained many of the objectives Roosevelt was advocating on the stump in 1912, and, as Stimson observed, many of the things he and Fisher and Nagel were urging in Taft's Cabinet in 1911.

It seems more probable that the events of 1912 were determined by something else. When the passion for service with which Roosevelt may have come out of Africa was thwarted by the fact that he found himself with nothing to do, he had in the interests of self-preservation to find a place where his services could be rendered. That, by the logic of history, was the place he had once so impressively occupied. No doubt the unhappy situation had been in the making since 1908. In that year, in obedience to "a wise custom" and the dictates of his own carefully scrutinized conscience, he frustrated his own high energies and greatest personal needs. He did so only after some "ugly qualms," a feeling that he might be "abandoning great work on a mere fantastic point of honor" — the precedent of Washington and his own word in 1904.

But there were other grounds than honor. He believed, as he told Trevelyan, in power; he did not think "any harm comes from the concentration of powers in one man's hands, provided the holder does not keep it for more than a certain, definite time, and then returns to the people from whom he sprang." History, he went on, the history of the first and second French Republics, the Spanish American republics, the Commonwealth, revealed that it was "a very unhealthy thing that any man should be considered necessary to the people as a whole . . ." Therefore in 1908, at the age of forty-nine, at the flood tide of his personal and public powers, he did what he could to return to the people from whom he had so spectacularly sprung. The decision, in the context, must be taken as a moving act of the will, but an act nevertheless against his own nature. Thus the delicate balance, retained so nicely whenever Roosevelt was in office, between his desire to serve the state and the need to act and control was, in the days of idleness, thrown out of adjustment. In 1912 the most natural urge, frustrated, before it was satisfied, by the decision of 1908, forced itself forward to spend, in one of his favorite phrases, and be utterly spent. The decision, in other words, when all the modifying circumstances are stripped away, was not so much required by the public as by a private welfare.

This interpretation does not diminish the interest of an election in which many men found themselves more deeply stirred than they had ever been before by a political situation. It only suggests that those who were stirred responded less to what Theodore Roosevelt said he stood for than what he seemed to them to be. His action, determined by private needs, provoked in others, inevitably, not so much a concern for large matters of public policy as an excitement of personal and private feelings. So many of the responses of those who had, until 1912, been Republicans indicate as much. It was not only that Theodore Roosevelt himself wanted to take a pistol and shoot down Elihu Root on the convention floor; it was not only that William Howard Taft, after a speech, returned to his Pullman car and cried. Citizens sang of "sifting out the hearts of men" at political meetings, and walked to the polls in "the gleaming raiment of saints in that day and hour." Candidates for the Presidency of the United States shouted at each other things like "puzzlewit," "egomaniac," "fathead." In the course of the campaign, George Walbridge Perkins sobbed in a hotel room as he listened to the draft of a keynote speech and Charles Nagel turned the picture of Theodore Roosevelt to the wall, thus saving the image for perpetual denial. "Rage and wrath . . . ran riot in men's hearts," it was said in 1912, and at the end, more than one "stood there heartbroken upon the shore at ebb tide." And when the campaign was over some did not speak to each other for a space of years and some never spoke to each other again. Men do not do this kind of thing because they disagree on a tariff schedule or fall out over the recall of judicial decisions.

That he could involve members of a political party in this kind of intense personal experience, that men like H. K. Smith, twenty years later, could find themselves "shaken once more by the wind of that struggle," reveals the awful power of Theodore Roosevelt. He had the hold of the hero. By his words and deeds he gave a defining and supporting frame for the aspirations of those insufficiently clear or strong to support their aspirations by their own endeavor. Men, in the hope of finding their better selves, attached themselves to him. In so doing, they transferred some of the responsibility for themselves to him and in turn created in themselves a compensating sense of responsibility for his own actions. Thus when he embarked on this remarkable adventure, those who believed he was sacrificing himself for a cause were exalted, and those who believed, like Robert Grant, that he was endangering a cause in his own subterranean interest, were appalled. Whether they yielded to exaltation or despair, those who did so were lost not so much in the works of the hero as in themselves.

Of course, some of those closely connected with these events escaped the toils of such intense private and personal involve-

ment. Stimson was one of these. No more than the others could
he avoid the pain of the moment. The horizon of his little
world did swim as he said, "You have made a mistake," to the
man who had put him in the public life he loved, who had invested the performance of public tasks with excitement and virtue, who had "a hundred times" touched him with "acts of personal kindness and compelling charm." But these considerations
did not deter him from reaching a decision at the first possible
moment, or from standing secure on that decision, in silence,
through all the months of turmoil that followed. Sometimes, in
ensuing years, he asked himself if he could have done anything
else; once at least he wondered if, had he been a private citizen,
he would have joined in the hallelujahs that went up from Armageddon.

It is possible, but it seems unlikely. He had, after all, in his
own early life, some knowledge of what can happen when a
commanding personality, under peculiar pressures, confuses the
satisfaction of his private need with what is wise for others. He
had discovered that on such occasions the shelter gained by trying to gratify the precise expectations of the demanding figure
was at best temporary. In that first struggle to become himself
he had found the painful confusion that sets in when the merits
of a proposition get entangled with ties of affection and loyalty
to the person who proposes it. From these times he had learned
that his survival depended not so much upon unquestioning fulfillment of the desires of one to whom he was devoted as upon
his ability to separate out the merits of a case and act on them
with becoming independence. Therefore he had learned the further fact that if one was sure of one's own ground, it was possible
to stand on it without doing or saying anything that imperiled
one's tenure in that quite different ground of common affection
shared with another.

So in 1912 he looked first not to his relationship with Theodore Roosevelt, but at the merits of the case presented. From
his survey he concluded there was "no real issue of public

policy" between Roosevelt and Taft, indeed, that Roosevelt was "making a campaign on false issues." He observed further, that Roosevelt had "deliberately left himself in the position where he must have known he would have been subjected to terrible pressure" from those who would "necessarily resort to him." Separating for himself so clearly the substance of the situation from the surrounding claims of personal affection, free as he made himself from any feeling of responsibility for his old chief's action, he enabled himself to say, with pain but without rancor, "You have made a mistake." He also, by his manner of saying it, enabled both himself and Roosevelt to meet together on their old common ground in later years. Not many could say, as he did, that in 1919 he lost a friend as close as the one he had lost in 1912.

What all this meant to him, personally, he kept in an envelope at Highhold. This envelope was filed with the other papers that covered the negotiations of a lifetime — the relief of Ainsworth, the settlement in Nicaragua, the work as Governor General of the Philippines, Manchuria, Overlord, Hiroshima and all the rest of it. One evening in the years of his retirement he showed the envelope to the maid who looked after him and Mrs. Stimson. "Louise," he said, "if the house burns down some night, come first and get this envelope." Inside there were four letters written to Stimson in 1917 and 1918 when he was in France in the First World War. They are the letters full of news and philosophic cheerfulness a man at the front receives from old, close friends at home. Three had been written by Theodore Roosevelt and one by William Howard Taft.[1]

[1] Material for this chapter was taken primarily from memoranda and correspondence in the Stimson Papers and from *Roosevelt Letters*, VII.

12

Town and Country

WHEN STIMSON returned to New York in 1913 he was
forty-five years old. At a casual glance he seemed, at
first, younger. It was not only that he was physically fit, "well
preserved." There was also in his face, in spite of the finely cut
hooked nose and black mustache, a boyish look, some evidence
of perceptions not fully assimilated, of strain and anxiety controlled but incompletely resolved. Otherwise he gave off an
impression, in air and manner, of one in early middle age who
had dealt successfully with large affairs. His one hundred and
eighty pounds, his erect carriage, gave him presence and a certain dignity. The effect of dignity was increased by the clothes
he wore. The suits were made by "a little tailor" named Sie-
gling, out of sober-hued materials. The white shirts came from
a man named W. L. Burke and the black, laced high shoes were
supplied by Louis Rosenthal. Each one of these men, from time
to time, received orders to make new products on the old patterns — "exactly as before" or "the same size and style as the
previous order."

The manner of his life was appropriate to the appearance and
the condition. The house at 275 Lexington Avenue to which
he returned was in the area left behind to solid, sensible people
by those who were moving steadily uptown. It was a plain, un-
comfortable house joined to the one in which Dr. Stimson lived
with his daughter Candace. When all four were in the city

they formed together the center of society for each other. Not a day went by but what Stimson went through the door that had been cut into the partition between the two houses to report his doings and to discuss private and public futures. Candace and Mabel Stimson exchanged news about the progress of the good works each was interested in and supported one another in their efforts to extend the impalpable influence of women in a masculine household that could more easily recognize than fully understand a woman's rights and privileges. To all these gatherings — with father, brother or sister-in-law — Candace brought a sophistication and wit, a sense of individual gaiety, that had apparently been strengthened rather than dulled by her decision to devote herself to others' welfare than her own.

At the dinner table on the 275 Lexington Avenue side of the house there were not often many who were not members of some branch of the family. The Stimsons continued to be earnest but "stern and fidgety and Victorian and unrelaxed" in the dispensation of formal hospitality. With those who were older and those who were younger than himself, Stimson could establish comfortable relationships. But with those his own age, if they were not relations or friends of his youth, he still moved uneasily and it is with contemporaries that one ordinarily maintains a social life. When nieces, cousins, aunts or uncles came to visit he would, after dinner, look through the paper or glance at a magazine, breaking into the conversation of others to read aloud a passage that interested him. Then, often enough, he would take to a sofa and drift off to sleep. When he and Mrs. Stimson were alone they discussed the day's affairs, read to each other before the fire, and in accordance with the habits of a lifetime, went early to bed.

Nor were there enticements in the city that drew him away from the domestic routines. Like most men in his position, he belonged to a good many clubs, but like a good many men he rarely went to them. His favorite, the Century Association, he found, was a good place "to keep appointments and that sort of thing." Two other organizations gave him a transitory pleasure. One was a dining club of lawyers, which included men like James Byrne, Henry Taft, Learned and Augustus Hand, Charles E. Hughes, Wickersham and C. C. Burlingham. These men were all old friends but he often came away from a meal with them in "a rather soggy condition." They were "all so fond of each other" that nothing happened; they just talked. Without intellectual contention there was "no excitement or stimulus to digestion." At another dining club — with men like Grant La Farge, Norman Hapgood, Simon Flexner and Finley Peter Dunne, and with such stated subjects to discuss as "Prostitution in Europe," or "Hookworm" — he found more to stir his interest, but neither there nor in the other diversions of the city could he find continuing pleasure. His real satisfactions lay elsewhere, forty miles to the east in the township of Huntington in Suffolk County, Long Island.

At Highhold he had, since 1903, slowly constructed the kind of environment he desired for himself. His land was in the area of West Hills, six miles from the village of Huntington. On the high ground along the spine of Long Island he had a hundred acres from which a man could look northward to see the Sound and look to the south to "catch the glimmer of the sun on the ocean 25 miles away." These acres lay in the center of farming country, in sidling meadowland broken up here and there by clumps of high brush and larger stands of hardwood. The men who had worked this land for years had taken the sense of wildness out of it, but there remained a feeling of open country, the soil and changing seasons. Over to the north, on the Sound, great houses were going up in 1903, but the West Hills in that year had been discovered by only a few prospectors from the city. One early visitor to Highhold found it "a desolate spot." The desolation slowly changed as the years went by and other men from New York moved in to build their homes there.

If Highhold was not, as its owner sometimes claimed, a farm, it was also not what is meant by "an estate on Long Island." Though there were gardens, they supplied only enough vegetables for the table and flowers for the house; though there were barns, there were in them only the cows and chickens necessary to supply milk, cream and eggs for domestic needs; though there were stables, the horses in them were without the high style of superior blood lines. The house itself, a low-lying frame structure without distinction in its original form, had acquired through several additions an amiable shapelessness. By 1914 a porte-cochere had been attached, a living room expanded, and a small room set aside for the accumulating memorabilia of the Stimson career — the flag of the Secretary of War, group pictures of his staff when he was District Attorney, signed photographs of Leonard Wood and William Howard Taft.

The house as it stood when Stimson came back from Washington had cost something less than $15,000 to build. Inside, as out, it gave forth a pleasant air of comfort, plain, unpretentious, but substantial. The rooms seemed filled with light and furniture and velour and chintz. Along the walls were likenesses in photograph and paint of various members of the family. Here and there a small oil or water color by one of the Wheeler relatives could be found, valued more by Stimson for its family associations than for any aesthetic value. On the bookshelves there were sets of Dickens, Thackeray, Emerson, Tennyson, Browning, Shakespeare, Longfellow, Lamb and Whittier. What was inside these books was better known — or at least more fully recalled — by Mrs. Stimson than by her husband. He was not a man to make use in conversation of the apt quotation or the literary allusion. Some of his friends believed that in these regions, if pressed, he could move with greater familiarity and understanding than he ordinarily revealed. Once, when he had been pressed, he said that his favorite novel was *Some Experiences of an Irish R.M.*, his favorite play, "*Hamlet* by Shakespeare," his favorite poems, which he recited to himself on sleepless nights, Gray's "Elegy in a Country Churchyard" and Shelley's "To a Skylark."

Like the furniture, the meals in this house were substantial
and well constructed. At dinner there were things like clear
soup, roasts of beef and lamb, jellies and, often enough, ice
cream and chocolate cake. At tea there were cinnamon toast
and little frosted cakes. The people who cooked and served
these meals, had, ordinarily, been in the house for years. In the
long summer two or three of them were brought with the Stimsons from Lexington Avenue; on week ends John Colliton's
wife frequently looked after the house. John Colliton had arrived in the year the house was built. For thirty years he kept
watch and ward over the grounds and animals and over Mr.
and Mrs. Stimson. A rugged man in body and spirit, he had a
great way with growing things and a greater way with
horses. He used to ride down to the station — three miles
away — leading a horse and carrying a pair of puttees to meet
the evening commuting train. He and Stimson would then ride
back together to what John Colliton called "the big house." As
automobiles were added to the transport system — a Maxwell
and a Chalmers had preceded the Cadillac bought in 1914 —
these were also given into John's care. He did in fact almost
everything; "Highhold," Stimson once said, was "the expression of John's personality rather than anyone else's . . ."

In the physical surroundings under John's care, Mrs. Stimson
set herself to produce the kind of life her husband desired.
This, in the circumstances, was not altogether easy. Highhold,
if not pretentious, was at least an establishment of some size.
Outside and within, it posed daily problems of maintenance and
personal relationships that often, during her husband's absence
in the city, fell to her lot for decision. Then too, though it lay
empty for some part of each month in the winter season, it had
to be kept in a state of instant readiness for occupancy. The
responsibilities involved in this kind of administration Mrs.
Stimson accepted and discharged, if not with ease, yet in such a
manner that her husband was left wholly untroubled by household cares. But she did far more than this. As one of his relatives remarked, Stimson acted frequently in the spirit of the

man in *Mademoiselle Modiste* who said, "I want what I want when I want it." When his wife much earlier had discovered his love of dogs, she accepted Punch and Tinkerbell into the family; when, in these years, he wanted his ride, she was ready in the sidesaddle on Vanguard. When gardens were to be laid out, paths to be cut, trees to be transplanted, stock in the pens and stalls to be surveyed, she and her husband went out together on these errands. At times, after dinner, if he came upon a passage in the *Times* he wished to read aloud she listened, and if he dozed off on the sofa, she fell silent. Her husband, as people who knew him well often noticed, could not bear to be alone and, if it were in the power of his wife to prevent it, he never was.

Because she set herself so steadfastly to appear as Mrs. Stimson, it was difficult for those near her to discover much about Mabel White. That she was "intelligent," "competent," "pretty," and, as time passed, "handsome" was universally agreed. That she was more a respecter of conventions than of persons, that she was without much humor seemed also true. And those who noticed her lack of ease in social situations noticed also that in the expressions of her own views on matters political or ethical, she was forthright and firm. But what lay beneath the resolute support she gave to the correct appearance of things was a matter of speculation. Some, for instance, believed she "hated horses," "hated camping" and "intrepidly" schooled herself because she "felt that it was her duty to ride well and to camp with her husband." Whether, in this activity as in others, she acted from the dictates of duty or the spontaneous requirements of her own nature, or a happy coincidence of the two, she never fully revealed to anyone — perhaps never even to herself, for she had discovered that she was "such a goose whenever I try to say what is in my heart."

Fortunately, in her relationship with her husband, such things taken on trust could be left for the most part unstated. If she devoted her days to the fulfillment of his rather precisely stated wants, he, for his part, found it equally important "to have her to take care of." Though, with its foundations in the nineteenth century, it seemed to younger friends "an extremely formal marriage," yet it was obvious "each was saying, we exist to take care of each other." They struck many observers as "the most completely dependent couple," possessed of some deep "inward devotion" to each other; they wanted more than anything else "an open fire in their study with both doors locked so that nobody could intrude."

Safe from intrusion they permitted each other, within the given outward formality they both valued, considerable freedom. More than once it was noticed, for instance, that his wife, no matter how much he treasured her support, "never influenced his thinking once." It was also noticed somewhat later that, on returning from a ride, she made it her custom to stop by the study he was working in "just to show him she had been out riding." If he was seriously engaged in thinking, these visits were not always successful. Whenever the rather laborious processes of thought were interrupted, he would give way to irritable expostulation. When the disturber of his concentration was his wife, he would be at least sufficiently gruff to force her to withdraw in silence. Then, brooding on his insensitivity, he would, after ten minutes, "think of some sweet little thing to do to make it up to her." These small contretemps and resolutions most fortunately occurred quite often in the intense relationship forced upon these two people by their own temperaments and the absence of children. They gave a natural unevenness to an existence that might easily, by simple circumstance, have fallen into too rigid lines; they provided easy opportunities for the exchange of normal tempers and affections within the outward structure of extreme formality. And they demonstrated that each was to the other indispensable. Without him she was uncertain; without her he was "lost, absolutely lost."

Thus supported by land, by a sufficiency of things and service and by his wife, Stimson, at Highhold, lived as he wanted to.

Every week end, for all holidays and for summers that began in the spring and ended in the fall, he and Mrs. Stimson came out to Huntington to seek the relaxation he found in the place. Some of that relaxation came from his concern to see that his trees were planted in the right place, that his hens laid larger eggs, that his cows gave thicker cream and that the proper amount of manure was put on his fields at proper times. He took great pleasure in all the small tasks required to maintain a place in the country.

Even more of his relaxation came from the horses, Vanguard, Aberdeen and Piedmont. Vanguard, the best horse he ever owned, stood seventeen hands, and the others were also great powerful animals, built to suit their owner's requirements. As a rider, one knowledgeable friend recalled, he was "in no great danger of falling off," but he lacked the grace and finish of a schooled horseman. The rapport he had with his mounts lay in the fact that they knew what he wanted, which was a sense of posthaste and romage across the land. Nothing delighted or refreshed him more than to ride for twenty miles in and around the De Forest reservation that abutted his land. At such times there was much cantering along wood roads, much crashing through underbrush, and much leveling off for great gallops over the open fields. The horses had, as a result of these stimulating experiences, hard mouths, somewhat independent judgments on questions of pace and remarkable endurance.

They could also jump, for one of their owner's greatest satisfactions was the hunt that rode over his and the adjoining lands. This was not a great organization of pink coats, horns and hunt breakfasts. It was built upon the interest of John Colliton, Stimson and John Leiper, a retired farmer who owned a pack of hounds, and it was made up of the men and women who lived in the neighborhood. For twenty years they rode together after foxes that were permitted to escape after they had been brought to earth. The pursuit of this quarry provided Stimson with some of the happiest hours of his life at Highhold.

As the years passed, the concern with Highhold extended naturally to a concern for the town's affairs. By 1914, because of both his public achievements and his local activities, he became something of a figure in the community where he had established his legal residence. He and his wife regularly attended the Presbyterian church. In the development of the public library, the "most important community institution," he played a direct and continuing part, as he did in the organization of a boys' rifle club. To many of the other endeavors in the town he contributed modestly; twenty-five dollars here and there from year to year. And he was ever vigilant to guard and protect the township from the encroachments of the outside world. Proposals to introduce "automobile roads through the center of the West Hills area" or in other parts of the community found him "unalterably opposed" because, he said, property would "realize its highest value from its availability for large country estates."

In less formal aspects of village life he also took some part. When a bobsled carnival was held, recalling that he had built the fastest double-runner at Andover, he and Mrs. Stimson contributed a cup for the winner. And then there were the yearly "Highhold Games," the neighborhood day on Thanksgiving to which the whole town was invited. The day opened when the owner, in knickerbockers, fired off his double-barreled shotgun. Then to music by the Nathan Hale Band, men shot clay pigeons, played Going to Jerusalem on horseback and rode in steeplechases, while children rolled downhill in barrels, ran foot races, or tried to see who could jump the highest. For all — men, women and children, to the number of one thousand — there were cider, sandwiches, ginger pop and doughnuts. To these occasions Mr. and Mrs. Stimson, it was said, looked forward "just as eagerly as do children to their Christmas tree."

It has also been reported that Stimson once said that the event was "a lot of trouble . . . but we like to keep it up because it is good for the community." Maybe he even said it, and if so, it was half a truth. One of his operating principles was that almost anything worth doing — from writing a veto message for a President's signature to dropping a fly in a trout pool — was "a lot of trouble." Life, as he used to tell his law clerks over and over again, was hard, and he did what he could to approach it in that spirit. It seems clear, as a neighbor said, that "he simply loved everything about" the Highhold Games; therefore the day itself, as with everything he loved to do, must be good for the community. This was his understanding of the categorical imperative.

For instance, when Felix Frankfurter, who had never been on a horse in his life, first came down to Highhold, it was obvious that it would be good for him to ride a horse. It was obvious also that Arthur Page ought to join in the hunt. Page had just moved to Huntington and scarcely knew Stimson; besides, as he pointed out, he had not jumped horses very much. "No man," said Stimson, "has ever lived who hasn't jumped a horse," and he took his neighbor off for a new start in life. "He felt," Page reflected, "rather proprietary about people who moved onto Long Island."

Actually he felt rather proprietary about people. It was the relationship he had been reared in, that he best understood. Implying as it did the possibility of fixed responsibilities and measures of control amid the unpredictabilities of human association, it was the relationship he fell into most naturally. In his time he helped a good many young men through school, college and graduate study. He also helped them to decide that the best school for them was Andover, the best college, Yale, and the best place for graduate study, the Harvard Law School. He believed this, of course, because he possessed the necessary evidence. He believed it so completely that once, when interviewing a young man who impressed him, he assumed incorrectly that the young man must inevitably have attended these three institutions.

This proprietary attitude took other forms as well. He was

to be found frequently jacking up people for their own good. When a hired man surprisingly left Highhold, he was told "you cannot expect to get on in life unless you show yourself willing and fair-minded in dealing with other people." Neighbor Blydenburg when selling off his wood lot was offered the unsolicited advice to "leave large oaks and chestnuts in such places as they will be desirable shade trees." Offsetting the loss of income would be the increase of "beauty and value." In Brooklyn, after seeing an annoyed subway guard close a door on the knuckles of a small boy, Stimson dealt severely with the offender and wrote a full report of the incident to the president of the Interborough Rapid Transit Company.

Institutions as well as men came under similar scrutiny. From his telephone bill he once deducted the cost of a carriage from Cold Spring Harbor to Highhold because, with his line out of order, he had been unable to summon his own conveyance. Laundries, building concerns, department stores and common carriers down through the years received communications similar in spirit. Through it all the Long Island Railroad offered the richest field for his endeavor — the lateness of the 8:04, the crowdedness of No. 149, the unpleasantness of an episode at Jamaica, the nonexistence of No. 30 on Saturdays. The tone of all these communications was frequently minatory. Conditions were "intolerable," "wretched"; they revealed a "negligence almost criminal." Correspondents were assured, "I propose to make it more trouble for your company to violate its contract than to keep it, even at considerable trouble and expense to myself." The tone almost always was also hortatory — a man, a company, a service "cannot go backward," "a standard once set must be maintained."

Partly, of course, the standards had to be maintained for private reasons — a man had legitimate requirements and expectations and it was an aggravation not to have them decently fulfilled. You had to do things, as a niece once said, Uncle Harry's way, and there were, as time passed and the record of achievement lengthened, more and more things, not unnaturally, to be done. But there were other reasons too; the individual was under obligation to act in support and protection of the standards men had devised to hold the community together. There were times when it was sufficient to encourage the others by example. One went to church in Huntington "dressed for Saint Bartholomew's" to sit among a saving remnant of ten or twelve, and one went every possible Sunday. At other times, determined by the exigency of the moment and the intensity of personal involvement, action was required where example could not serve. Undergraduates in the Bones family, engaged in high jinks on a transatlantic liner, were waited upon by an old Bones man and told that "this was not the way to conduct themselves in a public place." When friends — old friends, dear friends — obtained divorces, hospitality was denied them ever after.

There was, however, a limit to the exertion of the proprietary interest; a nicely calculated point at which one ceased to have the right to impose the private aim because it would do the public good. The location of this point Stimson once described to his old friend and classmate Irving Fisher. Fisher, like Stimson, had been disturbed that at one or two class dinners there had been a good deal of drinking. The economist was also, in one of his many tertiary interests, involved in the prohibition movement. He therefore proposed to Stimson that no liquor or wine should be served on the next occasion the class met together. The proposal "opened up a serious question" in his correspondent's mind: Yale dinners were precious to Stimson; they were "about the only place" where one was treated with "equality without any of the perquisites or handicaps of age or life."

Furthermore, these dinners were not held, he believed, to demonstrate the progress of the warfare against alcohol or to contribute to that warfare. The only purpose of the reunions was to "get into each other's real lives during the past five years." "We have a right to insist upon a dinner conducted" in such a way that "the real aim" is achieved, he believed, but there was no further right "to impose absolute prohibition." Nor was he any happier at the thought of letting those who wished to drink and could afford it to buy drinks for themselves. Such a procedure set up invidious distinctions of all kinds. Summing it up, he was in favor of a quiet reunion, but he was also "very loath to impose by force my preference on others. If there is a single man present whose personal pleasure would be increased by having wine for himself, let him have it without the slightest constraint." "The minute you introduce the principle of compulsion," not only was "the moral effect of example destroyed," but the point of the dinner was lost as well.

Stimson had very clear ideas about how things in the world — his own private world and the larger world outside — ought to go. By example, as in attending church or joining a Good Government Club, and by direct action, as in pursuing a monopoly with savage indignation or using the threat of a presidential veto to persuade reluctant congressmen — by these means he would do everything in his power to obtain his way. But he knew the limits of the wise and possible. Felix Frankfurter did not have to climb on a horse, though in the event he was certainly sensible to do so; members of Congress did not have to heed the threat of a veto. One was justified in doing all that was in one's power only so long as others had recourse against one, only so long as others had the opportunity to reject the example and to oppose the direct action. What his generation called the better element had neither the right nor the privilege of seeking by compulsion and restraint to make all men better in the same way. This element had, however, the obligation to demonstrate wherein it was better, to prove its truth by its endeavor, and it had the positive duty to strive to make a world that others would find better than the one they were living in. In private and in public, this is what the life of Henry L. Stimson was all about.

After March 3, 1913, the public life was, for a season, about the law. He returned to an office that was larger than the one he had left when he entered the public service in 1906, but which, thanks to the watchfulness of Bronson Winthrop, was the same in spirit. Part of that spirit derived from the partners' willingness to do without cases that did not interest them or appeal to them. As Stimson explained somewhat later to Frankfurter, they "stood outside the Wall Street group"; they did not "adopt the methods of others" and thus "we don't get lots of business we could." For one thing, the firm acted as though there were other things in life than the law. Winthrop used to say that except when a case was in court, the day began at 9:30 and ended at 5:30. Outside these hours members talked and thought of other things, as Winthrop made clear to a law clerk who once tried to talk to him about a case after dinner at his club. This attitude tended to discourage clients who were seeking high-powered counsel from firms whose law clerks went home by the light of the morning stars and where male stenographers were on call twenty-four hours a day. Upon occasion Stimson took more direct means to discourage clients. Once when some men from the West Coast appeared in his office with an appeal for his services, he turned them away, after listening to their situation, with these words: "I can just hear the gates of the jail clanking shut behind you."

The young lawyers attracted to the firm in the years before the First World War naturally shared in this spirit. Indeed the men at work at Winthrop and Stimson seemed, and not infrequently were, members of a large family. Albert W. Putnam, who arrived first in 1903, had served with Stimson in the National Guard; he was followed in due course by George Roberts from Yale and the Harvard Law School; by Bronson Winthrop's brother Egerton; by, for a short time, Felix Frankfurter; by Allen Klots, the son of one of Stimson's classmates, also from Yale and the Harvard Law School; and by Stimson's cousin, Alfred Lee Loomis, from Andover, Yale and the Harvard Law School. If not a family, there was about these young members, as Stimson said, the fellowship of club members. When he returned in 1913, he found, to his pleasure, that something of the spirit of the group he had put together in the Federal Building existed in the chambers at 32 Liberty Street. It was still in the days when clerks could get their training in the general practice of the law by working on many different kinds of cases; still the days when partners and clerks worked closely together in the preparation and discussion of cases.

The rewards for a practice of this kind were not primarily tangible. They came from the pleasures of setting one's mind to work on interesting problems in peaceful surroundings; they came from working with clients one respected and became fond of. They came from having the time to ride and sail and fish and play tennis and read a book and see your wife and do with yourself what you wanted to do on Saturday and Sunday. A senior partner of Winthrop and Stimson in the years leading up to the First World War obtained these ways of life by earning about $20,000 a year, while lawyers half a block away were earning five and ten times that amount.

Something of the tranquility of the office was lost when Stimson returned to 32 Liberty Street, for when he was at work on a case he always succeeded in creating a good deal of hubbub. One of the things that made him uneasy about the law was that he could not control the order of business coming in to him. Clients got into trouble at odd and inconvenient times; they were as likely to arrive in battalions as singly in properly spaced intervals. His way of dealing with this difficulty was to create his own environment by locking himself in his office and going to work on one problem. At such times too he would "concentrate"; that is, as Felix Frankfurter remarked, he would set his mind at one thing, like the needle of an old Victrola caught in the single groove of a record. Actually he was clearer about the symptoms of concentration — closed doors, scribbled notes, piles of books, long silences — than on the nature of the thing itself. He never understood, in the opinion of an associate, that the mind was not always at the mercy of the will. He never left it free to play "like a wand of light" over dark places, never permitted it the liberty to establish, by intuitive and unconscious procedure, interesting connections between things.

His solitary exercises would be interrupted now and then as a case was developing. A clerk or a partner, opening the office door at such times would be greeted, often enough, by sounds of anguish or indignation. Throughout his life when anxious or diverted from a line of thought, or frustrated by untoward agencies in his pursuit of some endeavor, Stimson would give way to gusts of anger or exasperation. He was not a profane man, but in the moments of wrath he would, as a friend of his once said, use "confound it" or "damn" as code words for all profanity. And in these angry outbreaks there was nothing vindictive or long continued. The moments came, as a colleague said, like summer storms, leaving behind a landscape refreshed and in contrast more attractive. And also after the indignation came, sometimes, words or acts of oblique and touching solicitude for those around him.

At other times a partner or two and several clerks would be summoned to observe the mind at work. They would sit around while Stimson paced the floor, thinking aloud, making observations, throwing out questions. Since the audience was not always asked to participate in the proceedings, the method struck observers occasionally as both luxurious and irritating. It also struck such observers, from time to time, that the concentrating lawyer betrayed a general confusion of mind, a blurred and fuzzy and groping intelligence that was disconcerting.

The intent of this elaborate process was twofold — to canvass every conceivable aspect of a case and to select the essential points and tactics to use when the case came on for trial. Preparation was everything, or almost everything. George Roberts remembers one case in which he and Stimson spent weeks pre-

Upper left: Candace Wheeler Stimson, mother of Henry L. Stimson and Candace Stimson

Upper right: At Phillips Academy

Lower left: The family about 1887

Lower right: Candace Stimson

Cyclists at Phillips Academy. Stimson is kneeling behind
the fourth boy from the left in the first row.

Opposite page: Drawings made by Stimson at the age of eight

The Pow Wow, Harvard Law School, 1890.
Stimson is sitting on the floor in the middle of the group.

Davis & Sanford

Mabel White Stimson

Roughing it

The young lawyer . . .

Elihu Root

Lewis Atterbury Stimson

. . . and the great teachers

Theodore Roosevelt

Bronson Winthrop

The United States Attorney, Southern District of New York, and his staff. Standing, left to right: Wolcott H. Pitkin, Jr., Goldthwaite H. Dorr, Felix Frankfurter, Thomas D. Thacher, Harold S. Deming, Emory R. Buckner, Daniel D. Walton, Hugh Govern, Jr., Robert P. Stephenson, Francis W. Bird. Seated, left to right: Winfred T. Denison, William S. Ball, Henry L. Stimson, Henry A. Wise, D. Frank Lloyd, J. Osgood Nichols, John W. H. Crim paring five or six possible lines for cross-examination. Stimson finally decided to use line B. He planned that at the sixth question of line B, he would ask something which if responded to in the affirmative would reveal that the witness was telling the truth, at which point a series of questions called B prime would be asked. If, however, the witness responded in the negative, it would reveal that he was lying. Then Stimson would proceed for five questions on line B squared, at which point Roberts would hand him, from a card file, a document that would reveal the witness had lied. It thus worked out in court.

This care in preparation Stimson had learned from Root, as he had learned from Root's partner, G. E. P. Howard, to look for "a green elevator case." The point of Howard's advice was that when in search of a precedent one sought for a case precisely identical — even to the color of the machinery — to the case in hand. Many clerks spent a great deal of time attempting to fulfill the injunction to go out and "find me a *green* elevator case." One other thing he had learned from Root — that when a lawyer appears in court his first efforts should be directed "at making the court *want* to decide for you." Whatever the nature of a case, "you set up your data — financial, human interest or economic — in such a way that you prepare the mind of the judge emotionally to decide for you. And only after that preparation do you come in with legal precedents — which you can always find — upon which you can hang the case." An obvious point, perhaps, "but many lawyers make the error of going in and arguing it out and this puts the whole thing on a purely intellectual basis — and therefore they do not do well in court."

Stimson did well in court. He underwent a transformation that the law clerks and partners working with him found dramatic. Where before he had revealed a sense of strain and odd confusion, where before his assistants had had to explain ideas three or four times slowly and in very simple language before he understood them, he suddenly emerged direct, clear and very simple in exposition. He also spoke with the cold assurance —

the almost majestic certitude — of a man who knew absolutely everything. The effect was cumulative. An office boy, riding back from court with one of the partners after Stimson and his opposing counsel Mooney had made their opening comments in a case, remarked, "Isn't Mr. Mooney a great lawyer, isn't he a wonderful lawyer?" "Yes he is," said the partner, "but Mr. Stimson is pretty good too." "Oh yes," said the boy, "he's pretty good but Mr. Mooney, he's a great lawyer." After ten days of the trial, the office boy and the partner chanced to ride back together again. "Say," said the boy, "that Mr. Stimson. He's a great lawyer." As one lawyer said, "Stimson needed a long trial — and the longer the case went on, the better, because cumulatively in the jury's mind there arose, over a passage of time, an implicit belief in the man's information and integrity. So that when at the end he came to say, 'The evidence shows,' they believed absolutely that the evidence did show because they believed in Stimson."

In the weeks after March 4, 1913, the firm waited with interest to see how the returning public servant would accommodate to legal practice. Sometime in May, Bronson Winthrop, feeling that he had not before "found the opportunity to express suitably [his] great satisfaction," sent his partner a letter saying he had missed him "while away more than I can say. I only hope the come-down won't seem too sudden and that you will like your old place in the future as you did in the past." Some months later George Roberts felt justified in telling Frankfurter that "Mr. Stimson is now working very hard and apparently is enjoying his legal life more than he seemed to at first."

Whatever measure of satisfaction he derived from his labors, he was as always hard at work. The reputation he had established as a trial lawyer in the District Attorney's office was remembered and for a year and a half he was frequently in court. None of the cases he brought to trial achieved great public notice and few, if any, involved the creation of precedents that have continuing significance. But one by the nature of its intellectual interest and its neatness deserves attention.

Late in the year 1913 a man named Inglis appeared at 32 Liberty Street with the following story. He was president of the American Blower Company, a Detroit concern that manufactured fans from an English patent that was superior in design to any American counterpart. The principal competitor of the American Blower Company was the B. F. Sturtevant Company of Massachusetts, of which E. N. Foss, late governor of the Commonwealth, was president. Foss, according to Inglis, had infringed the English patent in the manufacture of his own fans. More than that, he had obtained, in his own name and in the name of men under his control, a majority of the stock of the American Blower Company. From this position of strength he had, over a five-year period, tried to get Inglis to agree with him on such matters as prices, fan design and the division of sales territories between the two companies. He had also proposed, Inglis maintained, that American Blower hire away engineers from mutual competitors and that the Sturtevant company should make use of the trade name Sirocco, protected by British patents held by American Blower. Inglis had successfully withstood much of the pressure and built up his company as a manufacturer of blowers second only to B. F. Sturtevant in the country. But when he arrived at 32 Liberty Street the voting trust into which the Blower stock had been put was about to expire. Therefore Inglis feared that Foss would use his new freedom and his majority position to obtain a board of directors of his own choosing. Inglis was seeking, on behalf of the minority, to enjoin Foss and his colleagues from voting their majority stock.

It is well-settled law that a minority may act to protect the assets of their company from waste or injury by seeking an injunction against a majority intent on such wastage. However, in this instance, it was apparent that no such obvious intent could be proved by citing Foss's desire to obtain a board of directors favorable to himself, or by any other direct means. When Inglis had finished his story, Stimson said to George Roberts that there was not a chance to obtain an injunction on any of the traditional grounds. Yet Stimson was attracted to the case because, familiar as he was with corporate practices from his days in the Southern District, he had such contempt for the kind of business procedures Foss, by Inglis' testimony, had been employing. It occurred to him that it might be possible to proceed under the Sherman Act; to demonstrate that Foss, as owner of B. F. Sturtevant Company and as the controlling interest in the American Blower Company, was "conspiring to monopolize or to attempt to monopolize directly or indirectly, the manufacture and sale of or the trade and commerce in fans and blowers . . ."

This was not a simple task. First Stimson had to prove that a combination of the American Blower Company and the B. F. Sturtevant Company would produce a monopoly in the industry. Then he had to prove that Foss, by obtaining his own board of directors, intended to establish a combination in restraint of trade within the industry. By dint of his usual massive research and with the aid of thirty-five witnesses produced in court, he did establish the fact that the two companies together controlled 70 per cent of the total putput of the industry. He then, by using the extensive correspondence exchanged between Foss and Inglis in previous years, demonstrated how Foss had tried by agreements on price, divisions of territory and so forth, to improve his own position. He then showed how Foss if "allowed to get possession of the Board of Directors" could "sacrifice the business of the American Blower Company in the interests of the Sturtevant Company" by "innumerable methods impossible to detect or prohibit in advance." Finally, he argued that as in the past he had proposed "fake bids," "stealing competitors' employees" and "infringement of patents," Foss "intends to use his control of both companies to crush competition." "Never," he concluded, "has the design of the monopolist been revealed in a more cynical way than by Mr. Foss in the records of this case."

By these methods Stimson obtained from the court in the Northern District of New York a decree enjoining the defendants from voting their stock and restraining them from combining or conspiring to monopolize. On appeal, a decision was given in the Circuit Court which indicated both the weakness in Stimson's central position, of which he was well aware, and the great strength of the argument he had made in defense of this position. Minority stockholders, the judge held, could of course protect their interest against illegal acts by the majority if such acts could be proved, admitted or explicitly threatened. But in the present instance nothing illegal had been done or threatened by those who wished to vote the majority stock. The judge in the District Court had decided that because of his previous conduct, Foss was "likely to carry out the plans complained of." Sufficient protection for the minority, in this case, would result, the circuit judge believed, if the defendants were enjoined from wasting the property of American Blower and from acting to monopolize the blower trade, but were permitted within these restraints to vote the majority stock. Just as this decision was given, Foss fell into financial difficulties and was forced to sell the stock he had just acquired the right to vote. Inglis and his associates were the purchasers of the stock.

This case extended over three years. During two of those years Stimson "devoted a large part of his time" to it. He and Roberts worked between them "365 separate days" on the case. They traveled to Boston, Albany, Syracuse, Buffalo, Chicago and Kalamazoo to interview twenty-nine witnesses. They engaged in a great many conferences and "a vast amount of correspondence" since the case involved "difficult questions of corporate law, a complete study of the blower industry, and an interpretation of the Sherman Act." The suit turned out to be one "of unusual difficulty," which, in the event, prevented the control of an industry by monopoly interests. For this the firm presented a bill of $10,000, plus disbursements of $1413.67 for carfare and printing.

By the time the bill was presented, Stimson was thinking about different things than *Davidson* vs. *American Blower* and indeed different things than the practice of law. As Winthrop had feared, his partner discovered with the passage of time that "this is merely the same old grind." His energies and urges were always seeking outlets beyond the exasperating confines of concentration behind closed doors. And such outlets were ready at hand. On April 24, 1916, he wrote Gifford Pinchot that "on a sober calculation" he had spent over 75 per cent of his available time during the past year on "non-professional work." [1]

[1] Material for this chapter was taken from the Stimson Papers; conversations with members of the family, friends and law partners; *Federal Reports*, Vol. 243, Sept.-Oct. 1915, 170-171; Records of the U.S. District Court, Northern District of New York, *Davidson et al.* vs. *American Blower Company;* Records of the U.S. Circuit Court of Appeals of the Second District, *Davidson et al.* vs. *American Blower Company;* the files of Winthrop, Stimson, Putnam and Roberts.

13

Responsible Government

T HE "NON-PROFESSIONAL" work engaging Stimson's attention was, of course, politics. From the moment of Taft's defeat he had been at work trying to help those who wished to put the pieces of the Republican Party together again. Less than a week after the election, on November 11, 1912, he had written to Governor Herbert S. Hadley of Missouri that "those of us Republicans who are interested in the party as a progressive party [ought to] keep in touch with each other during these disintegrated times." Three weeks later, on December 5, 1912, while urging Lloyd Griscom in New York to "get in touch with our Western progressive Republican friends," he insisted that "The Republican party must be reorganized on a progressive basis if I am to stay in it . . ." And just before leaving Washington in March he gave "a little dinner" for Republican congressmen to discuss the possibility of holding a special Republican convention in 1913 or 1914. It was his hope, he said, that, in such a convention, uninhibited by the necessity of nominating a presidential candidate the party could act to put its house in order.

There were, he believed, three things that had to be done to restore order in the house. First, he wished, with Root, to revise the rules by which delegates were selected for national party conventions, those rules that had caused the turmoil in Chicago in 1912; he wished next to drive the existing leaders out of the places of power in the organization so the party "should not fall into the hands of the old or stand-pat statesmen"; and finally he wished to introduce a series of changes in the structure of both the state and the federal governments.[1]

What these changes were he described at various times and places in the year after he returned to private practice. His argument was that Republicans had been members of a party that "always had been [interested] in constructive progress," that from Federalists and Whigs they had inherited the idea that government was not a police force, but "rather an affirmative agency of national progress and social betterment." Republicans were men who believed in action to overcome present evils, who abhorred disorder and emphasized efficiency. They advocated a strong central government. The policy of waiting for Wilson to make a mistake was "impotent, and ignoble, and above all unrepublican." Something must be done even though an ancient barrier to effective action had been laid across the way by Jefferson and his friends, who, in their fear of official power, had introduced a "not thoroughly baked" diffusion of responsibility into our scheme of government.

The first thing was to eliminate the barrier. To achieve this purpose Stimson proposed three things: first, the short ballot, which, in the states, would permit a governor to choose most of his own subordinates; second, the executive budget, which gave the initiative for expenditures to a governor or a President and not primarily to legislatures, bemused as they were by purely local requirements; third, the right of officers from the executive branch of the government to seats and to the defense of their policies in the legislative body. The system of committee leadership, "a truly invisible government," had developed because governors, Presidents and their executive subordinates had been excluded from legislative chambers.

The sum of these reforms was the greater concentration of assignable responsibility and power commensurate with that responsibility in the executive arm of the government. Thus cor-

[1] H.L.S. to Lloyd Griscom, Dec. 5, 1912, to H. S. Hadley, Feb. 14, 1913, to George Smith, Apr. 5, 1913, to A. P. Osborn, April 21, 1913.

ruption, logrolling, malfeasance and inefficiency would be reduced; thus forward motion would be maintained in the work of
social progress. Republics tended to disintegrate through waste,
inefficiency and gross expenditure; this republic could save itself
not by "prating of the rights of the people" and "pandering to
the vanity of the crowd," but by working out principles of truly
efficient government.[2]

These three proposals — the short ballot, the executive budget
and the seating of executive members of the government in
legislatures to answer questions and give reasons — were the
specific expressions of Stimson's allegiance to the principles of a
strong central government. They were the product of years of
reading in works on American government, from the *Federalist*
to John Fiske and Herbert Croly. They were the product of his
actual work as a United States Attorney, a candidate for governor, and Secretary of War. Whenever he advanced into new
ground he took with him what he had learned in the past that
was useful. In 1914, when he spoke at Utica, he did not think
his propositions "insignificant"; on the basis of his reading and
thinking and experience, he looked upon them as indispensable
instruments for sound government in this country.

His efforts to rejuvenate his party in the first two years after
Taft's defeat were not attended by great success. Plans for a
special convention to revise the rules for the selection of delegates to Republican National Conventions came, in spite of
Stimson's agitation, to nothing. Though he tried to mobilize a
force to drive the Old Guard out of the New York State organization, though he told Barnes "to his face" he ought to go, the
state machinery, with Root's acquiescence, remained in the
hands of the conservative wing. Yet Stimson remained undis-
couraged. He spoke at many meetings of the party faithful,
urging his own reform program and reiterating that a government was not a police force, but an agency of social progress.

[2] See especially "Initiative and Responsibility of the Executive," an address before the Law Academy of Philadelphia, May 27, 1913; "Lincoln Day Speech
to Republicans," Utica, Feb. 12, 1914; New York *Tribune*, Feb. 13, 1914; "Responsible State Government," *Independent*, July 6, 1914.

In December 1913 he was one of the moving spirits that put the party on record at the Waldorf-Astoria in favor of the short ballot and, in his case with less enthusiasm, in support of direct primaries.[3]

The decision, in 1914, by a slight majority of the citizens to hold a constitutional convention in New York in the next year gave him an opportunity to push his ideas much further. Stimson was chosen a delegate at large while Root was made chairman of this convention in which the Republicans had a large majority. Before the convention met, Stimson, at Root's request, took a leading part in the preparation of the agenda for the deliberations. As always, he did his homework faithfully. First, he disagreed with Root about the composition of the committee to prepare the agenda. His old friend wanted lawyers; but a lawyer, Stimson argued, without much success, is "apt to be much more rigidly conservative in regard to any constitutional or even statutory changes. He is somewhat like an army officer in his dependence upon the existing order . . ." Then after the committee had been appointed, he set about educating the members in the kinds of changes he thought ought to be made in the New York Constitution. To this end he began a correspondence with Professor Henry J. Ford of Princeton, a student of municipal and state government, who had supplied him with some ideas when he was running for governor. He also sought the advice of Charles McCarthy, the principal intellectual support of Robert M. La Follette, because he had "rather gotten into the habit of looking to Wisconsin for matters that are progressive and constructive." Similarly he turned to William S. U'Ren in the progressive state of Oregon for information about systems "of proportional representation and preferential voting."[4]

---

[3] H.L.S. to Heber Wheeler, July 23, 1914, to H. J. Hinman, Jan. 14, 1914, to Elihu Root, Jan. 30, 1914; New York *Tribune*, Dec. 6, 1913.
[4] H.L.S. to Elihu Root, June 5, 1914, to Charles McCarthy, July 10, 1914, to W. S. U'Ren, May 3, 1915. Stimson's account of his purposes and actions during the preparations for and proceedings of the Constitutional Convention are given in his "Memorandum of Events of the Autumn of 1915" included in his Diary.

Having by these means prepared himself, he set out to prepare others. Letters went out to prospective delegates to the convention describing in detail the virtues of the executive budget, the short ballot and the right of members of the executive branch to a seat and a voice, but not a vote, in the legislature. By these means he built up a considerable following for his propositions, a following made more imposing when he succeeded in persuading Root to support his views. To his great regret, however, he failed to win the approval of the *New Republic*. "We are," he said, "fighting for a program of which Croly was the first prophet": the principle of concentration of responsibility and coordination between the two branches of government. The aim was to get rid of the "hallucination" that the separation of powers ought to be maintained "in its strictness." To achieve this primary aim, some secondary things had to be laid aside for a season, but Croly persisted in his clamor for things secondary as well as primary. He could not see that the convention might represent "a revolutionary turn against old false traditions." Stimson was saddened that "a man whose vision I found so helpful three or four years ago seems to be unable to rise beyond the disappointments of party politics."[5]

On April 6, 1915, the Constitutional Convention met at Albany to hear Mr. Root, in his opening remarks, counsel that "the burden of proof rests always upon the advocates of change." Five months later, on September 11, the convention adjourned. In the interval, for the better part of every week the members worked from 10:00 to 1:00 in the morning, from 2:00 to 5:30 in the afternoon, and from 8:30 to 10:30 in the evening. Stimson and some of his Washington friends — among them Wickersham and Parsons — lived together at 4 Elk Street during the

[5] H.L.S. to Felix Frankfurter, April 5, 1915. Croly was not the only dissenter, however. Joseph H. Choate, Winfred Dennison, Sereno Payne, Horace White and Jules Jusserand, among others, all differed with one or another of his propositions. Some feared the concentration of power in the executive that Stimson recommended; some believed executive participation in the legislative debates "wouldn't work"; some were annoyed at Stimson's assumption that since "human nature doesn't change" it was necessary to change institutions that had proved insufficient.

days the convention was in session. They were called "the federal crowd" and their residence was known as "the ice house" because, it was said, they had "built an ice house, got inside of it and froze everybody who came anywhere near them." Besides this group with experience in Washington, there were the local bosses, William Barnes, Lemuel P. Quigg, Platt's old lieutenant, and Fred Tanner. But there were others from both parties, young and old, who had fought all their lives for decent, effective government in the State of New York. Here were De-Lancey Nicoll, John Lord O'Brian, William Church Osborn, James R. Sheffield, Louis Marshall, Alfred E. Smith, Jacob Gould Schurman, Robert Wagner, J. B. Stanchfield and Seth Low.[6]

The discussion between all these men in committee and on the floor was a summing up of the political attitudes of thirty years. Indeed the massive volumes in which the records of the convention were kept are a remarkable source of information about the final reflections of a whole generation about their political experience and the philosophy developed out of that experience. They contain also — running throughout the hundreds of pages — one of the fullest and clearest statements of the liberal position in the Republican Party as it expressed itself in the first decade and a half of this century. Before the committees appeared Abbot Lawrence Lowell, President of Harvard and professor of government; Frank Goodnow, President of Johns Hopkins and professor of administrative law; William Howard Taft, President of the United States and professor of law; and others with comparable learning and experience. On the floor, Wickersham, Jacob Gould Schurman, John Lord O'Brian and Seth

[6] An account of the proceedings can be found in *Revised Record of the Constitutional Convention of the State of New York,* 1915, 4 vols. (Albany, 1916). See also the illuminating *Documents of the Constitutional Convention of the State of New York* (Albany, 1915). An admirable discussion of the problems dealt with in the convention when it met is to be found in "The Revision of the State Constitution," a symposium printed in *Proceedings of the Academy of Political Science,* Oct. 1914. Jessup, *Root,* II, Ch. 40, is devoted to the convention.

Low engaged in extended debate or delivered two-hour disquisitions on the art of government. Root, once, while describing
the Black Horse Cavalry of the public service corporations delivered in 800 words what some feel was the most moving
speech of his life; and at another time he spoke to a rapt audience on "invisible government"; and yet a third time he talked
for two hours on the short ballot. Stimson himself contributed a
three-hour speech in defense of the executive budget.[7]

This speech was the high point of his oratorical contribution,
but his influence at the convention can be better measured in
other ways. He was a tireless member of the Judiciary Committee that was concerned with the reorganization of the courts,
and a leading advocate, in the State Offices Committee, of the
short ballot and the extension of the powers of the governor. As
chairman of his own Committee on Finance, he was the architect of an amendment describing the procedures to be used in
the development of the executive budget. This proposal took
the initiative for the preparation of the annual budget and attendant appropriation bill out of the hands of the legislature.
He also devised the amendment which substituted serial bonds
for a sinking fund as a means of dealing with the state debt. His
intent in this amendment was to introduce greater order and efficiency in the way in which debts were retired and also to remove political officials from the temptation of speculative investment offered by the sinking fund.

His energy and interest did not go unremarked. The *New
York Times* on several occasions selected him for particular
mention and the New York *Evening Post,* in the past rarely enthusiastic about Stimson, remarked that he emerged as the intellectual leader "on the side of constructive imagination." Indeed,
it continued, to him "is due the credit for having first developed

[7] Barnes confided to Root at the opening of the convention that the "most
noteworthy feature" was "the intense conservatism of most of the Republican
members," but those of the liberal persuasion were frequently heard and their
influence on the final product of the convention was determining. Jessup, *Root,*
II, 289-90.

the idea which has become the central theme of the Convention's endeavor — an idea he embodied in the phrase 'responsible government.' "[8]

On the day after this was written he had the intense satisfaction of seeing both his financial amendments passed by large votes. As he wrote to his father on August 22, he had never "dreamed of [such an] overwhelming victory for so radical a measure" as the executive budget. Against him, he reported, all the forces "of the lower world" gathered "with infinite opportunity for misrepresentation to the dear people." After these forces had dwindled to four votes, he achieved " complete financial reform" with the power of the government placed, he believed, where it should be. Unexpectedly he became "quite a lion in the Convention," with others seeking his advice on many matters. The debate leading up to the votes on these measures had indeed been exciting. Stimson had been on his feet withstanding questions from all sides for three hours. In defending the executive budget he said that, unless the amendment carried, the spirit of mutual accommodation, "sometimes unpleasantly referred to as logrolling," would prevail in budgetary matters. Al Smith said the amendment did not go "to the root of the matter." Martin Saxe tried to eliminate the passage permitting the governor to appear in the legislature, while Robert Wagner accused Stimson of creating "a king, a superhuman being." Throughout the session Root had sat watching and waiting "with a view to taking a hand in the fight . . . if the critical stage was reached." But even Root was worn down by the drama of the occasion; he appeared to observers "a little excitable" and his hands were seen to twitch.

Shortly after the vote of August 19, the convention adjourned. It placed, at its termination, a series of amendments before the people for consideration. Among the most important were the short-ballot proposal reorganizing seventeen state de-

[8] *New York Times*, July 13, Aug. 5, Aug. 11, 1915; New York *Evening Post*, Aug. 18, 1915.

partments and leaving the governor, the lieutenant governor, the controller, and the attorney general as sole elective officers; a proposal to reorganize the intermediary courts of civil and criminal jurisdiction in New York City and to abolish county courts in four boroughs; a proposal to return control of various municipal activities and services from the legislature to local governments; a proposal to regulate manufacturing in tenement houses; and the two proposals of Stimson's committee for the abolition of the sinking fund and the introduction of the executive budget.[9]

Most delegates went home from Albany well pleased with the work of five months. It remained to obtain the approval of the people for their work. Most of Stimson's time from the middle of September until the election in the first week of November was spent in an effort to convince the electorate that the amendments should be ratified. He wrote letters to influential men around the state, he held interviews and sent articles to the newspapers, he went out tirelessly on the stump. Almost all of October was spent speaking in the upstate regions. His arguments were everywhere the same: History shows that republics do not die from without but from extravagance and corruption within. Twenty years before the state had been without debt, now it owed over $231 million, the highest debt in the Union. By the proposed amendments responsibility and power had been concentrated. Such concentration and definition were the only solutions for an effective government in a republic. Economy, efficiency and commonplace principles of business management were the key to sound administration.[10]

Though almost every paper in the state, save the *World* and the Hearst papers, supported the amendments, and though invitations for speakers and literature poured in from around the

[9] H.L.S. to L. A. Stimson, Aug. 22, 1915; *New York Times*, Aug. 11, Sept. 5, 1915.
[10] H.L.S., *Statement for the Committee for the Adoption of the Constitution*. The substance of this statement he repeated in many speeches, letters and interviews.

state, there were obvious signs of opposition and apathy that had to be combated. There were reformers who wanted more; "idiots" who did not understand that "if responsible government in the shape of this Constitution is rejected" there was little chance of obtaining it in any new constitution. There were Democrats who disliked a document fundamentally Republican in origin. Mayor John Purroy Mitchell and his followers were annoyed at some of the home-rule provisions. Labor was reported to suspect that the absence of a bill of rights carried with it a sinister meaning. But by the last week of October there was a growing confidence that both opposition and apathy had been successfully combated by the activities of Stimson, Wickersham, Root, Parsons and the others who went about from city to city arguing the merits of their case.[11]

The men who had worked so long and hard at Albany were therefore unprepared for the blow that fell on election day. By a vote of more than two to one the revised constitution was rejected by the citizens. The *New York Times* reported on December 24 that the majority against it was "larger than any previously recorded on any question or candidate, according to the Secretary of State's records." For this surprising result there were, in retrospect, as Stimson explained to Frank B. Kellogg on November 10, a good many reasons — Tammany's disapproval, the bitter attacks of Hearst's *American,* the combined resistance of policemen, firemen, teachers and public servants to the home-rule clause which prevented them from going to the legislature for favors, and the opposition of labor, in part caused by the defeat of Gompers in the contest for delegate to the convention. But the transcendent reason appears to have been, as Stimson belatedly recognized, the result of a remarkable political miscalculation. The leaders of the convention, with the confidence of the ill-informed, had decided to present the document not in the form of separate amendments to be voted upon individually, but

11 H.L.S. to Felix Frankfurter, Oct. 11, 1915; *New York Times*, Oct. 4, 5, 1915; H.L.S. to Frank Lennox, Oct. 18, 1915.

as a single whole to be accepted or rejected in its entirety. Opponents of any particular amendment therefore tended to vote against the total set of propositions. Stimson said after the election that he found the arguments raised against this method of presenting the changes "in block" had been the hardest to answer. He went on to say that neither he nor his fellows had recognized the changed sentiment in the state. "People now," he wrote an upstate friend, "do not want a constitution framed for them by their representatives — [they] want to pass on each section of it themselves." [12]

In spite of the shocking defeat in 1915, two satisfactions remained for many of the delegates as the years passed. By 1926 home rule, the short ballot, the judiciary reform measures and the executive budget had become part of the fundamental law of New York. Wickersham in that year estimated that 80 per cent of the thirty-three amendments rejected in 1915 had been accepted as part of the structure of government a decade later. The convention, Stimson and his friends could solace themselves, had served as an educational institution for the New York electorate and for New York men like Robert F. Wagner and Alfred E. Smith, who became leading spirits in state politics in the twenties. It also served as an inspiration to others. "Thirty states," Stimson remarked in 1926, "have followed our precise example." As Root said, they had all been engaged in laying a foundation and building up a structure.[13]

Another satisfaction the members of the convention had as the years passed — their memory of the event. At an anniversary dinner in 1926, Wickersham said that in his obituary he would like it said that the convention was the "most interesting and perhaps the most inspiring event that I ever took part in." Others apparently shared his feeling. Root, in thinking about his own participation, once was moved "almost to tears" by what

[12] H.L.S. to I. T. Deyo, Nov. 3, 1915.
[13] *Proceedings of the Reunion of Delegates to the Constitutional Convention*, Dec. 17, 1926; New York *Tribune*, Dec. 18, 1926; Jessup, *Root*, II, 308.

he "gruffly" assured a friend was "a bad cold." In later years it seemed to Stimson that the convention "and its importance in his life runs far beyond its meaning to the voter or the general historian." Some of this intense allegiance to the experience must come from the sense of action well, if belatedly, rewarded — the pleasure men can take in work of little immediate showing that continues beyond their own time and expectation. And another part must have come from the feeling, increased with passing years, that the men who had worked, in city, state and nation, so long and intimately had, at Albany, met together with a clear purpose for the last time. At that convention the constructive spirit that had been evolving in the Republican Party since 1901 reached, in New York, its last and highest tide. From that time forth the spirit these men — the Wickershams, Nicolls, Lows, Parsons, O'Brians, Stimsons, and the others — brought to public affairs did not change, but the world itself did.[14]

And even before the Constitutional Convention assembled Stimson had begun to involve himself in that changing world. In November 1914 he had written a friend that "my own views as to our own duty of supporting England are so radical that I rather hesitate to make them public for fear of being thought a jingo . . ." Actually he kept whatever radical views he may have held on the subject to himself until the spring of 1917. Publicly he argued in support of a more measured policy. His position was that the destructive influence of modern warfare had been gradually reduced by the slow development of neutral rights, which served as "buffers of civilization against the shocks of war." The task of this country was to strengthen these buffers by maintaining and defending its neutral rights. This continued to be his attitude until the Germans declared their unrestricted submarine warfare in 1917. This German action, in his opinion, made our entry into the war inevitable.[15]

[14] *Reunion Proceedings;* New York *Tribune*, Dec. 18, 1926; Jessup, *Root*, II, 308; *Active Service*, 65-74.
[15] H.L.S. to F. W. Whitridge, Nov. 2, 1914; H.L.S., "The Duty of Preparedness Today," speech at Carnegie Hall, June 14, 1915.

His early moderate public views did not prevent him, how-ever, from advocating in the existing contingency what was then called preparedness. As early as December 1914 he began a correspondence with the Secretary of War, Lindley Garrison, and with certain general officers in the War Department to dis-cover what he could properly say and do to rouse people to the needs of national defense. In January 1915 he made his first in a series of speeches that continued over the next two years. His points were these: Under the existing budget system, the interest of the armed forces would always be sacrificed to the interests of the pork barrel. Under the existing laws, a military establish-ment costing $100 million a year maintained a mobile continen-tal army only twice the size of the New York City Police Force. This army of 25,000, if it fired its available guns at the rate the guns were fired at Mukden, would consume its existing ammunition in a day's time. The primary problem confronting the country, Stimson insisted in 1915, was how to turn this army into an effective fighting force. His proposed solution was, first, to train more men. The Secretary of War had asked for an in-crease in the regular army and the expansion of the trained re-serve. Stimson supported the request in speeches and letters to editors throughout 1915. He also attacked Congress for disre-garding Garrison's program and for substituting its own recom-mendation for an increase in the militia, the National Guard. This device, attractive politically, had little military value. The control of the Guard, divided as it was between federal and state governments, prevented the development of a well-trained body of troops.[16]

Persistently as Stimson supported Garrison against the Con-gress and the administration of which Garrison was a member, he went farther than the Secretary of War as the year wore on. Tentatively at first, by proposing military training for young

[16] H.L.S. to L. M. Garrison, Dec. 10, 1914, to William Crozier, Dec. 10, 1914; *New York Times*, Jan. 17, Feb. 4, 1915; H.L.S., "The Military Needs of the United States," issued by the National Security League, March 1, 1915.

men in school and college, he began to advocate the doctrine "that every man owes to his country not only to die for her, if necessary, but also to spend a little of his life in learning how to die for her effectively." This, as he pointed out, was the prevailing doctrine in those "most advanced and modern democracies," Switzerland and Australia. By the end of the year, dismayed that Garrison, whom he had always considered "a sound Federalist," was exhibiting constitutional scruples over the government's power in this area, he was ready to assert that he shared in the growing feeling "that universal military training or universal liability to military training" was the real thing.[17]

Shortly after he expressed this view he came to Garrison's defense in the Secretary's effort to obtain a large continental army from the Congress. Under the leadership of Stimson's old opponent, James Hay, the House of Representatives in the first months of 1916 was still determined to make use of the National Guard as the vehicle for expanding our forces. When in February Garrison resigned, in large part because he had failed to win the President's support for his cause, Stimson gave out an interview in which he said the Secretary's departure was a "national calamity." He then, at General Crowder's request, prepared a series of letters to the *New York Times*, defending Garrison's proposals for the increase in the regular army and exposing the weaknesses of Hay's bill to "federalize" the National Guard.[18]

The events of these weeks produced in Stimson the beginning of his disillusion with Woodrow Wilson whose domestic program he had admired and whose stand on neutral rights he had respected. The passage in June of the National Defense Act which was a "hodge-podge of inefficiency and 'pork' masquerading under the name of a federalized militia," accelerated this process of disillusion. The end of his patience came when the

[17] H.L.S., "Military Needs"; H.L.S. to Enoch Crowder, Dec. 10, 1915; *New York Times*, Dec. 9, 1915.
[18] *New York Times*, Feb. 12, March 20, 21, 22, 1916; H.L.S. to Frank McCoy, Feb. 28, 1916.

ill-trained units of the militia were "hurried immediately into active service" on the Texas borders at a time when "the United States is in no real danger from poor distracted Mexico."[19]

Increasingly thwarted by what he considered the incompetence of the administration, he found himself further frustrated by the law practice that kept him tied to his profession when he wished to be out and arousing the country to its needs. One day in 1916 the never very secure banks that contained his exasperation gave way as he was discussing with clients and colleagues some points about the case of *Orth* vs. *Stieger*. On the streets below, the city of New York was welcoming Marshal Joffre. Sounds of a military band drifted into the window of the office where Stimson was pacing the floor and talking to his associates and clients. Stopping his conversation, he listened for a moment in silence and then burst out in fury at his listeners, some of whom had a greater and more direct interest in *Orth* vs. *Stieger* —"This case is a millstone — a millstone — around my neck!"

With such feelings rising within him, it is doubtful that he could for long satisfy himself or his associates or his clients in the practice of law. In the fall of 1916 these feelings found another outlet in the most unqualified attack he ever made upon a political opponent. Explaining why he would vote for Hughes, he explained that no one "could follow as I have Mr. Wilson's course in respect to national defense and retain faith in his convictions" about the need for military preparations. Had Wilson not said "with a laugh" that the discussion of adequate preparedness was "good mental exercise" which "had been going on ever since he was a boy"? Had he not said there was no need to discuss national defense "at a time when there was not enough ammunition in our coast defenses to last for forty-five minutes . . ."? Had he not surrendered his own Secretary of War to James Hay with his "hodge-podge" of pork? And, finally, "In the War Department . . . Mr. Wilson was not at the mercy of Josephus Daniels; instead, he had to assist him the courage and

[19] H.L.S. to the Editor of the *New York Times*, June 28, 1916.

intelligent patriotism of Mr. Garrison. His sin was against light." [20]

Openly contemptuous of the administration and aroused to clear and present dangers by Germany's declaration of unrestricted submarine warfare, he threw himself, in the first months of 1917, almost totally into the effort to prepare the country for war. He argued in February before the officers of the National Guard against the Hay Bill, which used the Guard as the primary instrument of defense. He spoke at New York University, in March, on the necessity of military service and the duty of the United States to send troops abroad if war came. He spoke of our urban civilization which took boys indoors and gave them "the idea that life is a choice of pleasures instead of a stern school of discipline." This idea went very deep with him. The "undisciplined" youth of New York, where the murder rate was three times that of Berlin and seven times that of London, would profit by six months of practice in "the rapidly decaying art of obedience"; they would in these months learn more that was useful "toward self-control which is essential to leadership among men" than from "almost any other education." In an article he prepared in February, he argued that universal military training would offset the insidious effect of indoor life "upon the fibre of body and resolution alike." As a nation we must regain those "hardy outdoor virtues which are the secret ideal of every right-thinking boy." Late in March, with Frederic Coudert and F. W. Walcott, he began a tour of the Middle West for the National Security League. There he repeated his requests for universal military training and, in addition, began to explain for the first time in public what he thought the war was about. It was a collision of two great systems of government. One system had been defined at Koenigsberg by the Kaiser when he said: "Considering myself the instrument of the Lord, without being misled by the views and opinion of the day, I go my way." This system was based on the theory that the citizen belonged

[20] H.L.S., "Why I Shall Vote for Mr. Hughes," New Republic, Oct. 28, 1916.

to the state, in which all rights inhered. The other system was based on the theory that man had certain inalienable rights, and that the individual man is the responsible source of governmental power and that all rights of government come from him.[21]

This view of the First World War Stimson never changed; in the spring of 1917 this view made the war a struggle, he believed, into which a man or nation could enter with "lofty faith and burning ardor."

While Stimson was still speaking words such as these in the Middle West, Woodrow Wilson delivered the message in which he asked the Congress to declare war upon Germany and her allies. Stimson returned home and applied immediately for a commission, which he received on May 31, 1917, in spite of an old injury that had left him almost blind in one eye. On the next day, a major in the Judge Advocate General's reserve corps, he was ordered to duty at the Army War College in Washington. He went to the capital immediately, but not to the War College and not in the Judge Advocate's office. "I was," he said, "unwilling to be an administrative officer; my ancestors, when in service, have been in the fighting branch; moreover I felt that my former attitude toward this war and our part in it, made it necessary that I should now evidence my faith by works, and show that I was willing to do what I said others should do, and stake my life for the cause."[22]

21 *New York Times*, Feb. 3, March 22, 1917; H.L.S. to G. A. Slater, March 26, 1916; H.L.S., "The Basis for National Military Training," *Scribner's Magazine*, April 1917; H.L.S., undated speech (March or April 1917), "The Issues of the War."
22 H.L.S. to Secretary of the Class of 1888, Yale University, May 6, 1918.

14

The Soldier

JUST BEFORE Stimson set out for Washington on June 1, 1917, Bronson Winthrop had given his partner the only severe lecture he had ever delivered in their long years together. The substance of it was that Stimson was worn out by his exertions in support of preparedness, utterly exhausted in body and spirit. He ought to go to a sanitarium, Winthrop thought, rather than to war. Sitting in the Army-Navy Club on Sunday, June 3, Stimson felt that "all in all, perhaps, I agreed with him." To his father he wrote that day "wondering why the devil I was here." The people he met seemed absorbed in their own affairs; he could discover no optimism, "no dominant purpose or spirit running thro the military establishment." In the "hot, gloomy, depressing" city, he developed the "most acute fit of the blue devils I have ever had."

Thus began a summer in Washington during which he worked as a staff intelligence officer at the War College. Before reporting for duty he went out every morning to drill with the guns at Fort Meyer and, after dinner, he studied the duties of an artillery officer. These exercises he undertook to prepare himself for the reassignment to duty he was trying to obtain. In the last days of August, after an interview with the Secretary of War and an unexpected conversation with the Chief of Staff, he received the orders he was waiting for. On the 27th he was appointed a lieutenant colonel in the Field Artillery, National Army, and ordered to proceed to Camp Upton, Long Island, for assignment to duty with a light artillery regiment.

Camp Upton on September 6, 1917, was a "habitation startling and impossible," it "wore an air of having just been begun and of never wishing to be finished." Under a "mournful sky," on half-cleared land blackened by recent fires, surrounded by "countless acres of mud," stood " a few white pine barracks and two huge tents." On that day Lieutenant Colonel Stimson and Private Dunbaugh reported for duty and "behold we were a regiment — officers and a man."

The regiment was the 305th Field Artillery attached to the 77th Division. Not until the end of October had sufficient enlisted men followed Private Dunbaugh into the ranks to bring the unit up to regimental strength. The recruits came off the streets of New York, for the most part, and from parents who had been born in Italy, China, Russia, Spain, Germany, Lithuania and England. The officers came down from the Plattsburg Training Camp. Among them were Lloyd Paul Stryker and Allen Klots, then a junior member in the firm of Winthrop and Stimson. By the first of November, as the regimental history reported, all these troops needed "were horses and guns to realize that we were, indeed, artillery."

A good deal had, in fact, been accomplished by November 1. Two weeks after he arrived, Stimson reported to Felix Frankfurter that at the camp there were "no drill grounds or quarters, no equipment," and no troops — "everything is noise, dirt and chaos." Confronting this situation, he found himself falling into the mood of a regular. He saw things "go wrong without protesting — enough." But he was very glad to be away from Washington and nearer to the Great Adventure. He was "much more naturally a soldier than a lawyer. I win my cases by tactics not learning, and my heart is in the one much more than in the other." And, if he did not protest enough, he did at least take action. From an old client he obtained fifty miles of wire for the communication system and from another he procured saddles long before the horses, "overburdened by the cares of life," appeared. By the middle of November he had obtained a single battery of "venerable three-inch guns" from a National Guard brigade. At times, he confided, he felt, pushing from behind in all this chaos, like a switch engine. These were the simpler times in the annals of American warfare when a regiment waited two months in idleness until a lieutenant colonel could "snare for us [weapons and] much other useful equipment," when a medical officer placing upon a deal table "with proud gestures, a tin of alcohol, a demijohn of castor oil, a few assorted pills, and gallons, literally, of iodine" could announce "himself open for business."

Three months after the first soldier reported for duty, on December 12, 1917, the regiment conducted its first target practice with the battery of three-inch guns. Lieutenant Colonel Stimson directed the exercise. As the red flag went up on the range and the executive officer raised his hand, the first shot was fired and "we had made a crossing." That night Stimson received new orders and left the regiment.

A week later he sailed from Hoboken for France. As the ship moved out into the Atlantic the images of that "curious chaotic day" rose in his mind: The pier, under the cold sky, closed off from the world by armed guards, the transport painted all over with weird designs, his wife's face trying to smile through her tears. He thought too of something else. Only a few weeks before, his father had died while walking out on the Shinnecock Hills. At the shuttingoff of this never-failing parental concern the son was swept by an "irrevocable sense of loneliness," by the feeling that even the "prosecution of the war seems less worth while since he is no longer here to take an interest in it." All these images and feelings crowded into the moment of departure; there was no other time he could remember of such deep emotions. Over the whole occasion there seemed to be "a sinister spirit brooding." Yet there were consolations. In his pocket was a letter written by Aunt Minnie. From the time he had come, a boy of eight, to live with her he had been, she said, a joy and a blessing. Once his mother had said to her, "You will be very proud of my little boy," and that prophesy had been fulfilled. She was glad he was about to serve his country and deeply thankful that no word of hers could send him forth or hold him back. And she would take care of Mabel and they would both be busy and happy in each other. There was another letter from his wife who believed in him utterly, who knew he was doing what was right and necessary and who wished only to be worthy of him and what he was doing. And there was a third letter from Theodore Roosevelt, who was "*extremely pleased*" that in this war "you have set the standard for American citizenship — and I am not talking in any exaggerated way."

Still and all, "the loneliness of going away into an entirely new and strange life for a wholly indefinite time of separation . . . gives me a sense of loneliness which is hard to get rid of at these times." However much he tried to get himself into "the unimaginative and stolid frame of mind of the good soldier ready to take what comes," that loneliness stayed with him across the gray Atlantic, throughout four days in the gloom of London and during two weeks in the curious mixture of sadness and brightness of Paris. There was not, in these cities, enough to do. While he was waiting assignment to troops in the field he could only call on old friends like General Wood or dine with relatives at Voisin's. Once he took a long walk around Paris, to look at the hotel where his mother and father had lived, and to visit the pension where he and his wife had stayed twenty years before. It crossed his mind as he walked through the Latin Quarter and past St. Etienne and on along the Seine to the Rue de Beaune that he was about to fight to preserve many other things than freedom — an old and very valuable civilization. But this did not reduce the "homesickness" nor alter the lonely evening in his hotel when he returned "without even your own servants and surrounding." What a comfort, he believed it would be, to see at this moment old John or Alma or Margaret and his wife at Highhold.

The days of waiting were over on January 14, 1918, when he was ordered to join, for instruction purposes, the 51st, a Highland Division of the British Army that was in the line near the Somme. Two days later he was on his way, reflecting, as his train bore him toward the Western Front, that this was the worst way to go to war, a man in his fifties, without the support of comrades of his own country or regiment, "to serve with strangers of a different race." Toward evening he got off at a small station where a British staff car met him. For the next two hours he drove through the darkness past transport wagons and soldiers moving forward to the front. Every now and then the flash of distant cannon quivered on the horizon and the sky lit up with the great glare of an exploding rocket. Once the driver turned and said, "We are within sound of the guns now." And then he was at the headquarters of the 51st Division, where he remained for one month, to learn what he could of the uses of artillery in combat.

In that month he discovered a great deal about the incongruities of the war that was fought from 1914 to 1918. There was the "desolate" and "gruesome" battlefield of the Somme — dead trees, shell holes full of water, flourishing villages reduced to flattened masses of bricks and stones. "The very land," he said, "seems to protest against the havoc which has been wrought in it." And then there was the weather; not once since he had been in Europe had the sun shone strongly enough to cast a shadow. Over the stricken landscape there was at all times fog and mist and drenching rain, a "never ending darkness and dampness that gets on one's nerves a little." And then there was the enemy, opening up at odd times of the day with 5.9 howitzers, breaking into the night with "the hum of motors interrupted with the crash of bombs." The German shells at first produced a "nervousness" he gradually got over. He learned that the firing, once opened, was so regular, it was possible to walk between falling patterns.

But the bombs were different; he had the awful feeling of being unable to respond. He never did get used to the idea that "you just have to sit there and take it," without "the sustaining power of an immediately pressing duty to perform." Summing it all up for Aunt Minnie, he said he had seen a lot of this gruesome process and had lost all his illusions if he ever had any. There was, he said, no hot-blooded excitement about this war.

But there were some redeeming features. The British had given him a man who unpacked his bags, drew his water, built his fires and nursed him with skill and care when he fell ill for five days of a liver complaint. At four thirty every day he took tea with the staff and at eight he had an excellent dinner with them, talking often far into the night. They talked of many things: of fifth-century Athens, of Robert Burns at a special mess on his birthday, of the medieval mind and of the trouble the General had with his delphiniums. Three years these men had been out there and Stimson, watching them, hearing them, wondered if he could have done it. Every now and then someone said, incidentally, a word about a wife or child, "And then I remember that in spite of their apparent indifference to the dangers that surround us, they are husbands and brothers too, and are probably thinking just as much about their homes as I am."

In the middle of February he was ordered to the Staff College at Langres to finish the instruction he needed before rejoining the 305th Regiment which was to arrive in May. For two months he worked harder, he believed, than at any time in his life since he had left Harvard. At the Staff school he lived for a time with Major George Patton and Major Stanley Rumbough and an old acquaintance, Willard Straight. The food was delicious, so was the Pomard, and the untouched French countryside shook him with its springtime beauty. But the course was so hard he wondered if he could, with all his application, pass it successfully. If he could, he would have, he knew, a really systematic military education built up on the solution of a series of practical military problems. But "constantly," as he worked away, there rose the vision of those grim Highlanders — Gordon, Seaforth, Black Watch, men of the 51st Division — marching back, in kilts, to the skirl of their pipers, into the line along the stricken Somme. He could not think his real duty was at Langres while they "are still protecting us with their lives." The opening of the Ludendorff offensive did nothing to change these thoughts and it was therefore with great relief that he went at the end of May, after completing his study, to join the 305th Artillery at Camp de Souge near Bordeaux.

The regiment, just arrived from the United States, remained at Camp de Souge for six weeks to finish its gunnery training before moving to the front. During this period Stimson acted as a staff officer at regimental headquarters, but he worked every day with the troops at the guns. One day when a fire broke out on the range and threatened to engulf the whole camp, Stimson from a high tower organized the fight which brought the flames under control. Later he was happy to learn from the mail passing through the camp censor that as a result of his work he had acquired "quite a reputation for generalship in the regiment." A worse circumstance occurred on another day. Stimson and Klots were controlling the fire of a battery from a wooden tower when the breachblock of a gun blew off, decapitating two gunners and setting fire to a caisson loaded with shells. "Without thinking for a second," Klots reported, Stimson rushed out of the tower down to the scene of the disaster and organized a party to put out the fire by throwing sand on the caisson. He then arranged for the removal of the dead soldiers and "took the precaution of having a little talk" with the crew of the artillery piece that lay next to the exploded gun before the men went back into action. For himself he was "glad to find that I could carry on myself, without perturbation, for it was a shocking incident." The peculiar smell of burning camouflage nets would always, he felt, be associated in his memory with the sudden scene of death.

Not long after, the regiment moved from the camp to the Bois de Gramont in Lorraine, hard by Neuf Maisons. There it relieved a French division that was going north to meet the tide of Germans flowing across the Chemin des Dames. Neuf Maisons was, as Stimson said, a quiet sector, or as one of the Frenchmen called it, a place for *"un père de famille,"* but it was here that the 305th heard "the first sounds of actual warfare," and here, on July 11 at 3:10 P.M., that Battery A fired what the regimental history called "the first shot [fired by] the National Army artillery" in the war. Battery A was part of the First Battalion which had been given to the command of Stimson when the regiment left Camp de Souge. For the next few weeks the commander of the First Battalion was, he reported years later, "wonderfully happy." With his own men, in a sector disturbed frequently by alarms and excursions, but not in the line of ceaseless destructive fire, he could bring his command along to the point where "it ceased to be a green unit." By the end of July the 305th as a whole was prepared for the days that lay ahead on the Marne, on the Aisne and in the Argonne Forest. At that time Stimson wrote his wife that he felt he was living "so much more deeply and fully — if more sadly than ever before." He felt as if he knew France from end to end. "I have travelled her," he wrote, "from Boulogne to Bordeaux, from the channel and the ocean to the Swiss border. I have wintered in Langres and summered in the Vosges, I have fought for her in Picardy and Lorraine . . ."

Next day he learned he would fight no more. He had been given a promotion and ordered home to command and train a new regiment of artillery. As he departed, his old regiment "watched him drive away that night with a grave sense of loss." Within himself he discovered strange, mixed feelings. He was leaving men who knew and trusted him, who were about to enter the heaviest fighting on the western front. He was not fitted "to do this elementary training" to which he had been called, in fact he was an inefficient teacher and "might make a

botch of it." On the other hand, there was the thing Theodore
Roosevelt had written only a little time before, on March 12,
that "having been at the front in danger, you will hereafter
accept any position to which your Commanding Officers assign
you, instead of protesting against it because it is one of less danger . . ." There was also his realization "that all the miserable feeling which I have been laboring under since I have been
over here and which made me wonder why I had suddenly
grown so old and sluggish was nothing more or less than constant homesickness . . ." And finally, "far and away and beyond all I shall see Mabel and have even a momentary letup
from the homesickness and depression which has been my
worst enemy during all these months. When I think of her
face, there is no reservation in my joy at going back."

For her, as for him, there had been, during all these months,
no discharge in the warfare of her feelings. Loneliness, pride,
anxiety, the love she could not bring in words to full expression,
worked constantly within her. On the day he left Neuf Maisons
for home, before she knew of his orders, she had been thinking of him "every minute of the day." She had walked around
Highhold in the fragrant Long Island airs and had seen here and
there a spray of goldenrod just out, and the scarlet leaf on the
shrub that suggested "memories of bygone times of love and
comradeship such as few married people I am sure can boast of."
She had not long to wait for more tangible evidences. Two
weeks after she wrote this letter, her husband "shinnied down
a ladder" from a transport off Staten Island into a waiting tug
which put him ashore at Bay Ridge. From there he got to the
subway and arrived at eleven o'clock in the evening to find his
wife waiting at 275 Lexington Avenue. For both the war was
almost over, but not quite.

He went off on August 31 to take command of the 31st
Artillery at Fort Meade near Baltimore. For three months he
did what he could to prepare his new troops for action. Far too
much time in the past, he felt, had been spent in training

recruits in the finer points of discipline and close order drill. Instead he concentrated on nine- and ten-mile marches and gunnery practice. But he placed emphasis on the military formalities — the regimental retreat every night and formal color guards which gave to new soldiers, he felt, a sense of the dignity of their calling. And he discovered many compensations in "leaving the tactics of the battle front." "The sense of responsibility for every detail of the life of 1500 men, and of the molding of their characters is one of the strongest feelings in life, and is the real reason why service with troops even in the lower grades is so incomparably more attractive to most manly men than even the higher forms of staff duty requiring much more intellect."

Whatever compensations could be found in the life at Fort Meade, they were abruptly ended by the signing of the Armistice on November 11. Four weeks later, after eighteen months in the Army, Stimson returned, on December 9, 1918, to civil life. The point of his service, as he had described it to himself at the beginning, was at the end described for him by others. The Stimson spirit, said the Baltimore *Sun*, could not be stifled by "the fumes of personal fear and sordid materialism." His life was part of "the record of those men who not merely talk but whose lives exemplify the things they talk about." [1]

[1] Baltimore *Sun*, Sept. 18, 1918. The material for this chapter was taken primarily from the Stimson Papers and C. W. Camp, *History of the 305th Artillery* (New York, 1919). Stimson's own accounts of his service will be found in "Artillery in a Quiet Sector," *Scribner's Magazine*, June 1919, and in *Active Service*, 97-98.

15

The End of Innocence

No DOUBT each period of history, if there are periods of history, is in itself the best of times and the worst of times, the age of wisdom and the age of foolishness, the season of Light and the season of Darkness. Maybe, therefore, the late nineteenth century is better left as a grain of mustard seed or a leaven which a woman took and hid in three measures of meal. But those who spent at least some part of their adult lives in this period will not leave it there. They report that then "the conditions were ideal — a sense of purpose and progress in the world," that then there were "wonderful new conditions," that then was "the happiest period of all humanity in the Western World in ten centuries," that then one felt "safe."

What life was like in such a time Henry Stimson felt he could never fully communicate to anyone who came of age when the time was over. To one who doubted that there was in human affairs a law of moral progress, he replied: "You have never lived in the period before the last war when we all believed it. Why it looked as if we only had to mop up a very few minor parts of the world." Three words, he decided in old age, described the spirit of this earlier time — serenity, novelty and innocence.

To a world distracted, to a society in which the charm of novelty has been annihilated by the storms of revolution, to those members of a generation who feel, as one of them has said, that in some sort of crude sense they have known sin — it may well be impossible, as Stimson surmised, to impart the sense of this previous world. Certain things combine to set it beyond the pale of later understanding. One is that feeling for a particular moral system of which Stimson spoke. All such systems tend, as time passes, toward obsolescence, and when obsolete, tend to arouse in later generations condescending humors or, at best, perplexity. It is clear, for instance, that the moral scheme of the late nineteenth century was designed to exclude or convert the energy produced by the excitement of the senses, that it invested man with full control and responsibility in the matter of his own behavior, and that it nourished the concern to be up and doing in the cause of righteousness. But beyond this the scheme resists analysis. It all came down, as Theodore Roosevelt said, to the fact that right is right and wrong is wrong or, as William S. Sims said, to the fact that each man had an innate sense of right and wrong. Bald and unqualified assertions of such absolutes may set the teeth on edge in more knowledgeable generations, but in the age that believed them it is certain that a great many men proceeded with the assurance of an inborn sense to decide the things that just weren't done and the things they knew they had to do.

Then there was the sense of time on which depends so greatly the interpretation given to the meaning of experience. Time was still an ever-rolling stream, flowing, as Newton said, equally without relation to anything. Borne on uninterrupted currents men could think not wistfully of how little time there was, but serenely that there was time enough — time for the survey of causes and the measurement of effects, time for satisfying accommodation to refreshing novelty, time for things to work themselves out, time for the cumulative results of selected small changes to take hold, time in which one slow, increasing purpose could work onward, and probably upward and possibly forever. In such continuing circumstances men in public life could really imagine that they fulfilled the requirements of

Edmund Burke — that they appeared as the representatives of their ancestors, their fellows, and their children's children. For men so circumstanced, how was it possible to imagine a radical, conclusive break in the continuities of existence? The great world, change and motion nicely regulated within the ringing grooves, would spin forever.

To the moral system and the sense of time was added the attitude toward power. Men who knew the difference between right and wrong could be trusted, and could trust themselves, to bring the power at their disposal within the limits of the useful and the good. Other, more important limits were further placed upon the use of power by the size of the occasions in which it was applied. In that serene world, responding to benign evolutionary energies, the occasions offered were for small adjustments. All that was required was simple maintenance — "to mop up a very few minor parts of the world." In such a context, small means — the exercise of only a little power — could be made to produce great effects — one regiment could keep the peace in a dominion. Ordinarily indeed the symbol was sufficient. Because somewhere there was a fleet in being it was enough, on a single cruiser in the harbor of a remote continent, to show the flag. And since men with practice in fitting degrees of power to the needs of an occasion understood the relation of force to policy, it was possible, more often than not, to dispense even with symbolic measures. Conscious that they could and would continue their policies by other means in the last resort, men sought ordinarily to achieve their limited objectives by conversation and negotiation. Power in these circumstances was something that could be exercised in calculated measure without diffidence or guilt or fear of absolute corruption, indeed with calm confidence, to maintain the necessary order in the system.

Not everyone, of course, shared in the conditions of serenity and innocence. There were those who saw things around them every day that made their blood boil. Not everyone, also, shared in the calm confidence that sufficient order could be retained in the system. Henry Adams in 1912 discerned "a continuous belt of dissolved society [stretching] round the world, from Sicily . . . to Pekin. . . ." Within the year he expected the disease to reach the heart of society, Central Europe. At seventy-five he was "rotting to pieces in every sense"; nevertheless the "damned world," he said, "rots faster than I." But those who discerned these signs and portents were removed, for the most part, from the dominant center of society; detached from their surroundings they could give free play to their powers of observation and imagination. They were not in charge of the times.

Whether, in the absence of the cataclysm, the great world would have spun down the same fixed grooves forever is an open question. At this distance it is clear that the dislocating energies of industry were spreading rapidly about the globe. It is quite possible that the men of the period could not have summoned sufficient resilience, wisdom and power to arrange peacefully the modifications accelerating change made necessary. In the years from 1880 to 1910 it is clear that they had surprisingly learned much about the nature of their complicated civilization. But it cannot be certain that they had learned enough to take full advantage of an opportunity to maintain their world in satisfying consonance with steadily and rapidly changing situations. The war that began in August 1914 precluded the opportunity and destroyed all the carefully controlled arrangements that held a serene and innocent time together.

Unhappily it did something more than that. It broke up the processes by which men had been accustomed to learn essential things about their environment. Intruding suddenly, like the act of some angry or indifferent god, upon the affairs of competent and responsible men, it befuddled, like all acts of God, the senses of competence and responsibility. Fracturing by violent means the continuities in life, it made it impossible to establish useful connections between the assumed order of the first decade of the century and the disorder of the third decade. Those who had prepared themselves to live in 1910 had little to bring down with them that could be made to fit the life of the twenties. In the interest of survival they had to rely upon the reflexes conditioned in a previous time. Thus had the Seaforth Highlanders that Stimson knew marched with their bonnets and their pipes and their rolling drums back into a line of battle a thousand miles long, where destruction, borne by invisible modern means, awaited them from the sky above and in the gases of the air around them.

For forty-seven years Stimson had lived in the world as it was before 1914. He had grown to manhood in its temperate zones, acquired from books and observation its philosophy, tested that philosophy in his works, and prospered, as his world had prospered, by his works. In 1917 he had fulfilled the last requirement of his time. In 1920 he was fifty-three and had to try himself with his contemporaries in a world they never dreamed of making.

PART TWO

The Exploded Dream

1918-1932

Wandering between two worlds, one dead,
The other powerless to be born. . . .

For the world cries your faith is now
But a dead time's exploded dream.

— Matthew Arnold

16

Normalcy

ONE DAY IN 1920 Root and Stimson were talking together in a room where there was, on the wall, a picture of Theodore Roosevelt. Glancing at this picture, in the course of the conversation, Root broke into his own train of thought to say, "You know, the more I think over it the more I feel that Theodore Roosevelt was the greatest teacher of the necessary elements of self-government that has ever lived. He was not original, that was not necessary . . ." Part of his hold lay, no doubt, in the fact that Theodore Roosevelt realized more than most men who have held his high office that the President is, perhaps more than anything else, an educator. In all his unqualified assertions, by almost every carefully limited action, he succeeded in masterful fashion in stating the nature of the essential problems confronting his society. His ability to involve others in thinking about these problems was, indeed, extraordinary. He had the great teacher's gift for lighting off the excitement that must subdue the pain inevitable in the learning process. Around him, as the years passed, there gathered a body of excited students.

But there was more to it than that. As long as Theodore Roosevelt lived there was always the chance that the things the students thought about might, in actual fact, be brought to pass. Before every single Republican National Convention from 1900 to 1920 he was looked upon and talked about as a possible candidate for the Presidency. For two decades he remained the makeweight in the dreams of liberal Republicans. Men who could not hope to obtain power for themselves and their ideas came to pin their hopes on him. Entangled with their personal attachment to him was their dependence upon him as the central energy which alone could do the things they wanted to do.

The blow of his death fell with stunning force upon his followers. There were those who "could think of nothing else for days," those who were moved beyond their power to speak, and those who cried "like a child." Nor, in retrospect, did the shock diminish. Long afterwards William Allen White recalled how he had tried "to get used to a world without Roosevelt in it," and longer afterwards Harold Ickes remarked, "Something went out of my life that has never been replaced."

There was in the responses of such men a direct and personal grief for the loss of the tremendous spirit that had given shape and substance to their hopes; also a sorrow for a time lost, and also for the loss of something of themselves. For the death of Roosevelt did not really prevent, as some believed, a possible future; it simply coincided with the end of a time. Men were deprived by his departure only of the illusion that there was, for those trained as they had been, work to do in the decade that followed. Those who had tried to lift the shame of the cities in the days of "Golden Rule" Jones or Tom Johnson, for instance, had small place in municipal politics in the days of Jimmie Walker or the mayor who wished to poke King George in the snoot. Those inspired by the Oregon or the Washington Idea to look upon the state as the instrument of social progress could not easily serve in a party that had defected to the heresy that the government was best which governed least. Then there were those who had pitched their case on the assumption that "no amount of commercial prosperity . . . can in itself solve the terrible social problems which all the world is now facing." There was little room for them in an administration where it was held that the business of America was business. Men who had taken for granted the existence of moral laws for social progress could hardly rest satisfied in a state of something called normalcy. During the first decade and a half of the century there had been a continuing discourse on the value of the new nationalism and the new freedom. Muckrakers, novelists, mayors, social workers, governors, editors, Presidents, political scientists, senators, college professors and reporters had, in one way or another, taken part in this continuing discourse on the promises of American life. In the era of wonderful nonsense, men trained in such disputation found it difficult, if not impossible, to think or act within the prevailing spirit of the community.

Some, like Albert J. Beveridge, just petered out in a reversion to stale provincialisms. Some, like Donald Richberg, attached themselves to such lonely dissenters as Robert Marion La Follette or Norman Thomas. The majority, retaining their original impulses and reflexes, withdrew into private affairs and communings. Sometimes they emerged to write letters to the newspapers, or to press their cases before legislative committees, or to cast votes for losing candidates at party conventions. They were, in this sense, like the bees of Samuel Butler, who earnestly pursued their familiar errands across a flowered wallpaper.

Stimson no more than any other of his time and place could avoid such actions. Upon his return from the war he naturally took up the efforts he had left off when he became a soldier. In September of 1919, he went down to Washington to argue the case for the executive budget before the House Appropriations Committee. In December he wrote a letter to the *New York Times* in support of the same proposition. And in the following month he wrote another important letter to the New York *Tribune* when the New York Assembly refused to seat Socialists who had been elected to that body. Said he: "Yet even I can think of some matters in which I believe our government can be improved, and I hope during the remainder of my life to be free to urge upon my fellow citizens the desirability of the changes and reforms that I think desirable. . . . If I believe this, what right have I to deny to the man who believes in Socialism or in a soviet government the opportunity of endeavoring to persuade a majority of the inhabitants of America that a government and a society framed according to his beliefs will be best for America — provided always he confines himself to the democratic methods of peaceful persuasion to accomplish his ends?" [1]

Soon after, he got caught up in the effort to make Roosevelt's old friend Leonard Wood the President of the United States. Much of his time was devoted to protecting the old soldier from the ineptitudes of his organization, which in its incoherence fairly expressed the confusions of the party. One of the leading organizers was John T. King, onetime garbage contractor for the city of Bridgeport, who was skilled in the small and shrewd maneuver. Another was William Cooper Proctor, a very rich and earnest man, an "idealist" who had led a "sheltered life." These two quarrelled all the time, and while they quarrelled Frank Hitchcock, Taft's Postmaster General, slipped into a position of increasing authority. In the situation Stimson, who agreed with Will Hays that Hitchcock was more of a conservative menace than King, though "not so raw and crude," did what he could to help keep order between the dissonant factions. He also did what he could to keep the General in a liberal posture until his defeat in the Chicago Convention in 1920.[2]

Following the defeat, Stimson then did what he could to maintain a liberal view of the League of Nations in the mind of Warren Gamaliel Harding. His own active interest in the League had begun in the late fall of 1918 and early spring of

[1] New York Times, Oct. 1, Dec. 7, 1919; New York Tribune, Jan. 16, 1920.
[2] "Memorandum," April 27, 1920, included in Diary; H.L.S. to Leonard Wood, June 15, 1920; Hagedorn, Wood, II, 324-72, contains a full account of the effort to nominate the General.

1919 when Root had sought his help in preparing the reservations the older man hoped would bring agreement between
Republicans and Democrats. Like Root, Stimson's primary objection was to Article X of the Covenant which pledged members to preserve the territorial integrity of all members against
external aggression. But he was opposed in principle to the
whole idea of the Covenant. Herbert Hoover, when dining
with Stimson in March 1920, had told him that in a conversation
with Wilson in Paris, the President had told Hoover that the
League needed "a great state instrument" like the Constitution
of the United States. Stimson remarked that it was the wrong
way to go about it, that "your plan was to develop the cause of
international law, in much the way in which the common-law
has developed as contrasted with codified or statute law."
When, a few days later, Stimson reported this conversation to
Root, the latter replied that Wilson might have known that the
Declaration of Independence and the Constitution "were only
successful because they embodied a long previous development."
"What a mess of it," Root concluded, "he had made." [3]

The hope was that the messy debate of 1920 could be resolved by the election of Harding, who had given some indication that he favored the League "with proper reservations as to
Article X." Accordingly Stimson wrote the New York *Tribune*
on October 9 that if the views of the Republican irreconcilables
were in fact the responsible views of the party, he would leave
the party. But he was prepared to vote for Harding because by
so doing he felt he would assist in achieving a world court and a
"loose association" without Article X. That, he was sure, was
what all progressives desired. Six days later he signed a statement with thirty other "prominent men" which took very
much the same ground. In so doing he felt, much later, that he
made a serious mistake, a "blunder," that he would "have done
better not to sign that letter . . ." By the time he reached these

[3] "Memorandum of Talk with E.R.," Dec. 22, 1918, in Diary; Diary, March 9,
13, 1920.

views he could recognize that "With the election of President Harding, all hope of American participation in the League soon died." [4]

While he was acting in these several ways in public affairs he was also, in the first years after the war, thinking about possible changes in the way these affairs were conducted. One night, he and Hoover had a long talk about John Maynard Keynes's book *The Economic Consequences of the Peace*. Hoover observed that "if you struck out the first chapter about President Wilson, and the last chapter where [Keynes] tries to bunco the U.S.," the author was about right on his views in between. The talk then turned to "responsible government." Stimson tried to convince his guest that cabinet members should "have the right to the floor of Congress. . . ." Hoover disagreed, but proposed instead an under-secretary in each department with a right to the floor who would serve as a liaison between Congress and the executive branch. Responsible government, he continued, produced poor administration; men rose because they impressed legislatures, not because they were administrators. It occurred to Stimson that Hoover "strongly distrusts" legislative bodies because "he himself is no speaker or debater." [5]

Wherever he went in those days, Stimson tried to stimulate interest in his theories of responsible government. In 1921 he worked out a set of propositions which included the ideas that the election of executive officers for a fixed time was inconsistent with human nature and democracy; that a system which permitted the election of an executive for four years, a senator for six years, and a representative for two years was "doubly wrong." And that the system of picking a chief magistrate in a campaign of four months was "unworkable" under modern conditions. He and Root discussed these propositions at great length, reflecting, as they did so, on the British, Italian and early American experiences. This was a congenial exercise which

[4] *New York Times*, Oct. 15, 1920; *Active Service*, 105-7.
[5] Diary, March 9, 1920.

ended with Root's conclusion that the question was not whether the existing American arrangement was right or wrong, but whether the evils produced were greater or less than those produced under the other system.[6]

It was with discussions of this kind that Stimson sought to satisfy his concern for public affairs in the first years after the war. His active life was lived elsewhere — in the law. On his return to practice he was mildly chagrined to discover that there were a good many of his professional friends who did not recall how successful he had once been as a lawyer; that there were, in fact, those in the profession "who knew not Joseph." New York, he reflected, was and always will be "a seven-day town." The blame for this situation, however, could hardly be laid entirely upon the city. As Stimson said later, private practice became, in the twenties, his primary concern for the first time in "more than a decade"; in actual fact for the first time in considerably more than a decade. Not since 1906 could he be said to have devoted his full attention to the work for which he had been trained.

It did not take him long, however, to re-establish his position as a leading trial lawyer. Soon after he returned to practice, he successfully prosecuted, at the request of the Attorney General of the State, a combination of plumbers and labor union leaders under the state antimonopoly laws. There followed, in rapid succession, the three largest and most interesting cases of his career. In the first, Stimson acted as counsel for the Cement Manufacturers Protective Association in the course of a suit brought by the government under the Sherman Act. The association, composed of the principal cement makers in the eastern part of the country, was a trade association formed to facilitate the exchange of financial and production information between the several members. The argument of the government was that the exchange of information and "the concerted adoption and observance of the trade practices," based on the informa-

6 "Memorandum of Conference with Elihu Root" in Diary, Jan. 20, 1921.

tion, constituted a "gigantic scheme" of concerted action against which "the dealers and public have stood and now stand defenseless." [7]

The trade association was one of the devices developed in the twentieth century to stabilize, by the cooperative activity of individual companies, the conditions within a particular industry. Skillfully manipulated, it could also serve as an instrument for giving cooperating companies the advantages of monopolistic conditions which could not be obtained by individual enterprise. The problem for Stimson, in this case, was twofold. To demonstrate first that some form of cooperative activity was necessary for the constructive development of the industry and to demonstrate second that in this instance the cooperative activity of the cement companies had not taken the form of combination or conspiracy in restraint of trade.

He began his task with the usual tremendous preparations. The history of the cement industry in this country from the beginning was carefully assembled. Production, pricing, financing and distribution figures for two decades were collected and incorporated in an elaborate series of charts. Stimson loved the clarity and finiteness of the chart as a means of presenting a case to a jury, and George Roberts worked for weeks to satisfy the exacting demands of this love. When the jury had been sworn, biographies of each member were prepared in detail. These included information about jobs, education, background and religion and also assessments of the individual members' feelings about the case.

To this jury Stimson had three principal points to make. First, in a time of inflation when everybody got hurt it was the human instinct to hold someone else responsible, in this instance the trade associations. His clients were, in 1922, the object of indiscriminate attacks caused by the general hard times. But the

[7] The history of this case in the courts is given in brief in *The Federal Antitrust Laws* (New York, 1949), 123 ff. The following account, like those of Stimson's other cases to be given later in this chapter, is based primarily on material in the files of Winthrop, Stimson, Putnam and Roberts.

real issue lay elsewhere, in a consideration of whether freedom
is inconsistent with intelligence — that is, information — or
whether intelligence is necessary for freedom. The purpose of
the trade association was to collect information from which men
could make sensible, constructive decisions about the safe conduct of their business. The purpose of the association was to
supply the data which changed industry from a game of poker
to chess. As one who believed that freedom was preserved by
rational decisions consciously taken, Stimson preferred chess to
poker.

His third point was that the government had to prove conspiracy and willful combination and that it could not do this.
First, none of the apparatus of industrial conspiracy was present
— no agreements, no pools, no division of business and territory. All that could be found was a tendency toward uniformity of times and places in the prevailing market prices. The
government argued this showed an agreement which they could
not prove existed. Stimson argued that it was the inevitable
result of competition in marketing a standardized commodity;
it was the result whenever there was perfect competition, as he
summoned expert witnesses to explain. With his charts he demonstrated that prices from company to company changed not
simultaneously, as must happen with prior agreement, but
over a period of days and weeks. He also showed that shipments by individual companies varied considerably from year
to year. He also met the government argument that where
prices remain level over a long period there is no competition,
by asking whether this meant that competition — over time —
must inevitably reduce prices to zero or a minus factor. He
thought not. Finally he said that the government's case was in
effect a statement that uniformity in an industrial price structure equaled a conspiracy. If this were upheld, he argued, every
industry was open to indictment at almost any time. The Sherman law did not intend, he said in closing, "to condemn American business to ignorance."

The jury, impressed by Stimson, but also impressed by the fact that the Lehigh Cement Company was ordinarily the first member of the association to announce a price change ultimately accepted by all other members, divided 7-5 in support of Stimson. A civil suit brought by the government against the association was tried a year later on the record made in the criminal suit. The judge in the District Court on this evidence dissolved the association and enjoined the members from entry into any further similar combination. This decision was reversed in 1925 by the Supreme Court, and at the same time, the criminal charges against the association were dismissed.

Before the final disposition of this suit, Stimson had become involved in quite a different kind of case. In the year 1911, Miss Emily Southmayd had made a will in which she had divided her money between certain charitable organizations and a number of nieces and nephews to whom she left $150,000 each. Four years later, upon the death of her brother, who left $900,000 to be divided among the nieces and nephews, Miss Southmayd executed a new will in which she withdrew the former bequests to her relatives on the grounds that they had already been amply provided for by her brother. To this will a codicil was added in 1919 leaving $30,000 to her executor, Allen W. Evarts, who had for long been her man of affairs. Two years later, when Miss Southmayd died at the age of ninety-three, some of the nieces and a nephew entered objections to her will on the grounds that she was "not of testamentary capacity" and had acted under the "undue influence of some person." The defense of the will was placed in Stimson's hands in the spring of 1922.[8]

The case involved one of those family altercations that violated his sense of decorum; it also took him far into those intimate domains of the personality which he always felt should be made impregnable against any intruder. Miss Southmayd

[8] Much of the interesting argument and testimony will be found in the *New York Times* from Nov. 11, 1922 to Dec. 23, 1922.

was, as Stimson said at the trial, "eccentric in some respects." As her brother had disapproved of college education, so she had disapproved of automobiles, telephones and central heating. She exhibited also a compulsive desire to protect her person and her possessions from dangers more imagined than real. No doctor could examine her; she shut herself away in a house where windows were never opened and furniture never dusted; she washed interminably the dollar bills that were left lying around her locked bedroom. Each year she burned the accumulated clothes she could not entrust to a laundress. From servants, guests at the summer hotels she frequented, and workmen who came to repair her house, it was possible to accumulate a striking inventory of the intimate and pitiful details of her aberration. It was possible also to document the sense of anxiety and gaiety with which she always looked forward to the visits from her attorney and man of affairs.

The first step taken by Stimson to protect the will made by this woman was to ask for a special jury. He did this on the grounds that it was very difficult to discriminate between the manifestations of the aged, the senile, the eccentric and the psychotic. He did this also because the case involved a conflict fraught with the public interest, a conflict between the ties of blood and the concern for charity. In such situations, as the Eno case indicated, "the jurors in probate contests are easily influenced by sympathy and prejudice. They are apt to substitute their own judgement for the testators . . ." By these means he obtained the special jury he requested.

More difficult was the task of deciding how to conduct the case. Before a decision was taken, memoranda were prepared on seven different points of law covering, among other things, the extent of the privileged nature of the attorney-client relationship, the use of opinions on rationality given by nonexpert witnesses, the nature of "undue influence," and the necessity for the proponents, that is Stimson, to assume the burden of proof for sanity. Most important was the memorandum in which testamentary capacity was defined as strength and clearness of mind about (a) the nature and extent of the property involved; (b) the nature of the act performed; (c) the names, identities and mutual relationships of the objects of bounty. Against strength and clearness of mind on these matters, extended precedent held that neither eccentricity nor delusion in other matters could necessarily demonstrate testamentary incapacity.

These memoranda provided the general framework within which the case developed. It was determined in a series of conferences between Stimson, Allen Klots and several law clerks to prove first the facts of the will by witnesses. Then Stimson would proceed with the aid of correspondence to demonstrate that Miss Southmayd, who until her brother's death in 1915 had relied on him for financial advice, had, upon his death, worked carefully with her lawyer in the conduct of her own affairs. Finally he would demonstrate by correspondence and witnesses that Miss Southmayd knew her nieces and nephews well; that she had provided for them until other provision had been made for them in her brother's will; and that she knew equally well the various charitable endeavors to which she had contributed throughout her later life and to which she had left the bulk of her fortune in her last will. The intent of these demonstrations was to show through the naturalness of the will the competency and freedom from restraint with which the testator had acted.

Having decided the strategy, Stimson and his colleagues devoted a great deal of time to a consideration of the tactics. They decided that it was necessary to allude to Miss Southmayd's eccentricities but to reduce the expected impact of her strange behavior in three ways: First, to suggest that opposing counsel would dwell at great length upon the eccentricities because they were the substance of his whole case. Second, to place them in harmless perspective as often as possible — to point out, for instance, that though Miss Southmayd gave a retiring servant a horse, this was natural since the servant was opening a livery stable. Third, to demonstrate that the eccentric behavior was of long standing — as early as 1883 she had thrown all the table silver into boiling water because a guest with a cold had walked by the table — and that this behavior had always been restricted within the sphere of an obsession to protect her self and her possessions from assumed contaminations of all kinds. Furthermore, the eccentricities had not prevented her from keeping accurate accounts or writing her lawyer sensible letters about changes in her stock holdings.

A further tactical consideration on which much time was spent concerned the opening. Should Stimson open only with the facts of the will as was first suggested? He thought not, for in so doing he would lose the advantage of presenting first his own case in its strongest light. His opponents had more impressive witnesses than he because Miss Southmayd had outlived almost all her friends who could have testified for her, while opposing counsel had a stream of servants who over the years had been in a position to watch most intimately her personal aberrations. So he decided to "open substantially before we rest" to create a feeling for "the complications in the case" and a predisposition for his side. In so doing he had to avoid either giving his opponent information he did not already possess, or using in his own first argument material he would have to repeat in his rebuttal.

Finally, as always before a big case was brought to court, Stimson prepared a list of witnesses, rating them as strong, weak or to "use only in extremity." For each of these witnesses and for the witnesses he expected his opponent to present he drew up projected lines of questioning. Thus prepared, he put together his opening statement in 134 pages. As always the statement of facts was clear and undecorated. From there he went on to a reconstruction of the life and personality of Miss Southmayd, equally clear and undecorated but containing in the spare recital of carefully organized evidence an increasingly dramatic momentum. She had feared both cats and dogs; she had heated her house with fireplaces; she had, as he set forth in precise descriptions, locked up, washed and burned her personal belongings. But the sphere of her aberration was carefully marked out and delimited. A butcher would testify that she knew what she wanted and carefully selected "high-quality stuff." A janitor would testify that she learned at an advanced age to operate an automatic elevator. A Valentine poem, written when she was eighty-seven, would be seen to contain good ideas and to scan. Into this narrative at various points were introduced often interesting touches — a summer boarder in a Maine hotel reported that a niece of Miss Southmayd's "would not let her putt though the niece putted and Miss Southmayd expressed a wish to putt." And then this whole elaborate and touching personal record was lifted out and clear of the circumstances in which Miss Southmayd had conducted her business affairs since she had begun, at the age of eighty-three in 1911, to be responsible for them. What was then presented was a woman learning at an advanced age how to keep adequate account of her estate, consulting an experienced lawyer to help her in the learning process, writing intelligent letters on how she might change her holdings and how, in the event of her death, she would dispose of them. Then Stimson rested.

The case he had prepared withstood the assaults of the opposing counsel whose efforts to show Miss Southmayd "lived in a cave," feared poisoning by a plumber and burned bouquets of flowers sent by relatives simply fell into a framework Stimson had prepared. At the summing up Stimson decided not to listen to the opposing counsel. So clearly had he thought through every step of the case that he did not wish to have his mind distracted by "irrelevancies, pot holes, and red herrings" which the adroit Mooney might, he feared, set for him. He went before the jury fiercely concentrated on his own position, indifferent to the claims and arguments of the other side, and won his case when after a three-hour deliberation the jury upheld the will. It was perhaps the most complete expression of his method as a trial lawyer.

In the closing days of the Southmayd trial, Stimson was asked by a man named J. C. Brydon if he would act as counsel for a special committee of bituminous operators. The committee was about to prepare a report on the coal industry to be submitted to the United States Coal Commission. This commission had been appointed by the President in September 1922 as a fact-finding body "with a view to aiding and assisting in advising Congress in matters of legislation which will ensure a supply of [coal]. . . ." The recent history of the industry had more than justified public concern. Three times in the years from 1916 to 1923 there had been critical shortages of bituminous coal, caused in principal part by industry-wide strikes in 1919 and again in 1922. The hope of the President was that the commission under John Hays Hammond could make some recommendations for the stabilization of peaceful labor relations in the industry. The special committee of bituminous operators was, in the fall of 1922, seeking Stimson's aid in preparing a brief for their interests that could be given to the commission.

After some days of reflection, Stimson, on December 1, 1922, agreed to take the job "on the understanding [his] clients wanted a constructive solution for all." For the next six months he devoted himself to a study of the industry. In his researches his old friend Goldthwaite Dorr and a young lawyer in the firm, Edgar Crossman, were his principal assistants. They went out into the coal regions — Illinois, Indiana, Ohio and western Pennsylvania — to investigate company records, to talk with countless people in company offices, union headquarters and in the mines; to take pictures of working and living conditions in those company-owned villages that needed "only castles, drawbridges, and donjon-keeps to reproduce to the physical eyes a view of the feudal days." The result was a series of memoranda, historical studies and, inevitably, charts on everything from wage scales and prices from 1846 to 1923 to the place of income and excess profit taxes in determining the margin of profit.[9]

[9] The full findings of the Coal Commission are to be found in *Report of the U.S. Coal Commission*, 5 parts (Washington, 1925). The recommendations are in Part One, 255-78. A shorter version is *What the Coal Commission Found* (Baltimore, 1925).

On the foundation of these elaborate findings a series of extended briefs was presented throughout the month of April 1923 to the Coal Commission. The central conclusions of these briefs were as follows: First, that the bituminous coal industry was stable and competitive "when not affected by abnormal conditions and artificial obstructions." Second, that in the past six years abnormal conditions had been introduced by the war and artificial obstructions created by both the United States Government and the United Mine Workers. As a result of the actions of these two agencies labor costs had risen so rapidly that they were no longer counteracted by improvements in machinery; they had risen so rapidly, in fact, that the labor costs on coal, which, in 1921, had been 67.7 per cent of the total cost at the mine mouth were, in 1922, 77 per cent of the total cost. Such wages attracted 200,000 additional men into the industry where they were kept, unneeded, by the artificial obstructions. Third, the principal source of disturbance in the industry was the United Mine Workers, "an arrogant minority — challenging the American Republic by its attempt to fasten a monopoly of coal labor upon American industry and by its attempt to fasten an irresponsible class supergovernment upon American political institutions . . ." The source of the union's strength was discovered to be a "campaign of intimidation and murder," an attempt to obtain high wages and short hours by strike and violence financed by the use of the "checkoff [that] is practically non-existent in any other industry." The object of this campaign was to enable the UMW to impose on all consumers of coal "an unreasonable burden of cost," to place in "the hands of the irresponsible leaders of this organization a power which they should never have, viz: the power to control the supply to the citizens of the United States of the prime necessity of life"; in other words, the object was to establish monopolistic conditions.

The "tactical center" of this case against the UMW in the brief Stimson presented was what had taken place in the town of Herrin, Illinois, where "on June 22, 1922, in the middle of a bright, sunny morning, the people of Herrin watched six Americans, survivors of the massacre, forced to creep on their hands and knees through the streets of Herrin in token of their subjection to the power of the United Mine Workers." In the town which had become a hissing and a byword "the fear of personal violence and perhaps death hangs over the community as it did in Pennsylvania in the days of the Molly McGuires," all because the South Illinois Coal Company had hired some shovel runners to operate the mine struck by the United Mine Workers. These shovel runners were to be looked upon, John L. Lewis said in his famous telegram, "in the same light as . . . any other common strikebreakers," and so the massacre had begun.[10]

Having used Herrin to demonstrate his conviction that the aim of the mine workers under John L. Lewis was to establish monopoly conditions in the coal industry by "massacre, arson, and insurrection," Stimson a month later went on to make recommendations for what he believed would be a "constructive solution for all." He wanted a solution which would, in accordance with American tradition, produce "a spirit of partnership in a common enterprise" and preserve the "high degree of individual initiative [which is one of our] most prized national characteristics."

To that end one had to begin with the recognition that three distinct sets of employer-employee relationships existed between the laboring man and the coal operators. In one of these the re-

[10] The Commission accepted "the massacre as a crime and the subsequent trials as a miscarriage of justice," but they assigned the general cause for the "Herrin disaster" to a state of mind created by bad conditions in the industry for which operators were in considerable part responsible. See *What the Coal Commission Found*, 234-36. Paul M. Angle in *Bloody Williamson, A Chapter in American Lawlessness* (New York, 1952) gives in his first four chapters an objective and a much fuller account of the Herrin episode than is contained in the above synthesis of Stimson's brief. On the specific matter of Lewis' telegram he offers powerful evidence suggesting that it was not the cause of the massacre and that Lewis never intended it be. He also gives substance throughout his account to the Coal Commission's opinion that the operators were in considerable part responsible for the general conditions that produced the incident.

lationship was determined by the terms of the UMW contract with owners, in another by the agreement between owners and company unions, and in the third between owners and non-union employees. No one, he believed, in the year 1923 should attempt to choose among the three a "best method." The existing industrial system, as human institutions go, was "a mere infant." It would be "stupid to suppose that the last word has been said as to the forms which relations of employer and employee should take under the system." "Let that form of relations survive," he said, "which can show itself most consistent with American ideals and of the greatest service to the industry." To that end he sought conditions stabilized by law that would permit "freedom of evolution of the three [existing] labor-employer relationships."

To stabilize conditions he proposed first the creation of state industrial commissions with the power to obtain information, particularly financial figures, from both companies and unions and the power to make the information public. Then he proposed the incorporation of labor unions, the continuation of existing contracts with the addition of provisions for compulsory arbitration at the request of either party, the adoption of a new code to govern working conditions and the abolition of "the key log," the checkoff.

There can be no doubt that these proposals represented precisely Stimson's real desires in the situation; but they represented also the extreme concessions that the most enlightened members of his group of clients could be persuaded to make. Indeed, counsel for one of his clients had expressed the "fear" that Stimson's policy "would lead to government control." This attitude of his clients had in part, as he told his old friend George Wharton Pepper, determined the way in which he had developed his case. He had been shocked by his investigation of the Herrin massacre; it affronted his deepest instincts for law and order. Moreover he soon reached the conclusion that the policy of the United Mine Workers was the fundamental evil, the "real issue" in the industry. That was why Herrin became the heart of his brief. But he used it also to achieve the unity among his clients that would give him a consistent "trial policy." He had at the beginning, he felt, to win the confidence of an industry composed "of small, combative units" unused to cooperative action. All the operators really agreed upon was their antagonism to the United Mine Workers. So his first briefs were designed in part to work up the "great satisfaction" among his clients which permitted him toward the end "to win their assent to certain policies of a more progressive and constructive character. . . ." Among these policies were the adoption of arbitration and automatic wage readjustment and the "voluntary publicity of accounts." [11]

He explained all this to Pepper "because I fear some of my old friends reading those early briefs thought I had relapsed into a hard-boiled reactionary." Some of his oldest friends, in fact, could not agree with his final recommendations. One was Felix Frankfurter, who objected to the proposal to incorporate the unions. Frankfurter approved of the Coronado case, which without incorporation made unions responsible to the judgment of juries. And also he felt the want of trust he sensed in Stimson's briefs created an unfavorable atmosphere for union maturity. Stimson replied that "our Anglo-Saxon history" suggested it was unwise "to expect classes to improve in self-restraint on a regimen of uncontrolled power." To make the conflict fair, unions like companies ought to be regulated by incorporation. Frankfurter then retorted, "How long have armed guards been part of the Ango-Saxon temperament and tradition? " Stimson replied that his justification for the armed guards used by operators lay in the English concept of the right to defend property from attack, and that he still was convinced that incorporation — on condition of the elimination of the checkoff — was the solution.[12]

[11] H.L.S. to G. W. Pepper, Aug. 2, 1923.
[12] Felix Frankfurter to H.L.S., June 10, 1923; H.L.S. to Felix Frankfurter, June

The Coal Commission itself was skeptical of some of Stimson's proposals. It too refused to accept the idea of incorporation and it rejected also the idea of compulsory arbitration. Otherwise the principal proposals of Stimson were included in its final report. Whatever Stimson or the commission felt turned out to be, in the event, unimportant, for nothing was done with the report when it was finally issued. But the briefs gave Stimson the fullest opportunity he ever had to work out and express publicly his attitude on the relations between capital and labor.

By his work in the cement case, on the Southmayd will, and before the Coal Commission in the years from 1920 through 1923, he established himself as one of the leading trial lawyers in New York. He did, also, something more than that. For his work in the antitrust suit he received a fee of $100,000. In the Southmayd matter he had argued a celebrated will case, like those which, in the days of his apprenticeship, had made the reputations for the great advocates of the time, and in the coal briefs he had dealt with a problem attended by questions of great public interest. He could feel that he had demonstrated, by these works, his ability to attain the highest success in a profession which circumstances theretofore had prevented him from achieving. He was also enabled to say in after years, like Root, that upon withdrawing from the public service he could make the money that would permit him to return to public service if the occasion arose. In the twenties, he became, for the first time, a rich man. But this was not primarily because of the money he made in his law practice.

It is true that his income from the law for the ten years from 1919 through 1928 was, on the average, in the neighborhood of $50,000 a year, but the development of his financial competence derived primarily from another source. In the

---

18, 23, 1923. For further explanation of his views — especially on the checkoff issue, which "incidentally we have put . . . on the map" — see H.L.S. to Elihu Root, Aug. 10, 1923.

nineties a wealthy patient of his father had deposited a sum of
money in a bank in his father's name instead of paying the bill
that had been rendered for medical treatment. This sum, becoming capital by the transaction, also became in Dr. Stimson's
eyes untouchable. He confessed once that during the nineties
he borrowed $5000 rather than take money from this account.
Save for one occasion it remained intact until his death in
1917. That one occasion, he also confessed much later, was
when he purchased the yacht *Fleur-de-Lys*, and with it years
of "happy loneliness." This fund together with Stimson's own
savings was managed in the twenties by Stimson's cousin, Alfred
L. Loomis, who had left the law firm to become a member of
Bonbright and Company. By his exceedingly skillful management, the holdings grew until Stimson attained a state of what
he called "financial freedom."

This freedom he used to obtain, so far as money could buy it,
precisely the kind of life he wished. Highhold became not
larger or more elaborate, but completely fitted out to supply in
detail even the smallest requirements of what remained a taste
— indeed a demand — not for impressive display or aesthetic
pleasures, but for perfect comfort. In the summer months
there were trips to Europe with Mrs. Stimson, and ordinarily
several other members of the family, in the most comfortable,
if not the most ornate, staterooms of the largest and fastest
vessels. In New York there was, at last, after the years in the
cramped quarters of Lexington Avenue, a well-built, large
town house on East 36th Street. There were also modest increases in the never very large amounts given to the fifty-odd
charities that claimed the interest of Mr. and Mrs. Stimson and
larger contributions to those members of the extensive family
who had fallen upon troubled or hard times.

As Stimson prospered in these years, so did the firm. It grew
in size and in the extent of its interests. A "considerable
amount" of its business lay in corporate financings, in the
representation of companies or underwriting bankers in the is-

suance and distribution of stocks and bonds. The firm also represented "as to financial and general matters" public utility companies, of which the largest was the Commonwealth Services Incorporated Company, and such other industrial clients as Bristol Meyers Company, Singer Sewing Machine Company, and the Alexander Smith Carpet Company. But the firm retained, even in expansion, the spirit of its founders. Young men on their arrival were not required to work in the managing clerk's office or at law research but could "start to practice law." They were given offices near partners working in their fields of preference — estate, corporate, tax or trial divisions. And they were expected still to work in conformity with "our expressed and actual desire . . . to conduct our law practice during office hours, which are 9:30 to 5:30 and, under press of unfinished business, if necessary, Saturday morning." [13]

In these friendly and civilized surroundings Stimson proceeded much as he had in the earlier days. From his office drifted the muffled sound of irritation when a secretary failed to hear what he had said in dictation or broke in to ask how to spell a French word he had used. There were also the visible and audible signs of the fierce work of concentration. There were, too, the long conferences in which the "slow mind" turned things over and over and the young men said "things two or three times in very simple language," the long conferences that preceded the days in court where the "dramatic transformation" occurred and "simplicity came into his thinking" and he was "riveted to the point." There were also quieter discussions with Bronson Winthrop to whom Stimson often turned for aid and counsel in preparing his harder cases.

But there was a subtle change from the condition of earlier years. The firm was larger and by its increase had lost, for Stimson at least, the sense of intimacy that had pervaded it before the war. He missed that *esprit*, that feeling of the band of

[13] Memorandum on the history of the firm, April 29, 1948, files of Winthrop, Stimson, Putnam and Roberts.

brothers that had buoyed him up in the District Attorney's office and in Winthrop and Stimson in 1914. The firm was larger to be sure, but Stimson also was older. In his fifties he was at the age when men are more fathers than brothers. And he could feel this if only in the fatigue that set in during the hours of the afternoon. Sleeping badly by night, chained to a desk and the work of concentration by day, his energy spent itself frequently by three o'clock. So all these things took some of the pleasure out of his achievements, and there was also another thing. "That is the law"; the law which is certainly, he reflected, "a jealous mistress." It was, of course, also a "noble profession," but one with which he had never "been thoroughly satisfied except as a means of livelihood." Feeling all this, he told his friends in Bones, he felt also that he was "not sure" that the whole period does not seem one of "marked anticlimax," indeed that the causes in which he was engaged were not "rather trivial and unsatisfying." Still he was prepared to go along, "grumbling now and then to myself," glad of an absorption that made him think "not too much about old age."

Not many months after he wrote these words he was provided with diverting absorptions of a more congenial kind.

17

Proconsul in the Philippines

TIME, IN THE twenties, no longer flowed equally; the great current had been broken up and discharged into an intricate system of channels. There were, in places, torrents like those that carried Lincoln Steffens over into the future where he could see that it worked. There were, in other places, backlashes in the current that bore men like Jay Gatsby and his friends ceaselessly back into the past. And there were also to be found whirlpools that spun so fast it was impossible to hang on to what D. H. Lawrence called the pure present. In some places there even remained quieter reaches where, on the surface of the stream, the current did flow equally as before. These quieter reaches lay, for the most part, in areas remote from the transforming energy of the industrial process: in agrarian regions, in retarded societies and in the dominions beyond the seas. Here, to all appearances, the rate of change in the twenties was about what it had been in the first decade of the century. And in the twenties, as two decades before, there was still in these regions work to be done.

There was, for instance, a dispute over the ownership of the provinces of Tacna and Arica between Chile and Peru that had begun in 1879. The attempt of the United States to resolve the issue by the extension of its good offices had involved the Secretary of State in a situation that "was giving him . . . more anxiety and trouble than any situation in the government." Feeling he needed "a detached mind" that could "study the situation afresh," he summoned Henry Stimson in April 1926 to provide a new analysis. Stimson's opinion that the issue could not be solved by plebiscite because "a fair plebiscite could not be held" in the province of Tacna became part of the extensive record of a quarrel that was finally settled in the administration of Herbert Hoover.[1]

Not long after he filed his advisory brief with Secretary Kellogg, Stimson traveled to the other side of the world to observe the situation in the Philippines. Returning in September 1926, after a visit of five weeks, he reported his findings during a lunch with Calvin Coolidge in the White House. The impression he made at that time apparently lingered in the President's mind, for six months later Coolidge summoned Stimson once again to Washington.[2]

On this occasion he was told that there was a "mission of 'important and emergent nature.'" If Stimson would not take it, the President said, "I really don't know who I can select . . . in the U.S." What, Stimson wanted to know, were the limitations; was he to assume that he was to be the President's eyes and ears, to report — nothing more? "No," replied Coolidge, "I want you to go somewhat further. If you find a chance to straighten the matter out, I want you to do so."[3]

"The matter" was a revolution in Nicaragua that had broken out in the following fashion. In 1923 the countries of Central America signed in Washington a treaty of amity by which they pledged themselves to refrain from interfering in each

[1] "Memorandum of Conferences at State Department," April 28, May 7, May 10, May 17, 1926, in Diary; H.L.S. to Secretary of State, June 3, 1926.
[2] Stimson's visit to the Philippines took place at the suggestion of Wood, then Governor General, who said that he wanted his old friend's advice. Stimson's views in support of Wood's administration and of continued United States sovereignty in the Islands will be found in the Diary, Sept. 22, 1926; "First-Hand Impressions of the Philippine Problem," *Saturday Evening Post*, March 19, 1927; and "Future Philippine Policy Under the Jones Act," *Foreign Affairs*, April 1927.
[3] Diary, March 31, April 1, 1927.

other's affairs and to withhold recognition from Central American governments established by revolution or *coup d'état*. In the same year Nicaragua, with the help of the United States, adopted new procedures designed to insure honest popular elections. Before this time, since the party in power had always been able to control the results of the suffrage by force, the only way in which a Nicaraguan government could be changed was by an uprising or a *coup d'état*. Indeed, for a century revolution had been "a regular part of their political system." The Washington treaties and the election law of 1923 appeared to lay a sound structure for the development of Nicaraguan self-government. Therefore, after the election of a new administration in 1924, the United States in August 1925 withdrew the Marine force which had been stationed in the country since 1912. No sooner had the Marines departed than a revolution broke out. It ended in the following year when, after the intercession of the United States, a new President, Adolfo Díaz, was elected by the Nicaraguan Congress. Díaz, a member of the Conservative party, was to hold office until the next popular election in 1928. The government of Díaz was recognized by the United States, France, Great Britain, Italy and Spain in addition to most Central American countries. Shortly after the new President assumed office, however, a revolution was raised against him by the Liberals under a politician named Juan B. Sacasa and a general, José Maria Moncada, who commanded the liberal armies. This revolution was three months old when Coolidge sent for Stimson at the end of March 1927. At that time, the rival forces had divided the country between them, the Liberals holding the territory on the Atlantic seaboard, the Conservatives controlling the western area.[4]

For one week, after accepting the President's request to go to Nicaragua as a "command," Stimson educated himself in the nature of the problem confronting him. After reading everything he could lay his hands on, talking with men in the State Department and men with business interests in Nicaragua, and discussing the situation at length with Root, he reached certain conclusions. The aim was not only to stop the revolution, but to stop it in such a way that the theoretical framework of self-government supplied by the Washington treaties of 1923 and the Nicaraguan election laws of 1924 was continued intact. To achieve this end it was first necessary, he believed, to retain in office Adolfo Díaz, the Conservative who had been recognized by the United States as the legitimately elected President; and second, to insure that a free and fair election would be held in 1928. The principal task, he believed, would be to gain acceptance of these terms by the Liberals. They resented the continued recognition by this country of the man against whom they were fighting and they had rejected already a proposal, "part promise and part threat," to lay down their arms in return for the assurance of a free election in 1928.[5]

Knowing this much, Stimson returned to Coolidge on April 7, 1927, with the following questions. Did Coolidge agree that since the United States had, in accordance with the treaties of 1923, recognized Díaz it "would be an element of weakness" to reopen the question? The President agreed. Was Coolidge prepared to accept the risk of having a Liberal returned to office in a free election of 1928? The President said he did not see how he could avoid doing so. What if Stimson found on his arrival that in the opinion of the resident American Minister every effort to stop the revolution short of force had been made; that armed intervention alone remained? Such intervention, in Stimson's view, "should be acquiesced in with very great reluctance." The President agreed but "made no other suggestion"; he was prepared apparently, as before, to let Stimson "straighten the matter out," if he found a chance to do so.[6]

---

[5] Diary, April 1-6, 1927; "Memorandum of a Conference with the President, the Secretary of State, Colonel Olds and Mr. Stimson, Thursday, April 7, 1927," in Diary.
[6] Memorandum of Conference on April 7, 1927.

Having carefully defined the nature of his endeavor and obtained a description of the means at his disposal Stimson, with his wife, set out on a cold, raw April 9 aboard the *Aconcagua*. For six days after his arrival on April 15 he talked steadily with American naval and diplomatic officers and with representatives of both the Conservative and Liberal parties of the country. While in the middle of these conversations, he received a cable from the State Department. Basing its conclusions on the assumption that the revolution was about over, the Department warned Stimson that his was not "in any sense" a mission of mediation. He was to take no initiative in seeking out the rebels and to hold no formal discussions. He was also to recognize that the United States hoped "to avoid . . . assuming the responsibility of supervising" the next election.

In reply, on April 19, Stimson reported that the actual military situation did not support the Department's optimistic view and stated that all his conversations indicated that the ultimate hope of peace rested upon "the absolute necessity" of supervising the 1928 elections. The Department, in return, accepted Stimson's view of things.[7]

From his continuing conversations Stimson reached several conclusions. Both sides were ready for peace, but neither side possessed the strength to achieve a dominant stabilizing position. American help was needed if an "indefinite succession of sanguinary revolutions" was to be avoided. This help could take the form of what he called "barren or naked American intervention" such as P. C. Knox had sponsored, from which Nicaragua could learn nothing. There was as an alternative a kind of intervention which would "endeavor to lead the country nearer to self-government." Such intervention would take the form of supervising elections. Not only was this philosophically sound, but it offered, he believed, the greatest in-

[7] Diary, April 20, 1927. The substance of the dispatches exchanged between Stimson and the State Department throughout the negotiations in Nicaragua is given in the Diary. Full texts may be found in *Papers Relating to the Foreign Relations of the United States, 1927*, 3 vols. (Washington, 1942), III.

ducement to the Liberals for settling the revolution. Their greatest fear was that Díaz would continue himself in office by controlling the next election.[8]

Acting on these assumptions, Stimson obtained Díaz' consent, on April 22, to six propositions. It was agreed that there should be an immediate grant of peace and amnesty, the opportunity for Liberals to participate in the existing government, the creation of a nonpartisan constabulary, trained by Americans, and the supervision of elections in 1928 and succeeding years by Americans. Using these proposals and Díaz' agreement as a basis for settlement, Stimson then turned to the Liberals. There followed ten days of complicated, continuing negotiations which revealed that the Liberals were prepared to accept every proposal except the continuation of Díaz in office. So firm were they in their insistence that the State Department suggested to Stimson "Even the elimination of Díaz as a last resort." He replied that the President of the United States had twice expressed his desire for a settlement worked out under Nicaraguan law and the Constitution. Stimson agreed with this proposition and therefore deemed the continuation of the duly constituted President indispensable to a wise solution. By his proposals Díaz would become "a mere figurehead" but his presence would underscore for Nicaraguans the integrity of the constitutional method and the continuities that could be achieved in constitutional government.[9]

But still some way had to be found to obtain Liberal agreement to the proposal. That way led past the politicians to the center of Liberal strength, the army commanded by General Moncada. On the morning of May 4, Stimson arose at five and set off for a place called Tipitapa. There under a thorn tree by a river he sat down alone to talk for one hour with Moncada. The military leader agreed in general with the settlement; he agreed to a constabulary under American control and admitted

[8] Diary, April 19, 1927.
[9] *American Policy in Nicaragua*, 64-72; Diary, April 22-May 2, 1927.

that no Nicaraguan could hope to pacify the country without the help of the United States. But he could not accept the retention of Díaz. It was a matter of honor; men had died on the battlefield because of this matter. For his part Stimson said the retention of Díaz was also a point of honor, the honor of the President and people of his own country which had recognized Díaz. They talked on. Moncada said he would not fight if the United States insisted. Stimson said he was authorized to insist. "If you will give me a letter," answered Moncada, "I will try to persuade my men."

Stimson withdrew to dictate a letter containing the terms, including a statement that general disarmament of both sides was a prerequisite for the peace. The sentence that Moncada especially desired stated that forces of the United States were authorized to take custody of all arms and to disarm forcibly those who would not voluntarily give up their weapons. Stimson then rejoined the General and for some time they discussed how the news should be broken to the troops. The conference then ended with an arrangement to meet again after Moncada had presented the propositions to his followers. In the meantime there would be no fighting.[10]

A week later they met under the "same old thorn tree." This time Moncada was accompanied by some political leaders who suggested that final settlement should await a plebiscite within the Liberal party. Stimson replied that he had waited three weeks "trying to talk with politicians and had gotten nowhere." He found it "very different talking to soldiers, and proposed to settle this with them." Turning to Moncada he arranged within a few minutes terms for the peace which were virtually the terms proposed in their first conversation. Next day he reported to the State Department that the document containing these terms had been signed by Moncada and eleven

[10] *American Policy in Nicaragua*, 78-79; Diary, May 4, 1927. This diary entry contains transcripts of the cables between Stimson and the State Department describing the armistice negotiations and terms.

of his twelve generals. "I believe," he concluded, "this marks definitely the end of the insurrection." [11]

On the following day Stimson went to the capital at Managua to receive a dove of peace and an honorary law degree from the University. Before crowds in a state of "wild jollity and excitement" he explained that the interest of the United States was that "here, as our friendly neighbor, there shall develop and grow up a successful, prosperous and happy nation devoted to peace and to the practice of orderly democracy and self-government. It is in that friendly spirit that the President of the United States has acted in what has been done here this month."

From Managua he drove out to Tipitapa to meet Moncada and his troops. To the soldiers he said: "I have come here to meet you and your officers today because I respect and admire you. Not only have you fought with bravery and devotion for the cause in which you believe but by your conduct since our meeting on May 4th you have demonstrated that you place the welfare of your country above any personal, party, or military success." Two days later, having informed the State Department that "the civil war in Nicaragua is now definitely ended," he embarked on the cruiser *Trenton* for home.[12]

Five weeks had passed between the time the President in the White House had asked him "to straighten the matter out" and the time when Stimson spoke in the tropic sunlight to the Liberal troops at Tipitapa. That interval, taken by itself, can stand as a wonderful small passage in the art of negotiation. By accurately calculating the play of rival forces in the situation, Stimson reached correct conclusions about what was possible. By stating the possible ends clearly and adhering to them without modification he gave, throughout, a firm base for negotiation. By creating, as before his juries, the gradual development of the feeling that he could be trusted, he facilitated

[11] Diary, May 11, 1927.
[12] Diary, May 16, 1927.

the acceptance of his intentions. These intentions, it will be recalled, were not only to stop the revolution, but to stop it in such a way that useful results would flow from the end of the conflict. His superior aims were to demonstrate that the essential continuities of self-government depended upon fair election and a respect for constituted authority. When he discovered that one of his aims, the recognition of the duly constituted Díaz, could not be achieved simply by discussion, he had the choice of giving it over or of retaining it by the use, real or implied, of force. The State Department, anxious to stop the revolution, indicated that as a last resort Díaz could be dispensed with. Stimson decided instead to make what he considered an indispensable point by demonstrating his willingness to use the force at his disposal. He thus brought off the resolution of the particular conflict within the exact context he had prescribed. The immense satisfaction he derived from these results, at the time, he revealed in the interesting statement he gave reporters at Norfolk on his way home. "We have succeeded," he said, "in quelling the bloodiest and cruelest revolution of modern times." Looking back on his work much later he said that he and Mrs. Stimson always felt that "hardly any single month in their lives was better spent."

' That month, taken by itself, yields the satisfaction that attends any dissonance nicely resolved. In any larger context it appeared to many people far less gratifying than to Stimson. Only eleven of Moncada's generals accepted the agreement reached at Tipitapa. The twelfth was Augusto Sandino. For six years this skillful, elusive man remained to fight from the jungle against Liberals and Conservatives and to excite the imagination and respect of those in America who wondered why United States Marines were still in Nicaragua. During the four years after the peace at Tipitapa 42 Marines and 3000 Nicaraguans were killed in the continuing action that began on the day after the peace was signed. These things happened, the St. Louis *Post-Dispatch* believed, because Stimson had "totally misjudged the Nicaraguan people." Eighty per cent of the country, in the opinion of Senator Borah, opposed the Peace of Tipitapa at the time. More temperate opinion held with the *New York Times* that "bad luck" had undermined an achievement of "the highest importance and promise." Sandino had been annoyed, it was said, because he had not been presented to Stimson. But it was in fact something more than mischance.[13]

The neat handiwork had been introduced into the middle of a disorderly situation that had persisted for a decade and a half. The first causes of the disorder were the economic and political immaturity of the countries of Central America. The United States had been directly associated with the unstable conditions in Nicaragua ever since Marines had been sent there, after a Nicaraguan request, during a revolution in 1912. By this association America had been caught up in a disturbing conflict of principle produced by its desire on the one hand for security in the Panama area, and its regard on the other for the sovereignty of small nations. In these circumstances the country could not bring itself to provide stability by "a thorough job of imperial administration," nor could it avoid the temptation to devise a "special recognition policy" in an effort to eradicate revolutionary activity in Nicaragua. It thus committed itself to a policy of what Lawrence Dennis called "in again, out again." In such a situation it was almost inevitable that neither Stimson nor anyone else could provide a fixed and permanent solution to the continuing problem. His neat arrangement, sound enough in theory, simply disintegrated in the immediately ensuing months, when it was discovered that the realities of American and Nicaraguan political life could not give it meaning.[14]

[13] *New York Times*, May 23, 1927; *Active Service*, 111.
[14] Lawrence Dennis, "Nicaragua: In Again, Out Again," *Foreign Affairs*, April 1931; St. Louis *Post-Dispatch*, Dec. 14, 1927; *New York Times*, July 27, 1927. There were, during the course of the negotiations and afterward, a good many people who did not like Stimson's handling of the situation. The greatest source of dissatisfaction lay in the anxiety over the means the American might

From his endeavors, however, came a possible basis for a constructive solution to the difficulties he had confronted. Though Sandino continued to disturb the population, the revolution that had engaged the whole country was stopped. The elections of 1928 and 1932 were held, as provided at Tipitapa, under the supervision of the United States and the results of these "fair-and-free" elections were accepted by the population. The training given the constabulary by the United States Marines, developed an efficient nonpartisan force. These things, in the opinion of one careful observer, "restored orderly self-government in Nicaragua, brought back peace and prosperity, and made it possible by 1931 to taper off the forces of occupation" ultimately withdrawn in 1933. In addition, Stimson had obtained the trust and respect of the leaders of both parties, as the cables, letters and visits to him in after years demonstrated. And for them he had stated in unmistakable terms the ultimate objective of his country — the creation in Nicaragua of a prosperous nation devoted "to the practice of orderly democracy and self-government." [15]

Shortly after his return to the United States he was offered a further opportunity to extend the practices of orderly democracy and self-government in a different, more remote territory. When Leonard Wood died in the summer of 1927, Calvin Coolidge had to appoint a new Governor General in the Philippine Islands. He thought, it is said, of General James G. Harbord, Jacob G. Schurman, General Frank McIntyre, Chief of the Bureau of Insular Affairs, ex-Senator James Wadsworth

---

use or did use to obtain his end. As early as May 9 the *New York Times* reported that government circles were "agitated" over whether Stimson used the threat of force. The continuing dissatisfaction over the settlement is well revealed in the debate over Senator Wheeler's resolution calling for a "sweeping inquiry" into the Nicaraguan situation. With a good many others he held that our Marines had "no business in Nicaragua." Such divisions at home made the steady support of any American policy in the Central American country virtually impossible.

[15] Bemis, *Latin American Policy*, 213.

and Henry Stimson. From among these he chose Stimson after two of the leading Philippine political figures, Manuel Quezon and Sergio Osmeña, urged his selection. Stimson accepted after the two, during a visit to New York, had assured him that they would work with him to give a stable constructive administration to the islands. Quezon in arguing his point reminded Stimson of his words as Secretary of War to Quezon in 1912 — that "he considered the promotion of the welfare of the Filipino people one of the grave national responsibilities of the United States." [16]

When the appointment was announced in December 1927, the general response was very favorable; only a few grumbled, like the St. Louis *Post-Dispatch* on December 14, that the new Governor General was "a man who has had exceptionable political preferment, but we aren't aware that he has distinguished himself in any of his numerous opportunities." Stimson himself shared, as usual, more of his opponents' forebodings than his supporters' confidence. As he set out in February with his wife and niece Eleanor Gamble he fell somewhat under the spell of Mrs. Stimson's mood. She was "always bored and depressed by a long sea voyage." On the *President McKinley* he read steadily about "the Philippine problem" and reached the conclusion, "I will require the patience of Job and the wisdom of a serpent and the help and blessing of the Lord to get through it without utter disaster." [17]

Though the task did not require quite such remarkable capacities or such impressive assistance, there were nevertheless difficulties. The organic law under which the Islands were administered was the Jones Act passed in 1916. It provided for an elected House and Senate with large legislative powers. Subject to the consent of the Senate, the Governor General, appointed by the President of the United States, had the power

[16] *New York Times*, Sept. 21, 28, 1927; Manuel L. Quezon, *The Good Fight* (New York, 1946), 140-45.
[17] H.L.S. to Mary Stimson, Feb. 18, 1928.

to appoint a great many of the local officials and, as well, the power to veto legislation and to supervise all departments and bureaus which were directly administered by Filipinos. To this act was affixed by the Democrats, as a kind of editorial comment on Republican attitudes, a preamble which extended a vaguely stated promise of eventual independence to the Islands.[18]

Under the Jones Act, two men had served as Governor General before Stimson. The first was Francis Burton Harrison, a sophisticated, imaginative and utterly charming man. He was also lethargic, or as one man said, "excruciatingly lazy." Partly from principle and partly from apathy he permitted the Filipinos from 1913 to 1921 to acquire more and more power over the government and the economy of the Islands. Believing completely in the justice of the Philippine claim for independence, he allowed Filipinos great freedom in the direction and misdirection of their affairs. As a result the system of American administration, built up under Republicans, disintegrated; the health services dwindled to the point where, in the opinion of many observers, the well-being of the community was endangered; and the finances and industrial structure were placed in precarious balance. As a result also the Filipinos tended to think more of the implied promise in the preamble of the Jones Act than of the procedures for American executive control presented in the Act itself. They tended to revere — indeed to love — Francis Burton Harrison. And it is quite possible that under his relaxed administration they discovered for themselves not only many of the pleasures but some of the perils and painful necessities of self-government.[19]

[18] Garel A. Grunder and William E. Livezey, *The Philippines and the United States* (Norman, Oklahoma, 1951), 154-56.
[19] Quezon, *The Good Fight*, 127-28; Maximo M. Kalaw, "Governor Stimson in the Philippines," *Foreign Affairs*, April 1929, 372-74. Quezon believed that future historians would discover that Harrison had made an "important contribution . . . to the policy which won for the United States the loyalty of the Filipino people." In the opinion of Stimson what he "wryly called 'the Harrison interlude'" produced only "disastrous consequences."

Into this situation in 1921 came Leonard Wood. By his energy and incisiveness he did much to restore the financial security of the territory and to place the health services on an effective operating base. He also acted to reduce the direct involvement of the government in the industries that had been established in his predecessor's time. By doing these things he took away much of the power of the Filipinos and returned to himself as Governor General the authority prescribed in the Jones Act. Partly because of what he did and partly because he was Leonard Wood he also antagonized most of the influential men in the government. From 1923 forward he acted without a cabinet because the legislature refused to confirm his appointments. For the next four years, although he achieved constructive results in economic and social areas, the political relationship between the United States and the Islands lay sterile — and something worse than sterile, for the relationship was disturbed constantly by irritating accusations and backbiting. This mission to the Philippines, when some things were pushed slowly forward against a sullen opposition and other things were decisively accomplished amid a cantankerous tumult, was unhappily appropriate to the career of Leonard Wood who never quite discovered how to fulfill himself or to satisfy others in the exertion of his own remarkable powers.

Thus things stood when Stimson arrived in the Islands on the first of March 1928. He arrived that day as the conservator of a great tradition. The foundations of that tradition had been laid by Elihu Root when he said in 1900 that the government about to be established in the Philippines was designed "not for our satisfaction or the expression of our theoretical views, but for the happiness, peace, and prosperity of the people of the Philippine Islands, and the measures adopted shall be made to conform to their customs, their habits, and even to their prejudices, to the fullest extent consistent with the accomplishment of the indispensable requisite of just and effective government." Just and effective government rested upon the rule of law and the maintenance of individual freedom which, in turn, rested upon certain principles that must be maintained even though they conflicted, in the first instance, with the laws of procedure and customs with which the Filipinos were acquainted.

To this tradition William Howard Taft had contributed when he reported in 1908 that "The national policy is to govern the Philippine Islands for the benefit and welfare and uplifting of the people of the Islands and gradually to extend to them, as soon as they shall show themselves fit to exercise it, a greater and greater measure of popular self-government. . . ."

To this tradition Stimson himself had added in 1912 when he wrote: "Until our work in the archipelago is completed, until the Filipinos are prepared not only to preserve but to continue it, abandonment of the Philippines, under whatever guise, would be an abandonment of . . . our responsibility to the Filipino people and of the moral obligations which we have voluntarily assumed before the world." In the spirit of this tradition Taft, Luke Wright and Cameron Forbes had acted as Governors General in earlier times, and in this spirit Stimson entered upon his new duties.[20]

Two ultimate objectives lay before him, he believed: First, to re-establish the government of the Islands as a cooperative enterprise. This meant the rehabilitation of the procedures and institutional forms that regulated the relationships between the executive and legislative branches of the government. Second, to rejuvenate the economic and industrial structure of the Islands. These points he made clear in his inaugural address delivered on the evening of the day he reached Manila. The speech with its description of "what we have to accomplish together," and its appeal for "the fullest possible measure of sympathetic and patient cooperation . . . under the organic law under which it is our joint duty to labor," set a tone which, in the opinion of the *Times*, may "go far in solving . . . difficult

[20] *Active Service*, 118-20; Grunder and Livezey, *Philippines*, 85.

problems." By his opening words, said a Filipino lawyer, he "gained our souls. He called us 'fellow countrymen.'" [21]

This was a good beginning, but as Stimson long ago had written to Winfred Dennison when the latter was serving on the staff of the Governor General in 1915, "after all, history is not often changed by speeches." "I am inclined," he had said, "to think your judgment is apt to err in seeing opportunities for speeches. The course of history is made up by a long patient series of humble acts which gradually form the opinion and character of a nation and not by dramatic utterances." Accordingly, on the day after his inaugural he set himself at a long, patient series of small and carefully designed acts. His purpose, at the outset, was to inform himself fully of the situation and to create in his constituents the feeling that he was trustworthy.

On March 2 at 11:30 in the morning he began the continuing conferences with his fellow countrymen that extended throughout his term of office. At that hour he met the two most powerful political figures in the Islands, Sergio Osmeña and Manuel Roxas. The third significant leader, Manuel Quezon, whom Stimson had visited in the hospital before he departed for his new office, lay ill in the United States of tuberculosis. The Governor General began by saying that he "did not intend to discuss" the question of independence. In fact, he "desired to draw the attention of the people here away from that thought to questions which were within my jurisdiction and were of practical importance." Others could freely debate the topic, but for himself it lay beyond the scope of his official powers, and in any case the "ultimate solution . . . would depend upon considerations far beyond the personal influence of either myself or of them." [22]

[21] *New York Times*, March 2, 1928. Stimson's fullest account of his own intentions and actions in the Philippines will be found in *Active Service*, Ch. 6, and in his *Annual Report of the Governor General of the Philippine Islands, 1928*, *House Document 133*, 71st Congress, 2nd Session.
[22] Diary, March 2, 1928.

With that out of the way, he stated his primary duty as he conceived it — "to protect the small man in the Islands." Unlike the United States, the Philippines possessed no educated, organized body of opinion to insure this purpose; it therefore devolved on the Governor General. Pursuant to this task it was necessary first to develop an effective executive office and the procedures that would enable the executive and the legislative branches to work closely together. Over a period of weeks Stimson, Osmeña and Roxas discussed cautiously how this aim could be achieved. One of the first needs in Stimson's mind was a staff of experts that would act as "the ears and eyes" of the Governor General. He made the point that if these experts, without administrative responsibility, could keep the Governor General informed of the needs and conditions of the government departments and bureaus, the Governor General could with confidence grant greater independence to the Filipino administration than if he were ignorant of conditions. A bill providing for such experts was before the American Congress while Stimson and the two Filipino political leaders discussed this matter. It had been opposed by the Filipinos because they feared the Governor General would use his experts as administrators to reduce the power of the Philippine Government. It had been opposed by many congressmen with ingenious arguments: it "casts reflection upon" the Congress and the Committee on Insular Affairs, and it was "an acknowledgement on the part of the committee and of the Congress of the United States that they are not sufficiently informed . . . to see what advice [presumably for the Governor General] is necessary." [23]

[23] Diary, March 2, 1928; *New York Times*, March 10, 1928; Washington *Star*, June 10, 1928; *House Report 771*, 2 parts, 70th Congress, 1st Session, Part 2, 1-2. Stimson, in the first five months in office, spent much of his time attempting to obtain the passage of the Kiess bill, the legislation designed to provide him with expert advisers. On March 24 in his cable No. 96 to Frank McIntyre, Chief of the Bureau of Insular Affairs, he urged the passage of the bill as "necessary." In letters to Arthur Page, March 21, 24, May 15, 1928, Page Papers, he sought ways to arouse men in the administration and in Congress to the support of the Kiess bill. In return he received assurances from the Secretary

If this bill failed, Stimson suggested that he might look to the Philippine legislature for money to obtain his experts. Once that had been done he would consider other ways to improve the executive-legislative relationship. He would appoint cabinet members, as Wood had not done, from the majority party; he would consider revivifying the Council of State, abolished by Wood, in which sat the Governor General, the Cabinet, and leaders of the legislative houses. He would like to try out his old project of having cabinet members sit in the legislature with the right to speak and the duty to answer questions. These were the political proposals Stimson, Osmeña and Roxas cautiously examined in the first months of Stimson's tenure.

With equal caution a set of economic proposals was also discussed. Together the three men investigated the possibility of diversifying crops, means to attract capital for electrical development, and ways to withdraw the banks and industrial corporations from the control of the national government and place them directly in private hands. Out of these talks Stimson discovered three things. Filipinos, for one thing, feared the large private corporation. Seeking to allay these anxieties, he told them of his work as a United States Attorney and explained the progress of "customer and employee ownership in the United States and of the change of standards of corporate management during the past twenty years." He also discovered the fear the Filipinos had of any reorganization of the land-holding procedures. At the time, no individual was permitted to own more than about thirty-two acres. This rigid limitation was the product of the Filipinos' experience with the large landowners, ecclesiastical and private, in the days of Spanish control. Any threat to the system of limitation raised the threat of domination. Yet all of Stimson's proposals for economic development involved

of War that the Department was "strongly in favor of enactment" (Dwight Davis to Arthur Page, March 29, 1928, Page Papers), but the opposition in the Congress was too great to overcome. Stimson had to obtain his end by other means to be described later.

necessarily some liberalization of these procedures. Finally, he discovered that the resentment against America was not a fabrication of a few contentious political figures designed to fill local political needs. To his surprise he found it derived in considerable part from a national racial sensitivity that "entered into all administrative problems."

As the first weeks passed, the discussions were broadened. Every day Stimson talked with officials and private citizens in his office; he became acquainted with the situation in each department of the government and with the nature of the difficulties of daily life in the Islands. He learned about rinderpest, leprosy, the effect of the marriage laws on the non-Christian tribes, the dreadful state of interallied shipping, the condition of the beef butchered in Manila. He discovered that 300,000 parcels of land were tied up in court by the law's delays, that the local market in pineapples was dead, that in Ifugaos the culture of rice was advanced, that in Solo there was trouble over fish traps. From the trips he took in the first four months — to Baguio and Cebu and round about the Islands — he also learned much. And in these first months he was determined not so much to act as to learn. He did not call the special session of the legislature as suggested to him; he did not set up the Philippine Research Institute — for study in biology, physics, chemistry and mathematics — when he discovered acquiescence rather than enthusiasm; he did not remove officials whose efficiency he suspected. He told them instead that he "was not satisfied," but would not act until he "personally [knew] more by actual observation" and urged them to "start afresh." [24]

But there were certain things he did do. He talked in his office to Filipinos alone, without the white man Wood had always had with him as a witness. When he heard his own church had refused membership to a Filipino he explained to the clergy that

---

[24] Evidence for these paragraphs was taken from Diary entries throughout March-June 1928; H.L.S. to Arthur Page, May 15, 1928, Page Papers; *New York Times*, June 2, 1928.

this "made a very unpleasant impression upon me" and wor-
shiped from then on at the Episcopal church. After reviewing
the Philippine cadets, he dropped into the rifle butts with them
and fired five rounds of five shots, scoring 5-4-3-4-5. When
the time came to open Malacañan for the social occasions expected from a Governor General, it was opened to Americans
and Filipinos alike. This, said Osmeña, was the best improvement made in the Palace during the Stimson Administration.
And when the Filipinos came, Mrs. Stimson, who had painstakingly learned the steps, danced the ancient *rigodon* with the
party leaders and with the Governor General, who had learned
the steps not quite so well. On all these occasions, public and
private, informal and official, Stimson said very clearly what he
was in the Islands to try to accomplish, what he would do, what
he would not do, and what he would have to think about before
he decided what to do.[25]

By these means he built up in the early months of his term a
reservoir of good will and confidence. As the astute and experienced Henry Misselwitz reported to the *Times* on March 18,
"the conservative manner in approaching the Governor General's tasks is reacting in a sound sense of security and desire to
cooperate . . ." There were among the Filipinos of both major
parties "staunch supporters," and in the businessmen "feelings of

[25] Diary, March 15, 27, 1928, Feb. 21, 1929; H.L.S., *Annual Report*, 2; *Active
Service*, 138-39. William Howard Taft wrote Stimson on May 18, 1928, "The
more you open Malacañan the better they will like it. They are a lovable
people . . . hospitality is part of the order of their being." It is quite probable,
however, that the opening of Malacañan and the other efforts of the Stimsons
to meet the Filipinos on equal terms did more than minister to the Filipino
sense of hospitality. Their acts and attitudes did much to reduce whatever
feelings of racial inferiority the Filipinos had hitherto felt or been made to feel.
How acutely sensitive the population of the Islands was on this point Stimson,
as he said, had not at first understood. Edgar Crossman, who served in the
Philippines with both Stimson and General Douglas MacArthur, reached the
conclusion that Americans from the beginning never understood how greatly
the question of race troubled the relations between this country and the Islands.
He also believed that the influence of Quezon derived in no small part from
the fact that, alone of the native leaders, he was three-quarters Spanish and
therefore had a hold over the population which retained much of its orientation
toward Spain.

amity." Stimson's thoroughgoing, though comparatively slow methods were meeting general approval.

Five months after he arrived, Stimson had an opportunity to test the strength and extent of this general approval. In the elections of June, which turned exclusively, Osmeña told him, on the issue of cooperation with the Governor General, the Nationalistic Party, committed to a program of cooperation, obtained a large majority of the seats in the legislature. This favorable result added greatly to the growing satisfaction Stimson had taken in his work as the weeks passed. Some of his pleasures were small and unexpected. "I can never," he wrote Aunt Kitty, "realize I am Governor General and an Oriental Potentate." It was a constant surprise to find in the domestic scene that "all I have to do is express a wish and it is taken as the law of the Medes and Persians." For a man who had come to want what he wanted when he wanted it, as a good many successful men no doubt come to do, this was a source of some gratification. So also were the dinners and receptions of the Palace. Not only were they justified by the demands of official duty, but also they fitted nicely into the organized form within which social intercourse could safely be pursued. And then the demands of official duty were not too exacting; always at the end of an afternoon there was time for two or three sets of tennis with the niece who had come along "to exercise Uncle Henry" or a round of golf with members of his staff.[26]

These staff members found the Governor General, in his predictability, easy to work with, save on the occasions when the steady routines were punctuated by moments of wrath, sometimes justified, sometimes inexplicable. They found that on trips of inspection the Governor General was tireless in the field, uncomplaining over primitive modes of transport or housekeeping, skillful at the art of climbing, and lost in rapture when possessed of rod or gun. They noticed also that while their superior was thoughtful and unquestioningly generous in all matters con-

[26] Diary, June 11, 1928; *New York Times*, June 7, 8, 10, 1928.

nected with money, he found it hard — indeed impossible — to concede a five-inch putt. Losing, especially in small contests, was in fact not something the Governor General did very well. Once a thoughtful aide, after hearing his chief speak frequently of his interest in tennis, arranged a game for him with a member of the Philippine Davis Cup Team. After the contest there were a few black and silent hours in the gardens of Malacañan.

But, for the most part, miscalculations of this kind did not interfere with the satisfying routines of the day. When the day was over, the staff discovered, the Governor General was wont to withdraw into the rather solemn privacy of his own quarters to review the day's events with his wife and niece. Mrs. Stimson had, inevitably, less to keep her occupied than did her husband. She traveled with him on his inspection trips, spent "a good deal of her time seeing the native life of the Philippines," assumed with her usual trepidation and organizing ability the duties as hostess, learned the local rituals and wore the traditional evening dresses, but, though always "gracious," she had little skill or desire to fit easily into a different way of life from that she knew. Besides she was very lonely, out of the familiar context of Highhold, and suffered much while in the Islands from physical discomfort and occasional illness. Yet, as always, she did faithfully and efficiently the things required of her by her husband and her husband's position.

This was not more than he expected. He brought to his task a mixture of feelings — a small but persistent sense of self-sacrifice, a far larger and equally persistent sense of solemn duty and obligation, and a wholly gratifying but carefully guarded elation that the call of duty coincided in this instance so precisely with the possibility of doing what he loved to do. These feelings he presumed extended naturally and identically to all those around him. He found it difficult to believe that those working with him were not acting a little irresponsibly if they went off to a club for casual entertainment in the evening while he took to his own quarters; he found it very near to a breach of faith if aides he had appointed and relatives he had brought with him fell into the human condition of love with its attendant occasional distractions while he and his wife stood faithfully at their positions on the far ramparts of their country. Things like this caused him to brood over "the strain and pressure of matters inside and outside the government, some expected and some unexpected."

There were times even in the Philippines, as everywhere else, when he felt with Job that his troubles were really more than he could bear. But these were brief moments. As he wrote to Allen Klots, "I had [as Secretary of War under Taft] a chief to fall back upon, a well-organized non-political department, and plenty of wise friends close at hand. Here I have none of these, and everything I say or do, and many things that I do not say or do, are under fierce scrutiny all the time. So far as support from Washington is concerned, it is so far away as to seem negligible." These things, coupled with the fact that Coolidge had given him no instructions, made the "sense of responsibility here infinitely keener" than it had ever been before. Such considerations, unlike the smaller matters, were not troubling at all. He had, in the Islands, come out from under the shadows of older, taller men, the chiefs to fall back upon, like his father, Theodore Roosevelt, William Howard Taft and Elihu Root. In accepting and discharging the infinitely keener responsibility to be found in a remote archipelago he had become, no doubt with shouts of momentary anger and brief morose indulgence in his own ordinary troubles, very much his own man.

The June elections had created a cooperative spirit in the Islands, but it was not yet clear what the Governor General and the legislature were going to cooperate in doing. Before the legislative body met, Stimson held a series of conferences with Osmeña and Roxas to develop a proposed program of legislation. He began by stating that his purpose in coming out was to organize the executive branch of the government so that it would be efficient and still increase the autonomy of the departments. To this end he needed in his staff technical advisers who would investigate the needs of the Islands and the ability of the departments to fulfill those needs. The failure of the Kiess bill in the United States Congress had prevented him from obtaining these advisers. Therefore, he said, the Filipino government must supply them. So strongly did he feel about this that, he told Osmeña, he would "withhold all future steps," including the appointment of cabinet officers, until the legislature provided him with the money to obtain advisers. Filipino public opinion was at least cool to this proposal, placed before the legislature as the Belo bill. There was a fear that the appropriated money might be misused and a greater fear that future Governors General might, through the advisers, build up an arbitrary "super-cabinet." Stimson firmly insisted that nothing would be done until the Belo bill passed and, thus stimulated, Osmeña and Roxas took it through the legislature in the first week of August. They were greatly aided by the efforts made by Stimson to allay suspicion. As he said: "The evident purpose of the statute is to provide for the employment of men whose duties will not be administrative . . . but will be limited to giving advice upon technical matters. . . . Administration is placed by law in other hands, namely in the heads of the six executive departments and their subordinates. To attempt to form a super-cabinet of administrators with this appropriation would be . . . clearly illegal." [27]

The passage of the bill was well received by the Manila press. The Philippine *Herald* said on August 9 that the Governor General's statement "will undoubtedly set at ease the minds of those who held misgivings." The *Daily Bulletin* on the same day called it "more than a law. It is a declaration and application of principles of government. It is a realization of things talked of." The *Tribune* also on the same day was prepared to accept the prophecy that the Belo bill was an important step toward responsible government in the Philippines, "simply because Stimson is Stimson."

With this issue out of the way the organization of the execu-

[27] Diary, July 3, 27, Aug. 8, 1928; *New York Times*, July 26, Aug. 10, 1928; Grunder and Livezey, *Philippines*, 180 ff.

tive branch and the development of mechanisms to increase co-operation between the legislative and executive branches went rapidly forward. A cabinet was appointed from the majority party; the principle of permitting cabinet officers to appear and speak in the legislature was confirmed; the Council of State created by Harrison and abolished by Wood was reconstituted. It included with members of the executive branch leaders from the two chambers of the legislature. Unlike Harrison, however, Stimson made it perfectly clear that this was an advisory body and not an executive agency. As a further step in his program Stimson brought over from the United States Edgar Crossman, a lawyer, and Earl B. Schwulst, a banker, as his first two expert assistants under the Belo law. By October the reconstitution of legislative-executive relationships was well advanced.[28]

During these same months Stimson was busy also at his second purpose — the development of the Philippine economy. In a message to the legislature he put forward a plan to attract private capital by changing the laws controlling corporate behavior, banking procedure and landholding. Most of these laws, he argued, had been introduced thirty years before from an America inexperienced in the direction of industrial development. They were now antiquated. Stimson's admitted conviction that attraction of private capital from the United States was the way to improve economic conditions and his interest in altering the land laws disturbed many observers. To allay these anxieties he revealed his willingness to move slowly toward his objectives. He was content to introduce a private public-service company to work alongside the government-owned utility as a demonstration of the benefits to be obtained. He was also clear in his

[28] H.L.S., *Annual Report*, 7-8; Grunder and Livezey, *Philippines*, 186; *New York Times*, Sept. 1, 1928. The meetings of the Council of State were not always devoted to immediate affairs of state. At times, after gathering the officials about him to discuss "policy," the Governor General would turn the meeting, according to Edgar Crossman, into a seminar on the development of democratic government. Going back to Magna Carta he would come up, in a series of "almost set lectures," through the evolving liberties of freeborn Englishmen and Americans.

conviction that private companies manufacturing rubber, for instance, should not be given the opportunity to create huge plantations. He desired only to make it possible, as a beginning, to hold somewhat larger parcels of land on short-term leases and to organize private farms more efficiently around a series of processing plants or centrals, as they were called.[29]

This economic program, reduced to laws liberalizing the restrictions on corporate financial practices and on property-holding procedures, became the primary concern of the legislature in the fall and early winter of 1928. Osmeña, Roxas and Quezon, who had returned from the States in July, worked out acceptable legislation in conference with the Governor General and bore the brunt of getting it through the legislature. This was not always an easy task. As the Philippine *Herald* said, there were a good many who believed the attempt to rejuvenate the Islands by outside (i.e., American) private enterprise was "premature" and "private operation of the public services was not the only way to improvement." What was needed was an "opportunity for self-improvement if there is to be growth and progress in the government." [30]

Reservations of this kind were strongly enough held in all political parties to reduce the modifications proposed in the bills to first steps rather than radical changes. Even so, opposition persisted. By amendment, attempts were made to emasculate the provisions in the corporation law designed to encourage investment. Delays over this amendment lasted until Osmeña came to Stimson in some uncertainty about whether he could proceed. The Governor General gave him his word of honor that the bill as drawn "in my opinion" would not violate the policy of the

---

[29] *New York Times*, July 17, 1928; *Active Service*, 140-42; H.L.S., *Annual Report*, 4-5; Diary, Sept. 21, 22, 24, 26.
[30] "Stimson Shows His Hand," *Nation*, Oct. 31, 1928. This article quoted the Philippine *Herald* and lent its own support to the argument that Stimson's "theories" might well blight independent Philippine economic development. Opposition to Stimson's ideas, the article continued, had been dulled because the "political leaders, appetites whetted by the sniff of political favors, seem to swallow any scheme. . . ."

existing land laws and would protect them. The time had come, he went on, when timid Filipinos had to trust somebody; suspicion and imaginary difficulties could no longer postpone action. The corporation act passed and shortly after the laws designed to establish a firmer banking structure also passed.[31]

In the course of the months of discussion over this legislative program Stimson and the Filipino leaders got to know each other very well. Respect and friendship between them all naturally and inevitably grew. With the Quezons Stimson had perhaps the closest association. Mrs. Quezon began to call him *mi viejo*, my old man, the affectionately informal greeting used from time to time for one's father. As the relationship with all these men and women ripened, the conversation between them turned, as Stimson had said it would not in his term of office, upon the inevitable subject of independence. In the closing months of his tenure such talk was spurred on by the introduction of the Timberlake Resolution to the United States Congress.

The intent of this resolution was to limit the amount of sugar imported duty-free from the Philippines, an intent which struck fear into the heart of every thinking Filipino and which, if consummated, would undermine the whole Stimson program. Once, in discussing this resolution, Quezon burst out with the assertion that if the United States would try to hold the Islands by force and yet deprive them of their major market, "he would quit politics and go home and teach his boy to be a rebel." Such an attitude upon the part of America, said Stimson, was "contrary to our whole history" from 1776 forward. On the other hand, the thing he feared was that Congress, remembering the long-continued demands for immediate independence by Filipinos, would at the behest of American special interests give the Filipinos immediate independence and "disregard the real harm and cruelty which this would do to them." And Quezon, Stim-

31 Diary, Nov. 3, 5, 8, 1928; Kalaw, "Governor Stimson," *Foreign Affairs*, April 1929, 378.

son recalled, replied, "If I could get a dominion government with free trade advantages, I would do so at the price of giving up all agitation for independence for thirty years. . . ." To which Stimson himself responded that, as Quezon knew, his "dearest hope [was for] a permanent connection between the Philippine Islands and the United States," but the time for "caveman methods" had passed. "It must be brought about on a basis of honorable marriage where," he went on, "the Islands like a woman are persuaded that it is for their best interest. . . ." [32]

Again and again they returned to this topic in the last days of Stimson's administration. One night at Malacañan, after dinner, Quezon walked up and down the porch in the moonlight saying, "What we need more than anything else is certitude. What we need more than independence is the knowledge that the situation as it now exists or could be made to exist will continue to exist. We are constantly being subject to changing administrations in Washington, changing attitudes on the part of the American people, changing procedures on the part of American businessmen here. Give us certainty and we will take dominion status. Give us certainty and we will take a dependent status. But for heaven's sake let's get organized so we can run the thing with some assurance that it will continue to run for a while and forget the independence issue." Then said he ruefully, "Like your President T.R. — if you quote me on this, I will say you lie." [33]

Certitude, some assurance that the thing would continue to run for a while, was not within the gift of the Governor General. As there were Filipinos in the Islands who distrusted attempts to stabilize their economy by the efforts of outside private enterprise, or who had a natural pride and trust in their own capacity to govern themselves, so there were Americans at home who were convinced — some by concern for special in-

[32] Diary, Jan. 6, 7, 1929.
[33] Conversation with Edgar Crossman, May 18, 1955.

terests, some by desire for votes, and some by the feeling that in the Philippines their country had stumbled and sinned in the dark — that the Islands should be given up. Among all these conflicts of interest and desire, the continuation of settled policy by any means was, in fact, impossible. What Stimson could do because he was Stimson, he did do. He re-established, by all the available evidence, "harmony and cooperation"; he awakened the people to the economic problem; he obtained the services of prominent Americans in improving health and education; he took the first step in a program of economic development; he reconstructed sound relations between the executive and the legislative branches. In so doing he laid the foundations for constructive administrations of the same kind that might follow.

For these things he obtained the gratitude of many in the Islands and at home. In the Philippines, as Roxas said in introducing him for the last time to a legislature that stood cheering, his accomplishments strengthened confidence in the altruistic purposes of America and laid the foundations for responsible government. In America, as the *New York Times* reported, most interested observers would conclude that his had been "a brilliant administration."

On February 23, 1929, the Governor General and his wife were driven on a "triumphal ride" from Malacañan to the pier. On either side were cheering crowds. At the dockside Quezon gave him a flag of his office and Roxas gave him a flag of the Islands. All the whistles blew at two o'clock throughout the city. Ten thousand "friendly brown faces" lined the pier to catch "a last glimpse" of the Governor General. As the *President Pierce* moved out into the stream he left behind "a happy year," a "job well done," and the last enchantments of the nineteenth century.[34]

[34] *Active Service*, 144-45; *New York Times*, Feb. 24, 1929.

18

The Secretary of State

THE BODY POLITIC apparently, like men and women, may succumb to the illness fashionable at the time. When, for instance, the Czar told Sir Hamilton Seymour that Turkey was a sick man, the country seemed down with the chronic invalidism that was so much in the Victorian vogue. The illness of the great powers after Versailles was of the modern kind; its etiology had been first clearly described in 1917 by the eminent contemporary physician in Vienna. Patients who had been exposed to severe personal shock sought to escape from unbearable reality. "They give the impression," he said, "that they are fixed to a particular point in the past, that they don't know how to release themselves from it. . . ." By this process the sick people tried to find refuge in some quiet corner of their earlier experience, to use responses that had worked successfully in better times. Ordinarily these fixed and obsolete responses proved unavailing against the existing painful reality. Therefore the patients took flight into carefully constructed illusions. These illusions, carrying images that would gratify the desires or allay the terrible anxieties, were designed to insulate patients from an awareness of what was actually happening to them. They thus served to prevent the sick people from learning anything about their environment or from doing anything useful to change their situation. As the physician said, men and women who responded to shock in this way were "alienated from both the present and the future"; they were, he said in one of his striking images, "marooned in their own illness."

The illness in which the powers of Western society lay in the decade after Versailles was, apparently, of this same order. Shocked by the force they had let loose upon themselves and by the conditions produced by the war, they fell back upon certain attitudes fixed in their past — *la sécurité*, masterful inactivity, isolation from the world's affairs. They sought also to organize the new and dangerous world by using many of the familiar methods that had served in a quieter past — reparations, balanced budgets, the gold standard and, in time, systems of balancing powers. When these attitudes and methods proved insufficient for the task at hand, the nations withdrew from danger by converting what at first had been a hope into an illusion. The illusion was that since no nation could face the prospect of further war, all nations were ready to accept the existing peace and that peace could be held together indefinitely by a new energy that would displace the force of arms. This new energy, deriving from a kind of universal conscience, was called world opinion. "What we rely upon," said Robert Cecil in 1919, "is public opinion. . . ." "The truth is," Sir John Simon told the House of Commons in 1932, "that when public opinion, world opinion, is sufficient to pronounce a firm moral condemnation, sanctions are not needed." So world opinion would make itself felt in discussion — in words that could be used to organize and support the peace.

What followed therefore, as Sumner Welles said, was a decade of endless conference — at Genoa, at Locarno, at Spa, at London, at Washington, at — most of all — Geneva. In what Flandin called *"l'atmosphère ouatée des Conciles,"* men talked as though they had the will and power to arrange a set of new conditions for Western society. They talked of many important things — money, geography, guns, boundaries, the flow of goods. Some few things they did settle. But when the talk reached topics that could not be resolved by the application of world opinion — topics having to do with national interests or national attitudes fixed at points in the past — then, to protect the faith in the illusion, things were left unsettled. After years of discussion for instance, a schedule for disarmament was at last drawn up, but the quotas for each nation were left blank.

As time passed and dangers left uncontrolled persisted, the nations, to protect themselves from further shock, drove ever deeper into their verbal universe. The talk became, in certain circumstances, more frank and positive. The nations were very clear, for instance, about the exact number of cruisers a country without money would be allowed to build if it had money. Then too, in desperation, they began to reaffirm things they had so frequently affirmed before. War, renounced as an instrument of policy in 1919, was at Paris ten years later specifically re-renounced.

By these procedures the sustaining illusions were held intact while, apparently, only the meaning of words was altered. By these procedures also was produced what Frank Simonds called the "simulacrum of a peace," and what Gustav Stolper thought of as an Age of Fable. Never in history, Winston Churchill remarked, had there been a period "when the gap between the kind of words statesmen used and what was actually happening in many countries was so great as now."

The pathology of this condition was recognized by some observers. There was the question, as Alice had said, "whether you *can* make words mean so many different things." It was, in fact, surprising how often these observers turned to the works of Lewis Carroll when they tried to explain to themselves what was going on around them. And indeed the peace signed in the Hall of Mirrors did seem, at times, sustained by manipulations of the looking glass. But those who perceived these things were not in charge of matters; they were, like Simonds or Stolper, detached students of events, or public figures like Winston Churchill, excluded by their perception from positions of responsibility. Those called to do business with this world had perforce to share, at least in part, in the sustaining illusions. If they were to hold the particular scheme of things together, they had, like any public servants, to accept the primary assumptions. Men at the conference tables had to fall in with certain attitudes fixed to particular points in the past, to concede the existence and power of world opinion, to acquiesce in the forcibility of right words. They had to accept these things to get a hearing at the tables. But by the same token such acceptance meant that no man in office would have it in his power to change conditions very much, to close the gap between what was being said and what was actually happening. Willy-nilly he would get caught up in the effort to maintain, by the only methods that could be agreed upon, the simulacrum of a peace.

As the year 1929 opened, Stimson was summoned from the Islands in the Pacific to take a hand in ordering the affairs of this world. On January 25 he received a cable from his law partner George Roberts informing him that the President-elect was considering him for either the Department of Justice or the Department of State. Stimson replied that he would not accept the former, but he would be willing to become Secretary of State because it might give him an opportunity to supply "a permanent solution" to the problem of the relationship between the United States and the Philippines. A month later he left the Islands and a month after that, on March 28, he took the oath of his new office before his old friend Chief Justice William Howard Taft.[1]

Herbert Hoover is said to have considered at least twenty men and to have offered the position to three others before turning to the Governor General of the Philippines. The reasons for the choice, besides Stimson's record and reputation, were the support of Root, Hughes and Taft and the fact that the President wanted a New Yorker in the Cabinet.[2]

[1] George Roberts to H.L.S., Jan. 25, 1929; *Active Service*, 155-56.
[2] Conversation with Arthur Page, March 18, 1955; Robert H. Ferrell, *American Diplomacy in the Great Depression* (New Haven, 1957) 35, note 4.

When the appointment was announced both the record and the reputation were subjected to careful scrutiny. Those who looked upon him as "the evangel of meddling in Nicaragua" felt that almost no one would be "less likely to allay South American distrust." Others asserted that there was ground for concern because "he is an internationalist in the same sense that Mr. Root and Mr. Hughes are internationalists." Yet, apart from his views and the feeling, as *The Nation* said, that he was "not a great man," there were reasons to approve of the appointment. It was very generally agreed that by his experience and knowledge he was better qualified for the office than most of his predecessors, and it was agreed also that he was "extremely able" and "of fine character." "When you think of him," said Harold Stokes, "you think of words that are the sport of cynics, like 'duty' and 'service.' Through his career the 'Stern Daughter of the Voice of God' has stood by his elbow laying on him the compulsion she laid on men of old." [3]

The first thing the new Secretary of State had to do after taking his oath of office was to get better acquainted with his President. Though they had known each other casually for ten years they had never worked together and really knew very little about each other. The President undertook to correct this situation by asking Stimson to spend the ten days after he assumed office with him at the White House. The spirit of the place had changed somewhat from the days when Archie Butt beguiled a summer evening for Taft and Stimson by playing records on the Victrola. The day began with the cheerless ritual of medicine ball and went on to a "disorganized" breakfast during which two big dogs climbed all over the President and ate, from time to time, off his plate. In the evenings there were long and earnest conversations about affairs of state.

In these talks the President revealed "what one might call temperamental impatience on his part." This impatience ex-

[3] Louisville *Courier*, Feb. 7, 1929; Kansas City *Star*, Feb. 8, 1929; St. Louis *Post-Dispatch*, Feb. 14, 1929; *New York Times*, Feb. 17, 1929.

tended through all things — from his desire to get the new Secretary on the job at once to his anxiety to lose as little time as possible on personal necessities. Try as Stimson did in those ten days, he never succeeded in changing his clothes after medicine ball as rapidly as the President did; he was "quicker than anybody . . . in or out of the Army." The mind of the President was also quick, quick to acquire new information and amazingly quick in organizing it. He knew little of the Philippines and rather shocked his guest by asking at the outset, "How long must we keep the Islands in order to do our duty to them?" But by the end of the visit, prodded by his guest and fortified by further study and reflection, the President had acquired a good deal of information and "As usual he brought some new and unusual viewpoints to the problem . . . after he got interested in it." [4]

Out of these ten days grew a mutual respect, meticulously defined when each spoke in public about the other in after years. They trusted each other's intentions and they trusted each other's word. But the ten days did not make them comfortable in each other's company. They were in fact quite different, with a difference that had been made clear early in their acquaintance. In 1917 Hoover, at Frankfurter's suggestion, had sought out Stimson to be his legal adviser in the Food Commission. Stimson, already in uniform, had, in refusing, explained why he felt "in honor" that he had to bear arms in the conflict he had advocated. This point of view, he discovered, "I couldn't make [Hoover] understand." "Very much put out," the Food Administrator replied, "You can kill a great many more Germans if you help me than you can alone as a single man in the war." [5]

He was attracted by such calculations, by the possibility of stating situations as problems in the economy of forces. When Hoover talks of "judicial machinery," Taft said, "he thinks it's

[4] Diary, Aug. 28, 1930.
[5] Transcript of H.L.S.-McGeorge Bundy conversation, May 29, 1946.

machinery." Like so many other men in his profession he proceeded in the belief that by the application of logical systems, by deductions from the measurable, statistically accountable data, the important matters in life could be held in place. Given the obvious and appropriate assumptions — as to why one dug ore or whether the starving should be fed — and given also the reliable data — as the thickness of the overburden or the consumption of wheat per man per day — this method of attack when used by a resourceful, powerful mind had brought to pass remarkable results, indeed, on occasion, miracles. This much was obvious in January 1929.

It was obvious also that a President in 1929 was confronted by larger tasks than those presented to a mining engineer, or a Food Administrator, or a Secretary of Commerce. The given assumptions to work from — about the place of the country in the world, about the nature of free enterprise — were subject to qualification and modification by public events and attitudes. The necessary data — the value of common stocks, the French spirit, the feelings of hungry men who could not be fed — were frequently more difficult to obtain and, at times, almost impossible to interpret. What a mind trained to calculate from known causes to measurable effects would do amid the imponderables of Presidential responsibility was not clear in 1929.

It was clear, however, that Herbert Hoover knew a great deal about a great many things, that he possessed an orderly, powerful intelligence, and that he derived his greatest satisfactions from organizing and building. His whole life had been dedicated to the release and control of energy in support of productive purposes. Something else was also clear: he was a figure at a distance, he had "a curious offish manner." This was ascribed, as it so often is, to "extraordinary shyness." It was also, perhaps, the product of his own method. To make his equations work it had been necessary, frequently, to exclude the awkward variables and unknowns of human response. Thus "you can kill more Germans" by other means; or, what is "our duty" to the

Islands, figured in months? For all its constructive urges, for all its decent commitments, there was something too statistical, something bleak and denatured in the spirit Herbert Hoover brought to bear on experience.

The limits placed upon a Secretary of State are in the first instance determined by his President, but there are other influences at work. One of these is the United States Senate and, particularly, the Chairman of the Senate Committee on Foreign Relations. In 1929 the Chairman was William E. Borah of Idaho. To him, upon Stimson's appointment, the *Outlook* extended its sympathy. "After all his service to Herbert Hoover," the magazine said, he was confronted by a Secretary of State whom he looks upon "as an imperialist and interventionist." Precisely what Borah's own views were at any given moment was harder to tell. He had made himself into a remarkable and unstable compromise between his provincial opinions, odd personal crotchets and fine intelligence. But he did have an abiding suspicion of Europe, a profound desire for peace and a settled conviction that any alliance would entangle this country in trouble not of its own making. In these views he fairly represented what most men in public life thought most Americans thought about foreign affairs on the occasions when they turned their minds to the subject. "Aloofness," as Anne O'Hare McCormick said, "is the attitude of our passionate choice." Our rejection of the League of Nations, she went on, "our readiness to give, lend, advise, but never to join is the struggle of a long isolated and independent people to evade to the last the political consequences of the rise to world power." Yet there was also a "vague but powerful emotion for peace, our strongest mass sentiment and a dim hankering for moral leadership. . . ." [6]

Within the frame of these views, so faithfully represented in Congress by the Chairman of the Senate Committee on Foreign Relations, and so fully accepted by the President of the United States, Stimson had to work out his policies when he entered the

[6] *Outlook*, Feb. 27, 1929, 340; *New York Times*, Dec. 5, 1929.

Department of State. It was, in 1929, a department that as Frank Simonds said, "we have never thought . . . was very important." The yearly budget was $15 million, or one-fortieth the sum of money given to the armed forces. The men in the foreign service were, as Simonds said, members of a "sweated industry," with the morale of men in such an industry. Underpaid, understaffed, hobbled by "antiquated organization," "bureaucratic traditions" and "lack of leadership," men in the Department, said the *New York Times*, "suffered grievously from the negative tradition . . . cherished for many years." In Washington there were not, it was asserted, very many "first-rate men," indeed not many men at all. In the whole Department there were, including everybody from the Secretary to chauffeurs, clerks, stenographers, and janitors, six hundred souls in 1929. And the few Foreign Service officers on duty had been trained too often in the limiting technical procedures of diplomacy. In 1929 there was, for instance, no one capable of giving sound advice on economic matters to the Secretary.[7]

Believing that he could not look to such an organization for help in more than routine affairs Stimson set about creating his own staff. He brought in with him, to the irritation of a good many observers inside and outside the Department, his military aide in the Philippines, Eugene Regnier. Regnier was a charming man, but a soldier ill-acquainted with the world of diplomacy. He was not, by the nature of his position or his understanding, empowered to assist in matters of policy, but the fact that he was constantly at the side of a Secretary who was very fond of him gave his word a real or suspected weight that disturbed more properly authorized counselors. Far more important was the contribution of another man Stimson appointed. The obvious and frequently reported choice for Undersecretary was William R. Castle, a career diplomat, then acting as Assistant

[7] Boston *Herald*, March 24, 1929; *Annual Report*, Civil Service Commission (Washington, 1929); Hearings Before the Subcommittee of the House Committee on Appropriations, 71st Congress, 2nd Session; *New York Times*, March 16, 1929.

Secretary for European Affairs. But Stimson, as always, wanted a man he knew well, a lawyer, and probably a graduate of the Harvard Law School as his chief assistant. So Felix Frankfurter and George Roberts were asked to find a man, on the theory that anyone who appealed to both of them would be remarkable. One day Frankfurter proposed Joseph Cotton to Roberts, who expressed his doubt that Cotton would even consider the position. But the offer was made and, surprisingly, Cotton accepted.

The qualifications of this gifted man were indeed remarkable. Professor Joseph Beal had said that the class of 1900 at the Harvard Law School was the best that had ever graduated and "Joseph Cotton was without any doubt whatever the best man in the class." "Five years either side of him," in the opinion of Learned Hand, "there was nobody like Cotton in the whole generation." He dazzled those who knew him best. None, they said time and again, was "more brilliant," "more versatile," "more imaginative" than he. To a swift and large intelligence he added powers of intuition that made his solutions to legal problems at once "strikingly original and yet tremendously simple." He was one of those vivid, singular men who lay their peculiar mark on everything they touch — "even a cable from Cotton needed no signature."

Witty, sophisticated, fully informed, altogether charming, he did not, he confessed, suffer fools gladly, nor even perhaps himself. Under a cloak of irony, it seemed to Thomas Lamont, he had hidden the gentleness and idealism of which he alone was ashamed. But another believed he "so deeply questioned the possibility of changing the world [that] he was very skeptical about his own usefulness in the world. He really didn't care about anything. He was a brilliant, disillusioned mind."

In the Department Cotton discovered great opportunity to use his extraordinary powers. He served as an accurate conveyer of information from the Foreign Service officers to the President. In him, able men like Francis White, the Assistant

Secretary of State for Latin America, Wilbur J. Carr, Assistant Secretary for Administrative Affairs, and Nelson T. Johnson, Assistant Secretary of State for the Far East, found a helpful ally. An able administrator, he presided easily over the Department when the Secretary was away. Familiar with large causes and quick to acquire new information, he was indispensable in the development of policy. Utterly self-assured and a friend of both the President and Secretary, he could explain each to the other at critical moments. During one of the testy arguments that broke out between Hoover and Stimson, Cotton sat lolling in a chair, smoking a corncob pipe. After ten minutes, during which the din steadily increased, Cotton broke in with, "How can you fellows be so silly?" The two men "stopped, looked angrily at him and then began to laugh at each other." He could do all these things and something more. As the unforeseen and ever deepening gloom settled in the next two years over the administration, Joseph Cotton was for the Secretary the only "steady, intelligent, cheerful refuge to which I could go with every big problem for discussion." [8]

With the appointment of Cotton to the staff that included Regnier, Castle, Carr and White, Stimson had put his professional house in order. He needed also, after arriving in Washington, to find a home for Mrs. Stimson and himself. One afternoon, looking at a house near the Shoreham Hotel with a real estate agent, he saw some distance away, half hidden by trees, a large house standing in an extensive ground. "I rather like that," he said. "Well, it's for sale," the agent replied. So they went over and looked at it and Stimson said, "Well, I like that, I think I will take it." The real estate man said the price was $800,000. And Stimson replied, "All right, I will take it." And so he bought Woodley, built by the uncle of Francis Scott Key,

[8] Conversations with Arthur Page, March 18, 1955, Felix Frankfurter, Oct. 29, 1954, Learned Hand, March 19, 1955; "Memoirs of J. P. Cotton," *Year Book* of the Association of the Bar of New York (New York, 1931); H.L.S. to F. M. Sackett, March 27, 1931.

the previous home of a senator, a commodore and a Secretary of the Treasury, the summer home of four Presidents.

It was a late eighteenth-century structure, high-studded, rambling, spacious. Without much architectural distinction the house was still both imposing and comfortable. Off to the south it looked out upon the natural beauty of Rock Creek and on to the city of Washington. Since the grounds — twenty acres in the middle of the District — reached out to Rock Creek Park, the head of the house could take his daily ride of ten or twelve miles without touching pavement. It was, as he said, as near as he and his wife could come to Highhold and both found it a place of comfort and consolation for sixteen years.

Thus supported at home and in the Department he went, in the first months, eagerly to his work. He soon learned that his days would be full. Three weeks after he took office he began one Thursday with a conference at ten o'clock with Silas Strawn, the United States delegate to a conference at Peking on Chinese tariffs. At 10:30 he held a press conference followed at 10:45 by an appointment with Dr. McLaren of the Williamstown Institute. Between 11:00 and 12:00 he received the Spanish Ambassador and a representative from the Bolivian delegation. They were followed by Senator Howell at 12:00, Congressman Keyes at 12:40 and General Allen at 12:55. After lunch at 2:30 he began to sign the official mail, a task he had finished by 3:30 when Congressmen Robison, Thatcher, Walker, Newhall, Kendall and Blackburn called upon him and talked for an hour. Elihu Root, Jr. appeared at 4:30 and remained until 5:00. Just before going home the Secretary called James M. Beck, then a congressman, in New York. That evening he attended a dinner given by the Chilean Ambassador in honor of the Chilean Minister of Finance.[9]

For four years the calendar was filled with days like this — with calls, conferences, talks with senators, ambassadors, con-

[9] *Appointment Book*, Secretary of State, April 11, 1928, Files of State Department, National Archives.

gressmen, delegations from missionary societies, private citizens with influence, newspapermen, committees from women's clubs, bankers, and around again to senators, ambassadors and congressmen. The appointments — ten, fifteen, twenty minutes — went on each day whether the Secretary had as his most pressing problem to decide where Alice Longworth should sit in reference to Dolly Gann or whether he had to decide what to do now that Japanese troops had occupied the city of Mukden in Manchuria.

And there were, even in the first months, a good many things to be decided. The New York *World* pointed out as he began work in his new position that before him lay "the following problems": friction with a dozen nations over our tariff and prohibition laws; Chinese extraterritoriality; Russian recognition; South American trade; Caribbean protectorates; Philippine independence; foreign debts; World Court; rivalry over raw materials, markets and credits; and, "overshadowing all, the freedom of the seas dispute and naval armament race with Great Britain." [10]

In one way or another Stimson had to deal with most of these problems before he left office. Virtually his first act as Secretary was to tell the House Committee on Ways and Means that proposed tariff restrictions on imports from the Philippines represented a "betrayal" that would damage "American credit throughout the Orient," and would raise once more all the ancient agitation for independence. His words, at that time, were a primary influence in warding off the tariff restrictions, but his efforts, continued over the next four years, to work out a permanent relationship between the United States and the Islands were unavailing. Shortly after he left office the desires of a majority, both in this country and in the Philippines, were satisfied by the grant of future independence extended to the Islands in the administration of Franklin D. Roosevelt. [11]

[10] New York *Herald*, March 25, 1929.
[11] *New York Times*, April 21, 1929; Diary, Aug. 28, 1930; *Active Service*, 148.

Unavailing also were Stimson's efforts to reduce the friction between this country and other nations over our tariff policy. For the most part he remained aloof from the tariff discussions that took place during the Hoover Administration; he vividly recalled the troubles visited upon William Howard Taft when he tried to achieve sensible revision. But when Congress in 1930 was considering a bill designed, in one of its framer's words, to make the nation "self-contained and self-sustaining" he expressed his doubt about the wisdom of this Hawley-Smoot tariff. How actively he opposed this legislation cannot now be documented; he himself left no record of his activity. But Felix Frankfurter remembers that for two days Stimson "fought like mad," unsuccessfully, to persuade Hoover to veto the bill.[12]

There were, as the paragraphs in the New York *World* had predicted, other sources of difficulty and friction in these years. An endless and unresolved argument went on with China over extraterritorial rights in the treaty ports on the Chinese mainland. The wisdom of recognizing Russia was under constant review. Stimson was opposed to recognition. Though he was impressed by Borah's argument that "the best way to cure communism in Russia was to bring it into contact with American capitalism," he could not bring himself to recognize a nation that was always "violating the fundamental tenets of international intercourse . . ." Throughout his administration, also, the question of America's entry into the World Court was steadily debated. The discourse brought the Secretary into close touch with the controlling intelligences in the Senate — Borah, Swanson, Joseph T. Robinson and George Moses, whom Root called "a mischievous monkey." It also involved him in a running argument with the President, who was convinced that the senators were using the Court issue solely "to put him in a hole." Suspicious that Borah wanted "to kill him politically," Hoover feared that if he supported the Court in the Congress of 1930

12 A. M. Schlesinger, Jr., *The Crisis of the Old Order* (Boston, 1957), 164; H.L.S. to Felix Frankfurter, Sept. 5, 1930, Frankfurter Papers; Conversation with Felix Frankfurter, Oct. 29, 1954.

his "enemies" would take the opportunity to force a special session on the question in 1931 in which the effort would be "to embarrass us . . ."

This attitude annoyed Stimson, who felt the case ought to be argued on its merits. He therefore undertook one day to explain to the President the nature of political leadership. Human affairs, he said, were "not like building a bridge" — not every stress could be projected and calculated; "in the movement of great currents of human opinions . . . you could make your plans only for a certain distance. . . ." Any effort "to foresee it all" led to an appearance of timidity and vacillation. From the law and the army, he went on, he had found that "In case of doubt . . . march toward the guns." When the infantry were engaged you supported them with your artillery as best you could. Kellogg, Coolidge and Root had already committed the infantry on the question of the Court — it remained for the President to see if he were "willing to take the hounding of the Hearst press for a year" and use his artillery to support the Court before Congress. These were not arguments or analogies that appealed to the President under the best conditions and, in the gloom and confusion of the year 1930, he could think of many reasons for not marching toward the guns that, he increasingly believed, had been specifically trained on him by selfish, ambitious senators. It is quite probable that no President could have done anything in 1930 or 1931 or 1932 to insure America's entry into the World Court, but it is at least equally certain that this particular President did little enough to bring this to pass.[13]

In another area the President and his Secretary worked more

[13] Diary, Nov. 7, 8, 12, Dec. 3, 12, 1930, July 27, 1932. The question of the World Court is interesting here especially because of the argument it produced between the President and his Secretary of State. Hoover was not moved in this instance, as Stimson's diary suggests, exclusively or even primarily by his dislike of the political consequences. Though he may not have completely agreed with W. R. Castle, then Under-Secretary of State, that the court was of "extraordinary unimportance," he hardly shared Stimson's enthusiasm for it. His judgment of the matter must appear more correct than that of his Secretary of State. In spite of his reservations he did place the Court before the Senate "if only," in the opinion of Robert Ferrell (*American Diplomacy*, 31), to "please Stimson and Root."

easily together. It was from the beginning one of Mr. Hoover's prime desires to reduce the confusion and irritation that marked the relations of the United States with the countries of Latin America. Toward this end, two impressive changes in general policy were made in the course of his administration. In 1930 Stimson ordered the publication of a memorandum prepared earlier by Undersecretary J. Reuben Clark. In this paper the author had decisively modified, if not repudiated, the Roosevelt corollary to the Monroe Doctrine — which sought to justify, on grounds of self-protection, America's intervention in Latin American affairs. In a much-quoted phrase derived from the memorandum, Stimson, in supporting this modification of a Rooseveltian policy he had previously advocated, remarked, "The Monroe Doctrine was a declaration of the United States versus Europe — not of the United States versus Latin America." The second change of policy ended the practice, begun by Woodrow Wilson, of withholding recognition from South American governments conceived in revolution by unconstitutional means. Whenever a new government demonstrated *de facto* control of the domestic situation, the ability to fulfill international obligations and the intention to hold elections, it would be recognized.[14]

The declarations of benign intent implicit in these changes of policy were, during the Hoover Administration, supported by certain definite actions. Not always was Stimson able, in pur-

[14] R. L. Wilbur and A. M. Hyde, *The Hoover Policies* (New York, 1937), 588; H.L.S., "The United States and the Other American Republics," *Foreign Affairs*, Supplement, April 1931; Ferrell, *American Diplomacy*, 221; Bemis, *Latin American Policy*, 220-23. The best studies of our relations with Latin America in these years are: Alexander De Conde, *Herbert Hoover's Latin American Policy* (Stanford, 1951); more briefly, Ferrell, *American Diplomacy*, Ch. 13, and Bemis, *Latin American Policy*, Ch. 12. What the Clark Memorandum meant exactly has been the subject of debate among diplomatic historians ever since, though its general intent seems clear enough. It may be noted also that the change in recognition policy did not meet universal approval. Norman H. Davis, an old Wilsonian, asked (*Foreign Affairs*, July 1931, 551), "Is it merely a coincidence that there have been more revolutions in the Latin American republics since Secretary Stimson adopted the policy of extending prompt recognition to revolutionary governments than there were in any other period of their history?"

suing his course, to create the favorable impression he sought. In 1930 he obtained for himself "some rather nasty remarks" and the nickname "Wrong-Horse Harry" by imposing an arms embargo on shipments to Brazilian rebels who ultimately won control of the country. In 1931 two statements he issued indicating the country's reluctance to protect our nationals in the interior of Nicaragua were sufficiently maladroit in timing and phraseology to arouse hostile comment throughout the press. But, on the other hand, while he was Secretary of State the essential friendliness of this country toward Latin America was demonstrated by such acts as the refusal to intervene when Haiti and El Salvador defaulted on their bonds, when Panama was shaken by a brief revolution, or when troubles recurred in Nicaragua. And at the very end of his term of service the Marines were finally withdrawn permanently from Nicaragua. Policies and acts like these, all taken with the approval and, at times, at the direct urging of Herbert Hoover, completed, in S. F. Bemis's words, "the foundations for Franklin D. Roosevelt's Good Neighbor Policy." [15]

The success of these endeavors derived in part from Mr. Hoover's firm intention to change the atmosphere of our relations with Latin America, and in part also from the skill with which Francis White, the Assistant Secretary of State for Latin American Affairs, conducted the negotiations that gave substance to the general policies. In many matters Stimson did not turn to officers in the foreign service in the Department for advice, but he relied heavily upon White in an area he knew little about and was not, in fact, much interested in. The Secretary of State, for his part, was in complete sympathy with the President's designs and gave constant encouragement and support to his able subordinate in the Department. The three men thus worked together in this area of international relations to produce one of the few successes in the foreign policy of the Hoover Administration.

The foregoing matters were all, in a sense, the minor con-

[15] Bemis, *Latin American Policy*, 221; Diary, Nov. 7, 1930.

cerns the *World* had predicted the new Secretary would have to deal with in his term of office. In its prescience the paper had also foreseen three other issues, grave matters attended by consequences of great significance for many nations in the world — the rivalry between certain countries for raw materials and markets around the globe; the economic condition of Europe; and the naval armament race between this country and Great Britain. With all three Stimson was to be directly concerned; with all three he was to render advice and take decisions that modified the atmospheres, if they did not alter the shape of the world he lived in. His first venture into these issues was his effort to resolve the conflict between the United States and Great Britain over the size of their respective navies.

19

Mathematical Reality

As the London Naval Conference of 1930 ended, a London clergyman prayed for "peace in our time, oh Lord — peace without conference." This meeting of the nations, Frank Simonds thought at the time, was something out of *Alice in Wonderland* while Admiral Sir Herbert Richmond, casting a retrospective glance, was put in mind of *Through the Looking Glass.* By the terms of the treaty finally agreed upon, Great Britain, in Winston Churchill's opinion, had made "formal acceptance . . . of definitely inferior sea power." But across the water Senator Hiram W. Johnson believed that, by the same terms, England had been left in a position to "wipe out the whole American fleet." Although the Washington *News* figured out that the London agreement "calls for upward of a billion-dollar . . . increase," President Hoover calculated that the country saved by the same agreement one billion dollars in six years. American naval officers were convinced that at the conference Japan had obtained concessions that "made it practically impossible for the United States to support its policies in the Far East. . . ." The benefits received by the Japanese in 1922 at Washington had been at London in 1930 "tilted further," it was said, "to her advantage." And yet in Tokyo the chief of the naval general staff was forced to resign because of the conference and the Prime Minister was assassinated for supporting the London Treaty. A good many other people, elsewhere, contented themselves with pointing out that the conference on naval limitation had produced an increase of 102,000 tons in new construction. Whether one is confused, discouraged or entertained by these considerations, as many were at the time, the proceedings of the conference still serve as a useful source of information about the nature of appearance and reality in the years after Versailles.[1]

The cause of the conference was real enough. Eight years before, at Washington in 1922, the maritime nations had tried to limit the navies of the world by limiting the tonnage in capital ships assigned to England, the United States, Japan, France and Italy on ratios of 5:5:3:1.75:1.75. In spite of Secretary Hughes's belief that the Washington Treaty "ends, absolutely ends, the race in competition of naval armament," the effort at limitation failed. The effect of the treaty was only to transfer naval competition from capital ships to other fleet categories — destroyers, submarines and especially cruisers.[2]

Seven times in the five years from 1922 to 1927 the nations tried to reach limiting agreements in these other fleet categories and each time they failed. But in their deliberations the nature of the principal difficulties confronting them was made very clear. Although there were many debates about the different kinds of fleets different countries needed to answer their different needs, the primary source of trouble could be found in

[1] Frank H. Simonds, *Can Europe Keep the Peace?* (New York, 1931), 255, 301; Herbert W. Richmond, "Immediate Problems of Naval Reduction," *Foreign Affairs*, April 1931, 374; Merze Tate, *The United States and Armaments* (Cambridge, 1948), 180-83; *Literary Digest*, April 26, 1930; George T. Davis, *A Navy Second to None* (New York, 1940), 344, 348; Ferrell, *American Diplomacy*, 101.

[2] Harold and Margaret Sprout, *Toward a New Order of Sea Power* (Princeton, 1940), 252; Tate, *United States and Armaments*, 138-40. At the time it was widely believed that the Washington Conference was a "diplomatic victory" in which the United States had demonstrated a way to control armaments while leaving the security of the great powers, as Hughes said, "unimpaired." Neither end was accomplished. But few men in 1922 had the perception of Raymond L. Buell who said in his *The Washington Conference* (New York, 1922), 328, 368, "As a result of the Washington Conference, the intervention of foreign powers in the progress of Japanese imperialism on the continent of Asia is more impossible than ever." The only way left, after Washington, to prevent Japan from endangering the world, he felt, was to make concession in the matter of immigration and tariff schedules and then to support Japanese liberalism with "the tremendous force of international opinion."

cruiser tonnage. England and, to a lesser extent, France believed they needed more cruisers than other countries, not as fleet support, but as defenders of the imperial sea lanes. The fulfillment of these excess requirements would naturally put in jeopardy the ratios set up at Washington. In the second place there was a confusing difference in cruisers: the United States, for instance, preferred to have a greater number of heavy cruisers mounting eight-inch guns; England preferred, on the other hand, to have a greater number of light cruisers carrying six-inch guns. The two countries had been unable to agree on the relative strength of these two different kinds of ships; they had therefore been unable to reach satisfactory conclusions on building programs that would give the parity between the two fleets that had been implied in the 5:5 ratio set at Washington.[3]

At Geneva, where in 1927 these matters were debated once again, the meeting broke up in bitterness. France and Italy had refused to attend and Japan had looked on while American and British experts drew farther and farther apart. After this failure there was, as Lord Cecil said, "a certain tension in Anglo-American relations which was very undesirable." In the next two years several actions on the part of both countries increased this tension until, on his return from the Philippines in 1929, it seemed to Stimson that the two nations "were really at each other's throats."[4]

Thus matters stood when Herbert Hoover, as he said, "took up the problem" in the first months of his Presidency. The problem, as he clearly saw it, was first to restore amity between England and the United States by re-establishing parity between the fleets of the two nations. Since he "had seen too many international conferences fail from lack of preparation," he proceeded to lay the foundation with his habitual thoroughness. First he authorized Hugh Gibson to give a speech in April 1929 at Geneva in which the Ambassador proposed "yardsticks"

[3] Davis, *Navy Second to None*, 305-37; Tate, *United States and Armaments*, Ch. 10.
[4] Tate, *United States and Armaments*, 164; H.L.S. to Lord Elton, April 5, 1938.

of combined ship characteristics — age, weight, speed, fire-power — that would provide a means to equate ships of different size with each other. These yardsticks would serve to measure the relationship between the British light and the American heavy cruisers that had caused the trouble at Geneva. It was, in the opinion of one student, "the blast which dislodged the key log in the jam" in which the two countries found themselves caught.[5]

A second circumstance assisted Hoover in his preparations. On June 7, 1929, Ramsay MacDonald, by temperament and stated objective predisposed to peace and disarmament, returned to power in England. Within two weeks the President, through Ambassador Charles G. Dawes, had begun to explore the possibilities of a naval settlement with the Prime Minister. These explorations, conducted in America for the most part by Hoover himself, with the assistance of Stimson, Cotton and Dawes, continued throughout the summer. By September the range of difference between the Prime Minister and the President had been reduced to the question of cruiser tonnage. At this point it was suggested that it might help to invite MacDonald to this country for conversations. On October 4 the Prime Minister came for a week of personal triumph. He captivated the public by remaining unruffled when James J. Walker introduced him as the Prime Minister of the United States; he beguiled the senators when he said to them, ". . . 'What is all this bother about parity?' Parity? Take it, without reserve, heaped up and flowing over"; he impressed the President and Stimson with his honesty and directness when they sat down to talk over the naval agreement in the rustic simplicities of Rapidan.[6]

---

[5] The Memoirs of Herbert Hoover, Vol. II, The Cabinet and the Presidency: 1920-1933 (New York, 1952), 340-41; Tate, United States and Armaments, 166.
[6] Hoover, Cabinet and Presidency, 341-42; Charles G. Dawes, Journal as Ambassador to Great Britain (New York, 1939), 1-82, describes in detail Dawes's negotiations in the summer of 1929; L. Macneill Weir, The Tragedy of Ramsay MacDonald (London, 1938), 228; Ferrell, American Diplomacy, 85; H.L.S. to Lord Elton, April 5, 1938.

At the end, on October 10, Hoover and MacDonald issued a joint statement in which they said they had looked at things in the light of the Briand-Kellogg Pact. They asserted that each was prepared to work to secure world peace though one of the countries "will never consent to become entangled in European diplomacy" and "the other is resolved to pursue a policy of active cooperation with its European neighbours." In this spirit and in this interesting conception of cooperative partnership the two had been brought so close to agreement that it seemed possible to call a general naval disarmament conference. At that conference other nations, it was said, would reach "mutual understandings" by "the same free and candid discussion of needs. . . ." Shortly thereafter invitations went forth to Japan, France and Italy to meet in London in January 1930. These countries had been kept informed of the developing negotiations between MacDonald and Hoover. They were aware that by October 10 only two questions had been left unresolved between them — whether England should have an advantage of 24,000 tons out of the combined fleet tonnage of over two million; and whether the United States should have twenty-one heavy eight-inch cruisers or a smaller number — fifteen to eighteen of these ships.[7]

Thus far the negotiations had been conducted, as Hoover had intended, with neatness and dispatch. For this the conciliatory spirit of MacDonald was, in part, responsible. He was genuinely anxious to give the United States parity if anyone could discover what parity between fleets composed of ships of different size really was. He had also been willing to reduce England's demands for new cruisers when Hoover argued that "he could perhaps worry along with his policing of the British Empire by extending the life of some of his older ships for a few years." But the tidiness of the negotiation was in greater part

[7] The statement by Hoover and MacDonald together with other papers bearing on the MacDonald visit will be found in *FR 1929*, III, 1-36. Further papers on the visit will be found in *FR 1929*, I, 112 ff. Tate, *United States and Armaments*, 173-75.

the result of Herbert Hoover's industry and freedom of maneuver. As for the industry, he made himself personally the master of the tortuous metaphysics of fleet tonnage; he became, in fact, completely at home in the intricate equations of arms limitation by number. MacDonald, on the other hand, "was not," as Hoover noted, "very good at figures." More important, however, was the freedom of maneuver assumed by the President. For one thing he did not, save on purely technical matters, have to pay much attention to the Navy since the Navy, as Hugh Wilson pointed out, did not really know what it needed. In England, where there was a clear imperial position and a foreign policy with some definition, the Navy could press carefully calculated needs upon a Prime Minister. In the United States, with small imperial position and a less discernible foreign policy, it was more difficult for the Navy to calculate its actual needs. This situation gave Hoover greater liberty to arrange the size and character of the fleet, not in recognition of the defense of sea lanes or the support of national commitments, but of simple parity with England. This explains, at least in part, the otherwise surprising fact discovered by Joseph Cotton in late October 1929. At a conference of government officials he found that neither the Secretary nor the Assistant Secretary of the Navy was really informed about the state of the negotiations then far advanced between England and the United States.[8]

In still another way the President had more room for maneuver, at this stage, than the Prime Minister. MacDonald had said

---

[8] Dawes, *Journal as Ambassador*, 77, 95; Hoover, *Cabinet and Presidency*, 341; Hugh R. Wilson, *Diplomat Between Wars* (New York, 1941), 248; Undated Memorandum (received by Secretary of State, Oct. 28, 1929) 500.A 15A 3/575, SD. On the question of naval cooperation Hoover asserted that he, unlike MacDonald, had no difficulties. The officers he consulted "supported what we were trying to do." Dawes suggests that this support was achieved only after a "struggle" in which the President emerged triumphant because, having "mastered the technical elements," he could not be misled. The Navy itself of course was divided over the question of cruiser size as the departure of Admiral Hilary Jones from the conference and the bitter recrimination directed against Admiral William V. Pratt within the Navy after the London Conference indicates.

to Dawes in the course of the conversations in September that "although in our talks . . . we assume that the discussion takes place between us two, that is really not the case. . . . A spirit photograph would show you unaccompanied, but round me would be the ghosts of the other nations." Hoover, thus unaccompanied, representing a nation and a point of view that would "never consent to become entangled in European diplomacy," could, he believed, proceed to solve the problem of naval competition with England out of any larger context; the satisfaction of the American requirement for parity could be taken as the primary, virtually the exclusive, objective.[9]

Whatever the causes for the success of the preliminary preparations, it was clear by November that Hoover and Mac-Donald seemed, in their own words, to have "substantially removed" the "obstacles in previous conferences arising out of Anglo-American disagreements." MacDonald may have had more doubts than Mr. Hoover about the durability of their tidy arrangements. He had delicately hinted that in arriving at naval agreements the navies of other nations had sometimes to be taken into account and, though not good at figures, he had once suggested that the conversations about parity were "an attempt to clothe unreality in the garb of mathematical reality." Nevertheless out of the talks between him and the President there seemed to be enough of real substance to justify the calling of a general conference.[10]

Until this time Stimson had joined in the developing negotiations at all important points but he had not served as a directing energy. When the invitations to the conference had been issued and Stimson had been appointed the head of the American delegation, he set seriously to work. Like Hoover he thoroughly prepared himself in the intricate computations of fleet tonnage as a preliminary to dealing with the questions posed by the differential of 24,000 tons between the two fleets and the exact

[9] Dawes, *Journal as Ambassador*, 79.
[10] Dawes, *Journal as Ambassador*, 79.

mutually acceptable number of eight-inch American cruisers, questions left undecided by the President and Prime Minister. For weeks he worked with the General Board of the Navy, informing himself about firepower, cruising ranges and armor belt. He was also, like his chief, completely committed to the view that his primary mission was the resolution of tension between England and the United States on the matter of parity. On the voyage to London he instructed the individual members in the lore he had acquired. It was a very strong delegation, including C. F. Adams from the Cabinet, Joseph T. Robinson and David A. Reed from the Senate and Ambassadors Hugh S. Gibson and Dwight W. Morrow. Dawes, who joined the group in London, remarked later that the delegates "are strong men and only capable leadership would satisfy them." Stimson, he reported, was "a safe leader, not afraid to take individual responsibility where necessary, without hesitation, and yet wise enough to patiently explain all he does to his delegation." Newspapermen, who because of Stimson's attitude toward the press were frequently left in ignorance of what was going on, reported from time to time that the delegation was divided within itself. The available evidence now suggests that on the whole it was, and remained, what Dawes called it, "a united delegation." [11]

It was also a delegation that went about its work in the grand manner. "Mr. Henry Stimson," in Hugh Wilson's opinion, was "essentially a grand seigneur and proceeds about his high duties with the pageantry and suite that such high duties conventionally call for." The Secretary had leased for himself the country house of Stanmore with its nine-hole golf course that could, as Eugene Regnier told Cotton, be converted to eighteen holes by an ingenious rearrangement of tees. The delegates took three floors of the Ritz while the technical advisers put up at the Mayfair. Recollecting moodily the earlier conferences at which they

[11] Eugene Regnier to Joseph Cotton, Feb. 7, 1930; David A. Reed to William Borah, March 5, 1930; H.L.S. to Herbert Hoover, Jan. 24, 1930, SD; Dawes, *Journal as Ambassador*, 125, 145.

had tried to present the American position with the aid of one stenographer, Wilson and Gibson concluded that this was the last meeting of nations conducted in the great tradition of the Congress of Vienna.[12]

A London fog on January 21 enshrouded the opening ceremonies of the conference to the consternation of those who sought for omens and to the continuing entertainment of Drew Pearson. But a sense of large possibilities and the sound of grave eloquence, befitting the great tradition, came through the murk. It was said that the nations were met together on "one of those rare occasions of history out of which . . . a long and permanent step forward on the road towards peace may be taken for all the nations of the earth." Words like these had been used in the spirit of invocation whenever the nations of the earth met together in the twenties. Nothing in the first days of the London Conference belied them. Thanks to Mr. Hoover's careful preparation, the resiliency of Mr. MacDonald and the clarity and firmness of Mr. Stimson, England and the United States proceeded rapidly to resolve their remaining differences. Informal conversations quickly produced a series of tentative agreements. On February 3, the Prime Minister said that if the United States would accept eighteen instead of twenty-one eight-inch heavy cruisers England would be prepared in compensation to let her build five more of the six-inch light cruisers than had originally been prescribed. These additional vessels would reduce the differential in cruiser tonnage to a mere 12,-000. In a further diplomatic stroke, it was agreed that even this differential could be eliminated by permitting either nation, at its own desire, to duplicate precisely the cruiser force of the other.[13]

12 Wilson, *Diplomat Between Wars*, 236.
13 Drew Pearson and Constantine Brown, *The American Diplomatic Game* (New York, 1935), 116-17; *London Naval Conference*, Publications of the State Department, Series 3 (Washington, 1930), 1, Diary, Feb. 3, 4, 1930. MacDonald had himself earlier offered the duplicate cruiser force to Hoover on the Rapidan.

These proposals were cabled to Hoover on February 4, and he replied the next day, " 'heartily approving' our detailed proposition." From that time forward, as Stimson later noted, "there remained only trivial differences between the British and the Americans, and these were easily adjusted in later meetings." The desire of the President to obtain a successful international agreement through careful preparation had been rewarded. Because of his knowledge, gained as Dawes noted "through months of intensive investigation," and because he was "a good tactician," Stimson had placed the United States "in a position of leadership" in the conference. By his statement on the cruiser proposal the Secretary of State had, further, pleased both American and British public opinion. Regnier reported to Cotton that the Secretary commanded the respect and affection of all he met and worked with. A Japanese delegate remarked that this was the week of smiles.[14]

What he actually said was that this was the last week of smiles. In the middle of February the ghosts of other nations came out of the spirit photograph and turned up substantial and unsmiling at the conference table. Unseen or unrecognized before, they had not been previously unheard even by the American delegation. In December 1929 the Japanese representatives, on their way to London, had stopped off in Washington to see the Secretary. As an earnest of their good intent they had told him that their country made it "the fundamental principle" to have "a strength insufficient for attack and adequate for defense." But they had gone on to say that the maintenance of this principle required that the 5:5:3 ratio agreed upon in 1922 should be changed, as applied to fleet auxiliaries including cruisers, to 10:10:7. Such a ratio had in fact become, as Reijiro Wakatsuki, a member of the Japanese delegation, told the Secretary at Woodley, a "national desire." Stimson replied that the expression of their conviction "would give a bad im-

14 Diary, Feb. 5, 1930; *Active Service*, 167-68; Dawes, *Journal as Ambassador*, 145; Eugene Regnier to Joseph Cotton, Feb. 7, 1930.

pression to the American people. . . ." But he went no further, apparently believing with the President that if England and the United States reached agreement, Japan, in Hoover's words, "would go along." [15]

Three days after the meeting at Woodley the French Ambassador at London had presented, on December 20, a note to the British which said, in effect, that what determined the strength of a cruiser force was not a mathematical formula but "Length of coastlines, size of colonial empires, [and] length of trade routes." So forthright was this statement that the New York *World* wondered on December 29 whether the conference was worth holding since the French were unwilling to accept a limitation of naval strength on the basis of principles adopted by Hoover and MacDonald. To such a query the President had already given his answer. If France or Italy proved irreconcilable it would be possible, he said, to "make it a tripartite agreement between the United States, Britain, and Japan anyway." [16]

In the second week of February Japan and France restated their positions in surroundings where the arguments could not so easily be disregarded. Wakatsuki went "so far as to say that he could not sign any treaty which did not contain" the principle of the 10:7 ratio. His words were reinforced by a cable from Castle in Tokyo to Stimson which said that "the 10–7 ratio has been for months insisted on as necessary for national safety. . . ." Since an election was shortly to be held, the Japanese government, as Castle reported to Stimson, was "unlikely to back down now." [17]

France, for her part, told England on February 13 that, in view of her coastlines and imperial position, she needed ten new

[15] Draft Minutes of Informal Conversations, Dec. 17, 1929, 500.A 15A 3/594, SD; Hoover, *Cabinet and Presidency*, 346.
[16] Giovanni Engely, *The Politics of Naval Disarmament* (London, 1932), 132; Hoover, *Cabinet and Presidency*, 346.
[17] Diary, Feb. 13, 17, 1930; Joseph Cotton to H.L.S., Feb. 8, 1930, 500.A 15A 3/655, SD; William Castle to H.L.S., Feb. 10, 1930, 500.A 15A 3/684, SD; H.L.S. to Herbert Hoover, Feb. 17, 1930, 500.A 15A 3/708½, SD.

eight-inch cruisers. The British, at a conference attended by Stimson, replied that six or seven would be sufficient. Tardieu said that this proposal was "not even in the zone of negotiation" and went on to claim, in the interests of national safety, a number of submarines that both England and the United States considered excessive.[18]

What these French and Japanese claims amounted to, obviously, was that both countries wanted more ships. Caught between the unlooked-for pressures of these national attitudes the delicate formulae for British-American limitations, which had seemed so secure in the vacuum surrounding the MacDonald-Hoover talks, showed signs of disintegration. At one point the British sought to reopen the cruiser question, making the claim that the yardstick used to reach the original understanding had been imperfectly graduated. The measuring rod had incorrectly indicated that an eight-inch cruiser was worth 1.4 of six-inch cruisers, whereas it now seemed that a more reliable figure was 2.36. Stimson, in perfect command of the figures and trained by experience to negotiation in a limited situation, steadfastly held MacDonald to the terms of the original agreement reached on February 3. But he discovered from this episode, among others, that the British building program depended not only on an understanding with America but upon the construction plans of other nations. He therefore set himself to see what he could do to bring Japan and France to satisfactory terms.[19]

There followed weeks of exploration and discussion in the course of which Stimson found out what a conference of the nations was like when it started to come apart. He noticed first that MacDonald, the chairman, was "not a good executive," that he was "not good at concentration on matters of primary importance and was also not good in delegating work of secondary importance to others." The Prime Minister, busy con-

18 Diary, Feb. 13, 1930.
19 Diary, Feb. 12, 1930.

stantly with an unruly House of Commons was tired, preoccupied with the possibility that his government might fall at any
time, and frequently uninformed on matters brought to the conference table. As a result the discussions began to slip out of
his control, as indeed some members of his own delegation
tended to slip out also.

As for the French, in addition to their intransigence in negotiation, they revealed other alarming characteristics. Once when
Stimson said to Aristide Briand that he could more easily sympa-
thize with French cruiser demands than with the excessive submarine proposals, the Frenchman had frivolously replied, *"sous-
marine c'est ma faiblesse."* On another occasion he threatened to
return to Paris "in despair" and not come back. Also the French
even in the best of times were not always available; every week
Tardieu and his suite had to return for two or three days to attend meetings of the French Chamber and then, in the middle
of things, his cabinet fell. For a time the conference was at a
standstill awaiting the formation of a new government in France.
Elections also limited, at first, the possibility of conducting sensible negotiations with the Japanese delegation, which in addition was divided within itself on everything but the 10:7 ratio.
Finally there was the "weak" Italian representation that had to
call up Mussolini every evening and that would take no step until the French problem was solved. Then, it was understood,
Italy would demand parity with France even though, as everyone knew, she was economically and physically incapable of
building a navy as large as that of France.[20]

As February gave way to March and March stretched toward
April, the conference, caught in the deadlock of the Japanese
and French demands, struggled aimlessly in the toils. Newspapermen looked on with "Disgust and bewilderment"; the London *Star* at the beginning of March reported the meeting was
dying and the *Daily Express* gave its opinion that the meeting

[20] H.L.S. to Herbert Hoover, Feb. 17, 1930, 500.A 15A 3/708½, SD; Diary,
Feb. 6, March 8, 10, 12, 1930.

was already dead. It seemed to Stimson during these days that things had reached "an impasse . . . which will require something drastic to be done." Nor was he much comforted by the assurances of Morrow and Gibson that they were in the trough of "one of those psychological waves which come at intervals in every international conference." [21]

In such atmospheres Stimson worked, as Dawes observed, never showing "the white feather or a slackening of effort because of discouraging circumstances." The principal source of discouragement, the prime obstacle to a five-power agreement, he discovered in time, was the attitude of France. That country, in her obsession for security, would not consider a reduction in either cruiser or submarine strength if she did not receive in return a political guarantee of her position in the Mediterranean. In the early days of the conference Stimson had not fully recognized the meaning of this French preoccupation. When Briand had murmured something in his ear about "a possible amplification of the [Briand-Kellogg] Pact" this had seemed to him to coincide with an idea he and Hoover had already talked over, the creation of a commission under the Pact to publish the facts surrounding any breach of the agreement. But ten days later, in the middle of February, he had learned a little more. "France," he wrote the President, "is beginning to talk about security and there is running in the background a possible Mediterranean Pact or our long-thought-of amendment to the Briand-Kellogg Pact." Though nothing specific had been mentioned, "I should not be surprised," he told Hoover, "if

[21] *Literary Digest*, March 8, 1930, 12; H.L.S. to Herbert Hoover, Feb. 17, 1930, 500.A 15A 3/708½, SD. Stimson was not much comforted either by Cotton's constantly cabled reports from Washington that Japan was responding to the Secretary's proposals "with indignation," that American interest in the proceedings was "waning," that there were frequent reports of "division" within the American delegation, and that some congressmen were writing the President to say Congress would not accept the cruiser proposals Stimson had announced. "Prominent Senators," said Cotton on April 1, 1930, were constantly saying what "they think you ought to do. I am getting pretty sick of it and I wish you would come back."

[Briand] brought it in finally as a quid pro quo for naval reduction." [22]

By the first of March the nature of the quid pro quo had become just a little more clear. Though Briand went on dropping hints about an amplification of the Pact of Paris, his colleagues, Aubert, Massigli and Tardieu, were more forthright. They wanted something with greater substance; they could not consider a reduction of their naval strength without an accompanying assurance of support for their position in the Mediterranean. An agreement between the nations to consult with each other in a breach of peace was not enough; there must be something beyond that. But none of the Frenchmen was very clear about exactly what the "something beyond" should be.[23]

In these clouded circumstances Stimson set out to find the necessary quid pro quo. He seems to have hoped, originally, that if England would agree to give a political guarantee to France he could then obtain from his own country consent to a consultative pact that would bind the nations at the conference to talk over ways and means to preserve peace when peace was threatened. During the first week of March he explored these possibilities. He soon discovered several discouraging things. It was revealed first that the British delegation was divided; MacDonald, disturbed by the precarious tenure of his government, was opposed to any offer of help to France, while his Foreign Secretary, Arthur Henderson, felt some more generous approach was desirable. But in spite of this division it was obvious that Britain was not prepared to give France the kind of assurances she required. Stimson also discovered that the President, though not opposed to the idea of consultative pacts, was opposed to entering a specific pact that would be given as a condition of French naval reduction. By such an agreement the United

[22] Dawes, *Journal as Ambassador*, 166; H.L.S. to Herbert Hoover, Feb. 17, 1930, 500.A 15A 3/708½, SD; Diary, Feb. 10, 1930.
[23] Diary, Feb. 6, 24, 27, March 7, 1930; Ferrell, *American Diplomacy*, 95-97.

States would appear to assume a moral obligation to come to French assistance in case of attack.[24]

Thus matters stood by the end of the first week of March. By his explorations the Secretary had uncovered imposing obstacles to the finding of an acceptable quid pro quo. He had also roused up, by his activities, a certain amount of hostility in his own country. Joseph Cotton cabled him on March 3 that "it is repeatedly asserted here you are personally in favor of expanding the Kellogg Pact by Presidential declaration" and, more serious, that because of all the talk of political guarantees the conference was "losing rapidly" the support of peace groups at home. In view of all the difficulties and dangers attendant upon further effort, the matter might have been left there. But Stimson had set out to obtain a naval treaty from the five nations at the conference and he could not bring himself to settle for less before every possibility had been examined.[25]

In the next two weeks of March he persisted in his conversations with the French and English. At the end of that time, on March 26, he issued what Dawes called "a memorable statement." It began with a reiteration of the essential position of the United States: the country, while in favor of consultative pacts in theory was opposed to a consultative pact that would be used to obtain a reduction in French arms. He then went on to say, "If, however, [the French] demand for security could be satisfied in some other way, then the danger of misunderstanding a consultative pact would be eliminated; and in such case the question would be approached from an entirely different standpoint." The same day the British, roused by Stimson's persistence, helped with the work by issuing the following statement: Though Britain would enter no new military commit-

24 Diary, March 8, 1930; H.L.S. to Herbert Hoover, March 11, 1930; Hoover, *Cabinet and Presidency*, 348. Hoover, in his account, says that when Stimson urged him to accept "a pact of 'consultation' as to measures to be taken in case of a threatened attack" he "was compelled to instruct him that we could not agree. . . ."
25 Diary, March 8, 1930; Joseph Cotton to H.L.S., March 3, 4, 1930.

ments, the Government was prepared "to amplify and to explain any part of the Covenant of the League of Nations, of the Locarno, or the Kellogg Pact which may be obscure or uncertain in the mind of any of the other powers." [26]

Neither Stimson's suggestion that a consultative pact could not be misunderstood if it were replaced by something else, nor the British offer of further textual exegesis resolved the doubts of the French. The Secretary of State therefore thought of two other ways to settle the problem. He suggested, first, that the conference might adopt a separate resolution asking all signatories of the Pact of Paris to agree at some other time and place to a consultative amendment to the Pact. This suggestion too proved unavailing. So in the last week of March Stimson tried yet again. At his instigation a proposal was prepared by the American delegation which read as follows: "The high contracting parties shall consult with one another fully and frankly as to what measures may be adopted to maintain peace among them; but neither this agreement to consult nor any consultation thereunder shall imply commitment on the part of the signatories . . . to employ military force or to take . . . coercive other action." What this stated, as Stimson said, was the American intent to favor "a pact if it clearly eliminated any obligation upon us to become entangled in European conflicts." But as a source of assurance to the French it hardly served; by the end of March all possibilities of satisfying the needs of this troubled country had failed, and with this failure the chance of a five-power treaty at London went glimmering.[27]

From the beginning there had been little or no chance. Neither England nor the United States could put themselves in a position to satisfy the French requirements and France could not bring herself to modify the requirements. Looking back seventeen years later at this event Stimson created the impression that he understood all this and therefore took no steps to

[26] Dawes, *Journal as Ambassador*, 170-72.
[27] Dawes, *Journal as Ambassador*, 175, 178.

resolve the situation. In fact, as the record shows, he tried indefatigably against mounting discouragements throughout the month of March. In his search for a formula he tested so many approaches that, as one unkind observer remarked, he "vacillated back and forth on the question of consultation as frequently as the French had commuted between London and Paris." He also advanced in so doing far into that realm where words were used by statesmen in an effort to close the gap between what was hoped for and what was actually happening.[28]

Yet the persistent effort to frame a consultative agreement was perhaps not wholly without point. It produced, in Dawes's opinion, a "psychological effect in demonstrating the sincerity of the American desire for agreement was very great. . . ." It may well have pushed the conference off dead center to move toward such conclusions as it would reach. Of Stimson's actions during these last days of March Walter Lippmann said, "I don't think [his] courageous and far-seeing move is appreciated in this country. But he's really saved our faces, and possibly the conference."[29]

In any event, in the first two weeks of April a series of decisions were quickly given form at London. Great Britain, Japan and the United States agreed upon a schedule for scrapping certain capital ships before 1936 and also agreed to end capital ship construction in that period. Agreements in other fleet categories, including cruisers, that had been reached between England and the United States on February 5 were without important change contained in the final treaty. In the cruiser category Japan was granted her desired 10:7 ratio in light cruisers and, by an engaging compromise, received what was called a 10:6 ratio but what was in fact the larger ratio in heavy cruisers. The same 10:7 relationship was extended to destroyers, while in sub-

[28] *Active Service*, 170; Pearson and Brown, *Diplomatic Game*, 146-47. These authors give (108-71) a heavily satiric account of the whole conference. They are jocosely condemnatory of Stimson throughout.
[29] Dawes, *Journal as Ambassador*, 178; Walter Lippmann to F. R. Coudert, April 3, 1930.

marines Japan obtained parity with England and the United States. Thus Japan for every practical purpose achieved her end at London of breaking the relationship that had been established at Washington between her fleet and the fleets of the other two great powers.

To these firm commitments was added a clause to enable England to maintain her historic policy of constructing a fleet as large as the combined fleets of any other two continental powers. Since neither France nor Italy had joined in the above arrangements it was acknowledged that Great Britain had the right, should either France or Italy embark on a naval expansion program, to increase her fleet to equal those of her continental neighbors in combination. This "escalator clause," in view of France's demands for cruisers and submarines, took much of the meaning out of the limiting agreements of the three big powers. Finally all five nations did agree to a set of regulations prohibiting unrestricted submarine warfare in the future.[30]

This treaty was signed at London on April 22 and consented to by the Senate at a special session in the summer of 1930. At the time it was not received with any great enthusiasm in this country. Many papers, including those as widely separated in opinion as the *Daily Worker* and the New York *Journal of Commerce*, were prepared to call the London meeting a failure. Many more — Republican like the *Herald Tribune*, Democratic like the St. Louis *Globe-Democrat* and independent like the New York *World* — were willing to believe that the conference was "a step in the progress [toward] the goal of disarmament and peace." This tepid response was reflected, even before the treaty was signed, in a cable sent by Cotton to Stimson on April 11, 1930. The President and Under-Secretary were "oppressed by the difficulty of changing the current of popular comment . . . mainly hostile to the London Conference into a belief in its suc-

[30] The complete text of the treaty is in *London Naval Conference*, Publications of the State Department, Series 6 (Washington, 1931), 203-20. A digest of the treaty is contained in Conference Series 4 (Washington, 1930).

cess. . . . We both deem it essential that you commence now to give to the news that comes out of London a clear note of exultation in your success." [31]

Clear notes of exultation over anything did not come naturally to Stimson, but it was not difficult for him to express satisfied confidence in the treaty made at London. Between the United States, England and Japan there was "to be no further naval competition or . . . rivalry . . ." he said in commenting on his work. In this assessment he was joined by Herbert Hoover, who believed we "had achieved our most important aim," parity with Great Britain. Neither man ever altered his view that the London Conference had been a considerable achievement. In part this was, no doubt, because both men, in the course of long and remarkable careers, had become accustomed to expect only success to attend their earnest efforts. But also each succeeded in reducing his principal recollection of the treaty to the limited dimension of the original intent. Certainly a President and a Secretary of State who in 1929 had found England and the United States "really at each other's throats" could take satisfaction from an understanding that restored mutual amity in 1930. [32]

But this particular understanding cannot be made to signify when placed in any larger context of international relations; the London Naval Treaty was not, in itself, as Stimson asserted seventeen years later, "an important step toward disarmament and lasting peace." What came out of all the talk at London was less a progress toward arms limitation than a further definition of persistent attitudes of mind which, within a decade, would make lasting peace impossible.

Out of the debates emerged, a little more obviously than before, the growing uncertainty of Britain about the part she would play in the Europe that developed after Versailles; out

[31] *Literary Digest*, April 26, 1930, 8-9; Joseph Cotton to H.L.S., April 11, 1930, 500.A 15A 3/838a, SD.
[32] H.L.S., "Radio Address on the London Naval Conference," June 12, 1930; Wilbur and Hyde, *Hoover Policies*, 592.

of them emerged, once again, the almost pathological attachment of France to the hope of guaranteed security; out of them emerged the undiminished determination of Japan to push herself into a commanding position in the sun; out of them emerged, as before, the inescapable involvement of the United States in the conditions of the world and her incapacity to share directly with others the responsibility for organizing those conditions. Finally, out of these debates at London emerged once again the desolating truth that not one of the problems produced by all these conflicting attitudes, nor even the attitudes themselves could, by so much as one jot or tittle, be modified by the dialectical method.

At London Stimson was, for the first time, introduced to the problems of negotiation at an international conference. The way in which he sought to solve these problems has not, either at the time or in later years, escaped critical notice. For one thing he was not good with the press; he seemed to feel that reporters always wanted to know more than was good for them, or for him, or for the welfare of the body politic. He therefore told them as little as possible, which ordinarily was very little indeed. And he had no very great success with his efforts to offset the unfortunate impression this created. Over the radio to America he gave out "one little word of caution" about "excited" reporters who came to him almost every day with the rumor of a crisis that was going to wreck the conference. Actually there was "nothing but hard work and friendly good will among the various gentlemen. . . . I therefore recommend that you be not troubled by reports of crises. . . ." [33]

[33] Active Service, 173; London Naval Conference, Series 3, p. 9. Stimson's relations with the press improved somewhat in the last two years of his administration after he introduced his "background conferences" with selected newspapermen. The Secretary believed that these weekly meetings held at Woodley "proved a great help in 1931 and after." A rather startling anecdote supports this view. In 1940 Stephen Early, so Louis Brownlow reports, believed Stimson "handled his press relations [as Secretary of State] better than any other" public man in Washington. Franklin Roosevelt, Early told Brownlow, was "pretty good," but Stimson was "so much better that it was nobody's business."

There was also the matter of communicating with the home base. Cotton's letters and cables suggest that men in the State Department were not always sure they knew what their chief was going to do next and Dawes believed that Stimson did not make enough of an effort to keep the President informed of what he was doing at the moment. In such an unsettled situation as the conference presented in the month of March, it was no doubt difficult to describe conditions and intentions clearly, but it seems equally without doubt that Stimson did not have the necessity for such description at all times in his mind. This failure of communication between the Secretary and President in large part accounts for the unfortunate moment when they issued, almost simultaneously, radically different declarations of the American intent.

And finally, in his efforts to find a proposition so full of substance that it would allay the anxieties of France and so devoid of meaning that it would find favor in Britain and America, he roused public concern and amusement in about equal parts. It is not, perhaps, an extenuating circumstance but only a fact that the methods used by Stimson in his inexperience were the familiar means used by statesmen of far more experience in the society of nations where it had become the custom to distract attention from the unobtainable by reaffirming the unnecessary or the irrelevant. It is not so surprising that on his first venture he accepted the customary measures as it is that from the failure of his efforts he learned something. He learned a great deal about the nature of the world he had been asked to deal with and he began to learn, sooner than most of those in authority in this country, that the customary measures would not serve.

For this reason, Early and Brownlow thought of proposing to Roosevelt in 1940 that Stimson should "take over, for the entire government, press relations involving foreign policy." For a description of this episode see *The Autobiography of Louis Brownlow*, 2 vols. (Chicago, 1958), II, 442-43. The Early assessment, as reported, seems, at the very least, surprising, and the job suggested for Stimson, at the very best, unsuitable.

20

Money, Credit and Psychology

I N A TIME when there was nothing safer than the Bank of
England the whole world seemed safe. The Bank was one
element in a general system. This system — if men respected
the gold standard, took care to balance the budget and did not
interpose too many obstacles in the free flow of goods and
money — was understood to be, for the most part, self-regula-
tory. The play of economic energies developed naturally in
response to laws general and unchanging. Such distortions, momentary and local, as occurred within this solid universe could
be brought under control by the manipulation of the discount
rate. Slight changes in this rate by an institution like the Bank of
England were enough, it was said, "to dispel disturbances in the
international movements of money with all their effects on exchange rates, credit positions, and the price level of commodities." So simple was this device, so much a matter of routine
was its application, that it could be used with competence "by
men who rarely cared to give much thought to economic or social theories."

The conditions of the time combined to support the friction-
less interaction of the working parts in this economic system. It
was natural that faith in the continuation of these conditions
should become, over the years, confused with faith in the working parts — the gold standard, the balanced budget, the open
channels for goods and money. It was also natural that men

should seek to fortify their faith by investing it with the rein-
forcement of moral commitments. The gold standard was referred to, for instance, as an Ark of the Covenant. Systems
that have worked for a long time, that have become encased
in a moral sanction, are seldom brought under careful analysis
by those who live within the systems. In a world where men
felt in the bone as in the flesh "safe, certain, secure," as Gustav
Stolper said, "economic forces were so much taken for granted
that few people troubled to give critical thought to them."

In the years from 1914 to 1920 this solid structure was totally
dismantled. Europe, it was said at the time, lay "in the fearful
convulsions of a dying civilization." A "world where progress
was a matter of course, moral standards were not seriously
questioned, and economic rules were immutable and general," it
was said twenty years later, simply "went to pieces."

If the economic consequences of the war and ensuing peace
were obvious to most observers, the essential causes of disaster
were far more difficult to discern. When Leo Pasvolsky was
told he could not know what the war had meant until he looked
upon the battlefields, he replied, "Have you seen the meaning
of the depreciated and oscillating exchanges, the disorganized
banking and currency systems, and the disrupted trade and commercial relations . . . ?" Only a few had been able to see
through to the existence of such meanings and even these few
could not fully understand what they saw. Events in the immediate future, as John Maynard Keynes said, would be shaped
not by the conscious acts of statesmen but "by the hidden currents, flowing continually beneath the surface of political history," yet no one, not even he, could predict the shape and
course of these subterranean currents.

How in such a society, laid waste, deprived of "psychological conditions, which it may be impossible to recreate," shaken
by economic energies at once invisible and unfamiliar — how
in such a society a new, changed world could be constructed on
new, different principles was the problem presented to men who

knew only a safe, certain, secure, self-regulating past. Keynes insisted that it was necessary to set in motion the forces of instruction and imagination. There are difficulties, however, in preparing a course of instruction out of such information as can be obtained about situations that are "almost wholly unrecognized." There are difficulties in trying to instruct pupils who by fatigue and bitterness had been brought to "the dead season of [their] fortunes" and who, having taken economic forces for granted, had never really thought about them. There are also difficulties in stimulating men to imagine a new community when the shock of the present has driven them to search backward for familiar psychological conditions that cannot be recreated. Men who have spent all their lives in the Book of Genesis cannot be snatched away at any moment of time and required, in ignorance of the origin of species, to construct a new world that will actually work on Darwinian principles within something less than six days.[1]

In such moods and conditions the men of 1920 set out to construct the new economy. They were confronted at the outset by two dominant and inescapable facts. First, virtually all the victorious nations were deep in debt to a country which in the past had owed them money, the United States. Second, the productive energy of Central Europe which had contributed so much to the earlier general prosperity had been severely

[1] The description of conditions, as given in the foregoing paragraphs, is derived principally from: E. H. Carr, *Conditions of Peace* (New York, 1943), Chs. 4, 5; H. G. Moulton and Leo Pasvolsky, *War Debts and World Prosperity* (New York, 1932), Chs. 1, 2, p. 369; John Maynard Keynes, *The Economic Consequences of Peace* (New York, 1920), Chs. 2, 5, 7; Gustav Stolper, *This Age of Fable* (New York, 1942), 1, 9. Keynes is especially interesting on the moral attitudes at work in the prewar world. The wealthy preferred, he says, the power which investment gave them over the pleasures of immediate consumption. Society, therefore, was "working not for the small pleasures of today but for the future security and improvement of the race" — that is, for "progress." The principle of accumulation of wealth based on inequality was "a vital part of the pre-war order of Society and of progress as we then understood it." This agreement upon the unequal distribution of wealth and the use of it to invest rather than to spend depended, he concluded, upon the "psychological conditions . . . impossible to recreate" after 1914.

damaged by the war. These two facts by themselves posed a problem of readjustment difficult to solve by the application of pure economics. And unhappily pure economics became entangled with considerations of politics and the human heart. The instinctive need of the European victors was to punish the nations that had cost them so much in blood and treasure. Therefore reparations were required of the defeated, thus adding to the load of debt in a debt-ridden system. The instinctive fear of the European victors was that the conquered would rise again. Therefore steps were devised to maintain the defeated nations in their crippled position, thus reducing their capacity to pay the required reparations. There was yet a further complication. As a self-respecting nation that sought to keep itself clear of "the mess" in Europe, the United States could not, unlike England after the Napoleonic wars, bring herself to remit the obligations of her debtors in the interests of a general good; she expected the money owed her to be paid. Also as a self-respecting nation that sought to keep itself clear of the mess in Europe, the United States did not join in the assessment of reparations from the Germans. In fact the country insisted that between the debts incurred by the expenses of the war and the debt assigned by reparations claims there was no connection.

Acting on these responses the nations put together a system that was designed to satisfy the urge for revenge, protect the future against the return of the marauder and restore the world's economy to the ancient stabilizing faiths of the balanced budget and the gold standard. The source of initial energy in this system was supposed to be Central Europe. The thought was that if Germany and her associated powers sent enough money in reparations to the victorious nations it would be possible for the victors to pay their debts to the United States and reconstitute their own industrial plants. Events soon demonstrated that there was not enough money in the defeated countries to make the system work. By the middle of the twenties, as Secretary Mellon said, the world had learned "the folly of imposing indefinite and impossible terms from the experiment with Germany. . . ." So a new approach was tried. The obligations of Germany were more fully defined and limited in the Dawes and Young plans and, as the Secretary of the Treasury proposed, "America, with its excess of capital . . . must aid by making private loans to Europe for productive purposes." Accordingly from 1926 forward American money — much of it loaned at short term — went into Central Europe in quantity. The results were gratifying. German industry began to flourish; the reparations payments were transmitted on schedule to the victorious allies who, in turn, sent on their debt payments to America. Throughout all Europe return was made to the gold standard, to stable exchanges, and to a time of industrial development.

There was only one difficulty. If the nations of Central Europe were ever to obtain real money of their own making to pay their debts and finance their industrial growth they, instead of borrowing from England, France and primarily from the United States, would have to sell the things they had made with borrowed money. And in the event they did not find a sufficient market for their goods. Tariff policies, limited purchasing power, fear of overstimulating the economic growth of defeated nations, all reduced the demand for German goods. For instance, the United States, committed by tradition and primal instinct to protection, erected impressive tariff barriers in 1922 and again in 1930, thus "doing everything in our power to restrict German sales of all . . . commodities in this country."

The result was that money, borrowed in increasing amounts, was used by debtor nations in part to supply working capital to produce goods that could not be sold abroad and in part to pay the enlarging charges on debts that were constantly growing "in snowball fashion." The foundation of the new economy was in part the capacity of certain countries, notably the United States, to continue lending money. This was but dimly understood. For one thing, few men were trained to investigate the operation of the total economic system. Then too most men in each country had superior local attachments and requirements that were being satisfied — the protective principle, the repayment of hired money, revenge, momentary peace of mind. Finally the ancient symbols of the gold standard and the balanced budget were being held in place. Thus not many perceived that the old allegiances and the old way of doing things were sustained by artificial means. And these few, unbemused by the classic moralities, clearly intent only on survival, were often enough, like Hjalmar Schacht, taken to be scamps. And so, when the capacity to lend without much prior thought ceased "almost overnight" in 1929, there were not many who could foresee the probable course of the hidden currents flowing beneath the surfaces of political history. And when in 1931 the currents reached and washed away the flimsy foundations of the structure, there were fewer still who knew exactly what had happened or what to do.[2]

There were of course premonitory symptoms. As early as May 1930 Briand had proposed a self-protective economic federation for Europe, but since it was based on a reaffirmation of the situation created by Versailles it only antagonized the Germans. In December 1930 Germany herself by emergency decree cut salaries of civil servants, doubled the taxes on beer and tobacco and raised income taxes in an effort to obtain more money from within her troubled economy. In February 1931 Philip Snowden gave one of the gravest speeches made by a Chancellor of the Exchequer in fifty years. And in March Germany and Austria drew together in a customs union designed to give mutual protection, but which in fact alienated the only

[2] The description of postwar conditions, as given in the foregoing paragraphs, is derived principally from Moulton and Pasvolsky, *War Debts*, Chs. 6-13, 17, 18; John W. Wheeler-Bennett, *The Wreck of Reparations* (New York, 1933), Ch. 1. Hjalmar Schacht gives an episodic account of the German, or at least of the Schacht, view of things in *Confessions of "The Old Wizard"* (Boston, 1956), 206-56. A description of the monetary situation in Europe in the twenties is to be found in *The Course and Control of Inflation* (League of Nations, 1946).

European country, France, that had the capacity to lend money. In April England closed its books with a deficit of £23 million while the deficit for Germany, it was predicted, would reach £35 million.[3]

These symptoms were duly reported. The Purport Books of the State Department began to fill up in the fall of 1930 with warnings of coming difficulty; in the early spring of 1931 these warnings turned to occasional predictions of disaster. Creditors, frightened by conditions, had begun to pull money and credit out of Central Europe. Once or twice on the pages of the Purport Books it was noted that Germany might not find the cash to meet the reparations charges, might seek a moratorium on her payments. Yet these symptoms, though duly noted, were not correctly interpreted. In Europe there was the natural tendency to set the evidence aside and, with Sir Samuel Hoare, to think "of the danger as one of the many that so often came and went in Central Europe." The United States, physically more remote from the scene of trouble, distracted by her own hard times, no doubt thought less than other nations about the meaning of events. On April 7, for about the first time, the Cabinet discussed the world economic situation. Montagu Norman of the Bank of England had come to Washington to report to the President the flight of money from England and Germany, and to give Stimson his view of "a very gloomy situation." There was, as a result, a listless discussion in the Cabinet from which no useful ideas emerged. The men in the Cabinet, like men everywhere, had no way of telling that out of the first few months of "sullen depression" in 1931 "amazing developments were to happen" in the latter part of the year.[4]

[3] Moulton and Pasvolsky, *War Debts*, Ch. 14; Wheeler-Bennett, *Wreck of Reparations*, 30-35.
[4] Purport Book 462:00R, SD; Viscount Templewood (Samuel Hoare), *Nine Troubled Years* (London, 1954), 13; Diary, April 7, 8, 1931. The State Department Purport Books, containing brief digests of incoming dispatches, give, in a kind of dramatic shorthand, the accumulating evidence of approaching collapse. It is hard to imagine how anyone reading these summaries could escape the recognition of what was happening; in these Purport Books also it can be

The amazing developments began only a few weeks after Montagu Norman's visit when word got around that the Credit Anstalt in Austria was in trouble. Loss of confidence in this great banking institution set off a panic that swept through Austria into Germany. No manipulation of the classic device, the discount rate, could bring this situation under control. Withdrawals of money and credit from the area increased as May turned into June. On June 8 Ramsay MacDonald cabled a letter to Stimson to say that he had been told by a German delegation that Germany was at the end of her rope. To the Prime Minister the situation appeared "awful." Germany, he said, was "a sort of economic advance post"; if she fell into bankruptcy and "surrendered to the forces of revolution either of the Left or to Right the state of Europe [would be] full of very ominous prospects." Only a moratorium on reparations and the continuation of American short-term credits could save their country, the Germans had told MacDonald.[5]

This communication from MacDonald served to confirm the dreadful tidings Stimson had begun to receive in his own country during the previous week. The run on the banks in Europe had put in jeopardy the short-term credits extended by American banks to Germany and the American bankers had carried their anxieties to the White House. The condition of these banks was indeed precarious. It was estimated that there was $700 million of American money in Central Europe and one report was that all but three of the big banks in New York had loaned to the area short-term credits that were greater than their capital and surplus combined. Whether or not the report was correct, it was obvious that the fate of American finance was intricately tied up, in the first week of June, with the uncertain fate of Germany. This brought the condition of all Europe home to the United States.[6]

---

discovered that the idea of a moratorium was at least discussed abroad as something necessary and possible as early as the winter of 1930-1931.
[5] Ramsay MacDonald to H.L.S., June 8, 1931.
[6] Diary, June 2, 1931; Conversation with Herbert Feis, Nov. 4, 1955.

On June 5 the President laid before Secretary Mellon, Assistant Secretary of the Treasury Ogden Mills and Stimson "a bold emphatic proposition" to place a moratorium on all intergovernmental debts. This, it was hoped, would not only relieve debtors of obligations they could not at the moment meet, but, as a dramatic and generous gesture by the principal creditor, would serve to restore the indispensable influence of confidence. The Secretary of the Treasury responded apathetically. Ogden Mills, whom Joseph Cotton called "the Village Snowden" after the Chancellor of the Exchequer whom the French called "Monsieur Non Non," was, at first cautious. It was said he needed the debt payments to balance the budget and that he wanted above all things to balance the budget. Stimson knew less economics than either of the men from the Treasury. Indeed it had come to him as something of a surprise that the flow of goods and the state of the exchanges could bear heavily upon the course of diplomacy. He had never cared for these things and when he took office he had known, he said, less about the economic condition of Europe than the average intelligent layman who lived with the New York newspapers. For instance, in 1929 he "didn't know anything about the Young Commission, its origin, its jurisdiction, or really have any accurate information about the reparations situation." He had, since 1929, tried to educate himself by reading and conversation, but inevitably events had progressed in that time more rapidly than his education. But he knew a crisis when it was upon him and so he was openly enthusiastic in stating that the matter "was one of psychology and credit" which might well be restored by the President's action. Hoover gratefully replied that he had himself "always believed in going out to meet a situation." [7]

[7] Diary, Aug. 28, 1930, June 5, 1931; W. S. Myers and W. H. Newton, *The Hoover Administration* (New York, 1936), 88. The President had been thinking about the condition of things early in May. On May 11, he asked Mellon and Stimson to study ways to relieve the pressure. They were, he reports (*Memoirs*, Vol. III, *The Great Depression: 1929-1941* [New York, 1952], 67),

But then, in the days following June 5, the President began to have second thoughts about how far he should go out. He first became alarmed lest the general moratorium would suggest a connection between reparations — which the United States did not collect from Germany — and the war debts which she did collect from other countries. Such a connection, in the President's mind, would drag us into "the European mess" by associating America with the punitive charges of German reparations as well as with the legitimate financial charges of the debt. That there was a connection in fact if not in pure logic — since our debtors used reparations money to pay their debts — was argued at length between Stimson and Hoover in two discussions that grew "quite tense." Then the President began to think of what it might mean politically to forgive, even temporarily, the payments on debts which had been made an article of American faith ever since his predecessor had pointed out that "they" had hired the money. Then he thought of the politicians, those men like Wright Patman of Texas who would later say, "I believe that [the people] are against it," or like Louis MacFadden of Pennsylvania who would speak of the tricks of international bankers, or like John Rankin of Mississippi who would say that if there were any moratorium it should be for those people who have Federal loans on their homes. "Why not grant a moratorium to those who sustain this Nation in time of peace and fight its battles in time of war?" Then the President thought of France and how with her morbid obsession she might object to giving up the unconditional German reparations prescribed in the Young Plan. Then he began to think the situation on short-term money "was not so bad as he had thought." From "private advices" he had heard that Germany owed on bonds no more than $300 million. Bernard

---

"unable to make any suggestion." On May 20 he talked with Stimson about the possibility of making a statement on the tariff and the debts. He recalled in his memoirs that when he first suggested the moratorium, Mills approved of the idea. Stimson recorded that Mills made the point that the President's power to do what he proposed was probably "limited" by former agreements.

Baruch, among others, had called Stimson to say he had seen "worse situations in the war which had come out all right." [8]

The President had all these things, and more, to think about, and as an elected official with final responsibility for the calculation of what was possible he naturally thought about them more than his appointed advisers did. And in those days the capital was a poor place to think. Out of Europe came daily reports of "tottering" and "revolution." From New York the bankers in panic "came crying down . . . and said that they were busted." No single man knew much and when he joined in conference he found that what he knew only conflicted with what others knew. In "the failure of anybody to understand . . . ," what was done was, after much talk, "done instinctively." It was also done in a temperature of 100 degrees by men who had, often enough, slept five hours the night before. One evening a three-hour argument at the Treasury Building ended indecisively just as a thunderstorm was breaking. Men who stepped into the rain were drenched to the skin after walking five feet. One of them walked on home because it "seemed like such a cooling and pleasant device after the dreadful period in Washington." [9]

In such an atmosphere it was hard for men to keep their "nerves ironed out." Stimson at times felt as though he were "sitting in a bath of ink." He felt also that the man at the center of these chaotic things seemed, after his first great forward step, "for a long time to be going backwards." To work with the President in these moods, the Secretary discovered was "terribly

[8] Diary, June 8, 11-15, 1931; Hearings, House Committee on Ways and Means, 72nd Congress, 1st Session, on H. J. Resolution 123, pp. 80, 104, 118. The estimates of the amount of American money lent in short-term credits to Germany varied greatly in this period. Mills, several days before Hoover reported that his private advisers placed the figure at $300 million, told Stimson the New York banks alone had extended $420 million of credit while Dawes placed the amount at $500 million in New York alone. The usual figure for the total American amount was $700 million.

[9] Conversation with Herbert Feis, Nov. 4, 1955. For an excellent description of all the complicating factors that had to enter into Hoover's calculations, see Moulton and Pasvolsky, War Debts, 320-22.

wearing . . . because the agony of going through so much fear and hesitation beforehand is a great burden." The natural uncertainties of Mr. Hoover served as an agenda for his advisers from June 6 to June 16. But as Mills, now converted, Eugene Meyer, Dwight Morrow, George Harrison of the New York Federal Reserve Bank and Stimson urged him forward on the course of his original desire, his plan began to take concrete form. All agreed that a two-year moratorium was economically more desirable, but this was taken to be politically impossible. The great figure of Borah, surrounded by a multitude of lesser, more dimly discerned politicians, loomed in the way. So it was agreed to limit the proposal to one year. It was also agreed that the moratorium would be announced without previous consultation with other nations to achieve the maximum psychological effect. To this idea Dwight Morrow offered substantial dissent. He believed that France, the only other important creditor nation that would have to share a sacrifice with the United States, ought to be included in prior discussions. Also he had studied France carefully at the London Naval Conference; he knew that with her dark concern over Germany she would resist the idea of altering the Young Plan by accepting the loss, even for a year, of the unconditional reparations. Support for this position was given in a letter from Ambassador Walter E. Edge who reported that France would resist any revision of reparations; that she looked on the United States as Uncle Shylock and that "The word SECURITY is the first and last chapter of the constitution of France." These counsels, in the end, went unregarded. The Secretary of State on June 18 told Paul Claudel, the French Ambassador, that he "couldn't say whether we would do anything or not," but he "could say that we would do nothing unless France shared in the sacrifice." And on the following day, after the moratorium had been decided upon, he summoned Claudel to tell him "what we were proposing to do." [10]

[10] Diary, June 10, 13, 18, 19, 1931; Walter Edge to Herbert Hoover, June 9,

On that day, June 19, the President, since Congress was not in session, called as many legislative leaders as he could reach by telephone to obtain their consent to the plan. To his gratification, surprising support was forthcoming. At noon on the 19th he told Stimson "to spring it on the representatives of the Powers." Two days later the moratorium proposal was announced to the world and it seemed, as John Wheeler-Bennett said, as though "the star of the west had arisen." [11]

At home and abroad there was "a great burst of applause," "a universal acclaim." The spontaneous enthusiasm in the United States suggests that the Administration had been distracted by the small, shrill voices; around the country there was, apparently, a majority waiting to be roused by some confident, commanding act. Overseas the response was even more rewarding. Stock and commodity prices bounced up in London, Paris and Berlin. Withdrawals from the Reichsbank, which had reached an historic high on Saturday, June 20, dwindled away on Monday, June 22, to nothing. When the President returned to Washington from a week end at Rapidan he was a "transformed man." For that day the effect of his act on the exchanges, on the nations, and on the hopes for the future seemed "magical." [12]

But, as Dwight Morrow had foreseen, there was an exception. In Paris, Edge reported, the tone of the response was "frankly hostile." Claudel, the French Ambassador in Washington, more gently told Stimson that while his country appreciated the American "spirit of solidarity," still the moratorium posed "many problems of the first order" which France wanted to think about. The Secretary of State replied that in a crisis of confidence and credit psychology was the big factor. For Claudel he drafted the kind of note the United

1931, 462.00R 296/4099, SD; H.L.S. Memorandum of talk with Claudel, July 18, 1931, 462.00R 296/4024, SD.
[11] Diary, June 18-20, 1931.
[12] *The Literary Digest*, July 4, 1931, 56-57; Diary, June 22, 1931; Moulton and Pasvolsky, *War Debts*, 324-25.

States would like to receive from France. It expressed "hearty accord" with the general proposition and reserved for further discussion only "details and technicalities." This, however, was not the kind of note France was prepared to send the United States. From Paris came an expression of fear that a one-year exception in the unconditional reparations would mean that Germany would never begin the payments again. Two weeks of frantic exploration went on before a solution was reached which would apparently continue the precedent of payment while in fact excusing Germany from the actual necessity of paying reparations for one year. During this interval the fate of the moratorium hung in the balance, and during the interval the first effects, like all effects produced by magic, began to fade away. Soon the decline in public feelings began to be reflected on the exchanges and the flight from the mark and the pound began again.[13]

It remained the conviction of the President and the Secretary of State that the haggling of France was in considerable part responsible for this return to the dead season of the world's fortunes. As Mr. Hoover said, "During the French delay, the spirit of panic had gained force and . . . severely depleted gold reserves. . . ." If this were true it was unfortunate that for a second time within a year the administration had miscalculated the influence on events that could be exerted by a French attitude that did not happen to coincide with American attitudes. There may be ways to gauge, in the long run, whether the desire of France for its special kind of security in the geographical middle of the mess of Europe was more or less noble than the desire of the United States not to get dragged into a mess to which she was already joined by the invisible cords of economics. But in the short run it seems obvious that efforts to reconcile rather than to disregard these conflicting points of view would have been useful.[14]

[13] Cable, Walter Edge to Secretary of State, June 23, 1931, 462.00R 296/4068, SD; H.L.S. Memorandum on talk with Claudel, July 21, 1931, 462.00R 296/4030, SD; Diary, June 21, 1931.
[14] Hoover, Great Depression, 72; Active Service, 206-7.

Yet in the actual event such considerations are no doubt beside the point — the delay caused by French hesitations, so annoying and disappointing to men desperately engaged in a search for measures to avoid delay, cannot be made a first or even significant source of failure. The moratorium was a reasonable effort to solve a problem; it can be made to seem, within the existing context of American political understanding and prejudice, an imaginative, even a striking, decision. But it can scarcely be taken as a marvel of American ingenuity. Men on both sides of the water had suggested it for a good many months. And it was in the larger revolutionary context of the time both timid and insufficient; one of those conventional maneuvers which in later times were said to produce too little and too late. The process of decay within a fundamentally unsound economic arrangement had gone too far to be arrested by such limited means or by their psychological side effects.

The psychological effects of the moratorium on Stimson, however, were beneficial. It was "an attempt at the bold executive leadership" that he particularly liked and understood. Throughout June he had been fully engaged in seeking to drive through a proposition that was clear and definite, in "crowded and exciting moments." Amid the ringing telephones, the come and go of ambassadors, bankers, senators and cabinet members, the crossfire of discussion between tired, driven men, he found himself in a situation that was quite like war. Against the background of what had gone before, this kind of purposeful action was particularly rewarding. He had in those months fretted away his energy among events and moods about which he could do nothing — what Cotton called the usual troubles and revolutions of South America, interminable discussions in preparation for a conference on silver that was never held, endless debates with French and Italians trying halfheartedly to reach the agreement they had failed to obtain at the London Naval Conference, complicated conversations about a possible meeting of the long-postponed conference of the nations on disarmament. He moved in an atmosphere where decisions as well as hopes were all deferred; where men, made sullen or stunned by depression, moved not so much in disillusion as without perspective or without direction. These were times and moods that Stimson by instinct and by training could least understand or accept.

To these official difficulties had been added a profound personal sorrow. In January 1931 the man on whom he relied not only for sage counsel and informed advice but for relieving humor and for the steadying sense that he was understood fell ill. When after two months of pain Joseph Cotton died, Stimson realized for the first time with full force "how different the world would be." Driving away from the funeral Stimson turned to his companion and said with tears in his eyes, "You know a good deal about this administration, but even you can't realize what a loss to the country Joe's death is. He is the only man who could do anything with the President."

The death of the Under-Secretary also emphasized further an official deficiency which Stimson had already tried to correct, the absence of a staff which could supply adequate information and assistance. In part this deficiency was caused by Stimson's predilection to rely upon the people he knew and chose; he did not, save in the case of Francis White and Wilbur Carr, turn often to the regular officers of the State Department for advice. But in larger part the deficiency was caused by defects within the Department itself. It was a small — really a tiny — organization, ill-prepared to deal with any of the great problems thrust upon it. This, to some extent, explains why Stimson sometimes turned to men like Mark Sullivan and Walter Lippmann for information he felt he could not easily get from within his own domain. It also explains why he looked, for additional staff, to the circles outside the Department with which he was familiar. But 1931 was not a good year to tempt men away from their own concerns to serve the state at personal sacrifice, and in the spring the Secretary searched far and wide for men to help him.

In the course of educating himself in economics he had read *Europe, the World's Banker* and in April he appointed the book's author, Herbert Feis, as his first economic adviser in the State Department. By May he had obtained the services of Allen Klots, Harvey Bundy and James Rogers. All three had graduated from Yale and the first two from the Harvard Law School. Klots, the son of a classmate, came from Winthrop and Stimson to become the "indispensable eyes and ears" of the Secretary; Bundy, as an Assistant Secretary of State, concerned himself at first with matters connected with foreign debts and loans, and Rogers also became an Assistant Secretary of State. They were all well-trained, intelligent, devoted men for whom Stimson developed a high regard, but, in the spring of 1931, they were all without experience in the world of foreign policy. Such experience was to be supplied by William R. Castle, who was appointed to Cotton's place. Castle had spent his life in the diplomatic service, he "knew the State Department game," he was a cultivated man. He was also, in the opinion of one who worked with him, bound by a "narrowness and obsolescence of outlook," and, in the opinion of another, "an insecure little man." Between him and the Secretary there was at first no tie of affection and, as time passed, no bond of trust.[15]

Amid the frustrations posed by the times, the tasks and the search for a new staff, Stimson found himself the victim of familiar symptoms. He described in such faithful detail the course

[15] Diary, March 30, 1931; H.L.S. to Felix Frankfurter, Feb. 11, 1931, Frankfurter Papers; conversation with Harvey Bundy, Oct. 29, 1955; Herbert Feis to author, Aug. 19, 1959; *Active Service*, 192-93. Among those Stimson considered, to some of whom he offered positions in the Department in the spring of 1931, were Nelson Perkins, Charles Curtis, John McLane, Charles Taft and George Rublee. The relations between Stimson and Castle at the time of the appointment of the latter are confused by the recollections of those who remembered what happened afterward. Stimson in *Active Service*, 192, suggests that Hoover was responsible for the appointment and, in the strongest language he ever publicly used about a man he worked with, calls it a "mistake." Yet, at the time, he told the President he was "prepared to recommend Castle" and told Root that Castle was a "very hard-working, well-poised and helpful associate."

of his twists and turns in the great clutch of insomnia that even his most devoted subordinates listened with diminishing interest and sympathy. Deprived of sleep he succumbed by day to feelings of debility, indigestion and "pained patience." Toward the end of a day members of his staff found him growing not only more "petulant" but also, occasionally, slower to respond and to organize his thoughts. But the confusion that set in about three o'clock was sometimes deceptive. Pierrepont Moffat discovered what others in the law had noticed before, that the Secretary was "a curious man in that while talking to him you have a feeling that he has not gathered the point you are trying to make, only to find it come out from a day to a week later, rephrased, redressed, but seized in all its details." From these frustrating days Stimson fled out to Woodley to clear his mind and spirit in long rides or in intense games of deck tennis. Members of his staff discovered that the spirit tended to clear more quickly if the Secretary emerged victorious from these contests.

But Stimson sought and found more sustained relief in travel. Before the excitement of the moratorium, he had planned to go to Europe to see and talk with the men he was dealing with by cable and correspondence. In the last week of the negotiation with the French over the precise terms of the moratorium he was already at sea on his way to Italy. On the boat he was told in a message from Castle that the French were trying to attach political conditions to their acceptance of the Hoover proposal while the Americans were insisting on acceptance of the moratorium in its pristine form. Stimson replied that in his mind "we should go too far if we sought to veto all side negotiations between Germany and the other European nations. . . ." He also repeated his conviction that the remedy for the crisis was psychological and that the influence of the United States would be greater if exerted "by suggestion and persuasion rather than by the imposition of hard and fast conditions." "If," he added, "the President's main purpose is achieved I believe the ratification by Congress will follow much more easily than he is sometimes inclined to believe." By July 6 he heard that the formula for the unconditional reparations had been worked out and the French had accepted the moratorium.[16]

By that date he had begun his tour of the capitals of Europe. In Rome he was exposed to the customary diversions of the time — the Forum bathed in artificial light at night, Titian's "Sacred and Profane Love" and a ride in a speedboat driven by Mussolini. He also talked with Il Duce in the enormous room. Everybody, the Dictator said, knew where Italy stood; she was for disarmament. He gave it as his opinion that a naval building holiday proposed by Mr. Hoover was possible. Later, at a pleasant dinner, the Foreign Minister Dino Grandi told Stimson frankly that the Fascist regime was transitory; was not really a possible permanent solution.

From the glisten of Rome the Secretary's party, attended by a guard of *carabinieri*, departed in Mussolini's private car. At the border the inattentive French put the travelers in the compartments of a regular railway coach and, in Paris, a single minor *fonctionnaire* from the Quai d'Orsay awaited them on the platform. But the unfavorable impression this created was in part dispelled by later conversations with the Prime Minister Pierre Laval and Pierre E. Flandin. The latter, a former Minister of Finance, proved "very intelligent and very frank" while in the former Stimson discovered an "able, forceful man, and I think also a sincere man." Laval talked to him, also frankly, about the difficulties caused him by the Cabinet in the moratorium negotiations; he assured the Secretary that while the French liked flags, music and soldiers they were not militaristic, and he explained that while Mussolini was "a bad boy who talked roughly," he "thought he was a pretty good fellow." When the party moved on to Berlin Stimson was appalled by the "atrocious" architecture and the "frightful" statuary. But he found in Paul von Hindenburg a fine old man who was much concerned

---

[16] Radio message, Castle to H.L.S., June 29, 1931, 462.00R 296/4170, SD; Radio message, H.L.S. to Castle, June 30, 1931, 462.00R 296/4220, SD.

to defend the Army against the charge of war guilt, and in Chancellor Heinrich Bruening he discovered a real friend. They had served, it developed, on opposite sides of the line at Cambrai in December 1917, and that led the German to say they must find "some other better way of solving international questions in the future." Stimson took up this same subject at a dinner attended by Bruening, Otto Dietrich, Minister of Finance, Wilhelm Groener and the Foreign Minister Julius Curtius. He told them how much his father had disliked the cold and clanking Berlin of the 1870's, explained how the distortion in the civil-military relationships in Germany had placed on her the major responsibility for the war and advised his audience to get in touch with the British on steps to take toward disarmament.[17]

These visits and frank exchanges supported the faith he had expressed to Grandi that one of the best ways to preserve the peace was through continuing conversations between responsible officials in different countries. But a more important immediate result of this trip to Europe was the part he was unexpectedly called on to play in what he later called "one of the neatest and most successful" negotiations of his career.

The negotiation began in Paris when he arrived on July 15. There he found that the moratorium of July 6 had already failed of its purpose. The flight from the mark had begun again and Germany was on the very edge of disaster. If Germany went down there was "no one in London, Paris, or New York [who] could declare . . . that they would escape the abyss." The British had already called a conference of the interested nations to meet in London on July 20. Conversations preliminary to this conference had already begun in Paris between representatives of the nations when Stimson arrived. From these conversations he learned that Germany had a position, France had a position, England had several positions and his own country had also a position.

The German position was clear and simple. As Bruening ex-

plained to Stimson the moratorium was not enough; Germany
had over a billion dollars in short-term credits which had to be
extended and she needed, in addition, more money. He went on
to explain that his country from the very beginning "had been
paying reparations . . . out of borrowed money" since she had
been unable to sell her goods abroad in any quantity. About this
statement Stimson felt "legitimate doubt"; for five years Germany had seemed prosperous, but he accepted the Chancellor's
description of Germany's desperate straits. The French position
was that England, France and the United States should lend new
money to the stricken country. This would serve to place
Germany even further in the control of the allies and, it was
said, Laval hoped to tie political conditions to the loan — an
agreement by the Germans to dissolve the Austro-German customs union and to give up the two pocket battleships that had
been planned. England's position was one of divided counsels.
Henderson, the Foreign Minister, was apparently attracted to
the idea of a loan while Montagu Norman, believing the Bank of
England already overcommitted, wanted, it was reported, a
complete re-examination and readjustment of the financial and
political settlements that had been made at Versailles. Nothing
alarmed the French more than such a proposal. As for the
American position, Stimson was prepared to consider a loan if
only because it was the only way to give Germany what everyone agreed she needed — new money. But when he told the
President of the French proposal, Mr. Hoover said the New
York bankers had told him it was impossible. Instead the President suggested a guaranteed extension or stabilization of the
short-term credits already outstanding in Germany.

   The task was to prevent any one of these conflicting positions
from assuming a dominance at Paris that would appear to fore-
close the possibility of the discussion of alternatives at London.
The British wanted all important decisions to be taken at the
conference they had called; the French did not want to see their
idea rejected out of hand, indeed they indicated they would not

go to London if this occurred; and the administration in Washington was anxious to have its own proposal serve as a guide for the London discussions. To keep the range of possibilities open Stimson did two things in Paris. First he prevented Dean Jay, the Morgan representative in Paris, from telling the Bank of France that American bankers would lend no money. When at a dinner Jay informed Stimson that Thomas Lamont asked him to carry this message to Emile Moreau, Governor of the Bank of France, the Secretary "blew up." He said he "had never heard of such a piece of God-damned folly" as the folly of bankers "in getting into a situation depending on psychology when the representatives of their Government were trying to control the psychology of the situation like this and that they could not take refuge in narrow banking axioms because banking depended on general psychology." In the middle of this disquisition Stimson was called from the table by a call from the President in Washington and to Mr. Hoover the Secretary went on: "If you want to help in the cause you are speaking of you will not do it by calling me up, but by calling up Tom Lamont and tell him he was the damnedest fool you ever heard of." Nothing was more certain to prevent the French from going to London than to give this information to Moreau. As a result of these conversations the French never did hear the attitude of the New York bankers toward their loan proposal and Stimson had the secondary satisfactions of seeing Dean Jay turn "white as a sheet" and of taking "one good chance to swat Morgan in the eye and I did it."

He also kept discussion open in another way. At a conference with Laval and others the thought occurred to him to use the simile of a bathtub with an unstoppered drain. There was no point in putting in fresh water until the hole was plugged. Stabilization of short-term credits was an indispensable preliminary step before additional credits could be considered. This simile could be construed in two ways. To the French it suggested that after stabilization came the probability of fresh credits to

Germany. With this idea in mind they joined the London Conference on July 20. It could also be interpreted to mean that the conference would do no more than stabilize the existing short-term credit situation. This was the desire of Herbert Hoover and also, it turned out, on Stimson's arrival in London, the desire of Ramsay MacDonald. Here was a further complication, for the President, having thought of the idea himself, was reluctant to have the British share in putting it before the conference.[18]

This was the state of affairs when the Secretary went to England on July 20. On that day, just before the conference opened, he summarized his own views of the situation in two cables to the State Department. First he said that, though he agreed "with the President's theory that existing credit levels should first be stabilized — we are in grave doubt of practicability of successful stabilization of credits." Secretary Mellon, who was with him, believed in fact that by itself it would only accelerate a run on German banks. The "indisputed evidence at the Paris Conference [was] that Germany requires fresh credit and could not recover even if present credits were stabilized." Second he said that the further doubt he had about presenting the President's plan to stabilize was whether "it can be fairly presented as solely an American plan inasmuch as British independently reached same view and were fully prepared with it when I met Prime Minister this morning."[19]

Mr. Hoover, who later recorded that "in view of the confusion among the leaders in Europe" it had been necessary for him to "take a strong hand" and come forward with a "new and drastic solution," was thoroughly alarmed by these two cables and by the suggestion in New York papers that in the simile of

[18] *Active Service*, 209; Weir, *Ramsay MacDonald*, Ch. 39. Evidence for this description of the negotiations in Paris is taken from Diary, July 15, 16, 17, 18, 25, 1931. These entries, beside the running daily account by Stimson, include memoranda of conferences and telephone calls written by Stimson and, in some instances, by Allen Klots.

[19] Cable, H.L.S. to Castle, July 20, 1931, 462.00R 296/4616, SD; Atherton to Castle, July 20, 1931, 462.00R 296/4598, SD.

the bathtub Stimson had endorsed a French loan plan. On the night of the 20th the President called Stimson to say he was considering a public statement of his own plan. Stimson replied that such a statement at the moment the conference was beginning might do irreparable damage by limiting the subject of debate and antagonizing the French. Reluctantly Hoover accepted this idea. Scarcely had he hung up when Castle called the Secretary to say Mills "rather insisted" on the President's statement. Again Stimson himself insisted that it would ruin the conference.[20]

Having secured his position Stimson went off to the conference Ramsay MacDonald called in his opening remarks "one of the turning-points in the history of the world. . . ." Chancellor Bruening spoke first on July 21 and "surely never before . . . was such a tragic story of misfortune and despair told by any European nation." When he sat down there was a feeling that "no more need be said." Stimson followed with the assurance that the United States would not "withdraw any short-term credits" and left the impression on all that his country "won't let Germany down." Then came Philip Snowden with his reputation for "consistent obstinacy" to say that he "commended the very benevolent action of America, but regretted that he was not in a position to go so far as Mr. Stimson." At this critical moment Stimson brought to bear the arts that Elihu Root had taught him. By careful cross-examination he drew from Snowden the admission that the stabilization of credits was a first and important step. Turning then to Bruening and MacDonald he obtained from both of them agreement on the same point. By this process of cross-examination he had achieved three objectives. First, he had prevented the free flow of the oratory of doubt and depression. Second, by drawing from all his witnesses

[20] Hoover, *Great Depression*, 73-75; Diary, July 20, 25, 1931. Mr. Hoover has fixed in his memory that he was the moving spirit in all the negotiations leading up to the " 'standstill' agreement" that was finally made in London. After European meetings that "got precisely nowhere" he suggested through Stimson, who "had gone to the South of France on a holiday," to the British that they call the conference in London.

a description of a stabilization program he had avoided the irritating question of whether America or England had thought of the program first. Third, by concentrating on this program he had prevented the French from coming forward with their loan proposal until it was obvious from the discussion that neither England nor the United States would seriously entertain such a proposition. After the session the idea of lending more money to Germany was dead "without having been killed" specifically by anyone. Tentative agreement was then reached on certain measures to provide the stabilization of the short-term credits — that is, agreement on the need to "stand still" instead of requesting immediate repayments.[21]

From this meeting Stimson went off to his hotel to be greeted by a group of reporters. They had word from Washington, they told him, that he had that day placed before the conference "a *new* American proposal"; the precise terms were said to be even then on the wires from Washington to London. Would he care to comment? Unaware of any "new" proposal and obligated, he felt, to say as little as possible about the proceedings of a conference meeting in executive session, Stimson was even more uninformative and brusque than reporters had come to expect him to be. He spoke of establishing a "bureau of denials." Soon after meeting with the newspapermen on the afternoon of July 21 he discovered what the new proposals were. They were simply the old Hoover plan of stabilization that the conference had talked about all day. Fearful that his Secretary of State might be drawn into the discussion of a loan, harried by private bankers who told him they could lend no more, assured by a friend of Ogden Mills in the Bank of England that the Bank would not consider a loan, anxious to put forward a plan of his own, Hoover had released the statement Stimson had earlier persuaded him not to make.[22]

[21] Weir, *Ramsay MacDonald*, 336-40; Diary, July 25, 1931.
[22] H.L.S. to Herbert Hoover, Aug. 11, 1931; Diary, July 25, 1931; *New York Times*, July 22, 1931; Hoover, *Great Depression*, 75-78. In the cable setting forth his view the President said the emergency was strictly "a short-term credit crisis" and, since there was no reason to doubt the basis on which the credits

The advices from Washington and the Secretary's comments in London created a certain amount of "confusion and consternation." Before the terms of the new proposal were disclosed, the French talked of going home, and on July 22 the *New York Times* reported that "Unfortunately the full benefit Mr. Hoover's proposals might have had on British public opinion today was impaired by Secretary Stimson's rigid ideas as to the amount of reticence his office imposes upon him." By the 23rd everyone had discovered that the American suggestions were actually those which the conference had already tentatively agreed upon — stabilization of credits. Stimson on that day, in the interests of further harmony, then explained to the reporters that both England and America had thought of the Hoover solution; it was after all, as he said, "an obvious measure." These observations restored the peace everywhere but in Washington where Castle gave out a statement in which he declared the whole idea belonged exclusively to Mr. Hoover.[23]

After this diversion the conference quickly completed its work. By July 24 it had agreed to extend for three months a

---

rested in the long run, "the first approach" was "the maintenance . . . of the present outstanding lines of credit."

[23] H.L.S. to Herbert Hoover, Aug. 11, 1931; *New York Times*, July 22, 23, 26, 1931. The confusion over who thought up the idea of stabilization — the standstill agreement — suggests the real lack of communication, in spite of many cables and telephone calls between London and Washington and, more specifically, between the President and the Secretary of State. The President, in his *Memoirs*, obviously felt Stimson and Mellon opposed his idea "lest we appear to be dictating [the conference] policies," and not because the British had also thought of what was indeed a very obvious idea. Castle in his Diary (as his view is given in Ferrell, *American Diplomacy*, 117, footnote 18) apparently believed Stimson put out the idea that the standstill was "an Anglo-American notion" to appease the French who were annoyed at Hoover's moratorium. The President, also in his *Memoirs*, indicates that both Mellon and Stimson "strongly urged" support of a further loan for Germany. He had to telephone them "emphatically" not to participate in such a loan. There is evidence in Stimson's Diary that he did not believe a standstill agreement without a further loan would help much, but at London, his Diary also says, he did his best to squelch the French loan plan. What these conflicting reports suggest is that Hoover and Stimson were not able to get across to each other what they were doing or hoped to do.

loan to Germany from the Bank of International Settlements; it
had also agreed to use the Bank as an instrument through which
the volume of credit extended to Germany by private banks
would be maintained. Finally, it recommended the appointment
of a committee to study further the credit needs of Germany.
These were the achievements of the London Conference. They
proved insufficient for the occasion. In the ensuing weeks Germany slid down into "chaos and disaster." Other nations were
pulled after her. The "August crisis" in England brought a
change in government and in September Britain left the gold
standard. One by one, as the months passed, countries around
the world, in a desperate effort to survive in the economic
wreckage, repudiated the faith of their fathers in gold.

In later years it was agreed that the London Conference of
1931 made no difference; it might as well have never met. Yet
there were moments of real meaning; it can remain as a kind of
parable of the times. On the afternoon of July 21 Charles
Dawes watched in the White House while Herbert Hoover
framed his statement on what was called the standstill agreement. The telephone rang continuously. The word came in
from Harrison in New York, Stimson, Mellon and Montagu
Norman in London, Hans Luther in Berlin. "Only first authority" was consulted by the President, who had around him Mills,
Castle, Morrow and Eugene Meyer. He was alert, competent,
compelling; "no one concerned with the whole situation in Europe had at his command," Dawes reflected, "more authoritative
information than did the President." And probably no one did.
But the information he had was not sufficient. When Dawes returned to his post a week later he found that the actual situation
at London during the conference had not been understood in
Washington. At a still later time it was discovered that no one
had been able to tell the President on July 21, over the telephone on which so many calls had been made, the exact total of
all outstanding credits. Mr. Hoover thought on that day that
the amount was five billion but it turned out, when the Bank of

International Settlements studied the matter, that the figure should have been ten billion. And how much of this amount was held by American banks no one knew for certain in June and July — some said as little as $350 million, some said as much as $700 million.[24]

These were the degrees of existing ignorance. A generation which had grown up taking economic forces so much for granted that few troubled to give critical thought to them had not had the time and perhaps the understanding to recognize what information was appropriate for its new needs, or to devise methods for obtaining this information or to create measures for the continuous organization and analysis of this information. In any given critical moment it was the natural custom to search out those informed by experience and on-the-spot observation. The extended recollections of an Andrew Mellon, the conditioned reflexes of a Philip Snowden, the opinion of a friend who worked in the Bank of England, the panic reactions of overextended bankers everywhere, were pooled together in the hope that not only wisdom but facts would emerge. There was, indeed, no better way, and by this process lesser men in other times had successfully manipulated the discount rate. But in the twenties and thirties there was more to it than the discount rate. At Versailles, at Spa, in the Dawes Plan, in the Young Plan and at Lausanne the men of these days, without full awareness of what they were doing, were putting together a crudely planned economy. For their purpose they could not even acquire enough information or create the means to interpret the information adequately. Perforce they had to rely upon the intuitive wisdom of men with obsolete experience to direct the scheme of things they were creating and, inevitably, such wisdom was not enough.

There are other suggestive things to be found in the proceedings of the London Conference of 1931. On July 20 Stimson had cabled the President that everyone at the discussions in Paris agreed that an extension of short-term credits was not enough;

24 Dawes, *Journal as Ambassador*, 366-67; Hoover, *Great Depression*, 78.

that Germany needed new money. Even the bankers in New York who could lend no more and feared for what they had already lent agreed to this. They begged Mr. Hoover to make a government loan. Yet after ten days of discussion and elaborate negotiation in Paris and London all the nations agreed to was a measure all agreed was not enough. This too was the custom of the times. Over and over again the nations of Europe, roused by the sight of clear and present dangers, met together in the decade after Versailles to discuss ways and means to set things right. Pursued as they were by separating anxieties, prejudices and objectives, they never were able in the meetings to do collectively the things they knew they had to do together — or even to do, at times, the things they claimed they had done in their meetings. Divided as they were among themselves they always failed to agree to take the steps they originally knew were necessary if they were to acquire a common safety in the dangers they shared in common. Stimson came late to this system of European conference and to a mood already established. Thus as at London in 1930, so again at London in 1931 he participated in an agreement that had died before it expired.

The mood of failure was already on all Europe in 1931 and found expression in one special symbol at London. At the conference table sat Aristide Briand, "the greatest orator in all Europe," the first statesman of France, the definer of the peace of the future, whose name was known around the world. In London Briand sat silent, gazing "listlessly before him with unseeing eyes," asleep at times, the great mouth "sagged a little open." He seemed a "derelict Demosthenes." In fact he was a very sick man. Within seven months he died, taking with him not only the hopes but the methods of those who tried to put the world together in the decade after the First World War. And as he was dying, an event in the East portended that the attempt of nations to solve their difficulties by the deliberations of conference and declarations of decent intent left unsupported by more than words had failed.[25]

25 Weir, *Ramsay MacDonald*, 340.

21

Manchuria

O N THE EVENING of September 18, 1931, there may have
been an explosion along the right of way of the South
Manchuria Railroad near the city of Mukden. Japanese military forces, stationed by treaty right in the railroad zone,
claimed that an explosion had occurred which placed the safety
of the railway in jeopardy. They therefore marched out of the
restricted area to pursue what they called bandits in Chinese territory. During the next six months while Western nations
sought to devise restraining measures the army of Japan spread
out over Manchuria. In March 1932 the state of Manchukuo,
unrecognized by Western nations, was created out of the conquered province. One year later this incident came to an uncertain ending when Japan, rather than accept the measured condemnation of the Lytton Report, withdrew from the League of
Nations.[1]

In reviewing this incident it is possible to select out for obser-

[1] There are many accounts of the Mukden incident and its attendant conse-
quences. See especially Sara R. Smith, *The Manchurian Crisis 1931-1932: A
Tragedy in International Relations* (New York, 1948); Henry L. Stimson, *The
Far Eastern Crisis: Recollections and Observations* (New York, 1936); Westel
W. Willoughby, *The Sino-Japanese Controversy and the League of Nations*
(Baltimore, 1935). Shorter accounts will be found in *Active Service*, Ch. 9,
and Ferrell, *American Diplomacy*, Chs. 8-11. Ferrell's description is enriched
by his study of Japanese documents bearing on foreign policy now on microfilm, in the Library of Congress. Most of the diplomatic exchanges between
the United States and other countries and the League of Nations produced by
the incident will be found either in *FR 1931*, III, or in *Foreign Relations of the
United States: Japan, 1931-1941* (Washington, 1943), I.

vation the insufficient behavior of particular individuals — the feeble equivocations of Kijuro Shidehara, the innocence of Charles Gates Dawes, the spineless temporizing of that "national and international disaster," Sir John Simon. Those who took an actual part in the incident or who, in later times, had to deal with some of its consequences have been moved, however, to think on larger questions of causality. Twenty years after it was over George Kennan, placing it in the long march of events in the Far East, concluded: "In the fabric of human events, one thing leads to another. Every mistake is in a sense the product of all the mistakes that have gone before it, from which fact it derives a sort of cosmic forgiveness; and at the same time every mistake is in a sense the determinant of all the mistakes of the future, from which it derives a sort of cosmic unforgivableness." Somewhere in the fabric no doubt there was a point dividing possible further hope from certain tragedy, but in the weaving of events in the Far East from 1900 to 1941 this point, Kennan believed, could not be placed precisely. It was "a vast and turgid process, involving immensely powerful currents of human affairs over which we Americans had little control or influence." [2]

Earlier, at the very moment the incident reached its closing, Hugh Wilson came to a somewhat different conclusion. Listening in March 1933 as Yosuke Matsuoka, shaken with passion, told the League that his country "was being crucified," he wondered for the first time if the course he and his colleagues had pursued for two whole years had, in fact, been all wrong. If nations feel strong enough to condemn, he reflected, they should feel strong enough to use force. While he was watching Matsuoka, taking his country out of the League and, in a way, out of Western society, the thought occurred to Wilson that condemnation creates a community of the damned who may later come together. Events, he decided, had started up a one-way street and he left the chamber troubled as he had never been troubled before. [3]

[2] George F. Kennan, *American Diplomacy 1900-1950* (Chicago, 1951), 49-50.
[3] Wilson, *Diplomat Between Wars*, 279-80.

Before the incident was over, indeed near its very beginning, Saionji was asked what he thought about it. Kimmochi Saionji was the last of the Genro, in theory the most powerful man in Japan. He alone had the right to place the name of a new Premier before the Emperor. Almost half a century earlier he had studied for ten years in Paris; he had lived in Berlin and Vienna and had toured the Continent to examine European constitutions. He was a friend of Theophile Gautier and Georges Clemenceau and was devoted to the works of Mill, Locke and Rousseau. When he was asked what to do while the Japanese army was sweeping through Manchuria, he replied, "there is no use in saying . . . 'I am at my wit's end.' This is probably one phenomenon of a transitional period. If one could only feel that this indeed is the time to put forth one's maximum effort one might even find it a very interesting period." [4]

Saionji, in a time of transition, was not well placed to ponder on forgiveness or the ultimate consequences of unforgivable things, but he was in a good position to state the mood of the occasion. At the time he spoke, wherever the culture of Mill, Locke, Rousseau, of party systems and constitutions, of private industrial enterprise and free exchange had penetrated — to London, Delhi, Berlin, Washington or Tokyo — the classic Western solutions, whether applied to problems of the counting house or to problems on a Manchurian plain, had come on for trial. And in this period of crisis and transition a favorable verdict, it might well seem, could be reached only by a maximum effort in the West.

Yet in the bomb that may have exploded at Mukden it was difficult to perceive a signal for maximum effort. For one thing it was a surprise and for another, as Tardieu said, "It was a long

[4] Takashi Oka, *Saionji and the Manchurian Crisis* (Committee on International and Regional Studies, Harvard University, Cambridge, 1954). This mimeographed study by Oka is based in principal part upon the Saionji-Harada *Diary* and the *Proceedings* of the International Military Tribunal for the Far East. The copy of these *Proceedings* now in the Harvard Law School Library was used in the preparation of this chapter.

ways off." Moreover there were few things, even for those prepared and on the spot, more difficult to understand than Japanese-Chinese relations in Manchuria. The relationship was imbedded in a tangle of history so confused that the merits of any particular issue arising in the province were almost impossible to assess. In this instance one could take the Chinese view that the Japanese had opened fire "without provocation of any kind," or one could take the Japanese view that their troops were acting only in self-defense, or one could assert, like Sir John Simon, that the technicalities were all with the Chinese and the moralities were all with the Japanese.[5]

There were other reasons to disregard the signal from Mukden. On the day it happened the American Ambassador to the Court of St. James's reported that the liquid resources of England were almost gone and that there were panic conditions in Amsterdam, Switzerland and Germany. Within the week England went off the gold standard and then the whole country was profoundly shaken by the news that elements of the fleet had mutinied at the Nore. "One must not expect anything in these times," Dawes concluded, "but be ready for everything." France, in a somewhat better economic situation than her neighbors, was entering a period of familiar political confusion attendant upon a change of government.[6]

If the European nations were ill prepared to heed the summons at Mukden, there was still the means available for collective action in the League of Nations. But historically events that occurred in far places had always caused the European delegates "pained surprise." The League to them existed "to put Germany in the position prescribed for it by the treaty of Versailles." Anything diverting attention from this end "had a tinge

[5] Allen Klots, Diary, March 28, 1932; Willoughby, *Sino-Japanese Controversy*, 32, 539-40; *The New Statesman and Nation*, Oct. 1, 1932, 364-65. The complicated story of Japanese treaty rights in Manchuria can be found in *Sino-Japanese Controversy*, Ch. 1, and F. C. Jones, *Japan* (Bristol, England, 1933), Ch. 4.
[6] Dawes, *Journal as Ambassador*, 393, 399.

of bad taste." Furthermore, delegates to Geneva had tended sometimes to get out of touch with their own governments. As Lord Cecil explained when he came to consider Mukden, "I was particularly awkwardly placed, without instructions and not even in close political alliance with the actual British Government." Finally, two of the countries most directly concerned with the Far East — Russia and the United States — were not members of the League.[7]

What, in these circumstances, was a country that in signing the Nine-Power Treaty had agreed with others to respect the territorial integrity of China, that had shared in the authorship of the Kellogg-Briand Pact, that for thirty years had put all its verbal support behind the policy of the Open Door, what was such a country to do when Japan marched out of the railroad zone into Chinese territory? Eugene Regnier was of the opinion that the Secretary of State at least didn't "like to get into the thing." He was, Regnier continued, "like a small boy at the edge of a pool which is cold, just not quite willing to get in there in one plunge and swim. . . ."[8]

The Secretary, for one thing, had his hands full of other matters. He was trying to persuade France and Italy to reach the agreement they had failed to achieve at the London Naval Conference; he was trying to prepare the American position for the forthcoming Disarmament Conference; he was trying to resolve some of the issues produced by the moratorium. There were a great many details to attend to in connection with the approaching visit of Pierre Laval and there was trouble in Salvador. Besides all this, the Secretary was an active member of an administration that was devoting most of its energy in September 1931 to devise means, within the frame of the President's economic and moral scruples, to support a disintegrating economic structure and to improve the lot of ten million unemployed. Finally

---

[7] Wilson, *Diplomat Between Wars*, 261-62; Robert Cecil, *A Great Experiment* (London, 1941), 222.
[8] Conversation with Stanley Hornbeck, Jan. 17, 1955. Three years earlier Hornbeck told Ferrell substantially the same thing. See *American Diplomacy*, 134.

he knew something of the condition of the other Western nations. The day before Mukden Ramsay MacDonald had sent him a cabled description of affairs in England and on the Continent. Reading this letter, Stimson said, was "like looking at a great flood breaking through a dam and having nothing but a hand shovel with which to make repairs." [9]

No doubt all these preoccupations caused the Secretary to hesitate about getting into this thing on the other side of the world. But also he brought to the occasion certain assumptions that suggested the wisdom of proceeding with caution and due delicacy. It could be assumed, first, that the incident was local, what he called "a mutiny." A mutiny did not necessarily demonstrate the existence of a plan to subvert a whole province; more probably it indicated that the relationship between civil and military elements in the Japanese government had once again been thrown temporarily out of balance. The history of the past decade suggested that, given time and appropriate support, the civilians, known to be temperate and liberal, would recover the position of dominance that they had held, if uneasily, since the end of the World War. Furthermore, it could be assumed that nations interested in the stability of the Far East would be able to mobilize world opinion as a means of limiting the incident by disapproving of it. Two years before when Russia and China had gotten into trouble with each other in the same region Stimson believed, though most others disagreed with him, that he had used the force of words and feelings to end the difficulty. In his mind therefore was the assumption that the earlier episode was "not the least significant evidence to show that the public opinion of the world is a live factor which can be promptly mobilized and which has become a factor of prime importance in the solution of the problems and controversies which may arise between nations." And finally, by virtue of his year in the Philippines and his negotiations with the Japanese at the London Naval Conference, he assumed he "knew

[9] H.L.S. to Ramsay MacDonald, draft of letter, Sept. 25, 1931.

something about" the Oriental peoples and what he called "the Oriental mind." [10]

All these assumptions were in his own mind when Debuchi, the Japanese Ambassador, reported that the incident was "a great surprise to him" and no doubt to the Foreign Office; he gave at the same time his assurances that his government was doing all in its power to "isolate" the situation. Translated into actual policy these assumptions meant, as Stimson said in often-quoted words, that he had "to let the Japanese know we are watching them and at the same time to do it in a way which will help Shidehara [the Japanese Foreign Minister], who is on the right side, and not play into the hands of any Nationalist agitators. . . ." This in turn meant that the influence of nations should be intruded "discreetly" to give Shidehara "an opportunity, free from anything approaching a threat or even public criticism, to get control of the situation." [11]

For three months this policy was pursued by the United

[10] Diary, Sept. 19, 1931; H.L.S., *Far Eastern Crisis*, 37; *New York Times*, Dec. 5, 1929; Secretary of State to Minister in China, Sept. 24, 1931, 793.94/1876c, SD. Stimson both in his diary and in many of his cables about the incident makes it clear that he believed he had a full understanding of "Oriental psychology." Mr. Hoover, in conversation on Nov. 2, 1955, exhibited a similar confidence in his comprehension of the same phenomenon. Beyond this the Secretary believed he and his associates "were habitually placed in the position of having in our hands earlier and more accurate information than almost any other country" about the developing crisis. If this was so it only demonstrated how little any country knew about the situation in the Far East and especially about the most important factor, the intentions of Japan. Edwin Neville, Chargé d'Affaires at Tokyo and the most useful source of information, had to content himself with reporting what he was told by the Foreign Office and with summarizing what he read in the newspapers and heard in talks with Japanese citizens. The impression on anyone reading the Purport Books and the papers in the State Department Archives for this period is that neither the Secretary nor his advisers could know much that was useful about what was going on in the Far East and especially in Japan.

[11] Memorandum by Stanley Hornbeck on conversation with Debuchi, Sept. 20, 1931, 793.94/1888, SD; Diary, Sept. 19, 22, 1931; Memorandum by Stanley Hornbeck on the "Mukden Incident," Sept. 20, 1931, 793.94/1889, SD; H.L.S., *Far Eastern Crisis*, 34. These Hornbeck memoranda are part of a series he wrote in the first days after Mukden in which he described the incident, examined the implications and suggested policies. Stimson was much influenced by these carefully worked out documents.

States, acting independently and in concert with other nations. Independently the country stated this policy on September 24, 1931, in identical notes sent to China and Japan. These notes used words like "regret" and "great concern"; they expressed the "sincere desire of the people of this country that principles and methods of peace shall prevail . . ."; they stated that the "American government feels warranted in expressing to the Chinese and the Japanese governments its hope that they will cause their military forces to refrain from any further hostilities." In the weeks that followed, public notice of the events continuing in Manchuria was reiterated in the same tones: the situation was "of profound concern"; this government was "constrained to call to the attention . . . the serious dangers"; it stated its faith in the "usefulness . . . of the established peace machinery of the world" and "once again" expressed "its earnest hope that Japan and China will refrain from any measures which might lead to war. . . ." [12]

During these months the Secretary also sought to exert the American influence by acting in concert with the other nations that contributed to the development of world opinion. Representatives of these nations at Geneva had first taken up the Manchurian question on September 21 in an atmosphere of "vivid and dramatic events," indeed of "indescribable excitement." Among the delegates, Norman Davis told Stimson, there was the feeling that the time had come "to do something perfectly wonderful," to ask the United States "to take a very dramatic step . . . and sit on the Council of the League and help compose this thing." The Secretary was not a man to believe that sound policy was produced by the colloquies of excited men caught up in scenes of vivid drama. Moreover he heard things that made him feel that the urge in Geneva was not simply to "compose this thing" by collective action but primarily to

---

[12] *FR 1931*, III, 58, 154, 281; *FR Japan, 1931-1941*, I, 9, 27-28. The diaries of both Stimson and Klots are filled with entries bearing on the development of this policy during the fall of 1931.

get the United States to bail the League out in its first big "test case." Hugh Wilson reported that among the excited voices there were those who recommended a resolution that since the League could do nothing the United States should "take it over," that the country should be forced to "assume responsibility for the future." [13]

These reports naturally caused the Secretary anxiety. He was afraid, first, that the Council of the League might, in a moment of high excitement, do something that would place in jeopardy his settled policy of letting the Japanese know he was watching them while at the same time giving Shidehara an opportunity, free of criticism, to get control of the situation. Furthermore, as Secretary of State for a country that had rejected the League in the days of innocence and hope, he was determined, as he said again and again, that on the day of reckoning the League would not leave this particular baby on our lap. [14]

The way to proceed in this situation, he decided, was to make clear at the outset that "We cannot participate, of course, in League action," but that we would "lend it all moral support that we can." These considerations governed the American behavior in the next three months. In September the Secretary rejected as "wild propositions" the invitation for an American representative to sit at the Council table and take part in the Council deliberations and decisions. In October he permitted Consul General Prentiss B. Gilbert to join the Council with permission to enter conversations only when they related to the possible application of the Kellogg-Briand Pact. Since the dis-

---

[13] Hugh Wilson to H.L.S., Sept. 24, 1931, 793.94/1944½, SD; *FR 1931*, III, 43.
[14] Diary, Oct. 5, 1931. Stimson throughout the fall was much disturbed that this baby would be "dumped," "deposited," "left" on our lap or our doorstep. In this he reflected the views of the President, who reported in his *Memoirs* that he had to meet some "international intrigue." Some "influential" Americans at home and a "coterie" of Americans who "derived great satisfaction from hovering around [Geneva] and feeling they were part of great events . . ." wanted the United States to join the League. These groups, as the President describes, were especially vocal when the question of sanctions was raised (Hoover, *Cabinet and Presidency*, 370).

cussions never dealt with the Pact, Gilbert, after a graceful inaugural remark, did not talk and in later sessions he was removed from the table to a chair at one side of the room where he sat as an observer. In November Charles G. Dawes was sent to Paris for the Council meetings, which he never actually attended. Instead he held conferences with individual delegates in his room at the Ritz. By these means the United States kept in touch with but did not participate in League action. As for moral support, on September 30 the League issued what Lord Cecil called "the usual resolution" expressing the belief that both Japan and China were sincere and would do all in their power to return to a normal relationship with each other. The Secretary gave his approval to this resolution since he had opposed the idea of League investigation on the ground that both China and Japan would be put off by "a lot of attachés or a commission appointed by anybody else." Inasmuch as Japan was "probably . . . sincerely trying to settle this matter," the thing to do was to try to get the principals in the dispute to sit down together alone to compose their difficulties.[15]

[15] *FR 1931*, III, 51, 154; Diary, Sept. 23, Oct. 8, 1931; Klots, Diary, Sept. 23, 1931; Cecil, *Great Experiment*, 223; Dawes, *Journal as Ambassador*, 417. The merits of the Secretary's policy as outlined in the above paragraph have been much debated. F. P. Walters, former Deputy Secretary-General of the League of Nations, gives perhaps the most dispassionate and informed assessment of the reasons for the American position and its consequences. In his *A History of the League of Nations*, 2 vols. (London, 1952), II, 472-73, he says that ". . . though the American government did much to encourage the organs of the League, the fact that it stood aside, sharing neither the rights nor the duties of the League powers, was a fatal handicap to joint action." Concerning Stimson's opposition to a League commission of inquiry, a special target for the Secretary's critics, Walters says that it was "a grave misfortune" which "led at once to a notable stiffening in the attitude of Japan both in Geneva and in Tokyo. Her greatest fear had been the establishment of a common front between the Council and the United States." Interestingly enough the dispatches of Edwin L. Neville, Chargé d'affaires at Tokyo, which now appear to support Walters' view, could, at the time, be cited in support of Stimson's policy. He reported (Chargé in Japan to Secretary of State, Sept. 26, 1931, 793.94/2050, SD) that the Japanese were responding favorably to Stimson's opposition to a commission of inquiry. He quoted Japanese papers as saying that any investigation "would aggravate the situation" — that the League should "remain passive for a time and calmly watch. . . ."

In October the League restated its beliefs of the previous months and set a time in November for the withdrawal of Japanese troops from Manchuria. Just before this resolution was passed the Secretary of State sent a supporting message to the two contesting countries expressing the hope that "they will find it possible in the near future to agree upon a method for resolving by peaceful means" their difficulties. In December at Paris the League Council passed another resolution which in effect restated the general propositions of September and October and in addition created a committee of inquiry — later known as the Lytton Commission — to investigate the situation. The day before this resolution passed, the Secretary cabled Dawes that he desired "to give to the public the impression of cordial support to the League Council resolution, if it is passed tomorrow. . . ." Dawes might make a brief statement in appreciation of the "long and patient labor . . . which has resulted in an agreement of the two parties to refrain in the future from aggression and to support an impartial inquiry." A statement similar in tone was, upon the passage of the resolution, released to the public.[16]

By the negotiations of these months the Secretary of State hoped to fabricate a world opinion that would support what he took to be the liberal intentions of the government in Japan and would serve to stay the course of the Japanese armies in Manchuria. These hopes were not fulfilled. On the day after the Council of the League passed its resolution of December 10 in Paris the Minseito cabinet fell in Tokyo. Three weeks earlier, the army of Japan that had started on September 21 to look for bandits had taken Tsitsihar, 370 miles northwest of Mukden. Three weeks later, on January 2, the army entered Chinchow, 175 miles southwest of Mukden. On that day it was, in effect, master of Manchuria.

The aims of the Secretary of State came to nothing, in large

[16] Willoughby, *Sino-Japanese Controversy*, 120, 177-78; Diary, Dec. 9, 10, 1931; Klots, Diary, Dec. 9, 10, 1931; *FR* 1931, III, 662.

part because most of his initial assumptions had been wrong. Twenty-seven years after the event this is obvious. The incident was not a local mutiny. It was the first act in an operation that had been planned to begin at an appropriate time and place, as Admiral Okada Keisuke has since testified, any time in the years between 1929 and 1931. When the Secretary of the Genro read the news of Mukden he remarked, "they've done it at last." On the first night Reijiro Wakatsuki, admitting he was at his wit's end, reported that his War Minister had said, "My power is insufficient to hold the Army in check." Three days later, persuaded to disburse money to send reinforcements to Manchuria, he in fact lost "whatever power of restraint [he] held over the Army." [17]

That army might perhaps have been restrained by the expression of a world opinion in some positive, tangible form. It could not be placed in check by a world opinion that revealed itself in separate but supporting notes, in statements of trust and concern, in the "usual resolutions," in the movement of a chair to the wall of a Council chamber or in restatements of trust and concern.

There is a good deal of evidence to indicate that the Secretary doubted the soundness of the assumptions he acted upon. He spoke much more harshly "about the outrage of it" in private to Debuchi than he did in public. As early as September 22 he said, "It is apparent that the Japanese military have initiated a widely extended movement of aggression only after careful preparation with a strategic goal in mind." Early in October he spoke of Japan as having run "amok." By the end of the month he remarked that the "essence" of the Japanese endeavor was to force China by military pressure to accept "certain disputed treaties." Three weeks later he saw that "the situation is in the hands of virtually mad dogs." [18]

[17] Ferrell, *American Diplomacy*, 123-30; Oka, *Saionji and the Manchurian Crisis*.
[18] *FR 1931*, III, 26; Diary, Oct. 29, Nov. 19, 1931.

And from the beginning he was not sure that world opinion would serve. To start with, it was hard to mobilize: "One is treading on very delicate ground when you have to consider the public opinion in China, Japan, the League at Geneva, and at home. It is pretty hard to avoid using a word which may arouse unintended repercussions in one or the other of those half a dozen localities." And even if one succeeded in obtaining some unanimity of opinion, "The peace treaties of . . . western nations . . . no more fit" the Asian governments "than a stove pipe hat would fit an African savage." [19]

How could a Secretary of State possessed of such second sight continue in policies that brought him, as he said in December, to "a very lame and impotent conclusion to our labors of the past few months." There is, for one thing, the conditioned reflex of anyone who has spent time in diplomatic negotiation. "You are always hoping," as Stanley Hornbeck remarked, "that something favorable will turn up," and often enough something does. But there were other considerations that governed the Secretary on this occasion. Of the two major powers in Europe France was unmoved by what she took to be a remote condition and England did not want to add to her difficulties an incident which, in Lord Cecil's words, would soon come to its own end. These countries, described by Leon Blum as paralyzed, were not prepared in the fall of 1931 to do more than frame the usual resolutions.

There was of course America, the country Massigli hoped would "take a very dramatic step." But the President of the United States was not ready to take the country beyond a "stand

[19] Diary, Oct. 9, 10, 14, 1931; H.L.S. to F. R. Coudert, Oct. 9, 1931. It is apparent also that Stimson was skeptical from the beginning that the United States, by participating directly in the League deliberations, could assist in mobilizing world opinion. In the first days he did not like the League "nagging" at him and he did not like the way the Council under Cecil was trying to "butt in." To Frankfurter he wrote (Oct. 15, 1931, Frankfurter Papers) his conclusion that the United States could "really do more effective work . . . if our relationship remains *ad hoc* . . ." — that is, if the country remained outside "regular League membership."

on moral forces alone in support of law between nations." This was not, he said, "isolationism." It was "a belief that somewhere, somehow, there must be an abiding place for law and a sanctuary for civilization." Citizens who had elected the President did not put it so eloquently, but it was apparent that, on the whole, they wanted no part of an effort, individual or collective, to restrain aggression in a far country. When, for instance, Prentiss Gilbert was sent to hold his peace at the council table in Geneva it was called a "Wilsonian delusion," a "sample of nitwit diplomacy," an error which if persisted in would produce "righteous repudiation." Even to wise and detached students it loomed as "an enormous step." In a time when, apparently, no one could make the maximum effort, even the half measure seemed to go too far.[20]

The situation was described by Stimson himself at a Cabinet meeting on November 14. When America rejected the League, he said, she "had deliberately chosen to rest solely upon treaties with the sanction of public opinion alone. . . ." This choice had been made "long before we came in." Thus the decision was either to let the country down or "to do the best we could with the force of public opinion and that alone." During the weeks after Mukden Stimson found himself, like the British Prime Minister, in front of a dam that was breaking up. For the better part of three months he made himself believe, because in the conditions there was little else he could believe, that the size of the repairs could be measured by the capacity of the shovel in his hands.

But even in these months he had thought about alternative methods whenever the Japanese had revealed a particularly flagrant disregard of public opinion. After they had taken Tsitsihar in November, he had raised the question of economic sanctions with the President. On the morning of December 6, a Sunday, as the ground forces of Japan were proceeding toward

[20] Diary, Dec. 6, 1931; Leon Blum, *L'Histoire Jugera* (Montreal, 1945), 47-48; Hoover, *Cabinet and Presidency*, 377-78; *Literary Digest*, Oct. 31, 1931, 3-4.

Chinchow, he raised the question again in conference with Castle, Rogers, Klots and Hornbeck. Hornbeck presented an analysis that showed Japan could not stand a boycott "more than a very few days, or weeks." All the men recognized "the danger of an embargo going further and leading to . . . war," yet Japanese collapse seemed more probable to all save Castle who alone opposed without qualification the idea and who, in his own opinion, was "pretty hard boiled" about it. That afternoon the Secretary took the question to a "much troubled" President.[21]

Ever since Versailles Hoover had felt that sanctions applied to a large nation meant war. They bred "incurable hatreds" and insensate opposition to any remedial action. He would not go around alone "sticking pins in tigers," and he had heard from a friend of Ogden Mills in England that Britain would not join the United States in such measures. Stimson knew from earlier conversations how the President felt and told him on December 6 that he "tried to start from the same proposition." He agreed that a boycott would generate ill will but he argued that this must be weighed against "the terrible disadvantages which Japan's action was doing to the cause of peace in the world at large and the danger that Japan was setting on foot a possible war with China which might spread to the entire world." Thus appealed to, the President did not seem, to Stimson's surprise, "absolutely and to the last resort against a boycott." But even if the Secretary correctly understood Mr. Hoover's response at this moment, it was nevertheless a temporary mood. The President, as he later indicated, was ready to go to war if the sanctuary of the country were directly attacked; he would not place the sanctuary in jeopardy by applying measures that would, he

---

[21] Diary, Nov. 7, 14, Dec. 6, 1931; Ferrell, *American Diplomacy*, 148. In November, though Stimson raised the possibility of an embargo, he was ready to "concur with [Hoover] as to the danger of a blockade leading to war." He was also glad that General Lassiter, in a conversation with Allen Klots, opposed economic sanctions. Klots, "a very close adviser of mine," had been "for taking a stiffer stand than I have." By December, however, the Secretary was clearly much more enthusiastic about using the "boycott."

was positive, lead inevitably to war. In his words, Stimson and he "agreed to disagree" on the subject of sanctions. In this situation the President's views naturally prevailed.[22]

So there Stimson was at the end of December. The nations had sent so many notes, as Will Rogers said, that "they have run out of stationery." Every morning, Rogers continued, some country wrote off an ultimatum and every time Japan put in another army. The Secretary of State himself, in his own words, was "getting very tired of being reassured of one thing by the Japanese Foreign Office and then having the army go ahead and do the opposite." The means at his disposal had failed and the likely alternative of economic sanctions had been withheld. What then, in his utter frustration, was he to do in those last days of December when the Japanese armies were at the gates of Chinchow, a city he believed the Japanese government had promised not to take? He decided to send no further notes ". . . but to leave them go their own sweet way and then lambast them if they do go to Chinchow."[23]

At the turning of the year, on January 2, they did go into Chinchow and he had then to determine the shape the lambasting would take. After a night in which he did not sleep much he

[22] Hoover, *Cabinet and Presidency*, 366-70, 377-78; Diary, Dec. 6, 1931. See also Wilbur and Hyde, *Hoover Policies*, 600-603. In his *Memoirs* Mr. Hoover makes Stimson appear at this time more positively and irrevocably committed to economic pressure than Stimson makes himself appear in his diary. "Economic sanction," the President recalled, "was [to Stimson] the magic wand of force by which all peace could be summoned from the vasty deep." By the same token Mr. Hoover describes himself as more intransigent against sanctions than Stimson makes him appear in his diary. The tangle into which they got themselves on this question probably came in part from a later clearly defined difference of opinion on the question of whether the United States should announce it would not use sanctions. Stimson thought not; it would take from him a threat he believed he could use to coerce the Japanese. Hoover thought the announcement should be made, as it later was, to avoid frightening Japan into a war. The argument is important primarily because it does reveal the essential difference between the two men in this matter. As the situation deteriorated, the President believed that anything beyond a stand on moral forces would endanger the immediate peace while Stimson, as time passed, believed something more substantive was needed to restrain the Japanese and, perhaps, to preserve a peace in the future.
[23] Diary, Nov. 28, Dec. 22, 1931.

got up at six on the morning of January 3 with his mind "clarified on what [he] wanted to do." The action he was about to take had been suggested to him by the President as far back as November 9 after the Japanese had taken Tsitsihar. Mr. Hoover had then said he was beginning to think that "his main weapon is to give an announcement that if the treaty [between the Japanese and Chinese that would end the incident] is made under military pressure we will not recognize it or avow it." This idea was not new in November 1931. William Jennings Bryan had used it to no purpose sixteen years before when Japan had presented China with the twenty-one demands. But in November 1931 the situation seemed to the Secretary "wholly different" so he took the President's proposal up with Klots, Castle, Rogers and Hornbeck. In that conference Hornbeck "advanced the rather common idea in the Department" that the remedy did not amount to much. So the subject was dropped for the moment. On December 22, however, it was brought to Stimson's mind again by a letter from Walter Lippmann. The commentator suggested that since "all resort to force is barred to us" it was unwise to take any measure short of it "but in that direction." Why not, therefore, do something that would leave Japan "indicted and on the defensive"? If Japan took Chinchow, why not try to persuade the signatories of the Nine-Power Pact to declare that they could not "recognize as legal any agreements which may result from Japanese action since September 18th"? Thus confronted, time and economic circumstance would work against Japan and, concluded Lippmann, "it would be fair to hope the military party would eventually be overthrown." [24]

The precedent from Bryan, the suggestion from the President, the recommendation from Lippmann were, no doubt, all in the Secretary's mind as he rose on the morning of January 3. At any rate he wrote out a draft proposal in his own hand which said, in effect, that the United States would not recognize a

[24] Diary, Nov. 9, 1931, Jan. 3, 1932; Walter Lippmann to H.L.S., Dec. 22, 1931.

treaty between Japan and China that had been reached by means that violated the Kellogg-Briand Pact — that is, by military pressure. That afternoon he presented the idea to his advisers who were, he believed, at first staggered. But by seven o'clock that evening all save Hornbeck seemed in agreement. The dissenter felt that the United States should go no further than to reserve the right to withhold recognition. At this point they all went home to consider the subject overnight.[25]

On the afternoon of the 4th, Klots, Hornbeck and the Secretary met again at Woodley. By the end of the afternoon they had put the draft of a note to China and Japan in a form that was "pretty nearly all right." After dinner Stimson took the drafted note to the President, who approved it. When the Secretary pointed out the dangers if Japan "called our position" and went on to take Manchuria, Hoover said he would take that risk.[26]

For two days more Klots, Hornbeck, Rogers, Castle, Stimson and, sometimes, Regnier, worked over the exact wording of the note. Hornbeck still tried "rather tenaciously" to soften the effect by "reserving the right to withhold recognition." The Secretary got into one of his rages. He was exasperated both by the reservation and by the careful study Hornbeck concentrated on each word before accepting it. But the difficulties were passed over and by the evening of the 6th there was a note on which all agreed. At the last moment Castle suggested "we should also notify the other members of the Nine-Power Treaty group, so that they could do the same thing. . . ." This was done and on January 7 the note was sent to China and Japan.[27]

The dispatch contained three sentences. The third and essential sentence read as follows:

But in view of the present situation and of its own rights and obligations therein, the American Government deems it to be its duty to notify both the Imperial Japanese Government and the

[25] Diary, Jan. 3, 1932; Klots, Diary, Jan. 3, 1932.
[26] Diary, Jan. 4, 1932.
[27] Diary, Jan. 6, 1932; Klots, Diary, Jan. 6, 1932.

Government of the Chinese Republic that it cannot admit the legality of any situation *de facto* nor does it intend to recognize any treaty or agreement entered into between those Governments, or agents thereof, which may impair the treaty rights of the United States or its citizens in China, including those which relate to the sovereignty, the independence, or the territorial and administrative integrity of the Republic of China, or to the international policy relative to China, commonly known as the open door policy; and that it does not intend to recognize any situation, treaty or agreement which may be brought about by means contrary to the covenants and obligations of the Pact of Paris of August 27, 1928, to which treaty both China and Japan, as well as the United States, are parties.[28]

The intent of the Secretary in sending this note, as has since been said over and over again, was to bring the inconclusive exchange of correspondence between Japan and the United States to an end "with a snap." And the dispatch did put a kind of logical period to the accumulating sentences. If for three and a half months the means have been condemned, it is, in the interests of consistency, natural to reject the fact accomplished by the means. For a time it seemed that the notes of January 7 might do something more. Debuchi came to see the Secretary and to drop a "cryptic remark to the effect that he thought he would have some good news for me before spring. . . ." He said other things that made Stimson "think that his people are getting more conciliatory at last." Furthermore, there seemed a possibility that the doctrine of nonrecognition defined

[28] *FR Japan, 1931-1941,* I, 76. This was the doctrine of nonrecognition — whether Stimson's, or Hoover's, or Lippmann's, or Bryan's or any of those others — Klots, Castle, Hornbeck — who had discussed it in the State Department. At least one man thoroughly familiar with the events of this time is reasonably certain that James Rogers first proposed the idea, while Rogers remembers proposing it but claims for himself no priority. Stimson who gave it its final form never specifically claimed the doctrine for himself, perhaps because it was popularly called his, perhaps because he did not care much. Mr. Hoover, recalling that "an attempt was made to stamp this as the 'Stimson Doctrine'" went to some pains to establish the fact that he "first proposed this idea (originally Bryan's)." See *Cabinet and Presidency,* 372-73.

in the note might be taken to have wider implications. When Allen Klots pointed out to a newspaperman that the doctrine was "in a mild form" an attempt to enforce good conduct on a nation that had signed the Pact of Paris, the *New York Times* agreed. "If Mr. Stimson's views prevail," the paper said, ". . . they will give to the Briand-Kellogg Pact a power and scope which few supposed that it had." [29]

But soon there were signs that the Secretary's views would not prevail. A few days after the notes were sent the Councillor of the British Embassy came round with an *aide-mémoire* to say that, while the new Foreign Secretary, Sir John Simon, "fully understands" the action of the United States, he would not follow suit because the British position was "somewhat different." The memorandum cited as a justification for this position the Japanese pledge of October 13 that they had "no territorial ambitions in Manchuria." On January 11, 1932, the British Government made this position public and on the same day the London *Times* commented that it did not seem the immediate business of the Foreign Office to defend the " 'administrative integrity' of China until that integrity is something more than an ideal." It also regarded as "at least doubtful" the possibility that the United States note would have the desired effect. Probably, the *Times* concluded, the drafting of it had been "influenced to some extent . . . by those considerations of domestic politics which are paramount in the States this year." [30]

The tone of the British response annoyed Stimson but the

[29] Diary, Jan. 11, 1932; Klots, Diary, Jan. 8, 1932; *New York Times*, Jan. 9, 1932.
[30] British Aide-mémoire, Jan. 11, 1932, copy in Stimson Papers; The London *Times*, Jan. 11, 1932. The newspaper, which in those days was virtually the house organ of the government, went on to cite other practical justifications for refusing "to follow Washington in rather a speculative lead." Stimson, as will be apparent, could think even at the time of some explanations for the British Government's position, but he never forgave the newspaper. On December 21, 1938, he wrote Henry Sloan Coffin, "The London *Times* is an old offender in regard to Manchuria. It was really more the cause of the original trouble than Sir John Simon." Walters, *History of the League*, 483-84, implies that Stimson's note might well have served as a useful rallying point for the Western nations. But in fact "one more chance of an effective common front had been stupidly wasted."

substance did not really surprise him. "Poor old England," he said at the first intimation of her defection, "is having so many troubles. . . ." Yet it made him "rather reflective." It took, he confided, "a good deal of courage to keep up the necessary firm front not to compromise the rights of one's government during a period of general depression and discouragement." The Japanese had counted on a failure of nerve, but he did not "propose to have some of my successors find that we yielded to it during this time." But he knew that with "No. 1 . . . backing out," the others would back out also. And so, except for an ingenious note on January 16 in which Japan stated its desire to respect the sanctity of treaties but pointed out that the disintegration of China altered cases, the rest was silence.[31]

Twelve days later, on January 28, 1932, the silence was shattered by the advance of Japanese marines into Chapei, a predominantly Chinese district in the city of Shanghai. This military movement and the alarms that for two days had preceded it were of immediate concern to all Western nations with holdings of their own in the International Settlement of the city. The actions set off two extended discussions in the Hoover Cabinet in which all the familiar phrases appeared: "the public opinion of the world," "the folly of getting into a war with Japan on this subject," "paper policies," "the safe course for us to follow," "fight for Continental United States as far as anybody." [32]

Had not the time come, Allen Klots asked, to decide "whether some show of force without any direct threat by accompanying soft words is not a desirable program?" The Secretary thought so; indeed, as Castle noticed, he was "feeling very belligerent, and nobody can blame him for his fury against the Japanese . . ." He proposed both to the President and to the British Ambassador that he serve notice on Japan that there was "no excuse" for the action and that substance should be

[31] Diary, Jan. 7, 11, 1932.
[32] Diary, Jan. 26, 29, 1932.

given to this notice by reinforcing the American military elements at Shanghai. By January 31 both Britain and the United States had increased their military and naval strength in the city and, as President Hoover said later, there was "no bluffing about this." At the same time the two countries invited other Western powers to join them in asking the Japanese and Chinese to settle their dispute in direct negotiations in the presence of representatives from other countries. The invitation was quickly accepted. As a result, by the end of the first week of February the Japanese, as Stimson said, for the first time since September 18 faced united diplomatic opposition.[33]

These new evidences of determination made the Secretary believe he had an opportunity to obtain the objective which, by his negotiations in the last three months of 1931 and by his notes of January 7, he had so far failed to obtain. On February 1 he laid before Ramsay MacDonald a set of five conditions for the settlement of the dispute. Four of these dealt with the situation at Shanghai while the fifth proposed negotiations between Japan and China "to settle all outstanding controversies between the two nations in the spirit of the Pact of Paris and of the resolution of the League of December 9. . . ." This fifth point was designed to introduce the Manchurian question for disposition. But when these five points were sent to the Japanese they categorically rejected the idea of including the subject of Manchuria in the Shanghai negotiations.[34]

In the course of the next two weeks Stimson and Sir John Simon frequently discussed on the transatlantic telephone what to do about the situation thus created. The Foreign Secretary from the beginning wanted to continue conversation with the Japanese in spite of their rejection of the fifth point on Manchuria. Stimson opposed this view. He did not think it was "dignified" to negotiate after Japan had "refused the essence

[33] Klots, Diary, Jan. 26, 1931; Ferrell, *American Diplomacy*, 178; Hoover, *Cabinet and Presidency*, 374-75; *Active Service*, 242.
[34] Transcript of telephone conversation between H.L.S. and Ramsay MacDonald, Feb. 1, 1932; Diary, Feb. 1, 4, 1932; Klots, Diary, Feb. 3, 4, 1932.

of our proposal." Beyond that, continued discussion would becloud the clear "moral disapproval that I thought we should otherwise show." While the two men were arguing out their differences in the first week of February, the Japanese Foreign Office indicated its belief that the assertions in the Nine-Power Pact about the integrity of China were obsolete and that the Chinese commercial areas should be put in the hands of other nations.[35]

Such propositions thoroughly alarmed the Secretary. On the 9th of February, with the approval of the President, he drafted a note which two days later he put to the British. His idea was that Britain and the United States should announce their intention to "remain firm on the Nine-Power Treaty" of 1922 and state clearly that "we do not propose to recognize . . . any steps which are an infringement on the policy which we then agreed to." In his mind as he made this proposal was the thought that under Article 7 of the Nine-Power Pact a violation of the Pact "gives to all of the [signatories] a right to communicate and to discuss matters of that sort. . . ." He seems to have thought also that if the Japanese refused to accept the idea of a discussion an opportunity would be given to consider the collective application of economic sanctions.[36]

From February 11 to February 16 Stimson and Simon discussed this proposal on the telephone. Simon was perfectly aware of the advantages of working with the United States

[35] Diary, Feb. 5, 6, 1932; transcripts of telephone conversations between H.L.S. and Sir John Simon, Feb. 6, 11, 1932. The bombing of Chapei and the Japanese assertion that the Nine-Power Pact no longer had any meaning were probably the last two steps toward Stimson's complete conviction that the Japanese were, by any half measures, incorrigible. "I have never," he wrote Root on Feb. 14, "felt the need of counsel and discussion so keenly as since this attack on Shanghai" (Root Papers). The attack reminded him of the German invasion of Belgium in 1914. If he could not reply with force of arms, at least he could try "to put the situation morally in its right place." Hoover then would avoid the obliquity placed on Wilson, who "did nothing to show the shame that we felt in regard to Belgium" (Diary, Feb. 8, 1932).

[36] Diary, Feb. 9, 1932; transcript of telephone conversation, Feb. 11, 1932; H.L.S., *Far Eastern Crisis*, 161-62.

during the continuing emergency at Shanghai. As he told Stimson, "Our interests are essentially the same." But he was far more interested in common action on the specific issue of Shanghai, where British interests were imperiled, than he was in a joint declaration of principles. Furthermore, his country was a member of the League and, as he said, if England called attention to the Nine-Power Pact it would look like "an absolute pronouncement of judgment in a matter which after all the Council of the League is considering."

For six days the telephone conversations continued. There were reiterated phrases from Simon: "go hand in hand with you," "do my best," "not decided whether we can actually join you on the same piece of paper or not," "best hope . . . the League of Nations," "make it a world statement." There were, on Stimson's side, also reiterated phrases: "separate duty to perform as a signatory of the Nine-Power Treaty," "not accept in the future changes which come from a violation of . . . treaties," "lose the moral issue." [37]

There were a great many reasons why the men engaged in these conversations in the very anxious days of February 1932 should find it difficult to understand each other. For one thing there was static on the telephone, for another the Secretary of State was never at his clearest in oral exchanges, especially in oral exchanges by wire, and for still another each man brought to the conversations somewhat different intentions blurred around the edges by somewhat similar hopes. It was, after all, a complicated condition with which they were dealing and, in dealing with it, they at times, in the opinion of Allen Klots who listened to the discussions, misunderstood each other.

But the primary drift of the talk became increasingly clear as the week progressed. Little by little Sir John, in Stimson's view, became "so lukewarm and dragged along so much that

[37] Transcripts of telephone conversations, Feb. 11, 12, 13, 15, 16, 1932. At one point on February 12 Stimson asked, "You see no reason why, on the general sharp issue of keeping alive the Nine-Power Treaty, your country should not stand with us." Simon replied, "I do not see any at all."

I became convinced that he was not going to go with me." The process, he remembered later, "was merely one of whittling down and gradually getting into cooler and cooler atmosphere of discouragements . . . until finally I became convinced that there was no use expecting them to go with me. . . ." Ray Atherton, Counselor of the Embassy in London, confirmed this feeling on February 16. The probability was, he said, that Britain would "content herself with participation in the League appeal. . . ." Thus the moment provided by Shanghai for joint action under the Nine-Power Pact had failed. "I think," said Stimson to Atherton, "she has let us down. You can tell him so." [38]

Did Sir John let Stimson down and, if so, what did he let him down about? These matters were in debate for at least a decade. It was possible to argue that the two had disagreed on whether the Nine-Power Pact should be invoked at all and it was possible to argue that they had disagreed only on when and how it should be invoked. It was even possible, by a skillful arrangement of chronology, to argue that they had not disagreed about anything. In the course of the debate all manner of things, some bland, some hard and some irrelevant, were said. But not much was said that served either to settle or to clarify the points at issue. In his later summation, for instance, Sir John felt free to assert that he and Stimson were not "at difference at any point. On the contrary, we acted in unison and with mutual agreement from beginning to end." Stimson, for his part, maintained that after his offer to walk openly hand in hand with Britain on the Nine-Power Pact, the British Government "preferred to take refuge in the inconspicuousness of League action among the flock of the European nations." Any attempt to prove otherwise, he said with a private wrath never publicly exhibited, was simply "another one of a sequence of

[38] H.L.S. to Hugh Wilson, Oct. 30, 1936; transcript of telephone conversation between H.L.S. and Ray Atherton, Feb. 16, 1932. As early as February 15 Klots entered in his diary that Simon was "beginning to welsh."

quite disingenuous if not mendacious red herrings which the Foreign Office has drawn across the trail of history. . . ." [39]

If consideration is limited to the actual evidence — details of negotiation like phrasings, timings and textual interpretations — then it is possible to blur, if not erase, the line dividing Sir John from Stimson. Yet a real difference lay between them; and it must appear that it lay in the region where things cannot be fully proved, in feelings about consequences, in ultimate intentions.

The Nine-Power Pact sought to preserve the territorial and

[39] Memorandum by Sir John Simon, Dec. 11, 1934; H.L.S. to Arthur Sulzberger, Nov. 21, 1938. In the Stimson Papers there is a good deal of material bearing on the negotiations between Simon and Stimson in the first three weeks of February 1932. This includes a letter written by Lord Lothian to H.L.S., Feb. 22, 1935; a letter from H.L.S. to Lord Lothian, March 15, 1935; Sir John Simon's memorandum, Dec. 11, 1934; a memorandum prepared early in 1935, almost a verbatim copy of Simon's memorandum, but bearing Austen Chamberlain's initials; an unsigned memorandum prepared in the Foreign Office on April 30, 1935; and numerous letters written by Stimson to American friends or colleagues in later years. The Foreign Office memorandum is useful because it served as the basis for the British Government's reply in defense of Simon to a question in the House on November 5, 1936; it is also useful because, since access to the files of the Foreign Office for the period was not granted, it remains the fullest expression of the official British position that is now available. Published defenses of Sir John's action may be found in his rather casual account in *Retrospect* (London, 1952), 190, in Sir John Pratt's letter to the London *Times*, Nov. 10, 1938, and in Pratt's *War and Politics in China* (London, 1943), 281-86. A British diplomat with experience in the Far East, Pratt takes the position, supported by his interpretation of a Foreign Office dispatch of February 16, 1932, and by his understanding of how the State Department worked, that there was no refusal to "go along" with Stimson. Contemporary British indictments of Sir John's general conduct of affairs during the crisis will be found in Arnold Toynbee, *Survey of International Affairs: 1932* (London, 1933), 540-58, and Wickham Steed, "After the Lytton Report," *Contemporary Review*, Dec. 1932. Stimson's published accounts of the episode, more circumspect than his private comments, are in *Far Eastern Crisis*, 162-64, and *Active Service*, 247-48. The typical British explanation of this episode is to be found most easily in Thomas Jones, *A Diary with Letters 1931-1950* (London, 1954), 399-402. Jones was for long a civil servant and Deputy Secretary to the British Cabinet. In the thirties as a retired government official he "moved constantly in political circles" and was an intimate of Stanley Baldwin, the Prime Minister. From his account of this episode it seems clear that he was thoroughly familiar with what may be called the British Government's party line on Manchuria. An excellent and painstaking summary, giving due regard to the claims of all parties, is in Ferrell, *American Diplomacy*, 179-83.

administrative integrity of China. Any country that invoked the Pact might therefore find itself with the necessity to do something real and specific. It might have to use means economic or military to contain the aggressive energy of Japan. This was at least a possible consequence. Nothing Sir John said at the time, or before or after, nothing his government did at the time, or before or after, suggests that he or his associates were prepared to accept this consequence. For reasons wise or foolish they sought in this instance to avoid the positive act and to let things go on the way they were going. Sir John himself at one time indicated as much. Stimson, he told Hugh Wilson, "had suggested taking such vigorous action that [he felt] it might lead to the use of the American and British fleets to enforce it." Neither Britain nor, he suspected, the American public was prepared to accept this risk.

Stimson may not have gone as far as Sir John in his assessment of consequences. He may simply have believed that the time had come to apply the instrument — the Nine-Power Pact — that had been especially designed to deal with such a situation as had arisen in the Far East. He may have thought that the Japanese would have been brought to terms by the discussion of the signatories provided for in the Pact or by a conference that might have grown out of the discussion. But certain things suggest that even if he believed in or hoped for these results, he could perceive and accept the possibility of larger consequences. Allen Klots was of the opinion that the Secretary was ready to run "a calculated risk of going to war with Japan, to take a strong stand during that period" although he was "the only man in the government who was prepared to do so." Much that Stimson had said or done in his years before 1929 and practically everything he said or did in the years after 1932 must, if consistency of character means anything at all, support this view. Whether Sir John acted with greater wisdom or greater folly than Stimson in the year 1932, nevertheless he acted differently. Whatever impressions he tried to leave at the time or later, he did not "go along"; he did not support the Secretary in taking the calculated risk which joint leadership in the invocation of the Nine-Power Pact involved.[40]

What then, in February 1932, was there left to do? the Secretary asked himself and Allen Klots in a conversation at Woodley. There seemed three possibilities: a note to China, a note to the League, or "to go on ourselves with the Nine-Power Pact." Klots urged a note in support of the League, which had the "machinery to judge Japan as the Nine-Power Pact does not." The Secretary preferred to go on alone. Next day and the day after he discussed the question with the President. They talked very briefly about an embargo and Mr. Hoover admitted his mind was "as much closed as possible" on the subject. They also considered the President's idea of telling the nations in the League that if they all subscribed to the Stimson note of January 7, the United States would join them in recalling diplomatic representatives from Japan. This was, the Secretary felt, "a long step towards combativeness for the President." [41]

On Sunday morning, February 21, the Secretary took a ride with James Grafton Rogers. "This damn Far Eastern matter" was on his mind. What could he do? he asked the Assistant Secretary. He didn't want to make a speech and he didn't want to send a note on the Nine-Power Treaty for fear of the "yellow-bellied responses" he would get in reply from the other signatories. Why not, Rogers asked, write a letter to someone? This proposal was discussed with the President and the Secretary's advisers in the course of the next twenty-four hours. Then on the night of Washington's Birthday Stimson, with Klots and Rogers around him, dictated the letter to Senator Borah "almost as it stood, with occasional suggestions and corrections from the others." [42]

In this letter Stimson began with a description of the origins of the Open Door Policy, its support for twenty years by in-

[40] Current, *Secretary Stimson*, 98; conversation with Allen Klots, Oct. 7, 1954.
[41] Diary, Feb. 19, 20, 21, 1932.
[42] Diary, Feb. 21, 22, 1932; Klots, Diary, Feb. 22, 1932; Feis's Memorandum, "The Secretary's Note to Senator Borah," Feb. 29, 1932, Feis Papers.

formal commitments and its acceptance, formally, by the nations in the Treaty of 1922. He then went on to suggest a new point; that the Nine-Power Treaty was part of a series of agreements bearing on disarmament and non-aggression, all of which were interrelated. Any modification of the terms dealing with the integrity of China automatically introduced the possibility of modifying the disarmament agreements, for instance those dealing with the battleship program of the United States or the fortification of Guam. Finally the letter restated the nonrecognition policy of January 7 and concluded with the assertion that if other nations would accept the policy "a caveat will be placed . . . which, we believe, will effectively bar the legality hereafter of any title or right sought to be obtained by pressure or treaty violation, and which, as has been shown by history in the past, will eventually lead to the restoration to China of rights and titles of which she may have been deprived." [43]

Next morning the Secretary took the letter to the President, who "pronounced it very good." He had only two suggestions. Would it not be well, for one thing, to put in a sentence relating to "the public opinion of the world" as the sanction behind the notes of January 7? The Secretary, arguing that this would create the impression that "under no possibility would we use any sanction of a boycott," persuaded the President that the sentence was unnecessary. Then Mr. Hoover asked, "with one of his rather shy smiles," if it would not be possible to say that the notes of January 7 had been sent at the instruction of the President. This was said. [44]

On February 24 the letter to Senator Borah — and to the five undesignated addressees, China, England, Japan, the League of Nations, and American citizens — was given to the world. There followed remarkable evidences of approval. From Roy Howard came the opinion that the Secretary was "the very

[43] FR Japan, 1931-1941, I, 83-87.
[44] Diary, Feb. 23, 24, 1932. On February 23 Feis made a note (Feis Papers) that "the question of the boycott and embargo against Japan may arise. . . . The President opposes it and holds the Secretary in check."

epitome of statesmanship," from the Chief of Staff, Douglas MacArthur, that the Secretary had hit a "master stroke." Summing up the domestic applause, the *New York Times* found that the Congress and the great majority of the press enthusiastically approved. From abroad came word through Norman Davis that the letter "had a very profound effect here" and promised to have "continuing effect upon the establishment of law and order in world affairs." The London *Times* spoke up with kind words too, and the *Economist* called it "one of the most important utterances of the time." [45]

There were some dissident notes. Some believed the caveat by which the integrity of China was to be restored had little support in history or fact. Cameron Forbes reported that both the French and British Ambassadors in Tokyo felt the Borah letter had "done a great deal of harm." Most alarming was the response of the President. When Stimson took over a sheaf of congratulatory cables to show him, he found Hoover at work on a statement that would, the Secretary believed, cut the foundation from under the letter. Mr. Hoover had become exercised about the reaction of the "big Navy people." He had begun to worry about the implied revision of the naval program. So the President wanted to give out a statement that the United States would not join in a boycott, nor would it, under any circumstances, go to war with Japan. Stimson persuaded the President to keep silent. But next day Lippmann wrote an article from Geneva which said that the Borah letter might create hopes in the League for further American action. Again the President became alarmed and again Stimson persuaded him not to make a public announcement. [46]

After the Borah letter there followed a train of loosely re-

---

[45] Diary, Feb. 25, 1932; Douglas MacArthur to H.L.S., undated memorandum; Norman Davis to H.L.S., March 1, 1932; *New York Times*, Feb. 26, 1932.

[46] Diary, Feb. 25, 26, 1932; Klots, Diary, Feb. 28, 1932. Feis, in his memorandum of February 29, said that both Borah and the President "wanted to immediately get out announcements to the effect that under no conditions would the U.S. join in a boycott and embargo against Japan. This move the Secretary managed to stave off after earnest argument with the President."

lated events. First, on March 11, 1932, the League of Nations, under Sir John Simon's urging, resolved to adopt the doctrine of nonrecognition. It thus embarked, in the opinion of Walter Lippmann, on "a fascinating and perhaps a momentous experiment," the effort to reconstitute itself by substituting the Kellogg-Briand Pact for the Covenant. Then the Secretary of State went to Geneva for the World Disarmament Conference. While there he explained to all the delegates he talked to that Japan seemed to be reverting to military feudalism, that she seemed ready to adopt policies similar to the "old Spanish ideas of exploitation of foreign peoples," and that her attitude was "exceedingly sinister to the general progress of the world. . . ." To contain her there should be simultaneous action by all signatories of the Nine-Power Pact and perhaps the League. To his regret and surprise he discovered "it was Mr. Hoover's view and not [my] own that was widely accepted among the diplomats of the major European powers." [47]

And while he was in Europe the views of the President were made both public and clear. "Very nervous about the feeling excited in Japan" during Stimson's trip, Hoover once again concluded that "the best way to prevent it" was to "come out and say that we were not going to boycott them." Therefore he apparently instructed Under-Secretary Castle to say what the Secretary had always been able to persuade the President not to say. Such as it was, the last small lever was taken away.[48]

[47] Walter Lippmann, *Interpretations 1931-1932* (New York, 1932), 207-9; *Active Service*, 258; Klots, Diary, April 27, 1932.
[48] Diary, May 16, 19, 1932. Castle's speech renouncing the boycott, the origins of which are still obscure since they are described differently by different people, caused a moment of tension between the President and the Secretary upon Stimson's return, but it was resolved by Hoover's frank explanation of why he had instructed Castle to make his speech. In Stimson's words, "He apparently had no thought of differing with me seriously." Yet Moffat thought the incident was another revelation of the "steadily growing difference of attitude Sec. and Pres." (Memorandum, May 9, 1932, Feis Papers). Castle's speech also increased the difficulties between the Secretary and his Undersecretary. Rogers, who had "done everything possible to dissuade C[astle] from" his

In May, after Stimson returned to Washington, the Japanese and Chinese agreed to terms of peace in the city of Shanghai. But in Manchuria the puppet government continued to extend its authority over the conquered province. So on August 8 the Secretary spoke out again to defend the Pact to Paris. War was an "illegal thing." The public opinion set against the doers of such illegality could be, if the public wished, "irresistible." In the next month Japan recognized Manchukuo and in October the Lytton Commission of the League found against Japan for virtually every action taken by her in Manchuria since September 18, 1931. Four months later, in February 1933, the League Assembly accepted the findings of the Lytton Commission, pointed out that a return to the status quo in Manchuria was impossible, refused to recognize the existing government of Manchukuo and recommended that the parties should settle the question through negotiations in which a League Advisory Committee would participate. In the next month, March 1933, Japan refused to accept the findings and proposals of the Commission and the Assembly. At Geneva Hugh Wilson looked on, sick at heart, while Matsuoka, in a shrill voice, took his country out of the League of Nations.[49]

The Mukden incident, as time passed, became part of a fabric of human events in which one thing led on to another. From Manchuria to Marco Polo Bridge to *Panay* to Pearl Harbor on down — a one-way street — to Hiroshima and Nagasaki. By its place in the sequence it could be taken as one of those points dividing possible hope from certain tragedy. Therefore it has

---

speech, reported the Secretary as "much troubled" on his return to the Department. Actually, in view of the President's supposed instructions, Castle could hardly have refused to speak, especially since he approved himself of the President's position.

[49] *Active Service*, 259; H.L.S., "The Pact of Paris: Three Years of Development," *Foreign Affairs*, Supplement, Oct. 1932; Willoughby, *Sino-Japanese Controversy*, 490-92. The Lytton Report is a publication of the League of Nations, *Appeal by the Chinese Government: Report of the Commission of Enquiry* (Geneva, 1932). Its principal author, it has been said, was the American member of the commission, General Frank McCoy.

received extended examination and analysis. And because its results — in the long run as in the short — were evil, the analyses have produced for the most part adverse judgments.

It has been said, for instance, that the Western case was lost in the first days when the League contented itself with "the usual resolution." For this pale response Stimson, by some, has been held in part responsible. By his first decisions he cooled off the ardors that might have accomplished something wonderful at Geneva. It has been said too that all his work in the first three months was self-defeating. He sought to support the liberals in Japan, to warn the Japanese army and to rally world opinion by using soft impeachments. What he achieved by these means was nothing, and even something less than nothing. Shidehara said that the Secretary proceeded along lines that made his own position "untenable." "The tone and the frequency of official notes" simply produced feelings in Japan that were "exactly what their military leaders wanted." [50]

It has been said too that Sir John Simon put on a sorry show throughout, and that by his temporizing in the matter of joint action under the Nine-Power Pact he ruined the possibility of useful activity after Shanghai. But still, it has been said, it was an error for Stimson to think that Sir John would or could do otherwise. The British had made their position clear in their response to the notes of January 7, 1932.

Besides this the British, whatever they might feel about the strength of purpose of the Secretary of State, had no great confidence in the resolve of the United States. "You Americans," Sir Ronald Lindsay had said, "can threaten, but you can never promise and you can never fulfill a promise." It was all very well to admonish and refuse to recognize situations created in defiance of treaties, but if the admonitions and refusals led on

[50] Sara R. Smith in her *Manchurian Crisis* makes the most compelling argument in support of the contention that Stimson helped to lose the case in the first days. Cameron Forbes in "American Policies in the Far East," *Proceedings of the American Academy of Arts and Sciences*, Jan. 1939, p. 13, quotes Shidehara and registers his own disagreement with the Secretary's policy.

toward other things like sanctions or even war, what then? Sir John and his government had every reason to believe that the Secretary, in Harvey Bundy's words, "could not deliver his President," and the President in turn was unwilling, and quite possibly unable, to deliver his countrymen. Such things as these a different Secretary of State might have understood better or taken into larger account in framing his efforts to obtain cooperation.[51]

And finally, it is said, that after the attempts at useful collective action failed, what Stimson tried to do on his own failed also. The doctrine of nonrecognition — whether his or Rogers', or Hoover's or William Jennings Bryan's — meant little at the time and nothing much afterward. By all his decisions and statements after New Year's Day 1932 "the United States took a position in Asia which left it exposed, without support, and embarrassed." To such an end, it has been held, came all the works of a Secretary who sought to conserve the American legacy, the legacy that was in his mind sustained by a great tradition and by a noble purpose.[52]

The Secretary, like others, subjected the incident, in later years, to examination and analysis. He wondered, for one thing, if he had "clung" too long to the policy of conciliation. Once — in 1936 — he thought so; the policy, he concluded, was "bound to fail once the army got the jump on Shidehara as it did on the very first night." But later he returned to his original premise — that his chosen course might have worked, that it was in fact the "best bet" if only because all other bets involved a choice between alternatives that "would lead to extremely unsatisfactory results."

He used to ask himself too, whether, since he was armed

---

[51] Conversation with Harvey Bundy, Oct. 29, 1955.
[52] H.L.S. to H. F. Armstrong, March 30, April 20, 1935. For a contemporary criticism of the doctrine see A. Lawrence Lowell, "Manchuria, the League, and the United States," *Foreign Affairs*, April 1932. For a later and more extended analysis of the practical failure of the doctrine see Robert Langer, *Seizure of Territory* (Princeton, 1947), especially pages 285-90.

only with "spears of straw and swords of ice," it had been at all useful to state the moralities of the situation, to make it clear that the United States "thoroughly disapproved the course of the Japanese." The course he adopted seemed in retrospect "very weak." But the effort at moral judgment at the best might have deterred the Japanese and at the worst it served to "lay a firm foundation of principle upon which the Western nations and China could stand in a later reckoning."

The questions raised, the judgments passed, have for the most part had to do with whether men did well or badly with what they had. A further question is whether what they had was sufficient for their desired purpose. The incident was, in fact, a demonstration, the first real demonstration, that against the simple act of violence, words, moral indignation and world opinion were not enough. Using these means the Secretary could claim that he "succeeded in engineering and leading a diplomatic movement against Japan" and that he left her "isolated" among the nations. Alone she may have been, but alone as the first member of a community of the damned. And she continued in her isolation an uncontained force. In pushing the contemporary presumptions — words, moral indignation, world opinion — to their outer limits, to their last logical conclusions, he had wound up like a man before a breaking dam with a shovel in his hands. Yet he left behind an image in the public mind, the image of a man in a time when the maximum effort was nowhere put forward who would do with all his might what there was left to do.[53]

[53] *Active Service*, 256-63; H.L.S. to H. F. Armstrong, April 20, 1935.

22

Malice Domestic and Foreign

M R. Hoover said of Henry Stimson that "His integrity of character, his loyalties, and his long experience in public affairs were a contribution to American life in its best sense." For his part Stimson held Herbert Hoover in personal admiration as one of the great Americans of his time. Nevertheless the two men did not, as President and Cabinet member, get on well together. When it was all over Mr. Hoover indicated that had he known Charles Francis Adams as well in 1928 as he knew him in 1933 he would have made Adams his Secretary of State. Beyond doubt, too, Stimson would have preferred to work under another President. Playing golf one day with Pierrepont Moffat he said, "I make no claim to the verdict of history but I do hope that those of you who are in the Department will realize all I was able to accomplish with a pacifist President." This coincided with Moffat's own views. In his opinion Stimson "would have gone down as one of the great Secretaries of State had he had a President who did not endeavor on every occasion to clip his wings. Mr. Hoover would move forward in jerks, become scared, and retreat." [1]

The fact was that the Secretary of State was usually prepared to do things in the field of foreign affairs that the President would not do. These things were bold, rash, wise, dan-

---

[1] Hoover, *Cabinet and Presidency*, 219-20; *Active Service*, 156, 283-85; Nancy A. Hooker, ed., *The Moffat Papers* (Cambridge, 1956), 40, 68, n.

gerous, commonsensical, depending on the point of view. Stimson could think about a consultative pact in London in 1930; he could pursue the possibility of a loan during the standstill agreements in 1931; he could consider sanctions in 1932. When the two men differed on these and other points they were wont to discuss their differences at great length and in the spirit of well-organized, impersonal debates over matters of policy. But as time passed, as each worked longer and harder, as the world of Herbert Hoover and Henry Stimson came tumbling down, it became increasingly apparent, even to them, that they were divided by more than transient differences of assessment and judgment on matters of policy. They were set off by fundamental differences in temperament — as perhaps the Quaker whose concern is to find sanctuary for the inner light is set off from the Presbyterian who contends that the righteous should be as bold as lions against the adversary. No mutual respect, no sustained and reasoned argument, no preservation of the gentlemanly decencies could subdue the clash of such different temperaments when fully roused by hard times. So in the last year of the Hoover Administration the strain placed on the carefully arranged relationship between the two men was greatly increased. Often enough they found themselves working not so much in a crossness of purpose as of spirit, in that uneasiness produced by the feeling of not being fully understood.

One of the things they worked on was disarmament. In the days of measured hope after Versailles, the League of Nations had set up the Permanent Advisory Commission on disarmament. For the next decade the subject was canvassed by a series of succeeding commissions, temporary, coordinating and preparatory. The matter proved complex. Not until 1930 was a tentative treaty drafted by the Preparatory Commission. This treaty was to serve as the agenda for a conference to meet at Geneva in February 1932.

Early in 1931 the President and Secretary of State began to

think about the conference. They looked upon it as "a very serious matter," but neither of them believed that the United States ought to take a directing part in the deliberations. As Stimson said, the country "having restricted our Navy and reduced our Army and being out of air range from Europe" would not take "a leading position." From time to time, however, in the course of the year they did discuss the kind of position the nation ought to assume when the conference met. Once the President suggested that the United States might propose a reduction of all fleets by 33 per cent. To Stimson this "took the wrong end of the problem." Disarmament was, under existing conditions, less a military than a political issue. The way to deal with the forthcoming questions at Geneva was "to get at the underlying problems which [stood] between France and Germany." The only hope for success lay, he believed, in trying to force the nations of Europe to settle their preliminary political disputes before the conference, in solving first "the question of the revision of the Versailles Treaty." [2]

Under the circumstances, neither the President nor the Secretary could summon up much enthusiasm for planning for the meeting at Geneva. Their views were reflected in the State Department. Joseph Cotton, at an early discussion of the subject, remarked that he was "against our going ahead with anything drastic." At another discussion Dwight Morrow told Stimson that in his opinion the treaty draft of the Preparatory Commission was "almost entirely unworkable as a basis for future disarmament." In addition the Army and Navy actively resisted any further reduction of their forces unless the countries in Europe took more definite steps to cut their military strength. The word received from Europe in the months before the conference met was scarcely encouraging. MacDonald was said to be cool to the idea of any formal discussion of disarmament. Stimson was given to understand

[2] Diary, Jan. 3, 5, Sept. 30, 1931, April 20, 1932.

that no nation was "making long and careful preparations" for the meeting. Dwight Morrow reported after a trip to the Continent in the spring that England and France were "not ready," and that the Admiralties in both countries "were behaving rather badly." He also said it was very doubtful that there would be a disarmament conference in the next year.[3]

Such intelligence naturally reduced the spirit of the planners, and when, in September, the subjugation of Manchuria began, the whole subject of disarmament seemed, in Stimson's words, "rather a mockery." Yet the conference was approaching; it was still "a most important matter and we have to keep up our face and our courage and go ahead and go through the gestures." But it proved very hard to go ahead under these conditions. There was even difficulty in finding people who would accept appointment as delegates to the conference. In the middle of December, six weeks before the opening day at Geneva, Stimson reported that there was "a danger of having a delegation where there would be no one to do [the routine work but] Hugh Gibson. In fact," he went on, "we are running right up close to the time to start in and the work isn't being done. . . ."[4]

One month later the situation was little better. "Here we are," Pierrepont Moffat wrote, "within 96 hours before the Delegation sails with the make-up of the Delegation itself still open, without any instructions, with no authorization from Congress, no appropriation, consequently no travel orders issued, and what is still more extraordinary nothing to do about it. . . ." Somehow enough was done about it in ninety-six hours to start a delegation on its way to Geneva where the conference opened on February 2, 1932.[5]

"A less opportune moment for a conference," said Eduard Beneš, "could not be conceived." Throughout the Western

3 Diary, Jan. 5, May 5, 12, 20, 1931.
4 Diary, Nov. 6, Dec. 14, 1931.
5 Hooker, Moffat Papers, 55.

world nations lay in economic paralysis. In France there was a government of the extreme right facing an uncertain election; in Germany there was a government shaken by elections three months past in which the National Socialist Party had made unexpected gains. In the Far East the new government of Japan, dominated by soldiers, had just consolidated its position in Manchuria by force of arms.

The atmosphere of the Disarmament Conference that met against this background of events "murky and confusing," was, as Sir Samuel Hoare told Ramsay MacDonald, "like [that of] a conservatory without the heat on." The essential spirit of the meeting was summed up in the person of its President, Sir Arthur Henderson. Turned out of his office as Foreign Secretary and out of his seat in Parliament by the general election in England a few months before, he arrived in Geneva a man so ill he had to deliver his opening address while sitting in a chair. He was in fact slowly and bravely dying.[6]

The circumstances in which the delegates met together seemed to some "artificial," to others "neurotic and incongruous." Among the smaller incongruities were the Afghans who strolled about hoping to pick up secondhand weapons cheap from countries that were about to disarm; among the larger was the brief adjournment of the conference on the morning of the first day to give the Council of the League the opportunity to consider the Japanese attack on the city of Shanghai. When the delegates got down to work the same sense of incongruity persisted. Plan after plan — Winston Churchill counted fifty-six — was presented to one or another of the commissions into which the conference had been subdivided. All these plans in time were lost to sight beneath waves of

---

[6] Templewood, *Nine Troubled Years*, 123; Wilson, *Diplomat Between Wars*, 263-65. Both these books contain admirable brief descriptions of the general atmosphere of the conference. For the contribution of the United States see: Tate, *United States and Armaments*, Chs. 6, 7; Ferrell, *American Diplomacy*, Ch. 12; Hoover, *Cabinet and Presidency*, Ch. 46. Pearson and Brown have their usual fun in dealing with the topic in *Diplomatic Game*, 185-207.

technical discussion. The conversation turned, especially, upon the distinction between defensive and offensive weapons. It was conducted with the detached skill men had acquired in ten years of debate on the subject. Old Claude Swanson sat, for instance, on the Sea Commission "blowing great clouds of smoke from his cigar and demonstrating in fervid Southern eloquence that battleships were the most defensive of all types of weapons"; shaped by his words they became "a symbol of the American home and family." Salvador de Madariaga argued, on the other hand, that "A weapon is either offensive or defensive according to which end of it you are looking at." And so it went for a good many weeks. Once the conference came close to a preliminary agreement that weapons "peculiarly aggressive" — tanks, heavy mobile guns and gases — should be abolished. This proposal had the virtue of almost satisfying German claims for equality in armaments; it was supported by the British and Italians. But when the French opposed it the conference drifted into a deadlock.[7]

At this point the President and the Secretary of State decided that the time had come for Stimson, who was actually the chairman of the United States delegation, to visit Geneva. On the way to Switzerland he stopped at Paris to soothe the feelings of André Tardieu, who had become annoyed with a speech Hugh Gibson had given to the conference. Ambassador Edge cabled the State Department that the conversations between the Secretary and the Premier had been successful. But he reported also that Pertinax had remarked that the United States was "so committed to the principles of nonintervention, that American statesmen are unable to practice any real diplomacy."[8]

While Stimson was at Geneva in the following week he did

---

[7] Templewood, *Nine Years*, 124-25; Wilson, *Diplomat Between Wars*, 268; Tate, *United States and Armaments*, 103-4.
[8] Diary, April 18, 1932; Edge to State Department, April 16, 1932, 500.A 15A4, SD. Several papers relating to Stimson's visit to Geneva are printed in *FR 1932*, I, 104-14.

what he could to overcome this weakness in his position by using his personal influence. He set up his household in a small château that was "a veritable gem." Only once did he leave to put in a brief appearance at the conference in Geneva. On this visit he discovered "they were debating a lot of abstruse propositions and the whole process seemed like a meeting in the air. . . ." After such an experience he preferred to invite the principal delegates to join him for discussions in the beautiful library of his temporary home. To all of these men he presented, as he had to Tardieu, the American position as defined by himself: that the conference was essentially "in the nature of a European peace conference"; that until political problems were solved there could be no hope of disarmament; that the part of America was not to initiate "but to act the part of the useful friend pushing from behind." In return he heard that the French had a plan of their own involving an international police force; that France, however, could not "budge" unless England gave them guarantees of security; that English public opinion would not consider a grant of security; that the conference was going badly and had no leadership; that Tardieu, facing elections, was in no position to do anything and was very discouraged. In all of these exchanges of view the subject raised two years before at London was raised again and settled as it had been before. Would the United States, he was asked in various tentative ways, give any thought to a consultative pact, and each time he was constrained to "squelch" the idea. To add to the discouragement Stimson fell ill and stayed part of each day in bed. In fact, Lord Horder, MacDonald's physician, said that "he thought I needed medical care more than his patient." [9]

Finally on April 26 Stimson, MacDonald, von Bülow and Bruening sat down together to see what could be done to break the deadlock between France's desire for security and Germany's desire for equality. They canvassed the possibil-

[9] Diary, April 16-25, 1932.

ity that Article 5 of the Versailles settlement, restricting German armament, might be lifted out of the treaty and superseded by a new agreement leaving the rest of the Versailles arrangements intact. It was proposed that Germany in return for her promise not to increase the size of her army for five years might be permitted to manufacture offensive weapons, a right she would renounce if others also did. She would also receive permission to reduce the number of years required for service in the Reichswehr from twelve to five. In effect these tentative propositions accepted the principle of German equality without immediately giving her such equal status. The breaking of the ancient deadlock between France and Germany appeared, on some such terms as these, at least possible. Therefore Tardieu, who had returned to the French capital, was asked to come back to Geneva. On April 28 he refused, pleading laryngitis, and Stimson heard that he was "quite seriously ill." Ill or not, he had heard from von Schleicher that the Bruening government was about to fall. He never did return to Geneva and thus as Stimson said just before he left on May 1, "We were left up in the air." [10]

There matters remained until Herbert Hoover in June, annoyed by a conference that persistently "engaged in oratorical futilities," gave instructions "in order that it should stop dawdling and come to realities." These instructions had been refined in the President's mind for over a month. On May 24 he had "sprung on" Stimson proposals to reduce world naval tonnage by about a third and to abolish tanks, aircraft carriers, mobile land guns above six-inch caliber and all military planes save scouts. Although he had told Feis that things at Geneva had reached "an acute pass," the Secretary of State argued against these proposals. He believed that the President's plan was "just a proposition from Alice in Wonderland," without reality and without a possible chance of acceptance in Europe. Accordingly, he opposed the idea when it was presented to the Cabinet.

[10] Diary, April 26, 28, 1932; *FR 1932*, I, 108-12.

He argued that not only was the proposal unacceptable in Europe, but in coming directly from the President to the conference it would seem an insult to England and France. It would in fact undo all the work toward international cooperation for which he, Stimson, had been working for two years. Only the month before he had, he believed, worked out a program of conversations between England, France and the United States that might produce some limited but satisfying advances in the field of disarmament.[11]

The President wavered for a week, but then returned to his initial view. He was moved by several considerations. First he tied up the depression, the war debts and the armament budgets into a single package. By cutting the cost of armies and navies, he believed, financial and productive energies in support of economic recovery would be released. He also felt a statement about the high cost of armaments would put him in a better position to insist on payments of the war debts from England and France. Then too he had heard that Senator Borah was going to attack him for failures of leadership and it seemed to him that a dramatic proposal to the Geneva Conference would reduce the severity of the charges of the Senator from Idaho. These economic and domestic considerations appeared, to the Secretary of State, to be the determining causes of the President's attitude toward the Disarmament Conference. "This," Stimson confided to his diary, "is a pretty difficult time to run international relations; over here nobody is thinking about anything except the domestic side of it. The President has been so absorbed in domestic troubles that he isn't able to give any time, and more than that the whole action when it

---

[11] Hoover, *Cabinet and Presidency*, 354; *FR 1932*, I, 180; Diary, May 24, 1932; Memorandum by Herbert Feis, May 16, 1932, Feis Papers. The Secretary had returned from Geneva in profound unhappiness, as Klots told Feis. When Feis in May gave Stimson a discouraging report on the state of the domestic economy, the Secretary replied that if he sent Feis to Geneva, Feis would commit suicide. Many of the papers dealing with the development of the Hoover proposal and its reception in Geneva are to be found in *FR 1932*, I, 180-322.

does come into my sphere is colored by solely his domestic problems." [12]

For whatever reasons, the President in the early weeks of June kept returning to his proposal for injecting spirit into the deliberations at Geneva. On June 18 Hoover, Stimson, Secretary of War Patrick Hurley and Rogers met to review once more the whole idea. The Secretary of State pointed out once again the dangers of the President's proposal and then followed "a slam bang argument." In the course of the debate Hurley spoke up in defense of the President's "sweeping proposal" on the ground that "it would probably break up the conference and the sooner it was broken up the better since it was wasting time." On somewhat higher ground Mr. Hoover insisted it would emphasize the importance we had attached to disarmament and would counteract arguments that the recently adopted Republican platform was not sufficiently liberal. So in the end it was agreed that the recommendation would be sent to Geneva, but as a concession to Stimson, who wished to preserve the reputation for being thorough and frank with people that he had labored three years to achieve, it was also agreed that the program would not be sprung as a surprise on the conference. Word would first be given to MacDonald and Edouard H. Herriot, the French Foreign Minister. [13]

In the next three days the Presidential points "were thrown into a coherent program, written and rewritten." These were not easy times, for "in draftsmanship [the President] is the worst possible man to work with." He was always "fussing over little things" and though his English was "not very good . . . he never leaves a thing alone after it is pretty well done." While the work of drafting was going forward, so was the work of preparing Geneva for the announcement. On June 19 Mr. Hoover talked with Hugh Gibson; he asked Stimson to lis-

[12] Hoover, *Cabinet and Presidency*, 353; Wheeler-Bennett, *Wreck of Reparations*, 34-35; Memoranda by Herbert Feis, June 20, 23, 1932, Feis Papers; Klots, Diary, June 20-24, 1932; Diary, June 7, 1932.
[13] Diary, June 18, 1932; Klots, Diary, June 18, 1932.

ten to the conversation and "to feel perfectly free to tell Gibson that he, the President, was a damn fool." The Secretary then assured the President he never said that sort of thing to another person. Together they explained the program to Gibson, who appeared delighted, and asked him to inform MacDonald and Herriot. So far, so good. But on the 20th word came back that Herriot was "dead set against any plan by the President" and that, as a result, Gibson and Davis in Geneva "are now scared to death of doing anything." Next day, however, it was learned that Simon and MacDonald looked kindly upon the proposal and it was discovered that the French objections had served only to make the President feel the need for more haste. So on the 21st the proposals went forward to Geneva. They were, in substance, much like those the President had first given to Stimson in May — the abolition of tanks, large guns, chemical warfare and air bombardment, the reduction by one third of all armies above the basic police ratio, as set for Germany at Versailles, of 100,000 men for each 65,000,000 of the population, and naval reduction of one third in some categories, one fourth in others.[14]

As Stimson and Hoover finished going over the last draft, the President, with a rare smile and in "rather shy hesitation," said he had been much troubled because he feared his Secretary did not approve of what he was doing. For his part the Secretary confessed he had been much troubled because he feared he was losing the confidence of the President. The President replied that he knew his Secretary was obliged to go slow and the Secretary said obstacles naturally looked bigger to him because he did not occupy so high a station. As for the matter in hand, he was now, he said, convinced that the only thing to do was go ahead.[15]

Next day — June 22 — the Hoover plan was, as the *Morning*

[14] Diary, June 19, 20, 1932; Klots, Diary, June 20, 1932; Feis, "Notes on the President's Disarmament Proposals," June 23, 1932, Feis Papers.
[15] Diary, June 21, 1932.

Post said, "delivered [to the Conference] a little in the manner of Moses unto the people in the desert under Mt. Sinai." Hugh Gibson, who had made the delivering speech, reported that it had been a tremendous day, "the biggest day we have ever had in Geneva." Grandi had made a grand speech, Matsudaira had made a good speech, Boncour had made a speech "as friendly as any Frenchman could have [made] in public . . ." and Sir John Simon, while leaving an impression of coldness, had promised to get together and make things succeed. The press of the nations, with one exception, was even more encouraging. Even in France, Léon Blum's *Populaire* urged his contemporaries to *"Dites oui. Dites oui sans nouveau retard"* to this *"coup de tonnerre."* Ambassador Mellon reported a "generally favorable" to greatly enthusiastic response in England. Frederic M. Sackett discovered a more measured but in general encouraging reception in Germany. John W. Garrett sent back word of "universally enthusiastic" applause in Italy.[16]

But in the end Patrick Hurley was right. The conference contemplated the Hoover propositions during the next four weeks before adjourning for six months. It reconvened in January 1933 when first MacDonald and then Franklin Roosevelt attempted to stimulate it with new suggestions. Nothing served. At Geneva the hopes for a new kind of world, sustained by twelve years in conversation, came by further discussion, at last, to their dead ends.

It is at least possible that Herbert Hoover foresaw this from the beginning. On the day after his recommendations were presented to the conference he called the Secretary "to know whether it wasn't time to begin to think of doing something to

[16] *FR 1932*, I, 215-18; Blum, *L'Histoire Jugera*, 16-18; Mellon to Secretary of State, June 23, 1932, 500.A 15A 4/1150, SD; Sackett to Secretary of State, June 23, 1932, 500.A 15A 4/1157, SD; Garrett to Secretary of State, June 24, 1932, 500.A 15A 4/1162, SD; Diary, June 22, 23, 1932. The French, with the exception of Léon Blum, were, apparently, "furious" at the Hoover proposals. The Secretary of State took the view that "France is such an odd stick in Europe today that we really cannot move entirely by her wishes," but he added that it was "a serious complication in my conduct of foreign affairs that the President should have such a strong prejudice and bias against France. . . ."

get the Conference adjourned." It is possible that having struck, by his message, a liberal posture for the coming campaign, having warned the nations that debts and military budgets were related, having headed in a Borah who was reported to be "off the reservation," he conceived that he had accomplished his ultimate purpose. Such, it cannot seem, was really the case. The President was forever offended, whether in the mine or at the conference table, by the dawdling, the oratorical futilities, the cunning evasions of human beings. He sought always to "cut through the brush" and "come to realities." No doubt he sought on this occasion to bring the conference at Geneva to its senses. The President also was forever offended "deep in his Quaker being" by the extravagance, the waste, the inhumanity, the utter senselessness of war. No doubt he earnestly desired, distracted though he was by the malice domestic of 1932, to make some signal contribution to the disarmament of nations.[17]

The trouble was that he had not cut through enough brush to come to all the realities. Military budgets, he had discovered, were part of a general economic problem that included war debts and the prevailing depression. He had not found that military budgets were also part of a political problem that included the irreconcilable attitudes of Germany and France. There was little or nothing in the European political situation that could be used to satisfy the precise and logical equation offered by Mr. Hoover. In such circumstances his recommendation was, as his Secretary had said, just "a proposition from Alice in Wonderland" — no better and no worse than all those other futile propositions that had been offered in support of a protective illusion. It was the kind of thing that happened in a conference that, as Beneš said, never should have met but which, as he also said, no government could suggest postponing "without creating a misunderstanding."

The travail of Europe was secondary for America in 1932 to the travail of the United States and of the President himself. In

[17] Diary, June 21, 23, 1932; Hoover, *Cabinet and Presidency*, 354.

that year, in a country with ten million unemployed, Mr. Hoover sought re-election. As always, he set about this immense task as if he alone must do it without the help of others, though others, in the nature of things, would help. Some men — Mills, Wilbur, Hurley, Hyde — he recalled later, carried on the fight night and day. Not so remembered was Henry Stimson. He "who had taken part in Republican political campaigns for many years past, felt that he must, as Secretary of State, be neutral. He was the first cabinet leader in history to take that view. He confined himself to a mild nonpartisan speech on foreign relations." [18]

The efforts which Stimson actually did make in the campaign of 1932 began with the convention in Chicago. There he had "quite a hand" in framing the platform plank which dealt with one of the great issues of 1932 — the repeal of prohibition. The President had with some reluctance agreed that something must be done about the liquor question, but he insisted that any referendum should not present a choice between the retention and repeal of the Eighteenth Amendment but between retention and submission of a new amendment for correction and modification. Both Ogden Mills and Stimson agreed with the President; they believed, in fact, that if the Democrats took the position for outright repeal "that will lose them the election." Stimson at Chicago spent his time first in framing a plank that would satisfy the President's desires on prohibition and then in fighting off a determined move led by Nicholas Murray Butler and the New York delegation in favor of outright repeal.

On other occasions he acted as a soothing influence on the men from New York who were in revolt against what they called "domination from Washington" as represented by Ogden Mills, who had been rude to them. He also discovered that powerful figures in the delegation, like Hilles who did not like Hoover, were "working their own hand for 1936" while for-

18 Hoover, *Great Depression,* 233. The best brief description of the campaign of 1932 is to be found in Schlesinger, *Crisis of the Old Order,* Ch. 33.

getting 1932. A "very ugly row" was finally settled when Kingsland Macy, Mills and Hilles met at Stimson's request in his room to hear words of apology from Mills. It gave the Secretary a twinge of nostalgic pleasure to find himself acting in New York politics as he "used to in the old days." [19]

On his return from Chicago Stimson heard from the President that "he was going to tax my utmost ability from September on," but in the meantime there was not much to do. At first there was apparently a kind of wan optimism in Washington — a hope based on the assumption that since Roosevelt was "not a strong character" a four-month campaign would "develop and prove that he has pretty well lost the confidence of business elements in the East." By the end of July the mood had changed to one of somber defeatism. This mood, the Secretary believed, was too apparent in the first draft of the President's speech accepting his nomination. In every paragraph he could find evidence of a tired mind and he was "pretty much discouraged by it." He was further distressed to find a few days later how much the President's early attitude had changed to "that stage of discouragement in which he always is before an issue or a combat." When Stimson went to see him on August 11 Mr. Hoover confessed that he felt "more depressed and troubled than I ever have been in my life. All my life," he continued, "I have been connected with the God-fearing people of this country . . . and I feel now that I have made a decision which will affront them and make them feel that I have betrayed them." The Secretary, understanding that the President referred to the plank on prohibition, tried to comfort him. But then Hoover said something which suggested that Stimson himself was not quite above reproach since he had urged a revision of the Eighteenth Amendment. Thereupon Stimson joined the issue. He observed that he came "from the God-fearing stock, the Puritan stock, of this country"; that his "earliest memories were of [his] grandparents and the generation after that who

[19] Diary, May 21, June 10, 13, 14, 15, 1932.

all stood for just the same thing he was speaking of; but that [he] knew that the people had gradually come to face the situation that the Eighteenth Amendment must be changed . . ." [20]

Not long afterwards, Stimson went off for a brief vacation with Mrs. Stimson at the Ausable Club. On the day of his return he had a "damned unpleasant interview" with the President. It had been decided that someone from New York ought to make a speech revealing that Roosevelt was "a failure as an administrator." Stimson, the President said, seemed the best man to do it. Two years before, the Secretary of State replied, he had been "dragged into an attack on Roosevelt" in the New York gubernatorial campaign. He had regretted it ever since and had determined he would not, in this election, make speeches that would again drag him into personalities. Such attacks did not come naturally, he went on; his "metier was to make a constructive speech about [Hoover]." The proposal was not fair to Stimson, his office or the President. He would not do it. But he felt unhappy at turning down the first campaign request the President had made. He knew the President was "much alone," that no one save cabinet members were speaking for him. He would, he said, in conclusion, think it over. And then he went off to the State Department where he found that "everything was going wrong all over the world": the Japanese were making up their minds to defy the civilized nations, Paraguay and Bolivia were at daggers drawn, Germany was inching up to a demand for equality of arms, the Peruvians had upset a boundary agreement of three years' standing. "So there is," he concluded, "a whole mess of trouble all over the world to run into and take all the benefit out of my vacation." [21]

But then for a time things went a little better. Mills, confessing that he had thought up the idea of Stimson's attack on

[20] Diary, June 27, July 5, 15, 29, Aug. 4, 10, 11, 1932. The President at first had believed that Roosevelt's nomination might well "bring on a panic, although he would probably be the easiest man to beat."
[21] Diary, Sept. 6, 1932.

Roosevelt, suggested a speech on foreign affairs instead. The President asked him, as the only man in the administration for whom Borah had any respect, if he would encourage the Senator from Idaho to take some part in the campaign. Shortly thereafter Hoover, indicating his approval of the draft of a speech on foreign affairs, suggested that Stimson give it in Indiana. Then, a few hours later, the President called to say that he had found that Middle Western farmers were thinking of nothing else but the price of hogs. So Stimson, rather "flabbergasted," was left feeling all dressed up and no place to go. On his own initiative he decided he would make a speech "in the East where the people knew something." On his own, he looked about for a place to speak. So great, he then found, was the disorganization of the Republican headquarters, that he had to change the date three times before obtaining a place to speak at the Union League Club in Philadelphia in the first week of October.

In the meantime "the poor old President" raised the question of an attack on Roosevelt again and "kept at" him until it was "perfectly impossible to refuse to make a speech which will to some extent attack Roosevelt." But in agreeing, he recorded his impression that "the bad judgment which is going on in the campaign is beyond all words, or rather I won't say that, but the people of the country are in a humor where they don't want to hear any reason . . . They want a change, and I think they are going to get it, but if they do get it, in less than a year they will be the sickest country that ever walked the face of the earth or else I miss my guess." [22]

Worse than the bad judgment was the mounting evidence of the total disorganization of the Republican machinery. Stimson spoke five times in the month of October. To help him prepare some of these addresses, a secretary to the President came over to tell him of Mr. Hoover's personal qualities — how he was loved by dogs and children, how he did not retain grudges

[22] Diary, Sept. 7, 19, 20, 22, 1932.

against people with whom he differed, how "his great knowledge of human nature . . . made him so effective in interviews with large groups," how he cut up some lamb chops for his granddaughter. On the other hand when Stimson set out to gather evidence for "that damn" speech on Roosevelt, neither he nor Allen Klots could find any useful information about the Governor's administration at either the State or the National Headquarters of the Republican Party in New York. And twenty-four hours before the delivery of this speech, the Secretary discovered that the air time originally scheduled on the radio for his talk at nine o'clock had been bought by the Democrats.

By dint of his own negotiation and his own money he obtained a new hour at 8:30. And so he gave his long-debated speech on Franklin Roosevelt before a handful of supporters hastily summoned by telephone to meet at the new hour at the Republican Club in New York. When he reported this to the President he discovered that, since the money had given out, Mr. Hoover was also buying his own time. A second speech he gave fared scarcely better when it was discovered that both he and the President had been scheduled on the same night in the same city; in haste his speech was shifted back to Washington. And a third speech, at Dayton, Ohio, was cut off the air prematurely because he had been misinformed about the time at his disposal.[23]

In these speeches he dealt primarily with foreign affairs. He described what the administration had achieved in limiting navies at London, in the development of good relations with South America, in the "direct method of international intercourse" between the statesmen of Europe and himself, in the

---

[23] Diary, Sept. 24, Oct. 4, 10, 12, 16, 17, 25, 1932; Klots, Diary, Sept. 22, Oct. 5, 17, 1932. Klots recorded that the help supplied by National Headquarters was "pathetic." By October 17 Stimson was ready to believe that unless help was forthcoming "the campaign was going to simply collapse." The "professionals" were obviously prepared to let Mr. Hoover fend for himself in 1932 while they waited for what might be the better days of 1936.

ratification of twenty-eight treaties of arbitration and conciliation, and in the efforts to give substance to the Kellogg-
Briand Pact. But he spoke also of domestic affairs. Where the
Democrats were willing to repeal prohibition and be done with
it, the Republicans wished to devise means to eliminate the sa-
loon and protect the dry states. Where the Democrats attacked
the "fundamental safeguard" that had been thrown around
American business, the Republicans understood that in this
time of foreign dumping a protective tariff was "absolutely
necessary." As for the general Republican program to deal
with the depression, it was "in its comprehensiveness, courage,
and originality . . . without precedent." In this connection
Stimson found it possible at last to speak of the Democratic candidate as "incredibly reckless" in his announcement that the Reconstruction Finance Corporation was diverting funds from the
small and forgotten people into the coffers of the financial institutions. By so doing Mr. Roosevelt not only "dealt a blow at
our recovery," but revealed that he could in time of national
crisis inflame class prejudice. When speaking of the President he
dwelt upon the sense of dedication, the powerful intelligence,
"the human sympathies of one of the most sensitive and tender
natures . . ." that informed the spirit of a man who was "no
perfunctory leader." The President, reading such comments in
the draft presented to him for his approval, jotted on the margin,
"If you believe it all, it is all right with me. I am glad if you do."
Of course, the Secretary of State replied, he believed what he
had said and the "personal tragedy" to him was that he found
such difficulty in making the President believe him in this regard.[24]

Near the end of the campaign Stimson put down, at the request of the *New York Times*, the reasons why he was a Republican. It was, he wrote in a draft, a time of national emergency, a time which required "certainty of action along fairly

[24] Speeches, Oct. 1 in Philadelphia, Oct. 18 in New York, Oct. 25 in Pittsburgh,
Oct. 29 in Washington, Nov. 2 in Dayton; Diary, Sept. 20, 22, 1932.

well understood even if difficult paths, rather than experiment and debate and trial of new courses." In such difficult circumstances "the general lines of procedure" involved "effort and sacrifice" and "disciplined support" for unpleasant measures. It was hard to avoid "the inevitable tendency to fly off after new experiments and short cuts on the part of men who are unwilling to make sacrifices." The Republicans with their flair for business, their interest in a strong central government, their concern for the established order, were superior to the Democrats in dealing with such times. They did not "fly off after new experiments." The Democrats were divided between the North and South. Their strength lay with the big city bosses who controlled the recent immigrant population who were by inheritance usually "agin the government." In the Democratic Party there were not only the reactionaries to the South, but the liberals of the North anxious to set afloat their "pet theories." Members of such a party under striking leaders — Bryan, Wilson — were admirable as critics in the good times, but unreliable as administrators in the hard times. This was not, perhaps, a persuasive election document and before its publication it was changed to a sober analysis of Republican legislation between 1928 and 1933, but it clearly stated the essential spirit its author brought to bear upon the moments of outrageous fortune in man's affairs.[25]

That this spirit would, in 1932, prevail at the polls Stimson never really believed. He knew that the Republican Party, considered as an organization, was a shambles. He knew that the President had been "immured" in Washington so long that "the people have lost touch with him . . . ," that the people themselves were "in a humor where they don't want to hear any reason." He had also known "from the beginning" that Franklin Delano Roosevelt would be a hard man to beat. So he had not been much moved by such things as Kingsland Macy's report that the Republicans would carry New York by a sub-

[25] Draft of letter, H.L.S. to Editor of *New York Times*, Oct. 30, 1932.

stantial majority, by the estimate that Coolidge's speech had changed a million votes, by the theory that the President was strong in the West. Indeed he had urged Mr. Hoover to go out to California and the President had resisted because he would have to support a candidate for the Senate who was against prohibition. He knew too that "the immense undercurrent is against us." Recognizing all these things, Stimson and his wife on election day were feeling "perfectly pessimistic." In such a mood the best he could do was to send the President a telegram congratulating him on his "magnificent" effort and "pointing out the educative effects it will have on the United States anyway." [26]

Then he and Gene Regnier and Mrs. Stimson sat by the radio to hear their estimate confirmed. Prepared for the event he may have been, but he was also fully committed to an attitude of mind that had been, taken as a whole, well and sometimes spectacularly well, supported by the four Republican Presidents whom he had directly served. When his wife remarked, as the results became overwhelmingly clear, that "a very unworthy element of the nation is coming into control," he had to agree that this was true. But, as he went to bed that night, only one problem came up in his mind, "the problem of cooperation for the future in order that the nation shall not lose by the transition."

[26] Diary, Sept. 22, 25, Oct. 4, Nov. 7, 8, 1932.

23

Shuffle Before the New Deal

TWO DAYS AFTER the election the problem of cooperation between the defeated and the victorious was raised by an unexpected agency. The British Ambassador appeared with a note about the war debts. In the communication it was recalled that in the fall of 1931 Mr. Hoover and M. Laval had suggested that it might be necessary to reach some new agreement on intergovernmental obligations during the period of business depression. Acting on this suggestion the British were now requesting a review of these obligations and a temporary suspension of the debt payments, the first since the moratorium, that fell due on December 15, 1932. Not long after the British Ambassador departed, the French Ambassador appeared with a note of similar import. These messages fell like "a bombshell" on the desk of the Secretary.[1]

There is a background against which the notes may be set. In the fall of 1931 Pierre Laval paid a visit to the United States that was looked upon as something of "a nuisance" in both Washington and Paris. Mr. Hoover feared Laval was coming over to pick his pocket at a time when the President was distracted by many other matters. On the other hand "everybody in France," Claudel told the Secretary of State, was afraid Laval would go wrong "so far from home on new untried land." It was therefore hoped that he would contrive "to

[1] FR 1932, I, 754-56; Diary, Nov. 10, 1932.

have matters opened but not finished." For the most part the French had their way, as the joint communiqué issued on October 25, 1931, by Laval and Hoover suggested. But the President did make, in the course of the discussions, a positive proposal about the debt situation. Acting on an idea put forward by Ogden Mills, he suggested that a European conference should re-examine the question of Germany's capacity to pay reparations. After such a display of Continental initiative it might then be possible to re-examine the question of all international debts on the basis of the capacity to pay during the depression. This idea, suitably qualified by the subjunctive mood, found its way into the Laval-Hoover communiqué.[2]

In the middle of 1932 the nations of Europe met at Lausanne and reached agreement on a revision of German reparations. They also reached a further "gentlemen's agreement" that this revision depended upon the willingness of the United States to accept changes in the existing European debt structure. It was in accordance with these understandings that England and France, on November 10, approached the Secretary of State with their proposals to review the debts and defer the payment due in five weeks. In view of this background it is quite possible that both countries looked upon their request as simply a realization of a normal expectation. There is a good deal of evidence to suggest that the English believed their proposal would be rapidly and easily accepted.

However, in this country other expectations had prevailed. Congress in approving the moratorium had also resolved that no

[2] Diary, Sept. 30, Oct. 9, 1931; *FR 1931*, II, 252. Stimson, unlike most others in this country and France, looked on Laval's visit as "a great opportunity" in which the chance was given to get after "the underlying and fundamental problems in the European question." Both Hoover and Harvey Bundy later believed that the Secretary was in a sense taken in by Laval, that he was "rather too impressed . . . as they sat together on the veranda, looking out, talking about policy. . . ." These judgments seem correct. "Laval," Stimson said in his diary, Oct. 23, 1931, "stands in a class by himself for frankness and directness and simplicity, and he is different from all other Frenchmen with whom I have negotiated in those respects."

other change should be made in the debt structure. This action of Congress was believed to reflect accurately the attitude of the country, and also of the President. Mr. Hoover may well have been prepared to consider the possibility of some re-examination of the general debt structure, but he certainly had no intention of permitting nations in Europe to modify their obligations at their own individual whim. In July 1932, he had told his Secretary that they had on this matter "no common ground . . . he thought that the debts to us could be paid and ought to be paid, and that the European nations were all in an iniquitous combine against us." As Drew Pearson said, in his jaunty way, talking to Herbert Hoover about war debts was as futile as negotiating with last year's leaves.[3]

And so the British note fell like a bombshell. On the day it was presented Stimson talked with Ogden Mills about the kind of reply that should be made. They agreed first that the President "would want to consult Mr. Roosevelt" and second that "we had no interest in the matter except to facilitate the transition period and to get the two administrations working harmoniously." These views they put to Mr. Hoover who was still in California where he had gone to cast his vote. The President was prepared to talk with Mr. Roosevelt but he indicated he could not accept the British proposal to defer the December 15 debt payment. In the campaign he had committed himself to a position from which he could not depart. He suggested that Mills and Stimson draft a letter inviting Roosevelt to come to Washington to discuss the subject. Such an invitation was prepared and sent out to Mr. Hoover, who by this time had boarded a train for his return to the capital. At Yuma, Arizona, on November 12, the President released a telegram he had just sent to Mr. Roosevelt. In it he asked the President-elect to come to the White House to consider the debt situation. He also proposed the creation of a new debt commission to review the whole subject. Then he went on to give a brief history of the foreign debts in which he fell away from the "magnanimous

[3] Diary, July 11, 1932.

tone" Mills and Stimson had urged upon him and introduced instead what seemed to those in the State Department rather peevish notes of self-justification. To this telegram Mr. Roosevelt replied accepting the invitation as soon as his health permitted. He added the thought that the ultimate responsibility for dealing with the problem raised by the British and French notes rested with those still in office. This rather jarred both Stimson and Hoover, who said he "did not like the ring of this disavowal of any responsibility. . . ." [4]

The tone in this exchange of telegrams gave the Secretary of State little hope that the remaining delicate matters closest to his heart, the negotiations with England and France on the debts and the transition from the Republicans to the Democrats, would be handled in a wise and judicious spirit. Much depended, he believed, on the temper of Mr. Hoover when he returned. From his telephone conversations he sensed that the "aroma of battle" was still in the defeated President, that he had "wrapped himself in the belief that the state of the country really depended upon his reelection." "I really believe," Stimson said to himself on November 14, "he believed it." The terrible results of the previous Tuesday therefore appeared to have come as "a tremendous jar" to the defeated man. How different, the Secretary of State reflected, had been the attitude of Taft who had watched with philosophic humor "poor Hilles' effort to make a vote a forecast which would show some chance of election." [5]

[4] Diary, Nov. 10, 13, 1932; Hoover, *Great Depression*, 178-79; Klots, Diary, Nov. 14, 1932.

[5] Diary, Nov. 11, 14, 1932. In the week after the voting Stimson thought a great deal about the effect of possible re-election upon a President. For three and a half years, he believed, the possibility was "constantly" on Mr. Hoover's mind, "constantly entered into his policy." The "whole attitude of mind was one so diverse from the one which I believe ought to be held as a principle, that it has been difficult for me not to show it sometimes." The desire for re-election "necessarily impairs his work. . . ." Perhaps, he reflected, a six-year single term would be better. "Curiously enough, I remember that that was strongly in my mind twenty years ago as the result of my observation of Mr. Theodore Roosevelt's great anxiety to be reelected in 1912, and the length to which he went to try to gratify that ambition."

Mr. Hoover upon his return did little to reduce the anxiety of his Secretary. At the station Allen Klots noticed the President looked tired and "pretty bunged up" and his eyes seemed inflamed. When Hoover, Stimson and Mills sat down to discuss the pressing issue that had brought them together, the auguries seemed little better. The President was ready to consider revision and the creation of a debt commission but he would not permit the December 15 payment to be deferred. As for Roosevelt, he would not see him alone. So many people had warned him that the President-elect would shift his words that he would insist on witnesses.[6]

The first thing to do was to prepare a position which would serve as a basis for a reply to the British and French notes and also as an agenda for the conversation that had been scheduled for November 22 with Franklin Roosevelt. From the 17th to the 22nd the three men worked together. Throughout that time Stimson also worked steadily in his own Department with Feis, Klots and Bundy. Never, Klots said to Feis, had the Secretary felt more strongly about any issue during his tenure of office. On certain important points Hoover, Mills and Stimson were in agreement from the beginning. The debts were taken to be part of a larger problem that included disarmament and the general economic condition of the world. Revision of the debt structure was undoubtedly necessary and for that purpose a special commission should be created which might work with the Disarmament Conference that was reconvening in January 1933 and with the economic conference summoned to meet in London in the spring of 1933. The creation of this commission and the revision of debts could not, however, be undertaken unless the payment of December 15 was forthcoming. On this point Stimson was less sure than the other two. He understood that with every congressman coming back "red hot" and "shooting his mouth off . . . against any concession . . . ," deferment of payment was politically hazardous.

[6] Klots, Diary, Nov. 16, 1932; Diary, Nov. 16, 1932.

But, doubting Great Britain's capacity to pay, he was at least prepared to look for some way in which the debt could be paid — either by pounds in London or nonnegotiable bonds — that would, while preserving the continuity of the contract, not break the back of Great Britain. He was the more interested in this because he believed the French, who could afford to pay, were using Great Britain's distress as a means of getting out of their obligations.[7]

All these main points were at least discussable among the three men. It was the way in which they would be presented to others that caused the most difficulty. Mr. Hoover and Ogden Mills wanted them embedded in a historical context that began in Woodrow Wilson's time. The President was especially aroused by the implication in the British note that in the Laval communiqué he had committed himself to the revision the British requested. He had heard also, while in California, of rumors he had made secret deals on the debts at the time of the moratorium. These rumors were said to have lost him the state. In the interests of getting the record straight he wanted to go over the old ground of the high-mindedness of the United States in separating reparations from debts, of the failure of nations to reduce their military budgets as he had suggested, and of the impossibility of any nation misreading the subjunctive, qualified clauses in the Laval communiqué. As first drawn, the draft he proposed to send to the British and French was long, complicated and argumentative. Stimson objected that it was drawn to satisfy domestic conditions, that it would serve only to irritate, that it would undermine the three years' work he had put into improving relations between the United States and Britain. Mills supported the President "in that we should strike back at the British." For three days they argued, debated, reconstructed, with the Secretary gradually reducing the hostile, argumentative tone by elimination and rearrangement of clauses. As they "battled" on it the Secretary slowly reached the con-

[7] Klots, Diary, Nov. 16, 1932; Diary, Nov. 16, 17, 1932.

clusion that without either of them realizing it the President was out to protect his past while the Secretary of the Treasury was equally interested in protecting his future. It was not a matter of their hostility to Europe so much as of their worry about their positions in the United States.[8]

Finally, on the 21st, the note, shortened and softened, was ready. Reading it in final form Herbert Feis concluded, "This is as devious a document as has entered the debt negotiations. Our diplomacy — under a most honest secretary—has been anything but most honest. It has been craven throughout the period from the moratorium." The next step was to discuss the general purport of the message with the President-elect and obtain his acceptance of the principal points — insistence on the December 15 payment and ultimately the creation of a commission to revise the debt structure.[9]

No one of the participants entered the conference on November 22 with confidence that its outcome would be satisfactory. The President, still bruised by the election, was naturally hostile in his feelings toward the instrument of his defeat. Besides that, he had heard so much about Roosevelt's "untrustworthiness" that he was "full of distrust of his rival." So he asked Mills to be present and Stimson to stand by in case Roosevelt brought John Nance Garner as well as Raymond Moley to the discussion. Roosevelt, for his part, though he opposed cancellation or postponement, did not really believe the foreign debts were very important. Then too he had heard that Mills remarked, "We now have the fellow in a hole. . . ." Finally, it may have seemed to him, as claimed, that the point of the conference was to "sidetrack the New Deal" by committing him to the theory that the depression was of international origin. It does not appear that all these fears were justified. Whatever Mills may have thought or said, Hoover was not the kind of man to create such a situation exclusively for the sake of a small, mean,

---

[8] Diary, Nov. 18, 19, 20, 21, 1932.
[9] Note by Feis on final draft, Nov. 28, 1932, Feis Papers.

The Secretary of War
with Leonard Wood,
Chief of Staff

The soldier, 1917

Highhold

Woodley

Opening the Highhold games

Mrs. Stimson on Vanguard

With
President Coolidge

With
President Hoover
and Dino Grandi

Governor General
of the Philippine
Islands

The Secretary of State and his staff. Front row, left to right: W. R. Castle, Stimson, Wilbur J. Carr. Back row, left to right: H. H. Bundy, Francis White, George Hackworth, James G. Rogers, Allen T. Klots

The Secretary of State is received by Mussolini, 1931

"Noted guests in Sutherlandshire." Left to right: Mrs. Stimson, Miss Ishbel MacDonald, Ramsay MacDonald and Stimson.

Aral-Photo

The Secretary of State confronts Sir John Simon, Geneva, 1932

The Secretary of State confers with Pierre Laval in a railroad car

Dr. Erich Salomon

The Secretary of State rides at Fort Meyer

not very clearly defined personal triumph. Furthermore, at that time no one knew the shape of the New Deal. It is doubtless true, however, that Hoover firmly believed that his solution for salvaging the republic was the only intelligent and useful one. Therefore what he looked for in the conference was not so much cooperation between two administrations in a time of transition as assent to prearranged policy.[10]

At the meeting on November 22 nobody, apparently, was much at ease. Mills and Roosevelt who did not like each other talked briefly about the campaign; the President lit a cigar and then the discussion began in halting fashion. But out of the stilted talk the Republicans gained the impression that they had "made some progress . . . in educating a very ignorant . . . well-meaning young man." They also gained the impression that the young man would cooperate in solving the debt situation the President's way, that he would "come out in favor of" the statement Mr. Hoover would issue when the conference was over.

The conference ended at six o'clock. A short time later the President told the Secretary of State on the telephone what had happened. Also, a short time later, there was a news bulletin on the radio which reported that Roosevelt believed the debts were the responsibility of the present administration. "This looks," said Stimson, "as if after having told the President at six o'clock that he would go with him, he had by six forty-five said something quite different to the press. This made a very unpleasant impression." Impressions equally unfavorable were to follow. Roosevelt was not prepared to work out with Mills a "harmonizing" set of statements for the newspaper. In the end he made public his agreement with Hoover that debts were separate from reparations and that debts should be paid, but he made it perfectly clear that any debt settlement in the next three months

[10] Diary, Nov. 22, 1932; Schlesinger, *Crisis of the Old Order*, 441-43. Schlesinger gives a full account, including the interpretations of the meeting made by both sides.

was the responsibility of the existing administration. On the general principles he was with Hoover, but the application of these principles "was not his baby."

Precisely what happened at the conference on November 22 will never be absolutely clear. Certain it is that Mills and Hoover thought Roosevelt had acquiesced in all their plans; equally certainly Roosevelt acted afterwards as though he had not. It may well have been the first of many occasions when Roosevelt as President created through innocence, guile, confusion, reluctance to hurt feelings or all these in combination the impression of accepting a position he never dreamed of committing himself to. It may have been the inevitable misunderstanding produced when men with quite different expectations met in mutual suspicion to discuss a matter together. In any event, if the old President had ever trusted the new President before, he never after this discussion really trusted him again.[11]

It remained to present the "devious document" which was a reply to the British and French notes of November 10. This was done at Woodley at two o'clock on November 23 when Sir Ronald Lindsay called upon the Secretary. Stimson prepared his caller for the tone of the note as best he could by saying the British had made it hard "for those of us who were fighting their battles" by mentioning the Laval communiqué and implying a charge of bad faith against the President and the government. Lindsay then read the note with consterna-

11 Schlesinger, *Crisis of the Old Order*, 441-45; Diary, Nov. 22, 27, 1932; Hooker, *Moffat Papers*, 77; Ferrell, *American Diplomacy*, 234-36; Hoover, *Great Depression*, 179-84. Most accounts of this incident are inclined to give Roosevelt at least the benefit of the doubt. Moffat, after talking with Stimson, Castle, Klots, Rogers and Ballantine, reported that "The strongest impression all obtained was a desire on Roosevelt's part not to make the President's path harder, and not to play politics with the situation. On the other hand, he did not want to be put in a position of making any definite commitment, until he had full responsibility." His evidence was all hearsay; none of his witnesses had attended the conference on the 22nd. Yet the summation seems not only the fairest but the most reasonable interpretation of Roosevelt's intention. It was probably and unhappily in the nature of things that Mr. Hoover from his position and in his own mind would extend Roosevelt's agreement on principles to a suggested commitment on the application of the principles.

tion. At the end, "terribly broken up," he remarked that it seemed that the United States was "deliberately trying to rub it in in our summary of the American policy in the most bitter way. . . ." The note could only produce the most unpleasant reactions at home. He, Lindsay, had been primarily responsible for drafting the British message and it had never entered his mind that it could be read as a charge of bad faith against the United States.

For almost an hour the two men talked and as they talked Stimson could see the three-year policy of good relations with England "tumbling in fragments around us." At last, sitting there in his study, watching Lindsay in his consternation and emotion, he "decided that I would make one final attempt to tone [the note] down even as it now stood. . . ." He told the Ambassador as much, but warned him he could do nothing to alter the decision to require payment on December 15. As soon as the British Ambassador had left, Claudel came in. Stimson handed him the note and, since the French Ambassador did "not read English very well," gave him the purport in his own words. Claudel listened in a very philosophic way and remarked it "was about what he had expected." [12]

The Secretary then hastened to the White House to reopen the questions he had already debated with Hoover and Mills for four days. Once again he endeavored to persuade them to cut out the pages dealing with the history of the debts and the pages attempting to refute the idea that the United States had made real commitments to Laval for revision. Mills, who saw only the mathematical and legal relations between the two countries, never yielded. Finally, however, comforted by the thought that he could give his arguments to the American press in a separate statement, the President agreed to a change in the note. The Secretary then took the text back to the State Department where Feis and Klots prepared in one hour a much shorter, less vituperative version of the United States reply to

[12] Diary, Nov. 23, 1932.

the British. This was sent to Sir Ronald Lindsay that night. Unhappily it was too late to transmit a similar revision to the French since Claudel had already sent to Paris the note given him by Stimson at three o'clock. Thus the American replies to the British and French notes of November 10 were published in quite different form. This untoward circumstance did nothing to increase the French enthusiasm for paying the December 15 installment.[13]

There followed two weeks of turmoil. Having insisted on the December 15 payments, in the note of November 23, the United States had to help England, virtually bankrupt, to devise means to pay the debt installment. Attention was also given to ways in which the revision of the debt structure, proposed in the note, could be brought to pass. About these two matters there were constant discussions both in the State Department and at the White House. Stimson urged Hoover to take the lead in beginning negotiations and not be "tied by Congress." The President resisted, recalling once again the fatal reference to the Laval communiqué. Harrison and Lamont came down from New York to urge the cancellation of the December 15 payments. Klots also urged this point upon the Secretary, who said he had suggested it originally to the President but that it was impossible. Word came in from England that Montagu Norman was aghast when he heard America would insist on payment; that Baldwin did not know, without asking Chamberlain, what England would now do; that Chamberlain, when asked, said England would not pay. Walter Lippmann gave it as his opinion that the whole thing had been handled in the worst possible way.

Edmund E. Day and John H. Williams, members of the

13 Diary, Nov. 23, 29, 1932; Klots, Diary, Nov. 23, 1932; Hooker, *Moffat Papers*, 78. The texts of the United States replies to England and France are to be found in *FR 1932*, I, 732-34, 756-57. Of the differences in these texts and the difficulties they produced, Klots remarked, "It just goes to show the danger of trying to word documents differently when we want to give exactly the same impression."

preparatory committee of experts for the World Economic and
Monetary Conference, returned from Geneva to report that in
Europe there was general agreement that three things had to be
done: (1) return to the gold standard, (2) revise the international debt structure and (3) eliminate trade restrictions in the
form of quotas and high tariffs. They also reported that none of
these things would be done, because they were all politically
difficult. Hearing this, Stimson "broke out," saying that "all
my difficulties" came from the timidity of governments in making certain great decisions "for fear that some administration
will be overthrown." The time had come, he said, "when somebody has got to show some guts." So he and Mills went off to
urge the President "to take some bold step" that would enable
the nations to "break out of the vicious descending spiral of
depression which we are in" and "settle the debt question. . . ."
For a time the President was roused by the possibility of a
"great state paper" but then he changed his mind. Stimson, he
said, was "ten million miles away from his position" — the
"debts were merely a chip on the current of ordinary prosperity." [14]

But still something had to be done about England's payment.

[14] Diary, Nov. 29, 30, Dec. 3, 4, 1932; Klots, Diary, Nov. 30, Dec. 2, 1932; Feis,
"Some Notes on Recent Turns in the Debt Negotiations," Dec. 2, 1932, Feis
Papers. Stimson, Klots and Feis all give accounts of the meeting with Day
and Williams. Feis said "they talked and talked." At one point Secretary
Stimson got up, "walked to the window, waved his arm, and said it is just
about time that someone had some guts in this matter." In the papers of all
three men there is striking evidence of the strain and confusion produced by
this "unforeseen" crisis. Everyone appeared locked into a dreadful situation
created by political, economic and psychic influences that seemed beyond
possible control. No one had enough information; counsels everywhere were
divided. It was proposed to make one more effort to get Congress to accept
default, to postpone part of the debt and accept interest-bearing notes
for the rest, to call in Roosevelt, and to try once more to find out from Lindsay what the British really felt and needed. The whole episode, Feis believed,
was "a type of perverse and unnecessary blundering that can defeat months of
effort." Tempers naturally were short. Once in a bitter argument Stimson
said to Hoover, "Today you impress me like a man who has . . . thus lost his
poise and his hold on these great events. Yesterday you had your hand on
the steering wheel and today you have taken it off."

It was suggested she might pay in negotiable bonds; it was suggested she might pay in nonnegotiable bonds; it was suggested she might waive the principal payment but retain the interest payments; it was suggested the payment might be postponed; it was suggested it might be cancelled. Several notes were exchanged between the United States and Great Britain. Then on December 11 the British offered to pay everything, if the United States would agree that such payment was not to be taken as a resumption of annual payments. This proposal came as "a great surprise and disappointment." It was agreed that if Britain met its December 15 obligation, a change in the debt structure would undoubtedly be made. But if England insisted on saying that this must happen as a condition of her payment, then the United States would have to reject the proposal. Walter Lippmann dropped in again to say things were going badly. Then Sir Ronald Lindsay delivered a message that "read like a bad translation of a French diplomatic formal note"; it was "a masterpiece of obscurity." And finally after two weeks of turmoil the British on December 15 paid in full without qualification; the French, who had the money, did not pay.[15]

This was not quite the end of the matter. The President wanted to explain his position on the debts in his annual message to Congress, but his draft of this message, Mills told Stimson,

[15] Feis, "Notes on Debt Negotiations"; Memorandum, Dec. 12, 1932, Feis Papers; Diary, Dec. 3, 4, 11, 13, 15, 1932; Klots, Diary, Dec. 12, 13, 14, 1932. For the exchange of notes between England and the United States on this matter in the first two weeks of December, see FR 1932, I, 758-80. The two crucial notes — one from the British on December 11, the other in reply from the United States on December 12, drafted by Stimson, Mills and Bundy — did not clear the air much. Klots considered the British communiqué "one of the most stupid, inept performances," worthy "of a shyster lawyer." Feis found the United States reply open to criticism "because of stiffness of tone, because of the way in which in the first sentence we quote back in a lawyer-like trick a sentence from the British note taken somewhat out of its text. . . ." Stimson on December 15 believed the President had been "pretty near the most sensible one in all the confusion . . . ," but he continued to believe, taking "the broad view," that suspension of the payment might well have been wisest for the world if not the country. Whenever he raised the subject, however, it met "violent antagonism."

was "bad, weak, unelevating and going backwards," a "new Wickersham report." For several days there were discussions while Mills, Stimson and others labored to alter what was taken to be the unfortunate tone. In the course of "the usual exchanges" the President referred to Stimson as "our friend who was for protecting every other nation except his own." Afterwards Hoover called the Secretary to say in a "shy voice" that Stimson "might not have realized that he was joking." [16]

After much discussion and revision the President's message to Congress emerged, in Stimson's view, as "really a good one." In the matter of the debts it stated clearly the President's view that debts, disarmament and the depression were all tied together. Mr. Hoover wanted to appoint a commission, a kind of interlocking directorate, to deal with all three problems. The hope was that this commission would "constitute a part of the Disarmament Conference and the Economic Conference" to be held in London. The President hoped that he could get Franklin Roosevelt to join him in some way in furthering this idea. He therefore sent a wire to Roosevelt on December 17 outlining his plan for a commission. The Secretary of State believed it would prove to be a "great contribution . . . for it brings together all the elements of the problem." [17]

Others were not so sanguine. Allen Klots, for instance, argued that any suggestion of a possible revision in the debt structure, unthinkable the year before, was a step forward. But he believed the message in which the idea was embedded was "a murky document," and he thought it was "ridiculous" to tie up debts and disarmament. Worse still it was a poor way to obtain Roosevelt's cooperation. It amounted "to handing him a plan and asking him to cooperate instead of getting his ideas first." [18]

Roosevelt felt almost precisely the same way. He indicated on December 21 that he could not share responsibility for as-

[16] Diary, Dec. 16, 17, 1932.
[17] Diary, Dec. 17, 18, 1932.
[18] Klots, Diary, Dec. 19, 1932.

sisting Hoover in creating the interlocking directorate. To both Hoover and Stimson this seemed the act of a very small man and left them "with nothing except to show that we have done our best." Others were not quite prepared to leave the matter in this posture. Within the Department both Klots and Feis believed that Roosevelt's attitude on the debts was better than Hoover's and they sympathized with Roosevelt's desire not to touch the subject until he had full authority. But they were also troubled that the Secretary's interest in a nice transition from one administration to the next had been thwarted by events. Stimson, they saw, was "disheartened and confused." "All the wires to Albany were down," he told them sadly when Roosevelt's reply came through.[19]

By chance, on the day after Roosevelt's rejection of the Hoover proposal was made public, Feis and Felix Frankfurter met together in Cambridge, Massachusetts, and reviewed the situation. Both agreed that the only thing to do was to bring the Secretary and the Governor together. Frankfurter, after the meeting, went on to Albany to see Franklin Roosevelt. That night he called Stimson to say that "suddenly out of a clear sky" Roosevelt had said, "Why doesn't Harry Stimson come up here and talk with me and settle this damn thing that nobody else seems to be able to do." The President-elect, Frankfurter went on, "feels very badly that all cooperative efforts had been broken off." Stimson replied that people in Washington "had gotten the impression that Roosevelt had his own plans and didn't want any cooperation." [20]

Next day the Secretary went round to tell the President of this "altogether . . . funny occurrence." Hoover "from the first" was against it. Mills came in and he was also against it.

[19] Diary, Dec. 21, 1932; Klots, Diary, December 22, 1932; Feis, "Memorandum, December 23, 1932," Feis Papers. When Stimson heard of Roosevelt's rejection of the Hoover proposition he was dismayed. The refusal to accept the President's dignified and unselfish suggestion made Roosevelt "look like a peanut." Coming home from the White House after Roosevelt's wire arrived Stimson and Mills "both felt that it was pretty much the end of the era."
[20] Feis, "Memo, Dec. 23, 1932"; Diary, Dec. 22, 1932.

Stimson simply presented the facts and did not "press the invitation at all." Yet it seemed to him incomprehensible "that we should take a position which would deprive the incoming President of the United States of important information about foreign affairs which he wishes apparently to get from me." [21]

Neither Frankfurter nor Roosevelt took the rejection of the invitation as final. Roosevelt in the last week of December passed on through Frankfurter a suggestion to see Stimson early in January. Frankfurter came down to Washington on the 28th and in a character sketch of the President-elect gave the Secretary "a much more attractive picture than we have been getting from the other side." Such stimulation caused Stimson to go again to the White House on January 3. He told the President he wanted him to "see [Roosevelt] and see him alone when he went through Washington on his way to Warm Springs." Mr. Hoover said that Roosevelt was "a very dangerous and contrary man and that he would never see him alone." In reply, the Secretary recalled how in the Philippines he had trusted the men who, he had been told, were members of a "treacherous race" and that these men had proved worthy of the trust extended, as men usually do. The President said he would think it over; perhaps Stimson could have some influence on Roosevelt. Next day, by lucky chance, the Secretary got a cable from Ambassador Edge saying he wished to resign; there was nothing for him to do in France because of the deadlock between Roosevelt and Hoover. Armed with this cable Stimson went again on January 4 to see the President who "finally yielded," provided Roosevelt would first ask Hoover's permission to see Stimson.[22]

On January 9 the Secretary went to Hyde Park. Looking about the house while waiting for his host, he discovered that it gave an impression neither of calm nor of simplicity. There was a feeling of confusion given off by the general furnishings which could not, he was sure, have met with his wife's ap-

[21] Diary, Dec. 22, 23, 24, 1932.
[22] Diary, Dec. 28, 1932, Jan. 3, 4, 1933.

proval. His thoughts were broken into by the arrival of Mr. Roosevelt, who received him with great cordiality. For six hours they ranged over the current problems of the world. The Secretary gave his account of the events in the Far East from September 18, 1931, and received, in return, the general approval of his host who had "a personal hereditary interest" in the Orient. From there they pursued the problems of disarmament, Philippine independence, Russian recognition, the economic conference, the recognition policy in South America and the international debt. On all matters the Secretary found the Governor receptive to his accounts, but he noticed that his listener tended to treat economic questions a little cavalierly. Still, the conversation laid the groundwork for further cooperation. As he drove back to New York Stimson reflected that "none of the President's forebodings" had been realized.[23]

Upon his return to Washington the Secretary put Feis and Bundy to work on a plan that would bring Roosevelt, Hoover, Mills and himself together again to discuss debt negotiations with England. The hope was that some way could be discovered by which conversations with the British could begin before March 4 without committing the members of the incoming administration to anything of which Roosevelt disapproved. Arrangements were made for the men to meet on January 20 in Washington. Before the meeting Stimson talked several times on the telephone to Roosevelt and once or twice with Moley in Washington. In these conversations he received the impression that the President-elect did not always follow the gist of the argument and that Mr. Moley changed positions rather casually.

The essential difference between the two parties was that the Republicans desired to make a reduction in the British debt not

[23] Diary, Jan. 9, 1933; H.L.S., "Memorandum of Conversation with F.D.R.," Jan. 9, 1933, included in Diary. Ferrell, *American Diplomacy*, 245, feels that some historians, notably Beard and Tansill, have given to this meeting "exaggerative exegesis." In his judgment it proved to be "an isolated incident of slight historical import." This judgment can hardly, with reason, be questioned, save for the fact that in this conversation Stimson made an impression upon Roosevelt that may have influenced the President when he was looking for a Secretary of War in 1940.

only part of a general solution to economic problems, but a concession for which the United States would receive a specific quid pro quo from England. There was some thought that the quid might be an agreement to return to the gold standard. The Democrats were not much interested in tying all these things together. So when Roosevelt, Hoover, Mills, Stimson and Moley met on the 20th a great deal of time was spent framing a communiqué which would satisfy both sides. Finally it was agreed to ask Britain to send representatives early in March to discuss the debt situation. In issuing the invitation it was "to be understood that any discussion of the debts which the British Government may wish to bring up must be concurrent with and conditioned upon a discussion of the world economic problems. . . ." [24]

This was perhaps not a great accomplishment but it enabled negotiations with the British to go forward. Otherwise the efforts at cooperation produced more difficulties than offsetting advantages. Herbert Feis noted that so many rumors flew about after the meeting that a further liaison between the two administrations was made almost impossible. "We [are] surrounded by endless small jets of dirty water," he reported, "and are not able to locate the points at which the pipe was leaking." Furthermore, the discussions did not improve the relations between the President and the Secretary. Mr. Hoover did not like the way in which Stimson had been working with and apparently for Franklin Roosevelt. Ogden Mills, "in one of his stormy moods," told Feis and Bundy that the President had said "he had never been so humiliated in his life." He felt "acutely the sense of being in the background." [25]

[24] Diary, Jan. 13, 15, 19, 20, 1933.
[25] Feis Memoranda, Jan. 24, 27, 1933, Feis Papers. One of the things that annoyed Mills was the "way in which the Secretary of State was now giving out material for FDR in a sense acting as his temporary Secretary of State." Stimson may well have contributed by his attitude as well as by his actions to Mills's annoyance. Castle, as quoted by Current (*Secretary Stimson*, 124), reports Stimson as saying at a press conference, though not for publication, "I am Roosevelt's acting Secretary of State." This, it seemed to Castle, "was almost the last straw." In his diary he said, "Poor Hoover feels that Stimson comes

Shortly another difficulty was added. Mr. Hoover still wanted to send or felt he ought to send another dunning note to France to protest once again the nonpayment of what Stimson called her "damn debt." The Secretary disagreed and so, as it fell out, did Roosevelt. On January 21 Stimson, Hoover and Mills, the last two "united as usual," argued it out. There was a considerable set-to in which "pretty hot words" were exchanged. Next day the President and Secretary went at it again over the telephone with no greater success. Stimson said he would not send the note unless requested, the President said he did request it and "we hung up the telephones both mutually angry." When Ogden Mills called Stimson a little later, the Secretary of State "gave him a blast on the subject of my whole troubles of the last two days. . . ." Mills replied that Hoover was "a very tired man" and ought to be allowed "to blow off steam." Stimson answered that he was tired too, that while the best thing Hoover could do was to blow off steam he still resented the President's "holding me responsible for a good many of his troubles."

And once again these two weary, sorely beset men, in mutual embarrassment, regretted what had been said and done. After the Cabinet meeting on January 24 Mr. Hoover remarked that they were all tired and said things they would not otherwise have said. Stimson agreed; amid expressions of regard and appreciation, the cloud under which they had labored was once again lifted.[26]

So it continued in the last six weeks. The Secretary remained in touch with the Governor at Albany, or at Hyde Park, or at Warm Springs, about the British negotiations, the coming World Economic Conference, the action of the League on the Far East. He talked several times with Cordell Hull after the latter's appointment had been announced. In these conversations he was disturbed by the thought that this thin, rather de-

---

very close to disloyalty and poor Stimson feels that his loyalty is a terrible strain on his conscience."
[26] Diary, Jan. 21, 22, 1933.

vitalized figure might not survive the burdens of his responsibility, and more disturbed by the indications he had received that Hull was prepared to let Roosevelt serve as his own Secretary of State.[27]

Before Stimson left office one piece of unfinished business came before him. On February 24 the Assembly of the League passed its resolution accepting the Lytton Report. In preparing the cable that would associate the United States with this action, he talked with the President who offered only one qualification. By force of "old habit," he proposed we should state that under no circumstances would we resort to sanctions. This, he believed, "would relieve the tension in Japan." After argument the President yielded his position. On the same day the British Ambassador arrived in the Secretary's office to ask how far the United States would go in supporting an arms embargo. This was going too far in the other direction. "We had delivered a great moral judgment," the Secretary said, "and the thing to do was to let that show its force and give its effect. . . ." An arms embargo at that time would be "a little bit like making a face at her."

Ten days later the Hoover Administration went out of office. Four months earlier, in November, on the morning after it had been defeated at the polls, the Secretary of State had awakened with "a greater sense of freedom than I have [had] for four years." On the evening of March 4, 1933, the Secretary and his wife went to the Bundys' for dinner with the Rogerses, the Feises and the Arthur Ballantines. They talked "a little about the crisis" but for the most part they talked of other things. After dinner they gathered around the piano and sang until almost midnight. It was a carefree evening among friends — "really the best time we have had in Washington." [28]

---

[27] Hull's own account (*The Memoirs of Cordell Hull*, 2 vols. (New York, 1948), I, 157-59) suggests that he wished to act with far more enterprise in his office and so informed the President before he accepted the appointment. Whichever account describes the truth of 1933, later events support the Stimson version.

[28] Diary, Nov. 9, 1932, Feb. 24, March 4, 1933.

24

Out of the Wasteland

THERE WAS always in the cellar — on Lexington Avenue, in 34th Street, at Highhold — a small store of liquor that had been made in the years before prohibition. The bottles stood there, almost untouched from year's end to year's end, as exciting symbols of the family ceremony and the very great occasion. From Highhold the Secretary of State had brought some of this small store to put in the cellars of Woodley. One night in January 1933 he went down to get a bottle of whiskey. It was at the end of the day in which he and the President had had their sharpest difference of opinion over the question of the French note on the debt payments. Returning from this distressing conference to the Department, Stimson had set to work with Bundy framing a suggestion for at least a postponement in the dispatch of the message to the French. When they had finished, the Secretary discovered he did not have "the willingness to go down to the White House again." Instead he sent Bundy, telling his emissary as he departed, "If you do not obtain the view I have been presenting to you here, I must resign." Then he went home to Woodley. Two hours later Bundy appeared with the news that the President, after an hour of discussion, had accepted the Secretary's recommendations. When the Assistant Secretary had finished his report Stimson went down into the cellar of Woodley and returned with the bottle of whiskey and two glasses. Pouring out the drinks he remarked that the occasion was one to celebrate.

444

At no other time in the course of those four years did Stimson speak of resigning his office. It is probable he never thought of it in his most private ponderings. Feelings of pride, of taste, of usefulness, were no doubt at work to prevent the thought. So also were the profound sense of commitment to the office of the Presidency and to the intentions of superior authority, and, finally, the almost primordial sense that the first duty of man was to finish the task begun. Not until the continuing arguments between him and Mr. Hoover had worn through the protective covering of matters of policy and reached to the raw edges of very tired personal feelings did he think, only for a moment and only at the very end, of leaving his position.

In the relationship there was a source of personal and private anguish for both. This anguish was the more acute because it could never be fully discharged in unqualified, irrevocable words or by summary acts like a resignation proffered or requested. The differences between the two were always in fact as well as by convention qualified. "I pined for a big stick more than he did perhaps but he pined for peace — at least as much as I, if not more." And so to Stimson, the President did remain one of the greatest Americans of his time. In the last years of his life when a man sought to commiserate with him on the President's "lack of understanding," he replied, "Don't do him an injustice. We were then fighting in the hopeless cause of working for peace when there wasn't going to be any peace and when we didn't have any weapons to compel peace and we both were helpless." As for the President, he continued to believe that the services of Stimson "were a contribution to American life in its best sense." Once, long after, he said he thought his Secretary of State deserved a better reputation than the one he had been left with. Perhaps he thought they all did. In the closing days of his administration he gave Stimson a picture of himself taken when he had been the Secretary of Commerce. On it had been written, "This will indicate my amiable character before I became President."

Beyond the private anguish, how much is to be found of public consequence in the differences between these two men? The foreign policy of the United States during their tenure of office was, as Pierrepont Moffat said, jerky and inconclusive. No doubt this policy reflected the incomplete resolution of the arguments that the President had with the Secretary of State on such matters as the debts, the use of sanctions, and disarmament. These arguments were, in turn, merely the reflections of a primary conflict between these two, never sufficiently resolved in these four years. The President, pushed to his final, instinctive responses, believed that the United States, as he had once said, ought, in the Pauline sense, to be in the world but not of it; he believed, in other words, that the country was, on the whole, a sanctuary, an island. The Secretary, similarly pushed, came increasingly to believe that the United States was, on the whole, part of the main.

The effects of this collision of personal attitudes cannot be disregarded. But there is more in the matter than a contrast in personal attitudes. Taken together the President and the Secretary expressed the divided heart which the whole country brought to the conduct of foreign affairs. There were, from the Atlantic to the Pacific, men who believed that the future of civilization depended upon active cooperation between the Anglo-Saxon races, or who believed that America should join the League of all the nations, or who believed in the words of Theodore Roosevelt, quoted by Dino Grandi to Stimson in 1931, that "the United States would be obliged, at least temporarily, to intervene in order to re-establish the balance of power in Europe, directing their efforts indiscriminately against any country or group of countries." There were also, from the Atlantic to the Pacific, other men — probably greater in number and certainly more articulate — who spoke up about other people's chestnuts in the fire, or who talked of the hired money, or who trusted that others would profit by a high example, or who, lost in their own troubled fortunes, had no time or thought for the decaying fortunes of others a long way off.

The divisions and inattentions and aberrations in the society produced a kind of national confusion that, left uninstructed, found expression, naturally, in policies jerky and inconclusive. Perhaps instruction, at the time, was impossible. What any administration can do to educate the electorate in the nature of its real needs, as opposed to its immediate desires, is still, in American politics, even in the best conditions, something of an open question. And these were the worst conditions: depression of the economic system and of the spirit; old things falling apart so fast time was not given to discover the things that were both new and truly needed; an administration which, having little confidence in itself, had lost confidence in others; a President confounded before public opinion, one of the few natural forces he could neither measure nor comprehend. In any case no single, clear, conclusive voice spoke up; no consistent course of action in the foreign field emerged. The country remained as fixed in its disengaged confusion as England was fixed in its spiritless improvisations, as France was fixed in its pursuit of the sense of security, as Germany was fixed in its need for a feeling of equality.

Men in these countries, benumbed by the national fixations, had contrived a world, to reuse the analogy worn threadbare in these years, as unreal as the wonderland of Alice. Anyone trying to do business in this world had, in some sort, to accept the given pretensions — the energy supplied by men-of-war that was somehow like the power of a mother's love, the conferences that ought not to have been called but could not be called off, the equation of the word with the thing and of the desperate wish with the actuality. People who rejected these and the other prevailing assumptions soon discovered that they could not keep in touch with the citizens of this world. When Winston Churchill spoke up in 1931 against the meaningless dialectic of disarmament—the distinction, for instance, between aggressive and defensive weapons — he was promptly called "the oldest old woman in Europe" and dismissed as someone too silly to talk to. It was therefore in the nature of things that those charged with the conduct of foreign affairs at this time would have to proceed from the common conceits: that the fate of nations turned on 12,000 tons of cruiser strength; that a flight of gold could, by the word of a conference, be brought to a standstill; that the full faith and credit of nations depended upon the exaction of a depreciated pound of flesh; that a territory must cease to exist when its existence was not recognized; that the force of unorganized public opinion was greater than the force of an army already in the field.

Stimson, for all his past experience and public service, had come to the State Department knowing only what any man who read the daily papers knew about the nature of the disordered world. As one charged with the conduct of foreign affairs in these times, as one committed to remain in touch with the citizens of this world, he naturally sought to act on the given pretensions and common conceits. For three years he labored within the existing sanctions until he reached the moment of doubt.

The nature of this doubt he explained to Theodore Marriner, Pierre Boal and Pierrepont Moffat on the morning of January 4, 1932. The day before the Japanese had entered Chinchow and made themselves masters of Manchuria by force of arms. On January 4 the Secretary stayed at home at Woodley to frame the communiqué in which he would announce the doctrine of nonrecognition three days later. His three callers broke in on his meditations in the morning to discuss with him the draft of instructions for delegates to the forthcoming Disarmament Conference.

The discussion proceeded with difficulty. The Secretary had a severe cold; his mind was on his own communiqué; and his attention was constantly distracted by telephone calls and messengers from the Department who brought new information about the Far East. In the free moments that occurred between the continuing interruptions, the Secretary tried at first to read the drafted instructions brought by his colleagues. Finally with some irritation he put them down and asked for an oral statement of the principles of disarmament. When Moffat had finished his presentation the Secretary thought for a moment and then said that he had been raised in the Anglo-Saxon school that dreaded the precise codification of principles. Then, almost to himself, he went on to wonder about the purpose of the armed forces. Did the Kellogg-Briand Pact so change human nature that only the defense of one's actual territory was essential? He was by no means sure, and then he went on to say that he had been forced to unlearn a great many axioms of his youth and that he did not have very clear-cut convictions as to the new order.

Things happened in the months after this conversation that began to resolve the doubts in the mind of the Secretary. Slowly he acquired convictions of clearer cut about the new order of things. During his last year in office it became more apparent to him that the new dispensations would not serve to break the political paralysis in the West or to contain the militant energies rising in the East. In part the means had failed because there was available neither the information nor the power of imagination necessary to enable men to deal with so precarious and so complicated a situation. But there were other reasons for failure. The new dispensations, Stimson slowly came to believe, were merely the sustaining fictions of frightened men, a method for satisfying themselves that it was not necessary or possible to do what they, often enough, knew they had to do. The old relationships between policy and power with which Stimson had been familiar had thus been thrown askew by those too tired or too decent or too scared of the consequences to use the power at their disposal. Surveying the chaos produced by these attitudes of mind Stimson concluded that the tragedy of 1932 in the politics of Europe had been produced by simple timidity. He concluded also that even those policies conceived in bravery must be continued in the future

as in the past by other means than faith alone — by force in being if not in use. These were old and simple truths deriving
from the castoff axioms of his youth.

So, in a time when no man in his office could do much, Stimson proceeded toward an understanding of what, sometime,
would have to be done. And he began to learn this thing in a
time when very few learned anything at all. Thus, in the years
that followed he did not misread the multiplying signs of the
times. And when all the prophecies were fulfilled he returned
to office in a time when a man who knew what he had learned
could do the things that were necessary.

PART THREE

The Struggle with Darkness

1933-1950

And I would do it again, but set down
This set down
This: were we led all that way for
Birth or Death? There was a Birth, certainly,
We had evidence and no doubt. I had seen birth and
    death,
But had thought they were different; this Birth was
Hard and bitter agony for us . . .

             — THOMAS STEARNS ELIOT

We forget that the human spirit, the spirit of goodness
and truth in the world, is still only an infant crying in
the night, and that the struggle with darkness is as yet
mostly an unequal struggle.

             — JAN CHRISTIAAN SMUTS

The only deadly sin I know is cynicism.

             — HENRY LEWIS STIMSON

25

On Borrowed Time

THE FIRST thought that occurred to Stimson as he woke up on the morning of November 9, 1932, was that he had regained his sense of freedom. The future, he suddenly felt, was "all up in the air." He had been out of his profession for five years and at sixty-five, he realized on that November morning, he did not feel very much "like going back into the harness again to the life of drudgery" he had known before. But unless he made "some reconnection with [his] profession" he would find himself, he knew, completely lost. For a time he considered making an arrangement with one of the Washington law firms, but the connection, when it was finally made, led back inevitably to 32 Liberty Street and Bronson Winthrop. He returned to his old associates, however, not as a partner but as a lawyer who rented "rooms and office facilities" from the firm. On October 1, 1933, he began in these rooms the kind of practice that would keep him decently active but not borne down by legal drudgery. He was retained as a trial counsel by a New York company in an appeal before the Appellate Division of the state courts and he appeared for a committee of the stockholders of the Tennessee Public Service Company to represent their interests in negotiation with the Tennessee Valley Authority over the purchase of the company plant in Knoxville. He also acted briefly as counsel for Wendell Willkie in some matters involving the future of the Commonwealth and Southern Company.

But, as always, his primary interest lay outside the law. For the next seven years he kept busy with other things, the kinds of things that made the papers call him an elder statesman. Not inappropriate to this august title was the manner of life he developed in the course of these years. He and Mrs. Stimson divided their time between Woodley, Highhold and an apartment in the Hotel Pierre. Frequently, in the early spring, they would go to Yeaman's Hall near Charleston, South Carolina, for a few weeks, and in the early summer, again for a few weeks, they traveled occasionally to the Ausable Club at the head of the Keene Valley in New York. In these two places he found the shooting, or climbing, or canoeing or fishing that had always been the sources of relaxation for him. In the separated cottages at each establishment the two could find also the privacy indispensable to their well-being, as they could find in the common dining room and along the porches of the main building the sense of the orderly, selected companionship each preferred.

In the late summer the two would go, almost invariably, to Scotland — to Sciberscross, Dabreavoch, Skelpick or Aultnagar. These were lodges and houses and moors and shootings that Stimson would rent for a month from Mrs. Andrew Carnegie or the Duke of Sutherland. Here he would take "the right of angling from the right or south bank of the Lower Borora on three days per week by two rods in accordance with the River Borora Agreements"; he would also obtain the right of search over 16,000 acres for partridges, night duck, black game, hares, rabbits, red deer and "a bag of grouse limited to 500 brace to be obtained without driving." He loved everything about these interludes — the ancient, comfortable houses, "the twenty-one-pound salmon," the weather on the moors, the sense of ritual and of a previous time passing into the present. Here with the special gun sight built to make accommodation for his failing right eye he could, as he said, practice the last virile sport that was left to him.

The journeys of these years — to South Carolina, Scotland, the Gaspé, the Keene Valley — were, frequently, impressive passages. The Stimsons, often enough, had friends to bear them company — his sister Candace, her nieces the Daggetts or the Jameses, old associates like Bronson Winthrop or Arthur Page. Baggagemasters were told off to give "special attention to your luggage on both the outward and the homeward passage"; the Lincoln followed the train down the coast to meet the passengers on arrival; officials stood by to expedite the search at customs. Nothing in these journeys was entered into lightly or unadvisedly. The space on the Cunarder was carefully selected with due regard for the fall of morning light through a porthole, for the number of steps to dining room and luggage hold. Only after floor plans had been submitted was the lodge in Scotland chosen. Questions were put about the incidence of black flies in the third week of June, the state of the mattresses at a Gaspé camp, the elevation of the house — which "makes a difference in climate and clothes."

Logistics planning for these ventures was made by Stimson; the execution was in the hands of Elizabeth Neary. It was she who went to see the man at the Cunard office so often that he once said he had never had so many questions asked about a berth even by a person seeking space for his own self. It was she who saw to it that the car and the station wagon were at the right pier at the right time or who put the customs officials at the alert. Miss Neary was Stimson's secretary. She was, Mrs. Stimson said, "one of those laughing, lighthearted Irish people" her husband liked to have around him. One of her secretarial associates in the law firm remarked that she was "pretty and talkative and blithe and witty which was the kind of environment he needed." But, she added, Miss Neary had a further advantage. "She worked for him for twenty years and it took that long to warm him up." In 1933 Elizabeth Neary had only worked for him for five years. She had come into Winthrop and Stimson in the middle twenties and stayed on there while

Stimson went to the Philippines and the State Department. Upon his return she again became his secretary and remained in that position until 1950. In that time she did all those things a devoted secretary is expected to do. She also did a good many things that were above and beyond the call of normal expectations. Receiving word that her employer wished to dictate a memorandum, she left on the moment the Christmas dinner she was having with her family. She was truly, as Stimson often said, indispensable.

If the scale of this life — the physical supports, the claims exerted, the services rendered — was appropriate to the matters large and grave upon which so much of the previous life had been expended, so were the continuing associations and concerns of the life remaining. As for the associations, everywhere Stimson went or came to rest he saw and talked with men who had spent their lives observing, thinking about or directing affairs of state. In New York it was Harrison, Mills, Bruening and John Lord O'Brian. In England it was Ramsay MacDonald, Anthony Eden, Sir Josiah Stamp, Sir Arthur Salter and Walter Layton. In Washington it was Feis, Lippmann, Hornbeck, Frankfurter, Hull, Rublee, Dean Acheson, and Sir Ronald Lindsay.

At first he was content merely to converse, to read and to write. He set out, at the beginning, to inform himself about the economic and financial problems that, in 1933 and 1934, seemed at the bottom of the world's troubles. He talked at great length with his classmate Irving Fisher about monetary questions and exchanged views on this subject with Stamp and Layton in England. In addition he read Warren and Pearson's book twice and distributed copies to various friends, among them, Ramsay MacDonald. From these investigations, he reached conclusions that enabled him to accept the monetary policies of the New Deal with greater equanimity than did many of his associates in New York.

It was well for him that he had already acquired a philosophic attitude on these matters when he visited London in July 1933 while the World Economic Conference was in progress. There he found that things in the American delegation were all at sixes and sevens. Raymond Moley had made his celebrated disrupting appearance and the President had already sent his messages repudiating the agenda Cordell Hull thought he was to discuss at London. Hull, the head of the delegation, was "worn out" and "wretched." The President had, he felt, cut at the bottom of his political faith and as for Moley, Hull told Stimson, "You can properly call him a son of anything you please." Then too, it was said, Senator Key Pittman, another delegate, drank far too much. "How on earth," the Prime Minister asked Stimson, "did Roosevelt ever send such a delegation to the Conference?" The members lacked information and initiative; they could act only on instructions from Washington. Because they gave out erroneous statements to the press about matters they did not understand, the British representatives had decided not to talk to them freely. Even the King was angry. Both he and MacDonald, the monarch told Stimson at a garden party, had been made fools of; the conference, in view of America's change of policy, should never have met.[1]

All these reports and confidences may have confirmed some of Stimson's feeling about the administrative high spirits and irresponsibility of the New Deal, but he was not unduly disturbed by what he took to be the ultimate implications of this adventure. In the first place, fond as he was of Hull, he believed he had brought much of the difficulty on himself. If it were true that Roosevelt intended to be his own Secretary, an impression Stimson had received from Hull the previous March, then the Secretary of State was "deliberately walking into an impossible position." As for the King, Stimson told him that he, Stimson, was a member of the opposition party whose only interest was the preservation of good relations between England and America. To MacDonald he said that the King ought to

[1] Diary, Oct. 18, 1933.

be told to stop making comments of that sort to any American. But on the essential point at issue, Roosevelt's "policy of reflation" and his insistence on freedom of action in monetary matters, Stimson told everybody that the United States was embarked on "a necessary experiment." The tone of the President's communications to the conference could be improved, he believed, but not their purpose.[2]

Having defended as best he could the actions of the new President, he turned shortly to the task of modifying some of the views of the previous Chief Executive. Throughout 1933 and 1934 Stimson and Hoover exchanged several letters on the state of the Union. The former President seemed to feel that the country might be moving toward some kind of authoritarian state. To comfort him Stimson replied that he had never been very apprehensive that a "turn to the right" in the United States would become "excessive." The National Recovery Administration seemed to be going up "into good-humored smoke" and while a good many of his friends were "all churned up" over Muscle Shoals and the Securities Act, even these friends seemed "inclined to lay the blame on the back of Congress rather than on the President." [3]

Some months later Stimson wrote again to say that he envied the "cheery pessimism" of Ogden Mills who was "happily engaged in leading assaults upon the fortresses of the New Deal. . . ." For himself he was using his microscopic influence to keep in touch with Hull, who was making "a good Secretary of State" and serving as a rallying point for the conservative elements around the President. By such tidings his correspondent refused to be comforted.[4]

Stimson, however, continued in his effort to bolster the spirit and faith of his old chief. He sent him the great speech, delivered on the seven hundredth anniversary of Magna Carta, in

[2] Diary, Oct. 18, 1933.
[3] H.L.S. to Herbert Hoover, Oct. 10, 1933.
[4] H.L.S. to Herbert Hoover, June 26, 1934.

which Elihu Root described the growth of the liberal influence in western society. He suggested that while it would be well in the immediate future for Mr. Hoover to remain in dignified silence, still there was, in the longer future, much he could contribute to the influence of the country. But Stimson could not agree, in spite of all the ballyhoo, that Americans had abandoned the philosophy of their fathers. "The industrial revolution," he concluded, "has made necessary changes in the methods and distribution of the profits of production; it is my bottommost faith that it has not made necessary changes in our old theories of individual rights against government." [5]

While continuing to discuss the future with Herbert Hoover, Stimson remained in touch also with Franklin Roosevelt. Once or twice in 1933 and 1934 he dined at the White House and talked about foreign affairs. Late in 1933 he wrote the President a long letter explaining that the Securities Act discouraged investment because, unlike the British act on which Roosevelt believed the law was modeled, it required extensive enumeration in great detail in every stock prospectus. Also by the terms of the law, again unlike the British act, the onus for error in any statement fell very heavily upon directors and underwriters. These features of the Act tended to discourage investment. Besides, while District Attorney, he said, he had found some provisions of the Interstate Commerce Act unenforceable because juries would not punish by jail sentence or large fine a single man or group of men for corporate misbehavior. Therefore the Securities Act, designed "to make somebody smart" rather than as a stroke of "constructive statesmanship," did not seem to be "adapted towards stimulating the recovery of a sick world." [6]

[5] H.L.S. to Herbert Hoover, July 12, 1934.
[6] H.L.S. to Franklin D. Roosevelt, Oct. 31, 1933. The original of this letter, as with other letters written by Stimson to Roosevelt and used in this chapter, is in the Roosevelt Papers at Hyde Park. Stimson had told the President the same thing in greater detail when he called on him five days before. He said he had tried "to get the standpoint" of all his advisers. He had read Warren's book twice, which was "more than anyone else had done," and besides he was "a

A year and a half later he wrote another letter to the President in which he gave the most complete expression in these years of his political philosophy. The occasion was provided by Roosevelt's irritable remarks, spoken at a press conference, about the Supreme Court's decision in the Schecter Case. These comments, Stimson began, had filled him with dismay. The National Recovery Act, which had been declared unconstitutional by the Court's decision, had, in general objective, the hearty sympathy of "rightminded men." It had tried to deal with the situation "thrown upon this country in common with the rest of the world by the industrial revolution of the past century, which so materially modified the workings of the doctrine of laissez faire." The problem, Stimson believed, was to discover the means to preserve "real competition while curbing the evils of cutthroat competition"; to secure stability in modern industry, prevent unfair practices and prohibit the exploitation of labor. This problem could be solved, in Stimson's view, by Roosevelt in ways that would not destroy the ancient continuities. He pointed out the way in which the Court historically had developed the law controlling the novel and expanding energies of the railroads, the intelligent flexibility with which it had handled the problems arising under the Sherman Act. Naturally there was criticism where the "rule of power must be developed by successive decisions on successive specific cases each varying from the others in its facts and in a constantly growing business." But a line of developing decisions permitted the possibility of growth and change — a continuing accommodation to a living, growing energy. Therefore to speak as if a single decision could overthrow this long, honor-

---

classmate and fellow member in Bones with Irving Fisher." This delighted Roosevelt. Stimson's letter to Roosevelt set off a long exchange of correspondence between Stimson and Frankfurter. The latter claimed the American Securities Act was in fact like the British act and that Stimson had mistaken the meaning of the history of the Interstate Commerce Act. After extended canvass of these matters over two months the two, in Frankfurter's words, ended the exchange like Carlyle and John Stirling, "agreeing in all things except opinion."

able adjustment to the growing needs of the country, to speak as though one decision could put the country back in the horse-and-buggy days, was "a wrong statement, an unfair statement and, if it had not been so extreme as to be recognizable as hyperbole, a rather dangerous and inflammatory statement."

As a second point, Stimson said he did not see how on the facts as given the Court could have made any other decision "without . . . leaving 'virtually no limit to the federal power.' . . . in respect to commerce and industry." He was a Hamiltonian, he approved of the countless decisions empowering Congress to control intrastate operations which directly interfered with interstate commerce, but if the Court adopted "any other rule than that the interference must be *direct*" it would, he believed, give the federal government an unwarranted control over all intrastate business. Such a result might well be fatal to the health of the republic. After "my long life of experience and observation . . . I have a stronger belief now than ever before in the necessity of the preservation of state authority. The longer I have lived in public life in Washington, the more clearly have I been impressed with the fact that Congress long since has practically reached the limit of its capacity under its present organization for keeping up intelligently with its legislative labor . . ." Greater duties would produce a transfer of its powers to administrative bureaus and the creation, in time, of an irresponsible bureaucracy. It was providential that the jealousies of the thirteen colonies produced the insistence upon the separate states which were still a bulwark against the central government.[7]

To this extended letter the President replied on June 7, addressing his correspondent for the first time as "Dear Harry" and suggesting that the truth lies "somewhere between your thought and my Friday statement. . . ."

It was all very well to see people and read books and write letters; the time came when Stimson believed he ought to act.

[7] H.L.S. to Franklin D. Roosevelt, June 4, 1935.

In the spring of 1934 a bill came before the Congress designed to give the President, for a limited time and within "careful restrictions," the power to enter into trade agreements with foreign governments. The purpose of the bill was to create as rapidly as possible, by changes in existing tariff schedules, a freer atmosphere for the exchange of goods between countries. Stimson, ever since he had made his first speech for the Taft Administration, had been interested in the subject of reciprocity and tariff reform. Increasingly he came to believe, as he wrote Herbert Feis on December 19, 1933, that "The doctrine of self-sufficiency is based upon narrow horizon, absence of historical study and a failure to realize how much of our present psychology is due to abnormal results of the war." In that month, he told Feis, he had "a far more understanding sympathy with Mr. Hull's position" than he had ever had before. He was also prepared to believe that if tariff reform were necessary in the existing emergency, it could only be obtained by an increased grant of authority to the President. He had watched the Congress, by treating the tariff as a local issue, devise, after long thought and longer debate, means "entirely ineffective" to deal with the existing economic situation. Nor did he fear that the grant of authority in the bill, qualified in extent and time, would endanger the Republic. "I have never been able to conjure up any real apprehension that the American people would be willing to carry through anything like a complete system of a planned national economy."

With such feelings he called on Cordell Hull to ask whether a speech in support of the pending bill "would do any harm." The Secretary was delighted and the talk, broadcast on the radio, was delivered on April 29, 1934. Democrats, as Arthur Krock reported, were tremendously pleased by this evidence of help from an unexpected quarter. To Hull it was one of the first indications that he and Stimson would always work "like double cousins"; to Roosevelt, in one of his expansive moods, it was clear that Stimson was "the chief influence" in the

probable success of the bill. Republicans, so Krock also reported, were as annoyed as the Democrats were pleased.
Though Stimson could not swing many votes since he had "no
party influence with them," he had "embarrassed the Republicans in their effort to take a party stand" against the tariff bill.[8]

The reform of the tariff, the commodity dollar, the decision
of the Supreme Court in the Schecter Case, the provisions of the
Securities Act, all these were a natural source of interest to a
man who had spent much of his life in American public service.
But as the months passed, these and the other domestic issues of
the time assumed secondary significance. He had, after all, been
a Secretary of State, and his primary concern, in time, became
again the foreign relations of the United States. By 1935 there
was much both at home and abroad to disturb the equanimity of
a man with such a concern. Meeting in the early part of the
year was a committee of Congress which in the opinion of Cordell Hull exerted an "unfortunate effect" virtually without paral-
lel upon the foreign relations of the country. The desire of the
majority of this committee, guided by its chairman, Gerald P.
Nye of North Dakota, was to demonstrate that America had entered the First World War at the direction of the bankers and
munitions makers. The intent was to demonstrate that if the
sale of munitions could be prevented, the country could never
become involved in foreign conflicts and thus would find it unnecessary to cooperate at all with other countries. By a series of
spectacular hearings the Nye Committee, it appeared, had communicated its desire and intent to the nation. At least the Congress thought so, for in the last days of August 1935 the first
neutrality legislation was passed.

By the principal terms of this resolution the President was
required, in the event of a foreign war, to prevent the sale of
arms to all belligerents. This legislation was "a startling break"

[8] Diary, May 18, 1934; *New York Times*, April 30, May 1, 1934; Irving Fisher
wrote him on May 2, 1934, after the speech on the tariff, to say he was "far
above" his party "whose attitudes on the tariff have been . . . very disgrace-
ful."

with America's past position, a reversal of the classic neutrality policy. It was also, in the opinion of the Secretary of State, an "invasion of the constitutional and traditional power of the Executive . . . ," an act that would deprive the government "of a great measure of its influence in promoting and preserving peace." Nevertheless the Secretary advised the President to sign the bill because he did not know what else to do "in all the circumstances."

Over the next two years the attitude of mind expressed in this bill was more specifically defined and elaborated by further legislation — which not only forbade shipments of munitions abroad but prevented the extension of private loans or credits to warring countries and limited the travel of citizens on ships of countries at war. The new neutrality, as defined in these laws, was the expression of the determination of the Congress to be quit of the mess in Europe once and for all, of the conviction that it was possible to abdicate from the common life of nations. These congressional views, it seems clear, were shared in by many and perhaps most of the American citizens the Congress represented.[9]

Against this view of things Stimson set himself in the year 1935. Before that time, diverted in part by domestic concerns and in part by his miscalculations of the staying power of Mussolini and Hitler, he had waited upon the course of events.

[9] Hull, *Memoirs*, I, 397-417; William L. Langer and S. Everett Gleason, *The Challenge to Isolation* (New York, 1952), 14, 15. Still one of the best ways to obtain both knowledge and feeling about what was happening in American foreign relations during the thirties is the study of the yearly issues of *The United States in World Affairs*, prepared by Walter Lippmann and others and published under the auspices of the Council on Foreign Relations. Although the appointment of Nye, an isolationist Republican, as chairman of the investigating committee was probably the result of "an oversight" and although it is impossible to calculate precisely the real weight of public opinion, it does seem probable that the Nye Committee in its findings gave expression to feelings shared by a majority of the citizens. Langer and Gleason, who have given the fullest and most careful analysis of "isolation" in this time, conclude that "The dominant feeling was overwhelmingly opposed not only to any involvement in foreign quarrels but to participation in any collective action to prevent or settle such quarrels."

But accumulating influences in the first eight months of the year caused him slowly to change his attitude. In March, while talking with the Canadian Minister about Hitler's plan to rearm Germany, he began to feel that "Everything seemed to be going to Hades." In May he told Moffat, who said he was not one of those who believed "in getting Germany back into the club," that it was impossible "that a great virile nation . . . could be held down permanently. . . ." It was of the first necessity to "stop these oscillations back and forth." Then in the summer followed the debate over the neutrality legislation and the mounting evidence of Italy's proposed attack on Ethiopia. These signs of "general deterioration" shocked him. As he wrote Hull on August 20, 1935, his thoughts were constantly with the Secretary in that time of "Italian crisis." In the ensuing weeks he saw and talked with many of his old friends who were interested and knowledgeable in matters of foreign affairs — Lippmann, Hamilton Fish Armstrong, John Foster and Allen Dulles. Several times he had long talks with Bruening who was living on Long Island under an assumed name. From the German he heard unsettling things about Goering and Goebbels and received a "very disturbing picture" of "the growth of the [German] army." [10]

These accumulating influences moved him to take some decisive positions in the fall of 1935. On October 11 he wrote a long letter to the *New York Times;* on October 24 he spoke on the radio about the President's neutrality proclamation and in the November *Forum* he published an article on the general subject of American neutrality. All three of these statements said, in substance, the same thing. He commended the President for the way he had proceeded within the meaning of the neutrality legislation to deal with the Ethiopian crisis. Then he went on to make two further points. First, he said, the urge for neutrality was "speaking with exactness" the wish to keep

[10] Diary, March 14, May 6, Sept. 19, Nov. 2, 1935; H.L.S. to Cordell Hull, Aug. 20, 1935.

out of war. But the way to avoid war was not to remain inert
after it had come. Isolation was, in the modern condition, impossible. "The real problem is to decide what methods of action
will best keep us out of war" at a time when "Civilized life has
suddenly become extremely complex and extremely fragile,"
when "the world has suddenly become interconnected and interdependent." And the second point was this. Not all had been
said that should have been said by the man who was "the natural
leader of the public opinion of his people," the man to whom
all turned "for information and guidance." "In this pending crisis
not a word has been said by our government to indicate to our
people the impelling moral reason why they should voluntarily
make the sacrifices involved. . . . Not a word has been uttered
to point out that Italy has violated solemn covenants. . . .
These questions stare the world in the face today, and in order
to steer our people successfully through this crisis I think
they will have to be faced by our government and an answer
given upon which our people can honorably stand." [11]

It was reported that officials in Washington were grateful for
Stimson's support of the administration's position but also that
they were "puzzled" by his comments on presidential leadership and his insistence on the moral considerations. "What more
would [he] have us do?" they were said to ask. Does he wish
to call a conference of the nations that signed the Kellogg Pact
or apply the doctrine of nonrecognition he had promulgated
during the Manchurian crisis? "They confessed," in fact, "mys-
tification." There is nothing to suggest that Stimson had such
steps, or any other specific actions, in mind. The call for leadership, the raising of the moralities, may suggest, however, something else — a change in Stimson's attitude of mind. There is
much in his diary and correspondence and actions in these
days to indicate that in his judgment the balance of possibilities
in the fall of 1935 had shifted away from continued peace and

[11] New York Times, Oct. 11, 1935; text of H.L.S. radio address, Oct 23, 1935;
Forum, Nov. 1935.

toward another war. And thus, as always when things seemed to be going to Hades, Stimson wished to speak out on matters of leadership and the duties of man in the days of approaching trial. His words were not so much a recommendation for a specific policy as an indication of his belief that the existing policies at home and abroad, if long continued, would lead to catastrophe.[12]

If such indeed was his judgment, nothing happened in the next few years to alter his view. In 1936 Hitler entered the Rhineland and civil war began in Spain. In 1937 there was the incident at Marco Polo Bridge and the sinking of the gunboat *Panay*. In 1938 Hitler entered Austria and then dismembered Czechoslovakia. In these same years Secretary Hull issued his eight pillars of peace — "as vital in international relations as the Ten Commandments in personal relations" — and the Undersecretary of State proposed a world conference to discuss five questions, and the President said "We are not isolationists except in so far as we seek to isolate ourselves completely from war." Over the waters in these years there were the Brussels Conference and the Hoare-Laval Agreement and Munich.[13]

The friends that came to Highhold and Woodley in these years brought with them unhappy tidings. From Bruening Stimson heard that Goering's activities might well drive the German people into war; from Jean Monnet, that "the Old Timer settlement" in England had "lost sight of the big political problem" in the Far East; from Sir Arthur Salter, that a situation was being shaped up which would make war probable within five years. Hearing such counsel Stimson was almost ready to conclude that the time for continued hope was really over. He was, he confessed to Lord Astor in 1936, disappointed with the

[12] *New York Times*, Oct. 12, 1935.
[13] Hull, *Memoirs*, I, 535-36; Langer and Gleason, *Challenge to Isolation*, 16, 19-20. Sumner Welles, *Seven Decisions That Shaped History* (New York, 1951), 74, says that had the President "been publicly supported by a few more men like Mr. Stimson himself, the American people might more easily have understood the gravity of the world situation. . . ."

twists and turns of the old diplomacy. We must, he argued, "bear in mind the necessity of educating and carrying along with us that public opinion upon which we depend." [14]

In the ensuing months he turned again to the work of education. Roused in October 1937 by the generalities in Roosevelt's "quarantine speech," he said two days later in the *New York Times* that there was no excuse for the American "seizure of nervous 'jitters,'" no excuse, except faulty reasoning, for the wave of "ostrich-like isolationism" and for the "erroneous form of neutrality legislation [which] has threatened to bring upon us in the future the very dangers of war which we now are seeking to avoid." In this communication he proposed stopping our trade with Japan and correcting the deep-seated error on which our policy was based — the setting of peace above righteousness. Supplementing this, he sent a letter to Franklin Roosevelt arguing that the influence of America and the President for leadership, moral and material, was great beyond computation and that such leadership should concern itself not only with immediate needs but long-term problems and solutions. Some weeks later he attacked, again in the newspapers, the assumption both "untrue" and "fantastic" upon which Louis L. Ludlow's proposed referendum on the question of a declaration of war rested. And then, as the year turned, he acted in the ways he could, by letter, speech and committee membership, to arrange an informal economic boycott on trade with the Japanese. [15]

In March of 1938 he invited six Republican members of the House and five members of the Senate to dinner at Woodley to discuss matters of foreign policy. Describing the state of the nation as he perceived it, he offered no special course of action except interest and courage. One month later he was telling members of the Hardware Manufacturers Statistical Associa-

[14] Diary, March 4, 26, 27, 28, 1936; H.L.S. to Viscount Astor, May 6, 1936.
[15] *New York Times*, Oct. 7, Dec. 22, 1937; H.L.S. to Franklin D. Roosevelt, Nov. 15, 1937.

tion that "we have not realized that we are living in an inter-connected world, a very much smaller world than the world we had before steam and electricity. I am one of those who believe that isolationism in a country in this modern world is not possible. But I won't even argue with it. . . . It is just damn non-sense." We had, in this contingency, been neither intelligent nor courageous. "We have just crept into our hole and tried to pull the hole in after us. We have a little ring of fresh-water statesmen who have tried to exclude the fact that there was a world outside the salt water. The quicker," he concluded, "we get over that and prepare to take responsibilities and back up statesmanship with responsibilities the better we will be." "Pretty soon," he wrote the Secretary of State a month later, he was "going to explode again." Looking out at the ships passing each day down the North River loaded with scrap for Japan he thought with rising irritation of the aid and comfort we were giving to that unfriendly nation. He was so "impressed by the barbarities of the Japanese bombings" and by the danger "to the world *and us*" if the barbarity went unchallenged that he was sure the country would back "still further expressions and non-military action" against Japan.[16]

But he did not immediately explode. Instead he became involved in the longest, hardest law case of his career — the Blaustein case. For most of the rest of 1938 he devoted himself with Allen Klots to the preparation of this most complicated and intricate corporate suit. Just as the year ended, however, he wrote the Marquess of Londonderry that while he would not criticize those who, like Londonderry, looked for new avenues leading to agreement with the Germans, for himself he believed the void dividing Germany from the United States and England was impassable. And so in the modern, connected, interdependent, shrunken world the different national aspirations, left unreconciled, would not permit the na-

[16] Transcript of remarks to the Hardware Manufacturers Statistical Association, April 28, 1938; H.L.S. to Cordell Hull, June 9, 1938.

tions to live together peaceably. If his assessment were correct, sooner or later those who believed governments were constituted to protect the rights and freedoms of the citizens would be driven to forcible resistance.[17]

Holding these views he found he could not, in spite of his labors on the Blaustein case, hold his silence as the year 1939 opened. On January 18 he sent a letter to Cordell Hull urging the President to lift the embargo imposed on May 1, 1937, by congressional resolution on the sale of arms to combatants in the Spanish Civil War. He argued that since the United States had recognized the loyalist government in Spain we had a time-honored right in international law to deliver munitions to this government. He also argued that the President had the power "without the action of Congress" to lift the embargo. "Mr. Secretary," he said, "the mere statement of this situation seems to me to show what a perilous path we are treading by our new experiment in fresh-water statesmanship." The "cowardly advocates of the new neutrality could not have chosen a more conspicuously unfortunate time to demonstrate the folly and danger of their emotional propositions." A letter similar in content if not in tone was printed in the *New York Times* on January 24, 1939. Maybe, said the paper in editorial comment, for the first time Stimson was giving the administration anxiety and inconvenience instead of holding its hand as heretofore. There was grave doubt in the State Department whether the President had legally the right to do what Stimson urged him to do, and graver doubt in and out of the Department that the President wanted to do what Stimson thought he ought to do.[18]

Six weeks later the busy advocate, in another long letter to the *Times*, laid down the basis of "an affirmative foreign policy for this government. . . ." Fascism, with its moral deteriora-

---

[17] H.L.S. to the Marquess of Londonderry, Dec. 15, 1938. A few months earlier he had written his old friend A. P. Proctor, "The war in Europe looks as though [it were] coming closer and closer and closer."

[18] H.L.S. to Cordell Hull, Jan. 18, 1939. The original of this letter is in the Roosevelt Papers at Hyde Park.

tion, brutality, destructiveness of individual freedom of speech and thought, constituted "probably the most serious attack" ever made on democratic principles. To attempt to forestall the Fascist aggression by soft words or inaction was the counsel of confused thinking, emotion or, "to speak plainly, undue timidity." How should "we conduct ourselves in this threatening world?" he asked. The answer, he believed, was to speak unwelcome truths, to alter the policy of dealing equally with both sides in the European alignment. "I am unalterably opposed," he said, to the doctrine that "we must sell to a nation which has violated its treaties with us as well as trampled upon the humanities of our civilization . . . as freely as we sell to its victim. . . ." [19]

These views he expressed more fully before the Senate Committee on Foreign Relations in April when the members met to consider the extension of the "cash and carry" provisions of the existing neutrality law. The point of his prepared statement was that in the present emergency the President, in imposing an embargo, should be empowered — as until 1935 he had always been empowered — to distinguish between an aggressor nation and a country attacked. He did not feel that any President, including the one then in office, would use this traditional authority to usurp power and he believed the proper and effective conduct of foreign affairs required this grant of freedom to presidential action. Having established his points he awaited the questions of the senators.

In the thirty-odd years during which he had appeared before congressional committees he had never quite lost the manner — chill, stiff, awkward — that settled over him in public situations. But by taking thought he had acquired some of the elaborate jocosity required for these occasions. And he retained the aplomb that derives from the determination to say what one means. So when the senators went after him he maintained the original lines of his argument intact and in good order. The

[19] *New York Times*, March 7, 1939.

point at issue, "and I am trying now to be philosophical on the differences between my old friend Senator Johnson and myself," was really only the "length of the viewpoint." When an enemy was "endangering us, step by step" he would not wait until the enemy "had killed off the last nation that stood between us and safety before I began to think hard and to take some economic action." But was there actually, asked Senator Robert R. Reynolds, anything happening in the world that imperiled the safety of the United States? When the witness replied that Czechoslovakia, Ethiopia and Austria appeared to undermine "the entire system upon which our relations to the world in the past have been predicated," the Senator asked if there were any difference between what Italy and Germany were doing and what England and France had done in the nineteenth century. Reynolds also inquired if the United States had not already encouraged England to stand against the aggressor "in every possible conceivable manner." "Well," Stimson replied, "I might possibly have thought, if I were trying, that we could have encouraged them more than we did. . . ." Had we not, he wondered, created the impression that we were observing matters from afar — as disengaged "as an hermaphrodite entirely or an impotent person . . . ?"

The mention of England put Borah in mind of Sir John Simon; had not the Foreign Secretary in fact let Stimson down? "Well now, Senator, I confess to have been perhaps disappointed. . . . but I have always felt — I think you will agree with me — that Sir John Simon perhaps was not entirely and in all respects similar to every other foreign secretary of the British Empire." And thus it continued: Reynolds admitted he was "sore with Britain and France because they are doing their best to lead us into another war"; Robert M. La Follette, Jr., worried about giving the power to the President to distinguish between an aggressor and an injured nation; Hiram W. Johnson feared that the effect of naming an aggressor nation and refusing to trade with it would be "to take us into war." Harsh things were said about the munitions makers and the propaganda that forced American entry into the First World War, about the British and about the "prejudices" of any American President and about many other things that came to the senatorial mind. But at the end Senator Lewis B. Schwellenbach asked the question that revealed the issue all but concealed by the three-hour discussion. "By and large," he said to Stimson, "you would favor the repeal of the present neutrality statute?" "I am inclined to think," responded Stimson, "that that would be the safest way, although of course that is subject to the judgment of you gentlemen. . . ."[20]

In the next few days of April 1939 Stimson learned something more about the temper of those numberless men and women in the country who spoke up in support of such senators as Reynolds, Johnson, Borah and Schwellenbach. He received letters which told him that he had lost the art of reasoning; that he was too old to sit as a member of the House Committee on Foreign Relations; that the Jews should fight their own battles the same as the Irish; that it must be easy to sit in Washington and declare war when you know you will stay there; that *Old Men* in certain key positions of their country suddenly become very brave; that, my dear sir, no foreign nations should be trusted since they are always waiting for us to play the part of the rich uncle; that we have been tricked in the past by the two so-called democracies; that the queer part of it was that the old fellows were always so quick to advise the wholesale murder of the young; that if you had shouldered a gun in 1918 I wonder if you would be so anxious. He was asked where he got off trying to tell the American people, of whom he knew nothing, about how to balk the dictators; where he was in the year 1918; why he had spent his life in the law representing British interests. Down upon him was called, not once but many

[20] *Hearings*, Senate Committee on Foreign Relations, 76th Congress, 1st Session, on S.J. Resolution 21, pp. 3-7. From the galleys of these Hearings Stimson struck out the reference to hermaphrodites and impotent persons.

times, the curse of God, and of a just God. From Reno, Nevada, came more measured opposition to his arguments. No war, said Herbert Hoover, was won by economic methods. Americans did not wish to be put in another war and Congress should take action to prevent us from engaging in European power politics or in any economic warlike acts without the approval of Congress itself.[21]

The year wore on while Stimson waited for the war which he expected "might come at any moment." Until September 1939 he did little but labor with Allen Klots on the preparation of the Blaustein case. This involved "an enormous amount of extra work." Yet he kept in touch with the larger events, exchanging letters with Key Pittman on the Neutrality Act, giving such advice as he could when Hull asked him in July what Republicans might support the administration's foreign policy, answering at the request of Thomas Lamont Senator Borah's speech on the need to retain the Neutrality Act after the war began in September 1939, and conferring with Alfred Landon on steps to be taken to repeal the Act. He was one of those, he said on the radio in October 1939, who believed the President and Mr. Hull were right. "In short my view is that the security, present and future, of the United States and of its people will be promoted by the repeal of the embargo and that such a step will not tend to drag us into war." [22]

By the end of the year his efforts to prepare the Blaustein case, which was coming on for trial, and his continuing activity in support of his public views had worn him down. He was, after all, seventy-two and he had worked with all his energy to prepare the Blaustein brief and to state his larger case to the American people. Beyond this he was frustrated by his divided concern for his client and for the state of the nation. During the Christmas holidays — bothered by insomnia, indigestion,

[21] Letters written to H.L.S., April 7-10, 1939; *New York Times*, April 8, 1939.
[22] H.L.S. to Key Pittman, April 25, May 1, 19, 1939; Diary, Jan.-Sept., 1939; *New York Times*, Sept. 15, 1939; Speech, Oct. 5, 1939.

vague but persistent feelings of disease — he came near the end of his rope. The arguing of his case in court as the New Year opened put a further burden upon him. He began to have trouble thinking clearly and quickly in his favorite moment of the cross-examination. To Felix Frankfurter he wrote that he was convinced at last that he was "a slow old man and that trial work is out for me." A week or two later he found he could go no further and asked Allen Klots to take over the management of the case in court. Throughout the spring he sat beside his younger colleague observing the course of the trial, but never once did he give direction or advice unless Klots asked his opinion. In February, during a brief recess, he went to Yeaman's Hall to sit in the sunshine and listen to the birds' spring songs, but he returned without much change in spirit. He felt, inert as he was in a dreadful world, a very old and useless man.

When the President asked him to lunch at the White House in May 1940, he went down for a pleasant conversation but heard nothing that gave him much confidence about the situation in Europe. And, on the same visit, what he heard from friends in the government about the confusions and uncertainties within the State Department increased his anxiety about the future. So in June 1940, as France was falling, he resolved to state his case once more and to state it in words of unmistakable meaning. Returning to Andover for the Academy commencement he told the boys that in that dark hour the civilization built up over four hundred years on principles of trust, respect, justice, fair play and above all on the Christian principle of the equal value of all human personalities was under attack; that in that attack the world was confronted by the clearest issue between right and wrong that had ever been presented to it. Looking into those faces he was filled not with pity, he said, but with a desire to congratulate those students that in this clear choice between good and evil they had been placed in a moment of great opportunity.

From Andover he went to his other old school in New

Haven. On the 17th of June he told the returning alumni that a system of universal military training was needed immediately. That night he went to his class dinner and the next afternoon he went off to see the Harvard-Yale baseball game. Before going to the game he told his niece Mrs. Daggett, with whom he and Mrs. Stimson were staying, that in the course of the afternoon electricians would move in to wire the house for a radio speech he would give that night. As the game was ending he went down to Mr. Daggett's office and dictated the remarks he would make that night on the radio. In the evening from the house on Prospect Street he set forth seven steps that should be taken in the national defense. Among these were: the repeal of the "ill-starred so-called neutrality act"; the opening of our ports to British and French vessels for purposes of repair; the acceleration by every means in our power, including, if necessary, convoy by vessels of the United States Navy, of the sending of war materials to England and France; the immediate adoption of compulsory military service. "In these ways," he concluded, "and with the old American spirit of courage and leadership behind them, I believe we should find our people ready to take their proper part in this threatened world and to carry through to victory, freedom and reconstruction." [23]

Soon after he had finished his speech the messages of congratulation and condemnation began pouring into the house on Prospect Street. Among them was a telegram brought by one of Stimson's grandnieces to him as he sat resting with his wife in the living room. It read, "Thank God you are not in the government." On the following day, back in his New York office, Stimson in a telephone call from the White House was asked by President Roosevelt to become the Secretary of War.

[23] Radio speech, June 18, 1940.

26

The Secretary of War

WHEN GEORGE DERN died in 1936 Harry Woodring was set up in his place as Secretary of War. Everyone knew, indeed the President himself had said, that this was only a temporary appointment; within a matter of months Mr. Woodring would be dispatched to some meaningless office over the water or even back to Kansas. And so for the next four years a good many people used up a good deal of time and energy in discussing what to do about the Secretary of War. To these discussions Jim Farley, Pa Watson, Missy LeHand, Steve Early and the Old Curmudgeon all made some contribution. Perhaps Woodring would go to Manila or Puerto Rico or Ottawa or Dublin and, if he did, perhaps Jesse Jones or Louis Johnson or Frank Murphy would take his place. In the beginning this was, for the most part, a matter of innocent scheming, the kind of corridor plotting that grows up around any man left with an uncertain future. Woodring was, to be sure, a little pompous but he had a kind of competence and a very pretty wife; he was also better, it was said, than Swanson who was 10 per cent alive, or Uncle Dan Roper who was befuddled or Ma Perkins who was both prim and a woman.

But as time wore on it was discovered that the office if not the man was increasing in importance. In these circumstances it was recognized that Woodring would not do, that there were "ups and downs" in his understanding and that he was, in fact, "a two-spot." The President was heard to say, "Harry [Woodring] is a nice fellow but . . ."; yet the President also told a funny story about the Woodring baby and said, "I am so weak at getting rid of people." Several men tried to help him. They offered their own services; at least one, Louis Johnson, thought he had been promised the position, and another, Harold Ickes, conceived the idea that all cabinet members ought to resign to help the President get rid of Woodring and one or two others. He was tired of these temporary appointments that had a way of becoming permanent. But the President continued to extend the hope that "everything would work out all right." As it turned out, things went from bad to worse. When the war began in 1939 it became clear that within the exact meaning of the neutrality acts of earlier years Harry Woodring was neutral in deed as well as thought. He resisted stubbornly and with some skill any effort on the part of the administration to contribute in any way to the effort of the countries engaged in the conflict against Adolf Hitler. In the War Department there was, as Assistant Secretary, Louis Johnson. He was not only anxious to oppose the Secretary's policies but also to obtain the Secretary's office. A struggle for power and place thus began in the Department which became a matter of almost public scandal. Officers as well as civilians inevitably were drawn into the conflict. By the late fall of 1939 the situation had, in Ickes' words, become "a holy show . . . with Woodring and Johnson each trying to outsmart the other." [1]

These unattractive matters coincided with the President's rising interest in 1940 as an election year. In time past he had occasionally thought of including a Republican or two in his Cabinet and usually at such times he had thought of Alfred Landon and Frank Knox as candidates. But the moments of insufficient crisis had passed without such dramatic action. Then, in the increasing turmoil of September 1939 he returned to his previous

[1] *The Secret Diary of Harold L. Ickes*, Vol. II, *The Inside Struggle* (New York, 1954), 24, 537-38, 552-53, 629, 718, Vol. III, *The Lowering Clouds* (New York, 1954), 14, 55, 64-65, 136, 179-81, 196; James A. Farley, *Jim Farley's Story* (New York, 1948), 115-16, 156, 241 f.; H. H. Arnold, *Global Mission* (London, 1951), 121-22; conversation with Grenville Clark, Aug. 17, 1954.

idea and drew up a possible program "to clear out both Woodring and Johnson. Frank Murphy will go to War, a place that he still wants. . . . Bob Jackson would go in as Attorney General, and Navy and Commerce would be offered to Knox and Landon." [2]

Though the plan in its specifics was laid aside, the mood behind the plan persisted into the spring of 1940. And then as the Democratic Convention drew nearer and the phony war in Europe ended, the President prepared himself to do the kind of thing he always found it hardest to do. He would reorganize his Cabinet. In the course of his preparations he received unexpected assistance from an old acquaintance, Grenville Clark.

Mr. Clark was a man who chose to serve the state as an independent citizen. He was no Baruch seeking to act, in the Brandeis phrase, as counsel for the situation; instead he appeared, in critical or confusing times, as a lobby for particular impulses of the national conscience. There were others not unlike him — George Rublee, Robert Bass, C. C. Burlingham, to name a few — in these years; men who bore a private and often invisible hand, here and there, in the public work. For a generation they had, sometimes individually, sometimes collectively, exerted subtle and interesting influences on the national life. The influence derived, in part, from the fact that they had known each other a long time — at colleges like Harvard and Yale, in the professions like the law where most of them worked, in the community life of the cities — New York, Washington, Boston — where most of them lived. Active in their independent, private errands or less often in minor appointive offices, they also had come to know a good many of the effective men in the government — civil servants like Hornbeck or Feis, military men like General McCoy, floor leaders in the Congress, cabinet members. Possessing confidence in themselves and in their views, they possessed also the confidence that they could walk into a room in the Treasury or the House Office Building and present clear positions that would be heard with respect. Acting

[2] Ickes, *Diary*, II, 718.

usually alone they sometimes gave body to their attitudes by organizing loose federations like the Plattsburg Training Camp Association or the Century Group to aid the allies. Altogether they were a useful and interesting element in the working of the democratic process.

Of them all Grenville Clark was perhaps the most constantly active and certainly the most dogged. He had been a moving spirit in the development of the Plattsburg Training Camps to prepare officers for the First World War; refusing to act as Assistant Secretary of State in the Hoover Administration he had nevertheless done odd jobs throughout the four years for Secretary Stimson. In the early years of the New Deal he took a hand in framing some of the economic and financial legislation, while in 1936 he had mobilized a group of lawyers against the President's plan to enlarge the Supreme Court. In the spring of 1940 he turned his persistent energies to the task of obtaining universal military training in this country. To this end he discussed matters with his friends, roused the alumni of the Plattsburg camps, called on General George C. Marshall, the new Chief of Staff, and took his case to James F. Byrnes, then floor leader of the Democrats in the Senate. From the General he learned that the Army was, for the time being, opposed to universal training and from Byrnes he heard that there was not a "Chinaman's chance" that a universal training bill would pass the Congress.[3]

This much he knew when he woke up one morning in the middle of May with the conviction that the only way to achieve

---

[3] Conversation with Grenville Clark, Aug. 17, 1954; Mark Watson, *U.S. Army in World War II, The War Department, Chief of Staff: Prewar Plans and Preparations* (Washington, 1950), 190-95. Watson reports, as does Clark, that Marshall "flatly refused" to urge the President to support the draft. But Watson suggests that Marshall's position was determined not by his feelings of military necessity but by his understanding of what was politically possible. He did not wish to make it seem that the Army was pushing the draft in its own behalf. In support of this is Marshall's recollection of a senator who told him that the draft was "one of the most stupid and outrageous things that 'the generals' had ever perpetrated on Congress."

his purpose was to obtain a Secretary of War who would "push it through." He needed, he decided, someone like Henry L. Stimson. This project he took immediately to Felix Frankfurter, then a Justice of the Supreme Court, who knew that the President was preparing himself to get rid of Woodring. Clark and the Justice considered other names — especially William J. Donovan and Lewis Douglas — but they always came back to Stimson. On the other hand they knew Stimson was not only "bored stiff" by the Blaustein case, but also, and more important, at seventy-two very weary. He had seemed to Clark earlier in May "a very tired, decayed old man." So the two arranged "a ticket" of Stimson and Robert P. Patterson, a former partner in Clark's firm, then a United States Circuit Court judge, who as Assistant Secretary would supply the necessary youth and energy.

This proposal was taken by Felix Frankfurter to the White House on June 3 where the President heard it with interest but with a reservation about Stimson's health. With matters carried this far Clark conferred with Stimson. The old man was at first very peeved that this "ridiculous idea" should have been put forth without his knowledge. But he promised to talk with his partners and Mrs. Stimson. An hour later he called back to say that, on conditions, he would accept the office if it were tendered. He would not take any part in domestic politics; he would do his utmost to obtain universal military training; he would not submit his speeches for revision by the administra-ation; and he would want his own subordinates — i.e., Patterson. Any one of these conditions would, he told Clark, disqualify him from further consideration. But they did not; the President wished only to be reassured about Stimson's health. So Grenville Clark went round to the Stimson family physician, whom he knew, to ask "an extraordinary thing." There was an extended pause before the doctor said that he had never done this before, nor would he do it now, he supposed, if there were anything wrong with his patient, but in truth there was nothing wrong. Stimson was tired because he was "terribly frustrated," but he was in very good shape. The word went back to Frankfurter and from Frankfurter to the White House and then, for several weeks, nothing happened. At last on June 19 the President called Stimson at 32 Liberty Street and a little later Stimson called Clark to tell him that "your preposterous plan has succeeded." The plan had been brought to final success with one of those presidential flourishes. Before talking to Stimson Roosevelt had called Knox to tell him that "War and Navy are now open"; Stimson would like one, he went on, and "which will you have?" Knox said he did not know enough about the Army. And what if he had preferred the War Department? "Oh," the President later told a friend, "I would have spun it along and worked it out some way." [4]

Reconstructing in later years the feelings with which he returned once again to office Stimson said of himself: "He was at work again, under a chief whom he was able to admire and like as a man, even as he respected him for his office. He was in charge of the United States Army, which for thirty years he had known and loved and trusted. And he had a good Chief of Staff. No man . . . could have asked more of fortune in a time of national peril." [5]

[4] Conversation with Grenville Clark, Aug. 17, 1954; conversation with Felix Frankfurter, Sept. 29, 1954; Diary, June 25, 1940. Stimson in his account, *Active Service*, 323-24, is not quite as precise in the statement of the conditions on which he would accept. Nothing is said, for instance, about not submitting his speeches for revision. But in general intent the conditions described are the same. That conditions substantially like those enumerated were attached to Stimson's acceptance is confirmed by George Roberts with whom he discussed the subject. Before Clark called Stimson to complete his "ticket" he had already obtained Patterson's consent. Patterson had won the President's regard in the immediate past by a curious chance. Only a week or two before the appointment was made, Secretary Woodring had showed Roosevelt a letter from Patterson offering to resign his judgeship and enlist as a private in the Army, or in any other capacity the Secretary chose. The news of the appointments stunned most observers, both those in favor and those opposed. Senator Burton K. Wheeler said the names ought to be pleasing "to the war mongers," and the *New York Times*, June 21, 1940, reported that Stimson and Knox had been "virtually read out of the Republican party" for their "act of party treachery."

[5] *Active Service*, 331.

These were the saving and enduring elements extracted by the sense of propriety and passing time; fortune in the immediate event contrived a more ordinary and natural situation. Stimson was first introduced to the raveled actuality on July 2, 1940, when he appeared before the Senate Committee on Military Affairs to give evidence of his fitness to hold office. In the committee room through those hours all the unresolved anxieties at play throughout the nation were held for a concentrated moment in unattractive suspension. The witness in himself represented the confusions of the time, a Republican, a servant of four Republican Presidents, seeking now a place in a Democratic cabinet. At the committee table were, by special invitation, other representatives of the besetting sense of cross-purpose in the country. There sat the great Republican politicians Arthur H. Vandenberg and Robert A. Taft, deprived on the day before and in the last moment of pandemonium at Philadelphia of the Republican Presidential nomination by Wendell Willkie who had never been in politics and was not even certainly a Republican. In the testimony some of the causes that produced such unusual effects were revealed. Stimson in his opening statement was clear enough: he did "not believe that we shall be safe from invasion if we sit down and wait for the enemy to attack our shores." To prepare for days of "unprecedented peril" was the first obligation. The time for such preparation would be given by the British fleet, maintained in being by American aid if necessary; the means would be supplied by congressional appropriation, the substance by universal military training.

Responding to this line of argument the senators first pulled some well-roasted chestnuts out of the fire. There were allusions to Wall Street lawyers, prominent bankers and foreign clients. But then Arthur Vandenberg asked if some of Stimson's proposals, like servicing the British fleet in our ports, were not acts of war and the witness replied that he preferred to call them legitimate acts of defense. In this connection, he said also, as he had in his opening statement, that what they might be was not his affair; the Secretary of War does not make policy in foreign affairs. Then came Robert Taft, fixed in his purpose to keep America isolated from the turmoils of Europe. With all the skill of his sharp, well-stocked mind, with that cunning in debate sometimes permitted by decent men to themselves when they think they are acting as instruments of a higher good, he went after the witness. For instance he said, "Then, as I understand you, you are in favor of joining in the war just as soon as you figure that the British have no longer a chance. . . ." But because he was Robert Taft he went on to matters of more substance. How could the witness argue that the Secretary of War simply administered his Department, that his general views would not have influence on the foreign and domestic policies of the administration? This was not only a new idea, it was contrary to the historical record and, in fact, impossible.

The Senator was of course correct; it was his awareness of this, and his fear that Stimson's views would carry real weight in the administration, that drove him on to those other mean and meaningless points of his. And because he was right, the witness in the chair before him, though he gave some ground, never really answered him. Possibly the Senator's manner and method were not, as Stimson said, "worthy of a son of William Taft," but on this occasion the witness was not perhaps acting in complete consonance with his own heritage and future record. In stating his views he was naturally anxious, as he put it, to do nothing that would embarrass Franklin Roosevelt or Cordell Hull. Also, as he said much later, he was, after all, trying to get confirmed in his office.[6]

---

[6] *Active Service*, 325-30; transcript of H.L.S.-McGeorge Bundy conversations, Sept. 9, Oct. 16 (mistakenly dated 1945), 1946; *Nomination of Henry L. Stimson: Hearing*, Senate Military Affairs Committee, 76th Congress, 3rd Session (1940). In thinking about his replies to Taft on the question of the influence a Secretary of War may have on matters of general policy, Stimson confessed that he had "had pangs." This did not mean he would have done it differently if he had done it over again, only that he was unhappy it had to be done that way. The things that governed were two: First, "The one straw in the maelstrom with which I was surrounded that I could cling to at all was national

What went on in this committee room in July 1940 was also going on throughout the country. In any democracy the concern to fulfill the immediate need tends to displace consideration of more remote requirements. And this tendency in the United States has, perhaps by accidents of history, become exaggerated. With its appetites and energies the country could acquire a great sense of opportunity — even a sense of the developing present — but not the feeling for the probable or possible future. When by the war in Europe an awareness of what might come was pushed out toward the nation, the American society, lacking a settled habit of cooperative consideration for the future, fell apart into anxious, hopeful, fearful, distrait, even — in certain times and places — perverse sections of opinion. For men in public life there was thus no simple way to fit nicely the requirements of the moment — to get elected, to control an uneasy minority, to get confirmed — to those ultimate requirements on which there was no agreement. Between what must be done in the actual today and what might be done in some range of alternative tomorrows, there was no obvious consonance. So men in public life had, in the interests of survival, to make some kind of terms with the occasion that was upon them, and so to make debating points or to present novel definitions of old authorities, or to give their word, sometimes again and again and again, on matters where no word could be given. Some men in doing or saying these things were, perhaps, more worthy and some less worthy of their heritage or of themselves. But still this is a society where one man is always as good as another, or at least no better than anybody else. And in the government of such a society the power of a public man to give life to his best

---

defense." He would represent only the requirements of what he understood to be the overriding national interest of that moment. Second, he did exercise influence and in that sense Taft "was quite right." But he exerted it in "full loyalty to the regular basis of the American Cabinet Office." He was "a member of a team and of course subordinate to the President. . . ." He would take positions the President was not prepared to take himself, but he would never take a position the President was unwilling to have him take.

intentions derives from the will of the people and in 1940 that will, divided by rival counsels and conflicts of opinion, lay almost paralyzed.

This national irresolution cut down the power of any member of the administration, as Stimson learned upon his confirmation as Secretary of War, to move with certain steps in definite directions. And there were other things that prevented him from doing clearly and well whatever he may have wished to do in his new position. To begin with, the War Department was not in a condition to conduct its own business. General McCoy said that "there never had been such a situation in the War Department in its history. . . ." In part this was simply a matter of morale. Ill supported through twenty years by insufficient appropriations, an object of popular indifference or misunderstanding for the same two decades, the spirit of the Army had gradually declined. And in the recent past this spirit had been further damaged in the holy show produced by the conflict between Secretary Woodring and Assistant Secretary Johnson. But there was also a further and more persistent source of administrative failure in the War Department. Nowhere within it was to be found a center of organizing and directing energy.[7]

To supply such a center in a military establishment is one of the great problems of any government, for it involves the successful reconciliation of the two opposing influences that meet in the control of an armed force. To achieve this end it is necessary to create an energy wise and powerful enough to provide effective military command but still dependent upon and responsive to the will of the civilian in the determination of the uses to which the military shall be put. The danger is always present, in the administration of an armed force, that an energy strong enough to command the means — which is the army —

[7] Stimson himself said that the situation, largely produced, in his opinion, by the conflict between Woodring and Johnson, was "absolutely the most shocking situation in the Army that had ever occurred. It was a tremendous advantage to me for anything I did would be a contrast." Transcript of H.L.S.-McGeorge Bundy conversation, Sept. 9, 1946.

will be strong enough also to dominate the civilian influence and thus to shape the ends — which is the national policy. It had been the custom to assume that this great problem of military administration — the successful accommodation of the civil and military influences within the structure — had been in large part solved by Elihu Root when, in 1903, he obtained the legislation creating the General Staff.

By this Act, it will be remembered, the General Staff had the power to prepare plans and to supervise the actions of the several military agencies working together to fulfill the requirements of these plans. In this way opportunity was provided for intelligent military direction. The principle of civilian control was sustained in the legislation symbolically by the fact that the first officer of the Army was called not the Commanding General but the Chief of Staff and by the fact that all his orders were issued in the name of the Secretary. This Act provided the Army with a more useful administrative mechanism than the Navy had ever been able to devise. It did two important things. It created a place within the operating organization where the ablest officers could think and where the product of their thought could be made to apply to the actual workings of the profession. Officers, by virtue of the General Staff experience, were given an opportunity, withheld in large part from naval officers, to discover the nature and influence of ideas. Furthermore, the General Staff brought the Secretary of War and the Chief of Staff more closely together through mutual consideration of ideas and policies, and thus provided some mechanism for the fusing of military and civilian influence in the administration of the Army.

But these advantages were offset by a cardinal defect in the legislation of 1903. The Chief of Staff was not given sufficient authority over his subordinates, the Chiefs of Arms and the Chiefs of Services, to make them work together in the fulfillment of his plans. By the terms of the Act the Chief of Staff could only supervise his subordinates and much time was spent

and many memoranda were written to demonstrate that supervise did not mean command, that it merely granted the Chief of
Staff the power to call attention to the requirements for cooperation set forth in the plans of the Staff. The word supervise had
been used deliberately by the congressional framers to prevent
the development of a dominant military interest, but it also prevented effective administration. The subordinate agencies with
their own jobs to do and, in many cases, their own budgets,
were relatively free to pursue their own purposes. Through the
years efforts had been made by General Orders and change in
regulations to enlarge the meaning of "supervise" but an experienced lawyer going through the literature of definition in 1940
reached the conclusion that no one could determine what power,
if any, the Chief of Staff really possessed. By 1940 the military
establishment had grown into a loose federation of agencies —
the General Staff, the Special Staff for services, the Overseas
Departments, the Corps areas, the exempted Stations. Nowhere
in this federation was there a center of energy and directing authority. Things were held together by custom, habit, standard
operating procedure, regulations and a kind of genial conspiracy
among the responsible officers. In the stillness of peace the system worked; but in the turmoil of war the system disintegrated
in 1917 as it did again in 1941. And it was not a system that
could be used to prepare an army effectively for war.[8]

The state of the Union and the state of the military establishment limited Stimson's power to act decisively. So in the summer of 1940 did a third influence — that of the President of the
United States. Franklin Roosevelt always saw to it that the authority he had perforce to delegate became in the distribution so
fragmented, so offset by counterweights that no single view, no
single man could achieve undue significance or influence. Over
years of maneuver he had devised many ways to achieve his pur-

[8] The unhappy history of War Department organization in the first four decades of the century can be found in great if somewhat murky detail in Nelson,
National Security. The weaknesses of the structure on the eve of conflict are
described in Watson, *Chief of Staff*, Chs. 1-3.

pose — the appointment of a Johnson to serve a Woodring, of a Welles to serve a Hull; the moving of the section administering soil conservation from the Department of the Interior to the Department of Agriculture; the creation of a new agency to do what an ancient department was already doing. Perhaps this was not so much a principle with him as an unconscious perception, a conditioned reflex forced on him by the efforts necessary to circumvent the portentous authority with which he had contended in his youth. At any rate the method had great virtues in a time when settled remedies had failed; it supplied the turmoil out of which new solutions arise and left opportunities open for experiment and selection. It also left the ultimate power of decision and direction in the hands of the Chief Executive as Franklin Roosevelt wanted, and as he especially wanted in military matters. He had an abiding faith in the necessity of the civilian control of an armed force and this faith in a principle was further supported by unhappy personal recollection. As an Assistant Secretary of the Navy he had not been favorably looked upon by naval officers who had therefore, disregarding the charm of his personality, taken such steps as naval officers can to limit his influence.

For these reasons, both high and human, the President was prepared to do what he could to retain control over the armed forces in his own hands. This meant that he would survey with special care the activities of the civilian Secretaries and that he would make certain no centers of real power developed within the two Departments that did not derive their strength directly from him. And in 1940 he was not ready to offer support to any such center, for he was in his own mind uncertain of what action to take. Profoundly moved by the events in Europe, disturbed by the cries of those who wished to intervene, bedeviled by the evangels of isolation, troubled in an election year by the undiscernible intentions of the great majority, genuinely puzzled, no doubt, by what a nation committed only to its own defense could or ought to do in such defense, the President, like the country, seemed in that summer to wait uncertainly upon events.[9]

What influence such moods and conditions exerted upon the conduct of the business of the government Stimson discovered as soon as he took office in the second week of July. The War Department was, as his friends told him, in "a situation . . . that is perfectly horrible." By their quarrels, their bickerings, their "daily combats" and their maneuvers, Woodring and Johnson had made it a "notorious," battleground. As one consequence much of the work in connection with the procurement of munitions and equipment which ordinarily was the province of the Secretary of War had fallen, in "a very singular situation," into the hands of the Secretary of the Treasury. The task of procurement was further shared with the National Defense Advisory Commission, an independent agency recently created by the President without a single directing chief. To make matters worse the Congress, though in session, met only intermittently and the President was out of town for much of the month of July.

One morning the feeling swept over Stimson as he was rising at 5:30 that it was broiling hot, that life was bad, that he had been forcing himself to spread all his energies over a whole field he did not yet understand, that everything was falling between contesting interests and authorities and was, therefore, falling behind. "Pretty soon," he concluded, "too late." Feeling thus, he wrote in the first gray light of dawn what he called a letter of distress from a sorely pressed friend to Felix Frankfurter. "If I was not overworked and could sleep and were younger and a few other things I might get through, as it is I don't know. . . ."[10]

[9] Eliot Janeway, The Struggle for Survival (New Haven, 1951), 51 ff. and Watson, Chief of Staff, 5 ff., have interesting things to say on the subject of Roosevelt's administrative methods.
[10] H.L.S. to Felix Frankfurter, July 23, 1940, Frankfurter Papers. Of all the things that distressed Stimson in the first months, the thing that troubled him most, apparently, was that he could not get a good understanding of his job.

Whether he could get through or not was one thing; what he had to try to do was another and far more obvious matter. A few days after he wrote Frankfurter, he set about what he took to be the first order of business. On this business, the President, he wrote, "dallies." He had not been able to think up a new job for Louis Johnson and, since there was no indication that the President cared to think very hard on the subject, it appeared that the Assistant Secretary might remain for a long time in the position already offered to Robert Patterson. Stimson reflected on the troubles caused him in the State Department by an Undersecretary not of his own choosing; he bore in mind the conditions on which he had accepted his new office. In the third week of July he drafted a letter for the President to present to the Senate. It nominated Patterson as Assistant Secretary of War. He sent it over to the White House with the additional information that since the appointment of Patterson would "greatly facilitate and expedite the organization of my office," he "earnestly" hoped that the nomination would be sent to the Senate "on Monday." Louis Johnson left within the week.[11]

Into his place came Robert Patterson, the first of the remarkable talents that were added to the Secretary's staff in the ensuing months. Though he came to the War Department from the Federal bench, he was scarcely of the judicial temper. Around his waist he wore, as a perpetual reminder, the belt of a German soldier he had killed in the First World War. He loved a job to do and he flourished in the feeling of combat. First as Assistant Secretary and then as Undersecretary he gave energetic, single-minded, at times stubborn direction to the material development

---

In his first conversation with Marshall, the General sought to explain his plan of organization. "I am ashamed to say," Stimson said later, "that they were so, I won't say complicated, but I was in such an ignorant state that I didn't grasp the whole thing at all clearly in that evening's conversation. . . . I just remember a rather crowded and tiresome talk which I wasn't yet up to." When the President, in an unlikely role, tried to explain on a very hot day the financial problems of the Department, "Again I fell behind." (Transcript of H.L.S.-McGeorge Bundy conversations, Sept. 9, Oct. 16, 1946.)

11 H.L.S. to Franklin D. Roosevelt, July 19, 1940, Roosevelt Papers.

and support of the Army. Procurement was a field in which many diverse interests could legitimately find a place, in which the merits of conflicting principles and needs could be argued persuasively and interminably. It was a field in which many good men in Washington in these years lost heart or job or reputation. Into this area Patterson came not in the spirit of enlightened compromise, of what was, all things considered, the judicious, the wise, the best possible thing to do, but in the spirit of a man who knew what the Army had to have and what he had to do to get it. A force so unqualified by reasonable doubt, so directly and exclusively mobilized in support of a single purpose can accomplish great things, and the Services of Supply was one of the great accomplishments of the War Department in these years.

A few months after Patterson took office John J. McCloy arrived, at the suggestion of George Roberts, to bear a helping hand at all those points where the lines of the organization chart do not quite meet. He was first a special assistant and then was appointed in April 1941 an Assistant Secretary of War. Within a few weeks the services of this happy man were coveted in all those corners of the government where his vitality, his acute sense for the location of real influence and his consuming delight in the successful operation caused him to turn up on his errands for the Secretary. As time passed, these errands were attended by ever larger significance — the passage of the Lend-Lease Act, the relocation of the Japanese on the West Coast, the administration of military government in conquered areas, the future of Germany after the war.

And after McCloy, in October 1940, came Robert A. Lovett first as special assistant and then as Assistant Secretary of War for Air. What in this man appeared to be, at first assessment, a kind of frailness was in reality a refinement of special gifts. His clear intelligence had been civilized by a variety of experiences and by the great feeling he had for the human situations in which the mind was put to work. Lacking the bottomless source of energy possessed by McCloy, he brought to his office the dedication of one who had flown airplanes at the beginning. Usefully modifying this dedicated spirit was the sense of what was really possible and the sense of what was really ridiculous. He was, in fact, one of the funniest of men, full of brief sophisticated witticisms, rueful humors and a perception of incongruity that expanded in the bureaucratic circumstances where such perceptions ordinarily wither away. He was, in other words, both sure in action and wise in counsel.

To these three Harvey Bundy was added in the spring of 1941. He came to do odd jobs — to search out the matters that had been left almost finished; to talk with all those people who have a point that is just not quite big enough to engage the immediate concern of the Secretary. As time passed he became the moving spirit in the development of scientific information in the Department and in the coordination of matters connected with the atom bomb. For his undefined position he had the requisite capacities: he was a well-trained intelligence, a quiet, discreet man, adroit in negotiation, and he was not puffed up. And in this position he acquired power in the Department — the power, a colleague said, of a French king's mistress, who had no authority but great influence.

There was another civilian on the staff of the Secretary. Miss Elizabeth Neary came down from the firm a few weeks after Stimson arrived in Washington to act as his secretary. What she supplied to the administration of the Department is hard to describe. She sat just outside Stimson's office and waited for his summons. One day the buzzer on her desk rang and it was not a ring that suggested, "Come any time you are not busy, dear," but indicated that she should come at once. Into the office she went to find McCloy, Lovett, General Marshall, General Somervell and four or five other general officers sitting before the Secretary in dead silence. The Secretary, as she entered, held up his hands and framed a space in the air that was about the size of a page of typewriter paper. "Where," he shouted at her, "is that paper that is like this?" Miss Neary asked what it was about. "I don't know what it's about," the Secretary bellowed at her, "it's about this size and I want it. Where is it?" For a time there was a good deal of noise in the room until Miss Neary said, "I think it may be here." Walking over to the Secretary's desk she opened the top drawer and pulled out a typewritten sheet which she then gave to Stimson. He shouted, "of course, that's it. Why wasn't it here to begin with?" There was a further moment of strained silence around the circle until Lovett laughed, and Stimson turned on him to ask the reason for his laughter. "Well, sir," the Assistant Secretary for Air replied, "after all, she has just done a rather remarkable thing. You held up your hands and she said 'It's right here.'" Then everybody laughed and the Secretary said, "Of course she can do it. She's psychic." Miss Neary did remarkable things of this kind for four years in the service of the Secretary of War.

And so did the other members of his staff. These men had grown to man's estate in their own right; they did not recoil in dismay like law clerks before the portentous presence or the irritable outburst. They knew exactly what to do. Once when McCloy was at the White House with James V. Forrestal he was called to the telephone by the Secretary. "Where," Stimson asked him, "are my goddam papers?" "I haven't got your goddam papers," McCloy replied and hung up. And Forrestal, overhearing, remarked with rueful wonder that things were not the same in the Navy Department. They were not the same in very many other departments.

Stimson never mastered the great instrument of government administration — the intercommunication system or squawker. He would hit the key for the man he wished to speak to and then lean back and talk so that his voice came to his listener with the sound of boiling water. Subordinates formed the habit of saying, "Yes sir," and of running forthwith to the Secretary's office. One day Stimson by mistake hit both McCloy's and Lovett's keys at the same time and both appeared simultaneously at the Secretary's door. This so disconcerted him that he ordered them both out of his sight. Both withdrew, one to drop into General Marshall's office next door and the other to have a word with Miss Neary outside Stimson's door. In a moment Stimson went in to see Marshall. On his way he collided with Lovett at Miss Neary's desk and asked what he was doing there when he'd been told to go; proceeding in to the General he met McCloy and asked what he was doing there when he'd already been kicked out. Unruffled, the two withdrew, reflecting as they did so that it was a rare Secretary who could throw two Assistant Secretaries out of two different offices two minutes after they had been sent for.

And there was one morning when Lovett, unsent for, entered the Secretary's office when the latter was at work on a paper. He received the same blast that had flattened so many innocent law clerks who had intruded upon a Stimson caught in the toils of a refractory brief. After gently closing the door upon the rising gale, he saw McCloy coming along the corridor on his way to work. "Good morning, Jack," he said cheerfully. "The Secretary wants to see you right away."

It was not only possible for these men to say and do all these things, it was also necessary. This is the way the Secretary got through. Too often in the past young men had been bowled over by the inexplicable moment of indignation; too often older men had been put off by that positive, at times, it seemed, that overweening presence. Here he was, in his seventies, an old and lonely person, still saying life was hard, still preparing to go grimly on his way. And then these men around him in the Department airily brushed aside the symptoms and broke through the stiff plating almost into intimacy. They made him feel useful and wanted and understood. So when they sat, at tea, on the sofa at Woodley, earnestly and patiently explaining to a disbelieving Mrs. Stimson all the things that made her husband impossible to work with, he sat there laughing until the tears came into his eyes.

The fact is he was understood and he was wanted and he was useful. No man in those times gathered abler men about him or created better conditions for men to demonstrate their ability. The members of that staff were of the first class and therefore they did first-class work. They shared with the Secretary and no doubt derived in measurable part from him the burning desire to get on with the national defense with speed, efficiency and probity. Simply because they were all there working together other men of the first class were selected and drawn in — to write procurement contracts, to develop policies for the administration of captured territories, to prepare budgets, to develop logistic plans, to bear a hand with all those other things necessary to prepare an army and sustain it in the field. The work in any institution is done by innumerable men up and down the line; the tone and manner and sense of purpose are set by the man at the top.

In the War Department there are in fact if not in theory two men at the top. There is the Secretary and there is the Chief of Staff, who in 1940 was George Catlett Marshall. Those who served with him ordinarily speak of this man in superlatives — the wisest, the finest, the best, the greatest. For his peculiar position he had certain great and unusual assets. He possessed a thorough knowledge, historical and contemporary, of the Army as a military instrument, an institution and a society. He recognized the nature of the civilian influences — as exerted both by the executive and the Congress — that were of necessity brought to bear on military policy and decision. Years of experience had not perverted either his understanding or respect for these necessary influences. He had known of a Secretary of War who could only get to President Harding in a poker game arranged by Charles Dawes; he had looked on while President Coolidge treated his Chief of Staff "like a schoolboy"; he had watched while President Roosevelt "was dealing with the Navy as sort of his command." He had been caught in the cross fire between Secretary Woodring and Assistant Secretary Louis

Johnson. He knew that among the Derns and the Goods "very few are going to come in like Mr. Root and go to the nub of the whole thing." He also knew that a Quartermaster General or a Chief of Engineers, because they dealt with the legislative appropriations, could become more powerful than a Chief of Staff. He had sat with Pershing when he could not get rid of a disloyal, inefficient Quartermaster General and an incompetent Chief of Engineers because "they were dealing with Congress in relation to money." He had discovered that it was possible to reach a point where a Chief of Staff was so second fiddle that he could hardly do business on an effective basis. No doubt such occasions had touched the soldier's pride and strained the soldier's faith; still he could say that all this was in the nature of men and things. When he became the Chief of Staff he could deal with bureau chiefs, congressmen, corps commanders, the President, with knowledge and understanding but without rancor, subservience, slyness or disillusion. In return they trusted him. Other qualities for his position he also had. He was clear, he was firm, he was fair, he was, within familiar contexts, a good judge of men, he could acquire and digest information and he could make up his mind.[12]

Still one can be an excellent military administrator and not be wisest, best, greatest. There was apparently something else — what some called his character and others his moral stature. The General, as Vannevar Bush said, had his ambition under perfect control, but it also appears he had brought all other desires under such control. After two weeks of sitting for a por-

[12] Transcript of a conversation between H.L.S. and George C. Marshall, April 18, 1944. The occasion was a discussion of the place of the Secretary in the single Department of Defense that was then being considered. Marshall wanted an arrangement whereby the Chief of Staff could go directly to the President to state "in writing" the requirements for the security of the nation. Secretaries of the armed forces, lacking information, swayed by political considerations, tended historically to fail in stating these requirements clearly. It had to be done in such a way that the President would be made really aware of the situation in the armed forces. "In time of war he takes it and in time of peace he leaves it, but he cannot get away from it."

trait commissioned by some of his admirers, he said a gravely courteous goodbye to the painter and walked away without looking at the picture. Yet he was not dull or incurious or merely accommodating; he was a man of passion who could be greatly roused — but not to pointless rage. There are few, if any, human achievements as impressive as a passionate energy so regulated by the purpose of the will that it can be placed, almost naturally, in the ordered service of commitments superior to self.

The task to which General Marshall had committed himself in the years from 1939 to 1945 was the development of an effective army, first in peace and then in war. In this task he shared responsibility with others. The administration of a modern army includes everything from the selection of a disembarking port for an invading force to the renegotiation of a contract for shoes. At one extreme the interest is primarily, if not exclusively, military; at the other the interest is primarily, if not exclusively, civil. And in between are innumerable problems — like the training and use of colored troops, like the administrative policies of an occupying army — where the division of interest is not obvious, where military and civil energies meet and interact with a subtle relationship.

Laws have been passed to define, in general terms, the nature of this relationship and many devices — the morning conference, the coordinating committee, the joint board — have been created to give it administrative expression. But if the Chief of Staff and the Secretary of War do not share a common interest, it is difficult if not impossible to sustain the relationship in a way that gives meaning to the law or single-minded direction to the Army. The history of the War Department in the time of Dickinson and Baker and Weeks and Woodring proves as much. Both General Marshall and Secretary Stimson were determined to work together. The General felt "very keenly and continuously the need for civilian advice on all kinds of problems confronting the military." On his part the Secretary, in principle and by virtue of his experience, believed that the purpose of his office was to give direction to military action and balance to military judgment through the exertion of civilian influences. To achieve their purposes they both knew it was first necessary to share the same information. Each from the beginning was at great pains to pass whatever he knew through what was called "the door that was always open" between their adjoining offices. When Ordnance was in trouble, or when new plans were being discussed in the Joint Chiefs of Staff, Marshall brought the news to the Secretary. When Stimson learned from his own scientific advisers the meaning of radar in the Battle of Britain, or arrived at some understanding with Secretary Hull, he took the information in to Marshall. Through that open door, it was said, "they were always walking back and forth to each other." Out of this constant exchange of information between the General and the Secretary they and their staffs, as one staff member said, were informed "by a large and continuous understanding of the war." Normal expectations suggest that this is how it should be, but this was not, in every armed force, how it really was. James Forrestal, for instance, obtained in part his understanding of the many things Admiral King never told him by inviting John McCloy frequently for lunch.

The fact that Marshall and Stimson shared the same information did not mean that they always reached identical interpretations of the data supplied, nor that they were always in complete agreement about whether the military or civilian judgment should dominate in a given situation. The General, for example, was at first as reluctant as most soldiers to accept the idea that scientific development might produce significant changes in weapons systems. The Secretary was more ready than most Secretaries to believe he could unerringly select the best rifle design or the coastal town that gave easiest access to the interior for an invading army. There were thus times when the Secretary would deliver carefully prepared lectures, speaking, with pointed forefinger, as from some slightly raised eminence of greater age and of a previous experience that had been attended by impressive consequences. And the General, for his part, would express his measured regret that the Secretary, with all those other things he had to do, required of himself the further burden of attention to purely military considerations. But in the end they always, or almost always, worked themselves out to a common ground.

The official relationship they established as a matter of principle was buttressed by other, more personal considerations as time passed. They had something of the same intense feeling for the United States Army; they shared a common understanding of what the word "duty" meant. Most of all, perhaps, they looked to the same sanctions for what was honorable and decent in human action. In their arguments they were drawn together, as one man who served them both once said, by the moral sense they held in common.

Whatever the cause or causes, they worked together and thus brought the contending influences — civil and military — that worked within the War Department into a consonance. What this meant cannot be measured out precisely. Like the effect of the men Stimson appointed to his staff, like all those other impalpable elements in successful administration, the exact meaning is incalculable. Yet it may be said that throughout an organization that had been almost paralyzed by conflict, these two men introduced a sense of single purpose, a sense that remained alive and at work through eighteen confusing months of preparation and four years of actual war.

27

"The Old War Department Machine . . ."

THE SECRETARY introduced men of great ability into the War Department in the first nine months of his tenure, and he established an atmosphere in which able men could work with confidence together. It does not follow that in the eighteen months from July 1940 to December 1941 great things, or even all things necessary, were accomplished. Neither the time nor the place permitted such results. There were divided counsels over what was necessary and, in matters where necessities could be agreed upon, there was doubt about what was legally, or politically, or physically possible. And whatever was done was done in the spirit of waiting — of waiting, depending upon the point of view, for the thing that would certainly happen, or that might happen, or that could never really happen here. That in such conditions there could be action, simple and direct, by any one man or agency was improbable; that the effects of such action as could be taken would be reduced, qualified, offset, undercut or misunderstood by other men in other agencies was all but certain.

Consider the circumstances in which men worked. The heavy bombers in the late summer of 1940 are a case in point. At the time of the conversations in July and August leading up to the trade of the old destroyers for British bases it had been agreed that to the ships would be added five bombers. But the conversations had been conducted in various places by various officials. When the final agreement was drawn in the State Department the five planes, by an awkward oversight, had been omitted. No one then cared to reveal this omission by a public correction. But the British, fighting on alone, still wanted the planes. The President said he would see what he could do and asked the Army what arrangements could be made. It was then that he was told that within the continental limits of the United States there were forty-nine heavy bombers. When he heard this his "head went back as if someone had hit him in the chest. . . ." In time it was worked out that the British would get the promised bombers in return for British motors that would be put into American planes that were grounded for lack of engines.[1]

But the administration was left with the questions posed, in the year of the Battle of Britain, by forty-nine heavy bombers. How could the companies be persuaded to build more? How could one "try to stir the country — the business people of the country — who are still asleep"? Were the companies to be told to stop building the commercial planes that were the primary source of their income? And if, by concentrating exclusively upon military planes, the companies were to derive all their profits from this kind of work, what was the place of profit in building the national defense and what was an excess profit? And if building more planes meant building more plants, what was a reasonable and attractive rate of amortization for these plants? And if the workers in these private plants building planes on government contract struck the plants, what did one do with the strikers? All these questions and more came up in connection with airplanes in 1940. In the search for answers to these questions the President, the Army, the Congress, the Advisory Commission on Defense, the Treasury, the aircraft industry, and the unions all took a hand. Each brought to the nego-

---

[1] Diary, Sept. 10, 12, 14, 17, 21, 27, 1940; H.L.S. to Cordell Hull, Sept. 14, 1940; Watson, *Chief of Staff*, 126-27, 306. Also omitted by error from the final agreement on the destroyer deal were a quarter of a million Enfield rifles. The rifles were ultimately sent on to the British.

tiations a separate and different point of view, a separate and varying weight of influence.

Then there was the natural working of the democratic process as it revealed itself in these times. A senator "with his hair standing on end" could command the time of a Secretary because two general officers from his state had been put on the retired list. A senator could prevent a lawyer from drawing up contracts for army suppliers because the lawyer was "personally obnoxious" to the senator. Shell casings in the amount of $70 million remained for a time unpurchased because a "headless" committee without legal authority could not make up its mind. There was a delay which "amounted to a scandal" in the building of certain camp facilities because of "one of those typical squabbles" over what agency had the right to spend the money. Then there were those who tried to settle things by going in the back door of the White House with a funny story and a purely personal opinion. And there were those who went in the front door with a carefully prepared statement that was said to represent the best thinking of the Department. And there were those who tried to get the ear of Bill Bullitt or Felix or "the inevitable Harry Hopkins, without whose wise counsel we cannot resolve anything, either in relation to peace or war." And even if by one of these means or another, or by all in combination, things were resolved, then was it necessary to say so? Was it necessary or wise to explain the full meaning of the American troops that landed in Iceland in July 1941, or to announce that elements of the fleet in the Pacific had been shifted to the Atlantic in the spring of the same year? [2]

From these prevailing atmospheres it is difficult to isolate and classify the traces of individual influence. What any man did became, through conference or compromise, subtly melted

[2] Diary, Oct. 16, Dec. 3, 11, 1940; Ickes, *Diary*, III, 629. The Stimson Diary entries from August to December 1940 are an invaluable source of information about the problems of industrial mobilization and the deficiencies of government organization in this period.

down into the alloys of what finally was decided or what actually occurred. But what Stimson tried to do and how he tried to do it is easier to determine. He came to his task with three purposes in mind. He wished to introduce order and system into the administrative environment. He wished to prepare the country in body and spirit to deal with certain danger and possible war. He wished to have those in final authority make it clear that in the conflict already begun by others the country had made a choice of sides and stood ready to support the choice with action. That action, up to a point not yet fully determined, could take the form of all aid short of war. As time went by he wished increasingly to have the point determined and to make clear that if the point were passed, action would take the form of war itself.

Order and system were in the first months the first concern. There was, to begin with, his own domain, the War Department that, as Stilwell reported, was "just like the alimentary canal. You feed it at one end, and nothing comes out at the other but crap." Stimson put it another way. He said that much of his time was spent "in tightening up the strings and trying to get the old War Department machine hummed up and ready to go on with less squeaking." The tightening began at the top. In the General Staff there was so much deadwood that, in Lovett's opinion, the place was a positive fire hazard. This wood was slowly cut away by Stimson and Marshall and replaced by stouter timber. Moreover, the General Staff which had gradually been drawn into administrative activity, had to a measurable extent lost sight of its original purpose to think and to plan. The Secretary therefore took an active part in the development of a new section to supply reasonable and clearly planned objectives toward which the collective military energies could work. He also acted against considerable service opposition to give the air arm increasing independence in directing its own fortunes.[3]

[3] Joseph W. Stilwell, *The Stilwell Papers* (New York, 1948), 44; Diary, May 23, 1941; conversation with R. A. Lovett, Sept. 15, 1955.

Beneath the General Staff lay a large and complicated hierarchy of bureaus, divisions and sections. These agencies supplied the goods and services that supported the Army. They did these things within the classic bureaucratic sanctions — duplication, overlap, joint cognizance. The size and shapelessness of this hierarchy was a source, as Stimson's friends believed, of continuing frustration to him. He could never lay his hands firmly on all the slowly moving parts; he could never have the feeling, as he did in 1911, that he knew all that was going on, that he was "running the whole show." But he did what he could to snap "the whip over the Department and [to get] the various agencies and bureaus working as fast as I could." His method was to see as many officials in the course of a day as there was time for and to ask as many questions as he could think of. Since he had known the Army a long time and since he was supplied with excellent advice from his staff, he could think of a good many questions.

By these means he discovered interesting things. Once he asked how many tanks the Army had and received two entirely different replies from the same agency. He put a man on the job to find out the correct answer and to see that this would not happen again. He also learned that the officer in the Quartermaster Corps who had charge of construction had handled all the negotiations for the new program "without a taint of scandal," but also without the energy to get enough buildings built. Therefore, after a conversation between Stimson and Marshall, the officer was replaced by Lieutenant Colonel Brehon B. Somervell in December 1940. In the spring of the next year he found that the Signal Corps was lingering in continued uncertainty over a design for a radar instrument. He talked with Alfred Loomis and Vannevar Bush and Karl Compton, satisfied himself that the device was a good one, and ordered it — the first Army radar — into immediate production. By such "dippings down," as he called it, multiplied a hundred times, he kept in contact with his organization and made his touch felt throughout the hierarchy. It was not always a light touch; by the manner as well as the matter of his downward dips he left an impress. Coming from one of the interrogations in the Secretary's office, a colonel remarked, "I never heard the Lord God speak before." [4]

There was much in the way of tighten-and-tinker a man could do in an antique mechanism that no one cared to reconstruct in a time of rising trouble. But there was also, in such a time, much else to do. The Secretary wished to make the influence of the Army felt in an orderly and systematic way in the determination of national military policy. He held the view that he was the principal responsible military adviser of the President, that recommendations on policies of "strategic national defense" should come up through the Chief of Staff to him, and after discussion between him and the Chief of Staff, should be taken by the Secretary to the President. No recommendation should go to the President, he told Marshall, until it had "passed through and received the critical attention" of the Secretary of War. On this position there was a difference of opinion, and Stimson recognized it as "a delicate matter." The President, he admitted, "should have the constant right to consult directly" with the Chief of Staff, but still he felt that in the hierarchy the Secretary stood between the Chief of Staff and the President.

The matter was indeed delicate; it posed, in theory, one of the most perplexing problems in the administration of an armed force in this government. Stimson and Marshall argued it out by the hour. The Secretary would maintain that sound administrative practice dictated that the official responsible for the Army should have the right to represent the Army to the President. Marshall would maintain that a Chief of Staff also had the right to communicate directly to the Commander-in-Chief. Besides, he knew from history that Secretaries of War were not always, in fact not often, capable of representing the Army very clearly or accurately before the President. "But you, sir,"

[4] Diary, Dec. 11, 1940, June 11, 19, 20, 1941; conversations with V. Bush, Jan. 28, 1956, and Frederick Osborn, March 17, 1955.

he would say to Stimson, "are dealing with yourself." The General had to think of all those other Secretaries, those gone before and those to come.[5]

For his part the President agreed with Marshall. The view of the Chief of Staff was in accord not only with the Presidential inclination to talk with anybody in a department or out of it who interested or entertained him, but it was also in accord with Mr. Roosevelt's profound conviction that the President, as Commander-in-Chief, of necessity possessed the right to confer at all times and on any subject without regard to the rights and duties of the Secretary of War — and sometimes even, without regard to the sensibilities of that official. In August of 1941, for instance, he took General Marshall and Admiral H. R. Stark off to talk with Churchill at Argentia, leaving both Stimson and Knox, amid a rising tide of rumors in Washington, in total ignorance of the event.[6]

Though much can be said on both sides, it must seem that in theory the view of Roosevelt and Marshall on the matter is correct and that it is, in practice, the inevitable result. In time of crisis the Chief of Staff of the Army with his expert knowledge and the President with his exclusive authority for final decision tend naturally to work directly together on all military matters. But in this instance Stimson, if he did not obtain the order and system he desired, still exerted more influence on military matters than most other Secretaries and certainly more

[5] Diary, Nov. 25, 1940; transcript of H.L.S.-George C. Marshall conversation, April 18, 1944. The problem is not as simple as these two paragraphs make it seem. Neither Stimson nor Marshall for one moment wished to limit the access of the other to the President; the difference between them was, more precisely, over the kind of question each could raise in the Presidential conversation. The issue at bottom was over what was meant by policies "of strategic national defense." Stimson was certainly inclined to believe he should have a greater hand in these policies in the strictly military way than most Secretaries. On the other hand, he was also more useful in this complicated relationship than most Secretaries. Marshall told Stilwell that the President was "hard to handle," that Stimson as a "buffer" between Roosevelt and Marshall "stands up courageously on the big questions."

[6] Diary, Aug. 6, 7, 11, 13, 1941. Stimson apparently first learned positively of the Argentia meeting from Halifax, the British Ambassador.

than either Knox or Forrestal in the Navy Department. This was because he had the complete trust of both Marshall and Roosevelt, who saw him constantly — and because the General told him everything. Returning from Argentia, for instance, Marshall went directly to Woodley and told Stimson all that had happened.[7]

In another area Stimson had more success. He felt that any recommendation having to do with "the formulation of a general policy" should be based on conferences between the Secretary of the Navy, the Secretary of War and the Secretary of State. Soon after he arrived in Washington he invited Frank Knox and Cordell Hull to meet with him on matters of joint interest. By the end of 1940 these conversations, continued throughout the war, were formally organized into stated meetings. These meetings did not always prevent odd things from happening. Once the Navy asked the Army to have 6000 troops ready on seventy-two-hour notice to go to Martinique, and nobody could ever discover why the request was sent or who in the Navy Department had sent it. Another time the State Department by telephone asked the War Department to hold up a troopship sailing to the Philippines and then a few hours later canceled the order, again by telephone. Cordell Hull never found out why either order was given. These things happened. But the conferences between Stimson, Hull and Knox reduced their number and, more important, permitted the three men to present recommendations of policy, commonly agreed upon, to the President. Whether the President acted on these recommendations remained, throughout the war, quite another matter.[8]

It was a matter that disturbed Stimson considerably. In his experience Presidents took the advice of cabinet members seriously; he was not prepared for and did not like what he called "the present happy-go-lucky snap-of-the-moment" administrative method of Franklin D. Roosevelt. As he looked

[7] Diary, Aug. 14, 1941.
[8] Diary, Oct. 14, 18, 30, Nov. 1, 1940.

around him in 1940 and 1941 he could see a great many different agencies — the National Resources Planning Board, the
National Munitions Control Board, the Interdepartmental Committee for Coordination of Foreign and Domestic Military Pur-
chases, the Advisory Commission to the Council of National
Defense — which seemed to be doing not only each other's
work but also a great deal of the work of the traditional departments of War, State and the Navy. He also found, upon his
arrival in Washington, a "very singular situation." Many of
the decisions affecting the defensive strength of the nation were
in the hands of Henry Morgenthau. In part this was because
Morgenthau was Secretary of the Treasury, in part it was because he was an old, close friend of the President and in part it
was because he possessed a greater sense of urgency than did
his other colleagues in the Cabinet. In any event he had been
conducting most of the negotiations with the British Purchasing Commission. Since what was sent to the British determined
what was left over for the growing American army, Stimson
believed the British negotiations should be placed in the control
of the War Department.[9]

Things like this made Stimson determined to work for
greater order and system in what he called over and over again
the "haphazard" direction of the nation's total war effort. He
persuaded the President first to place the British negotiations in
his hands. From September 1940 on he worked with his old
friends Sir Walter Layton and Sir Arthur Salter on the arrangements which ultimately led to the plan to equip ten British divisions with American material. And this in turn led to a survey
of the prospective material needs of the Army, Navy and the
British together with "a chart of possible emergencies" so that
"we will not make the decisions, these vital decisions, as to what
we give or do not give to the British too haphazard and under
the emotion of a single moment."[10]

[9] Diary, Sept. 10, Nov. 25, 1940; Hull, *Memoirs*, I, 902; Watson, *Chief of Staff*,
300.
[10] Diary, Sept. 10, 24, 1940.

Having achieved this much, he raised with the President the inadequacies of the Advisory Commission to the Council of National Defense. This commission had an ill-defined cognizance over industrial mobilization. Yet it had no legal existence and no presiding officer so it lacked a sense of direction and real power of decision. The Secretary in the fall of 1940 "rolled up [his] shirt sleeves and went for them," but his arguments at first failed to impress the President. Roosevelt preferred to leave William S. Knudsen, Edward Stettinius, Sidney Hillman and Leon Henderson to work it out among themselves. By December, however, the Secretary was absolutely convinced that the "defective" commission was the principal reason why "industry was not working at the rate it should work. . . ." He decided to go to the President on the matter again, but before doing so he organized his views and sought support from Knox, Forrestal, Jesse Jones and William Green. Thus buttressed he went with Patterson, Knox, and Forrestal to lay their recommendations before Roosevelt on December 18, 1940. It took some time: "Conferences with the President are difficult matters. His mind does not follow easily a consecutive chain of thought but he is full of stories and incidents and hops about in his discussions from suggestion to suggestion and it is very much like chasing a vagrant beam of sunshine around a vacant room." [11]

Two days of argument produced a new commission composed of Stimson, Knox, Knudsen and Hillman. There was some talk on the first day of making Knudsen the director but on the second day the President decided that Hillman and Knudsen should act as associate directors. This seemed to "jar" Knudsen, but Stimson was at the moment satisfied. For one

[11] Diary, Oct. 16, Dec. 14, 18, 1940. There were seven members of the Advisory Commission, but the four mentioned dominated the commission deliberations. Roosevelt, however, dominated the commission. When Knudsen asked, "Who will be the boss around here?" the President replied, "I will be the boss." Matthew Josephson, *Sidney Hillman: Statesman of American Labor* (New York, 1952), has in Chapter 21 an extended account of the tribulations of the commission.

thing the solution, by precluding a separate labor board, honored the necessary "principle of concentration." He also liked and trusted Hillman and expected that the labor interests would cooperate as they had abroad. On the issue between appeasement and carrying on the war he looked, he said, "for the upper classes to be rather on the side" of the former and "the common people [to be] pretty strong on the moral issue." Finally, in the interests of concentration he believed, as he said, that the chief figure of the two associated chairmen would be Knudsen because he represented "management which has the initiative of production." [12]

This new commission with enlarged powers became in January 1941 the Office of Production Management. It worked about as well as any committee under dual authority could. When in the summer of 1941 many of its powers were claimed by the newly created Office of Price Administration and Civilian Supply, Samuel Rosenman thought of trying to solve the continuing problem by creating a new board composed of the four members of OPM and of Henderson to represent the consumer, Hopkins to represent the claims of Lend-Lease and Wallace to represent a "new economic warfare board." At that time Stimson took a position from which he never again receded: the only "proper solution" for industrial mobilization was to "concentrate authority in one man." [13]

This proposition the President continued to resist. In part this was because of Roosevelt's predilection for what Stimson moodily called "government on the jump." He wanted personally to be free of the weight of old or settled authorities. "God, Jim," Hull once cried out to James Farley. "You don't know what troubles are. Roosevelt is going directly to Welles and Berle. . . . He doesn't consult with me or confide in me and I have to feel my way in the dark." Stimson was equally

12 Diary, Dec. 20, 1940; "Memorandum of conference of December 21, 1940 — First preliminary meeting of Messrs. Knox, Knudsen, Hillman and Stimson," in Diary.
13 Diary, Oct. 16, 1940, July 1, Aug. 15, 1941.

unhappy about things "which ought to come up from the bottom rather than down from the top." Two thirds of his troubles, he concluded in November 1941, had come from "the topsy-turvy, upside-down system of poor administration [by] which Mr. Roosevelt runs the Government." [14]

But there was quite probably another and higher cause for this administrative topsy-turvydom. The President did not want to turn the War Department or any other single agency into a "gigantic Bourse where all political and business interests would meet a hundred times a day. . . ." Such an instrumentality, in which money, power and political interest were all concentrated, might give greater efficiency to the direction of the defense effort but it might also in time come to dominate the economy and perhaps even the government of the United States. Once, for instance, in defending the influence of a civilian agency that Stimson had blamed for retarding the work of defense, the President had replied that he was determined that there should be "no boom of rising prices" as a result of the industrial mobilization and "no depression of prices after the war — if there is a war. . . ." Such things Stimson admitted he had "not so clearly in mind as [Roosevelt] had." [15]

[14] Diary, Nov. 7, 1940, Nov. 12, 1941; Farley, *Jim Farley's Story*, 233. The Diary is at every point in these years overloaded with entries condemning the Roosevelt topsy-turvy system of administration. But it should be noticed that on December 1, 1941, Stimson, "Looking at it . . . in as detached a way as I can," concluded that "the only fault I have to find with the President is that he is so irregular in his habits of consultations." By this he meant the way in which the President would talk with his advisers and then "suddenly he stops and makes his decisive decision without calling us into conference again."

[15] Janeway, *Struggle for Survival*, 43; Diary, Dec. 18, 1940. The Diary from August 1940 to December 1941 contains countless entries about the problems of industrial mobilization before Pearl Harbor. They suggest, among many other things, the continued interest of Bernard Baruch in the possibility of cleaning up the administration of the arsenal of democracy, and the President's continued reluctance to give Baruch too large a hand in the cleaning-up process. Stimson's own account of the developing industrial mobilization is given in *Active Service*, 351-55, 380-81. Robert Sherwood, *Roosevelt and Hopkins* (New York, 1948), Chs. 7, 13, gives a brief, clear description of the "defensive agencies" created in 1940 and 1941 to organize industrial production. Josephson, *Sidney Hillman*, Chs. 21-22, emphasizes, naturally, the problems of organized labor in

He had in mind order and system and he had also in mind the second purpose with which he had come to Washington, the preparation of the country in body and spirit to deal with the war — if there were a war. To this end, in the years 1940 and 1941, he threw all the force of his personality and all the weight of his extended argument behind the major endeavors of the time: the transfer of the old destroyers, the passage and the extension of the selective service law, the passage and effective administration of the Lend-Lease legislation. Wherever he found the administration or the Congress or the people hesitating over some action that in his mind would expedite the preparation of the Army to fight, he appeared intransigently in the interests of expedition.

He opposed the efforts of Thurman Arnold to raise the threat of antitrust proceedings against industries engaged in the manufacture of military material. Not once but several times he tried to stop production of commercial planes in 1940 and 1941. Not once but again and again he tried to persuade Knudsen to discontinue the annual model changes in the automobile industry. He argued that changes in the laws designed to encourage industry to expand plant facilities should not wait a single moment upon the creation of nice adjustments between amortization schedules and excess profits taxes. When Army officers, chastened by years before Congress, limited their requests for arms to the amounts required to equip each soldier in training, he pushed

---

the period before Pearl Harbor. Though his admiration for his subject, often stated in rather lyric prose, is virtually unqualified, Josephson creates in these chapters a useful impression of the kind of labor difficulties encountered during the period, and a fair enough description of Stimson's attitude toward these difficulties. A description that strains to brighten up the dull surfaces of the whole subject of prewar industrial mobilization is Janeway, *Struggle for Survival*, Chs. 1-10. Concealed within the gossipy accents is a certain amount of information and some real insight into the problems. Donald M. Nelson, *Arsenal of Democracy* (New York, 1946) is a very serviceable report, containing among other things the fullest account of the unusual contribution of the statistician Stacy May to the defense effort. Watson, *Chief of Staff*, Chs. 5, 6, 10, 11, gives a solid description of the ways in which the rearming of the Army was organized.

them into enlarged requests by pointing out the necessity to take replacement needs into account.[16]

Concerning labor there was the same singleness of purpose revealed. It was true he considered working men "pretty strong on the moral issue." It was true that he believed that industrial peace, collective bargaining and responsible trade unions were indispensable instruments of national well-being. Indeed he went to New Orleans to give what the surprised *New Republic* called "a brilliant affirmation of one important part of the New Deal philosophy." But he argued day in and day out that labor should not in the existing emergency be permitted, at all times, to operate within the relaxed confines of that philosophy.

When Roosevelt and Hillman sought to delay the shift from the forty- to the forty-eight-hour week in government arsenals in 1940, he pushed them into an immediate change. When in May 1941 he received reports that Communist elements were reducing production in industries manufacturing for the national defense, he said that if he were still a district attorney he would "proceed under the statute which gives us the right to prosecute conspiracies to defraud the United States." When a strike broke out in the North American Aviation Corporation in the spring of 1941, he took the lead in recommending that the government "take over the plant under the general powers of the President as Commander-in-Chief." At the same time he directed General Hershey to inform draft boards that "strikers would lose their deferred status." This was "one of the best weapons that we have left . . . and I decided that it was a good plan to slap it in at once . . ." Near the end of 1941 John L. Lewis threatened to

[16] Diary, Aug. 2, 5, 9, 19, 23, 26, Sept. 17, 19, Oct. 4, 17, Nov. 26, 29, 1940. Stimson's continued contribution to the developing defenses of the country is well described throughout the pages of W. L. Langer and S. E. Gleason, *The Undeclared War 1940-1941* (New York, 1953). They remark (page 265) that in his testimony before the committee considering the Lend-Lease legislation he was, unquestionably, "the most effective member of the Administration 'team.' . . ."

strike the entire coal industry on the question of the closed shop. The President's view was, essentially, that if strikes did occur the Army should be used in policing actions at the individual mines. Stimson's attitude was that the Army, at the first outbreak of trouble, should be used "as a whole over the whole situation." To use the military as a kind of local constabulary to police "sporadic outbreaks" was "all wrong"; the thing to do was to move in on the entire industry with an "overwhelming display of strength." Argument over this issue produced "the hottest debate at Cabinet that we have ever had" in which the Secretary "talked out to the President more than I ever have." To some it seemed he talked out far too much. Arguing "almost with tears in his eyes," he persisted until Roosevelt was obviously impatient. When the meeting was over Stimson came away "rather discouraged." An exchange of telephone calls moderated the tension between President and Secretary, but it was John L. Lewis who resolved the debate. When he retreated from his position the general strike in the industry never took place.[17]

In his desire to prepare the body and spirit of the country in a time of danger Stimson was obviously less sensitive than many of his colleagues to the possible side effects of the mobilization of national energy. He was not much concerned by the thought that some of the New Deal social gains would have to be set aside for a season. He was not much disturbed by the idea that

[17] *New Republic*, Dec. 9, 1940, 775; Diary, Aug. 2, 6, 1940, May 27, June 6, 8, 9, Nov. 14, 23, 1941; Josephson, *Sidney Hillman*, 544-45, 562-64; Ickes, *Diary*, III, 642-43. Stimson, at the time, considered his actions in the North American case "one of the most important days of my service here." He was moved to take action by the continuing report that "a rather sinister group of Communists were getting control of the situation." Josephson takes the view that the coal strike was avoided when Roosevelt "capitulated to John L. Lewis completely" by appointing a committee of Lewis, Myron Taylor and John Steelman to settle the affair peacefully on terms favorable to Lewis. Stimson, on the other hand, believed as the episode ended that the President "gradually fenced Lewis into a corner from which he can't get out." The attitude of the Secretary of War on the use of government troops "surprised and discouraged" Ickes, who was also discouraged that Stimson was so slow "in grasping what the President had in mind."

the War Department might become a great Bourse. He was not much afraid that, in the existing emergency, an overwhelming display of strength by the Army against a resistant industry would subvert the democratic process that had long endured. He did fear that the country might be left powerless to defend its own life and its democratic birthright in a world that was tearing itself to pieces. Therefore he was single-minded in the task of preparing the body and spirit of the country to cope with the conditions of the world.

28

The War Begins

BEYOND THE wish to introduce order and system, beyond the desire to prepare the country, was the third intention with which he came to his task: to have those in final authority make it clear that in the conflict already begun this country had chosen sides and stood ready to support the choice with action. In July 1940, when he took office, the conflict was, for all practical purposes, between Germany and England; and by September, after the Battle of Britain, the American choice appeared beyond all reasonable doubt to be Great Britain. There remained only the problem of supporting action. What form that action ought to take was made clear in the fall of 1940 by the events occurring along the sea lanes of the North Atlantic. On these lanes merchant ships were sinking at a rate which by the Navy's estimate would starve out Great Britain within six months. The United States, in the Secretary's opinion, would not permit England to fall in this way. "The only thing that can be done," he said in his Diary on December 3, 1940, "and the thing that we eventually shall do, will be to convoy . . . from Canada . . . with our own destroyers."

"Eventually," as things were moving in those months, was a long way off. In the meantime Stimson threw his support behind all the half measures taken in 1941 to increase the power of the United States to protect the sea lanes between North America and Great Britain: the introduction of the patrol system in April, the shifting of fleet elements from the Pacific to the Atlantic in May, the peaceful occupation of Iceland in July, the orders to shoot at sight in patrol zones in September, the arming of merchantmen in November.

Though he supported all these actions and legislations he was not satisfied with them in either their substance or their spirit. They were half measures, insufficient to the needs of the occasion. Again and again, therefore, he spoke out in favor of stronger actions and fuller explanations. Before he spoke he had counted the cost. "This emergency," he said in his Diary on December 16, 1940, "could hardly be passed over without this country being drawn into the war eventually. . . ." To be drawn into such an enterprise by the suction of several qualified commitments, shaped by calculation, never fully explained, was against his whole nature. When you knew what you had to do you did it and said why you were doing it.

So on several occasions in the year 1941 he went to the President with his own propositions. The first time was in the spring when Mr. Roosevelt seemed to his associates to have withdrawn into a kind of torpor. The President may have been exhausted by the effort he had just made to obtain the Lend-Lease legislation. Some part of his spirit may have been damaged by the crude and terrible accusations that had been thrown at him in the course of the debate over that legislation. He may have correctly calculated that the people had been subjected to all the strain they could, for the moment, stand. He may with his sensitive instrument simply have taken in too many signals from the people and thus fallen into a numbing confusion of his own. To Stimson he appeared "tangled up in the coils of his former hasty speeches on possible war and convoying as was Laocoön in the coils of the boa constrictors." [1]

The Secretary therefore spent much of the month of May in trying to extricate the President from the coiling entanglements. On the 6th he gave a speech in which he said he was "not one of

[1] H.L.S. to Harry Hopkins, May 12, 1941, WD.

those who think that the priceless freedom of our country can be saved without sacrifice." He proposed active naval support for beleaguered England and he closed with the statement of his belief: "Unless we on our side are ready to sacrifice and, if need be, to die for the conviction that the freedom of America must be saved, it will not be saved." Such observations "seemed to place the United States on the very brink of war." The President had read the speech and approved it but "that did not mean that he was willing or ready to go so far himself." So the Secretary kept pushing him. On the 9th he wrote Harry Hopkins that the state of things was in "deterioration," that the President should do something to "give him leadership again. . . ." He should not use only words but he ought to announce that a squadron from the Pacific was on its way to the Atlantic. Three days later he wrote in the same spirit again to Hopkins.

Then, toward the end of the month, he went directly to the President himself. On the 24th he took to the White House a "rough imaginary resolution of Congress" which read, in substance, as follows: Because certain aggressor nations were seeking to destroy the historic freedom of the seas in an effort to impose on free and independent democracies a system of conquest and servitude abhorrent to the principles of free government, and because Congress, recognizing that a defense of democratic nations was vital to this country, had authorized the United States to assist the nations by furnishing supplies, therefore the President should be authorized to use the naval, air, and military forces to prevent the control of the sea by the enemy and to secure the successful delivery of supplies and munitions.

He suggested this resolution, he told the President in an accompanying letter, because "The American people should not be asked to make the momentous decision of opposing forcefully . . . the evil leaders of the other half of the world possibly because by some accident or mistake American ships and men have been fired upon by soldiers of the other camp. They must be brought to that momentous resolution by your leadership in explaining why any other course than such forceful resistance would be forever hopeless and abhorrent to every honored principle of American independence and democracy." Next day, May 25, he sent the President yet another letter in which he urged once again the announcement of the arrival of the "first units of the Pacific fleet" in the Atlantic. This would indicate "more loudly than any words" the purpose to defend the Western Hemisphere and to carry out the objectives of the Lend-Lease Act.[2]

The President, Samuel Rosenman noticed, was heartened by such counsel but he followed the recommendations imperfectly. He did, at the end of May, give a speech in which he said "all additional measures necessary to deliver the goods [to England] will be taken," but the following day, at a news conference, he denied that he was considering any new step.[3]

Therefore in June, after the Germans attacked Russia, Stimson wrote the President to recommend that "this precious and unforeseen period of respite should be used to push with the utmost vigor our movements in the Atlantic theater of operations." And when in the next week the President called him to report a favorable shift in the Gallup Poll Stimson replied that beyond the poll there was the "power of leadership . . . if he would lead, the whole country would follow." That was possible, the President agreed, but he felt mean, had no pep and had been running a temperature for several weeks.[4]

[2] H.L.S., radio speech May 6, 1941; Sherwood, *Roosevelt and Hopkins*, 293; H.L.S. to Harry Hopkins, May 9, 12, 1941, WD; H.L.S to Franklin D. Roosevelt, May 24, 25, 1941. Stimson was not alone in his desire to rouse the President to greater acts of leadership. Ickes, for instance, wished "to join in some written representation to the President that we are experiencing a failure of leadership that bodes ill for the country." (Ickes, *Diary*, III, 512.)

[3] Sherwood, *Roosevelt and Hopkins*, 298.

[4] H.L.S. to Franklin D. Roosevelt, June 23, 1941; Diary, June 30, 1941. Before writing the letter of June 23 Stimson had talked with Marshall and officers in the War Plans Division. To his relief they agreed with him in the conclusion stated above. "As you know," he told the President, "Marshall and I have been troubled by the fear lest we be prematurely dragged into two major op-

A little later, in the days just before American troops entered Iceland, Stimson went to the President again. He should speak "face to face" with the Congress in announcing the landings and point out that "you have done your best to serve the cause of peace and how events have proved too strong for you." He should say also that if Congress approved the protection of Iceland the territory could be made into a base from which our forces would be in a position "to powerfully check and control these attacks of the Nazi submarines." Unless "we add our own every effort to the efforts of those free nations which are still fighting for freedom . . . we shall ourselves ultimately . . . be fighting alone." [5]

The President, in reporting the landings in Iceland, did make his statement forcefully instead of putting it in by "the back door," and he did say that the route from Iceland to the United States would be made safe for shipping. But to neither Knox nor Stimson in the following weeks did it seem that Roosevelt would "make the frank statement on the subject" of making the Iceland route safe by convoy operations. The whole situation, Stimson told Knox, reminded him of the vacillating days before Sumter, of "the pulling back and forth, trying to make the Confederates fire the first shot." [6]

---

erations in the Atlantic, one in the northeast and the other in Brazil, with an insufficiency of Atlantic naval . . . strength." The rash attack of Germany on Russia had relieved this anxiety, "provided we act promptly." The prompt act desired was the "Iceland project."

[5] H.L.S. to Franklin D. Roosevelt, July 3, 1941; Draft Suggestions for President's Report to Congress, July 6, 1941.

[6] Diary, July 6, 7, 8, 21, 1941. The President had at first prepared a statement on Iceland that seemed to Stimson to be "about everything that it should not be." When the Secretary saw Frankfurter and Hopkins on July 6 he told them so and said, "The President must be frank." Hopkins later told Stimson that after the Secretary's "intervention" the President's speech had been rewritten to emphasize the "protection of the North Atlantic." In the weeks after the message Knox had orders prepared to convoy merchant vessels, including "shipping of any nationality," from the United States to Iceland in accordance with the meaning of the President's statement on Iceland on July 7. The orders were issued by the Commander-in-Chief, Atlantic Fleet, on July 19, 1941 but, as Stimson said, "The President refused to make the frank statement on the subject which Knox wanted him to do and I am afraid he is

Not long after, the first shots were fired. On September 11, the President announced that ships carrying supplies to Britain were being convoyed and that German or Italian men-of-war entering our defensive zones would do so "at their own risk." Five weeks later the destroyer *Kearny*, south and west of Iceland, was torpedoed but not sunk. Two weeks after that, on October 31, the destroyer *Reuben James* was torpedoed and sunk in the North Atlantic with a loss of over one hundred men. In the fall of 1941 these attacks were somehow fitted, as no more than natural consequences, into the general context of a time of extended strain.[7]

The sources of extended strain lay not only in the Atlantic. For well over a year there had been indications that Japan was preparing to fill the vacuum in the Pacific created by the disintegration of the power of England, France and the Netherlands. From the moment Stimson arrived in Washington he had taken the position that firmness rather than cajolery would be necessary to stay the Japanese hand. In the early fall of 1940 he proposed to the President a full embargo on Japan with British vessels, "perhaps backed up by a flying squadron of our own" stationed near the oil fields in the Dutch East Indies, to discourage the Japanese from further expansion. A little later, on October 12, 1940, he suggested that the American fleet should move "across the Pacific by a non-provocative route" and accept the British invitation "to establish itself at Singapore." By this means the United States forces would command the Japanese sea lanes and would be given a "Heaven-sent opportunity" for a naval action away from Japanese bases "if the

---

going to get troubles from that." For a good account of the occupation of Iceland and the organization of the convoy system see S. E. Morison, *History of the United States Naval Operations in World War II*, Vol. I, *The Battle of the Atlantic September 1939-May 1943* (Boston, 1947), 74-79.

[7] Morison, *Battle of Atlantic*, 80-81, 92-94. The President's announcement of September 11 followed an attack by a German submarine on the U.S. destroyer *Greer* on September 4, 1941. The two torpedoes fired missed their mark but, arguing that the attack on the *Greer* was "piracy," Roosevelt made his public announcement of the shoot-at-sight policy.

Japanese should be foolish enough to attack Hawaii or the American coast." [8]

Such recommendations arose from Stimson's belief that Japan had yielded to a firm policy at Shantung in 1919, at the Washington Conference in 1922 and at London in 1930. He remembered also that from 1931 onwards, where it had been impossible to construct firm, consistent policies, the Japanese had not yielded. But at least until the summer of 1941 his counsels went unregarded. About the first of the year Cordell Hull had begun his apparently interminable negotiations to explore with Ambassador Kichisaburo Nomura a possible common ground on which Japan and the United States could meet in the Pacific. Though there were many points at issue the principal obstacle to agreement was and remained China. In sum, the United States in accordance with its historic policy wished Japan to get out of that country while Japan wished to stay in. As early as May 1941 Hull came to believe that "everything was going hellward," but he continued to negotiate with due caution and soft words until July. In that month Japan occupied the southern part of French Indo-China. From this base she could threaten all the surrounding area, the Philippines, Thailand, Malaya and the Dutch East Indies. It was then that Hull hardened his heart, concluding that "nothing further . . . can be done with that country except by a firm policy and, he expected, force itself." This view was made clear to Nomura when the President told him in August that if Japan pursued a further course of conquest by force or threat "the United States will be compelled to take immediately any and all steps which it may deem necessary toward safeguarding the legitimate rights and interests of the United States. . . ." [9]

[8] *Active Service*, 383-85; Diary, Oct. 8, 1940; H.L.S. to Franklin D. Roosevelt, Oct. 12, 1940. It seems probable that Stimson got the idea of sending the fleet to Singapore from a naval officer, Jules James, who married one of his nieces. In 1946 he noted that the "man hole" in the idea was the "superiority in air power of the Japanese fleet" which neither he nor the Navy knew about.
[9] Diary, May 27, Aug. 8, 1941. The course of Hull's negotiations with the Jap-

From that point forward this country applied rising pressure, economic and diplomatic, upon Japan, but the negotiations continued. They continued for several reasons. There was still the chance, as there always is in diplomacy, that something would turn up. Furthermore, by continued negotiation it seemed possible to gain the time necessary to build up the force of B-17's in the Philippines. These planes, just coming into production, made it possible to put effective American power into the archipelago. On September 12 nine of the bombers arrived at Manila. Within a few months, it was estimated, enough more could be added to create a positive deterrent force. Therefore in September, October and November the negotiations between the United States and Japan in which no one had much confidence continued.[10]

So matters stood in the fall of 1941. An earlier consent — something between an unconscious impulse and a clear decision — to render aid short of war to the democracies had by a logical progression brought the United States, in the Atlantic, into a confused area of warlike measures without war. In the Pacific the apparent decision of Japan to expand its sphere of control placed in further jeopardy the interest and policy to which the United States had historically committed itself. But at what point this process of expansion, continued as it had been spasmodically for a decade, could really be said to endanger the safety and fair name of the United States was difficult to figure out. To some, no doubt, it would be when the expanding energy reached Thailand and to others, no doubt, it would be if, and not until, the energy touched some piece of land that was the property of the United States.

The result in the fall of 1941 was a time of waiting. One

anese in 1941 is reported in great detail in Hull, *Memoirs*, II, Chs. 71-74, 77-80. A more rounded account of Japanese-American relations in 1940-1941, conceived in both sympathy and understanding, is Herbert Feis, *The Road to Pearl Harbor* (Princeton, 1950). The position adopted by Stimson as early as January 1940, and sustained throughout, that Japan should and could be forced to change its course, is fully described at appropriate places in the narrative.
[10] *Active Service*, 388; Diary, Sept. 12, 1941.

waited, as Stimson had said in May 1941, "for the accidental shot of some irresponsible captain on either side," or, as he said in July, one pulled back and forth like Lincoln before Sumter, "trying to make the Confederates fire the first shot," or, as he said in November, since "the Japanese [were] notorious for making an attack without warning," one asked how, when negotiations failed, "we should maneuver them into the position of firing the first shot without allowing too much danger to ourselves." [11]

To reduce the danger to ourselves, in the time of hanging fire, it was necessary to reinforce the defenses of the United States in the Philippines, in Panama, along the sea lanes of the Atlantic, in Iceland, at Wake Island, at Pearl Harbor — wherever around the whole globe the troops of the United States were stationed. It was also necessary to put weapons in the hands of those nations — Russia and England — already struggling for survival in war. And in the fall of 1941 there were, whatever principles of division and distribution were adopted, not enough, not nearly enough, weapons to go round. On August 29 the Secretary of War told the President that the requirements of the two fighting nations alone were so great that, as a practical matter, there were two choices: "Either to go to war at once and change the set-up of production so as to get the benefit of the speed which could be obtained by a war psychosis; or else have the program so delayed that the war would probably be over before we got through with it." [12]

Commanders around the globe who had to make do with weapons that were in short supply had also, like the men in Washington, like the people elsewhere in the country, to live on short rations in other less tangible ways. There was the wear and tear of waiting for the thing (not defined) to be done at the time (not specified) perhaps (but not probably) to them.[13]

[11] Diary, May 23, July 21, Nov. 25, 1941.
[12] Diary, Aug. 29, 1941.
[13] One example of the short supply: In the spring of 1941 the War Department

In the last week of November the negotiations with Japan were still going on, but they were going on badly. There was a consideration of a six-month and then of a three-month truce. So little hope for anything was held out that on the 24th a "quasi alert" was sent to the Pacific commands. Next day word came in, through the broken Japanese code, that several divisions of Japanese troops were boarding ship at Shanghai. On the 26th Hull believed that Japan was "poised for attack" but he made one further "honest effort to keep our conversations going." He gave some proposals to the Japanese but his pessimism continued. While Nomura and his fellow negotiator Saburo Kurusu took Hull's recommendations off for study, the Secretary of State confided to Stimson and Knox on the 27th that the matter "is now in the hands of you and Knox — the Army and the Navy." [14]

On that same day the Secretary of War took some part of the matter into his own hands. He suggested to the President, who like Hull believed the "talks had been called off," that a "final alert" should be sent to the Pacific to put the forces on the "qui vive for any attack." The President agreed. And so that afternoon Stimson, Knox, Admiral Stark, Chief of Naval

---

allocated 180 B-17's to the Hawaiian Department. By December 7, 1941, twelve of these planes were in actual service in Hawaii. Another example: In November, 1941, the President asked the Army to divert some Kitty Hawk fighters (P-40's) to the British in the Middle East. In reply the Secretary said that all the planes of this type that would be produced through July 1942 were already allocated by prior commitments to our own forces and to Russia and England. "In other words," the Secretary added in longhand, "there ain't no Kitty Hawks for the poor Army to give you." H.L.S. to Franklin D. Roosevelt, Nov. 12, 1941, WD.

[14] Diary, Nov. 25, 27, 1941: Watson, *Chief of Staff*, 450, 505; Hull, *Memoirs*, II, 1083; *Hearings Before the Joint Committee on the Investigation of the Pearl Harbor Attack*, Congress of the United States, 79th Congress, 2nd Session, Part 11, p. 5421. Hereafter referred to as *Pearl Harbor Hearings*. Stimson's testimony appears in Part 11, pp. 5416-63. Hull did not remember using the phrase attributed to him by Stimson in the last sentence of this paragraph. Indeed he doubted he said it. Whether he said it or not he appears to have had no more confidence at this time than Stimson that his negotiations would turn out successfully. The detailed negotiations of the last ten days of November are clearly set forth in Feis, *Road to Pearl Harbor*, Chs. 39, 40.

Operations, and General Leonard T. Gerow of the War Plans Division sat down to work out a text for the final warning. General Marshall was away for the day at troop maneuvers. The two military men revealed in discussion a "not unnatural" tendency "to seek for more time." Stimson replied that he too would like more time but not at the cost of the humiliation of the United States or at the cost of "reopening the thing which would show a weakness on our part." He then called Cordell Hull to obtain an exact statement of the existing situation. With this statement in mind he introduced some qualifying phrases in the text which then served as the basis for the "final alert" prepared in the War Plans Division and sent under General Marshall's signature to the Pacific commands.[15]

The first sentence and the last seven words of the second sentence in the alert were written by Stimson himself. He approved the rest. The message, Number 472, read:

Negotiations with Japan appear to be terminated to all practical purposes with only the barest possibilities that the Japanese Government might come back and offer to continue. Japanese future action unpredictable but hostile action possible at any moment. If hostilities cannot, repeat cannot, be avoided the United States desires that Japan commit the first overt act. This policy should not, repeat not, be construed as restricting you to a course of action that might jeopardize your defense. Prior to hostile Japanese action you are directed to undertake such reconnaissance and other measures as you deem necessary but these measures should be carried out so as not, repeat not, to alarm civil population or disclose intent. Report measures taken. Should hostilities occur you will carry out the tasks assigned in

[15] Diary, Nov. 27, 1941; Watson, *Chief of Staff*, 509; *Pearl Harbor Hearings*, Part 11, pp. 5423-24. One of the reasons Stark and Gerow wanted "more time" was stated in a memorandum Stark and Marshall had sent to the President on the same day, November 27. They had pointed out the pressing need for delay to build up reinforcements in the Philippines. It should be noticed that the Army alert, because of the modifications introduced by Stimson, was "less positive" than the Navy message sent the same day to the Pacific commands. The Navy alert began, "This dispatch is to be considered a war warning."

Rainbow Five so far as they pertain to Japan. Limit dissemination of this highly secret information to minimum essential officers.

This message was sent on November 27.

To the alert, Lieutenant General Walter C. Short, the commanding general of the Hawaiian Department, replied as follows:

Report Department alerted to prevent sabotage. Liaison with Navy [as prescribed in your radio message] four seven two twenty seventh.[16]

This reply, like the others received in answer to the final alert, was passed through the Secretary's office where Stimson put his initials on it.

In the next ten days, while the Japanese in Washington were preparing an answer to Hull's propositions of November 26, there was a good deal of inconclusive activity. At the beginning of the period it was feared that the troops put aboard ship at Shanghai on November 25 might be used in an attack on Thailand. While the troopships steamed south the President debated three courses of action: to do nothing, to send an ultimatum or to fight at once. Stimson said he preferred the third thing, but on November 28 it was decided the President would send a

16 These dispatches are given among other places in *Pearl Harbor Hearings*, Part 3, p. 1026, Part 11, p. 5424. General Gerow's account of the session at which the warning dispatch was drafted appears in *Pearl Harbor Hearings*, Part 3, pp. 1019-37. His recollection is much like that of the Secretary. He recalled that the first sentence of the warning was put in at Stimson's insistence, after the telephone call to Hull, if not in Stimson's own handwriting. By one of those fatalities that surround Pearl Harbor, Short received two more messages from the War Department about the same time he received the final alert. One of these, though warning of hostile action at any moment, advised him not "to alarm civil population" by any defensive measures he might take. The other warned that "subversive activities may be expected." These two messages confirmed the General in his preoccupation with sabotage. Brief but illuminating descriptions of the measures taken to build up the defenses in the Pacific and to inform commanders about the state of the Japanese negotiations throughout 1941 are to be found in Watson, *Chief of Staff*, Ch. 13, and T. B. Kittredge, "The Muddle before Pearl Harbor," *U.S. News & World Report*, Dec. 3, 1954.

warning letter to the Emperor and also a message to Congress "reporting what we would have to do if the danger happened." [17]

Then the Japanese convoy put in at Indo-China near Saigon, and there was "a little bit of respite." The President talked again of some kind of message to Congress and of a speech to the country. Harry Hopkins from his hospital bed sent word to Knox and Stimson that they "should not let what they call the Appeasers pull the President back." Stimson worked with General Marshall almost every day to put more supplies and planes into the Philippines. And so they came to December 7, the day the Japanese were to make a reply to Hull's proposals.[18]

In the morning Knox, Hull and Stimson met in the State Department and "talked the whole matter over." They all felt, as Hull said, that the Japanese were "planning some deviltry." The information received from the decoded MAGIC intercepts indicated that the Japanese had been holding up their reply "until now in order to accomplish something hanging in the air." Therefore the three men sat "wondering where the blow will strike."

About noon, before the Japanese representative called on Hull in the State Department, Stimson returned to Woodley. He was finishing his Sunday dinner when President Roosevelt called him to say "in a rather excited voice" that the blow had been struck at Pearl Harbor. The exact way in which the news was communicated, Stimson later told a friend, was as follows: "Harry," the President said. "Come down here at once. The Japs have struck." Stimson then asked if the blow had fallen somewhere in Southeast Asia. To which the President replied, "Southeast Asia, hell. Pearl Harbor!" Though the news came as "an excitement indeed," it brought, at first, "confident hope of a major victory." The forces at Hawaii, the greatest Ameri-

[17] Diary, Nov. 28, 1941.
[18] The events of these days, filled with uncertainty and confusion, are described in the Diary, Dec. 1-7; Hull, *Memoirs*, II, Ch. 79; Feis, *Road to Pearl Harbor*, Ch. 41.

can base, would probably inflict "very heavy damage" on the attacking enemy. Not until the evening, when he went with the rest of the Cabinet to the White House, did Stimson learn something of the real truth about the attack. Then, with the others, he listened to the President read the draft of his proposed message to Congress. Though it was "a very effective document," it seemed to the Secretary of War that it was no more than an expression of "just indignation . . . at Japan's treachery." He and Hull had looked for more — a placing of the incident in a wider context, a statement of broad statesmanship. As "gently" as they could, they argued with the President, but the message remained virtually unchanged.

Still, on the night of December 7 there was for Stimson a feeling of "relief." The long months of waiting and indecision, the years, in fact, during which America had lain "half asleep," "self-imprisoned," were finished. And the end had come in a way that "would unite all our people." [19]

Yet the end had come in such a way that there were questions. Some of these questions were left until the war that began at Pearl Harbor was over. It was then asked whether the Roosevelt Administration had not tried, as the sole object of its negotiations in 1941, to put us into a war in the Pacific that would get us into the war in Europe. It was even asked whether, in pursuit of this purpose, Pearl Harbor had not somehow planned that way. Had not officials in Washington deliberately withheld "practically all of the vital information concerning the developing Japanese situation" from the com-

---

[19] Diary, Dec. 7, 1941; *Active Service*, 391, 394. The sense of release from inhibiting confusion and of satisfaction in a people united continued. On December 15 Stimson wrote to his British friend J. S. Muirhead that "ten days of unremitting high pressure work . . . has been like a tonic to me." Everybody felt the same, even the "isolationists were howling for war," recruits were flooding offices and the strikes were over. Both Frances Perkins and Frank Walker noticed that on the night of December 7 Roosevelt, "in spite of the horror that war had actually been brought to us," felt "calmer" and "more relief than he has had for weeks." See Frances Perkins, *The Roosevelt I Knew* (New York, 1946) 379-80.

manders in Hawaii? There is nothing to say about the allegations implicit in these questions except that they are not true.[20]

The administration had three objectives in its negotiations with Japan in 1941. It sought to divide the Axis powers that had signed the pact of September 27, 1940; to prevent the expansion of Japanese power in Southeast Asia; to restore all the things that are meant by the Open Door in China. Evidence is available to suggest that the administration had considerable success in obtaining the first two objectives — on which immediate peace in the Pacific depended — until July 1941. Then, it has been said, by insisting on the third objective, by hardening its heart in defense of all those moralities that had accumulated about the idea of the Open Door, the administration lost its previous advantages. Unwilling to modify this "morally inspired position," increasingly inflexible in the defense of it, the administration thus crowded the Japanese into a position from which they could only fight back. War, in other words, might well have been avoided if the administration had proceeded in elastic negotiation to adjust the immediate necessities; if it had not proved intransigent on the ultimate intention to free China. No one knows. It can be argued that given time and elastic negotiation the immediate difficulties between Japan and the United States could have been resolved. Ambassador Joseph C. Grew so argued and he was on the spot at the time. It can and should be argued, as George Kennan does, that sentiment and a fixed conviction of moral duty are in themselves inadequate bases for a foreign policy. It can be argued that nothing in the previous ten years of Japanese history gave much if any prom-

[20] Readers who wish to make up their own minds on the validity of these allegations should see Charles A. Beard, *President Roosevelt and the Coming of the War, 1941* (New Haven, 1948); Charles C. Tansill, *Back Door to War* (Chicago, 1952); and Robert A. Theobald, *The Final Secret of Pearl Harbor* (New York, 1954). For brief refutations see S. E. Morison, "Did Roosevelt Start the War?" *Atlantic Monthly*, Aug. 1948, and Kittredge, "The Muddle before Pearl Harbor." Much fuller understanding of the developing policies and negotiations in the two years before Pearl Harbor can be obtained in Langer and Gleason, *Undeclared War*.

ise that the country, any more than Hitler's Germany, would respond favorably to elastic negotiation. What would have happened if things had been done differently must be, in the light of all the variables, an unanswered question.[21]

But from the things that were done the war came. Stimson had a hand in these things. From the very beginning, before most others in political office at the time, he had believed in the firm rather than the elastic response. He believed in this for two reasons. First, his understanding of history and his personal recollections convinced him that Japan would yield only to direct pressures. Second, he believed that what was involved in the East was not only national interest but principle, the underlying moralities of the thing. On such matters, whatever the consequences, there could be in his mind no compromise.

[2] The most reasoned and sensible statement of the position described in this paragraph is to be found in Paul W. Schroeder, *The Axis Alliance and Japanese-American Relations, 1941* (Ithaca, 1958), 200-216. After careful survey of the available literature he permits himself (page 216) "the modest conclusions that the kind of policy advocated by Grew presented real possibilities of success entirely closed to the policy actually followed and that it was by no means so immoral and unprincipled that it could not have been pursued by the United States with decency and honor." Schroeder (n. 22, p. 214) makes some very interesting critical comments about the limitations of the attitude held by Stimson. In this same connection one should also read the imaginative book by Robert E. Osgood, *Ideals and Self-Interest in America's Foreign Relations* (Chicago, 1953). In speaking of the beginning of our modern troubles with Japan — Manchuria — he says (352-53) that we should either have decided that Japan's action was both a breach of morality and a danger to our national interest, in which case we should have used strong measures not excluding force, or we should have decided Japan's action did not endanger our interests, in which case regular diplomatic devices would have served. In the event, what we did was to take a vigorous moral stand without regard to the practical consequences. The measures taken were "pitifully inadequate" while the public was encouraged to believe in their adequacy "in accordance with the wishful supposition that world opinion alone could alter basic power conflicts." Somewhat the same rigidity was at work, in Schroeder's opinion, in 1941. My own view is that, all things considered, it is probable that no attempt at accommodation, no set of elastic negotiations, would have prevented Japan's continued threatening expansion in Asia until, in time, it reached some vital American interest like the Philippines. For ten years the country had taken advantage of every opportunity offered. This is not to say that the Western powers had acted wisely at all times in their dealings with Japan in those ten years.

With these larger questions there were also others which had to do with the immediate event. To what extent, for instance, were those in Washington responsible for what had happened at Pearl Harbor? On this matter of general or collective responsibility the Secretary of War said, "No one in Washington had correctly assessed Japanese intentions and capabilities." He, "like everyone else," had been "painfully surprised by the skill and boldness displayed by all branches of the Japanese war machine from December 7 onward." Moreover, "Washington had not adequately appreciated the importance of keeping its field commanders fully informed." And, finally when the majority report of the Joint Committee of Congress to investigate Pearl Harbor "by no means exonerated War Department officials, . . . the responsibility which it inferentially placed on him, as head of the War Department, he was quite willing to accept." [22]

Beyond responsibilities collective and inferential there was also a possible responsibility individual and particular. Of all the countless causes of this remarkable disaster, one certainly was that Pearl Harbor on that Sunday morning lay at Alert Number 1. It lay, in other words, in the standard defense against sabotage "with no threat from without." The fact was that General Short had misinterpreted the message designed to put all the Pacific commands on "the qui vive for any attack."

For this misinterpretation was he himself alone responsible? An Army board of investigation in 1944 thought not. The board members held that the "final alert" of November 27 was in its phrasing ambiguous. They called it the "Do-Don't message." They also believed that General Short's reply stating that he had alerted his department to prevent sabotage should have

[22] *Active Service*, 384-85, 391-93. Watson, *Chief of Staff*, Ch. 15, has an excellent summary of events leading up to Pearl Harbor and of the day itself. He reaches (498-99) nine conclusions of which the most important are (*a*) the attack was a complete surprise caused by the miscalculation of Japanese intentions, (*b*) much secret information with "implications, crystal clear *after* the tragic fact," was not transmitted from Washington to the field, (*c*) nevertheless enough was sent to warrant the belief that Pearl Harbor like San Francisco "was alert to its own peril."

revealed to the War Department the extent of the General's mis-understanding, especially since, on the basis of existing informa-tion, "positive directives could have been formulated to put the [Hawaiian] Department on Alert Number 3." Reviewing these points, the board members concluded that "The difference be-tween alerting those defenses in time by a directive from the War Department based upon this information and the failure to alert them is a difference for which the War Department is re-sponsible, wholly aside from Short's responsibility in not himself having selected the right alert." [23]

Who then, in the War Department, was responsible for this difference? General Gerow was the head of the War Plans Di-vision which had actually sent out the final alert of November 27. He had taken a hand in framing the alert. He had seen Gen-eral Short's reply. When he failed to recognize in this reply that General Short had misinterpreted the message of Novem-ber 27 and thus had taken no corrective step, he had been, he later said, "in error." [24]

The Secretary of War had, in his conversation with President Roosevelt, been the instigator of this final alert. He too had taken a hand in framing the message. He had actually written some of the words that were said to contribute most to the am-biguity of the alert. Had he also, therefore, been "in error"? Was he in some sort a sharer in the direct responsibility assigned by the Army Pearl Harbor Board to the War Department?

There were, of course, extenuating circumstances. The Do-Don't message was no more ambiguous than the times. It did describe the situation quite precisely. Of all the commanding generals in the Pacific, only General Short misconstrued its meaning as far as the setting of the alerts was concerned. In the ordinary course of events the Secretary of War would have taken no part in the composition of the message. He did so only

[23] *Pearl Harbor Hearings*, Part 3, p. 1035; *Supplement to the General Report of the Army Pearl Harbor Board*, 1-2.
[24] Watson, *Chief of Staff*, 509.

because General Marshall was away on troop maneuvers. Also, in the ordinary course of departmental procedure he would not have been expected to take action upon receiving General Short's unsatisfactory reply. It was routine for him to initial a copy of this reply but it was also routine for the War Plans Division, as the originator of the first message, to deal with Short's response.

These were some of the extenuating circumstances. Yet, given all the facts, a prosecutor less experienced than Stimson would have little trouble in convincing a jury that the Secretary had started something he did not wholly finish, that in so doing he contributed directly to the "difference between alerting those defenses in time by a directive from the War Department . . . and the failure to alert them," and that for this difference he was, therefore, in some part responsible. This is a finding never explicitly stated in an official report. But the line of argument, once started, does not appear to lead to any other conclusion.

The Secretary of War had a different view. He felt, to begin with — and with much justification — that the message of November 27 "presented with the utmost precision the situation with which we were all confronted. . . ." Therefore, "we assumed that when [General Short] had been [thus] warned . . . it would not be necessary to repeat that warning over and over again during the ensuing days." And quite apart from this was the position of General Short as an outpost commander. He was "like a sentinel on duty in the face of the enemy." It was not his "to speculate or rely on the possibilities of the enemy attacking at some other outpost instead of his own. It is his duty to meet him at his post at any time and to make the best possible fight that can be made against him with the weapons with which he has been supplied." In this duty, he concluded, "the commanders in Hawaii failed." [25]

This view excluded the Secretary of War from any part of

[25] *Active Service*, 392; *Pearl Harbor Hearings*, Part 11, pp. 5424-25, 5428-29.

the responsibility for the direct consequences of the message of November 27. The analogy between the outpost commander and the sentinel is not, perhaps, wholly exact; the explanation given will not, probably, satisfy everyone. It has in fact been suggested that Stimson took this view from one of a variety of motives: because in so doing he could protect General Marshall from attack for the errors of his subordinates; because he was in this way "passing the buck" to an officer in the field; because he could save himself from blame. Nothing is beyond all doubt in the domain of motive. It is conceivable that in some deep, private recess, concealed from himself and others, he found it impossible, after all his schooling in the imperatives of duty, to believe that a duty left unperformed might be a duty of his own and thus he displaced his share of responsibility on others. But the less recondite explanation appears the more correct. He believed what he said. Nothing in his whole career suggests that on such a matter he could possibly have done otherwise. Those who knew him best, who saw him at the time, who talked with him afterwards, have no doubts on this subject. Concerning the message of November 27 and the position of General Short, he simply thought he was right.[26]

It is inevitable that in the individual interest efforts should be made to personify the causes and quantify the responsibilities for Pearl Harbor. But such efforts have done little to reveal

[26] Current, *Secretary Stimson*, 188. On page 391 of *Active Service* Stimson speaks of the "preposterous charge" made in the Army Pearl Harbor Board report that General Marshall himself might bear some of the responsibility for General Short's failures. To offset the effects of this report Stimson himself started an investigation of his own conducted by Lieutenant Colonel Clausen. Clausen's report, consisting principally of interviews with and affidavits from various officers involved in the Pearl Harbor attack, though massive, does not in fact clear up any of the real issues left unclear by the official investigations. The Proceedings of the Army Pearl Harbor Board are reprinted in *Pearl Harbor Hearings*, Parts 27, 28, 29, 30, 31. Stimson's testimony before this Board is given in Part 29, pp. 2063-87. An account which includes much of this testimony and which gives an unfavorable interpretation of Stimson's actions, both before and after, in connection with Pearl Harbor is found in Current, *Secretary Stimson*, Ch. 8.

why things turned out as they did. The misapprehension of General Short is still only a single item in what is apparently an inexplicable sequence: The massive miscalculation of the Japanese intention by all those in high authority, the arrival of the unarmed B-17's, the submerged submarine detected at the harbor gate at 0350 hours, the morning ride of General Marshall, the unregarded message from the mobile radar unit that picked up the track of Japanese planes 132 miles from Oahu, and all those other things right down to the boy, the undelivered telegram and the bicycle. Not even a system schemed out in total depravity to produce all the wrong things at all the wrong times could have organized such compounding error and misfortune. As Robert Sherwood said, "Millions of words have been recorded by at least eight official investigating bodies and one may read through all of them without arriving at an adequate explanation of why, with war so obviously ready to break out *somewhere* in the Pacific, our principal Pacific base was in a condition of peacetime Sunday morning somnolence instead of in Condition Red." [27]

If there is no adequate explanation for all the things that happened on December 7, there are at least precedents. Some are small and merely suggestive, like the embalmed beef in 1898. Some are large but lack dramatic impact, like the destroyers in 1917. In the spring of that year U-boats were sinking about a million tons of merchant shipping in the western approaches to the British Isles every thirty days. The figuring was that England would be "brought to her knees" by the autumn. At this moment, April 1917, the United States entered the conflict with "over one hundred" vessels on the Navy list that were "suitable" to fight the submarine. In the first month of the war the United States Navy found itself able to put only six destroyers into the western approaches.

Other precedents have both size and dramatic impact. There was, in the early days of the Civil War, the "panic flight" of the

[27] Sherwood, *Roosevelt and Hopkins*, 434.

forces commanded by Irvin McDowell from the field of Bull Run. And, farther back in time, there was the surrender of William Hull's entire army at Detroit in the first month of the War of 1812.

The precedents suggest that when wars begin, the country, in "annoyed surprise," as Melvin Johnson said, often sends "our men out to fight and die with two strikes against them." The precedents suggest that what occurred at Pearl Harbor might, with individual variations, have occurred at any other American base and to any other American commander on that Sunday morning. The destruction of the heavy bombers on the ground at Clark Field in the Philippines also suggests as much.[28]

Pearl Harbor, like all the other installations, was a single part in a far larger system, the military establishment of the United States. This system is designed primarily to adjust and reconcile the conflicting impulses — civil, financial, military, political — that are at work in the administration of an armed force in a democracy in time of peace. Since the impulses do, in fact, often conflict, the central agency in the system, the War Department, is a place of compromise, of unsteady accommodations between opposing interests. In the administrative works there is, therefore, much slippage and lost motion. The same things are done, or partly done, or done twice over or never done at all by different men in different places because of differences not wholly reconciled. Then too, because in peace the civil, financial and political interests tend to dominate, the supply and influence of military energy diminishes. It is a process that produces, ordinarily, the imprecise and sometimes the inappropriate transaction. Such disorders as there may be in the central agency are naturally sent throughout the system to the last and farthest outpost. Some of the transferred confusions have to do with supply, the quality and quantity of goods and weapons; some have to do with personnel, the size and disposition and training of the forces; and some are of the spirit.

[28] Melvin M. Johnson, Jr., and Charles T. Haven, *For Permanent Victory* (New York, 1942), 7.

The shape of this military establishment is determined by the shape of the larger whole of which it is a part, the process by which the conflicting impulses in a democratic society are brought together for adjustment and reconciliation. The process has its own slippage and lost motion, the play in a system designed to accommodate an infinite number of variables with a saving grace. In this process, malice domestic is reduced only "with all deliberate speed"; the great decisions on restraints of trade or action are left tentative, for revision by the rule of later reason. It is a process as uncertain as the human feelings. But out of the play and over time general intentions do evolve, inexact but useful expressions of a national inclination. The trains, however, do not always run on time. Public opinion working within the evolutionary process resists clean organization and the ordered aims of sound administrative practice. It also resists exterior distraction. The public imagination, preoccupied with internal conflicts, has limited power to act on events outside the process or on the possible future. The circumstance preferred is the isolated present.

In the best of times the process does not lend itself to the single-minded prosecution of the unqualified act. Especially it is not the process to determine precisely when, where, how and why an act so unqualified, so abnormal, so hostile to the democratic process, as a war should begin. Never in the transition from peace to war has the country been able to reveal its full intentions or its full strength. And the months before Pearl Harbor were not the best of times. Distracted by sudden shifts in fortune, confused by recurrent choices between apparent present safety and some ill-defined ultimate necessity, baffled, as always, by the abstract relationship between force and policy, the country seemed to have lost the power of decision. Whatever conflicts of opinion existed — between the annual model and a business as unusual as all aid short of war, between faith and fear — went unresolved. And the irresolution was transmitted to Washington and from Washington to the last and farthest outposts. What was produced in these months was not a fortress America but a thin and improvised arrangement. So all along the perimeters of defense too few men stood to the guns in short supply waiting for something sudden to happen sometime, perhaps, to them.

What did happen on December 7 was, of course, not planned. Some men had indeed done all in their power — personal and official — to see that it would not happen that way, and the Secretary of War was one of these. Since July 1940 he had exerted his one-track will to put military energy into the War Department, to concentrate the energy in the country exclusively upon the build-up of the national military power, to explain clearly what he believed the turmoil in the world outside was all about, and to define what he took to be and what did become the ultimate necessity. What in his words and acts he represented was, however, only one of the impulses legitimately at play in the democratic process. Not until December 8, 1941, did he appear as one having a majority.

29

Decisions Seven Days a Week

A THOUGHTFUL friend once came in to tell the Secretary that when the affairs of his office were in hand he would have to spend no more than four hours a day at his desk. But, as the Commentaries so often said, in war those in charge have all things to do at one time. And when a war begins as this war began, all things are not in hand; they come streaming through the consciousness of superior authority distorting the sense of time and the sense of scale. For two years after December 7, 1941, where so much was necessary at the very moment, it was difficult to discriminate between the useful, the futile, the possible, the incredible, the wise and the simply inevitable.

The first of the first things was, however, obvious. In spite of the efforts of the two preceding years, it was still necessary, as George Marshall said two days after Pearl Harbor, to "fight the fact that the War Department is a poor command post."

The principal reason it was a poor command post was that the lines of authority and responsibility had become, over time, twisted and tangled. To straighten these lines out a study group under Lieutenant General J. T. McNarney recommended in February 1942 the creation of three new commands — the Army Ground Forces, the Army Air Forces and the Services of Supply or, as it was later called, the Army Service Forces. The commanding officers of these forces were to act under broad grants of independence and authority within their own domains but each also was to act under the supervision of the Chief of Staff, who was specifically assigned responsibility for the strategic direction and control of operations and the determination of over-all military requirements. This system of administration, placed in effect on March 9, 1942, by Executive Order 9082, continued throughout the war.[1]

In the deliberations leading to these recommendations the Secretary took some part. From the time he had assumed office he had been interested in the development of the air arm. He had in 1940 rejected the advice of those who had advised him to get rid of General Arnold; he had then selected Lovett and supported both the Assistant Secretary and General Arnold in their efforts to expand Army air power. And in the reorganization of 1942 he was, in the opinion of Lovett, the determining influence in the creation of the separate air command. In at least two other instances he acted to shape the nature of the reorganization. General Marshall and John McCloy proposed to him the substitution of "a single chief of staff for the two officers who represent the Army and Navy now." This suggested means to coordinate the separate arms he rejected as too "radical"; it would, he said in recalling the history of Root's reforms for his advisers, create such "bitter opposition" that the purpose would be defeated. The better way was to work out "*ad hoc* methods" of getting better cooperation between the Army and Navy. Later he modified this view sufficiently to support the idea — first suggested by Marshall — that Admiral William D. Leahy should be appointed as an informal unifier of military opinion for President Roosevelt. This was done in 1942 when Leahy became Chief of Staff to the Commander-in-Chief.[2]

[1] Ray S. Cline, *U. S. Army in World War II, The War Department, Washington Command Post: The Operations Division* (Washington, 1951), 90. For a detailed discussion of this reorganization see Nelson, *National Security*, Ch. 8.
[2] Conversation with R. A. Lovett, Sept. 15, 1955; Diary, Jan. 27, Feb. 7, 10, 25, 1942.

Stimson also acted to "keep the [McNarney] committee from going astray" in its desire to change the title from Chief of Staff to Commander-in-Chief. Though he admitted that "the error is largely one of nomenclature," he believed the change would be an unwise departure from "the old principles" that he had learned from Root. The title "Chief of Staff" made it clear that the senior officer of the Army had no real independence of command, that he spoke only in the name of the constitutional Commander-in-Chief, the President, or the Secretary of War acting for the President. The Secretary's interest in this matter was to prevent the "old trouble," the building up of a "commanding general" beyond the easy reach of civilian authority. The members of the McNarney Committee after several days of argument accepted his views.[3]

On another matter of greater substance he was not so successful. Article 6 of Executive Order 9082 read as follows:

The Secretary of War is authorized and directed to prescribe such functions, duties, and powers of the commanders of the various forces and commands of the Army of the United States and the agencies of the War Department and to issue from time to time such detailed instructions regarding personnel, funds, records, property, routing of correspondence, and other matters as may be necessary to carry out the provisions of this order. Such duties by the Secretary of War are to be performed subject always to the exercise by the President directly through the Chief of Staff of his functions as Commander-in-Chief in relation to strategy, tactics, and operations.

By this article the Secretary of War was assigned administrative responsibilities of impressive magnitude, but he was also taken out of the line that ran through military matters. Historically the office of the Secretary of War had served as one of the "interposing layers" between the President and the Chief of Staff. By Executive Order 9082 General Marshall was specifi-

[3] Diary, Feb. 7, 10, 1942.

cally given direct access to Roosevelt on matters relating "to strategy, tactics, and operations." In accepting this situation Stimson, as has been said, revealed qualities of "high character, statesmanship, and unselfishness." But he found it difficult as an old soldier, as a former Secretary of War and as a man with acute feelings of responsibility for his office and his own person to keep at all times within the new limits set upon his position. Not always consciously, indeed, more often than not, quite unconsciously, he acted to extend his influence beyond the prescribed confines of Executive Order 9082. Thus he conversed frequently and often usefully on military matters with the Chief of Staff, who, out of his great respect for the office and the man, left open opportunities for such conversations.[4]

Out of the conversation between these two in the first days came a series of decisions, all forced and in great part shaped by the needs of dreadful occasions; some that produced immediately useful results, some that were attended by continuing anxieties, and one at least that was heartbreaking.

An immediate necessity was to find an officer to go to China. Consideration was given, at the suggestion of John McCloy, to General Hugh Drum. Drum, the senior line officer in the Army, came down to Washington from his headquarters in New York in the first week of January with the expectation that he would be offered an opportunity to do great things in Europe. Instead he was told that there were plans to send him to China. The Secretary said that this was not "a happy-go-lucky mission leading nowhere"; it was instead the "fulfillment of a policy and of principles" Stimson had believed in for many years. He went on to give Drum the impression that in China there would be a major theater of operations. Further questioning by Drum in other places in the Department led him to believe, however, that not everyone shared the Secretary's view. General Marshall seemed to have a much smaller mission in mind. After a good deal of discussion Drum reached the

4 Nelson, *National Security*, 350-51.

conclusion that the plans for the China-Burma-India area were "nebulous, uncertain, and indefinite." This kind of careful investigation and candid judgment pleased neither the harried Chief of Staff nor the Secretary. There was a conference between Drum and Marshall "in which apparently both men lost their tempers." Marshall came away from the argument feeling that Drum, in asking for a clearer definition of the task assigned, was in fact asking whether the position was large enough for an officer of his rank and talents. This feeling was transmitted to the Secretary, who also came to believe that Drum "did not think the role in China which I had offered him was big enough for his capabilities."

This ended the negotiations with General Drum. Marshall then proposed to the Secretary four men, among them Joseph Stilwell. Though Stimson was at first skeptical of Stilwell because he had seen him sitting in his office one day with his head down, a two-hour talk between the two at Woodley resolved the Secretary's earlier doubt. Impressed by the unequivocal spirit of the old foot soldier, by his simple assurance, after all of Drum's questioning, that "I'd go where I was sent," Stimson soon came to prefer Stilwell to the others. So on the day after the talk at Woodley, in Stilwell's words, "Henry said he had been stimulated, and that George should keep his eye on me, because I might be a commander. So George told him, Hell, that's just what he'd been telling Henry."

Ten days later Stilwell's orders were written out, and, after "a fatherly talk" in which the Secretary gave him the "hand of destiny stuff," he was sent on a mission from which, the Secretary of War believed, all difficulties seem pretty well cleared out of the way. Perhaps the Chief of Staff and Secretary were too impressed, in the days when it was "hard as hell to find anybody in our high command who's worth a damn," by a soldier who was willing to go anywhere and fight. Without any doubt they miscalculated, like almost everybody else, the nature of a post where the relatively sophisticated intelligence of a Hugh

Drum might usefully have supplemented the more earthy talents of a dedicated general of infantry. In the opinion of the British officer, J.F.C. Fuller, Stilwell was "an outstanding American soldier, wasted on an all but impossible job and one for which, temperamentally, he was unsuited." Also, in the opinion of Fuller, "few generals have been so disgracefully treated."

Still, in rank atmospheres, in a theater where few achieved even local success and none great reputation, General Stilwell made himself felt as a trainer and leader of troops, a resourceful tactician, a brave and honest man. These were the qualities for which the Secretary of War and the Chief of Staff were looking when they selected him and which they believed sufficient for the ill-defined task at hand. For these qualities Marshall and Stimson supported him during thirty-one months against the subtle resistance of the Chinese, the rival claims of the air arm, the diminishing regard of a President with whom Stilwell "never made his number" and the unhappy history of the China-Burma-India theater caused by inadequate means and divided counsels. In the end this support and his own rather inept statement of his case profited the General nothing and he was brought by the request of Chiang and the acquiescence of Roosevelt to his recall and to what the Secretary of War thought of as his "terribly sad ending." [5]

At the time Stimson had talked with Stilwell about his selection for the Chinese mission, he had also raised another topic, the situation on the West Coast of the United States where Stil-

[5] Diary, Jan. 1, 2, 6, 11, 13, 14, 23, 24, 1942; *Active Service*, 538-41; C. F. Romanus and Riley Sunderland, *U.S. Army in World War II, The China-Burma-India Theater, Stilwell's Mission to China* (Washington, 1953), 63-76; Stilwell, *Papers*, xxiii-xxiv, 49-53; conversation with John J. McCloy, Sept. 14, 1955. For Stimson's views on the purpose of the China mission, see "Memorandum for the Chief of Staff," Jan. 6, 1942, in Diary. An example of Stimson's continued support of Stilwell is given in his letter to Roosevelt, May 3, 1943, WD. "I know," he said, "of no other man who is anywhere near as good." The Secretary had had to deal with so many others who were prompt "to shuffle off responsibilities for evil fortune" that Stilwell's acceptance of responsibility for difficulties was refreshing.

well had been stationed at the time of Pearl Harbor. General De Witt of the Fourth Army had been "clamoring for the evacuation of the Japanese of the area surrounding the intensely important area at San Diego, Los Angeles, San Francisco, and Puget Sound. . . ." It was De Witt's fear that the members of the Japanese communities, many of them American citizens, were acting or were about to act as enemy agents. There were reports of "suspicious signalling," of enemy submarines, and of unidentified radio transmissions." Spot raids by the FBI in February 1942 had produced, it was said, rifles, maps, shotguns from the homes of enemy aliens. These raids and flying rumors, it was later claimed, so roused the public "that it was ready to take matters into its own hands." No doubt, as Stilwell had believed in December, a good many of the reports were not unlike a "two-pound bundle of crap," but by February both General De Witt and the citizens of the West Coast, with the memory of Pearl Harbor, were terribly alarmed.

The General asked the War Department to remove all Japanese — every alien and citizen alike — from the sensitive areas. Stimson was reluctant to do so for two reasons: first, he felt that De Witt was given to exaggeration and, second, he recognized that a forced removal of the Japanese would "make a tremendous hole in our constitutional system . . ." For several days he examined the matter, thinking of Homer Lea, talking with McCloy, who had visited the West Coast, and conferring with the Justice Department. While he pondered, the excitement and tension in California rose steadily. Reports flowed in suggesting that, unless the Japanese were removed, the situation might well get out of hand. In such a pass the Secretary, after conferring with the President and the members of the Justice Department, gave his approval of the evacuation plan which affected about 100,000 Japanese, 60,000 of whom were American-born. McCloy remembers that Stimson, in view of the state of mind of the commanding general and the West Coast, accepted the necessity to move the Japanese, but he was less sure that he had the right to make them move until reports of riot made him feel that he could act to protect, under the Constitution, the rights of minorities. In the Foreword he prepared for the army report on the operation, the Secretary argued from a somewhat different premise, a premise no doubt longer held and more fundamental in his character. That Japanese, regardless of their individual loyalties to the United States, were thus treated he found more than unfortunate. But, he added, "in emergencies, where the safety of the Nation is involved, consideration of the rights of individuals must be subordinated to the common security." [6]

About this decision the Secretary remained not uncertain but unhappy. He took such steps as he could to see that the evacuation of the Japanese was conducted with due regard for their feelings and their comfort. When he got wind of a project "hatching up" in California to keep the Japanese "huddled up" in temporary assembly camps so they could be used as cheap

---

[6] Stilwell, *Papers*, 31-36, 57; Diary, Feb. 3, 10, 11, 1942; *New York Times*, Feb. 21, 1942; *Final Report Japanese Evacuation from the West Coast 1942* (Washington, 1943), 9-10. The mechanics of the removal and relocation of the nisei are described in great detail in the *Final Report*, also the reasons which appeared to justify the evacuation. Some of these reasons are odd, viz., (34), "The very fact that no sabotage has taken place to date is a disturbing and confirming indication that such action will be taken." Morton Grodzins in his careful study of the episode, *Americans Betrayed: Politics and the Japanese Evacuation* (Chicago, 1949), concludes that the evacuation and the supporting court decisions that followed were a "fundamental" policy change in the handling of minorities, a change reached not by meeting the issue "but by sliding around it." Eugene Rostow, "Our Worst Wartime Mistake," *Harper's Magazine*, Sept. 1945, asserts that by its decision the Supreme Court converted a "piece of wartime folly into national policy. . . ." The most reasonable assessment will be found in Mr. Justice Jackson's dissenting opinion in *Korematsu vs. U.S.* He held that "It would be impracticable and dangerous idealism to expect or insist that each specific military command in an area of probable operations will conform to conventional tests of constitutionality." His duties, he felt, did not require him to make a military judgment on the wisdom or necessity of the evacuation order. But he did not think any court "may be asked to execute a military expedient that has no place in law under the Constitution." See *The Case for the Nisei*, Brief of the Japanese American Citizens League, 140-43. The issue in February 1942 was whether the evacuation was a "military necessity." In view of the available evidence, as presented by a commanding officer, and the nature of the times, Stimson decided the evacuation was "common sense," though on any other grounds, he said (Sept. 15, 1942), "It may be hard to justify it."

labor in the harvest time, he wrote an angry letter to the President about "that patriot" Governor Olson whom he believed behind the project. In the beginning, he told Roosevelt, Californians had been "hell-bent for rushing these unfortunate Japanese out of the State. . . ." The Army had considerable difficulty in seeing that great injury and injustice were not done under pressure of that feeling. Now the Californians wished to make use of these people for their own convenience. He did not want anyone to "blow first hot and then cold without any reference to the safety or welfare of these unfortunate people . . ." and, in the event, the Japanese were moved out of the assembly camps with the dispatch and ease permitted under the circumstances.[7]

In these same February days that Stimson was reaching his decision about the evacuation of the Japanese he and the Chief of Staff were called upon to consider a situation even more unfortunate. In the Philippines the armies fighting under General Douglas MacArthur were proving unable to deal with the greatly superior force of the Japanese. Placed in a hopeless circumstance, Manuel Quezon sought some way to save the Islands from what seemed further pointless warfare. On February 8 he sent a message in which he proposed as a means of ending the hopeless struggle the neutralization of the Islands. The independence, which by the Tydings-McDuffie Act had been fixed for the year 1946, should be granted the Philippines immediately. On the acceptance of this condition the forces of both Japan and the United States would be withdrawn from the archipelago. In an accompanying message General MacArthur described the "violent resentment" of the Filipinos against the United States and warned that Washington must "figure on the complete destruction of this command" at any time. He seemed to go "more than half way" toward supporting Quezon's position.

These reports and proposals came in to men who knew what

[7] H.L.S. to Franklin D. Roosevelt, July 7, 1942, Roosevelt Papers; Diary, July 7, 1942.

war was like and who waited, remote from the scene of action, only with the power of decision. They reached a Secretary of War bound, by the recollection of past achievement, to those Islands he was without present means to help. They reached a Chief of Staff who a few weeks before had remarked that military training and education were "good things for any man to have as part of his experience but that ten minutes of combat duty was ten minutes too much." After these messages came in they turned to each other to work out the necessary reply. Each agreed that the forces under General MacArthur had to remain in action. Together they went to the White House on February 9 to explain their position to the President and to Sumner Welles, acting for Cordell Hull who was ill. Stimson gave his views "standing as if before the court," and when he had finished, the President "said he agreed with us." Marshall and the Secretary then returned to the Department to work out the messages that would contain the order to continue the defense of the Islands. When these were completed they returned to the White House to put the message in final form in a conference with the President, Welles, Admiral King and Admiral Stark. At the end of the day the dispatches went out to MacArthur and Quezon in the Philippines.

Early in the discussions between the Chief of Staff and the Secretary about the nature of the response that should be made to Quezon and MacArthur, Stimson had said, "There are times when men have to die," and the response in its final form was designed to give the meaning of this particular time. A common front had been formed against the predatory powers seeking to destroy individual liberty and freedom of government. America was the most powerful member of this coalition. In the Philippines, American forces were not engaged merely upon a mission of delay with military consequences. There it was mandatory to establish "once and for all in the minds of all peoples complete evidence that the American determination and indomitable will to win carries on down to the last unit." There was also the pledged word of the United States. Until

the promised independence in 1946 the country had undertaken
to protect the Islands "to the uttermost of our power." "So
long as the flag of the United States flies on Filipino soil as a
pledge of our duty to your people, it will be defended by our
own men to the death."

Receiving these declarations Quezon and MacArthur replied,
in the General's words, that Filipinos and Americans could be
counted on equally to "hold steadfast to the end." This response came as a relief to all those in Washington who had
taken part in the decision. But it did not supply much solace.
"During the watches of the night," the Secretary kept "thinking of the people locked up in Corregidor." His heart went out
especially to Quezon, to that "volatile character" wracked by
"illness and the strain of the battle." He reflected how hard it
must have been for his Filipino friend in such straits to reply so
bravely to the "rather severe telegram" asking him to hold
fast. And so, on his own, he sent to Quezon and MacArthur a
further message taking cognizance of their "superb courage"
and "fidelity." [8]

[8] Diary, Feb. 8, 9, 13, 1942; conversation with George Roberts, Sept. 14, 1955.
The text of messages exchanged between the Philippines and Washington are
to be found in the Diary. For an extended account of the episode, see *Active
Service*, 394-405. Fuller descriptions and judgments on the events leading up to
the defeat of the forces in the Philippines will be found elsewhere. Courtney
Whitney in *MacArthur, His Rendezvous with History* (New York, 1956), 27,
believes the administration "never intended to send [reinforcements] and concealed the fact that they would not be sent." This "deception," deliberate or
not, was the product, in Whitney's opinion (36-37), of a "major strategic
blunder," the insistence of the " 'Europe-first' concept that not only set up an
automatic military priority for Europe but also assumed unnecessary defeats
in other vital areas of the world." Louis Morton, *U.S. Army in World War
II, The War in the Pacific, The Fall of the Philippines* (Washington, 1953),
390-91, gives a different view. "Despite the fact that Allied strategy called for
the defeat of Germany first, the bulk of the troops and supplies sent overseas
during the early part of 1942 went to the Pacific." The requests for supplies
"were received in Washington with the greatest sympathy. . . . No expense
was too high, no effort too great to relieve the embattled garrison." General
Marshall "undertook to impart this sense of urgency" to the efforts to supply
the beleaguered forces. But the Japanese hold in the Southwest Pacific was
"too firm." "The story of the attempt to break through the Japanese blockade,
like the entire story of the campaign in the Philippines, is one of heroic efforts
and final failure."

These were some of the larger and hard decisions — the dispatch and support of Stilwell, the removal of the Japanese from the coastal regions of the West, the orders to fight on at Corregidor — that filled the first days of the war. In the long months of the next two years the decisions — large, small, simple and hard — continued. There was the problem of production. Stimson twice acted to protect industries engaged in making war materials from Thurman Arnold's desires to "fire a number of indictments" under the Sherman Act. He also spent a good deal of time trying to insure a steady flow of raw material to all the war industries by strengthening the organization of the War Production Board. At first, together with Knox, Patterson and Forrestal, he sought to persuade Donald Nelson, the Chairman of the War Production Board, to make the necessary changes himself. But he soon formed the impression that Nelson was a man with a "fictitious" reputation, surrounded by weak men, "terrified" by the bluster of his associate William M. Jeffers. When the altercations within the Board blew up into the row which produced the resignation of Ferdinand Eberstadt in February 1943, Stimson reached the conclusion that Nelson was incapable of giving direction to the industrial defense effort. "For two and a half years," he said, "the whole production organization has been bungled." It was time to bring in Bernard Baruch. The Secretary called first on Hopkins, who seemed "converted," but the President, ill with a toothache, delayed until Stimson went to him and pointed out the "great disintegration of morale" caused by the delay. Roosevelt's response was not "very satisfactory" but he did report that he had asked Baruch to take Nelson's place and Baruch had temporized. As the Secretary left this conference Pa Watson followed him out to say that he was "dead right" and must "push the President on." Thus encouraged, the Secretary summoned Baruch to the Pentagon and got him to promise he would accept the position if it were firmly offered. Baruch's promise was relayed back to Watson by the Secretary but without much confidence because he believed it was "a difficult decision" at which the President "always balks." The temporizing of the President was doubtless increased by his feeling that Mr. Baruch would not necessarily solve all the difficulties. And, in the event, Nelson continued in authority, or at least in office until October 1944. From this time forward Stimson tended to leave matters of industrial production more and more in the hands of Patterson. Bored by the nature of the problem, exasperated by the continuing confusions in the organization designed to deal with the problem, he turned the negotiations over increasingly to the subordinate in whom he had complete confidence.[9]

There was also the problem of manpower. In the fall of 1942 he supported Marshall's request for a larger army than the Bureau of the Budget and those concerned with the supply of domestic labor thought either wise or necessary. He also tried unsuccessfully to keep the selective service agency completely separate from the agency controlling the allocation of civilian manpower. His argument was that, by a long and painful evolution since the Civil War, the Army had produced "a system which today selects men for the Army to the general satisfaction of the people of this country." Regulating civil manpower was different; it involved matters of profit, industrial need, political expediency and social theories. The two did not mix. "Manifestly that controlling authority [over manpower] cannot be in the hands of either the one or the other of these two ultimately competing systems." But he lost his point. And when Paul McNutt was put in charge of the Manpower Commission at the end of November 1942 he almost lost McCloy as

9 Diary, March 2, 3, 14, July 20, Sept. 10, 1942, Feb. 15, 22, 1943. For Nelson's version of these events and his bitter feelings about the Army, see his *Arsenal of Democracy*, 385 ff. Other accounts are in John D. Millett, *U.S. Army in World War II, The Army Service Forces, The Organization and Role of the Army Service Forces* (Washington, 1954), 211-12, and Sherwood, *Roosevelt and Hopkins*, 699-700. Sherwood believes it was Hopkins who persuaded Roosevelt to give Nelson another chance.

well. The President, at McNutt's request, told the Secretary that "after very mature thinking" he had decided McCloy should represent the War Department on the Manpower Commission. When Stimson passed the word to the White House that he did not intend to have McNutt thus "dictate my own handling of my own Department" the matter was dropped.[10]

A great deal of the Secretary's time was taken up in negotiations of this kind. When representatives of the Federal Communications Commission came round to claim that the Army radio transmitters broadcasting news and music to troops in Alaska were established in violation "of policy and precedent," he had to spend several days in "one of those ever recurring New Deal troubles which arise among 'the cherubs.'" He pointed out that most of the programs were arranged by the soldiers themselves, that the radius of the average transmitter was five miles, and that there was no possibility of rivalry with commercial interests in those gloomy, rainy, inaccessible spots. When he heard that Archibald MacLeish of the Office of Facts and Figures was going to give a speech about alleged discrimination against Negroes in the Army, he spent an hour with Mac-

---

[10] Diary, Oct. 22, 23, Nov. 4, 5, 29, Dec. 9, 18, 1942; H.L.S. Memorandum for the President, Nov. 5, 1942, in Diary; Franklin D. Roosevelt to H.L.S., Dec. 18, 1942. Stimson told Marshall that if on McNutt's initiative the President was prepared to select McCloy, "I was ready to resign." Stimson's position on manpower in 1942 was determined in great part by his concern that the Army would not have enough men. On October 23 Marshall told him that "our divisions are going out to the front undermanned" and that nine divisions preparing for action had a strength of 45,000 instead of the normal 135,000 men. Two weeks later the Chief of Staff was "very much wrought up" because a proposed limitation of the Army might "very well paralyze our 1943 effort." This overriding interest in military manpower was not shared by others in and out of government. For unfavorable comment on Stimson's attitude toward both industrial mobilization and manpower, see Current, *Secretary Stimson*, 202-10. The burden of these pages, and of other critics quoted in these pages, is that Stimson with a zealot's concern for the Army was quite prepared to dislocate the economy, damage the public interest, and, in some cases — as to save newsprint by giving up Sunday comics — to threaten the civil liberties in the interest of military necessity. Nelson also, *Arsenal of Democracy*, 360-61, was annoyed by the Army's attitude toward funny papers but he says he objected less to the Army's effort to get top consideration for their programs than for its "many unfair methods of needling anyone who stood in its way."

Leish, "pointing out" how "this crime of our forefathers had produced a problem which was almost impossible of solution in this country and that I myself could see no theoretical or logical solution for it at war times like these. . . ." When a "new tempest in a teapot" blew up over the Army's school to train officers for duties in occupied territories, he had to protect the commanding officer against charges of fascist intent. The effort was not to train officers for proconsular duties, he argued in the Cabinet, but to prepare them to undertake administrative obligations that they would legitimately assume in the control of occupied territory. In making his point he had, he felt, all "the typical difficulties of a discussion in a Roosevelt Cabinet" but he did think he "got away with it." The school continued, but later he argued in vain that the evidence of history supported the use of the War Department as the agency through which the administration of occupied North Africa should be conducted.[11]

Inside as well as beyond the War Department there was also work to do. In these months he spent a great deal of time before he found a Surgeon General who was satisfactory alike to the military, the President and the medical profession. He pondered the removal of a Chief of Ordnance because of what he called a "lag" in the production of guns. He investigated a new and supposedly more sustaining kind of diet for soldiers in combat. He took a hand in drafting the Army's position on liquor at army bases since he was "an old bird at this thorny proposition" who knew how much dynamite there was in the antisaloon sentiment. And one day he acted to change the phraseology in the footnote of a version of the Scriptures distributed to the troops in which a Jewish synagogue was described as a house of Satan.[12]

To all these numberless negotiations, great and small, the

[11] Diary, Jan. 24, Aug. 27, Nov. 4, 6, 1942, May 13, 1943. For Stimson's full views on the Negro in the Army see *Active Service*, 461-64.
[12] Diary, Oct. 20, 21, 1942, May 3, 1943; H. L. S. to Franklin D. Roosevelt, May 12, 1943.

Secretary brought unchanging qualities of mind and spirit. There was first his absolutely unqualified commitment to the object of victory and the Army as the great instrument to secure that victory. "I am the one man — or rather the highest man — in the Government whose duty it is to see that the United States Army is equipped," he remarked to himself on New Year's Day, 1942. Against the claims of a rival service, the needs of the domestic economy, the arguments of those who wished to preserve social gains, the request from farmers for labor to harvest their crops, the unceasing requisitions from allies across the seas, against all these, "I have," he said, "a steady fight all the time to hold my own for the United States Army." Steadily he fought for that institution to which he was bound not only by the logic of his situation, but by ties of memory and temperament.

The depth of that devotion was left, ordinarily, unstated, but it revealed itself frequently to his associates in odd moments and in unpredictable ways. Once the Chief of Staff proposed that Frederick Osborn, the very tall, very thin, very useful chairman of the Army and Navy Committee on Welfare and Recreation should be commissioned as a general officer. "Oh," said the Secretary, "you can't do that." "Why not?" Marshall asked. "Well," the Secretary replied, "he'd look too funny." And at another time he was in Panama on an inspection trip. To get a better view of the installations protecting the machinery at one of the locks, he had climbed high up the steep side of a canal cut. While he was thus engaged an Army transport came into the lock. From his eminence he could look across and make out the faces of the men on deck. By chance he himself was recognized and the bugles blew to the attention. In this unexpected moment, as the ship bearing soldiers to the war in the Pacific moved in absolute silence through the lock, he took the salute from the ranks along the rails while the tears poured down his cheeks.

There were other qualities he revealed in his negotiations.

There were times when he was fretful and deeply stirred by the thought of the difficulties surrounding him; there were other times when he was roused to sudden, unqualified dicta and ultimata. In the fretful times it would come upon him that he was an old man, very probably a man misunderstood and undoubtedly a man frustrated in the discharge of his immense duties by the inanity or the wilfulness or the slyness of others. "But it is the kind of thing," he would then confide to himself, "which reduces to a reductio ad absurdum our system where a man who is conducting a great department and supervising the organization and equipment of the biggest army that the United States ever had, and thirdly, is being consulted every day seven days a week on the conduct of a war in all the three great areas of the world, should have his equilibrium upset by the demand of an alumni association that he should make them a speech. It is perfectly preposterous." The causes of these reductions to the absurd, these perfectly preposterous matters that destroyed the equilibrium were, invariably, no larger than requests for speeches or rumors by "loose-tongued" outsiders about why Cordell Hull gave up playing croquet on the Woodley grounds.

Graver occasions brought forth the old man who was justified in the unhesitating opinion or the irrevocable judgment because he had seen it all, or almost all, and because he was right. Thus when he once heard of a memorandum in which it was reported that the President proposed to discuss with Winston Churchill the turning over of reinforcements prepared for MacArthur to the British his "anger grew" until he called up Harry Hopkins and said "if that was persisted in, the President would have to take my resignation. . . ." Thus when the President once seemed about to interfere in the interior administration of the War Department he was again prepared to make it a matter for resignation. Thus when he was placed under what he took to be very heavy pressure to appoint men prominent in political life, like Fiorello La Guardia or Frank Murphy, as general officers in the Army he said he would have not one "make-believe general" and held to this line in spite of the clearly stated annoyance of the President.

Thus too when he heard that Wendell Willkie was going to make a speech criticizing the arrangement made between Eisenhower and Admiral Jean F. Darlan, he called Willkie without consulting anybody to say that if he made that speech "he would run the risk of jeopardizing the success of the United States Army in North Africa. . . ." He had decided, in making his case, to put it "pretty blunt and strong" and when Willkie "at once flew into a terrific rage" he was afraid he had made it too blunt and strong without sufficient explanation. Still he ended as he had begun and told his listener that if he persisted in making the speech he planned to, "my respect for him would be gravely diminished." Willkie did then alter the speech to suit the Secretary's demands and, after the tempers had cooled, both men re-established with grace the old relations of mutual respect.[13]

These moments — whether of sudden unshakable judgment or of lingering fretfulness — were the exception and not the rule in the conduct of the Secretary's business. Ordinarily he moved into the negotiation of an issue slowly, clearly, carefully. His chosen instrument was the memorandum, followed often enough by the supporting memorandum and the supplementary memorandum. These papers, solidly founded on data, closely argued, were pervaded by the Secretary's knowledge of the past and his sense of history. In considering the reorganization of the Department he began with Root; in dealing with the assimilation of colored troops he started from his father in the Civil War; in recommending means to administer an occupied province he took as his point of departure Cuba; in suggesting the way to handle liquor on army posts he went back to the regulations of 1910. From "the history of the thing" he led in measured steps up to the present contingency. These means of approach, the weight of the personal and official past, the or-

[13] Diary, Dec. 25, 1941, May 17, Nov. 16, Dec. 18, 1942; H.L.S., Memorandum for the President, April 6, 1943.

derly marshaling of information, the unhurried reasoning from these causes to these effects gave depth and impressive perspectives to the positions taken. They gave support and a kind of awful dignity to what Marshall called "the buffer" which the Secretary put between the Army and the views of those seeking from outside to influence the Army. They served as briefs for the Secretary himself as he strove to introduce system, order and reason into an administration he came to believe operated far too frequently by insight, intuition and the work of cherubs at the back door.

There were times when the extended preparation of these memoranda took Stimson's time and attention away from other things his associates asked him to consider and there were times when the men to whom they were sent appeared too busy to digest them fully. Based, as they were, primarily on precedent, observable fact and logic, they did not always take into account other elements that enter into the formation of policy, nor did they always appeal to others, like the President, who acquired his information and made up his mind by rather different means. But there were times, as in the first conference of the President with the Prime Minister, when a Stimson memorandum became the indispensable agenda for discussion and there were other times when his carefully organized essays became the statements of official policy.

One other thing the Secretary brought to his negotiations — that which, after all the years, he had become. Men who had known Stimson a long time felt that during the war the waters flowed above their source. In earlier times, too often, he seemed under strains and pressures, as though an earnest youth were forcing himself by acts of will and self denial into some pattern of advancement and assumed maturity. Evidences of this had persisted well into middle age. Earlier also, "a New England conscience on two legs," he had at times no doubt walked in the isolating chill of Puritan rectitude, as a Pharisee among the publicans.

Now, after seventy-five years of experience, he had apparently found how it would be with him at any swelling of Jordan. He could therefore forget himself. Beyond the need for further testing, beyond the reach of temptation large or small, fixed in his final devotions, he could put his whole life, without further self-inspection, at the service of the event. What this meant in an administrative way is hard to say. Like heat, it is known by its effects. The President, who worked with him day in, day out for four years, said he could trust him with anything. That, as he told some members of the Democratic National Committee who wished to get rid of Stimson, was "a great thing to have in the War Department in the middle of a great war." Another man, who worked for three years in the Pentagon but never saw Stimson in that time, described how great a thing this was. "You will never get it down on paper," he said, "but every day in the War Department people did not do certain things and did do certain other things in a certain way because Stimson was in the office of the Secretary." [14]

[14] Diary, May 28, 1943.

30

King, Marshall, President
and Prime Minister

I

THE QUALITIES of mind and spirit brought by the Secretary to his work were thoroughly tested in two great negotiations he undertook in the first two years of the war. The first had to do with the development of means to deal with the German submarine. The Army became involved in this essentially naval problem by an accident of history. Twenty years before the war the control of land-based planes had been assigned by mutual agreement to the Army while the Navy was given control of aircraft based on the sea. In 1941, therefore, the Army had command of all the land-based bombers. Planes of this type, the British had already demonstrated, could be used effectively in antisubmarine warfare. In the spring of 1942 the armed forces of the United States needed every kind of weapon they could find to fight the submarines that were sinking about a half million tons of merchant shipping every month in the waters along our East Coast. The Navy in this crisis asked the Army for the loan of some of the land-based bombers. At the end of March 1942 Army planes flown by Army aviators were fitted into the naval antisubmarine commands along the Eastern seaboard.[1]

The fact that planes under his jurisdiction were thus engaged in this important mission caused the Secretary of War to turn

[1] Morison, *Battle of Atlantic*, 240-41; *Eastern Sea Frontier War Diary*, July 1942, Ch. 4.

his attention to ways to increase their effectiveness. He first bent all his energies to get the aircraft equipped with radar. From his cousin Alfred Loomis he had heard of the part played by this device in the winning of the Battle of Britain. By conversations with Loomis and with Vannevar Bush, director of the Office of Scientific Research and Development, in the early spring of 1942 he greatly enlarged his understanding of the possibilities of this device. Another man in the same period gave him further information. Just after Pearl Harbor Robert Watson-Watt who had contributed to the development of British radar came over to this country with news of recent British experiences with the instrument.

Any strange device that alters the familiar procedures tends to disturb the military society and Watson-Watt was the kind of man, and especially the kind of Englishman, to disturb American military circles. As he talked about radar in Washington he was therefore not always listened to by a very attentive or respectful audience. But, among others, the Secretary of War listened to him. What he learned from all his sources of information was confirmed on his inspection trip to Panama in March 1942 where he found planes with crude radar instruments able to detect the approach of ships at some distance from the Isthmus. On his return to Washington he and Bundy took a plane equipped with an improved radar out to sea. Fifty miles away, "out of sight of the naked eye," they picked up "three ships and ran them down." To watch the approach of the plane to these ships "until we were right over them and I could look out at the little window . . . and actually see the ships right under us" was "interesting and wonderful." [2]

[2] Diary, March 14, 23, 27, 30, April 23, 1942; conversation with Harvey Bundy, October 29, 1955, with V. Bush, Jan. 28, 1956. The development of radar was, of course, already well along in this country by the time the Secretary of War became interested in the subject. As Vannevar Bush says in his *Modern Arms and Free Men* (New York, 1949), 38-39, "In Great Britain, and also in the Army and Navy in this country, progressive officers and civilians, working in government laboratories and with industry, reduced the basic ideas of radar to workable form before the war started." After the war began in Europe the

So excited was Stimson by this experience that upon reaching his office he wrote out what one associate called "the closest approach to an order" he ever gave to General Marshall and General Arnold. They were sent off on a flight similar to the one the Secretary had taken, but the results were somewhat less satisfying. The Chief of Staff, harried by the necessity, in the spring of 1942, to bring all the traditional means of warfare under his control, was reluctant to consider anything that would introduce new variables to think about. Indeed throughout the war he never was quite prepared to accept easily at first the contributions, like DUKWS, of the new technology.[3]

But the Secretary pushed ahead. On April 1 he appointed Edward Bowles of the Massachusetts Institute of Technology as his "special consultant for the purpose of getting RADAR upon a thoroughly sound and competent basis." Calling together Arnold, Lovett, Bundy and the Chief of the Signal Corps he put them to work first to get planes equipped as soon as possible with existing equipment and then to develop some new and improved devices. Shortly after, he established at Langley Field an experimental unit, "virtually a laboratory for the study and application of the several instruments which are based upon electronics and which will be necessary to work together for the killing of the submarines."[4]

Within a short time there were results from all these varied

---

pace of development naturally quickened. By the time of Pearl Harbor radar sets were used in both the Army and the Navy, but full exploitation of the device had to wait upon the refinements developed by our scientists in the months after we entered the war. For a further description of the Secretary's trip to Panama, see W. F. Craven and J. L. Cate, editors, *The Army Air Forces in World War II*, 6 vols. (Chicago, 1948-1955), I, 300. Panama defenses, though better than those of many other bases, were not strong. Watson-Watt after a visit in January wrote a "blistering report" of them. Craven and Cate say handsome and well-deserved things (I, 291-93) about the contribution of Watson-Watt, but as Watson-Watt wryly indicates in his *The Pulse of Radar* (New York, 1958), 311, the admiration of the Army Air Forces for his work came after rather than during his initial visit and first remarks about the inadequacy of our radar equipment.

[3] Diary, April 24, 1942; conversation with V. Bush, Jan. 28, 1956.
[4] Diary, April 1, 6, May 20, 1942; conversation with R. A. Lovett, Sept. 15, 1955.

efforts. As early as March, ten pre-production models of the new ten-centimeter radar sets, put together at the Radiation Laboratory at M.I.T., were installed in B-18's that were in service along the East Coast. By the end of May General McNarney reported to Stimson that ninety more B-18's would within a short time be equipped with radar devices and trained for antisubmarine work. The numbers increased throughout the year and in the fall Army planes in Europe under Ira Eaker contributed to the antisubmarine warfare by bombing the yards at Cherbourg and by flying patrols over the Atlantic from North Africa. The success of these radar-equipped planes on their missions in 1942, the contribution which they made to the searches along the East Coast, the precision with which they could follow their targets at sea, all gave the Secretary increasing confidence in his conviction that the plane could be further developed into a primary weapon against the submarine. Based near the narrow waters through which the submarines would pass in leaving or returning to their home ports on the Continent they could be used — not to patrol great wastes of sea — but to search out and destroy the enemy in confined spaces.

This forced development of radar within the Army was perhaps the most brilliantly executed effort of the Secretary in his continuous attempt to make available to the Army the products of science and technology. In the opinion of many of his associates his greatest contribution as Secretary lay in opening up the resistant military to the flow of scientific ideas and applications. His understanding of possibilities, his choice of men like Bowles and General Stephen G. Henry to direct the military effort in this intellectual field, his persistent pressure for experiment and the acceptance of the products of successful experiment, all these combined to exert his enlightened influence upon the kind of war the Army was able to fight because of the introduction of new means in the fields of weaponry and communications.

The achievement was made the easier for him because he

had for a long time followed with interest the imaginative scientific investigations of his cousin Alfred Loomis. It was also made easier by the fact that the brains and energy of scientists and engineers in this country had already been mobilized to develop these new instruments of war to the point where they could be used effectively. But the achievement was made possible, in the first instance, by the attitude of mind he brought to the subject. The nature of morality of course was fixed and permanent; but ideas and their applications changed. Once an old cavalry officer wrote him from the Army and Navy Club that he was burned to a cinder by the "destruction of our fine old cavalry." He laid it to that foot soldier McNair and prayed that the Secretary would interfere to retain the horses during and after the war. To him Stimson replied that some of his "oldest and choicest recollections are pervaded with the smell of horse sweat and saddlery . . . that goes with a good cavalry unit," but it did not do, he told the old officer, to get bitter. "Nearly all of us have to see some of the things we love remorselessly replaced in the modern mechanized world — a world that is just as repellent to me as I think it is to you." [5]

The Secretary of War achieved a striking success in equipping Army planes to fight the submarine. It was another matter to gain acceptance from the Navy for his ideas of how these planes could be used to fight the submarine. For this there were several reasons. The Navy was convinced that the sovereign remedy against the submarine was the convoy system. The unquestioning commitment to the convoy was nourished by the memory of its success in the First World War. And this memory was fortified by the further recollection of the time, money

[5] This assessment of Stimson's attitude toward and contribution to scientific development is based on conversations with Harvey Bundy, Oct. 4, 1955; R. A. Lovett, Sept. 15, 1955; Alfred Loomis, Sept. 16, 1955; and V. Bush, Jan. 28, 1956. For an account of the contributions of science and engineering to the war, see James P. Baxter, 3rd, *Scientists Against Time* (Boston, 1946). Chapter 3 contains a brief account of the development of American radar and its use in antisubmarine warfare.

and effort that had been wasted in that war on the exploration of other means — the North Sea Mine Barrage, the independent search and attack at sea, the patrol system, "the hunting," in Woodrow Wilson's words, "of the hornets in their nests." The suggestions, some imaginative, some silly, some necessary temporary expedients, had never helped very much. Coming too often from impetuous civilians or excited politicians they involved frequently a dispersion of force or the massing of great weights to achieve a small effect. In the end the solution had always proved to be the convoy system.

It was true that since the First World War the plane had been introduced as a new instrument, but the plane, in this context, was not to be taken as an independent weapon. It could be used to patrol and it could be used to supply air cover for convoys — that is, it could be fitted in as a supplementary element in the existing system, the system which had served before. Electronics and planes, no more than the mystery ships or the bombing of Zeebrugge in the First World War, would change it. So for compelling reasons of history the Navy in 1942 was ready to stand pat on the matter of submarine warfare.[6]

It is at least a reasonable conjecture that the Navy was moved in this matter, wittingly or unwittingly, by more than considerations of history. The plane, if not a novelty, was certainly not as customary an instrument for the seagoing officer as was the ship on which the naval society had from the beginning been built. The use of aircraft, not as a subordinate element in an existing system but as a primary weapon of search and attack, therefore posed some immediate and difficult operational problems. Many arguments could be found to demonstrate that it would be unwise to try to solve these new problems in a time of great danger. And if the problem were in fact solved, if the plane became a dominant weapon in the war against the submarine, other problems more remote but real

[6] For the attitude of the Navy toward airplanes in 1942, see Morison, *Battle of Atlantic*, 237-51.

would be posed. These would have to do with the revision of custom, mental attitude and the sources of power in the naval society, perhaps even with the problem of institutional survival in a society which from the beginning had been built upon the ship. Few laborers in any vineyard willfully devise and refine the instruments of their own technological unemployment or the destruction of their ways of life.

Of the correctness of the Navy's views on how to fight the submarine, no one was more convinced than the Commander-in-Chief of the United States Fleet. He was a remarkable officer and a remarkable man. Not since the Army of Northern Virginia had an American military force depended so much upon a single commander as the United States Navy, in the year 1942, depended on Ernest Joseph King. If not the only officer who could have retrieved the physical and spiritual disaster that befell his service on December 7, 1941, he was the officer who did. When, as he is supposed by some to have said and as he certainly believed, the time had come to call on the sons of bitches, he was sent for to construct out of a demoralized service the fighting force that in the last two years of the war became incomparable. He had a cold, clear intelligence that could, in prose of simple elegance, give unmistakable expression to his exact purpose. Behind the bleak and fixed composure some intense spirit burned away, a spirit fed by incalculable devotions to individual concepts of self and the service. Above and beyond all these was resolution — grim, harsh, ruthless and whatever else it is or can be made to seem — but above all, resolution.

These indispensable virtues were naturally qualified by counter-influences. Something of the inflexibility of the will invaded the workings of the mind. Comfortable within the confines of existing doctrine, the Admiral tended to find sanctuary in the dispatch of orders. Many military problems are solved this way, but not all. The war against the submarine, for instance, was, in one manifestation, a contest between systems of information, an intellectual exercise demanding the collection, organization, interpretation and dissemination of many different kinds of data. Since what was learned from one source altered or enlarged the meaning of things learned from another source, there was a place not only for commands but for a pooling of ideas and understandings. Officers in remote stations needed, at times, more from the central intelligence than the limited security which comes from specific orders about what to do in a particular situation. They needed also relevant information from which they could derive a general comprehension of their own situation as it related to other situations. This the Admiral, so long indoctrinated in the naval assumption that information is to be retained as classified, did not at first perceive. His perception may have been blunted by a further consideration. To increase the knowledge of officers on remote stations might well serve to give unwanted increase to another great naval assumption, the initiative of the subordinate. For the spirit that so unquestioningly trusted itself extended trust to others with some reluctance. The urge for certitude revealed itself in an unceasing effort to bring the environment within the compass of personal control, direct and absolute. Thus in the year 1942 Admiral King sought to bring all the disparate far-flung elements, all the scattered bits of information, all the shifting actions of the war beneath, upon and above the surface of the sea, under his own command. The urge for certitude revealed itself also in efforts equally unceasing to hold the naval society inviolate, impervious to outside influence, fixed and intact, within his own proud stewardship, for the future.[7]

It was therefore on a service confirmed in its belief in the convoy system and commanded by Admiral E. J. King that the Secretary of War sought to impress his own ideas of how to fight the submarine in 1942. He began on March 28 by sending

[7] Admiral King's own account of himself and his active service is given in Ernest J. King and Walter Muir Whitehill, *Fleet Admiral King* (New York, 1952).

Lovett and General Arnold to discuss with Admiral King the ways to use aircraft against the "present submarine attacks on the Atlantic coast." Four days later he went to give the President, "whose ideas as to RADAR were hazy," a description of the new devices. Then, some days afterwards, he called on Frank Knox to tell him about radar and discovered that he "didn't know very much about even what the Navy was doing in regard to it." To the Secretary of the Navy he then explained that the devices were new, that neither the Army nor the Navy understood much about them, and that, therefore, "they meet the fate of all young infants." In such circumstances, Stimson went on, it was necessary to do what he had already done, that was "to put in all my personal influence and pressure on it to get the thing to go at all." [8]

Throughout the rest of 1942 he tried to keep the problem of the antisubmarine war before the highest authorities. As time went on he talked not only of the new uses for aircraft, but, as well, of changes in personnel, attitude and organization that would, he thought, improve the situation. "Disgusted at the handling of the matter by the Navy," he spoke with Harry Hopkins in June about ways to rouse the naval officers to the "great occasion." The same day he told the President he ought to get rid of that "terrible old fusspocket of a society man," Admiral Adolphus Andrews, who, he thought mistakenly, was the principal source of trouble. Four weeks later he proposed to Frank Knox a reorganization of the East Coast defenses that would put all the forces — Army and Navy — under a single unified command. Toward the end of the year he went again to the President with the claim that the Navy had failed because

[8] Diary, March 26, 27, 28, 30, April 1, 2, 21, 1942. See also Craven and Cate, *Army Air Forces*, I, 546-53, for other indications of Army pressure and Navy resistance as interpreted by the Army. The quotations cited above from the Secretary's Diary may well give a false impression of the Navy's attitude toward radar. Great and successful efforts had been made in the year before Pearl Harbor to equip surface combat vessels with the device. Stimson's concern for the installation of the improved instruments in planes led him to overlook or discount what the Navy had achieved in this area.

of the "conservatism and lack of imagination of the higher Navy command." To get at the "plenty of brains lower down," it would be necessary to do what he had done with radar, "pick out the best man in the Navy for the purpose and give him charge." This would only happen, he said, if the President himself intervened.[9]

As the New Year opened the Secretary himself went to the Navy. In January he laid a proposition before the Undersecretary of the Navy James V. Forrestal; Vice-Admiral R. S. Edwards, Chief of Staff to Admiral King; and Vice-Admiral F. J. Horne, the Vice-Chief of Naval Operations. To these men he suggested the creation of the "killer groups" that had been thought of by others. These groups, composed of escorts, small carriers and planes, guided by "the best of our electronic and sonic devices," were to seek out and destroy the enemy submarines that hunted in "wolf packs." Since the location of these packs could be determined precisely by the fixes obtained from the radio messages exchanged between the submarines and the commander in Germany, the use of killer groups could not be considered a dispersion of energy. To this proposal the naval officers replied "as usual" that the solution to the problem was the convoy system. At least, the Secretary of War argued, experiment on a small scale was possible. The naval officers thought not; there were no escort vessels available. But, the Secretary suggested, with 169 new escort vessels to be added to the fleet in 1943, perhaps six could be spared for an experimental venture. The conference ended on this note and three days later Stimson wrote Forrestal he was not "hopeful" that anything would be done.[10]

For a year the Secretary had done what he could by the example of his own air force, by appeals to higher authority and by direct arguments with officers — civil and military — in the

[9] Diary, June 7, Dec. 27, 1942; H.L.S. to Frank Knox, July 7 and Sept. 8, 1942, WD; Frank Knox to H.L.S., July 10, 1942, WD.
[10] Diary, Jan. 25, 1943; H.L.S. to J. V. Forrestal, Jan. 28, 1943.

Navy. Throughout that year about a half million tons of merchant shipping had been sunk every month. In February 1943, 312,004 tons and in March 1943, 567,401 tons of shipping were sent to the bottom. In spite of these losses and in spite of the general concern caused by the losses, no great change had been made in the methods of dealing with the submarine. The reason was that, in spite of the arguments of the Secretary, the primary cause of the sinkings in these months was not so obviously a failure of method as of means.

That same fusspocket Adolphus Andrews was the Commander of the Eastern Sea Frontier whose waters stretched from Maine to Florida. In all the months of 1942 these waters were the scene of violent submarine warfare. To meet the enemy in the first stages of the conflict Admiral Andrews had at his disposal — from Maine to Florida — about twenty small craft without the speed to overtake or the armament to fight a surfaced submarine. He had also about a hundred planes, scouts and trainers, almost all of which were either unarmed or insufficiently armed. The forces grew, but they grew exceeding slow. In the Eastern Sea Frontier as elsewhere in 1942 the Navy, committed to diverse actions from Bora Bora to the Western Approaches, met the several enemies on all the waters and in the air with insufficient means. No argument from a Secretary of War, no intervention by a President could alter this fact. Under such conditions the naval officers could say with complete justification that what was needed was more ships and planes and they could argue with a show of truth that ships and planes for the convoy system were all they needed.[11]

---

[11] Morison, *Battle of Atlantic*, Appendix 1; *Eastern Sea Frontier War Diary*, Dec. 1941, Jan., Feb., March 1942. This War Diary gives an extended account of the difficulties produced for Andrews by insufficient means throughout 1942. It may also be said that although the submarines were able to destroy almost at will along the East Coast in the early days of the war, primarily because the Navy lacked the means to withstand them, a secondary cause of the U-boat success was the Navy's initial difficulties in developing an effective convoy system. The capacity of the submarine to operate along the East Coast of this country so effectively had not been foreseen.

As the year 1943 opened, however, the conditions had some-what altered. The supply of physical means had increased and, it was obvious, would continue to do so. But, even with the en-larged forces, the sinkings continued at an alarming rate. There were growing criticisms even within the naval service and the President was known to be worried over the fact that the Navy proposed "to be purely on the defensive" in using convoys throughout the year. In these circumstances the Secretary of War decided to exert his influence by employing a new ap-proach. On the suggestion of Edward Bowles, on whose wis-dom and judgment he had learned to rely, he proposed to leave the Navy to its preferred task of using planes to give air cover to convoys while the Army would undertake a new and sepa-rate mission of hunting and destroying submarines at sea. Land-based Army planes manned by Army aviators would attack at "specific places" like the entrances to the Bay of Biscay and exits from the North Sea. Under general naval cognizance the Army force would be placed "under the direct operational com-mand" of an army officer who would be granted "freedom and initiative" to move at will into areas threatened by subma-rines.[12]

The Secretary proceeded with great care to work out the de-tails of this proposal with Bowles, Arnold, Bundy, McCloy and Lovett. He wanted "to get my own Department thoroughly together and behind me . . . before I took it up any further with either the Navy or the President." When the details were arranged the Secretary began his effort to get the plan accepted. Bowles gave a report to the Atlantic Convoy Conference which met in March to discuss the critical situation in the war beneath the sea. In this report Bowles stated that the convoy system

---

[12] S. E. Morison, *History of the United States Naval Operations in World War II*, Vol. X, *The Atlantic Battle Won, May 1943-May 1945* (Boston, 1956), 28; Diary, March 10, 11, 25, 1943; H.L.S. to Franklin D. Roosevelt, March 26, 1943. The Secretary's proposal was directly based on a massive report prepared by Edward Bowles in which he supported his principal contentions with argu-ment and statistics.

was "a most inefficient procedure" and that, in his opinion, air-craft could be effectively used "in carrying the attack to the enemy wherever he may be found." Soon after Bowles's argument before the naval officers Stimson prepared a letter describing his plan to the President. He and Bundy and Bowles and Lovett worked several days on this letter. At one time they thought of giving "a general exposition" of antisubmarine warfare; at another time they wrote out, in their irritation, an extended history of the "departmental quarrels" that had arisen between the Army and the Navy on the subject. Both these attractive proposals were thrown out by the Secretary as "unlikely . . . to get across [to] the President's crowded and volatile mind." The real issue was whether to make the proposal "big and formal," which might scare everybody into opposition, or whether to run the risk of a small, acceptable proposition that would get "nowhere owing to its lack of strength." What the letter finally said, in effect, was that the Army already had an "offensive anti-submarine air unit" which if "dressed up with the modern improvements" and placed under Army operational command could be put into action six months before the Navy "will have perfected its system of defensive convoys." [13]

With this carefully prepared letter in his hand Stimson called on the President on March 26, 1943. After Roosevelt read it the Secretary of War produced some charts. These charts, a record of merchant sinkings in 1942, revealed with "striking effect" that when the Army bombers began operations on the East Coast in May 1942 they "were effective in driving away the submarines" to other areas. The President "followed the demonstration" and acceded to Stimson's interpretation "with-

[13] Diary, March 24, 25, 26, 29, 1943; H.L.S. to Franklin D. Roosevelt, March 26, 1943; Morison, *Atlantic Battle Won*, 27. General Marshall, who would have the main work of getting the agreement of the Navy to any Army proposal, argued strongly for caution — for keeping the proposed force small and "experimental." Otherwise the Navy would resist "any further intrusion of the Army" and the President, "in spite of his protestations," would not "force [the Navy] to come along."

out contradiction." After further discussion, "finally the President's mind focused on exactly the point which I thought it would, namely that he thought we might start an experimental autonomous air force as a task force on some particular part of this Atlantic problem." The Secretary suggested as "the particular part" the Bay of Biscay, and read the President, in support of the argument, "the British scientists' study on the use of air at that point." [14]

When this was agreed upon the President, "thinking aloud," said, "I don't want to go over Knox's head." He suggested that Lovett and Stimson should talk with the Secretary of the Navy and "the way he spoke," Stimson believed, "indicated very clearly that he recognized the futility of discussing the matter with the admirals." Thus reinforced, Stimson sent off to the Secretary of the Navy his proposal for a "Special Anti-Submarine Task Force" under the command of an Army officer. In a discussion of the subject on April 1, Frank Knox appeared "congenial and cooperative," though he did wonder if the Navy "wouldn't think that we were setting up an independent command right in the middle of their submarine work in the Atlantic." [15]

Four days later the Secretary of the Navy replied formally to his colleague's proposition. Thanking Stimson for his "continued and vigorous interest," he indicated that in time the Navy would have planes enough to do itself what the Army had suggested. This letter was based on an enclosed memorandum

[14] Diary, March 26, 1943. It is quite probable that Stimson attributed the "driving away" of the submarine from the East Coast too exclusively to the action of the radar-equipped Army bombers. The introduction of these bombers coincided with the strengthening of the surface forces in the area, which permitted the development of a strengthened convoy system. Admiral Karl Doenitz, the commander of German submarines, attributes the withdrawal of his U-Boats from these waters to a combination of "strong air and sea patrols and the introduction of the convoy system." See Admiral Karl Doenitz, *Memoirs* (Cleveland, 1959), 250. The same author, it should be noted, describes (218, 232-34) in considerable detail the special threat to submarines posed by radar-equipped planes.

[15] Diary, March 26, 31, April 1, 1943; H.L.S. to Frank Knox, March 31, 1943.

written by Admiral King, who had read Stimson's letter. The Admiral began with the philosophic observation that the submarine was a "unique" weapon which, however, had proved vulnerable to attacks mounted by an "intimate coordination of air and surface craft." Therefore it was planned to add killer groups to convoy escorts when forces became available. As for Stimson's proposal, experience had revealed the necessity for a single information center and for unity of command. Therefore the Admiral was led to conclude that whenever long-range land-based bombers became available they should be placed under the operational control of the Headquarters of the Commander-in-Chief of the Navy.[16]

In this communication Admiral King clearly recognized that there were other ways to deal with the submarine than by the convoy system. Perhaps he had known this all along and had simply waited until there was some promise that the necessary forces would become available; perhaps he had succumbed to the pressure of events and arguments. In any case it is clear that in his memorandum the classic lines of argument had been shifted. It was no longer a question of whether the convoy was enough; it was, much more, a question of how planes when available should be commanded.[17]

To the Secretary of War the answer to this question was obvious. He could point to the immediate availability of the planes under Army command in the Eastern Sea Frontier. He could point to the success of the British Coastal Command that had been organized, he believed not quite accurately, on the same principles he was proposing. Therefore throughout April he pressed both Roosevelt and Hopkins to support his venture against Admiral King's opposition. In the middle of the month he invited Hopkins to his office to hear from Bowles a

16 Frank Knox to H.L.S., April 5, 1943, WD; E. J. King to Frank Knox, April 5, 1943, WD.
17 Morison, *Atlantic Battle Won*, 28, says Admiral King intended to use escort carrier groups "to sweep the convoy lanes and kill submarines" just "as soon as they could procure the necessary ships and aircraft."

long demonstration of the Army's position. Next day the President's adviser called to say he had been "much impressed"; the President, to whom he had talked, would, he believed, "have to make a strong decision on that matter against the Navy." Stimson then set Marshall to argue out the case in the Joint Chiefs of Staff. There, it was said, the General "scared them all out of their wits" by saying that if the two services went on fighting over this matter they would end by producing a separate air force.[18]

At first the pressures applied by the Secretary promised success. Not only had Hopkins encouraged the belief that the President would make a "strong decision" but Marshall appeared to be making headway with King. The General, in citing the "entirely wrong method" by which the Navy had handled Army planes in the South Pacific, had caused the Admiral to retreat "in confusion." Following up this advantage, the General had then talked about sensible arrangements in the Atlantic and seemed "in a fair way to win there." For a time it seemed Admiral King had been driven "to his last breastwork." After attacking Stimson's proposition on April 5 until it was "whittled . . . down to nothing," he now appeared about to give. The Secretary of War was ready to believe that "we shall get our little task force going somehow."[19]

But the Admiral did not give. He said that antisubmarine warfare was part of the war at sea and that naval officers, not army aviators, understood the war at sea. He said that the British Coastal Command was not what Stimson thought it was, but a makeshift produced by the failure of the Royal Air Force in the fight against the submarine. He said that command relations between the Navy, where command went with the function to be served by a group of weapons, and the Army, where command went with the kind of weapon, would be hopelessly confused if such a proposition as the Secretary's were adopted.

[18] Diary, April 5, 6, 8, 14, May 6, 26, June 14, 1943.
[19] Diary, April 5, 14, 28, May 6, 1943.

This argument about command relations was gradually extended in the months of April and May to include a general discussion of command relationships between the Army and the Navy in the whole matter of antisubmarine warfare. This was the chosen ground of Admiral King, for he was a master of the dialectic of military organization.[20]

For two months he and General Marshall sought ways by which the Army air power could be fitted into the new antisubmarine organization, the Tenth Fleet, that Admiral King had created. The efforts came to nothing when it proved impossible to supply in the same organization the freedom of action desired by the Army and the control of operations sought by the Navy. By June Stimson reached the conclusion that there would be nothing "but further trouble between the Army and the Navy over these vital problems of jurisdiction." Therefore, in that month, the Army withdrew from the war against the submarine. Their planes were turned over to the Navy in exchange for planes that could be used for other military purposes. To Stimson it seemed on June 15 that what Admiral King had done was to reject the Army's proposal and then "to hurry hell-bent to raise his own force as quickly as he can, to duplicate our efforts." [21]

In all this matter there were, of course, two sides and two sides with real substance, as anyone who has read the histories of the Army and Navy on the subject must recognize. This account, too brief perhaps, may not sufficiently reveal the nature of this fascinating situation. The problem contains so many different elements, so intricately related — forces available, new and changing instrumentation, geography, the skill of the per-

[20] In spite of all the favorable signs in the spring of 1943 there was, in fact, no chance that Admiral King would be overborne and none at all that he would give. As S. E. Morison, *Battle of Atlantic*, 243, says in his account of the Navy's action in this matter, "But Admiral King had no intention of permanently sharing with the Army what he considered to be a naval responsibility. . . ."
[21] Diary, June 14, 15, 1943; H.L.S. to Joseph T. McNarney, June 25, 1943.

sistent enemy; it contains so many subtle variables — weight of a successful past, service pride, force of character — that the complex truth is difficult to get at. Then, too, a judgment on the merits of the case must rest, in the end, on certain assumptions about things that did not happen or that might have happened otherwise.

From the study of such a situation it is possible to arrive, perhaps, at no more than a set of impressions. The impression here is that the Secretary may well have oversimplified the problem of antisubmarine warfare; he may have claimed a too exclusive competence for his chosen weapon; he may have been unduly moved by an ancient distrust of "the Admirals." But in those critical months he was more imaginative and dogged in the development and more correct in his understanding of the full use of the radar-equipped plane than the Admirals seemed to be. The difference was a state of mind. His attitude was that in a time of actual crisis there was still more that could be done with novel means of demonstrated power; the attitude of the Navy was that within a familiar context everything possible was being done.[22]

The Navy got more or less what it wanted because, having more at stake, it was the more resistant. The Secretary of War, in seeking to use the Army plane as an independent weapon

[22] For the most useful accounts of this long negotiation as viewed from one side or the other, see Craven and Cate, *Army Air Forces*, II, 402-11; King and Whitehill, *Fleet Admiral King*, 463-70; Morison, *Atlantic Battle Won*, Ch. 2. Morison's account cites several instances in which the Army's assumption of superior wisdom and its interest in independent action strained the patience and complicated the task of the Navy. To his account is appended a set of notes designed to correct "certain statements" made by Stimson and Bundy in *Active Service*, 508-18. These notes do correct some details in Stimson's narrative and offer also alternative interpretations for some of the facts Stimson presents. Neither individually nor in sum however do the notes support the conclusion reached that "The essence of the matter is that General Arnold and Mr. Stimson wished to apply their incorrect notions of the British command system and antisubmarine tactics in an area stretching from Newfoundland to Brazil, so different from the British Isles that even a correct application of the British system would have been a mistake." In the matter as proposed by Stimson there was no such essence.

against the submarine, was striking with an alien force not only at classic naval doctrine, but, it has been suggested, at the separate foundations on which the naval society had been built since time out of mind. If Admiral King had not opposed such untoward influences with all the power at his disposal he would perhaps have been something more than a human being and certainly something other than a naval officer. That, when freed from the threat of Army interference, he at last acquiesced in the new technical dispensation and explored to the utmost the possibilities of the planes under his command demonstrates how great a naval officer he really was. In the last years of the war the stream of new instruments, most of them developed by the Office of Scientific Research and Development, that were fitted imaginatively into a new kind of weapon system by the Navy virtually eliminated the submarine dangers to our shipping and naval forces.

In this future success of the Navy the influence of the Secretary of War was significant. By his expedition in the matter of radar he contributed to the demonstration of how useful planes could be in the war on the submarine. By his persistent pressure and argument, by his final threat to establish an "autonomous" force, he accelerated the changing attitude of the Navy. Other influences — the public concern, the accumulation of forces, the growing annoyance of the President, the continued sinkings — contributed also in degrees unmeasurable to this changing naval attitude. At the least his own claim that he "put a new spirit" into what he called the "indigestible bunch of senior admirals at the top" is justified and it does not appear unreasonable to support his further claim for some of "the credit for having accomplished this revolution in submarine warfare." [23]

Perhaps he could have done more. One participator in the long negotiations believes that he was "right on his facts and wrong on his tactics." By attempting to set up an autonomous army command and by arguing from the British experience and

[23] Diary, March 16, 1942, June 15, 1943.

the premise of administrative procedure, he played, it was said, right into the hands of Admiral King who had his own convictions about the British and about administration. What he should have done was to proceed by delicate hints steadily dropped before the President so that Roosevelt could have slowly modified, through his own influence and through Frank Knox, the attitude of the Navy.

If it is difficult to assess and measure the weight of the influences at work in a negotiation that did take place, it is impossible to assess and measure the influences and results in a negotiation that never happened. But it may be said that neither the President with all his skill nor Frank Knox with all his bravery was always effective in making their views felt in the Navy. Stimson himself believed that the President "never dares buck the Navy when the Navy is obstinate." Admiral King was not a man to respond to delicate hints and subtle pressures; more than once he protected the immediate interests of himself and his service from the civilian influence. No more than Admiral King was the Secretary of War a man of delicate hints and subtle pressures. In this negotiation he had employed the methods he had found useful time and again in a lifetime of 75 years.[24]

II

The second great negotiation in which the Secretary took part during these years had to do with the time and place and character of the second front. In the first days after Pearl Harbor Winston Churchill came to Washington to meet with Franklin Roosevelt in a set of conversations that were called, in wistful spirit, the Arcadian Conference. At this time many significant decisions were taken about the structure of allied command, the allocation of material and the disposition of forces. Above all it was decided that the disintegration of strength in

[24] Diary, March 25, 1943; conversation with V. Bush, Jan. 28, 1956.

the Pacific would not divert the primary attention of the new allies from the war in Europe. It was also decided but not so incisively stated that the Churchillian concept of the European war would prevail. What this meant was that a direct attack on Germany by way of France would be subordinated in the planning to the fabrication of a constricting ring around the Axis powers. Germany and her allies were to be slowly squeezed to death by action on such perimeters as the Mediterranean shore rather than summarily smashed by attack across the English Channel.[25]

This view of things, sustained in Arcadia by the majestic presence of the Prime Minister, the more compelling because of the dangers he had already passed, lost some of its attraction upon his departure. When in February 1942 the Army reached the conclusion that the British Isles offered an appropriate base from which to launch an air and ground attack against the Continent in the spring of 1943, the President was at least prepared to listen. Throughout the month of March the Army's case for a cross-Channel invasion into France was argued out before Roosevelt by the military spokesmen, Marshall, Eisenhower and Arnold, and by Stimson and Hopkins. The advocacy of the Secretary of War was persistent and unqualified.

In the first place, the implied concentration of force was "proper and orthodox" warfare. In the second place, the early commitment to this massive concentration would give those in authority the reason and the will to resist the anguished appeals for help from theaters that were secondary to the great purpose. In the third place, the mounting of a second front on the continent of Europe was the quickest, surest way to reduce the

---

[25] Accounts of this conference are given in Sherwood, *Roosevelt and Hopkins*, Ch. 20; Winston Churchill, *The Second World War*, Vol. III, *The Grand Alliance* (Boston, 1950), 645-81; Trumbull Higgins, *Winston Churchill and the Second Front, 1940-1943* (New York, 1957), Ch. 5. Higgins' book, based on extended investigation among documents, official histories, biographies and periodicals, gives a good account of all the negotiations bearing on the second front through 1943. Stimson's own account is in *Active Service*, 415-48.

terrible pressure on beleaguered Russia. And finally, Stimson was impelled to his position no doubt by force of temperament and training. In court, as in the field, he had proceeded to victory not by economy of means, not by subtle pressures adroitly and obliquely applied, but by the massing of overwhelming weight, in argument and evidence, against the central position of the enemy.

So in the month of March, by discussion and by letter, he sought to prevent "further dispersion on the already over-extended world front," to shift from the "rather dilettante pace" of preparations, to take "the initiative out of the hands of Churchill where I am sure it would have degenerated into a simple defensive operation to stop up urgent rat holes," to force "a powerful attack through Great Britain into France." He sought also to prevent the Navy from endangering his objective by wasting too much of its substance in a "step by step creeping movement" in the South Pacific. And he sought finally to counter those qualities in the President "which endear him to his own countrymen" but which militated "against the firmness of his execution . . ." "We cannot," he said to himself, "make our offensive diversion this summer [1942] unless we have the courage, even the hardness of heart, to reject appeals for other good purposes." [26]

Mr. Roosevelt, subjected to such arguments by his principal advisers, reinforced by optimistic estimates from the War De-

[26] Cline, *Operations Division*, 154-55; Diary, March 5, 6, 8, 24, 25, 27, 30, 1942; H.L.S. to Franklin D. Roosevelt, March 27, 1942. In suggesting the possibility of a "summer" offensive Stimson was accepting the most optimistic proposal of the Joint U.S. Strategic Committee which had a plan for a "British-American air offensive beginning in the last two weeks of July 1942, to be followed by an assault with ground forces six weeks later." See Cline, *Operations Division*, 151. D. D. Eisenhower, *Crusade in Europe* (New York, 1952), 42-48, says that many believed the cross-Channel plans at this time were "madness." He lists, besides himself and Marshall, Spaatz, McNarney, Hull and Wedemeyer as the few, some of the "very, very few," who thought otherwise. A full description of the evolution of the planning for the cross-Channel operation is in the admirable Maurice Matloff and Edwin M. Snell, *U.S. Army in World War II, The War Department, Strategic Planning for Coalition Warfare, 1941-1942* (Washington, 1953), 177-87.

partment, slowly came round. On April 1, after two and a half hours of discussion in which General Marshall set the course of the talk while Stimson and Hopkins held "the laboring oar," the President "made a decision" which, in the Secretary's mind, would "mark this day as a memorable one in the war." The decision was to subordinate other plans to the fulfillment of the objective of a cross-Channel operation. The intent was to follow a possible preliminary attack in the fall by a full-scale invasion of the Continent in the spring of 1943. Three days later Marshall and Hopkins left for London to convince the Prime Minister of the wisdom of this plan. In spite of the reluctance of the British military, the resistance of Churchill himself and the "preoccupation in Great Britain with dangers on all sides," the Americans apparently made their point. Upon his return Marshall told the Secretary that after "very serious trouble" the decision to invade France had been agreed upon.[27]

The agreement, such as it was, did not last long. What Churchill really had in mind at the time of his discussions with Marshall and Hopkins is not entirely clear but it is obvious that from the beginning his heart was not in this operation. His con-

[27] Diary, April 1, 20, 1942. In the minds of both Marshall and Hopkins there was no doubt that at the meeting with Churchill and his military advisers on April 14 the British had accepted the American proposal. See Sherwood, *Roosevelt and Hopkins*, 536-38, and Cline, *Operations Division*, 159. Arthur Bryant, *The Turn of the Tide* (New York, 1957), 286, quotes General Sir Alan Brooke, then Chief of the Imperial General Staff, as saying at the time that at "a momentous meeting" the British accepted "proposals for offensive action in Europe in 1942 perhaps, and in 1943 for certain." Bryant himself suggests that this was acceptance "in principle," the view apparently held by Churchill. The Prime Minister in *The Second World War*, Vol. IV, *The Hinge of Fate* (Boston, 1950), 324, says that although he preferred alternative attacks in North Africa and Norway, he was ready to give the American idea "a fair run." He then goes on to say: "But I had little doubt myself that study of details — landing craft and all that — and also reflection on the main strategy of the war, would rule out" the American proposal. For an explanation of the landing-craft situation in 1942 — which was indeed unsatisfactory — see Matloff and Snell, *Strategic Planning*, 192-94. In Albert C. Wedemeyer, *Wedemeyer Reports!* (New York, 1958), Chs. 8 and 9, there is an interesting account of the Marshall and Hopkins mission by a man who obviously distrusted the "trained" negotiators of the British as much for their method as for their presumed intent.

cern for imperial commitments around the world deterred him from accepting the excessive concentration of force implied in the American plan. To this concern were added the deterring personal memories of the landing at Gallipoli and the dreadful warfare in Picardy and at Passchendaele. Before his eyes rose the recurring vision of the Channel waters running with English blood. Thus, unpersuaded in his heart, he wavered in the late spring of 1942, returning constantly in his broodings to the possibility of a landing in North Africa. The President, oppressed by the division between his principal military advisers and his principal ally, also wavered. Stimson did not waver.

In April and May he and Marshall successfully stood off threats to send planes to Russia and reinforcements to Australia on grounds that such a "tidbit of help" would "imperil our Channel attack this summer and fall." A larger threat occurred in June when "trouble that is now on the ocean" came on to Washington in the shape of Winston Churchill. The Prime Minister had been preceded early in the month by Mountbatten who had supplied Roosevelt with many arguments against the proposed venture. On June 17, just before Churchill arrived, the President gave evidence that he had been swayed by Mountbatten, that he was "going to jump the traces" in the forthcoming conversations; therefore Stimson prepared a long, carefully arranged letter to steady his superior. He spoke of England's series of "uphill defensive campaigns with insufficient resources and almost hopeless logistics." He spoke of our own "fresh and unwearied leaders and forces." He spoke finally of "a steady, rapid, and unrelenting prosecution" of an attack across the Channel as the surest road to the ultimate defeat of Germany.[28]

28 Diary, April 25, June 17, 19, 1942; H.L.S. to Franklin D. Roosevelt, June 19, 1942; Bryant, *Turn of Tide*, 317. In the conference on June 17 Marshall and Stimson worked hard to hold the President in line. To the Secretary of War it seemed, however, that "King wobbled around in a way that made me rather sick with him. He is firm and brave outside of the White House but as soon as he gets in the presence of the President he crumbles up." "A few words of

Whatever impression this letter may originally have made on the President, its effect was greatly reduced upon the arrival of the Prime Minister. Deeply disturbed by the news of the fall of Tobruk, Churchill began his talk with the President on June 21 with "a terrific attack on Bolero," the code name for the Channel build-up. Though, as Marshall told Stimson, Roosevelt stood "pretty firm" on the 21st, it was clear in a conference Stimson attended on the 22nd that the President had been greatly influenced by the Churchillian argument. To the horror of his advisers he threw into the discussions the idea of putting a large American diversionary force into the Middle East somewhere between Alexandria and Iran. Churchill followed up with the observation that he had not found "a responsible soldier of his Staff" who thought Sledgehammer — the preliminary cross-Channel attack — was possible in 1942. Stimson, taking himself as "the focus" of these "suggestive attacks," replied that he and the War Department knew as well as anyone else that the main operation could not take place until 1943. He knew also that "we could only be ready next spring by making every effort now to go ahead [and] that if we were delayed by diversions [he] foresaw that Bolero would not be made in '43 and that the whole war effort might be endangered."

Altogether it was, for the Secretary, "a very unhappy meeting." The President seemed most irresponsible; "he was talking of a most critical situation and in the presence of the head of another government with the frivolity and lack of responsibility of a child." Part of this was, Stimson believed, the effect of Mr. Churchill. The two men were "too much alike in their strong points and in their weak points. They are both brilliant.

---

cross-examination" from Stimson served, it seemed, to put the Admiral in "a rather indefensible position." It may be understood that King had at this time less interest in the Channel project than the Secretary of War. Even Marshall himself was not as intransigent as the Secretary could wish. In April he gave momentary thought to the defense of Egypt which caused Stimson to say the Middle East was "the very last priority." See Matloff and Snell, *Strategic Planning*, 200-202.

They are both penetrating in their thoughts but they lack the steadiness of balance that has got to go along with warfare." But the results of the discussion were not completely unsatisfactory. Though the Army was asked to prepare plans for an invasion of French North Africa, it was apparently agreed that the cross-Channel operation would remain the prime obligation for study and preparation, at least until September 1, 1942.[29]

With that presumed understanding the British party returned to London. But in less than a month a dispatch came in indicating that the Prime Minister was "going back on Bolero" and reviving the Gymnast plan of North Africa. Both Marshall and Stimson were "stirred up" over these constant decisions "which do not stay made." The General proposed a showdown in the form of a plan to "turn our backs" on the British if they would not go through with Bolero, and to take up the war with Japan. Stimson approved a memorandum sent by Marshall, Arnold and King to the President in which this proposal was forcefully made. He hoped it would drive the British from "their fatuous defeatist position." Just before the memorandum was submitted the Secretary reread Field Marshal Robertson's description of the planning for the Dardanelles and was struck by the way in which history was now being repeated by the "fatal decision to

[29] Diary, June 20, 21, 22, 1942; Higgins, *Churchill and Second Front*, 125-32. Certainly Stimson and Marshall believed an agreement had been reached to proceed on the cross-Channel proposal pending a review on September 1. There is not much in Churchill, *Hinge of Fate*, 379-88, or in Bryant, *Turn of Tide*, 325-28, to support the idea of such a specific commitment, though both indicate agreement that possibilities for a landing in 1942 "should be further studied." On the other hand, both accounts suggest the great reluctance of the British to consider a cross-Channel operation and their preference for North Africa. Brooke, on meeting Stimson, reported that he was "exceptionally charming," a "fine administrative brain," but of "limited strategic outlook" because he was for "breaking our heads in too early operations across the Channel." The code names for the Channel attack were: Bolero, the build-up; Sledgehammer, the 1942 landing; Roundup, the 1943 large-scale landing. In discussion the three separate stages sometimes lost their separate identities. Stimson used Bolero loosely at times to mean any part of the operation. He also seems to have invented a code name of his own by combining existing names into "Roundhammer."

go half-baked" into proposed expeditions to North Africa and the Middle East.[30]

Three days later he took Robertson's book to the President and begged him to read it as part of the argument in favor of Bolero. Roosevelt assured Stimson he was still "sound on Bolero" but did not like the manner of the threat to go off to the Pacific. Instead Roosevelt declared he was going to send Marshall and King to London to argue out the matter of the second front once more. On the same day General Marshall himself had "a thumping argument" with Roosevelt in which he hoped he had "knocked out the President's lingering affections" for North Africa and the Middle East. Next day King and Marshall left for London.

One week later, July 23, they reported that the British had "definitely refused to go on" with the second front in France. On hearing this, Stimson went at once to the White House and discovered that Roosevelt was about ready to accept this decision, and the proposed alternatives for 1942 that seemed "to be the result of a fatigued and defeatist government which had lost its initiative, blocking the help of a young and vigorous nation whose strength had not yet been tapped by either war." These thoughts, together with an indictment of the British for violating an understanding and a recommendation to continue the build-up for Bolero, he put that day in a memorandum to the President.[31]

[30] Diary, July 10, 12, 1942; Churchill, *Hinge of Fate*, 437-40; memoranda from G. C. Marshall, E. J. King, H. H. Arnold to the President, July 10, 12, 1942, WD. Stimson believed that both Sir John Dill, head of the British Military Delegation, and his staff were in favor of Bolero. A message from Dill to Churchill, July 15, 1942 (Churchill, *Hinge of Fate*, 439-40) suggests as much. For a full account of the threat to turn away toward Japan, see Matloff and Snell, *Strategic Planning*, 267-73.

[31] Diary, July 15, 23, 1942; H.L.S. to Franklin D. Roosevelt, July 23, 1942. Roosevelt made up his mind finally on July 25 after a cable from Hopkins in London urging an "immediate decision" one way or the other. See Gordon A. Harrison, *U.S. Army in World War II, The European Theater of Operations, Cross-Channel Attack* (Washington, 1951), 30-1. Other accounts are in Sherwood, *Roosevelt and Hopkins*, 610-611; Walter Millis, *Arms and the State* (New York, 1958), 110-11.

On the following day he returned to the President to say that he felt in his soul that to accept the British proposal to go into North Africa would destroy Bolero for 1943 and throw us on the defensive. And one day later, July 25, he wrote another memorandum in the same vein and took it himself to the White House. When the President told him he had accepted the British proposal to land in North Africa in the fall of 1942, the Secretary again argued against the idea, and "cross-examined him" to see if the President realized that North Africa would certainly hold up Bolero. Following this discussion Stimson did not read the memorandum he had brought with him since the President did not seem to be "in a mood to discuss the matter." But he left the paper, which ended with the conclusion that "this is a fundamental mistake," for Roosevelt to read himself.[32]

Further reflection did not alter Stimson's opinion. Convinced that the British had "lost their nerve," dismayed by "the evil of the President's decision," he was brought to hope for victory only because of his "belief that there is a Power in the universe that makes for righteousness and that Power cannot allow such a clear issue of right and wrong to go the wrong way." But throughout the summer of 1942 things seemed to him to continue down the wrong way. Watching the forces originally assembled for an expedition across the Channel being diverted to support the new operation in North Africa he found it sad to "see these premonitions which I have had from the beginning becoming realized and I am doing all that I can to make sure that no big hazard is lightly run into." Increasingly disturbed by these recurring premonitions, he could not avoid communicating to the Chief of Staff his "very grave misgivings as to the hazards of the whole plan strategically." So often in these months did he reveal his anxieties to General Marshall that, as he once said to himself, "I really think he got rather tired of me." [33]

[32] Diary, July 24, 25; Memorandum, H.L.S. to Franklin D. Roosevelt, July 25, 1942.
[33] Diary, July 26, 27, Aug. 25, Nov. 9, 1942.

All these pursuing doubts and fears were once changed into exploding anger by something the President said on an August day in the Cabinet meeting. Roosevelt had begun by saying that he was disturbed by newspaper reports that he and Churchill were running the war without regard to the advice of his military advisers. As a matter of fact, he went on, he had never departed from such advice except when the Army and Navy differed on some matter. Stimson gained the impression that he was trying to "prove to the rest of the Cabinet that he meant what he said," but the Secretary of War also concluded that the President was exercising his "happy faculty of fooling himself." To put the record straight he went back to his office to write a letter rehearsing once again the shifting negotiations that had led to the change in the President's unequivocal instructions for "an attack by American ground forces in Europe in 1942." In the course of these negotiations, the Secretary stated, the question of whether the substituted North African campaign was wise was "never submitted to or passed upon by [Marshall] or your other military advisers." And the result of all this negotiation was simply to delay the invasion of the Continent until 1944.

Before this letter was sent Stimson took it to General Marshall, who, upon reading it, begged the Secretary not to send it on to the White House. After a good deal of discussion Stimson yielded to the Chief of Staff, who, he believed, took "an even severer attitude towards the President" than he himself did. But he withheld the letter only after obtaining from Marshall the assurance that the General would not permit the North African expedition to go forward if it seemed headed for disaster.[34]

And thoughts of disaster persisted in the Secretary's mind throughout the early fall. He feared on the one hand that "all the best men in the Army, even Marshall," had become so insistent that the North African venture must not fail that they would lose sight of the "very much more important objectives" and thus further delay the attack on Germany by air and ground forces. He feared on the other hand that the expedition to

[34] Diary, Aug. 7, 10, 1942; H.L.S. to Franklin D. Roosevelt, Aug. 10, 1942.

North Africa might not be strong enough to succeed, and as the days passed this fear increased and was more frequently expressed. On the night of the landings in November he lay sleepless during the early hours of the morning in one of his "bogy fits," shivering at the thought of what would happen if the Germans had made an arrangement with Spain "to come through without opposition and shut the Straits of Gibraltar on us." [35]

When the operation proceeded, on the whole, favorably, he felt himself again free, in the spring of 1943, to return to the persistent support of his great objective — the cross-Channel invasion. There was little or no resistance to this objective on this side of the Atlantic — the Chief of Staff, the planners in the War Department and the President were united in their desire for the invasion of the Continent from the British Isles. But the English themselves continued in their reluctance. In May the Prime Minister came over to discuss the further development of the war and before his arrival Marshall and Stimson talked at length about the best way in which to meet his expected arguments. The Secretary believed it would "be the same story over again. The man from London will arrive with a program of further expansion in the eastern Mediterranean and will have his way with our Chief . . ." He looked forward with dread to Churchill's "eloquent and vigorous presentation of cases that are themselves unstable and dramatic rather than military." [36]

Some of these expectations were fulfilled. On the first day of the discussions the British did appear to try "to divert us off into some more Mediterranean adventures." But as the conversations went on, the President, fortified perhaps by a telephone call from Stimson and supported at all times by the lucid explanations of his Chief of Staff, continued to resist the British claims. In fact on May 17, as he told the Secretary of War, he found himself coming to the conclusion that he would have to "read the Riot Act to the other side." In the event this proved unneces-

[35] Diary, Sept. 30, Nov. 9, 10, 1942.
[36] Diary, May 10, 12, 1943.

The door that was always open

The Secretary of War draws the first order number in the nation's first
peacetime draft. October 29, 1940

John J. McCloy, Assistant Secretary of War, and Robert A. Lovett, Assistant Secretary of War for Air, after taking the oath of office. April 22, 1941 ·

Winston Churchill speaks to the troops at Fort Jackson, South Carolina. In background, left to right: Field Marshal Sir John Dill, General Sir Hastings Ismay, General George C. Marshall, Secretary of War Henry L. Stimson, General Sir Alan Brooke, Chief of Imperial Staff, Great Britain

The Secretary of War and General Dwight D.
Eisenhower somewhere in England

The Secretary of War and General Omar N. Bradley somewhere in France

The Secretary of War with Harvey H. Bundy, Lieutenant Colonel Kyle,
Aide-de-camp, and Major General C. R. Huebner, somewhere in France

President Truman awards the Distinguished Service Medal,
September 21, 1945

Relieved from active duty, September 21, 1945

HENRY LEWIS STIMSON

United States Attorney, Southern District of New York, 1906–1909; Secretary of War, 1911–1913; Delegate-at-large, New York Constitutional Convention, 1915; Lieutenant Colonel, 305th Field Artillery, Colonel, 31st Field Artillery, United States Army, 1917–1918; Special Representative of the President to Nicaragua, 1927; Governor General of the Philippine Islands, 1927–1929; Secretary of State, 1929–1933; Secretary of War, 1940–1945 sary; after several days of negotiation and compromise the cross-Channel operation was agreed upon and a tentative date in the following year was determined. As General John E. Hull of the Operations Division told Stimson, the conference had gone better than in previous years, the British had been "less over-whelmingly successful with their projects" than theretofore. But the Prime Minister was obviously not as pleased with the results as were the Americans. On the last night of the discussions he and the President had disagreed over some point. After a period of deadlock Churchill said suddenly that he would yield if in return Roosevelt would let him take Marshall for a trip to Africa. To the annoyance of the Chief of Staff who told the Secretary he didn't like being traded "like a piece of baggage," the deal was made. Both Marshall and Stimson believed the Prime Minister intended to work on the Chief of Staff to get him to accept some desired "excursions in the eastern Mediterranean," but neither believed he would succeed, and he did not.[37]

Some months later Stimson had an opportunity in London to work on the Prime Minister himself. At dinner with Churchill and Eden on July 12, 1943, the Secretary pointed out the politi-cal danger to Roosevelt of delay or of "further penetration of the eastern Mediterranean" in default of a cross-Channel opera-

[37] Diary, May 17, 25, 27, 1943. The conference was a trying meeting for all. Marshall and General Sir Alan Brooke argued steadily in behalf of their op-posing views. How uncertain was the agreement on the Channel operation is revealed in Brooke's summary, Bryant, *Turn of Tide*, 515. Brooke, in say-ing he got about what he wanted, cited the continued operations in the Mediterranean in return for the concession to Marshall "that we should go on building up forces for the liberation of France at some later date, and not quite so early as he wanted." That it might be later than sooner, Brooke also recog-nized because Admiral King, "the inconvertible," was more concerned with an-other area. Brooke "knew well," he said, "that shipping and landing craft would continue to be sucked into the Pacific, irrespective of requirements for the war in Europe." It was perhaps because this preoccupation of the Admiral's would unfavorably affect the Army's plan that Brooke concluded that King, "the old crustacean," was an abler strategist than Marshall, though the latter had the greater "grandeur of character" (*Turn of Tide*, 504). *Wedemeyer*, page 218, gives his position that although the conference was "disappointing and frustrat-ing" it did at least produce a "commitment from the British for the cross-Channel operation in 1944."

tion. Though Eden spoke of the "rosy" possibilities of stirring up trouble in the Balkans, Churchill renewed his pledge to the Bolero project and Stimson left much cheered up. But upon his return to this country he wrote a long letter to the President in which he betrayed his continuing anxieties. His visit to England had convinced him we could not "rationally hope to be able to cross the Channel and come to grips with our German enemy under a British commander." The Prime Minister and the Chief of the Imperial Staff were too cool to the whole project.

The difference dividing the British from the Americans on this matter was, he continued, a difference of faith. The British believed in a series of attritions; the Americans believed in massing immense vigor and power at central points. No invasion commanded by a halfhearted man could succeed. It was a time for a resolute leadership that would silence timid or hostile voices both here and abroad. He spoke of the precedents of Cold Harbor, Spottsylvania and the Wilderness; he spoke of Wilson who had been forced to choose a "virtually unknown" general and of Lincoln who had to "fumble" through trial and error to find the great commander; and he spoke then of General George C. Marshall. Marshall by skill and character was best fitted to furnish the military leadership necessary to bring the two nations together. He saw no other alternative.[38]

When on the same day the Secretary took this extended letter to the White House the President, after reading it, said that it announced conclusions he had just reached himself. Shortly afterwards, the Joint Chiefs of Staff came in and, while Stimson remained, the President went "whole hog on the subject of Roundhammer" (Stimson's name for the cross-Channel operation) and said he wanted an American commander. To the Secretary it seemed that King, Marshall, Arnold and Leahy were "astonished and delighted" by the "definiteness" of the Commander-in-Chief. He came away with "a very much lighter

[38] Diary, July 12, Aug. 10, 1943; H.L.S. to Franklin D. Roosevelt, Aug. 10, 1943; *Wedemeyer*, 236-37.

heart on the subject of our military policy than I have had for a long time." He only hoped the President would hold up in the conferences he was about to have with the Prime Minister.[39]

Those conferences took place in the third week of August 1943 at Quebec. For two days Stimson himself attended the deliberations and found to his delight that matters were proceeding in the direction he desired. Once just before lunch Churchill took him out on the parapet of the Citadel to tell him that he approved of the project now called Overlord. Furthermore he had himself suggested Marshall as the commander in spite of the fact that much earlier he had promised the position to General Brooke. When Stimson returned to Washington he felt that at last "My great dream seems to be coming true and it is not impossible that the agreement in respect to the command of Overlord may widen out into giving Marshall supreme command in all the European theatre." In support of the dream he penned another memorandum to the President reviewing all the command problems posed by the acceptance of Overlord and suggesting that Marshall should be appointed General of the Armies. Such rank, he knew, would be accepted by the Chief of Staff only if General of the Armies J. J. Pershing gave his consent.[40]

And so the plans for Overlord went forward in the fall of 1943 and word went out around Washington that Marshall would be given the command. Yet once again at the end of October it seemed to Stimson for a moment as though all his hopes would fall to the ground. Churchill, he heard from General John R. Deane in Moscow, had sent Eden to Stalin with a very pessimistic summary of the situation in Italy. This summary, prepared by the British general Harold R. L. G. Alexander, was unaccompanied by a rebuttal that had been written by

[39] Diary, Aug. 10, 1943; *Wedemeyer*, 241-42, gives a slightly different account of this meeting.
[40] Diary, Aug. 12-Sept. 6, Sept. 16, 1943; Memorandum, H.L.S. to Franklin D. Roosevelt, Sept. 16, 1943. Churchill had offered the command to Brooke only about a month before. See Bryant, *Turn of Tide*, 540-41, 575.

General Eisenhower, but it was supplemented by a Churchillian comment suggesting that Overlord might, in view of the Italian situation, have to be abandoned. "Jerusalem!" the Secretary wrote in his diary. "This shows how determined Churchill is with all his lip service to stick a knife in the back of Overlord . . ." The apparent apostasy made him "feel more bitterly about it than I ever have before." [41]

But the plans for Overlord still went forward and until the end of the year the great dream was held intact. What it lacked of complete fulfillment was taken from it at Cairo in December 1943. There it was decided by the President that Eisenhower and not Marshall should have command. Marshall had never put himself forward for the task, had never, in fact, spoken out clearly about his own desires in the matter. To Stimson this was the selfless denial of a cherished object by a man who had learned to rule his own spirit. When the General exploded he was terrific, but he seldom exploded and "never does so," Stimson had written, "in his own personal interest." Thus when the President asked him at Teheran what he wanted, Marshall "dug his feet in and said that it was not for him to say what should be done." But he did add that if he took command of Overlord the office of Chief of Staff should be filled by Eisenhower. For the rest it was not for him to say; and so the President had to say that he had thought it over and that Marshall should remain as Chief of Staff and Eisenhower should take command of Overlord. The General accepted it and went out and told the meeting of the Combined Chiefs of Staff about it immediately afterwards. To one observer it did not seem that Marshall was a "very disappointed man" but to Stimson it appeared otherwise.

[41] Diary, Oct. 28, 1943. Churchill, *The Second World War*, Vol. V, *Closing the Ring* (Boston, 1951) 243-47, gives Alexander's summary in full and notices that Eisenhower described the summary "as giving a clear and accurate picture." A further complication is added by General Deane's own conclusion that at this time the Russians seemed to have lost their early enthusiasm for a cross-Channel attack because of growing confidence that the Red Army could "move into Berlin without benefit of the squeeze from the west." See Harrison, *Cross-Channel Attack*, 121-22.

"I know," he said to himself, "what was the deepest ambition in his heart and it was to command the invasion into France." Any other impression was the product of the General's "matchless power of self-sacrifice and of self-control." [42]

Disappointing to the Secretary and to Marshall as this decision may well have been, it was undoubtedly taken on larger grounds than either man, by virtue of the position of each, could hold in view. It was, if the favorable issue of events means anything, also wise and correct. It also in no way damaged the essential purpose of both Stimson and Marshall and, it should be added, of Roosevelt. That purpose was the invasion of France. Not long after the President returned from Teheran he asked the Secretary for lunch at the White House. To Stimson he gave a full account of the negotiations that had taken place in the remote city and then concluded "in his charming way," "I have thus brought Overlord back to you safe and sound on the ways for accomplishment."

Thus ended the negotiation that began in March 1942. From the beginning the plan for an attack across the Channel had been, as Sir John Dill noticed, the "first love" of General Marshall and of the Secretary of War. Perhaps it remained for both the only love. Late in the spring of 1943 the Chief of Staff told Sir Alan Brooke, "I find it hard even now not to look on your North African strategy with a jaundiced eye." Not everyone shared the affections of Stimson and Marshall. From the first days there were those who believed that the plan for a preliminary attack in 1942 to be followed by an irresistible assault in 1943 was neither wise nor possible. Winston Churchill and Sir Alan Brooke not only doubted, they skillfully opposed. The President, caught in a score of opposing considerations, blew hot and cold and lukewarm. American officers working on the initial

[42] Diary, Dec. 16, 17, 18, 1943; Forrest C. Pogue, *U.S. Army in World War II, The European Theater of Operations, The Supreme Command* (Washington, 1954), 23-33. The President as late as November 15, while on the way to Cairo, had thought that "Marshall should be commander-in-chief against Germany commanding all British, US., French and Italian troops."

plan became, in time, uncertain "that it represented the wisest strategic course that could have been charted." There were, in fact, all kinds of obstacles — political, military, logistic — which stood in the way of successful consummation. To Stimson and Marshall, not without experience in military calculations, it apparently seemed that these obstacles — what Winston Churchill called "landing craft and all that"— could be set aside if the venture were prosecuted with a single-minded, urgent devotion. It may be difficult to accept their assumption as correct; there is now no way to prove it was not. For in the event the men, agencies, services and nations engaged did not come together in a single-minded, urgent devotion to the venture.[43]

The steadfastness with which the Chief of Staff and the Secretary of War pursued their first love had, however, its continuing effect on operations. Bolero, Roundup, Sledgehammer, Roundhammer, Overlord, whatever it was called in its several parts or in its sum, served from the beginning as a makeweight in all the strategic discussions. It acted as a saving principle for the testing and limiting of ideas proposed for other ventures, as a rationale for the conservation of energy and the organization and distribution of men and material. In his dogged, unquestioning, interminable support for his chosen plan the Secretary of War tried the patience of a President, irritated a Prime Minister and even at times wore out his welcome with his Chief of Staff. But he also was one of those, the few, who through thick and thin gave body and continuing shape to a postponed but ultimate purpose, a purpose that served to excite and direct the spirits of all those responsible for our military fortunes in years of uncertainty and wearing doubt.

[43] Diary, Dec. 18, 1943; Cline, *Operations Division*, 145, n. 3; Bryant, *Turn of Tide*, 508; Harrison, *Cross-Channel Attack*, 113.

31

The War Continues

I N THE LAST two years of the war changes took place in the life of the Secretary. Some of these changes were of a kind that happen to any old man. In 1943 Dr. Gamble died and there was "now no one left of the group of four brothers-in-law" who had married the four handsome White girls and "who had been so closely united for so many years except myself." Then in the first months of 1944 Fred Solley, his closest friend in the undergraduate days at Yale, died and then Candace, the sister who had for all his years brought such sparkle and grace and supporting love to her brother, also died. In the same months Bronson Winthrop was brought down with a paralyzing stroke. These matters fitted, in a sentence or two, into the pages of his diary describing the endless negotiations of these years. Fitted in also on June 7, 1944, was the observation that "sixty-eight years ago today my mother died and now that Nan is gone there is no one left except myself to remember it." There was in fact almost no one left to remember some of the things he could remember. Even "a dear old friend" like Augustus Hand was only "almost a contemporary."

It was not only sister, classmates and dear old friends. Around him in the Department there were men who were wearing out. In 1943 General Miller White, General Blanton Winship and General H. H. Arnold all suffered acute heart attacks. Coming out of Walter Reed Hospital one day in December after visiting one of these officers the Secretary reflected that "A great many of our best men are breaking down under the strain of the war." Then recalling Theodore Roosevelt's General Order requiring physical exercise for officers on duty in Washington he took up with Marshall a scheme to get men in the Pentagon out into the open air each day. But the strain of war could not be lifted by light exercise. Six weeks after the death of Candace, Frank Knox, "so similarly situated that we seemed like side partners," died of a heart attack, and then later Sir John Dill and then Pa Watson. At the end of 1944 Cordell Hull took his tired body off, after his resignation, for seven months in Bethesda. That November night, reflecting on the "tremendous loss . . . personally and officially," Stimson felt both solemn and absolutely alone.

In his loneliness he wondered if perhaps it was not time for him also to depart. He knew that some others thought so. There were always reports going around Washington that he did not appear in the office in the afternoon, that he could not get through the paper work, that he fell asleep at conferences. Such remarks had not appeared to trouble him much. Once when he was at Walter Reed having a wart cut out of his back he heard the surgeon murmur to his assistant, "The Secretary has a very tough skin." Stimson called out, "I have to if I am to remain Secretary of War." In fact the skin was not so very tough.

After Hull resigned Stimson invited to lunch a man he knew would tell him the truth, a man who only a year before had thought of seeking the Secretary's office for himself. Did the President, Stimson asked Harry Hopkins, want "a younger man now to finish up"; was he getting annoyed at Stimson's continued frankness and persistence in argument? There was no use in putting these questions to Roosevelt who would only reply with a funny story, but the Secretary "did not want to be in the position where I might be dragging on beyond the time when the President would want me." To these queries and concerns

Hopkins replied that Stimson alone in the Cabinet had "national commanding stature"; that he was wanted, should remain and should speak out as he always had.[1]

This, in the fall of 1944, was reassuring and so was the word from the doctors. His circulatory system was no younger than the rest of his body, but with a little forethought, a little special care, it would serve. So at times he came to his desk a little later; usually he left a little earlier. Every week end he tried to get off to Highhold for the two days without which, he once said, he could not have lived through the war. He replaced a hard-mouthed mount with a well-trained Tennessee walking horse; he selected only understanding opponents for the deck tennis court; he broke up his routines with a week in Florida, ten days in the Carolinas, two weeks at Ausable. Such parings and taperings in a schedule were not hard for a man who had always shaped the patterns of life by force of habit and will. What was hard, as always, was to reverse the course of a spirit which, left unattended, turned inward to dwell on private woes and petulances.

Roused by the concern for a second front the Secretary could, even at seventy-six, work, study, write and argue for weeks with a sense of satisfied, if rather grim, well-being. But if he had to divert his attention to such matters as a conflict between the Red Cross and the Army Emergency Relief over the collection of funds, or the protest of a private at his treatment in an officer candidate school, or the request of Edgar Ansel Mowrer to go to North Africa at what seemed an improper moment, or the one hundredth description by Cordell Hull of the difficulties of working with Sumner Welles and Franklin D. Roosevelt, then the Secretary lost his sense of well-

[1] Conversation with John J. McCloy, Sept. 14, 1955; Diary, March 12, 1943, Dec. 5, 12, 1944, Jan. 1, 1945. About the same time Jesse Jones, who did "not think highly of the President's Cabinet as a whole," told a newspaperman, "There is one great man, however. Make no mistake about it, Henry Stimson is a statesman. They can talk all they want to about his age, but he's the outstanding man in the Cabinet."

being. He would brood upon the small things that frustrated him in his major endeavors; he would develop a "stubborn attack of indigestion," come down with insomnia, feel tired, misunderstood and put upon by meddlers and little men. Since war even more than peace produces meddlers, protesting privates, small bureaucratic squabbles and cabinet members with wounded feelings, there were a good many days when the Secretary returned home in need of special treatment.

At Woodley Mrs. Stimson, on these afternoons, listened to the bill of particulars with sympathetic interest, responding with appropriate sounds of outrage or regret. Such great comfort as she had given for fifty years by falling in with the prevailing mood sustained her husband in these wearing times. Others — Lovett, Bundy, John McCloy, Katherine Bundy, Ellen McCloy — could bring to Woodley their independent cheerful spirits to jar the Secretary out of his self-induced malaise: What worked best was the surprise assault, simple and direct, against the most sacrosanct propositions. Leaving the Pentagon one day Stimson saw Vannevar Bush and stopped to ask him to play deck tennis that afternoon. "No, sir," said Bush, "I can't." Shaking his finger, Stimson replied, "Why won't you play with me? I know; it's because you are afraid I'll trim you." "No," said Bush, "I know full well you'll trim me, but that's not why I won't play you. If you will live the kind of moral life I have and avoid these dissipations, when you get to my age you will be in as good condition as I am." There would then be no need to ride horses or play deck tennis to stay in shape. The Secretary thought this was so funny that he spoke of it again and again over the following years.

Such indispensable contributions to his well-being — the extraordinary comedy of Lovett, the open, free expression of lively spirits and affection by Ellen McCloy or Katherine Bundy, the jaunty brushing aside of small burdens too earnestly assumed — the Secretary repaid not in kind but in full measure. Whenever a member of the staff went off on a foreign mission, Stimson would telephone the waiting wife or drop in on her on his way home with the word that he had seen a dispatch or had talked on the scrambler and thus could report the husband alive and cheerful. When Congress decided that only cabinet members would be assigned official cars, he brought down from Highhold one of his own automobiles for a staff member who could not afford one. When Patterson thought he ought to resign, as he often did, to enter the Army as a foot soldier, the Secretary and Patterson would talk and talk, long into the evening, until the matter was talked out.

Changes occurred in the third year of the war not only in the private but in the official life of the Secretary. Of greatest moment to him was the fact that, increasingly, the purely military matters were moved steadily away from his office. In part this was the result of the reorganization of 1942 which took the Secretary, in strategic concerns, out of the line between the President and the Chief of Staff. Stimson, it will be recalled, never approved of this alteration and never really accepted it; to the end he insisted that he was the "constitutional adviser" to the President on military matters. In part too this change of position was the result of the President's discovery that he liked, as one observer remarked, "to play soldier," to talk with men in uniform without the distraction of other civilians in attendance. But in the largest part it was the inevitable product of the situation. As Stanton, for instance, had found it impossible to stand between Lincoln and the generals, as Baker and Daniels had not been able to fit effectively between Wilson and the military, so Stimson and Knox discovered that they could not find a tenable position between the President and the officers on military matters. They did not have the requisite information that bore on the total military or the total political situation, for one thing. For another, considerations of time and administrative convenience worked against the introduction of a *tertium quid* in the deliberations on policy. Thus, as time went on, Stimson, Knox and Hull found themselves frequently pushed to the periphery of those discussions out of which came the grander strategy of the war; at times, to their chagrin, they found themselves, in their weekly meetings, talking only to and for themselves and, not unnaturally, talking especially in the case of Hull who was farthest removed, with the bitterness that comes with frustration.

The extent of the erosion of the Secretary's influence on purely military matters is suggested in the long talk he had with Marshall on February 27, 1945. They discussed the forthcoming campaign against Japan, which, as Stimson said, was at that date "a new problem for me." He had "never studied it" and "wanted to find out what the staff was doing." This shift of influence did not go unnoticed, either by the Secretary or many others, though it remained for William Bullitt to put it in its crudest form. He breezed in one day to ask the Secretary how he liked to be "a mere housekeeper of the War Department."

The comment was about as fair as it was considerate of an old man's feelings. Though he did not take a hand, as he no doubt would have liked to do, in the selection of the Omaha beachhead or enter directly in discussion of the correct disposition of the troops in Italy, the Secretary nevertheless still exerted an influence on the character of the war that was being fought. This influence revealed itself in many ways, large and small. When General Somervell, "whose strong point is not judicial poise . . . ," gave some indication of a desire to reorganize the Department in such a way that it would become the efficiently controlled domain of General Somervell, he intervened. Admiring the Chief of the Services of Supply as a man with the temperament of Leonard Wood he nevertheless, with poignant memories of thirty years before, recognized the need to contain the General's zealous energies within a sphere of appropriate size.[2]

Then there were the countless and recurring situations

---

[2] Diary, Oct. 1, Nov. 20, 1942, May 20, 27, Sept. 21, 22, 1943. The question at issue was whether the old "technical bureaus," Ordnance, Signal Corps, etc., should be abolished.

created out of collisions between rival prejudices or personalities. Stimson entered into these with the unperturbed incisiveness produced by forty years of experience with such collisons. Did someone, as someone usually did, want to get rid of General Hershey because this time he had at last caused too much trouble by his talking? On the whole the General, it seemed to the Secretary, was doing a good job in an impossible position. To replace him with someone unfamiliar with the task would create new difficulties. Still he was opinionated and talked too much. The thing to do was to "tell him to keep his mouth shut." [3]

There were also, almost daily, larger matters: the problem of manpower, which the Secretary sought for four fruitless years to solve by advocating day in, day out before the President a National Service Act to allocate all manpower; the problem of inflation, which he wished to solve by the extension of ever greater control over prices and the rationing of goods; the problem of the size of the Army, over which he and General Marshall had a real argument in the first months of 1945. To increase the number of divisions as the Secretary wished would endanger, in the Chief of Staff's opinion, his carefully developed plan for the piecemeal replacement of existing divisions in the field. After the two had it out in a "red hot time," Stimson went to the President, who agreed to study the possibility of an increase in the Army. Arguments like this between the Secretary and the Chief of Staff took place rarely in these last two years. More often they supported each other unquestioningly as each pursued his own separate but related duties.

And where the Chief of Staff steadied Stimson by his frankness about all the military matters within his sphere of interest, Stimson steadied the Chief of Staff by relieving him of all but military duties and by his presence. As the war went on the insulation that protected the inner feelings of the General sometimes frayed away and there would be minutes of exploding anger at rumors in the press, at congressmen, or even at com-

[3] Diary, Oct. 11, 1943.

ments made in time past by the Secretary. At such times the tremendous faith each extended to the other would work through the hours of conversation until the General could return, his anger burnt and purged away, to his great concerns.[4]

The Secretary had, in spite of his changing task, some great concerns of his own. They centered for the most part on the problem of how the war would end and of what would happen afterward. To the consideration of these questions Stimson came slowly and, at first, reluctantly. When in March 1944 McCloy remarked that it was time to think about plans for a peaceful future, the Secretary found he could not get "churned up" over the idea. There was still a war to win for one thing, and for another, recalling his disillusion of twenty years before, he could not "help feeling very pessimistic about it now." To achieve anything constructive he would have to "set myself up as a sort of a master mind in this madhouse of Washington" and he felt "unequal to that." The mood persisted through the spring. In April General Marshall asked him something about the postwar military policies and he confessed that the whole thing for him was "artificial." He had the kind of mind that worked on one thing at a time and he was working on the winning of the war. Furthermore, by his calculations, the terminal boundaries of the conflict coincided almost exactly with the foreseeable limits of his own life, so he would leave the matter to those who would have some future to live in.

But then things happened that brought the image of the future into the line of sight of even those eyes that could see only a little way ahead. The change began in the small hours of June 6, 1944, when the Secretary heard on a portable radio given him

---

[4] Diary, June 29, Dec. 28, 1943; Jan. 3, 10, 11, 1944; Jan. 2, 4, 9, 10, 11, 15, Feb. 20, 1945; Memorandum, H.L.S. to General Marshall, May 10, 1944, WD. See also, for the National Service Act: a letter to the President on Dec. 28, 1943, signed by Stimson, Patterson, Knox, Forrestal, Land and Vickery; Stimson's notes for a hearing in executive session before the Senate Military Affairs Committee. These are in the Diary for the dates mentioned. See also transcript of speech of Feb. 18, 1945.

by Candace that "one of the great crises of the world"— a crisis that "played a great part in my own life"— was beginning on the Normandy beaches. This day and the days that quickly followed raised the question of what to do with a conquered Germany.[5]

For two months inconclusive discussions of the question went forward in Washington. By the end of August 1944 the Secretary had drawn two disturbing conclusions from these talks. First, as he told the President, although American troops were about to enter Germany, they had been given no instructions on "vital points" in their mission. Second, he had found around him "a very bitter atmosphere of personal resentment against the entire German people . . . and I am very much afraid that it will result in our taking mass vengeance on the part of our people in the shape of clumsy economic action." [6]

To put the discussions on a more constructive basis he prepared, on August 25, a brief for his conversation with the President in which he suggested a "lopping off of sections rather than a general partition" which would leave Germany "as a self-supporting state." In addition he proposed an orderly process for the determination and punishment of the individual Nazi officials. His purpose in so doing was to separate the particular guilt of the party from the more general guilt of an acquiescent society. He hoped that he could thus prevent the application of punitive measures of a clumsy nature.

Vivid in Stimson's memory was the fact that his father, in 1872, had left Berlin because he was appalled by the arrogant insensitivity he had found in the German capital. In middle age Stimson himself had fought against the German armies, and in old age he had returned to take a part in another war against the German nation. Yet in the fall of 1944 he said, "The question is not whether we want Germans to suffer for their sins." The

[5] Diary, March 15, April 12, 1944. Stimson's account of his negotiations in connection with the plans for postwar Germany is given in detail in *Active Service*, 568-83.
[6] Diary, Jan. 5, 6, Aug. 25, 26, 1944.

only question was "whether over the years a group of seventy million educated, efficient and imaginative people can be kept within bounds" if they were "reduced to a peasant level with virtually complete control of industry and science left to other peoples." Even if this were possible, it would not in the long run be good economically or spiritually for the rest of the nations. "Prosperity in one part of the world helps," he said in remembering his years as Secretary of State, "to create prosperity in other parts of the world." Therefore the Ruhr should not be destroyed but placed under effective allied control. To enforce poverty on a people who had been "outstanding for many years in the arts and the sciences" would not only disrupt the economy, it would destroy the spirit of the victim and debase the victor. In fact "it would be just such a crime as the Germans themselves hoped to perpetrate upon their victims — it would be a crime against civilization itself." [7]

Thoughts like these the Secretary put before the President on August 25 when he presented his memorandum with the recommendation that Roosevelt appoint a committee to prepare plans for the postwar treatment of Germany. Following this conversation the President put the matter in the hands of Hull, Morgenthau, Hopkins and Stimson. As these men began their deliberations in the first week of September, the Secretary was disconcerted to discover that he found himself a "minority of one." Morgenthau wished to "wreck completely the immense Ruhr-Saar area," Hopkins was ready to prohibit the manufacture of steel and, to Stimson's great surprise, Hull seemed ready "to jump all the principles that he had been laboring for in regard to trade for the past twelve years." There were arguments more "difficult and unpleasant" between these men than in all the past four years. Though "of course there were no personalities," they were "irreconcilably divided."

[7] Diary, Aug. 25, 1944; Brief for Conference with the President, Aug. 25, 1944; Harvey Bundy, "Memorandum of Conference with the President," Aug. 25, 1944; H.L.S., Memorandum to Franklin D. Roosevelt, Sept. 15, 1944, in Diary.

Returning from one of these meetings Stimson confided to Marshall that "Army officers have a better respect for the law in those matters than civilians who talk about them and who are anxious to go ahead and chop everybody's head off without trial or hearing." And, somewhat later, he reported that he, the man in charge of the department which did the killing in war, was "the only one who seemed to have any mercy for the other side." [8]

In time Stimson and Hull reached agreement on most matters, but the division among the four men continued so great that on September 6 they took their differences to the President. Roosevelt was tired and distracted; he wondered, first, if James Byrnes would make a good High Commissioner for Germany, and then turned off to his fear of revolution in France and finally to his conviction that the Germans could live from soup kitchens. His own ancestors had lived successfully and happily in the absence of many luxuries that were now deemed necessities. From such considerations the President went on to a description of pioneer fare in the America of the previous century. [9]

During the next week the exchange of views and memoranda continued and out of it came no resolution of the differences. The most irreconcilable was the Secretary of the Treasury who wished to shoot all leaders of the Nazi party without trial and to dismantle the German economy. So disturbed was Stimson by these views of his old friend and supporter that he sought out Felix Frankfurter. Over dinner he outlined his own attitude and asked for his guest's reflections. It comforted him greatly that

[8] Diary, Sept. 4, 5, 1944. Before presenting these views to his colleagues, Stimson, in the course of a week's vacation at Ausable at the end of August, sought out Paul Wolfe, a long-time summer resident, to ask his opinion. Wolfe was a minister and "a very able man." He strongly opposed "indiscriminate economic punishment," and supported Stimson's general attitude toward the problem.

[9] Diary, Sept. 5, 6, 1944. Cordell Hull prepared a memorandum for the President on the suggested treatment of Germany. On all points save those dealing with economic policy Stimson agreed. Hull wished to reduce the German standard of living to a subsistence level and eliminate the German economic position of power in Europe. Harry Hopkins with "minor reservations" approved of the memorandum. See Hull, Memoirs, II, 1608-9.

Frankfurter, "a Jew like Morgenthau," approached this subject with "perfect detachment" and expressed frank astonishment at the idea of shooting Nazis without some kind of trial.

Matters stood thus unresolved when the President went off to Quebec on September 11 to meet with Winston Churchill. With him he took a memorandum from Morgenthau and several counterproposals prepared by Stimson and McCloy. But the Secretary watched him go off in no very confident mood. Roosevelt seemed "tired out" and "distinctly not himself." Moreover he was unprepared by either "study" or "training" to deal with the "very difficult problem" of how to keep Germany from running amok again without imposing measures which would simply provoke the wrong reaction.[10]

In the next few days nothing in the news he received from Quebec gave him much comfort. First he heard —"an outrageous thing"— that Morgenthau had been summoned to the conference; then he heard that Lord Cherwell, "an old fool," had gone over completely to "the Morgenthau proposition." Finally he heard that Roosevelt and Churchill had accepted "the 'Carthaginian' attitude of the Treasury." It was, it seemed to him, "a terrible thing to think that the total power of the United States and the United Kingdom in such a critical matter as this is in the hands of two men, both of whom are similar in their impulsiveness and their lack of systematic study." And there they were in a great conference with "nobody to advise them on this crucial problem except 'yes-men.'" It was at this time that he put down in a memorandum for the President his judgment that the Morgenthau plan would be "a crime against civilization itself."[11]

[10] Diary, Sept. 7, 9, 11, 1944. Memorandum, H.L.S. for the President, Sept. 9, 1944. It seems clear that Roosevelt, worn out, after years of unimaginable strain, both physical and emotional, was often in these months "distinctly not himself." See, for instance, Perkins, *The Roosevelt I Knew*, 390-96.

[11] Diary, Sept. 14, 15, 16, 17; H.L.S., Memorandum to Franklin D. Roosevelt, Sept. 15, 1944. Morgenthau, it appears, was not summoned to Quebec to talk specifically about Germany; he went primarily to take part in discussions about the postwar economic situation of England.

On the 20th of September Morgenthau returned to Washington to give Hull and Stimson an account of what happened. He did it "modestly and without rubbing it in." Churchill, when first confronted with the plan to dismantle Germany, "blew up," claiming it would "tie the British nation to a dead corpse." But later, under the persuasion of Roosevelt and Cherwell, he not only accepted the plan but dictated the celebrated memorandum which recommended converting Germany "into a country primarily agricultural and pastoral in its character." [12]

It is possible that neither the President nor the Prime Minister knew exactly what they were doing in this matter. Certainly the account Churchill has given appears to describe very little that actually took place. He was, after all, under very heavy pressure to obtain economic help from America in the postwar world and the Secretary of the Treasury must have appeared as the primary source of such help. Something of the same concern for England may have distracted the President from the nature of the memorandum he had signed. When, on his return from Quebec, he saw Stimson, "he grinned and looked naughty and said 'Henry Morgenthau pulled a boner.' " Then he began to explain that he did not want to turn Germany into an agrarian state; all he wanted was to save a portion of the proceeds of the Ruhr for Britain. "Mr. President," said the Secretary shaking his finger, "I don't like you to dissemble to me." When Roosevelt asked what he was talking about, Stimson read him parts of the memorandum written at Quebec. Hearing this Roosevelt was "frankly staggered," said he would never use a word like "pastoral," and added that he had "no idea how he could have initialled this." [13]

[12] Diary, Sept. 20, 1944; notes made by John J. McCloy on meeting in Secretary Hull's office, Sept. 20, 1944. Hull's recollection (*Memoirs*, II, 1614) was that Morgenthau returned "wildly enthusiastic over what he had accomplished. . . ." Hull, in addition to his bitter opposition to the plan of Morgenthau, was further put out by the fact that the President had, in effect, taken the whole matter out of the hands of the State Department.

[13] Diary, Oct. 3, 1944; conversation with John J. McCloy, Sept. 14, 1955. Churchill, in *The Second World War*, Vol. VI, *Triumph and Tragedy* (Bos-

Whether the two men knew what they were trying to do or not, there was small chance that they could fulfill the terms of the memorandum. Anthony Eden and his followers in England violently opposed Churchill's decision when they heard about it and, in this country, when the proposal became public a wave of resentment supported those in the government — Hull, Stimson, McCloy, Hopkins — who were against the idea. Therefore the principle embodied in the Morgenthau plan was dismissed from further consideration.[14]

What to do with Germany, however, remained a problem. The task, in the fall of 1944 and the spring of 1945, was left largely to the State Department. But Stimson, principally through McCloy, kept in touch with the deliberations and, in one important issue, acted decisively. The Army in Europe, very successful for two years, appeared to feel it could easily add the civil administration of Germany to its other tasks. Walter Bedell Smith as Chief of Staff for Eisenhower was ready to take charge of the civil affairs in the German zone. To such a solution Stimson was firmly opposed. He sent McCloy to Europe to explain to Eisenhower why a Deputy Chief of Staff for Civil Affairs was

---

ton, 1953), 156-57, says that at first he opposed the Morgenthau attitude toward Germany but "in the end we agreed to consider it." Though he "had not time to examine [the Morgenthau plan] in detail," he did not feel it was "unfair to agree that [German] manufacturing capacity need not be revived beyond what was needed to give her the same standards of life as her neighbours." Concerning Churchill's interest in postwar assistance from the United States, John L. Snell, *Wartime Origins of the East-West Dilemma Over Germany* (New Orleans, 1959), 87-88, says that the Prime Minister "had come to Quebec in quest of assurance that the United States would extend financial aid to Britain even beyond the end of the war. . . ." He then goes on to describe the nature of the accommodation made between this country and England and concludes, "All of this may seem to suggest that Churchill was in effect bribed to accept the Morgenthau Plan. In a literal sense, he was not. There was no need for Morgenthau to make an offer and for Churchill to accept. . . ." But when the thing became a matter of choice Churchill quite naturally felt as he told Eden, "If it is between the British and German people, I am for the British. . . ."

14 John J. McCloy's notes, Sept. 20, 1944. The press, after Drew Pearson broke the story, was almost universally condemnatory of the Quebec proposals on Germany. How Pearson obtained the information is still, as are the sources of so much of his information, a mystery. Stimson at one time believed some person in the Treasury Department, in glee over their triumph, had told the columnist.

necessary and to prepare the way for General Lucius D. Clay to take the new position. Clay had been carefully selected for this post as a man who knew military procedure well enough to be acceptable to the Army and who, as Byrnes's assistant, was thoroughly familiar with larger matters of policy and administration.[15]

In the closing months of the war, as plans went forward for the postwar world, Stimson took positions on two other matters. When he discovered in March 1945 that the State Department was devising a world organization which would act, among other things, as trustee for the island bases in the Pacific he entered his strong objection. We had stood always for peace and freedom in the Pacific; at large cost in life and treasure we had recaptured these bases from an aggressor who had stolen them for aggressive purposes. If we announced that we proposed to hold the bases, gained in painful struggle, to protect the future peace and freedom of the Pacific no one could object. This position he defended, with extended descriptions of American diplomacy in the Pacific from 1922-1939, and with sufficient success to take the matter out of the realm of decision at the conference in San Francisco.[16]

He was less successful with another and larger issue at San Francisco. At a meeting in January 1945 to discuss preparations for this meeting he had taken a strong position against what he understood to be the general intent of the State Department to create a world organization before "we have . . . ironed out the realities." At the end of the First World War, he recalled, there was a proposal that England and the United States should guarantee the security of France as the pillar of Western Europe. When this guarantee was not forthcoming the League of Nations had no adequate foundation. Between England, France, the United States and Russia there were existing issues in 1945 that must be solved before any new international instrument

[15] Diary, March 31, 1945.
[16] Diary, March 28, 29, 30, 31, April 2, 1945.

could have a firm foundation. As an example he cited Russia. She would claim, no doubt, that her own self-defense would depend "on relations with buffer countries like Poland, Bulgaria, and Rumania, which will be quite different from complete independence on the part of those countries." Such claims presented problems and therefore he suggested that "fundamental problems" should be discussed and if possible resolved "before you endeavor to set up principles in a world organization which may clash with realities." This view, maintained steadily in the spring of 1945, did not carry much weight with the State Department nor with the new Secretary of State, Edward R. Stettinius, Jr., whom Stimson considered kind, pleasant, inexperienced, uninformed, well-intentioned, but without much firmness of decision or character. By May 15 he could foresee that his plan of a four-power agreement on realities to precede the creation of a world organization had no chance at San Francisco where delegates were "babbling on as if there were no . . . great issues . . . in our hands." [17]

These problems — Germany, the island bases in the Pacific, the nature of the organization within which the nations would be brought together — were those to which Stimson gave much time and thought when he turned his attention to the postwar world. His primary energy, however, was directed in the closing months of the war to the solution of one other, greater problem.

[17] Memorandum, H.L.S. for Secretary of State, Jan. 23, 1945; Diary, May 15, 1945. It should be noticed that the American representative at San Francisco knew next to nothing, because of the belief that complete secrecy was necessary to insure the success of the Manhattan Project, about the atomic bomb.

32

Second Coming in Wrath

THE SOURCE of greatest concern about the nature of the postwar world first entered the mind of the Secretary before the war began, on the afternoon of November 6, 1941. Vannevar Bush came to his office to tell him about S-1. S-1 was the thing Winston Churchill called Tube Alloys, the thing that became the Manhattan Engineer District, and then, finally, became the atomic bomb. Five weeks after Bush's visit, nine days after Pearl Harbor, the Secretary had a "particularly important meeting" with Bush and Vice President Wallace at which "certain experiments" to develop a "diabolical" new invention were discussed. While these experiments proceeded in the first months of 1942, Stimson served with Wallace, Marshall, Bush and James B. Conant as a committee to advise the President on all questions relating to the study of nuclear fission.

This committee did little save provide a means for the dispersion of the responsibility, which no man wished to hold alone, for the building of a bomb. The actual administrative supervision of the experimental work was conducted by a subcommittee which included Bush as chairman, Admiral W. R. Purnell and General W. D. Styer, the man who suggested General Leslie R. Groves as the officer in charge of the project. Groves was appointed in September 1942 at the time, as Bush said, "when the matter came to the construction of large facilities" and was therefore transferred to the cognizance of the War Department. This transfer placed the matter specifically within the jurisdiction of the Secretary of War.[1]

From that time forward Stimson remained fully informed about and in constant touch with the evolution of the Manhattan District project. He read carefully the stream of progress reports, he talked frequently and directly with General Groves, he had practically daily conversations with Harvey Bundy, who became in a sense his liaison officer between the War Department and the developing enterprise. Though Stimson did little in the way of direct administration, he found during the first three years of the war that a good deal of his time was spent in dealing with matters connected with the building of the bomb. It fell to him especially to devise ways to keep the work going forward within the spell of secrecy that had been laid upon it. He had, for instance, to head off an effort to bring an antitrust suit against the Du Pont Company which was doing

[1] Diary, Nov. 6, Dec. 16, 1941. Though Stimson seems to have heard about the atom bomb project for the first time on November 6, 1941, preliminary investigations and plans had, of course, been proceeding for some time before. The nature of these preliminaries and the part taken by various American and European scientists is told in Baxter, *Scientists Against Time*, 419-33. Henry De Wolf Smyth, *Atomic Energy for Military Purposes* (Princeton, 1946), is still the fullest and best account of the administrative arrangements and the physical installations created to build the atomic bomb. Though I have seen some of the correspondence and memoranda (in the Stimson Papers and in the War Department files) bearing on the history of the Manhattan District, I have by no means seen all or even the greatest part of the material that will no doubt someday become available for investigation. Though I have talked with four men intimately connected with one or another of the parts of the total activity — two of them in positions to know virtually everything of importance that happened — they have, I think, felt free to tell me only a fraction of what they know or remember. I do not believe, however, that whenever it may become possible to declassify all the sources of information there will be much added to what is already known about the crucial subject of how and why and by whom it was decided to use the bomb against Japan. Anyone who studies carefully *In the Matter of J. Robert Oppenheimer, Transcript of Hearing Before Personnel Security Board* (Washington, 1954), hereafter referred to as *Oppenheimer Hearing*, will discover a good deal about the history of the decisions taken in the making and using of the bomb. A useful summary of available information is Louis Morton's "The Decision to Use the Atomic Bomb," *Foreign Affairs*, Jan. 1957. Morton prepared this study for the Office of the Chief of Military History. This essay also appears in *Command Decisions*, Kent Roberts Greenfield, editor (New York, 1959), 388-410.

"important work for us" on S-1; he had to persuade labor leaders not to organize some of the laboratories; he had to cool off the rising temper of Henry Morgenthau who at first refused to authorize a deposit of twenty million dollars in a Federal Reserve Bank unless he was considered "fit to be trusted with the secret" of the uses to which the money was to be put; he had to prevent an investigation by a congressional committee that "wondered why at this stage of the war that kind of a size plant would be under construction. . . ." [2]

He had also, with Bush and Marshall, to go to the leaders in the House and Senate in the year 1944 to obtain $600 million to continue the project. Up to that time the work had been financed out of funds appropriated for the general purpose of conducting the war. By the fall of 1943, however, questions began to be asked about the large expenditures that had been made for unspecified and secret purposes. Therefore in February, Stimson with Marshall and Bush went before the House majority and minority leaders and in June repeated their appearance before the leaders of the Senate. They described the Manhattan Project, indicated its military significance, laid out the budgetary requirements and asked the members of the committees to keep the matter secret. On each occasion the leaders agreed to break the way through the appropriations committees and to keep the matter in absolute confidence, which all but one succeeded in doing.[3]

These negotiations, with civilians, cabinet members, members of Congress, which led to the construction of the bomb under the existing condition of secrecy, represent, in the opinion of some men closest to the Secretary in these years, a remarkable

[2] Diary, Sept. 9, 1943, June 1, Oct. 17, 1944; transcript of telephone conversation, H.L.S. and Andrew J. May, Nov. 27, 1943. The progress reports were presented by General Groves. Once President Roosevelt lost one of the reports in the White House and for some time Groves was "just beside himself" until it was finally discovered.

[3] Diary, Feb. 14, 15, 17, June 10, Oct. 17, 1944; Memorandum, Vannevar Bush to Harvey Bundy, Feb. 24, 1944; H.L.S. to Kenneth McKellar, Sept. 9, 1946, to Elmer Thomas, Feb. 17, 1947.

accomplishment and a further demonstration of his greatest contribution to the war effort. Philip Murray, Henry Morgenthau, Sam Rayburn and all the others trusted him. It was, as those things go, a clean war, in the judgment of Vannevar Bush, who believed that this was in part true because the moral rigor and integrity of the Secretary permeated the entire defense structure. He stood, in Bundy's phrase, as "a moral force against all the conflicting claims and interested parties."

There is a telephoned exchange that supports these views. In 1943 Senator Harry S. Truman had become interested in an atomic installation at Pasco, Washington. He wanted to have his committee look at it.

> STIMSON: Now that's a matter which I know all about personally, and I am one of the group of two or three men in the whole world who know about it.
>
> TRUMAN: I see.
>
> STIMSON: It's part of a very important secret development.
>
> TRUMAN: Well, all right then ——
>
> STIMSON: And I ——
>
> TRUMAN: I herewith see the situation, Mr. Secretary, and you won't have to say another word to me. Whenever you say that to me, that's all I want to hear.[4]

There were relations with men outside as well as inside this country. In May 1943 a Combined Committee, with Stimson as chairman, was created to supervise these relations between the United States, England and Canada. It was primarily a raw materials allocation board designed to provide a smooth flow of necessary material from Canada and the Congo to this country.

[4] Transcript of telephone conversation, H.L.S. and Harry S. Truman, June 17, 1943. Truman in his *Memoirs*, Vol. I, *Year of Decisions* (New York, 1955), 10-11, gives a version slightly different in phraseology but identical in meaning. James F. Byrnes, *Speaking Frankly* (New York, 1947), 259, admits his surprise that "Congress was willing to appropriate approximately two billion dollars without demanding more information."

Few differences of opinion disturbed the work of the Combined Committee in this practical matter but there was a division between the Americans and British on other questions of policy. There was the "very touchy" issue of the exchange of information between the two countries, and allied to this was the question of "political riders for the future" providing for continued exchange of information after the war in connection with the peaceful uses of the atom. Winston Churchill, mindful of the British coal problem, was insistent in his demand to "tack on" such riders to existing agreements. Stimson was equally firm — he "fought tooth and nail," it was said, so "that no administration could commit a future government to a line of policy as important as this in time of war." The Stimson views carried, but only after Churchill had tried "to come in the back door" at Quebec with some propositions from which the British finally withdrew.[5]

Stimson was also active in the delicate negotiations leading up to a complete exchange of the information necessary to expedite the use of atomic energy in the war. In June 1943 he went over to see Churchill on this question. In London he met Bush and the two discussed the position they would take in their conference with the Prime Minister. The Secretary quizzed and cross-examined Bush on "all the positions we had taken on the exchange of information." The Secretary acted at times as a man in vigorous opposition to Bush's views and once turned on him to observe, "That's the argument of a police court lawyer." On their way to Downing Street Stimson said, "I think you are the man to make the presentation." "You mean," asked Bush, "all my point of view?" "Yes," said Stimson. In the ensuing conference it became clear that the Prime Minister knew little about some things in the situation and had been misinformed apparently on others, but before Bush and Stimson left London the basis had been made for the "complete interchange of in-

[5] Conversation with Harvey Bundy, Oct. 29, 1955; conversation with V. Bush, Jan. 28, 1956.

formation between the British and Americans at the level of what each needed to assist in the development of the bomb." [6]

In the Manhattan District there were for the Secretary interesting matters of administration, of policy, of international negotiation. There was also, in the District, the matter of nuclear energy itself. Throughout the record of Stimson's life in these years as set down in the pages of his diary there is a running litany that has to do with S-1, the "most secret," "the dreadful," "the terrible," "the dire," "the awful," "the diabolical." How much this thing was on his mind was revealed by his treatment of congressmen and government officials who came to inquire about the strange rumors they had heard. He would turn on them with the stern injunction that they must seek no further, frequently with the flat assertion, as one of his aides noticed, that he was "one of a group of two or three in the whole world who knew about it." There were of course, as time passed, many more than two or three, and to some of these Stimson talked more about S-1 than he talked about anything else. He would drop in on Lovett, Patterson, McCloy or Bundy at odd times during the day for a half hour's discussion; he would take one or another of them home for a conversation after dinner in the study at Woodley. Then, in the first days of 1945, he asked Arthur Page to come down to the Pentagon where Page was "given an office with practically nothing to do." As the days passed it slowly dawned on Page that he was there to listen to the Secretary who wanted someone constantly by his side, "someone that he knew, that he could trust, that had no stake in the game with whom he could talk about the atom." [7]

These anxious canvassings, these reiterated communings, dwelt always upon the ultimate implications of atomic power. On the question of whether this power should or should not be applied within the particular context of the war the Secretary

[6] Conversation with V. Bush, Jan. 28, 1956.
[7] Conversations with Gordon Grand, Nov. 3, 1955, with John J. McCloy, Sept. 14, 1955, with Arthur Page, March 18, 1955.

said no single word. From the beginning, apparently, he was prepared, in the appropriate circumstance, to drop the bomb. John McCloy thought that at the outset he might have "gotten down on his knees" and made his decision and closed out the issue in his mind. Perhaps he did it that way, but the image may conceal the variety of possible influences at work in the taking of this particular decision.[8]

The nature of the first influence is in part conjecture, an assumption about the conclusions the Secretary of War had reached after his endless explorations into the use of power in the ordering of man's affairs. For over fifty years he had, by the judicious use of whatever force was available to him, sought to achieve saving solutions for particular problems. In his father's house it had been the self-respect and will of a young man; in the courtroom the fully documented case and the prepared mind; along the line of the Somme a 3.4 mobile field piece; at Tipitapa the invisible weight of the country; in Malacañan Palace the powers of office and colonial tradition; at Omaha Beach the massive accumulations of the Army of the United States. Out of such various occasions he could discover that power did not of itself corrupt, that it was subject to the skill and intent of the user. Put to evil ends by the evil or the incompetent, it could tear down or destroy; that was the risk. Directed toward wholesome solutions by responsible men it could stabilize, build up and, if not itself create, at least support creation; that was the opportunity.

Beyond all this, power when available but renounced as an instrument of policy — out of fear or guilt or presumptions of kindness — had, in his time, produced meaningless confusions and then the perilous circumstance. Fifteen years earlier he had found himself powerless to alter what he believed the turning point of modern history on the Manchurian terrain. Ten years before, he had watched iniquity grow out of the feeble remon-

[8] Conversation with Harvey Bundy, Oct. 4, 1955; conversation with John J. McCloy, Sept. 14, 1955.

strances of the thirties. Four years before, he had entered a war as the responsible Secretary of an armed force thrown, by lack of means, upon a long and wearing defensive. Here, in 1945, after two decades of uncontrollable aggression, was an available force commensurate with the apparent needs of the occasion, a force that could put an end to an evil situation that would otherwise continue.

There was a second influence. The Secretary, like everyone else who had to do with the making of the bomb, was engaged in a developing process. Any process started by men toward a special end tends, for reasons logical, biological, aesthetic or whatever they may be, to carry forward, if other things remain equal, to its climax. Each man fully engaged over four years of uncertainty and exertion in the actual making of the weapon was moved, without perhaps a full awareness, toward a predictable conclusion by the inertia developed in a human system.

The workings of this tendency were described by Robert Oppenheimer. He said that there was of course "a great deal of discussion . . . about the desirability of using the bombs in Japan." But the "hotbed" of such talk was Chicago. "At Los Alamos I heard very little talk about it. We always assumed, if they were needed, they would be used. But there were places where people said for the future of the world it would be better not to use them.

"The problem was referred to me in a capacity different than director of Los Alamos. We did everything we could to get them out there and as fast and smooth as possible." [9]

This apparently is the nature of the tendency. The more remote the place or the direct interest, the smaller the urge for the special climax and the greater the concern for the longer future. The nearer to the thing itself the firmer the assumption of need and use in the immediate contingency. Chicago was farther from the bomb than Los Alamos and Los Alamos, on questions of need and use, was farther from the bomb than

[9] *Oppenheimer Hearing*, 33.

Washington. In a process where such a general tendency has been set to work it is difficult to separate the moment when men were still free to choose from the moment, if such there was, when they were no longer free to choose.

The process in question had been set in motion, or at least started to its special end, when the Secretary of War, acting for all those in authority, told General Groves in October 1942 that his mission was "to produce [the bomb] at the earliest possible date so as to bring the war to a conclusion." Any time "that a single day could be saved," the General was then told, he should "save that day." By the middle of 1945 the necessary days were accomplished and the time had come for this particular course of human events to reach its predictable climax.[10]

Yet the predictable climax is not always and beyond all doubt inescapable. Neither of the two influences so far described is necessarily irresistible. Those who are prepared to apply power wisely and responsibly can also recognize that there are times when it is the part of wisdom and responsibility not to apply it at all. And the inertia in a human system may be diverted from its natural path by chance or by the intervention of the intelligence, or of the will or of the feelings. In the decision to drop the bomb, therefore, there was a third influence at work: the interpretation, that men of intelligence and feeling could still feel free to make, of the existing condition of things. Did the situation in the spring of 1945, as they might understand it, justify a determination of immediate need and use?

In reaching this determination there were certain general considerations to take into account. There was first the new weapon, unsettling in the secrecy of its development, awful in all its unproved connotations. There was also the war in the far Pacific, a war that had its beginnings at Bataan and proceeded by way of Corregidor, Guadalcanal and Iwo Jima to the unnatural exercise of annihilation and suicide at Okinawa. That war still continued. There was the consideration that when centers

10 *Oppenheimer Hearing,* 171.

of life and culture — Coventry, Berlin, London, Tokyo, Cologne — had become legitimate military targets it might be better to end a war now by atom bomb than later by the more conventional holocausts. There was, finally, the general proposition, with much support from history, that men controlled power more successfully if they understood it and they understood it more completely after they had used it.

There were also particular considerations in the spring of 1945: the weariness of nations four and six years at war; the difficulties of redeploying troops from Europe; the intelligence reports that, at the extremity of their pessimism, suggested that Japan might be capable of "several years of resistance . . ."; the uncertainty of the effect of the experimental weapon, either in demonstration or in actual use; and finally the estimated casualties, a half a million to a million, in the projected invasion of Japan.[11]

Not all men who could claim a legitimate concern with the

[11] *Active Service*, 617-19. A fuller survey of the situation is contained in a summary, prepared for Stimson in the War Department in 1946, of the strategic plans and military prognostications existing in the spring of 1945. A copy of this summary is in the Stimson Papers. Morton, "The Decision to Use the Atomic Bomb," 20, says that intelligence estimates on June 30 reported that "there are as yet no indications that [the Japanese] are ready to accept" unconditional surrender. On the other hand they might surrender "at any time" if proper terms were offered, such terms to include the retention of the Emperor. The estimate of casualties given here is Stimson's own. Other estimates are lower, varying from "several hundred thousand" to the half million General Marshall predicted to the President. See Truman, *Memoirs*, I, 417. P. M. S. Blackett, *Fear, War and the Bomb* (New York, 1949), 132-34, appears to imply that the bombs may have been used in an attempt to forestall Russia's entry into the war. I have found no real evidence in support of this implication. I have seen a War Department memorandum, undated and without the author's name, which appears to be a rough agenda for a discussion of Russia's position and attitude in the late spring of 1945. As one of several considerations — trusteeships, the advantages to us of a stable Japan in dealing with Russia — it also lists the effect of S-1, pointing out the advantages to us if Russia did not have her entry into the war as a bargaining point. This memorandum suggests a possible discussion of all reasonable considerations attendant on the bomb. It does not suggest the bomb was dropped to forestall Russia's entry and nowhere else have I found evidence of such a suggestion. The exclusive concern of those involved, on the evidence I have seen, was the closing of the Japanese war as an end in itself.

matter were in a position to take all the considerations, general and particular, into account and not all of them looked at the matter from the same point of view. Some, in the spring and early summer of 1945, concluded that the bomb should be used in a demonstration on an uninhabited atoll; some concluded that it should be used only after a preliminary and specific warning that would contain "some information about the nature of atomic power"; some concluded that the bomb should not be used at all.[12]

The Secretary of War wanted the final decision to rest upon an orderly canvass of the available evidence and a reasoned interpretation of the existing considerations. He wanted also to have prepared an explanation to be made public at the time the bomb was used, if it were used. Finally he wanted to have ready a set of proposals for the national and international control of atomic energy when the war was over. These natural desires assumed a new significance when on April 12 the President suddenly died in his house at Warm Springs. Into his place came Harry S. Truman, an untried quantity, ignorant of the existence of the atomic project until, on his assumption of office, the Secretary of War told him. To provide the orderly canvass of the situation, to assist the new President in his enormous decision, the Secretary took the following step at the end of April, ten weeks before the first bomb test: he appointed a committee "charged with the function of advising the President on

---

[12] Byrnes, *Speaking Frankly*, 261; *Oppenheimer Hearing*, 34. It should be noticed that many of the objections to dropping the bomb or to dropping it without warning were most clearly stated after the recommendation to drop it had been made to the President on June 1. See for instance the Franck Report, submitted to the Secretary of War on June 11, 1945, and published in the *Bulletin of the Atomic Scientists* (hereafter referred to as *BAS*) May 1946. For an excellent description of the various steps taken by scientists at Chicago to influence the policies governing the use of atomic energy both for military purposes in the war and for constructive purposes after the war, see Alice K. Smith, "Behind the Decision to Use the Atomic Bomb: Chicago 1944-1945," *BAS*, Oct. 1958. It may be noticed here also that officers in the Air Force believed Japan could be reduced to the point of surrender without invasion or use of the atomic bomb by using conventional means of air bombardment. See Ralph E. Lapp, *The New Force* (New York, 1953), 46-47.

the various questions raised by our apparently imminent success in developing an atomic weapon." The "first and greatest problem" for this committee, he later said, "was the decision on the use of the bomb — should it be used against the Japanese, and if so, in what manner." [13]

This body was called the Interim Committee. Members, besides Stimson who served as chairman, were George L. Harrison, the deputy chairman, James F. Byrnes, Ralph Bard, William L. Clayton, Vannevar Bush, Karl T. Compton and James B. Conant. Three of these members — Bush, Compton, Conant — were men of science who had followed the development of the weapon from the beginning. James F. Brynes had known of the existence of the Manhattan District since 1943. George L. Harrison had come into the Pentagon before the Interim Committee was fully organized to work specifically on the problem of using and controlling atomic energy. William Clayton, Assistant Secretary of State, probably knew very little about the subject before his appointment to the committee and Ralph Bard, Undersecretary of the Navy, certainly knew nothing about the subject before he attended the first meeting of the committee. [14]

To assist this body an advisory panel of scientists was appointed. The members were J. Robert Oppenheimer, Arthur Compton, Ernest Lawrence and Enrico Fermi. All four were physicists who had worked at one place or another on the development of the bomb. [15]

The Interim Committee held its first meeting at 10:00 in the morning on May 9, 1945. All members were present except James B. Conant. General Groves and Harvey Bundy also attended the session, which began with an explanation by the Secretary of the "basic facts." There followed one hour of "talk over the whole subject" before Stimson went off to meet with

13 *Active Service*, 616-17. Diary, March 15, April 25, 1945; Memorandum, H.L.S. for the President, April 25, 1945.
14 *BAS*, Oct. 1958, 295, 297.
15 For a description of the work of the Advisory Panel, see Arthur Holly Compton, *Atomic Quest: A Personal Narrative* (New York, 1956), Ch. 4. A wonderful brief account, informally given from memory by Robert Oppenheimer, is in *Oppenheimer Hearing*, 34.

a senatorial committee that had just returned from an inspection of Nordhausen, Dachau and Buchenwald. The others remained while Groves and Harrison took them "further into details" of the subject.[16]

Three weeks later the Interim Committee met again for two days on May 31 and June 1. On the first day the members were joined, from time to time, by the men on the advisory panel of scientists. On the second day, in the morning, the presidents of four companies that had taken part in the manufacture of the bomb attended the session. At the end of that day, June 1, the committee recommendations on the use of the bomb were presented to President Truman.[17]

Exactly what took place in the two days of discussion is not known. No official record of the proceedings has been made public. There are, however, accounts available — some general statements, some small fragments — taken in later years from the memory of a few men who participated in the meetings.

The Secretary of War gave two descriptions of what happened. He said that the talk "ranged over the whole field of atomic energy, in its political, military and scientific aspects. . . ." The members "carefully considered such alternatives [to dropping the bomb] as a detailed advance warning or a demonstration in some uninhabited area." The Advisory Panel of scientists "reported that 'We can propose no technical demonstration likely to bring an end to the war; we see no acceptable alternative to direct military use.'" At the end of the two days the committee recommended that the bomb should be used as soon as possible in the war with Japan, without warning, and against a target that would reveal its "devastating strength." [18]

Arthur Compton in his account recalled that the meeting of

16 Diary, May 9, 1945.
17 Diary, May 31, June 1, 1945; Truman, *Memoirs*, I, 419. Though June 1 is the date usually given in accounts of the episode as the date when the decision was transmitted to Truman, it is possible that the correct date is a few days later.
18 H.L.S., "The Decision to Use the Atomic Bomb," *Harper's Magazine*, Feb. 1947, 100; *Active Service*, 617.

May 31 was "the occasion for [the] fullest consideration of whether and in what manner the bomb should be used." He said further that throughout "the morning's discussions it seemed to be a foregone conclusion that the bomb would be used." At lunch that day he raised with the Secretary the question of arranging "a nonmilitary demonstration of the bomb in such a manner that the Japanese would be so impressed that they would see the uselessness of continuing the war." Stimson then opened the subject for a general discussion of those at the lunch table. One proposal after another was, in the course of debate, discarded. Then, after the meal, the Interim Committee went into executive session without the members of the Advisory Panel.[19]

Ralph Bard has recalled no "intensive exploration" of the question of the use of the bomb at the meeting on May 31. Indeed he came away with the impression that the committee "approved a decision that had already been made." Robert Oppenheimer's memory of the occasion supports this impression. He could not recall a discussion about the use of the bomb on that day and he is certain that "the recommendations which the Committee adopted on June 1st were not based upon discussions with the Panel at that first meeting." [20]

To these accounts based upon later recollection may be added a matter of fact. The report in which the Advisory Panel said it could propose no acceptable alternative to direct military use was submitted to the Interim Committee on June 16, 1945. This was two weeks after the committee had recommended to the President the dropping of the bomb.

Two questions appear to be raised by the conflicts of testimony. Any answers, based as they must be upon insufficient evidence, must be provisional. What most men remember about any event is transmuted by time; what any man would remember of such an occasion must be subject to special transforming in-

[19] Compton, *Atomic Quest*, 220, 238.
[20] *BAS*, Oct. 1958, 297.

fluences. The first question is whether the Interim Committee really did consider possible alternatives in the way of a demonstration or warning on May 31. The date of the opinion of the Advisory Panel suggests that it may not have done so; the recollections of Bard and Oppenheimer suggest that it did not do so, at least in their presence. It will be remembered that Arthur Compton said he raised the subject at luncheon. Mr. Bard had left at the end of the committee's morning meeting to attend ceremonies at which Mrs. Frank Knox was given the Medal of Merit that had been awarded to her husband. After the ceremonies Mr. Bard was the host at a luncheon in honor of Mrs. Knox. Furthermore, it will also be remembered, the Interim Committee after luncheon went into executive session without the members of the Advisory Panel. At the end of the session the committee asked the Advisory Panel to render an opinion about the possibility of a demonstration, a request which led to the panel report submitted on June 16.

It therefore seems that there were times, when neither Bard nor Oppenheimer were present, when the men on the Interim Committee could have discussed alternatives to dropping the bomb and from the descriptions supplied by Stimson and Compton it seems there were times when they in fact did. It remains true that the formal presentation by what was called the Franck Committee of the reasons why the bomb should not be used and the Advisory Panel's opinion on demonstration were not received and therefore not considered until two weeks after the committee recommendation to drop the bombs was made.[21]

The second, and larger, question is whether the decision to

[21] Diary, May 9, 1945; Compton, *Atomic Quest*, 238-39. One should certainly read, in connection with this examination of the two questions propounded, Mrs. Smith's painstaking article in the *BAS*, Oct. 1958. The questions examined would not have been raised in the form here presented had it not been for her investigation. James B. Conant, writing to McGeorge Bundy, Nov. 30, 1946, says on this matter, "I have in mind the fact that the Interim Committee and its advisers certainly considered the practicability of (*a*) giving a warning, and (*b*) giving a demonstration."

drop the bomb had, in effect, been reached before the committee met on May 31. Ralph Bard has said he received the impression that the committee "approved a decision that had already been made." Arthur Compton has said that in the morning's discussion "it seemed to be a foregone conclusion that the bomb would be used." Bard received his impression, he recalled, at his first meeting of the committee. It does not reduce the force of this impression to add that the first meeting took place May 9 and not May 31 as he remembered. Nor does it reduce the force of Arthur Compton's impression to add that after the morning meeting he raised the subject of alternative methods.[22]

Indirectly what these men recall is supported by the entry in Stimson's diary for the day in question. He describes only the committee discussion that dealt with the future control of atomic energy after the war. And there is further support for their impressions in the phraseology of earlier entries in the diary. On May 30, before the committee met, he says, for instance, that he and Bundy, Harrison, Groves and Marshall "talked over the subject very thoroughly of how we should use this implement in respect to Japan." On May 10 he said that he and General Marshall had talked on "rather deep matters — the coming program of strategy for the operations in the Pacific where I wanted to find out whether or not we couldn't hold matters off from very heavy involvement in casualties until after we had tried out S-1." On March 15 he had told the President that certain matters about the future control of atomic energy should be "settled before the first projectile is used. . . ."

"Tried out," "how . . . use . . . in respect to," even "before . . . is used" are not clear indications of a firm decision. They are not incontrovertible evidence even when put together with the fact that General Marshall, the Secretary and Gen-

[22] *BAS*, Oct. 1958, 297. Stimson's Diary, May 9, 1945, is the authority for Bard's attendance on May 9. Bard's confusion over dates merely puts him on an equal footing with almost everyone else who is asked to remember precisely what took place in this month.

eral Groves, like any sensible military planners, had "carefully worked out" the "strategy for the military use of the bomb" some weeks before the Interim Committee met. But taking all things together it is reasonable to suppose that the Secretary of War was, in the first months of 1945, acting within a developing assumption that the bomb would be used. It is also reasonable to suppose that the men working with him were acting upon the same kind of assumption.[23]

In the months immediately preceding May 31 six of the eight men on the Interim Committee had lived with the knowledge of atomic energy for a long time, five of them had been directly at work on the development of the project. They had lived with and continued in the spring of 1945 to live ever more intensely with all the surrounding information and attitudes — the intelligence reports, the continuing war, the stated doubts of some that the bomb would go off, the stated doubts of others that it should be used at all, the coming invasion plans and the projected casualties. All these things — some, facts; some, opinions formally presented; some, attitudes informally talked about — had been in the environment in the spring of 1945. In varying states of prominence and priority, they were forced into the observation of those involved, by the pressures created as the environment closed down upon the point of decision. No doubt those involved were moved by the inertia in any human system, but no doubt too they were being moved toward a conclusion by the continuing action of their intelligences and feelings upon the evidence presented.[24]

[23] Diary, May 10, 30, 31, June 1, 1945; Compton, *Atomic Quest*, 220-21.
[24] Admiral Leahy, among others, had expressed doubt that the bomb would work. So had another government official described in the Diary, March 15, 1945, as James Dunn, though this seems almost certainly an error in transcription. Whoever the official was, he expressed the fear that the President had been sold "a lemon." Some indication of why the men involved would have tended at any time before June 1 as well as afterward to resist the proposal of a demonstration can be found in J. B. Conant's letter to McGeorge Bundy, Nov. 30, 1946. He said, ". . . even the success of the test at Alamogordo Proving Grounds did not give 100% assurance that the first bombs used in combat would actually be successful; that there was certainly in the minds of the In-

They did not go into the meetings of the Interim Committee on May 31 cold. They had attitudes already developed — independently and by informal collaboration on a common task. The Interim Committee was appointed to give their opinions ordered form, some corporate structure, as the need for a defined decision was presented. The effort to give the decision this kind of support, to invest it with the sanction of a formal judgment reached by orderly procedures, a canvass and resolution of all considerations at some given moment in time, was the expression of the natural desire to make all human acts and decisions appear not only wise but the product of system and right reason. The Interim Committee, insofar as the special matter of using the bomb was concerned, was, in a sense, a symbolic act to demonstrate with what care this enormous conclusion had been considered. That in its actual proceedings, as so far reported, there should be some real ambiguity is less surprising than the fact that in its symbolism it should have so closely verified, all things considered, the actual process of decision.

In this process of decision the Interim Committee acted technically in an advisory capacity. The responsibility for the recommendation remained with Stimson alone just as the responsibility for the ultimate decision rested on President Truman. The recommendation as given in the first week of June was not, in the immediately ensuing weeks, accepted without further consideration. On June 18, for instance, there was a meeting of the Joint Chiefs of Staff at the White House to discuss the strategy to be used in ending the Japanese war. On this question

terim Committee or at least those most cognizant with the development of the weapon a conviction that it was only a matter of probability that the first bombs used would be successful." One of the difficult technical problems was the actuation of the bomb at a thousand feet by an untested mechanism. Nothing, in Conant's words, "would have been more disastrous than a prior warning followed by a dud, and this was a very real possibility." Byrnes, *Speaking Frankly*, 261-62, says that before recommending the use of the bomb the members of the Interim Committee had considered both a prior warning and a demonstration. The reason for eliminating the first was the fear the Japanese might move American prisoners of war into the area; the reason for the elimination of the second was the one described by Conant.

there was still a division of opinion. Officers of the Navy tended to feel that Japan could be reduced by naval blockade in support of intensive aerial bombardment; officers in the Army favored the invasion first of Kyushu and then of Honshu as the surest means of victory. At the conference on June 18 General Marshall made the case for invasion, which President Truman accepted. But the President was anxious to consider all possibilities. Toward the end of the meeting he asked McCloy what views he had. McCloy had gone to the White House to represent the Secretary of War who, the night before, had reported that he felt so ill and used up that he would send his Assistant Secretary instead. But, in the event, Stimson unexpectedly appeared and so, during the discussion, McCloy remained silent. On the direct appeal of the President and in the understanding that Stimson always wished him to speak his own mind, McCloy then raised the possibility of a political solution, an offering of terms that might liquidate the conflict without further extensive military effort. He spoke then also of the new force — the bomb. Every man in the room was aware of the existence and meaning of the new force, which in all the earlier discussion had remained not only undefined but unmentioned. When McCloy spoke the word that had so far been left unspoken there was a sense of silence and of shock. As the Assistant Secretary finished with his line of argument the President expressed his great interest in the possibility of a political solution, but after further investigation of the subject the proposal was laid aside. Laid aside also was the suggestion to warn the Japanese that the country had an atomic bomb before the bomb was dropped. Governing in the decision perhaps was the uncertainty that the "thing would go off." So in the end the recommendation of the Interim Committee was accepted and acted upon.[25]

Whether or not the recommendation or the action taken upon it was wise or necessary is still a matter of debate. It is now

[25] Conversation with John J. McCloy, Oct. 15, 1959. Morton, "The Decision to Use the Atomic Bomb," gives a brief account of the June 18 meeting.

known that the intelligence reports did not fully reflect the state of things in Japan with absolute accuracy. There was, as far as these things can be assessed, a greater inclination to surrender than had been supposed. Furthermore, in the opinion of men who, after the war, conducted the United States Strategic Bombing Survey, Japan would have succumbed without invasion and without the atom bomb to aerial bombardment by conventional means. Findings of this kind can shift the lines of argument in the continuing debate; they can increase the irony invested, as in most human decisions, in this particular decision. They cannot be taken to alter the situation in which the Secretary of War actually found himself. In the context of a continuing war, supported by informed advisers insofar as anyone in this matter was informed, and from data insufficient but the best available, he decided the bomb was needed and should be used.[26]

If, as suggested above, there was in the proceedings of the Interim Committee some ambiguity, there was in the early spring of 1945 much more that was also paradoxical. In those months, for instance, the Secretary of War was calculating the moment when the bomb should be needed and used. But he was also try-

[26] The summary of strategic plans cited in footnote 11 reports that in July 1945 the most optimistic military estimate of the date of Japan's surrender, given by General Arnold at Potsdam, was October 1945; the pessimistic estimate "anticipated several years of resistance." In the planners' minds in the summer of 1945 was the recent error in predicting Germany's collapse in the fall of 1944. The summary indicates the general feeling that the immediate use of the weapon would shorten the war at least by months and possibly by years. Robert J. C. Butow, *Japan's Decision to Surrender* (Stanford, 1954), 231, concludes, on the basis of later and fuller evidence, that the Japanese "decision — in embryo — had long been taking shape." What the bomb did was to create an "unusual atmosphere" in which the Emperor could emerge to work a "political miracle." In support of the conclusion that conventional bombardment would have achieved much the same end in much the same time, it may be said that the B-29's were putting the equivalent of one atomic bomb into Japan with their TNT raids every two or three days. It should be recognized that the decision taken by the Interim Committee was not final in the sense that the President could, if he chose, disregard it or change it as conditions changed. In the next two months there were, in fact, further discussions on the matter, but Stimson's recommendations remained unchanged by any of the arguments raised. Though Truman has emphasized that the decision was his alone, it is a fair conjecture that Stimson's opinion weighed heavily with him.

ing to end the war before the bomb was used by seeking to modify the intransigent condition, imposed by others, concerning the elimination of the Japanese Emperor. In pursuing this purpose he was almost alone among those in authority. Right down to the final message before the bomb was dropped, the message sent to Japan from Potsdam, he sought in every way he could think of to qualify the terms by proposing "a constitutional monarchy under her present dynasty." To Cordell Hull this proposal seemed "too much like appeasement of Japan" and so it seemed to the then Secretary of State James Byrnes. The view of the Secretary of War was not accepted in July of 1945 or before, though it ultimately prevailed. In the opinion of one thoroughly informed investigator, "Although it cannot be proved, it is possible that the Japanese government would have accepted the Potsdam Proclamation immediately had Secretary Stimson's reference to the imperial structure been retained." [27]

There was further paradox in these months. When the B-29's went out on their first raids into Japan the Secretary of War, against much opposition, struck from the target list the city of Kyoto, a cultural and religious as well as an industrial center. He also extracted from Robert Lovett a promise that the B-29's would conduct "only precision bombing" against purely military objectives. His aim, he said, was to maintain "the reputation of the United States for fair play and humanitarianism" because that reputation was "the world's biggest asset for peace

---

[27] H.L.S., "Memorandum for the President," July 2, 1945; Joseph Grew to H.L.S., Feb. 12, 1947; Truman, *Memoirs*, I, 428; Hull, *Memoirs*, II, 1591-94; Butow, *Japan's Decision*, 140. Grew was at the beginning the principal architect of the effort to continue the modified imperial structure. He had support from Eugene Dooman and Arthur Ballantine in the State Department. What he wished was to state his proposition to the Japanese in May, which seemed too early to most officials, including Stimson. Truman says (416) that he believed the Grew proposal a "sound idea," and apparently Byrnes was at least thinking of the idea until the moment of his departure for Potsdam. Why it was set aside at Potsdam is not entirely clear. Grew heard from one man who was at Potsdam that if Stimson had not been there the conference "would have ended without any warning having been issued to Japan."

in the coming decades." And then he found that the precisely dropped bombs fell on soldiers, industrial installations, dwellings, private citizen and child alike. He therefore summoned General Arnold to hold him to "my promise from Lovett" and to obtain from the General "the facts." The facts were that in the crowded Japanese cities it was "practically impossible to destroy the war output" without also destroying "civilians connected with the output." Therefore he had to say that the promise he had extracted should be honored "as far as possible." [28]

The antithesis set up in the relation of right to might, of force to policy, the Secretary of War had lived with for a long time. Rigid though he might be in his definition of the old moralities, dogmatic as he certainly was on matters of personal conduct, he had nevertheless learned that a paradox was not resolved by cutting off one end of it. Between opposing interests it was necessary to calculate, at best, the basis for an unstable equilibrium, for a resolution only "as far as possible." Such calculations Stimson had made and accepted in his dealing with all the appalling anomalies of warfare as it had developed up to August 6, 1945. Thus when the occasion arose he was ready to make one further calculation. By the application of the ultimate destructive force, he trusted, there would be produced as soon as possible and as far as possible the optimum conditions for a constructive peace.

The capacity of this quite unambiguous man to tolerate, indeed to expect, ambiguity in the administration of man's affairs permitted him in the year 1945 to hold the two opposing possibilities presented by atomic energy steady in his mind. Of the necessity for the military application of this energy in the appropriate circumstance he apparently had no doubts; on this matter he rarely spoke with his associates. Of its application to the peaceful ordering of man's affairs in the future he spoke over and over again in his endless discussions. This energy, he

[28] Diary, March 5, June 1, 1945; H.L.S. to Harry S. Truman, May 16, 1945, in Diary.

told them, "touches matters which are deeper even than the principles of present government." It would produce with absolute certainty "a new relationship of man to the universe." It would take everyone "right down to the bottom facts of human nature. . . ." And among these bottom facts, he recognized, was the awful fact that for the first time the destructive urges of human beings were armed with the power totally to destroy. From what he knew of the way in which men had used the forces previously at their disposal — the will, the intelligence, the steam engine, the electric motor, the gun — he had no very confident assumption about an ideal future. As he told President Truman, the rate of technical development so far surpassed the rate of moral advancement that "civilization might be completely destroyed." [29]

These intimations did not deter him from the use of the new power to end a destructive war; in fact he believed that such use would, among other things, bring home to all people the nature of the energy they had thenceforth to live with. That force, comprehended, could like all forces be made subject to the intent of the user. What lay open, as he said, was "opportunity," a new "advantage" to be seized. Nuclear energy could be turned to stabilizing and constructive ends in peace. How this result could be produced became his last great preoccupation and endeavor.

In a memorandum to the new President on April 25, 1945, he made his first propositions clear. Our part in the development of this "most terrible weapon ever known in human history" placed a "moral responsibility upon us . . . for any disaster to civilization. . . ." On the other hand it gave "the opportunity to bring the world into a pattern in which the peace of the world and our civilization can be saved." One month later, on

[29] H.L.S., "The Decision to Use the Atomic Bomb," 100. The warning of complete destruction was made in the impressive memorandum, written April 25, 1945, in which Stimson acquainted the new President for the first time with the full meaning of atomic energy. Michael Amrine, *The Great Decision* (New York, 1959), 125, suggests that Stimson had real doubts about dropping the bomb. I have found no evidence to support this.

May 31, at the meeting of the Interim Committee, the Secretary spoke continuously about ways to use nuclear energy for other things "than killing people." He wanted the members to get started immediately "talking and questioning" about methods "to take advantage of the changed relation of man to his universe." He wished them to begin to figure the means by which "the peace of the world would be helped in becoming secure." [30]

Out of such deliberations, supported by independent ponderings, came the views which in the following five extraordinary months he sought to fashion into national policy. There were several parts to his program. His first concern was to end the war in Japan as soon as possible on terms that would not arouse "fanatical resistance." To this end he proposed a warning of impending destruction before dropping the bomb; an indication that the Emperor could, under conditions, remain and an assurance that, once purged of militaristic influences, Japan would be given, also under conditions, industrial and commercial opportunities in the new world. His next concern was to obtain the "proper handling of Germany so as not to create such harshness . . . as to make it impossible to lay the foundations of a new Germany. . . ." In dealing with these two great enemies he would not, as a first premise, seek to repay exactly; vengeance was not ours. "When you punish your dog," he told President Truman, "you don't keep souring on him all day after the punishment is over." [31]

[30] Diary, May 30, 31, 1945; conversation with Arthur Page, March 18, 1955; *Oppenheimer Hearing*, 34-35. The Interim Committee was concerned, in addition, with the public announcement of the use of the bomb and the future of atomic energy and, also, with proposing ideas for the legislative control of the new energy. It is at least possible that in the framing of his April 25 memorandum and, indeed, of his whole attitude toward the future control of atomic energy, Stimson was influenced by certain ideas originating in the Metallurgical Laboratory at Chicago, ideas expressed in the Jeffries Report and in a memorandum prepared by Professor Franck in late 1944 and early 1945. For the possible relation between these papers and Stimson's ideas, see *BAS*, Oct. 1958, 291-94.

[31] Diary, July 2, 3, 1945; H.L.S., "Memorandum for the President," July 2, 1945, in Diary; H.L.S., "Memorandum of Conference with the President," Aug. 8, 1945, in Diary. These views on the treatment of the conquered were con-

The next part of his program, the last concern, was the playing of "the royal straight flush," the "new control . . . over the forces of nature too revolutionary and dangerous to fit into the old concepts." The new finding "really caps the climax of the race between man's growing technical power for destructiveness and his psychological power of self-control and group control — his moral power." The new energy could not be brought within the now obsolete schemes — nationalism, secret diplomacy, the balance of power. It required a direct and open approach, an offer for the mutual limitation and control of "the use of the atomic bomb as an instrument of war," an "exchange of benefits of future developments. . . ." The stumbling block was how to deal with Russia. The problem here, he knew, was that a closed, arbitrary system, directed by a single irresponsible authority, could not for long survive at peace in a free and open society. At first he thought to use the offer to share the atom to exact from Russia changes in the structure of her government that would introduce the classic political freedoms and civil liberties. But the behavior of Russia immediately after the defeat of Germany and the attitudes of the Russians as they were exposed to him at Potsdam in July convinced him that such alterations could not be forced through a rigid system, because of a bargain struck, in some given moment of time.[32]

The risk must be taken, he therefore concluded, of going to a Russia in its existing form with propositions to stop further development of the military applications of nuclear energy, to impound existing weapons, and to devise a covenant for exchanging the benefits of future development in the interest of industrial and humanitarian purposes. These propositions he insisted should be put forward, discussed and acted upon not by all nations or by an organization of nations, but only by

sistent with what Stimson had been saying from the moment he began seriously to think about the end of the war.
[32] Diary, April 25, May 31, June 6, 1945; H.L.S., "Memorandum for the President," Sept. 11, 1945. Stimson's own account is given in *Active Service*, 634-55.

those directly concerned — Russia, England and the United States. Only by agreements worked out first by these three could there be a peace "that has some chance of being kept and saving civilization not for five or for twenty years, but forever." To place nuclear energy at the discussion and disposal of a group of nations acting without collective sovereignty and without either the means or the responsibility for the production of nuclear energy would produce chaos. Once the essential centers of power had been stabilized and controlled through negotiation between the three powers, peace, thus fortified, could then grow unforced and naturally through a concert of all nations. In these atmospheres, opportunity would be given for the gradual modification of a Russian system that, to live in amity with other freer nations, would have to change.[33]

The risk in all these proposals was obvious to Stimson. He recognized the fears of those like Morgenthau who wished to pastoralize Germany; he sympathized with the feelings of those like Dean Acheson who wished to eradicate the imperial system in Japan. But he himself feared more the repressed fury of the dog who had been soured on all day long. And as for Russia, he understood the desires of those like James Byrnes who wished to go into conferences with the new weapon showing on his hip as an instrument of policy. He also was moved by the arguments of men like Averell Harriman who said that Russia was and doubtless would remain intransigent.

On the other hand, in the present circumstances the hope to rely on the new weapon on the hip, on the creation of an independent national military superiority, would not serve. It was now necessary to continue policy by other means. "Unless we now develop methods of international life," he told a group of friends at the Ausable Club, "backed by the spirit of tolerance and kindliness, viz: the spirit of Christianity, sufficient to make international life permanent and kindly and war impossible, we will with another war end our civilization."

As the initial contribution to this indispensable spirit he was

[33] H.L.S., "Memorandum," Sept. 11, 1945.

prepared to share the first fruits of this new knowledge of good and evil. The risk was obvious, but among all the enormous risks of the times it seemed the least. His experience verified this judgment. Acting in the spirit of trust he had eliminated the Black Chamber — the decoding agency that monitored dispatches between embassies in Washington and their home governments — when he had been Secretary of State. In the same spirit he had talked with Quezon and Roxas without other witnesses when he was in the Philippines. The thing he had discovered first in Bones had been confirmed in every office, public and private, he had ever held. "The chief lesson I have learned in a long life," he told President Truman, "is that the only way you can make a man trustworthy is to trust him; and the surest way to make him untrustworthy is to distrust him and show him your distrust." Therefore in the year 1945 he would trust the Russians to join in the administration of the power to totally destroy, which was also the power to create.

These views he set forth in memoranda, in committee discussion, in casual conversation during the spring and summer. In July he went to Potsdam where Truman, Churchill, Attlee and Stalin were meeting together. There he received a message from George Harrison, acting chairman of the Interim Committee. The message said that a large child had been born. If the baby had been brought to birth in Washington the sound of its screams would have been heard from Harrison's farm in Upperville, Virginia, and the light in its eyes would have been seen at Highhold. This, as Stimson told President Truman, was Alamogordo. Then he and Bundy went round with the official report of the explosion to Churchill who, sitting there in his zipper suit, looked up from the pages to say that gunpowder was trivial; electricity was meaningless; this was the second coming in wrath.

At Potsdam also the Secretary, who did not have a direct part in the official negotiations, rendered advice on the statement sent to Japan, argued once again for the retention of the imperial structure in modified form, took some part in the arrangements for the drop on Hiroshima and Nagasaki and presented once again his suggestions on how to contain the new forces of wrath. There must be a full exploration of how the American head-start in atomic energy and the Russian desire to participate could be used to remove "the basic difficulty" posed by the antithetical character of the American and Russian systems. That these difficulties could, with care and time, be removed was not "an idle dream." [34]

Having said and done these things, he returned to the United States with the feeling that the purpose for which he had entered the government in June 1940 had been fulfilled. What there lay ahead to do could be better done by a younger man. He prepared to leave Washington on September 20. But there remained one further thing. On September 18 President Truman asked him if he would remain through Friday the 21st to attend a meeting of the Cabinet on the question of the control of nuclear energy. Bone-tired, ready and more than ready to leave, his plan of departure already set in train, he admitted that the request came as "a sore blow." But he "would be there if I could walk on my two legs."

Friday, the 21st of September, was the Secretary's seventy-

[34] Diary, July 17, 18, 19, 20, 22, Aug. 18, 1945; H.L.S., "Memorandum for the President," Sept. 11, 1945; conversation with Harvey Bundy, Oct. 4, 1945. What Stimson saw of the Russian obscurantism and repression in Potsdam at first so depressed him that he began to think that he and his Interim Committee which had been "so set upon opening communications with the Russians on the subject [of atomic energy] may have been thinking in a vacuum." But he soon reverted to his only hope, dictating a memorandum for the President on the necessity of introducing freedom of speech with Russia and encouraging her by extending the opportunity to share in the benefits of atomic energy. In the pages of the Diary is a clear indication of how much the news of the Alamogordo test cheered everybody up and made Truman a "changed man" who "stood up to the Russians in a most emphatic and decisive manner." This would appear to justify the decision, rarely noticed in accounts of Potsdam, to postpone the conference for two weeks so that the United States representatives could negotiate with greater confidence that the bomb would work. See Diary, June 6, 1945. A dramatic and illuminating description of the Alamogordo test is given in a memorandum prepared by General Groves for the Secretary of War on July 18, 1945. This memorandum is included in Herbert Feis, "The Secret That Traveled to Potsdam," *Foreign Affairs*, Jan. 1960. Feis, who based his account on the yet unpublished Potsdam Papers in the State Department, gives a fuller account of the proceedings of the Potsdam Conference than is provided here.

eighth birthday; it was also his last day in Washington. At ten thirty in the morning he met to say goodbye with Patterson, Lovett, Bundy, McCloy, Dorr, Harrison, Bowles, Martyn and his aide Colonel Hyde. At eleven, as the others were leaving, the Chief of Staff came in. For one hour Stimson and Marshall remained alone in the Secretary's office talking. At noon Robert Oppenheimer arrived to discuss "certain final technical problems" about the atomic bomb. After this the Secretary went to the General Officers' Mess where, at a lively lunch, he received a "huge" birthday cake. Then he went off with Mrs. Stimson to the White House. Before "a very large flock" of military and civilian officials the President read the citation for the award of the Distinguished Service Medal which he then presented to the Secretary of War. Following this ceremony Stimson and the President went to the meeting of the Cabinet where, at the President's request, the Secretary gave his views on the control of nuclear energy.

The members of the Cabinet, as one of them said, had an "imperfect knowledge of the subject"; they were, as another said, "green." To them the Secretary, speaking extemporaneously, began by saying that whether Russia obtained control of the necessary secrets of production in a minimum of four or a maximum of twenty years was not nearly as important to the world and civilization as it was to make sure that when the Russians did get the necessary knowledge they would be willing and cooperative partners among the peace-loving nations of the world. If, he went on, we failed to approach them directly now, if we merely continued to negotiate having this weapon ostentatiously on our hip, suspicion and distrust would grow with the years. On the conditions he had made before, he therefore proposed that we should go at once to Russia with a suggested arrangement to control and limit the use of the bomb and to exchange the "benefits of future developments whereby atomic energy may be applied on a mutually satisfactory basis for commercial or humanitarian purposes." There was no offer to "turn the bomb" itself over to Russia, but there was a proposal to stop all work on military applications of the energy if England and Russia agreed to do likewise.

The Secretary reiterated his belief that this approach to England and Russia should be direct, without recourse to the United Nations organization. After the nations that had won the war had agreed to methods and means, "there will be ample time to introduce France and China into the covenants and finally to incorporate the agreement into the scheme of the United Nations." It was true that what he recommended was a gamble on the good faith of Russia. Since he was skeptical that any tangible results could be obtained by international debates in the United Nations, since he was certain the old schemes would produce in time the war of total destruction, he was ready to gamble on this good faith "as the most realistic means" available.

There followed an hour of discussion. Henry Wallace was "completely, everlastingly and wholeheartedly in favor" of the Secretary's proposal. Dean Acheson gave his "general agreement" and Robert Hannegan expressed his respect for the Secretary's judgment. But Fred Vinson said he was opposed to sharing "any part of our knowledge of atomic energy" and James Forrestal remarked that "trust had to be more than a one-way street." Since most of the members were green and had imperfect knowledge the talk was inconclusive and at times beside the point. But the subject had been fully opened up and the Secretary had once again made his own position absolutely clear. It was, thought Henry Wallace, "one of the most dramatic of all cabinet meetings in my fourteen years of Washington experience." To him it seemed that "Stimson was one of the wisest men ever to serve as a presidential adviser." "If there was one thing which Stimson understood above everything else," the Secretary of Commerce reflected, "it was the importance of moral leadership." [35]

[35] For accounts of this meeting see Diary, Sept. 21, 1945; Truman, *Memoirs*, I, 525-27; Walter Millis, ed., *The Forrestal Diaries* (New York, 1951), 94-96; *New Republic*, Feb. 17, 1947, 26-27. See also, Diary, Sept. 18, 1945; H.L.S., "Memorandum for the President," Sept. 11, 1945.

When the meeting ended, the Secretary went out in his black limousine to the National Airport. There, without his knowledge, his civilian staff and all the general officers in Washington had assembled. They had formed up in two long lines. As the Secretary and Mrs. Stimson walked down the lines he received the nineteen-gun salute. Then the band played "Happy Birthday" and then it played "Auld Lang Syne." As he reached the end of the lines he stood for a moment looking back into the faces of the men who had for four years of war served with him. Then he turned, shook hands with General Marshall, and followed his wife up the steps into the waiting DC-3. The plane then bore him off toward the sanctuary of Highhold.

33

"Having Done All . . ."

In the summer of 1943 the Secretary of War had set out on a trip overseas. While abroad he was going to inspect American troops based in Great Britain. He was going to hold conversations with British officials about the plans to invade the Continent and about certain matters related to atomic energy. Then he was going to North Africa to look at the battlefields and to talk with General Eisenhower about forthcoming operations in the Mediterranean. Before his departure these various inspections, visits and appointments had been fitted together into a demanding three-week schedule.

In these three weeks the Secretary demonstrated that he was still, at seventy-six, a good traveling companion. He was always on time and he was always the same. The other members of his party — at meals, in drawing rooms after dinner, during the long hours in the air — talked steadily about anything that occurred to them. Ordinarily he just listened. Sometimes, at an appropriate moment, he broke in to recite a few lines of light verse or to tell some anecdote out of his remarkable past. Sometimes, too, he spoke to his junior aide, who had been to Yale, about the college and especially about Bones, that had "shaped" his life. But for the most part he remained quietly outside the stream of conversation.

The planes, the great houses, the private train put at his disposal, he used apparently without thought and without remark. He went "quietly along, doing what anybody ever asked him to, in a very full schedule" because, it seemed, "his primary notion was that he was there to serve."

At the very beginning of that trip it had appeared that the very full schedule would be thrown askew. The plane put down at Newfoundland to refuel. Before it could get off the ground again a heavy fog settled down. The report was that the party would be held at the base for at least twenty-four hours. There they all were, beginning a trip carefully planned ahead for three weeks. Most officials in the Secretary's position, it seemed to one man, would "have gotten disturbed and gone calling up people and ordering stuff and so forth."

Stimson, on receiving the news, said that he had always heard there was good fishing in Newfoundland. So they found a man who took two or three of the party to a small stream where all day the Secretary cast his line in silent satisfaction. In matters where men were the responsible agencies, error or imprecision would be greeted by exasperation and the gnashing of teeth. Acts of God and nature, the inevitable, had to be met with acceptance.

In the fall of 1945 the spirit of acceptance was necessary. For four years there had been the ordinary strains of war and, in the last six months, the extraordinary strains of the ending of this war. These the Secretary had dealt with, for a man his age, surprisingly well. Men who worked closely with him for the first time in 1945 were impressed by his force and vigor. To Arthur Compton it seemed that he had a "spirit so strong it kept him alive and alert." But he also had a body and a body that at seventy-eight was wearing out. All during the spring he was under the constant and careful supervision of the doctors. Not infrequently after a day of conferences or a brief inspection trip he would put himself in the hands of the medical men for a thorough examination. They exerted an increasingly strict control over his diet, his exercise, his periods of rest and work. The President had not, at first, even asked him to the Potsdam

Conference, for fear the old man could not stand the strain. The trouble lay in the circulatory system and primarily in the heart. Yet the heart had responded to treatment and to excitement and to the sense that there were still things that had to be done before the war was over.

From the moment he reached the peace of Highhold, however, things changed. Forthwith he found he was in a "real fight to find out whether I was going to rescue my poor tired old heart which was uttering vigorous protests at the way I had treated it." Confined immediately to his bed he became "as much like a polyp as possible." For a time the transformation appeared to work; the prospects looked slowly better until suddenly, in the third week in October, he suffered an acute coronary occlusion. For the better part of six weeks he lay practically immobilized in his bedroom before there were reassuring signs. By Christmas it did seem possible to predict a "good recovery, eventually." And in the meantime there was the ideal spot for the needed therapy, Highhold, where there was "nothing to think about except the welfare of our horses, cows, chickens and pigs. . . ."

To such treatment he responded in time and with his return to a measure of health there was, inevitably, a renewal of the concern for larger, public welfares. The career so long devoted to the national interest could not by the act of retirement be disengaged from the continuing affairs of the nation. There was first a request for his advice from General Marshall who was ready to set out on his mission to China. To the General, in time, went forward one of the long, carefully prepared familiar documents. Very few white men, the patient wrote from his sick bed, had ever understood the Chinese political mind. The only way in which Marshall could hope to succeed was to limit his mission to matters purely military. The aim should be to convince China that she must do the fighting "necessary to eject such Japanese as she does not wish to have around." If ever he was clear on a political fact it was that the American people at the present time would not support the use of American troops to put the Japanese troops out of China. For the rest, though his knowledge of the Communists was superficial, he believed their "hold on people underneath them is sounder than [Chiang Kai-shek's] hold over his people."

This was the first of continuing levies made upon his time and wisdom by the men still in Washington. They asked him how he felt about a pending wool bill, about the unification of the armed forces, about a proposed ordinance for the control of the Japanese economy, and about a reduction in the funds for the Voice of America. On each occasion he replied, as in the past, with the carefully prepared, well-documented opinion. The wool bill was "shocking," a repudiation of the whole economic policy so carefully built up by Cordell Hull in his fifteen years "of great work." As for the unification of the armed forces, every precedent taken from the history of the Second World War demonstrated that the integrity of our military strength depended on the creation of a single Department of Defense. In Japan "all we want to do" is ensure our future security and peace "by limiting her sovereignty to the island empire, by disarming her people, and by developing in her people a democratic desire. . . ." The proposed ordinance imposed an extreme regulation of industry and business that would defeat the purposes the United States was trying to accomplish. The Voice of America was also an instrument in support of the purposes we were trying to accomplish. The solution to its difficulties lay not in the reduction of its financial means but in the improvement of its programs.

From Forrestal, Patterson, Truman and Kenneth Royall, on these occasions, he received words of thanks for his "splendid letter," for his "thoughtful, restrained, and persuasive" message, for "the best letter that had been written in defense of the bill." From Marshall he heard, in response to one of his frequent communications to the then Secretary of State, "your constant support continues to be my sole stock in trade and I feel I can always count on you for immediate action."

Others in these years also hoped they could count on him.

From his old Party there were continuing requests for his support and advice. Although he had "always remained an enrolled Republican" and planned to vote for Thomas E. Dewey as Governor in 1946 he felt, he told a member of the Republican State Committee, that it would "be more in keeping with the past and my previous relation with [Roosevelt and Truman] if I did not come out into partisan activities now." As time passed he became more positive in his declarations. When Kingsland Macy asked him for help in 1947, he replied that he was not unaware of the valiant work some Republicans were doing to solve the problems of the modern world. But, on the other hand, "I not only believe that certain Republicans were primarily responsible for the errors that led to the tragedy of the interim war period and the coming of another great war, but I have heard far too many of my present Republican friends emit sentiments which flavor too strongly of isolationism than I like to hear." Consequently he felt "very shy about such a Republican blast as you give me in your letter." Finally, in a letter to a delegate to the Republican convention in 1948 who had asked his advice, he said that he was fearful about the views of "my old party." It seemed reluctant to take "bold and forthright views" on the crucial matters of strengthening the western democracies in Europe and, he also might say, of strengthening our own democracy at home. He hoped, "but with its terrible background of history and the things that it did immediately after the First World War our party has a long distance to go to fulfill the active duty of world membership even at the present time." His only advice could be that his correspondent ought to be sure that men who sought the nomination "who have been silent as to views on issues on which they were so wrong some time, are right now and honestly right." That was as far as he could go in his thoughts and "perhaps it is a little too far."

Of far greater importance to him than the immediate future of the Republican party was the development of sound national attitudes toward two of the great issues of the postwar world.

He spoke out clearly on his own attitude toward these issues. In January 1947 he wrote an article in defense of the Nuremberg Trials. The legal justification for these procedures lay in the Kellogg-Briand Pact of 1928 which had outlawed war. Therefore the trials were not a matter of *ex post facto* law. The Pact had not been enforced before the Second World War because we lacked the courage to enforce it. But a legal right is not lost merely because temporarily it is not used. When in the war we chased the criminal and caught him we had the obligation to try and to punish him in a trial unprecedented but not illegal. In "just such cases as this one . . . the law becomes more nearly what Mr. Justice Holmes called it: 'The witness and external deposit of our moral life.' "

On the other issue, the future of the control of atomic energy and the future of a world in which atomic energy existed, he also spoke out in sorrow if not discouragement on his eightieth birthday. Reluctantly he had to conclude that to his dictum about trusting men to make them trustworthy must be added the qualification that "this does not always apply to a man who is determined to make you his dupe." Before we could make friends with the Russians as they had revealed themselves since 1945, it would be necessary to convince them that they had nothing to gain and everything to lose by assuming that our society was dying. Because of this sad finding, the policy of a common control of the atom must wait a change of heart in Russia. But that change of heart would not be produced by strong-armed methods and preventive wars. It could only be brought about by the ceaseless concern of a resolute America with the rebuilding of a strong and satisfied Europe. If we could make "freedom and prosperity real in the present world," communism was no eternal threat. In time the spirit of Soviet Russia would modify itself. The future depended not "on the tattered forecasts of Karl Marx" but on us.

And when this threat of communism was raised once in a different form in the closing months of his life, he spoke out in the last public statement he would make. There was, he said in the *New York Times* on March 27, 1950, an established method for investigating and weighing charges of disloyalty against government employees. If the interest of Senator Joseph McCarthy of Wisconsin had been to ensure the loyalty of these employees in the Department of State, he would have had resort to these means. "The fact that the accuser has wholly ignored this well-established method indicates that his interest is of a different character." Since in the present state of the world the denial could not always overtake the accusation, the present charges damaged the innocent and protected the guilty.

The real motive of the attack, it seemed, was to discredit the Secretary of State of the United States. The "extraordinary record" of this man would no doubt put him beyond "danger from these little men." But the matter was above "the rise or fall of individuals"; what was at stake was the effective conduct of our foreign policy. "The man who seeks to gain political advantage from personal attack on a Secretary of State is a man who seeks political advantage from damage to his country."

The President and the Secretary of State were trying to give wise leadership in a time of changing conditions and grave world tension. This effort would require of those in the democratic process "widespread and earnest public consideration of the great problems now before us, so that the ultimate decision will surely reflect the basic steadiness and faith of our people." Considering all this, he said in his last words, "This is no time to let the noisy antics of a few upset the steady purpose of our country or distract our leaders from their proper tasks. This is rather a time for stern rebuke of such antics and outspoken support of the distinguished public servants against whom they are directed."

The public services and interests were supplemented in these years by a more personal endeavor. In the spring of 1946 he began to work on what he called a "pilot biography," an account, primarily, of his public life and service. To help him investigate the large accumulation of records from the past, he obtained the assistance of McGeorge Bundy, the son of his old friend and colleague Harvey Bundy. Working together for over a year and a half at Highhold they organized the evidence drawn from the written word and the unfailing memory. The product was the book *On Active Service in Peace and War* where one can find so much that was seen and done and believed by Stimson as he constructed his long career. At the very end of the book he set down in his own words a kind of summarizing interpretation of the meaning to him of that long career. He had lived, as any active man must, in a world where at the same time there was good and evil, sinfulness and decency, the reality of war and, that greater thing, the hope of a faithful peace. In a world where every man had to live with all these things together the mainspring was hope; the only deadly sin he knew was cynicism.

The composition of this record of public service, the continuing interest in public affairs, the running flow of correspondence to public officials, all took place within a slowly closing circle of private actions. The old man could feel each year, each month, each week, almost each day the gradual but the steady whittling down of age. After his recovery from the first coronary occlusion in the fall of 1945 he had looked forward with hope to the time when he and Mrs. Stimson could together pursue the comfortable, pleasant rounds of honored retirement. To this end he had arranged to take a room in the new offices of his law firm at 40 Wall Street. There would be no return to active practice, simply an availability for occasional consulting, for the rendering of advice and counsel on matters that interested him. He had also taken an apartment at Fifth Avenue and 70th Street where, it was expected, he and Mrs. Stimson could establish "a center of interest" and entertainment for them and many of their younger friends in the city. Then too he had looked ahead to trips, north in summer, south in winter, as brief diverting changes from the normal activities in New York and Long Island.

The steady invasion of arthritic pain, the gradual reduction of energy interfered with the fulfillment of these expectations. Only rarely, perhaps five or six days in all between 1945 and 1950, did he go down to the office in Wall Street. Only a few times, and then only as a convenience, did he and Mrs. Stimson use the apartment on Fifth Avenue. Only once did they go south in the winter. For a few weeks in 1947, in Florida, he sat in the sun, putted on a small golf green, and bought a little rowboat where he "could sit and be comfortable in the beautiful little lake." But the whole excursion seemed, on his return, something less than worth it. Such pleasure as could be discovered in brief trips away from his ordinary daily concerns he found in his visits to the Ausable Club, a source of relaxation and delight in these years as in the past.

But the real sanctuary that remained was Highhold. There he and Mrs. Stimson could walk out to look at the peas, beans, potatoes and corn growing in the garden and at the six cows, the four pigs and the 200 chickens in the barns. There they could make their daily visits to John, the last horse in the stable, and to Patsy, the pony bought for visiting children to ride. For Stimson, crippled by arthritis, there was now no more riding. Once or twice he climbed on John's back but the effort and the pain were too great. A friend gave him a smaller, quieter jenny but experiments with this animal proved equally unsatisfactory. Finally a small wooden horse was built, in the hope that Stimson could use it to strengthen his weakening limbs. But here again the effort produced only pain. Philosophically he gave up the greatest joy in his life.

But under certain conditions he could still pursue the supplementary joys. From a wheel chair with a very light gun he was able from time to time to do a little skeet shooting and there was always, sometimes also from a wheel chair, fishing. He would go out to the Southside Club on good days for an hour or two of casting and return usually with enough fish to satisfy himself that the excursion had been worth it. Then too in the afternoons, both good and bad, there were long drives around the island with Mrs. Stimson.

What remained to them was a rather cheerless regimen. Yet in their private lives there were still mitigating influences. They were wonderfully well taken care of by Walter Olmstead who drove their cars and by Louise who attended to their needs about the house. Every week end Allen Klots and his wife came for a dinner, bringing news of the law firm and of matters in the world outside that would interest Mr. and Mrs. Stimson. The Pages, the Bundys, the McCloys, the Lovetts came out to Highhold from time to time with their jokes and their stories and their news of what was happening. From New Haven the Daggetts would come over frequently to report on members of the family. All together these younger people brought life and cheer constantly into the household of the old couple.

And the old couple still had each other. They read and talked and remembered and exchanged their firm opinions together, and together they supported each other in the observance of those sustaining rituals they had built up over a half century and more within a common bond.

Still, with all these supporting loyalties and affections, the tempo steadily diminished. In the spring of 1950 both husband and wife "were very tired and worn out." It became ever harder "to carry the load even of short friendly conversations." By the fall Stimson had to write a friend that they both had been in need of cheer. It was lonely, bleak, to be confined to Highhold, without the strength to talk to friends and relatives, with nothing much to do but keep up with the correspondence of condolence. But still they were pulling along and perhaps "sooner or later, we hope to be on our feet again."

One day in October his niece Mrs. Daggett came over from New Haven to take him out to fish. He took his wheel chair and they went down to a small brook and he sat down and cast his line. To his delight both he and his niece caught some fish. It was a pleasant fall afternoon. And in the evening, before their excellent dinner, he and his wife sat down with the Old Fashioned cocktails the doctor had prescribed. They went as usual early to bed. Next morning he went fishing again, this time with Walter Olmstead, at the Southside Club. After lunch he took a short nap before calling Walter once more to say that he and Mrs. Stimson would go for a drive. Walter brought the car around and they started out, but after only a short distance — about a quarter of a mile — Stimson began to feel in distress. They turned around, came home, and Walter and the nurse carried him up to his bed. Mrs. Stimson sat down beside him and took his hand. He looked at her, called her name, and died.

In the private letters, in the editorials, in the selected readings from the Testaments, in the published comments of great contemporaries the same points were always made. Trust, truth, justice, virtue, the reign of law, the call of duty, the shining example, the active service. He had been a forthright gentleman, a great trial lawyer, a courageous soldier, a dedicated public servant, a statesman who would live in grateful hearts. He had been a fort and a foundation stone. He had been set upon a rock. For he had taken the shield of faith against the fiery darts. Wherefore he had been able to withstand in the evil days, and, having done all, to stand. After all the doings he had left all the words — justice, duty, honor, trust — as he had found them — solid, quite solid. And his hands were steady until the going down of the sun.

Bibliographical Note

Index

Bibliographical Note

MUCH OF the information in this book was taken from personal letter collections. The primary source was the Henry L. Stimson Papers now in the Yale University Library. It is a massive collection begun in the days when the mail was still the principal instrument of communication and when correspondents seemed under some sort of moral obligation to keep everything. The papers contain copies in letterpress or carbon form of outgoing mail and originals of incoming letters dealing with matters both public and private from the time Stimson entered the legal profession in 1891 until his death in 1950. Added to this extensive correspondence are receipted bills, checkbooks, engraved invitations, income tax forms, certificates and scrolls of membership, deeds, lists of charitable donations — in short, all the records of the private activities of a long and varied life. Supplementing this body of material are the Diaries. Entries describing the early years, from 1906 to 1930, are, though extensive, for the most part episodic and retrospective. This is in general true also of the entries from 1933 to 1940. For the period 1930-1933 in the State Department and for the period in the War Department, 1940-1945, each day in Stimson's life is described in some detail. These entries were dictated, ordinarily, in the early morning after the day described. The Diaries are a mine of information about the way in which decisions are made in matters of public policy and they will remain indispensable documents for the study of our foreign policy in the Hoover Administration and of the conduct of the war in the administrations of Franklin D. Roosevelt and Harry S. Truman. The Stimson Papers also contain a transcript of the extended conversations between Stimson and McGeorge Bundy while they were writing *On Active Service in Peace and War*. The transcription of these informal discussions, which cover all kinds of public and private matters, is not always exact, but considering the difficulty of capturing any informal conversation in shorthand, the typed account is surprisingly ungarbled and the occasional errors are easy to discover. This record, though also retrospective, is especially useful because of Mr. Bundy's skill and persistence as an interrogator and because Stimson permitted himself fuller and freer expression of views on men and events than he sometimes did in his published works. Finally, there are in this collection notes and copies of Stimson's many speeches, magazine articles by and about him, his testimony before many congressional committees, newspaper clippings without number, a good many government reports and documents bearing on matters that interested him, and the records of various organizations and associations of which he was a member. Citations in the footnotes are always to correspondence and papers in this collection unless otherwise stated. This material has been well organized and catalogued by the staff of the Yale University Library. I am grateful especially to James T. Babb, the Yale University Librarian, and Howard B. Gottlieb, the Librarian of Historical Manuscripts, for their assistance and forbearance over several years. I am also and particularly in the debt of Arthur W. Page and McGeorge Bundy for the freedom given me to look for and to interpret in any way I wished the information to be found in the great collection under their trusteeship.

Other personal letter collections now on public deposit were also used. In the Library of Congress search was made through the papers of William H. Moody, Elihu Root, Theodore Roosevelt and William Howard Taft. In each case some material of value was discovered, but for the most part the letters found were also to be found in the Stimson Papers. The same is true for the Stimson material in the Franklin D. Roosevelt Library at Hyde Park which I looked at on microfilm kindly supplied by Herman Kahn, the Director of the Franklin D. Roosevelt Library.

Other useful information was taken from collections still in private hands. To Harvey Bundy, Goldthwaite Dorr, Herbert Feis, Felix Frankfurter, Allen T. Klots and Arthur W. Page I am under obligation for material — letters, memoranda, diaries — that permitted a much fuller understanding and more complete account of Stimson's career than I could otherwise have obtained.

ARCHIVES

Stimson's educational record and some other information about the educational institutions he attended was obtained from the archives of Phillips Academy, Yale University and the Harvard Law School. Information about his legal career and his principal cases was taken from the files of Winthrop, Stimson, Putnam and Roberts. The Department of Justice files were used in preparing the account of Stimson's work as United States Attorney for the Southern District of New York. These files in the National Archives are a rich source of material too rarely used by historians. I am very grateful to Bess Glenn for the care and patience she took to see I got the papers I needed from this file that was left in disorder by an earlier generation. The files of the Department of State that I used are now in the National Archives. Many of the documents in this source are now printed in the continuing government publication *Foreign Relations of the United States*, but a good deal of useful information in the way of memoranda, position papers and background studies bearing on particular events remains unpublished. My search in these files was much facilitated by the wise suggestion and kindness of E. Taylor Parks. The records of the Office of the Secretary of War that were used to describe Stimson's work from 1940-1945 are now in the Office of the Secretary of Defense. Rudolph A. Winnacker, who, among many other tasks and duties, has these records in his charge, expedited my researches and generously amplified my findings out of his larger knowledge of the period in question. He also read and corrected the chapters dealing with the conduct of the war.

INTERVIEWS

The information drawn from published and unpublished sources was supplemented by interviews with the following men and women: Mr. and Mrs. Harvey Bundy, McGeorge Bundy, Vannevar Bush, Mr. and Mrs. Grenville Clark, Edgar Crossman, Mr. and Mrs. David Daggett, Goldthwaite Dorr, Herbert Feis, Felix Frankfurter, Gordon Grand, Elizabeth Neary Hill, Herbert Hoover, Stanley Hornbeck, Rear Admiral and Mrs. Jules James, Allen T. Klots, Alfred Lee Loomis, Robert A. Lovett, Mr. and Mrs. John J. McCloy, J. Robert Oppenheimer, Frederick Osborn, Arthur W. Page, Albert W. Putnam, George Roberts, James Grafton Rogers, Mrs. Henry L. Stimson. The conversations with all these people were of incalculable benefit to me. Some remembered important things about the Stimson family beyond the reach of genealogical records; some recalled incidents in Stimson's career more revealing than any of those described in his correspondence; some described feelings, arguments, influences at work in the formation of policy or the administration of public affairs not to be found in the minutes of conferences or the published accounts as amended. Such sense of life and actuality as may be found in this study derives in large part from the fullness and frankness of the testimony of these people. To all I am in debt, and to some of them I am in very substantial debt. Mrs. David Daggett, a niece of Mrs.

Stimson, helped me greatly to understand the kind of family life the Stimsons lived and supplied me with much information to support descriptions of that life. Alfred Lee Loomis, the son of Stimson's aunt, an associate in the law firm, Stimson's financial adviser and one of his most valued consultants during the war, gave me evidence about his relative's career I could have obtained from no one else. Robert A. Lovett and John J. McCloy and Harvey Bundy contributed, in a way no search through correspondence or official records could, to my feeling for how the War Department worked in the years from 1940 to 1945. In addition Harvey Bundy illuminated for me many things I might well have missed in my subject's reticent personality. The same is true of Allen T. Klots who from the beginning guided me also in useful directions, explained hard points of the law and enlarged my feeling for the legal profession. I am grateful to him for all this, and for his continuing interest and many kindnesses in my behalf. The footnotes will reveal how much I have relied on the remarkable memory and insight of Felix Frankfurter whose continuing faith in the value of this venture has sustained my own during the inevitable moments of doubt. All these men, in addition to their contributions of supplying evidence and hospitality, have read the manuscript in whole or in part. For their comment and correction I am very grateful. My colleagues in history, John M. Blum, Richard W. Leopold and Samuel E. Morison, have also read the manuscript in whole or in part. So have my father G. A. Morison and my brother R. S. Morison. From the judgments and corrections of each I have greatly profited.

PUBLISHED WORKS

The books, government reports, periodicals and newspapers that have been of most substantial use in preparing this work are cited in the footnotes. I wish here only to record my admiration for the remarkable series, *United States Army in World War II,*

prepared under the general editorship of Kent Roberts Greenfield. My study of the enormous subject of the war was greatly
simplified and expedited by my use of the volumes in this series.
The footnote procedure adopted was designed to provide sufficient information about sources with a minimum of discomfort.
Like all compromise solutions it has its defects, but I hope it will
be found, in general, to have served its purpose.

The book produced from all the above sources of evidence
was written with the help of Constance Cone Walker, Nancy
Bradish Vivanti and Bettina Cleveland. Among them, at different times, they did research, transcribed dictated notes, prepared the manuscript for publication and checked quotations
and citations. Without them the work could not have been done;
with them it was done with continuing satisfaction and pleasure.

Index

Index